THE ARCHITECTURAL
REPRESENTATION OF ISLAM

MUSLIM-COMMISSIONED
MOSQUE DESIGN
IN THE NETHERLANDS

Eric Roose

ISIM DISSERTATIONS

ISIM / LEIDEN

AMSTERDAM UNIVERSITY PRESS

Cover illustration: The first two sketches for the first purpose-built mosque in The Netherlands. Bashir/Wiebenga, 7-10/16-10-1951, Archive NAi

Cover design and lay-out: De Kreeft, Amsterdam

ISBN   978 90 8964 133 5
E-ISBN 978 90 4850 879 2
NUR   761

© ISIM / Amsterdam University Press, Amsterdam 2009

Alle rechten voorbehouden. Niets uit deze uitgave mag worden verveelvoudigd, opgeslagen in een geautomatiseerd gegevensbestand, of openbaar gemaakt, in enige vorm of op enige wijze, hetzij elektronisch, mechanisch, door fotokopieën, opnamen of enige andere manier, zonder voorafgaande schriftelijke toestemming van de uitgever.
Voor zover het maken van kopieën uit deze uitgave is toegestaan op grond van artikel 16B Auteurswet 1912 j° het Besluit van 20 juni 1974, Stb. 351, zoals gewijzigd bij het Besluit van 23 augustus 1985, Stb. 471 en artikel 17 Auteurswet 1912, dient men de daarvoor wettelijk verschuldigde vergoedingen te voldoen aan de Stichting Reprorecht (Postbus 3051, 2130 KB Hoofddorp). Voor het overnemen van gedeelte(n) uit deze uitgave in bloemlezingen, readers en andere compilatiewerken (artikel 16 Auteurswet 1912) dient men zich tot de uitgever te wenden.

All rights reserved. Without limiting the rights under copyright reserved above, no part of this book may be reproduced, stored in or introduced into a retrieval system, or transmitted, in any form or by any means (electronic, mechanical, photocopying, recording or otherwise) without the written permission of both the copyright owner and the author of the book.

The Architectural Representation of Islam

Muslim-Commissioned Mosque Design in The Netherlands

PROEFSCHRIFT

ter verkrijging van
de graad van Doctor aan de Universiteit Leiden,
op gezag van Rector Magnificus prof. mr. P.F. van der Heijden,
volgens besluit van het College voor Promoties
te verdedigen op woensdag 6 mei 2009
klokke 16.15 uur

door

Eric Reinier Roose
geboren te Middelburg
in 1967

Promotores
    Prof. dr. A.J.J. Mekking
    Prof. dr. M.M. van Bruinessen (Universiteit Utrecht)

Overige leden
    Prof. dr. M.S. Berger
    Prof. dr. D. Douwes (Erasmus Universiteit Rotterdam)
    Prof. dr. A.C.A.E. Moors (Universiteit van Amsterdam)
    Prof. dr. P.J.M. Nas
    Dr. H.P.A. Theunissen
    Prof. dr. D.J. de Vries

Contents

Acknowledgements 7

Introduction: The Representation of Islamic Architecture in The Netherlands 9
On the Origin of Styles by means of Cultural Selection 9
Religious Construction, Mutual Contrasting and
Reality Representation 26
Towards the Representational Analysis of Mosque Design 32

1. Hindustani-Commissioned Mosque Design in The Netherlands 39
Varieties of Islam among Hindustani Communities 40
The Mobarak Mosque, The Hague 50
The First Taibah Mosque, Amsterdam 66
The Second Taibah Mosque, Amsterdam 83

2. Moluccan-Commissioned Mosque Design in The Netherlands 93
Varieties of Islam among Moluccan Communities 94
The Wyldemerck Mosque, Balk 96
The Bait Ar-Rahman Mosque, Ridderkerk 107
The An-Nur Mosque, Waalwijk 120

3. Turkish-Commissioned Mosque Design in The Netherlands 131
Varieties of Islam among Turkish Communities 132
The Yunus Emre Mosque, Almelo 134
The Sultan Ahmet Mosque, Zaanstad 156
The Wester Mosque, Amsterdam 163

4. Moroccan-Commissioned Mosque Design in The Netherlands 181
Varieties of Islam among Moroccan Communities 182
The Al Fourkaan Mosque, Eindhoven 186
The El Islam Mosque, The Hague 198
The Essalaam Mosque, Rotterdam 210

Conclusion: The Architectural Representation of Islam in The Netherlands   237
Design Interpretation and Diverging Realities   237
Overcoming the Clash of Classifications   245
Towards a Dutch Mosque Design?   248

Notes   257
Selected Bibliography   295
Samenvatting in het Nederlands   309
Curriculum Vitae   316

Figures   319

Acknowledgements

First: the International Institute for the Study of Islam in the Modern World (ISIM), with its unique diversity of academic disciplines, methodological interests and regional specializations, formed a stimulating environment without which some of the ideas in this study would definitely not have developed. Next: I am hugely indebted to all the designing and commissioning parties, or their representatives, who patiently answered my meticulous questions about the materials and information they so graciously provided. Without their cooperation, this dissertation would have been completely impossible. I would like to mention, in no particular order: Ergün Erkoçu, AbdelUahab Hammiche, Cihan Bugdaci, Hibatunnoer Verhagen, Abdul Hamid van der Velden, Abdul Rashid, Naeem Ahmad Warraich, Karim Mahmood, H. Hendriks, Paul Haffmans, Roy Kasiem, Mohammed Yunus Gaffar, Peter Scipio, Frank Domburg, Ghani van den Berg, Sufyan Ollong, D. Gaasterland, Hamid Oppier, Ismael Ririn, Hamid Samaniri, Boy Barajanan, Astorias Ohorella, Ibrahim Lessy, Türker Atabek, Nejat Sucu, Henk Slettenhaar, Ine Mentink, Ingrid Pelgrum, Ahmet Altikulaç, Bedri Sevinçsoy, Wim Vugs, Hans Florie, Kees Rijnboutt, Üzeyir Kabaktepe, Marc Breitman, Nada Breitman, Mohamed El Bouk, Piet Vernooy, Dolf Dazert, Haci Karacaer, David Boon, Jacqueline Slagter, Amar Nejjar, Ali Belhaj, Ahmed Arabi, Ahmed Ajdid, Joris Molenaar, and Wilfried van Winden. I also thank Marcel Decraene, Antje van der Hoek, Marcus Klomp, Henk van de Schoor, Jeroen Westerman, Marcel Maussen, Martijn de Koning, Nico Landman, Hans Theunissen, and Diana Wright for pointing me in the direction of crucial archives, articles, literature, websites, contacts, and organizations. Finally: a word of gratitude goes out to Berber den Otter, for enduring the four years of monomaniacal and near-obsessive behaviour that came along with this project. As meagre compensation, I dedicate this dissertation to her.

Introduction:
The Representation of Islamic Architecture in The Netherlands

On the Origin of Styles by means of Cultural Selection

In 1950, the first plan for a Dutch mosque to be built as such was developed by a Pakistani Muslim missionary group to The Netherlands. At the time when this first mosque plan entered the scene, knowledge on the subject within architectural design schools was mainly produced by a small number of standard Dutch works on the history of world architecture, written by influential Dutch architects-cum-teachers in the preceding decades on the basis of international literature. Although the authors differed in their attitudes towards the desirability and application of Oriental elements in contemporary Dutch architecture, they generally assumed that it was the non-structural and non-functional aspects of Islamic buildings that gave the latter their place in history. One of the founding fathers of Dutch architectural education, E.H. Gugel, in a much-repeated architectural chronology, effectively placed 'Arabian architecture' just between what was thought of as the Byzantine and Romanesque style periods. He deemed it not to have added any 'constructive' elements to the historical development of world architecture: it merely copied classical forms, with only a further detailing of decoration patterns.[1] According to W. Kromhout, the main difference lay in the fact that 'they [the Muslims] saw the conspicuously decorative in everything, whereas we [the Dutch] saw the constructive. They used building elements because they thought them beautiful, providing the opportunity for hundreds of aesthetically pleasing decorative-architectural applications, while we used them in a purely constructive development'.[2] In H. Evers' view, Islamic buildings had been created 'from the passionate imagination of the fanatical Oriental', the 'uncivilized conqueror driven by the need to be conspicuous', and through their richness of form and color gave the impression of a 'soothing of the senses' more than of being 'deeply touched'.[3] J.H.W. Leliman found that 'notwithstanding the many regional adjustments and periodical changes the architecture of the Mohammedans was subjected to, all varieties were branches of the same tree, expressions of one and the same fantastic, exceptionally sensual, almost intoxicating art'.[4] And J. Godefroy even went so far as to place 'Mohammedan art' in a phase of constructive degeneration.[5]

The phenomenon of Islamic architecture, believed to represent a singular religion and divided into a number of building styles related to the Arab, Persian, Moorish and Turkish culture areas, was widely regarded as completed. As such, H. Sutterland positioned it with other pre-modern building styles in the irrational, decorative, ornamental and symbolic phases of the evolution of the built environment towards the contemporary rational, sober, simple, honest, pure and constructional ideal.[6] Whereas the association of Islamic areas with the Arabian Nights tales had, in earlier centuries, already led to the phenomenon that the Dutch saw Islamic building elements as pleasantly diverting to the senses, mainly to be used in garden tents, cigarette kiosks, beach paviljons, colonial exhibitions, exotic zoos and theaters,[7] from the turn of the century they came to be seen as useful for the newly invented cinemas as well. Mixed with arcadian scenes in the façades of buildings called 'Alcazar', 'Luxor' or 'Alhambra', they were explicitly meant to evoke an idyllic atmosphere.[8] Finally, in the 1950s, their capacity as outstanding representations of make-believe earned them a place in the fairy-tale forest of the children's theme park 'De Efteling', as a moated, two-towered Islamic palace with a Fakir flying on a magic carpet.[9]

However, mosque design actually commissioned by Muslims in The Netherlands proved to be a different matter and quickly became a subject of heated architectural debates. In general, Muslim immigrant communities were known to be culturally dispersed but assumed to be religiously consistent, whereas Dutch Christian communities were known to be religiously dispersed but assumed to be culturally consistent.[10] Eventually, Muslims in The Netherlands came to be recognized as members of individual ethnic or culture groups, with Surinamese, Moluccan, Turkish and Moroccan Muslims represented by their own architectural style characteristics while sharing a basic Islamic belief system and liturgy. In this line of thinking, when municipalities were confronted with mosque plans, some saw the conspicuous use of building elements from the Muslim countries of origin as an unwanted and unnecessary intrusion on Dutch culture. Instead, Dutch Muslims were supposed to find ways to process their basic Islamic liturgical requirements into designs that on the outside would appear largely as Dutch buildings and not as transplanted Arabian Nights palaces. On the other hand, other municipalities found that although mosques were indeed thought of as mere practical places of Islamic liturgy, the introduction of building elements from the Muslim countries of origin would be a way for Dutch Muslim immigrants to feel at home in Dutch society, as well as a way to enrich Dutch culture. Whatever the exact contents and outcomes of these discussions, the fact is that Dutch mosque design was essentially viewed as a measure of to what degree its Muslim patrons, in their expression of a singular religion, chose to refer to their original cultures. Since the patrons, whatever their design requirements, also seemed to stress that their Islam was universal, their supposed stance on the manner of inclusion of a layer of 'cultural' building elements beyond the basic religious necessities came to be seen by the Dutch public as a stance on the manner of their inclusion in Dutch society. Whether the architectural visibility of Islam was to be monoculturally rejected, multiculturally stimulated, or pluriculturally solved, most Dutch parties seemed to regard the issue of Dutch mosque design as an issue of the culture clash and not of some internal religious dispersion.

  To be sure, a number of illuminating studies of purpose-built mosques in The Netherlands have been published, but these generally aim at an analysis of the history of establishment, the political and public turmoil, or their position in discourses of the negotiation of space and place, without delving into particular motivations behind the particular architectural choices of particular Muslim patrons.[11] Only two – unpublished but much-referred to – studies have treated the relation between Dutch mosque designs and their patrons in a more concrete way. Importantly, in their MA theses, both Barbara Dijker and Wendy Wessels interpreted the Dutch empirical data within the methodological framework of a popular international publication on the subject, prominently present on the bookshelves of – and heavily influencing – many Dutch architects, architectural teachers and architectural students. In this publication, Martin Frishman and Hasan-Uddin Khan by and large formally assigned Islamic architectural history to a limited number of building types corresponding to a limited number of Muslim 'regions'. In effect, their publication continued and extended the older notion of a limited number of circumscribed Muslim culture areas being characterized by their own recognizable building styles. Within Frishman's and Khan's overview, India and Pakistan were characterized by the Mogul style around a formal type with triple domes and a large courtyard, Malaysia and Indonesia by the Southeast-Asian style around a formal type with a pyramidal pitched roof, Anatolia by the Ottoman style around the formal type with a massive central dome supported by half-domes, and Spain and North Africa by the Almoravid/Almohad style around the formal type with a hypostyle hall with a flat roof and open courtyard.[12] **(Figure 1)** Based on this classification, Dijker understandably assumed that in the Dutch context 'our' Surinamese, Moluccan, Turkish and Moroccan Muslims shared a basic liturgy but needed to architecturally circumscribe themselves as consistent culture groups towards each other. Subsequently, she showed them to have been using, in their mosques, what she saw as the Indian, Indonesian, Turkish and Moroccan building styles. Any divergences from these ideal-types were explained by the author by the relevant patrons' need to be more recognizably Islamic in a non-Islamic society or from their architects' individual creativity.[13] Similarly, Wessels assumed that the Moroccan, Turkish and Surinamese mosques in the region of Utrecht had been based on the Moroccan, Turkish and Indian building styles as well. She, in turn, explained the empirical deviations from these ideal-types mainly from the rules and regulations placed upon them by municipalities, and from the inhabitants' desire that they be made to fit their Dutch surroundings.[14]

At first sight, the identification of these authentic cultural building styles and the consequent need to explain any empirical deviations in The Netherlands in terms of modern factors seem plausible enough. Beneath the surface, however, the Dutch empirical field is much more varied than can be described, let alone explained, by any consistent typology connected to cultures to begin with. Even when only cursorily surveyed, it can be seen that the 'Indian style' has been combined with elements from specifically non-Hindustani buildings, whereas both the 'Indonesian style' and the 'Turkish style' have been materialized in quite conflicting ways. Strangely enough, the 'Moroccan style' was conspicuously rejected in several Moroccan-commissioned projects, while the 'Mamluk style' was used, even though none of the mosque communities involved came from a Mamluk-associated region. Meanwhile, when confronted with the media, most patrons orally classified their own chosen forms or materials as typically 'Dutch' in some way and someone else's as completely 'un-Dutch'.[15] On the other hand, some patrons could never be bothered to explain anything in spite of heavy public speculation, leaving the observer even more confused in a matter that was initially imagined to be quite straightforward.

As yet, despite the obvious precariousness of the issue for the general public, there are no in-depth, published studies on the motivations of the

Muslim mosque patrons involved. Knowledge on that particular subject has been mainly produced by a small group of young, engaged Muslim architects united in the design bureau MemarDutch. The latter was established after two of its members – under the name of Memar – graduated *cum laude* in 2003 with an alternative Dutch mosque proposal for a Moroccan-commissioned project in Rotterdam that had led to a great controversy among local non-Muslim communities. They called their alternative the 'Polder Mosque', and it was specifically aimed at 'transparent design' and 'integration architecture'.[16] **(Figure 2)** Since then, their perspective has been referred to in all major Dutch newspaper articles,[17] magazine articles[18] and exhibitions[19] on the subject. Although their alternative was never executed, they may be regarded as quite influential and authoritative among a large part of the public, leading to what might be recognized as the start of a stream of prize-winning – although uncommissioned and unexecuted – modern design alternatives by architectural students in The Netherlands.[20]

In 2006, MemarDutch members Ergün Erkoçu, AbdelUahab Hammiche and Cihan Bugdaci published a printed article that summed up the argument their bureau had spread over the different public media in the years before. In this, the authors basically presented existing Dutch mosque designs as a sign of arrested development. They suggested Muslim immigrant communities in The Netherlands were emotionally stuck to copies and pastiches of their premodern cultural building styles caused by nostalgia for the mother countries or by the need to show an ostentatiously Islamic identity. Moreover, they suggested the Dutch, non-Muslim architects involved used an Orientalist perspective, resulting in the Arabian Nights architecture that had characterized the 'make-believe' buildings of earlier times. 'Because mosques are built in the styles of local architectures, the variety is large. [...] Therefore, it is amazing to see that mosque architecture in The Netherlands and the other Western European countries passes over any local architectural styles. [...] At the end of the 1980s a style developed in The Netherlands that strongly based itself on historical examples, partly because the first generation of Muslims looked for a connection with its roots, coming from a wish to secure their own identity. Currently, [...] mosque boards mainly choose Dutch architects, [...] often leading to buildings that copy Oriental forms. These are materialized with bricks, concrete and wood and executed with contemporary techniques: instead of creating a Dutch building style, Disney-like Efteling architecture comes into being. In reaction, [some] architects [...] leave this kind of historicizing construction behind. They incorporate Dutch characteristics in Oriental looking mosques. The result, however, leaves much to be desired.' In the authors' vision of the future, 'it is especially the young architects who oppose this homesickness architecture. They wonder how they can apply the Islamic idiom in a Western context. Some, including MemarDutch, present modern designs in which it is not the tradition but the function and the incorporation into the urban context that determines the form of the mosque. [...] Because Muslims identify themselves less and less with their home country, the need for a typical target group mosque (e.g. for Turks or Moroccans) will decline. The ethnic boundaries that still divided the ancestors will thus be crossed. The Netherlands is at the beginning of [...] its own mosque architecture'. As an illustration of that development, the authors described their Polder Mosque as 'attractive to a large public', whereas the Rotterdam Essalaam Mosque and the Amsterdam Wester Mosque were respectively evaluated to have 'a non-inviting appearance for non-regular users' and 'an outdated architecture with a questionable suitability for the building's current use'.[21]

Indeed, that same year the bureau presented a new, commissioned design for the thirtieth anniversary of the Moroccan Annasr Mosque in Rotterdam. **(Figure 3)** According to a newspaper reporting on the celebration: 'In the words of Erkoçu, it is a liberal building that fits its surroundings. It will definitely not look like the Oriental-like mosque located at a short distance [the Mevlana Mosque]. The building appears transparent through the lavish use of glass, and that is exactly what the mosque board states it wants: transparency.'[22] Explicating his design on a professional-architectural website, Erkoçu stated that 'in the *zeitgeist* of the 21st century, architecture demands a mosque to have a modern and dynamic design. Important elements are not only its users, but also the urban context in which the building is placed'. Within the design, he incorporated 'the central Islamic principle of Dawa (invitation to Islam)'. In his account, the architecture was made open and accessible by, among other things, the lavish use of glass. This made sure that people would feel invited to visit the mosque from its surrounding streets and the opposite square. He explained that the entrance formed the central point of Dawa. This public zone between prayer space and outside world was intended to invite to a debate and to the creation of understanding between Muslims and non-Muslims.[23] In effect, with this design it was suggested that Islamic architecture in The Netherlands had finally entered the modern age, with a new generation of Dutch-born Muslims tolling the bell of physical and social integration and the end to the culture clash in architecture.

Even so, the flow of 'traditionalist' mosque applications in The Netherlands still seemed to proliferate. When the Essalaam Mosque, the Wester Mosque and the Taibah Mosque came to be associated in the media with international Islamic missionary organizations that were deemed to be fundamentalist,[24] the authors extended their earlier explanations of the resistance to progress that had been encountered. Besides the nostalgic search for identity among some Muslim patrons and the Orientalist tendency among some non-Muslim architects, there was also the paternalistic ideal of multiculturalism among some municipalities and the socially rejecting attitude among some mosque boards with foreign sponsors. In the introduction to a debate on the subject, organized by MemarDutch for the Netherlands Architecture Institute (NAi), they stated that '[...] the immigrants' culture manifests itself more prominently. This development is supported by the idea of multiculturalism, which supposes immigrants to integrate into society by maintaining their own cultural norms and values, stressing their "being different." This aim at cultural diversity seems to be strongly intertwined with a paternalistic tendency. It is often only superficially about the interest of "other" cultures, and more about social aspects as emancipation, integration and pacification of immigrants. The architectural framework of reference is determined by the experiences in the country of origin. This often results in buildings that radiate a medieval mosque idiom and, as such, are clearly recognizable but at the same time show a frightening lack of architectural quality and conceptual inventivity. They appear neither to refer to classical mosque architecture, nor to be able to give a new stimulus to the mosque typology. [...] At the same time, the static culture and closed spatiality of many mosques creates an appearance of hidden conspiracy, leading to distrust. The image of the mosque as a capsular space, with its own, non-transparent regime, severed from society, appears to be realistic in a number of cases and frightens many people.'[25] In effect, the authors implied that the use of pastiches of building styles from the original Muslim culture areas may be directly connected to a tendency towards social segregation in traditionalist Muslim communities. On the other hand, they implied the use of a contemporary Dutch building style – like the Annasr's – to be the ultimate proof of being a modern, liberal Muslim community.

This approach largely corresponds to – and has arguably been based on – a more general approach in some well-known international studies on the subject of modern mosque design. In an overview of contemporary mosques, Hasan-Uddin Khan found that 'in the past, regional architectures were substantially affected by local conditions – climate, available materials and technology – and tempered by cross-cultural exchanges of design ideas among builders and craftsmen brought together on a particular project by the patron or the ruler. With the progressive diffusion of cultures on a worldwide scale, it is no longer possible to build within what might be called a purely regional mode. [...] The vernacular, in which buildings are defined by a traditional indigenous language, and historicist models, that refer back to styles generally regarded as "classical" in Islam, [...] act as reminders of a glorious past and reinforce the ideas of community and traditional values in Islam. [...] A third trend is the reinterpretation of different models into some kind of cross-cultural manifestation. The borrowing of styles, methods of construction and decoration combined with a local model or one adopted from elsewhere [...] presents a self-conscious search [...] leading in most cases to eclecticism and in some to an interesting synthesis. The fourth category is of being modern, the overriding concerns being originality and dealing with the twentieth century. Design, image and technology point to a break with the past so as to portray the modern Muslim in a progressive light. This is the domain of the formally trained architect (in the Western sense) and the educated client'.[26]

Khan elaborated on these views in a publication with Renata Holod. In the eyes of the authors, mosque designs in the West are characterized by 'making references back to regional Islamic traditions, the external architectural form being influenced in most instances by a single dominant style from a particular country or region [...]; in this sense, the design may reflect the self-identity and aspirations of the group that takes the initiative in the project. [...] Many of the earliest examples were directly based on a historical Islamic model, a few were modernist in nature, and the later ones attempted to achieve some kind of synthesis between the two.' However, in their eyes 'the link with the past is not a real one, but a wilfully manufactured myth which has allowed for the realization of the new expression [...]. The insistence on the part of many clients on the inclusion of a dome has forced architects to undertake the design of a form which no longer lies at the center of design achievement, either formally or technically. The results have been mixed. [...] The ubiquitous images of Ottoman, Mamluk, Safavid or Mughal monuments now familiar from the popular media, the postcard, the travel poster and the printed page have played a crucial, though as yet unstudied, role in anchoring the idea of the dome in the popular nostalgia for the "authentic"'.[27] James Steele also firmly rejected such '[...] clichés of dome and minaret [...]. [As for the dome] all pretence of structural integrity [has] been forfeited for visual impact. Similarly, the minaret makes no pretence at being useable, existing for its symbolic value alone. This syndrome of relying on elements to convey legitimacy rather than intrinsic merit, or creative, spatial interpretation, is not restricted to insecure architects in the West whose tenuous grasp of history compels them to do so [...]. One important function of this particular study is to demonstrate to those responsible for mosque construction in areas which do not have an indigenous tradition to draw upon, that the problem is complex, but that the wide range of solutions need not include pastiche.'[28]

In a study of American mosques, Omar Khalidi found the latter ranged from 'traditional designs wholly transplanted from Islamic lands', via 'reinterpretations of tradition, sometimes combined with American architecture', to 'entirely innovative designs'. 'Mosques and Islamic centers that try to replicate the original mosques of the Islamic world lack both the qualities and materials of traditional architecture. The distorted expressions of many of these buildings, their garish colours, and use of prefabricated industrial materials all deny the authenticity of the old monuments they aspire to imitate. Their generally crude aesthetics is also related to the low esteem in which a professional architect is held among American Muslims. Since the cost of re-creating a monumental mosque is beyond the financial means of the community, the clients will settle for a rough replica that any architect can provide simply by referring to photographs. [...] The results are always imitative and unimaginative buildings passing for "authentic" Islamic architecture and they can be found in the United States from coast to coast. [...] Attachment to traditional design principles is, however, by and large restricted to first-generation immigrant Muslims. Their descendants and American converts, who will eventually constitute the majority of the Muslim population, will probably tip the scales in favour of more innovative architecture.'[29] In the meantime, Akel Ismail Kahera offered an explanation for the American patrons' apparent love of the past. 'When building a mosque, the diaspora community ascribes emotional value to the utilization of a well-known convention or an influencing custom from the Muslim world. [...] However, there are problems with the indiscriminate use of a well-known convention or an influencing custom. In attempting to replicate extant features from the past, the architect invariably produces a de facto facsimile whose aesthetics are severely compromised. [...] In the American mosque, image is appropriated in an anachronistic manner; it is used as a display of ornament without regard to time or context. Image is essentially concerned with satisfying an emotional condition that has historical efficacy for the immigrant Muslim community. The appropriation of a familiar image vividly evokes a mental picture or an apparition that closely resembles an extant form, object, or likeness emanating from the past.'[30]

In the context of Europe we see the same argument. Ihsan Limon recognized three kinds of Islamic immigrants exerting their influence on mosque design in the European diaspora. In his account, only a few had fully assimilated to the majority population, a small number had orientated itself to both the majority and the own group, and most had identified completely with their own ethnic origins and not at all with their new surroundings. However, none of their designs had used the 'pure-cultural ('*in Reinkultur*') mosque types' as shown in the literature on Islamic architectural history. From Limon's perspective, they generally looked like hybrid forms, consisting of European architecture mixed with building elements from the countries of origin. As the main aspects responsible for the backward attitude of Muslim mosque patrons towards mosque design, the author mentioned 'a weak sense of I and a strong sense of We; formalism, in which the form, the ceremonial and a false morality ('*Scheinmoral*') are the essentials; the imitation culture ('*Nachahmungskultur*') of the home countries, leading to the lack of a critical perspective, creativity and the courage for experimentation; folk culture, folk art and folk Islam; a lack of orientation, a tendency towards tradition and a crisis of identity, caused by the cultural erosion in the countries of origin and incoherence between the Superstructure (imported, confusing, western culture of the upper class) and the Substructure (traditional, eastern culture of the lower class), among the Turks expressed in the backward orientation towards the Ottomans; emotionalism; no capacity for open conversation and conflict avoidance, leading to speechlessness or actions behind the scenes; a mistrust of state institutions, interviewers, researchers, and all outsiders; the non-culture ('*Unkultur*') of religious, political and ethnic particularism; personality cult etc.'. Moreover, in his eyes the 'myth of returning' influenced mosque design in causing 'culturally determined' nostalgic reactions among the first generation, expressing the need for a sense of security. 'The nostalgic illusions express themselves subjectively as an overvalorization and even glorification of the historical and religious past, and at the same time as a negative evaluation of the diaspora surroundings. […] [As for] the architecture of mosques, this is expressed in stubbornly clinging to a number of traditional building elements (minaret, roofshapes, entrances etc.), in the interior decoration of the men's prayer room (mihrab, furniture etc.) and in the naming of mosques. [Furthermore,] since they have experienced discrimination, marginalization, spatial segregation etc. from the sides of politics and the majority population, […] religiosity as a defensive, compensating attitude has led to a higher demand for newly built prayer halls and has also influenced their architecture.'[31]

Nasser Rabbat chose to interpret the myriads of contemporary Islamic building elements from the viewpoint of post-colonial criticism. In his account, Islamic architecture was not the ahistorical phenomenon that Western Orientalists had once made of it in their hegemonic historiographies and quasi-Islamic buildings. As he saw it, the application of non-Islamic historical frameworks and periodizations 'has led to the disregard for the architecture's autonomous evolution, […] needlessly privileging the role of the patrons in the conception of architecture and its signification to the detriment of the designers and builders. […] No single model – or unique cultural reference for that matter – can be induced as the sole inspiration behind any of the famous examples of Islamic architecture. Different tensions were at work. The people and groups concerned seemed to have adopted, borrowed, resurrected and invented at every stage, and then reapplied the creative process to the next work. The buildings they constructed […] referred to multifarious cultures, traditions, ideals and images which their patrons, designers and builders considered suitable, representative, or desirable for themselves and for their cultures. […] Not only were divergences from a putative norm common, but the very idea of overarching conformism or an underlying essentialism do not seem to provide an adequate explanation for any of the bold and innovative buildings dotting the historical landscape across the Islamic world'. When moving on to *contemporary* Islamic architecture, however, the author notably changed his narrative from 'innovative' to 'static'. 'Some experiments seem to have led to nowhere, and were dropped either immediately or after a few trials. Others were felt to be more satisfactory and were adopted for longer stretches of time. And still others became cultural standards, used over and over again, some even surviving the "pre-Modern" periods to become iconic markers in the revival of "Islamic architecture" as a design category pursued by many practitioners today. The cases of the arch and dome as carriers of cultural meanings are such examples. Not only did they complete the transition into modern times with hardly a change in their significance, but their use has expanded to permeate all religious structures built by Muslims in the last century. […] the defamed Orientalist view that identifies Islamic architecture with sedate, static and supra-historical forms […] has been unfortunately and, possibly unwittingly, been resurrected by some of the contemporary essentialist theoreticians and practitioners looking for easily definable or loudly expressive architecture.'[32]

Following Rabbat's perspective, Nebahat Avcioglu saw the 'standstill' in American and European mosque design as a continuation, by Muslim minorities themselves, of Western-Orientalist modes of Islamic-architectural representation, originally set up to deny productive or creative hybridity to the subject. Starting her treatment of modern Islamic architecture with Orientalist buildings built to look like mosques, she then moved on to actual prayer halls by actual Muslim patrons. 'Despite the buildings' reliance on technology, materials, and skills, a certain essentialism about these mosques continues to hold the space of Islam (or for that matter Muslim cultures) as fixed and presents it as either unchangingly distinct from the "West" or identical everywhere in the "East". Even the most recently built mosques have failed to produce an alternative representation. [...] Indeed more and more purpose-built mosques in Europe and North America, mostly funded by the Wahhabi sect (Sunni fundamentalists from Saudi Arabia), do seem to strive towards a "seamless national [Muslim] identity" inspired and guided by the colonial sense that the dome and minaret were the undisputed signs, not only of Islamic cultures, but Islam itself. [...] Indeed when [...] the chairman of the Islamic Centre of Ocean County in the United States was asked to describe the project for a new mosque the first thing he declared was: "We will have a minaret" and "We will have a dome". [...] formal reductionism, transcending all questions of style, design, technology, culture, history, or modernity, has now become the orthodox principle of a singular Muslim identity. [...] Since the minaret and the dome were claimed as divine properties of a mosque, any rejection of them was seen in opposition to Islam. Indeed for most practicing Muslims, and particularly those living in the West, even the sheer idea of a mosque lacking a minaret and/or a dome has now come to present a challenge of an existential kind. [...] There is no one methodology for understanding the long catalogue of minarets from Manhattan to Ayvalik but it is clear that most contemporary mosques no longer involve the makings of "a place of worship and collective social activities", but rather [...] they are in the service of "a monument" symbolizing power as culture. The existence of a minaret in this case is a neutral, easily manageable, generic trope, neatly tidying so many different cultures, habits, climates, and traditions. Within such a context it becomes apparent that legitimizing narratives for building minarets are not simply based on religion or historicity, but on sheer appearances, taken at face value, constructing a social and political reality based purely on themselves. [...] alternative solutions, aesthetically creative and non-conformist mosques employing modernizing elements, with or indeed without domes or minarets, do exist. [...] Their forms are contemporary and modern; here I am using this adjective not as a European prerogative but as a shorthand for a set of tendencies betraying an autonomy that, both thematically and formally, presents an outward-looking cultural productivity. These mosques have none of the identity politics trappings; they are not conceived as religious signposts. [...] These mosques foster a sense of cultural context and artistic concentration, and can be seen as not only contesting the modes but also the dominant forms of representation.'[33]

Christian Welzbacher also accused Western mosque patrons of self-Orientalism. Following Avcioglu's approach, he too began his treatment of modern Islamic architecture with Orientalist buildings built to look like mosques, only then moving on to actual prayer halls by actual Muslim patrons. 'Muslim immigrants confirm European clichés, taking on the "foreigner" role of their own accord. [...] The dome and the minaret [...] thus become visible symbols of the opposite of integration.'[34] He found that most of the new European mosques, regardless of who built them and who paid, and despite the fact that some presented themselves as centers of 'European Islam', strictly avoided any independent development of the Muslim tradition. 'Across Europe, minarets are rising into the sky. All these buildings are the products of a traditionalist approach. They appear to reveal how much those responsible long for their home countries. In this way, the architecture of Euro-Islam becomes a symbol of the diaspora situation in which most European Muslims find themselves. They came as guest workers, live at the lower end of the social scale and have a minimal acquaintance with the language, culture and religion of their adoptive countries. This will only change with the Muslims of the third or fourth generation – and that, too, may have an impact on architecture.' Once, Welzbacher thought he had finally found the emergence of a form of Euro-Islam that was 'of its time, above suspicion, capable of overcoming the hostile cliché of the "foreign"', since the design for the 'Islamic Forum' in question showed a 'cubic volume, abstract details, [and a] playful development of traditional forms'. But then the patron, who had presented himself as a spokesman for an 'open' religion, seeking dialogue with non-Muslims as a way of bringing about the integration of a decidedly 'modern' Islam into Western society, appeared to be connected to a 'fundamentalist' organization and quickly fell out of grace among the authorities and the confused public. However, what baffled (*sic*) Welzbacher even more was that the traditionalist picture did not change when one travelled to those parts of Europe where Islam was the main religion or, for that matter, to Turkey. 'Tradition, repetition, imitation, even here in an Islamic motherland.' The prevalent model in Islamic countries *not* being modern, effectively invalidated the argument that architectural traditionalism in mosques was merely used as an expression of a Muslim cultural or religious identity in a culturally and religiously diverging society. The author therefore formulated the question 'Does the self-willed historicism that seems to hold Islamic religious architecture in its thrall lie in the religion itself?'[35]

Notably, whereas most studies of the material and immaterial expressions of contemporary Muslim communities in the West seem to concentrate on concrete community members and their leaders, the studies of their mosque designs as treated above seem to largely consist of a normative architectural *critique* of the objects involved. They critically evaluate the quality of the objects from the perspective of the author, they draw their factual information on design processes mainly from the perspective of the designer, and they generally attempt to devise some kind of chronological typology in which the objects find a meaningful place within an ongoing, unstoppable process of architectural progress. Whereas domes and minarets were seen as appropriate in their 'original' contexts, either as ahistorical categories or as dynamic signs of hybridity and innovation, they are now seen as hampering further Islamic-architectural evolution. It is as if Muslim mosque patrons in the West were somehow disconnected from history, or at least were to be studied within the framework of a completely different age or mindset in which they are steered solely by the emotional need for a recognizable Muslim identity in an estranging non-Muslim environment. Once they adapt to their new social contexts, their mosque designs are supposed to adapt to their new physical contexts.

What these studies generally seem to lack, however, is a fundamental basis of research among Muslim patrons themselves, as well as a genuine interest into the possible rationality behind their current architectural preferences. The only author who made a point of consistently and interestedly connecting diaspora mosque designs to particular examples from Islamic architectural history was Sabine Kraft in a study of German mosques. However, these connections were still largely based on the author's own architecture-historical associations and not of those of the patrons involved.[36] More often than not, studies of modern mosques in the West seem to regard patrons as a force to be countered or educated, driven by a lack of taste or historical knowledge and by the need for cheap, populist recognizability. Gulzar Haider, a well-known Pakistani-Canadian architect who designed several mosques in North America, wrote some articles on the relationship with his patrons. 'It is not easy to untangle the complex network of individual and collective memories of first-generation immigrants. Little wonder that whenever a Muslim bank or an airline publishes a calendar of mosques, their torn pages start to appear in the mosque committee meetings. I have also the unique honour of having received a childlike paste-up calendar made of cutouts collected by a member of the community who owns an auto-body repair shop.'[37] During design sessions with his clients, he said he sometimes felt 'like a volunteer nurse in a room full of Alzheimer's patients at various stages of their condition'.[38]

In fact, the architectural critical perspective as inherently used in these studies can only lead to seeing the overwhelming majority of contemporary Muslim mosque patrons, except for a few members of what has already been defined *a priori* as the avant garde, as backward. Paradoxically, the anti-Orientalist mode of representation as applied above, relegating the average Muslim mosque patron, both in the East and in the West, to the category of self-Orientalist nostalgia – without ever having thoroughly or even interestedly studied him or his architectural preferences – may be an extreme example of Orientalism. It essentially continues the Western evolutionary notion – 'colonial' if you will – of the 'universal' development of architecture towards a higher level. By claiming that Islamic architecture has (or *should* have) its own autonomous development, 'just like non-Islamic architecture', it wilfully inherits the Western methodological pitfall of normative architecture criticism posing as objective sociological analysis, defining all designs – and their producers – that incorporate supposedly dysfunctional elements as 'traditionalist', and those that do not incorporate such frivolous symbolism as 'advanced'. Inevitably, it steers analysts towards a gross disinterest in, and therefore systematic neglect of, the possible dynamics and intricacies within all contemporary domes and minarets. Furthermore, it leads them to keep uttering their surprise at the interminable 'pastiches' chosen by Muslim patrons, without ever rising to the challenge of understanding the latter as purposeful social agents. And, lastly, it stimulates researchers to keep creating fictitious schemes of development – from the traditional to the modern, from the East to the West, and from the local to the universal – based, not on any in-depth research of actual design processes, but on superficial surveys of rows of decontextualized images.

In contrast to this, I propose to stop studying the architectural history of mosques as a glorious premodern development, subsequently arrested by defamed Orientalists, and now waiting to be pushed forward by modernizing architects in the face of unwilling patrons. Why should there be a methodological discontinuity between studying premodern mosques and modern mosques, with the assumption that the diversified and hybrid combinations of domes and minarets of the past were 'creative innovations', whereas those of the present are 'impure pastiches' and 'romanticist revivals'? Why should there be a methodological continuity between studying architectural look-alikes by non-Islamic colonialists and the actual mosques by contemporary Muslim patrons, in the sense that they would have been subject to the same social mechanism? In fact, why should contemporary Muslim mosque patrons insisting on 'domes and minarets', in the West or the East, be any different from their historical counterparts, except in the minds of those with an evolutionary agenda? It is instead my contention that Orientalist buildings should be taken out of the mosque equation, and that Muslim-commissioned mosque design should be studied as a never-ending story ruled by the same social processes now as it ever has been in the past. To be sure, that does not mean that I deny Islamic architecture, as opposed to non-Islamic architecture, the capacity to evolve. It merely means that I deny that there is such a thing as architectural evolution in the first place. If we really want to understand why, in spite of all attempts by designers to propagate different types of mosques, most mosque patrons still cling to domes and minarets, we have to let go of the architectural critical approach and the artistic ideal and ideology of the modernizing designer that it embodies. It is time to stop projecting phases of architectural backwardness on unresearched Muslim communities, and to concentrate on developing a method with which we can analyze the role contemporary mosque designs were meant to play by their patrons themselves. To approach the latter as rational beings instead of Alzheimer's patients emotionally hanging on to airline calendars, it is important that we find an alternative way of thinking, one that does not make the usual assumptions about the history of Islamic architecture, and its unstoppable but hampered evolution.

An interesting basis for this alternative way of thinking can be found in the perspective developed by Yasser Tabbaa. Tabbaa firmly dismissed the interpretative value of extant positivist and regionalist studies that merely explained Islamic art as having developed smoothly within a predetermined set of religious prescriptions. In these studies, architectural forms had either evolved stylistically out of earlier forms, as if they were subject to some sort of a natural process, or as emanations of culture areas, as if everything were either 'Persian', 'Turkish' or 'Arabic'. Instead, Tabbaa found that 'Islamic art rather underwent fairly abrupt transformations that were largely prompted by internal or external challenges to the central Islamic polity or system of belief. These political and theological challenges elicited visual or architectural responses and reactions that were intended to buttress the system of belief or power, to embody a new concept, and to establish its difference against the challenging force. [...] Art, like cultures and religions, defines itself against its opponents, and the more intense the conflict, the sharper this self-image. In Islamic art this axiom has been successfully applied to conflicts between Byzantium and the early Muslims or between the Umayyads and Christians of Spain, since such interfaith conflicts were perceived as defining moments in Islamic history. Much less has been done, however, with the political upheavals and sectarian schisms that have divided Islam since early times, and the impact of these conflicts on the development of Islamic art has barely been touched. [...] Can we, by problematizing instead of glossing over ruptures, disjunctions, and discontinuities, arrive at a better understanding of the meaning of change in Islamic architecture?' For a case study, the author focused on the Sunni revival, 'the theological and political movement that sought to reaffirm traditionalist Islam and reject rationalist thought while declaring allegiance to the Abbasid caliphate and opposing all its enemies, in particular the [Shia] Fatimids'. For example, '[...] *muqarnas* vaulting, imported to Syria by Nūr al-Dīn and to North Africa by the Almoravids, reflected a symbolic allegiance to the Abbasid caliphate and embodied some facets of Ash'arī theology regarding the atomistic and occasionalistic nature of the universe. Importing this symbolic form from Baghdad to the revived Sunni world also reflected the renewed allegiance of these dynasties to the center of legitimization and the safeguard of orthodox Islam.' Consequently, the Shia Fatimid patrons in Egypt strongly opposed these architectural symbols of the Sunni revival, thereby contributing to their sectarian-religious significance.[39]

It appears that Tabbaa, through his innovative perspective on Islamic architectural transformation, offers a way out of the essentialist notion of periodical and cultural style development around some basic Islamic liturgical requirements, while still avoiding the pitfall of normative architectural criticism posing as objective sociological analysis. If, against extant art-historical beliefs, religious architecture in the Islamic world never simply 'adapted itself' to 'its time' or 'its region' but instead dynamically followed politico-religious alliances, there is no basis for the expectation that contemporary Dutch mosque design will simply adapt to its time or its region; there is no reason to be surprised at the empirical phenomenon that it does not; and there is certainly no need for the invention of all kinds of unresearched reasons why it does not. For Tabbaa's perspective to become applicable to a broader historical and geographical scope, we need only to broaden its paradigm.

Religious Construction, Mutual Contrasting and Reality Representation

In order to do so, we can learn much from anthropological studies that treat the built environment as an aspect of ethnic and cultural dynamics. A theoretical model particularly applicable to the study of religious buildings can be extracted from the works of Fredrik Barth, who has always been strongly opposed to the premise that cultural variation is discontinuous and that there are consistent ethnic groups who essentially share a common culture.[40] Much of Barth's fieldwork among different communities on several continents was aimed at the social organization of cultural differences and the creative construction of cosmologies, in which cult buildings occupied important space. He found that what is often presumed to be a coherently structured ethnic group with a coherent communal will and a coherent culture, is, in fact, a divergent whole of community leaders who continuously use 'the cultural stuff', including internally diverging sub-traditions as well as chosen sub-traditions from neighbouring cultures, in the production of social boundaries.[41] These 'sub-traditions' form diverging interpretations of, among other things, what superficially seemed to be a fixed cosmology with a fixed cult building representative of an ethnic group as a whole. One of the many consequences of Barth's findings is that researchers should not study the supposed architectural essence of a culture group's temples as proposed by random members, covering over the unavoidable internal architectural variations by generalization or tidying them away by a consistent typology. Instead, they should study the way that specific cult leaders continuously shift forms and connotations of diacritical temple features, divergently defining social boundaries by producing contesting constructions of the group's religious system. Internal cultural inconsistency is a ubiquitous feature, and it should be a major component of description rather than a difficulty to overcome: architectural variation within what is assumed to be a single culture group should emerge from analysis as a necessity. Further, the analyst should look at elements of the temple buildings of neighbouring culture groups, not as if they were either disconnected or simply borrowed, but as conscious transformations of each other: the whole of culture, including the built environment, is in a constant state of flux.[42] When we translate Barth's local analyses to the arena of mosque design in The Netherlands, the focus of attention should be the competing ways in which contesting community leaders within a seemingly consistent Muslim culture group architecturally substantiate their religious constructions through the strategic use of internally diverging 'cultural' building elements and the incorporation of selected external 'cultural' building elements. It should not be some supposedly shared and consistent religious building style which is said to be representative for the culture group as a whole. Instead of assigning certain Dutch mosques to the typological category of, for example, the Indian building style, we should study the divergent ways that individual Hindustani-Islamic community leaders imagine Islam to arise from their particular designs, playing out ever-present internal differences in Hindustani mosque architecture as well as incorporating specific building elements from what we may think of as other culture groups in whatever way they see fit.

Another approach that might help soften the myth of cultural consistency in architecture is discernable in the research program initiated by anthropologist Reimar Schefold, architect Gaudenz Domenig, and urban sociologist Peter Nas at a 1997 Leiden conference on the transformation of houses in Indonesia.[43] Schefold, Domenig and Nas propose a new vision of the built environment as a continuous re-interpretation of an architectural heritage whose origins are shared with related cultures. Whereas Barth's work mainly touched on transformations between immediately neighboring communities, Schefold, Domenig and Nas take the whole of insular Southeast Asia as a starting point. In their view, traditional houses and settlements in Indonesia are extremely varied and all have their own specific history, but in local analyses change and variation are often neglected. It seems to be common to discuss a single, particularly impressive house as if it were representative of the houses of a whole ethnic group. However, by disregarding other house types encountered in the same region, we get a biased picture which suggests that the type singled out has remained static through the centuries without undergoing any major changes, and that that same region does not show multiple diverging developments of that particular building tradition. In many cases, the variety of house forms will reflect successful attempts at distinguishing one community's buildings from neighboring ones in an enduring process of what could be called 'mutual contrasting', albeit by means of pseudo-traditions which have little to do with past indigeneous developments. Various and sometimes quite divergent interpretations result, which can initially confuse the anthropologist inquiring into the significance of a certain element.[44] In the case of Dutch mosques, the findings of Schefold, Domenig and Nas mean that we will have to search explicitly for changing and contested interpretations of what is presented as a fixed 'cultural' building style, and the way that diverging interpretations by different communities in a process of mutual contrasting can lead to diverging variations in what was formerly seen as a typifying architectural structure.

For example, what observers imagine to be a typically Indonesian mosque tradition and building style could be divergently vested with meaning by different Moluccan patrons for the sake of distinguishing their communities from each other, leading to diverging types in their minds, although to the observer there are many similarities in the formal characteristics of their respective buildings. Instead of abstracting or typologizing the latter once more into some singular, shared building style, we should take the opportunity to study the process through which Moluccan-Islamic architectural changes are produced.

Obviously, despite the apparent fluency of architectural 'traditions', changes and variations do not come about arbitrarily, and community leaders do seem to prefer looking for building elements to be transformed rather than inventing totally new ones. In his fieldwork, Barth expected to find that some kind of longer-term criteria of consistency did seem to operate within the great variety of sub-traditions, and he saw challenge in trying to ascertain its 'canons of coherence and persuasiveness'.[45] Similarly, Schefold, Domenig and Nas maintained that underlying the rich diversity in architectural traditions there still were fundamental correspondences 'rooted in the ancient heritage shared by all the peoples in a region'.[46] As an answer to this methodological problem of the complex relation between fluctuation and consistency, between the 'flux' and the 'fix' of architecture, between transformation and tradition, the Leiden architectural historian Aart Mekking moves from the local and regional to the global level and offers a possible theoretical explanation.[47]

In regard to the relation between tradition and innovation in the architecture of churches, Mekking found that in each case earlier building elements had been 'received' in order to be recognizably incorporated in the new building commission. Besides the figurative sculptures and paintings inside and outside a church, the forms of the building itself proved to have a symbolic meaning as well. A church was in fact a contemporary politico-religious statement cast in stone, as the older meanings of the received building elements in the new prayer hall had been replaced by meanings attached to them in later times. The large differences in character and completeness between the countless examples of reception of the one building in the other had nothing to do with a disinterested or flawed way of looking, but with the position of the patron and the function of the 'copy'. Sometimes whole buildings were copied, while at other times very specific parts of multiple buildings were incorporated, in order to come to a new meaning as desired by a patron. That way, church patrons strategically positioned themselves inside or outside the politico-religious system prevalent at their particular time and place. As a consequence, the existing tendency of researchers to iconologically analyze the sculptures and paintings of a church while merely explaining its forms as practically and aesthetically motivated, proved incorrect. Applying these findings to Dutch mosque design, we should not participate in the popular criticism of 'those domes and minarets' as if they would no longer have a material function in the Dutch context. The much-heard questions whether, in light of amplification technology, the call to prayer would 'still' necessitate a minaret or not, or whether, in light of the local climate and roof span technology, the prayer hall would 'still' necessitate a dome or not, are irrelevant to the explanation of a patron's motivations. The material function or dysfunction of building elements has not had – and will not have – a determining influence on the decision to incorporate or reject them, since they would never have had a purely non-symbolical purpose in the first place.

As an alternative methodology, Mekking establishes architecture as the materialization of a mental construction: to describe and explain it, he uses the concept of the built environment as a representation of reality. Apart from those aspects of building that are subject to physical laws, architecture is nothing more than a proposal to see reality in a certain way, using specific building elements related to the variables form, material and function. Although certain combinations of building elements and their meanings are often presented as traditions fixed in time and space, they are by definition subject to change because the representations themselves are intrinsically subjective, just as form, material and function are put to subjective use. Since with each new representation a new topical meaning is attached to certain elements, the visible characteristics of what is presented as an architectural tradition, and the content of its meaning, both, will each time differ from before. However, the meanings that were attached to these building elements by earlier builders and observers always play a role during the conceptualization of a new building since nothing is created *ex nihilo*. In this process, patrons always aim first at a certain experienced or mentally constructed reality, while only afterwards do their thoughts go out to finding suitable building elements from earlier representations with which this reality can be represented. This mental connection may, but does not have to be, an explicit or outspoken one. To Mekking, one of the most important characteristics of architecture as a representational medium is that it enables a patron to make a profound statement towards particular target groups without resorting to rationalization or verbalization. Either way, for an accurate description of a building and the explanation of its current meaning, it is vital to distinguish between the recently built proposal to see a certain reality, and the underlying ones: a building always represents a *present* reality by way of referring to *earlier* representations through a specific *transformation* of one or more of the latter's constituent elements as found suitable by the patron. When this is translated to the case of Dutch mosque design, we must be especially cautious of the view that mosques are expressions of the static building traditions that observers generally make of them. Whenever a design is described using terms like 'traditional Mogul', 'classical Ottoman', 'typically Moroccan', 'referring to Mamluk architecture' or 'based on a mosque in Dubai', there is bound to be a transformation that does not fit in such a singular scheme, possibly having been missed, pragmatically neglected, or even frowned upon by the observer as being the result of a bad copy or pastiche. In concluding that a certain 'traditional' building or set of buildings must have served as an example to be 'mimicked' or used as a 'source of inspiration', we must not be satisfied with a mere reference but must ask exactly *why* that particular building or set of buildings was chosen in the first place, and exactly *how* the transformation of *which* of its building elements was meant to create *which* meaning in a new context.

According to Mekking, the classic architecture-historical analysis and description of the built environment generally gives a false impression of uniformity and precision. Architecture is narrowed down to a factual account, supported by the formulation of a number of objective criteria for comparing 'a' and 'b' in the sense that they could be objectively placed within a single category or not. One complex of such objective criteria consists of 'style characteristics', basically a tool for the observer in establishing which building elements are 'of the same style' and which are not. They arose from the assumption that before their introduction in the 19th century as 'laws' for architectural design in the West, they would have been applied as building criteria anywhere in the world. From the 19th century onward, built representations of earlier realities in widely differing contexts came to be evaluated by architectural historians along the lines of the style idiom. However, the purpose and meaning of a building cannot possibly be explained by stylistic criteria if it was not conceived with them in the first place. Style concepts should not be used as objective criteria but should only be seen as possible building elements themselves, to be consciously interpreted and transformed in a new building. In consequence, there is no such thing as a 'Romanesque', a 'Renaissance' or a 'Modernism' unless it is thought of as such in constructing a new representation. Turning to the Dutch-Islamic context, when mosques are referred to using a style concept, for example 'Mamluk', this notion may have had no relevance whatsoever to patrons themselves. In that case, the style classification only serves to provide observers with a false grip on reality, basically preventing any further interest in the matter. On the other hand, when several mosques can be shown to have been consciously created with the notion of a style in mind, for example, 'Ottoman', we must also realize that the idea could very well have had completely diverging meanings leading to completely different results for individual patrons. If so, to classify them all as 'neo-Ottoman' would therefore also only lead to a false sense of having mastered the empirical complexity.

Mekking not only argues against the use of the concept of 'style' in current architectural history as if it were an objective means of analysis, but is also highly critical of the use of the notion of 'context', as if this too could provide a set of objective criteria for description. The basically accurate idea that the relation between building elements and meaning depends on the context in which this relation is placed during the conception of a building, has all too often led to contextual stereotypes. The reference to empty notions such as 'Western modernity', 'non-Western society', 'Swahili culture', 'the Islamic worldview', or 'Calvinist Holland', presented as objective and uncontested contexts of architecture that need no further interrogation, prevents proper analysis. The absoluteness of these general contexts, as if they were some kind of physical characteristic of the building, can frustrate any attempt to gain insight into possible and probable relations with buildings from other times and places. What we used to think of as separate building traditions from separate periods and cultures, were really the results of any building element, from any period or culture deemed suitable for transformation by a patron, being incorporated in the new representation with new meaning in a new context. As the specifics of the latter determined the choices for specific constellations of building elements, and thereby the meaning of the whole representation, geographical and historical generalization only obscures a view of the motives leading to these choices. Thus, in the case of mosque design in The Netherlands one should be wary of the tendency to 'explain' a Dutch mosque merely by placing its architectural characteristics in the context of a 'Hindustani region', 'Moluccan tradition', 'Ottoman period', 'Moroccan culture', 'Dutch modernity', or 'post-colonial Orientalism'. The conception of each building must be analyzed as a specific constellation of building elements in a specific context, and if patrons themselves claim to represent a wider notion such as 'Islam', 'Pakistan', 'The Netherlands', or even 'the Orient', the researcher should study their particular view, which is bound to have entailed very particular choices for very particular reasons.

In Mekking's approach, as an important side-effect of the unavoidable re-use of representations since nothing is created out of nothing, a limited number of basic representational themes keep cycling through time and space with appearance, disappearance and reappearance, cutting across assumed boundaries of geography and history. In consequence, architectural novelty is relative and there is no such thing as 'progress' in architecture. To Mekking, this absolute, much-used concept is intrinsically meaningless anyway since the basic non-existence of objective 'laws' means the non-existence of objective criteria with which we could measure such a development. The Western-invented idea of the 'evolution' of architecture from the 'traditional' to the 'modern' merely serves to glorify certain contemporary design preferences. The separation of 'structure' from 'decoration', or 'rationality' from 'symbolism', is no more than an art-historical idea, and a 'modern' building should be analyzed in exactly the same way as a 'traditional' building: all these concepts have no analytical value whatsoever but should be studied as representations in their own right. In relation to the architectural history of Dutch mosques, any suggestion as to the fact that Muslim patrons in The Netherlands have been moving from 'traditional' towards 'progressive' mosque types or the other way around, although presented as an objective architectural conclusion, is a representation of the reality of the observer and not an empirical reality.

Towards the Representational Analysis of Mosque Design

Assuming that contesting community leaders, in a process of mutual contrasting, can produce diverging constructions of a religion by consciously transforming self-chosen building elements, the analyst of mosque architecture should refrain from making any attempts at categorizing his empirical field into quasi-objective historical and geographical types. If he wishes to understand the reasons why Muslim patrons chose certain building elements, especially when combinations seem mixed up, confusing, cheap, fantasy, or fake, he should leave existing analytical concepts far behind and start studying the patrons and their rational constructions of their own realities. Architecture is but one of many ways of representing reality, and the consistent typologies so far devised for the study of Islamic architectural history say less about the realities of patrons than about those of the typologists involved. The whole idea of boundaries between the 'traditional' and 'modern' periods in Islamic architecture is a mere representation itself, since contesting Muslim community leaders have always produced internal divergences and outside similarities in processes of mutual contrasting, no matter the scale or nature of their group, or the context of their group against other groups. Thus, in the representational analysis of mosque design, there is no place for analytical concepts like 'traditionalist', 'historicist', 'pseudo', 'hybrid', 'eclectic', or even for 'the invention of tradition', since all of these presume previously existing categories that were really never that authentic, consistent, traditional, uncontested, or uninvented to begin with. Building elements from earlier contexts have always been selected, interpreted, transformed, twisted, and combined in whichever way a certain Muslim patron in a certain new context deemed suitable. There is even no point in analytically thinking of them as traditions undergoing some kind of process, as if they were still a tangible part of an objective empirical reality. Here, we will merely speak of building elements as recognized by a specific Muslim patron, possibly interpreted as a tradition by him but only in the way and for the particular reasons he required. The analyst should realize that all Muslim patrons meaningfully and by definition establish a pragmatic transformation of building elements to a new context, even if they claim to 'stand in an age-old tradition', but also that all Muslim patrons meaningfully and by definition make use of earlier representations, even if they claim to 'leave the past behind'.

More specifically, a concrete methodology can now be devised with which to analyze the relation between mosque designs and Muslim patrons in terms other than previously used periods and cultures, covering the architecture-historical transformations and politico-religious alliances as found by Tabbaa as well as those in a more contemporary context. It is my contention that, in order to understand the motivations of its Muslim patron, a Dutch-Islamic prayer hall should first and foremost be seen as the patron's subjective representation of a reality in religious terms, saying 'we are Muslims', before anything else. However, although the general ideal is that Islam itself is universal and that divergences in building elements in Dutch mosque designs should be regarded as stylistic variation and not as internal religious contestation, such a preconceived idea should not be used in representational analysis. Looking at Dutch mosque designs as if they would merely say 'we are Hindustani/ Moluccan/ Turkish/ Moroccan/ Dutch Muslims' does not bring us any closer to an understanding of the empirical complexities. As Barth already showed, internal variation within what seem to be consistent culture groups is ubiquitous and should form a major component of description, with different community leaders expressing their contesting religious constructions in transforming cult buildings. And as

Schefold, Domenig and Nas already showed, the architectural varieties within what we consider one consistent culture area reflect successful attempts at distinctions in an enduring process of mutual contrasting. Subsequently, in representational analysis a Dutch mosque design should not be seen to say 'we are Muslims with such-and-such a culture', as if it used fixed cultural characteristics, but to say 'we are Muslims with such-and-such a religious view', using selected and transformed cultural elements to express a specific construction of Islam in direct contestation of specific other constructions of Islam. To identify the latter we first have to gain an idea about any experienced or desired oppositions and alliances of a specifically religious nature that might have governed a particular patron's choices. In effect, we must not resort to the standard works on Islamic architecture but to non-architectural studies of Islam in The Netherlands, which already have convincingly shown that each of the supposedly consistent Dutch Muslim culture groups is divided into Islamic varieties strongly contesting each other on an explicitly religious level.[48]

Subsequently, the inclusion of specific building elements by the patron should be analyzed in the light of the construction of Islam he required to be represented. In this, he will have chosen those elements that in his perception were most suitable and strategic to recognizably define the religious boundaries with those contesting constructions of Islam that were deemed relevant by him. Meaningful choices may lie in spatial divisions, elevations, ground plans, decorations, construction techniques, measurements, colors, location, orientation, ritual, naming, financier's or designer's background, referring to categories of religion, period, culture, nation, ethnicity, style, spirituality, geometry, or aesthetics and to particular buildings from other times and places. All of these choices and references are based on contemporary associations which may, but do not necessarily have to be, explicit or outspoken. Moreover, they could, and probably would, deviate from any meanings as produced in the contexts of their original representations. Whether a current association is 'correct' or not in relation to the originating context or whether a transformation of a building element remains 'true' to its predecessor is, in representational analysis, an irrelevant question. In a very basic sense, all materialized building elements are mentally constructed fixes of an incoherent flux of architecture and therefore should never form a-priori research categories, despite the fact that we used to think of them as 'traditions'. To us, 'building traditions' only should exist as notions used in the conception of mosque designs to the degree in which the patron thought he recognized them, although he may present them as predetermined, fixed and generally applicable in order to legitimize his choices. All the while, what we imagined as consistent building traditions from separated Muslim culture areas and style periods would have been selected, combined, transformed and included in whichever way a patron required in representing a specific religious construction in a specific context.

Building elements that have explicitly *not* been included in the mosque under study may be extremely important as well. In representational analysis, in the constant process of religious construction, mutual contrasting, and reality representation, a newly proposed prayer hall is always a particular choice from among an incoherent array of building elements, and it therefore, by definition, always rejects those that are thought to trigger associations with the religious construction that is to be opposed. For the analyst to grasp the choices in a particular mosque design these rejected elements must be known. This means that the whole design process, instead of just the artificially isolated end-product, is an important entry into the representational motivations of our subjects. As a consequence, the sketch history of the design, especially including the sketches with building elements that did not make it or that replaced previous building elements, is to be reconstructed as much as possible before a conclusion is reached on the patron's representational motivations as they are expressed in the end-product. Although, of course, any oral explanations by the patron involved of the meaning of his mosque are important, we must realize that in representational analysis such explanations are themselves mere representations. By definition, they were made in a differently defined context and for a differently defined target group, for instance, the architect, the municipality, or the media as the mirroring categories who were supposed to see the mosque as the materialization of the ultimate Islam and not that of a contested version. The analyst will always have to make his own reconstruction of his subjects' representational motivations instead of taking their explanations, if available at all, for granted. As a consequence, in this study, a design's sketch history is seen as the most objective source of information, and sketches and reference images are treated as important research materials and not as mere illustrations of expressed experiences and opinions.

In line with the representational approach, the following chapters will not conform to any selection of objects on the basis of preconceived geographical or temporal style characteristics. Instead, they will cover Hindustani, Moluccan, Turkish and Moroccan Muslim patrons in The Netherlands, explicitly thinking of themselves as culture groups but in daily life highly disagreeing on whether and how to use the 'cultural stuff' in their specific constructions of Islam. Each of the four chapters will contain three case studies, specifically selected on the basis of their connections to the Islamic varieties that have been shown – in the previously mentioned non-architectural studies of Islam in The Netherlands – to contest each other within their self-defined culture groups. A short – largely unreferenced since later extensively explicated – description of the (planned) buildings' history and the ways they have been interpreted until now is followed by an introduction to the history of the varieties of Islam as they relate to the patrons involved. Because the latter can only respond to each other in time, the first mosque in The Netherlands as well as one of the latest has been selected from each self-defined culture group. Case studies will follow the design process from the first contact between Muslim patron and municipality or architect to the latest stage of design or construction. Statements made by patrons, architects and municipalities on their mosque in the media or, if they were available, during personal interviews, will be compared to a chronological treatment of archival materials – sketch proposals, photographic references, literature studies, meeting reports, building permit applications, neighbourhood objections, municipal discussions, professional evaluations, and construction adjustments, to the degree that they can shed any light on the outcome of the design in question. Importantly, these statements will be interpreted from the viewpoint of the representational approach. This means that I will form my own reconstructions of the realities and representational motivations of the patrons, architects and municipalities involved, using the design process as the most objective source of information. The intention is to explain empirical complexities which, with a mere typological analysis of the confusing field of objects or with a mere discourse analysis of the even more confusing verbal explanations of subjects, would remain fundamentally inexplicable. Finally, in the conclusion to this study the twelve separate case studies will be viewed in comparative perspective, with the intention of extrapolating general tendencies from recent architectural history that might shed some light on present expectations of future developments.

The chronological presentation of case studies will show that sketch negotiations between patrons, architects and municipalities can go on for several years due to mutual reality divergences and representational miscommunications, but also that Dutch constructional-bureaucratic procedures can have an enormous influence on the speed of design processes. Following a national law on spatial regulation (Wet op de Ruimtelijke Ordening or WRO), municipalities devise zoning plans that prescribe specific functions and measurements for specific municipal areas.[49] In a patron's application for a building permit, detailed drawings and functions of the proposed building must therefore be included. If the relevant municipal department of urban infrastructure decides that the application is up to a certain standard of technical quality, the application may be taken up for consideration. Next, the department will see if the urban delimitations (*'stedelijke randvoorwaarden'*) have been taken into account, consisting of detailed constructional rules and measurements for the requested spot as based by the department on situational particularities like sight lines and heights of adjacent buildings. If so, the case will be referred to the municipal sub-council for urban infrastructure, consisting of assigned and specialized political representatives from the general council. The sub-council then advises to the general council on the matter of the design's acceptability within the zoning plan. The general council must decide if it is necessary that the zoning plan be changed or that an exemption procedure (also known as the 'Article 19 WRO' procedure) be started by mayor and aldermen. If so, the latter have to make the mosque plan publicly accessible with the opportunity for inhabitants to file objections. When, after having considered the objections, the municipality decides to go through with the project, this decision must then be evaluated by the provincial authorities. If the latter decide to give the necessary 'statement of no objection', the municipality may, but does not need to, supply the applicants with a building permit. All the while, an important part is to be played by the municipal Aesthetics Commission (*'schoonheidscommissie'* or *'welstandscommissie'*), consisting mainly of experienced, municipally-appointed architects and architectural historians, in evaluating the appropriateness of proposed materials and forms. There is no objective standard for this evaluation and decisions basically depend on the opinions of individual members, their ability to reach a certain consensus, and their esteem for the applicants' architect. The municipality may, but does not need to, follow their advice, whether the latter was positive or negative. All in all, since at any particular stage of decision-making a certain amount of normative evaluation and interpretation is necessary, there are many instances in which a proposed building or parts of it can be delayed, quickened, approved, or rejected according to the objectified architectural preference of subjective individuals concerned. The following case studies will show that mosque design proposals can evoke completely deviating reactions among, but also within, municipal departments, councils and commissions, making it very difficult to predict the reception and speed of a particular plan even if there is an official municipal policy on the subject.

1. Hindustani-Commissioned Mosque Design in The Netherlands

The first purpose-built mosque in The Netherlands was opened in 1955 in The Hague by a Hindustani-Islamic missionary community from Pakistan. Initially, since their Mobarak Mosque supposedly did not incorporate any 'cultural' building elements from their home country, it was regarded as physically integrated into the Dutch environment, a genuine 'modern Dutch villa'. For years after it was not even recognized as a mosque, let alone the first one. Only when two turrets were added on the entrance portal, almost a decade later, was the building described as a 'Pakistani mosque' in Dutch newspapers. After an extension at the back of the building that was kept completely in style, a minaret was recently added that supposedly gave the mosque its final, distinctively 'Mogul' image. As the minaret was constructed with Dutch bricks similar to the main structure, it was thought a successful attempt at integrating two distinct 'cultural' building styles. However, when studied in-depth, a more explicitly religious construction arises from its design process. The 'modern Dutch' quality of the building appears to have grown more from persistent municipal control than from any cultural adaptation required by the patron, even if this was later claimed to be the case by the patron himself. Moreover, many of the particular building elements that were produced in the original 'modern Dutch villa', as well as in its later additions can, on close inspection, be linked to a certain building in the home area of the community that had a much more specific religious meaning to it than merely being Hindustani-Islamic.

In 1985, the second mosque around a Hindustani-Islamic missionary community was built in Amsterdam-Southeast. Although this community had mainly come from Surinam preceding its independence from The Netherlands in 1975, the community's Pakistani connections were maintained in The Netherlands as tightly as in the colony. The Taibah Mosque was the first to undergo professional architectural critiques. The design's characteristics were generally attributed to the architect, who was seen to have successfully combined traditional Islam with modern Dutchness, and who was under the impression that he had built the first real mosque in The Netherlands. This assumption was not so strange, since his patron would have fervently denied any Islamicness on the part of the Mobarak missionary community altogether. From the Taibah's design process, it appears that although the building was described as a modern Dutch transformation of both a generally-Islamic building tradition and a Hindustani-Islamic building style, it can actually be seen as a transformation of particular building elements as recognized by the patron in some very specific buildings within and outside the Hindustani culture area, and representing a construction of Islam fiercely contesting that produced in The Hague.

Following a change in community leadership, the Taibah building has recently been drastically enlarged as well as given an almost completely new design. Although most observers seem confused as to what exact style it is they are looking at, some have assumed that it represents the old Islamic culture even more than its predecessor through the increased usage of 'cultural' building elements and the abandonment of the 'modern Dutch' approach. However, when looking at the design process, this design included specific building elements as identified by the new patron in a specific building outside the Hindustani culture area even more than its predecessor. As such, it was meant to surpass its earlier representation in an ongoing competition with contesting constructions of Islam embraced by other Hindustani-Islamic community leaders. On a different scale, the resulting transformations of these building elements were explicitly imagined as modernizations for a Western audience by the patron himself. Whereas the complexity and the dynamics of these representational processes seemed to leave most writers on architecture in The Netherlands indifferent, calling all Hindustani patrons' mosque designs 'Mogul' – combined with the prefixes 'modern' or 'traditional' according to the taste of the author – the continuous production of internal religious opposition has been shaping Hindustani patrons' mosque designs in The Netherlands all along.

Varieties of Islam among Hindustani Communities

For the Islamic divergences within what many architecturally interested observers in The Netherlands still think of as a coherent Hindustani-Islamic culture group to become even remotely intelligible, this first description also has to be the longest. The story begins centuries ago in the northern part of the South Asian sub-continent. Here, amidst deep-layered beliefs in ancestral saints as mediators between the living and the gods, Sufi missionaries had spread Islam on the basis of their intimate connections with the divine for hundreds of years. Reverence for these Islamic holy men and the Holy Prophet Mohammed as their physical and spiritual ancestor and – in effect – the ultimate saint, was widespread throughout the Islamic parts of the sub-continent, and had been incorporated by Sultans and Mogul emperors alike as a tool of politico-religious control. Importantly, the northern part, also called Hindustan, had never been as strictly controlled as the more central areas, so local religious leaders, or Pirs, here had always retained a large amount of land-based political power around the medieval saintly tombs they inherited. With the slow decline of Mogul rule from the 18th century onward, these leaders had been able to enhance the legitimization of their religious power by moving from being Sufi teachers to living holy men themselves. Where before they had derived authority merely from the saintly shrines on their estates, now they were attributed, by virtue of their ancestors and ultimately of the Holy Prophet himself, special powers of their own.[1]

However, things started to change with the abolishment by the British in the 19th century of what was left of the Mogul empire. In reaction to the subsequent politico-religious void, a number of Islamic revitalization movements sprung up which contested the religious traditions and political powers of the Sufi Pirs. Rival leaders of the Deobandi School aimed at reforming the saintly cults into a more purist Islam, partly grounded on Sufism but doing away with what they saw as the idolatrous worship of Mohammed, living holy men, and saintly shrines at famous mausoleum-mosques. As a later Deobandi Mufti explained about the role of the mosque in Islam: 'Three mosques, the Masjid-al-Haram [at Makkah], the Prophet's mosque at Madinah and the Masjid-al-Aqsa at Jerusalem have an exalted position in view of their […] religious sanctity. No other mosque has such an exalted position. […] a journey especially to visit any other mosque in the belief that one would earn a special reward (any more than his attendance at the local mosque) is not permitted. […] During the days of ignorance people used to undertake pilgrimage to places which they, in their blind faith, considered holy. This led to distortion of the faith and people started worshipping others than the one God. The holy Prophet plugged the sources of such a distortion so that such excursions do not serve as a step towards the worship of any other than the one God. […] [One] should not have a false notion that

[...] a visit to the Shrine at Ajmer would get him as much reward as a Haj pilgrimage.'[2]

The traditional leaders reacted in defence, especially Ahmad Reza Khan (1856-1921) who created a strong current with his Brelwi School, named after his hometown Bareilly, now in Uttar Pradesh. His teachings centered on Mohammed as the most important figure and source of Islam, a mediator between Muslim and God, and the ever-existing Light, or Nur, that lit the dark world of unbelief. This 'Nur of Mohammed' was derived from God's own light, and had actually existed from the beginning of creation. Mohammed's Nur had been sent down to earth through all prophets from Adam onward, culminating in Mohammed himself as their Seal. The very world had been created for the Prophet, and designed for his glory. In short, Mohammed was revitalized as the ultimate saint, and his birthday and heavenly ascension as the most important Islamic celebrations. Later saints derived their sanctity from him and the annual celebrations of their deaths, or Urs, were stressed. Just as Mohammed, they had a corporeal presence in their tombs and could actually hear the prayers of believers.[3] As a later Brelwi imam said in a Dutch publication, aimed against the purists: 'The Prophet and the Saints may always be honoured, even after their deaths. When Prophets leave the earthly domain, their miracles are not over, and when the Saints leave us, their wondrous acts are not over either. The hadith clearly states that [they] live in their sacred resting places. [...] [They] say that it is Kufr (unbelief) and Shirk (polytheism) when one builds a dome over the grave of a saint, burns oil lamps for those who worship and serve in mausoleums, and pledges donations for the souls of the dead. [...] [But in fact] No Islamic learned man has ever said that it was polytheism or unbelief to build a dome or a mausoleum, or to visit a mausoleum.'[4] Moreover, the living Pirs were confirmed in their physical and spiritual descent from the saints, and in their right to control their estates and the saintly shrines thereon. They were believed to be able to mediate between saints and followers and to have special spiritual powers, while their images were highly revered. The Sayyids especially, the claimed physical descendants of Mohammed, were given much respect.[5] Both Deobandi and Brelwi leaders call themselves leaders, not of sects, but of the mainstream Muslims, while each call their opponents a party of unbelievers. Members of the Brelwi School actually use the title Ahl-I Sunnat Wa Jama'at, a classical name for the Sunni community in general, for themselves, while they consistently use the title Wahhabi for any purist opponents.[6]

The nominal stress on the 'Sunni' character of the Brelwi School was also used in opposition to another religious community that had sprung up in the region in reaction to the British having stirred up the status quo. The community was created by Ghulam Ahmad (ca.1835-1908) from Qadian, Punjab, who claimed to have been sent by God as a Saviour to restore Islam to its original purity. He regarded the actual worship of saints and saintly tombs to be a corruption that had opened up Islam to encroaching Christian and Hindu tendencies, and required that the first vow to be made by any Muslim be that he abstain from Shirk.[7] As Ahmad's successors would state in their descriptions of a 'typical' mosque: '[...] No god except God is permitted to be worshipped in a mosque. [...] Hence the idols and images which some people worship are not allowed to be brought into the mosque [...]. There are no statues, pictures, memorial tablets or relics of saints. The services are free from all artistic and emotional distractions. There is no music or singing and no lighting of candles, [and] no [...] incense.'[8] This choice of words was no coincidence, since saintly images, memorial tablets, relics, incense burning, candle lighting and devotional singing were all fairly standard elements of saintly mausoleum-mosques in the region. Nevertheless, Ahmad's own religious thought itself was also firmly vested in medieval Hindustani ideas.[9] In his teachings, he made much use of Sufi notions of the divine light descending from God to believers on earth.[10] Ahmad proclaimed himself to be the Promised Messiah, or Masih, after Jesus. Jesus did not reside in heaven, waiting to return at the End of Days, but had been taken from the cross alive, ending up in Srinagar, Kashmir, where his tomb was located. Ahmad also claimed to be a reformer of Hinduism. But, most importantly, Ahmad claimed to be the next Prophet or Mahdi after Mohammed, presenting himself as the spreader of God's Light on earth. Since Mohammed was seen as the Seal of the Prophets by the reformists and as the all-transcending saint by the Brelwi Pirs, Ahmad's claims evoked strong reactions by all contemporary Islamic communities. However, he managed to assemble a small group of adherents and the Ahmadiyya movement came to life when, in March 1889, his followers pledged allegiance to him in the city of Ludhyana. Importantly, by claiming not to be a mere religious leader, with or without divine-ancestral powers, but the next Prophet and effectively the only Muslim holy man, Ahmad essentially eliminated the very basis for existing leadership in the region. In this light, the fanatic fervour with which both Deobandi and Brelwi have since fought the community is not surprising.

In 1876, Ahmad's father had built a white mosque in Qadian with the Mogul characteristics of triple domes and a forecourt, in his struggle to reclaim the landbased authority that he traced to an aristocratic kinship with the old Mogul emperors.[11] Although Ahmad held a divinely inspired sermon in this Al Aqsa Mosque, and although it would eventually come to be seen as one of several blessed buildings and important Ahmadiyya design examples, at that time Ahmad explicitly presented himself as less power-driven and materialistic than his father. Therefore, immediately after having been commissioned by God in 1882 to be the Reformer of the age, Ahmad decided to commission his own prayer house. As the Ahmadiyya story goes: 'The very first task he addressed was the building of a mosque like his Master, the Holy Prophet Muhammad. Under the Divine Command of God, around 1883, he laid the foundation stone of the Mubarak Mosque in Qadian, India. Upon laying the historic foundation of this Mosque, he received several revelations. One of these revelations was as follows: [...] "Both blessor and blessed is this mosque, and everything blessed takes place in it." Remarkably, when the numerical value assigned to each of the [Arabic] letters present in the revelation is considered into a total figure, the number attained is 1300. The Mubarak Mosque was completed, in the Islamic Calendar, on the 26th day of Shawwal in the year 1300.'[12] So it appears that Ahmad wished to represent his claim to be the next purifying Prophet after Mohammed also in architecture. Notably, whereas most Pirs' communities centered on the domed shrines of their ancestors, the new Prophet's structure never included either dome or shrine. Although the white building appears to have been renovated and added to several times, and although it no longer forms a clear, free-standing structure, it seems to have originally incorporated a simple protruding entrance portal with turrets and rising canopy, flanking wings, corner turrets and crenellation. **(Figure 4)** Indeed, Ahmad specifically meant his new mosque to be the starting point for the spread of a purified, true Islam around the world, literally, 'laying the foundation stone of Islam's Renaissance and a superior world order'.[13]

Ahmad made heavy use of the notion of the divine light that was to light the dark world around him. As he declared at the creation of his Movement in 1889: 'The community shall be a lighthouse so high as to illuminate the four corners of the world. The members thereof shall serve as models of Islamic blessings.'[14] In 1891, he elaborated on his intentions to spread the light to Europe and America. 'The rising of the sun from the West means that Western countries, which have for centuries been in the darkness of unbelief and error, shall be illumined by the sun of righteousness, and shall share in the blessings of Islam.'[15] That his community saw their Founder as the source of this blessed light is envisioned in their representation of a rising sun with Ahmad's statement 'I am the light of this dark century'.[16] In the Dutch mission a photo-collage on Qadian describes events: 'The land of Qadian is a sacred land and one which Allah has chosen to be the center from which Islam would spread all over the world and prevail over all other religions. Indeed, it was upon this town that all heavenly light and blessings were focused on Friday, 13 February 1835, when the founder of the Ahmadiyya Movement, the Promised Messiah and Mahdi, Hazrat Mirza Ghulam Ahmad was born; and again it is this sacred soil of Qadian which is the last resting place of the great spiritual son of the Holy Prophet Muhammad.' Moreover, Ahmad also materially substantiated this representation of Divine Light in his plans for the construction of a white minaret in Qadian, specifically meant as a lighthouse. This 'Minaret of the Messiah' would literally and spiritually, according to Ahmad, fulfill a prophesy by Mohammed saying that 'the Promised Messiah will descend by the White Minaret to the east of Damascus'. Although Ahmad interpreted this tradition symbolically, meaning that 'the Promised Messiah will come when there will be light throughout the world and distance cannot keep things hidden from view', and that 'the truth of Islam will tower up like a minaret and attain a height which will establish its superiority over all other faiths',[17] the photo-collage in the Dutch mission states about his minaret that 'it was also his practice to fulfill every prophesy in its literal form as well'. After colonial authorities put aside the objections by the mainly Hindu inhabitants, the foundation stone was laid on Friday 13 March 1903. However, due to lack of finances, the minaret itself could not be built in Ahmad's lifetime.

Ahmad died in May 1908. Nur al-Din, an erstwhile follower, was appointed by the elders of the movement as his successor or Caliph al-Masih. Under Nur al-Din, missionary activities were expanded to other countries, which resulted in conversions in Southern India, Bengal, Afghanistan and England. For his installment in 1910, he laid the foundation stone for the third most important Ahmadiyya mosque in Qadian, the white Noor Mosque or *Mosque of the Light*. **(Figure 5)** Nur al-Din clearly wanted to place himself in the divine tradition of his forebearers. His mosque appeared as a transformation of the main façade features of the Promised Messiah's Mubarak, combined with those of the Al Aqsa, into a consistent structure with a canopy with turrets over the main entrance and corner turrets at each end of the main façade.

When Nur al-Din died in March 1914, however, the movement's latent conflicts in leadership as well as religious doctrine came to the fore. As soon as Ahmad's son, Mahmud Ahmad, was elected leader, another faction was created under Muhammad Ali. The first group called itself the Qadiani, after their headquarters and birthplace of the Founder, while the second based itself in Lahore and was named after their new headquarters. In Muhammad Ali's Lahori version, Ahmad was a spiritually gifted reformer, a Messiah indeed, but not a Prophet in Mohammed's unique sense. While in Qadian his claims to Prophethood were stressed, in Lahore his statements suggesting the contrary were regarded as more important. The Lahore movement was much more decentralized into regional departments, with headquarters only having a worldly, coordinating role.[18] Mohammed was restored to his original significance as the Seal of the Prophets, and spiritual leaders did show much reverence for Ahmad but now merely as the latest in a line of God-sent saviours like Al-Ghazali, Abdul Qadir Jilani and Moin-ud-Din Chishti.[19] Although many of these Sufi saviours – as well as their tombs – were revered among the Brelwi communities in the Hindustani region as well, the Lahore-Ahmadi had a difficult time pressing their case and refuting any associations with the perceived Qadiani blasphemy. In fact, most non-Ahmadiyya Muslims do not seem to make any distinctions between the two schools whatsoever.

In Mahmud Ahmad's Qadiani version, however, the figure of the Founder and his birthplace, including its architecture, came to be seen as central and all-important, and he and his successors retained the title of Caliph al-Masih or Successor to the Messiah. In the Qadiani organization, the Caliph represented the highest power, with followers pledging obedience to him as they had done in the founding days to Ahmad. Mahmud Ahmad himself claimed that he had become Caliph not only because he was chosen but also as a result of divine appointment.[20] Moreover, between 1914 and 1916, he constructed the Minaret of the Messiah for which his father had laid the foundation stone. Bright lights were fixed to the top 'to dispel darkness and to show that the age of heavenly light and spiritual advancement has arrived'.[21] Note that the upper lights were pointed *away* from the minaret, lighting its surroundings and thereby materializing its Lighthouse representation in opposition to the rather common use of lights brightening a minaret itself. The minaret with its rays of light was depicted on the Ahmadiyya flag and all the movement's major publications. **(Figure 6)**

Mahmud Ahmad himself was elected for life, and his approval was necessary for any new plan of action. In January 1944, he enhanced his already quite powerful political status by the religious claim to be the one and only Promised Reformer whose birth had been predicted by the movement's Founder.[22] After the partition of British-India in 1947, and the ensuing formal split of the Punjab into Muslim and Hindu sections, the headquarters was forced to move from the now-Indian Qadian, first to the now-Pakistani

Lahore, but soon after, in August 1948, to the specially built town of Rabwah, whose name was meant to provoke an association with the hill where Jesus was given refuge by Allah according to the Koran. Only a few members of the movement remained in Qadian to preserve the historical monuments of the town and maintain it as a religious center for Hindustani followers.[23] Although the Founder's birthplace was to remain an important religious reference point, regularly visited by the spreading missionaries in fulfilling Ahmad's vision of a world-wide Islamic Renaissance starting from Qadian, it was mainly in Rabwah that they received their education and instructions. In fact, it was effectively with Mahmud's move from Qadian to Rabwah that the Qadiani-Ahmadiyya movement, as opposed to the Brelwi and Lahori competitors, came to be forcefully and consistently represented in architecture. Consecutive Ahmadiyya mosques in Rabwah all clearly incorporated the main building elements from the Noor Mosque in Qadian, which itself had formed a more consistent transformation of the Qadiani Mubarak and Al Aqsa. When the missionaries then spreading out into the rest of the world to preach the Ahmadiyya Islamic message, many – though not all – of them took the diacritical features of this ultimate Qadiani representation with them.[24] Some made combinations with the Minaret of the Messiah for an even more recognizably Qadiani result, with 'the first mosque in Spain since 500 years', the Basharat Mosque in Pedro Abad (Cordoba), as an extremely obvious example.[25] **(Figure 7)**

However, next to the Punjab as a direct supplier of Hindustani Muslims to The Netherlands, an indirect source was Surinam, a Dutch plantation colony in South-America where slavery had been abolished in 1863. Since many of the former slaves, mainly from West Africa, did not wish to remain as workers on the plantations, colonial authorities had to search for other employees. In 1872 a treaty was reached with Great-Britain to hire workers from British India.[26] The main region of acquisition was what is now Uttar Pradesh, where problems of housing and food formed strong push factors, besides motives of escaping the caste-system, family-problems, and adventure. Among the Hindustani immigrants, Muslims formed a percentage of 17.5. The first years consisted of hard work and harsh circumstances, but after the first 5-year contracts had ended, in 1895, the authorities induced workers to stay by creating special educational facilities and possibilities for ownership of land. The Hindustani remained a closed community within the socio-cultural hierarchy in colonial Surinam, but managed to acquire a certain position mainly by agricultural activities. Between 1873 and 1916 a total of 35.000 Hindustani came to Surinam, of whom 11.000 eventually returned to British-India. Between 1916 and 1940, also called the 'period of establishment', the Hindustani community raised its level of existence by investing in agriculture, the small crafts industry, and in the transport and distribution sector. In the end, they became part of middle class colonial society.[27]

In 1929, a number of Hindustani-Islamic communities combined forces and instituted the Surinaamse Islamitische Vereniging or SIV. However, with the shipments of Hindustani Muslims to Surinam, the basic divisions along the lines of Ahmadiyya and Sunni religious organization were not left behind. Whereas in the literature these first shipments of workers are sometimes categorized as 'uneducated' and 'therefore' almost ignorant of Islamic norms and values with only later influences from Pakistani teachers stirring up internal animosity from the 1960s,[28] this seems to be something of a simplification. Even in the process of 'establishment' they were split up into factions around existing Hindustani-Islamic differences.[29] Soon after the institution of the SIV the organization became linked to the Lahore-Ahmadiyya movement, leading to the foundation of three rivalling, anti-Ahmadiyya groups in the 1930s.[30] In 1950 these groups were united in the fervently anti-Ahmadiyya SMA, Surinaamse Moslim Associatie, or Ahle Sunnat Wal Jamaat. Not coincidentally, this particularly 'Sunni' denomination was also the one chosen by the Brelwi School as mentioned earlier. In fact, it was a Brelwi missionary Pir who had convinced them to unite, Maulana Mohammed Abdul Aleem Siddiqui.

Aleem was a member of a well-known Sufi-clan from Meerut, now in Uttar Pradesh, who moved to Pakistan after the division of British-India. He traced himself directly to Abu Bakr, whom he represented as the Prophet's most beloved Companion and purest of his successors, having provided the plot for the Prophet's Mosque in Medina and his later resting place. In fact, the Siddiquis claim the right to control this holy place of Islam and contest Saudi custodianship. They base themselves firmly on the writings of Ahmad Reza Khan, who fought those who tried 'to turn off the light of love for the Holy Prophet'.[31] In the Taibah community's representation, the story is more or less told as follows. 'In 1892 Muhammad Abdul Aleem Siddiqui was born in Meerut. At that moment, Maulana Sajjad Jamaluddin Al Afghani, a direct descendant of the Prophet himself, died. It was as if the successor had now come. Aleem's father was a great Sufi of the Qadriyyah Order, and so he became. He announced himself to the greatest Islamic teacher of that time, Ahmad Reza Khan in Brelwi (sic), who became his mentor. After having visited Mecca and Medina in 1919, the presence of the Prophet gave him the inspiration to start with his worldwide mission. He brought spiritual light to the hearts of thousands, and was loved for the divine light that manifested itself in his person. He fought for the independence of Pakistan and moved to Karachi with his family in 1949. In 1950 he visited Surinam, where Muslims were harassed by Ahmadi, who were supported by the colonial government. The Maulana inspired the Muslims to assemble and create a Sunni association, the SMA, resulting in the later construction of the first authentic Islamic House of God, at the Kankantriestraat. In 1954 the Maulana died and was buried near Aisha in Medina.'[32]

In the Taibah community's representation, the story of Noorani Siddiqui, Aleem's son-successor, is told more or less as follows. 'He was born in 1926 in Meerut and received from his grandfather and father the spiritual leadership of the Qadiriyyah, Naqshbandiyyah and Chistiyyah Sufi Orders. From his father, he also received the Caliphate of Ala Hazrat Ahmad Reza Khan. When the Pakistani Muslim League did not rise against the Ahmadi, Noorani created his own Sunni political party, the Jamiat Ulema-e-Pakistan (JUP). He called his political ideology Nizam-e-Moestafa, as in the example of his beloved Prophet "Mohammad Moestafa Sallallaahoe alaihi wa Sallam". He arranged for the constitution of Pakistan to be set up as an Islamic Republic, and had the Ahmadi declared non-Muslims. Noorani followed in his father's missionary footsteps and went to those areas where Ahmadi were supported by colonial governments to weaken the power of true Islam. The debates of Noorani with Ahmadi brought back the light in many houses of misled people who returned to Islam. In 1964 he started visiting Surinam.'[33] Here, Noorani was confronted with the fact that after his father's death some of the Brelwi member communities of the SMA had begun leaving the organization again.[34]

Noorani then aimed at countering Ahmadiyya missionary activities in the world by co-founding the World Islamic Mission or WIM in 1972/3 during a Hajj to Mecca.[35] After he had induced the Pakistani government to declare the Ahmadiyya heretics by a parliamentary resolution in 1974,[36] animosity among Hindustani Muslims in Surinam rose even higher. When Surinam was to become independent from The Netherlands, the SMA briefly tried to have the new constitution declare the Ahmadi as non-Muslims. Just as his father had managed to unite the competing Brelwi communities in Surinam in organizing the struggle against a common enemy, Noorani attempted to get them back together again in much the same way, emphasizing the religious differences between the Brelwi and Lahori visions even more. Although both groups strongly focused their Islam on Sufi saviours, with the Lahori effectively presenting their Promised Messiah Ahmad as merely the latest and greatest in a series of reforming mediators between Muslims and God, the prominent role they bestowed on their Messiah was still firmly rejected by Noorani. Consequently, Mohammed himself, as Light of God and Seal of the Prophets, gradually became more important in the production of a recognizably Brelwi construction of Islam in the face of the Ahmadiyya contestants. Whereas the SMA mosque that was built after Aleem's death still used the onion-shaped domes and ringed turrets that many mosques and Muslim graveyards in Surinam incorporated, whether Lahori or Brelwi, its successor explicitly used building elements as identified in the Prophet's holy places by a new community leader under Noorani's guidance. Later, that same leader came to have a profound architectural influence in The Netherlands in much the same way. However, the first Hindustani Muslims to actually build a mosque in The Netherlands were Qadiani-Ahmadi, directly come from the Hindustani region itself, so it is to them and their prayer hall that we first have to turn our attention.

The Mobarak Mosque, The Hague

Under the leadership of Ahmad's son, Mahmud Ahmad, which lasted for more than 50 years, the Ahmadiyya movement's missionary activities were expanded almost world-wide. He had been sending missionaries to the Netherlands for lectures and discussions on Islam, beginning in 1924, and in 1947 a stationary missionary post was established in The Hague. It was continuously manned by a head missionary and one or more assistants who gave lectures with the aim of banishing misunderstandings about Islam and propagating the Qadiani beliefs. Next, a monthly magazine, Al-Islam, appeared in 1948, and in 1954 the Koran was translated into Dutch. Ahmad's successor also stressed the importance of constructing missionary posts and mosques around the world. Thus, it is no surprise that, already in February 1950, 3 years after the arrival of The Netherlands' first Ahmadiyya head-missionary Qudrat-Ullah Hafiz, reports of a future mosque in The Hague started appearing in local newspapers. Apparently, a municipal council member, Schuermann, pressing for post-war reconstruction of destroyed parts of The Hague, had complained about the insufficient width of the sidewalk at the entrance of Oostduin Park during discussion of the budget of the department of Reconstruction and Urban Development.[37] Alderman of Reconstruction Feber's answer, according to the official 'Handelingen' of the Municipal Council, was that a house would arise on that particular location, which the council member was sure to appreciate[38] – although one newspaper reported the alderman to have said that it would *astonish* the council member.[39] A few days later, the press started reporting on negotiations between the municipality and the Ahmadiyya mission on the construction of a mosque, and its possible location on the Oostduinlaan.[40] And indeed, four months after that, Hafiz officially announced to the press that a piece of land on the Oostduinlaan had been bought, and that the first mosque in the country was soon to be built under supervision of Mahmud Ahmad, the movement's leader in Pakistan. It was also announced that the construction would be financed by the women of the movement worldwide, and was intended to form a connection of enduring and deep friendship between The Netherlands and all the Muslim countries in the world.[41] The press generally covered this announcement under the headline 'First Mosque in The Netherlands', with a short introduction to the Ahmadiyya mission, its headquarters and its history.[42] Sometime afterwards, reports appeared that the plans of the mosque had been finished and that '100.000 guilders' had been collected.[43]

An interview on the subject with Hafiz was published by several newspapers. Hafiz stated that the first mosque in The Netherlands would rise as soon as Rabwah headquarters and the municipality had accepted the plans designed by 'the The Hague architect Z. de Lyon'. An 800 square meters plot of land had been bought from a private property-owner,[44] and the building was to cost 100.000 guilders. With that amount, 'a sparkling white mosque' would be built, to hold 200 people, with a meeting-room holding another 200.[45] However, De Lyon appeared to be a follower with technical experience but not an actual architect under Dutch law. Unfortunately, this first sketch seems to have been lost, but in the following weeks, while the land was plotted out, several somewhat vague newspaper reports appeared on the mosque's lay-out. It would have two levels containing the actual prayer-room, a lecture room and living quarters for the missionary and his family, and it would be adorned with 'some small minarets' and 'a modest central dome'. A design was on its way to headquarters in Rabwah, where the leader would have to give his permission for the 100.000 guilders to be spent on the proposed construction.[46] However, this press statement seemed a bit early, apparently caused by the early mission's understandable unfamiliarity with the difficult Dutch building procedures and – not unimportantly – with the relatively high costs of design, materials and construction in The Netherlands. Moreover, when the original estate had sold its land in pieces, the properties themselves had been vested with the obligation to build nothing else on it than 'a villa', thereby keeping the neighborhood exclusive and the prices high. Each successive owner was bound by this obligation. However, Hafiz' lawyers subsequently arranged for the mosque to be exempted from this obligation by the estate owners' successor.[47]

Nevertheless, in that particular area the zoning plan stated that the edge of this – high-status – park was only to be built on by half-open housing – in essence, expensive, free-standing constructions or villas. This was clearly stated in the buyer's contract,[48] but perhaps the mission did not fully realize that any exception would be hard won. In addition, all kinds of strict, detailed construction rules applied, like the non-allowance of flat roofs, the minimum distance to adjacent streets and houses, and the allowance for trees and shrubs. The mission needed a local specialist, and new head-missionary Bashir, apparently the main patron in this phase of the mosque design process, decided to go to the The Hague architect J.G. Wiebenga. Now Wiebenga was not just any architect, having designed many buildings in what was seen as the modern-Dutch style of New Construction, in which he had played such an important role that he had even come to be renowned as the 'Apostle of New Construction'.[49] The fact that Bashir hired a famous architect means, assuming this had not been a municipal condition, that the community leader wished to present the first mosque in The Netherlands as a major architectural event, although that does not necessarily mean, as we will see, that he wanted to conform to any preconceived idea of 'modern Dutchness'.

On 7 October 1951, he presented Wiebenga with his formal requirements, to be translated into a crudely drawn sketch.[50] **(Figure 8)** The building elements produced in this sketch were clearly taken from both the Founder's and his successor's mosques in Qadian, just as had been done in the case of consecutive mosques in Rabwah. As shown earlier, Ahmad's Mubarak Mosque and Nur al-Din's Noor Mosque would provide strong diacritical features for many Qadiani-Ahmadiyya missionaries spreading over the globe from Rabwah, in order to materialize a recognizable architectural representation of their view of Islam. In light of earlier references to the 'sparkling whiteness' of the future mosque at the Oostduin Park, its 'small minarets' as a possible reference to entrance and corner turrets, and of its 'modest central dome' as a possible reference to the – misinterpreted – canopy above the entrance, it is probable that the first sketch made by De Lyon had been an early version of the 7 October sketch as found in Wiebenga's archive.

In reaction, Wiebenga explained the Dutch rules to Bashir. With all the requirements of the area's zoning plan, costs could easily rise quite high. On Wiebenga's advice to sell the plot and buy an existing house, Bashir instead decided to go ahead as he had planned and returned to Wiebenga the next day, starting intensive contacts and negotiations on the design, which resulted in a changing series of sketches.[51] First, Wiebenga wanted to get the customary Dutch approval for ground plans and volumes, taking in mind Bashir's comments, but not yet including elevation sketches.[52] However, the missionary then specifically asked for façade drawings.[53] Apparently, while preferences were initially mainly formulated in terms of practical requirements, size and costs, elevation forms were more important to the patron than the architect had estimated. Wiebenga decided to study some literature on the subject.

The particular book to which Wiebenga's notes can be traced was no exception to the decoration-over-function approach to Islamic buildings within Dutch architectural faculties, mentioned in the introduction. 'Mohammedans' essentially were tented nomads, who had merely taken pre-Islamic civilization and developed its architecture into decorational schemes.' […] in construction forms the static feel for the constructive task of separate building parts and their internal relation is missed. The unstable and unleashed, always aimed at the fairy-tale-like, fantasy of the Arabs, was much more attracted to the colorful and picturesque of an extraordinary form creation, than to the strictly proportioned rhythmic of Greek-Roman temples and palaces.'[54] The architect Wiebenga himself, of course, was raised and versed in this climate of 'rationalism' versus 'decoration' and had been admired for his modern-Dutch designs to begin with. He extracted some notes on the architectural forms in India from Hartmann, coming to the general conclusion that here the 'Persian School' applied.[55] However, the architect began on 16 October with a proposal for what was in essence a duplex housing designed in 1949 for the Van Voorschotenlaan,[56] only now with a minaret in place of a chimney.[57] **(Figure 9)** To materialize this minaret he devised an inauspicious variation on the Indian 'helmet-shaped dome', as he had called it in his notes, which he had apparently found in the 'Indian' images of his book. In line with contemporary Dutch views, he had imagined Islamic architecture as a decorative layer over 'rational design,' with this decoration to be placed into one of four regions. In this case, since his patrons were Hindustani Muslims, he presumed that the building style as normally associated in the Dutch professional-architectural literature with Hindustani-Islamic culture would be valid for Hindustani-Islamic design in general.

The resulting 'Dutch-Hindustani-Islamic type' fitted the architect's reality but not his patron's. Wiebenga's first plan totally deviated from Bashir's ideas as expressed in the first rudimentary sketch. This deviation should be seen as the direct result of the fact that the Ahmadiyya community leader never conveyed that he required Islam – and consequently his mosque – to be specifically defined in religious opposition to the versions of other Hindustani-Islamic community leaders from his home country, rather than in mere cultural opposition to other Muslim areas. On the contrary, he forcefully presented his view on religion in the media as uncontestedly Islamic and his view on architecture as typically Hindustani. Left largely in the dark, Wiebenga subsequently changed his first proposal to a sketch with a different minaret-dome on 20 October, followed by a sketch with a separate minaret using the first dome again on 22 October. **(Figure 10)** Understandably, these sketches remained essentially based on Wiebenga's idea of a 'modern Dutch' structure with only a decorative layer of Hindustani-Islamic building elements, not on his patron's representation of Islam and the building elements the latter associated with it.

Bashir then came to Wiebenga with a sketch made on 12 August 1952 by the Pakistani architect H.R.Wahid from Rabwah. **(Figure 11)** This made use of the main building elements we saw in the Qadiani mosques of Ahmad and his successor Nur al-Din that had arguably served as a basis for consecutive Rabwah mosques as well as for Bashir, although they had been abstracted into a more 'modernist' version. Like its Rabwah models, it had no minaret. Of course, in Wahid's design the Kiblah faced towards Mecca, accounting for a slightly turned prayer hall and a subsequently asymmetrical façade scheme. Wiebenga, however, had always hoped to use the slightly-off south-east wall, which saved costs and architectural objections from the municipality.[58] All in all, according to Wiebenga Wahid's design would not be up to municipal standards and he calculated that the construction would cost more than budgeted for.[59] Subsequently, Wiebenga changed Wahid's design into a new proposal, realigning the Kiblah to street lines, adjusting the Mihrab into the base of a minaret and generally changing the design into a 'modern Dutch' villa with a barrel-vaulted roof and attached chimney as he had done before, although he did incorporate the Qadiani form of the turrets as proposed by Bashir and Wahid. **(Figure 12)** The architect apparently expected that the envisioned corner turrets, façade scheme and flat roof would not pass municipal scrutiny, which, as we will see later, was not uncalled for. He wanted to send this design to Rabwah for approval, but apparently his patron would not agree to his plan.

On 29 October different façade sketches were sent to Rabwah and subsequently accepted.[60] **(Figure 13)** This design notably included translations of Bashir's early drawing's façade elements like the arched and turreted entrance portal – here in the form of a barrel-vaulted second layer, corner turrets on the flanking wings, and crenellation. Again, it had no minaret. The community leader seems to have insisted on the inclusion of the building elements that he recognized in his Founder's mosque in requiring a representation of a specifically Qadiani construction of Islam, rejecting Wiebenga's idea of a 'modern Dutch' structure with some general Hindustani-Islamic decoration. On 25 July 1953, the design was ready to be submitted to the Aesthetics Commission. **(Figure 14)** However, it took another year-and-a-half for any mosque design to be accepted by the municipality, as Aesthetics kept rejecting plans and asking for rigorous adjustments like the elimination of the four corner turrets.[61] In Z. de Lyon's words: 'I can imagine that the Aesthetics Commission has objections against the proposed plans, although by now it starts appearing that the nature of these objections seems to apply to other than purely architectural aesthetical considerations.'[62]

In effect, Wiebenga was slowly but strictly steered back towards his familiar designs for contemporary houses, as they reappeared, after some experiments with other regional-Islamic forms and decorations he found in his literature, in a drawing of a 'Duplex' with an arched entrance portal and two minaret-turrets on 19 December.[63] **(Figure 15)** Wiebenga summarized: 'These authorities could not agree with the plans and required that another plan should be made. Mr. G.A.Bashir and the architect J.G.Wiebenga asked for information for the reasons why the plan could not be approved, and also pleaded to suggest some changes so as to improve the plan in the eyes of the authorities. But without any success. A totally new plan was asked for. The opinion was that the design did not suit the surroundings and did not harmonize with the architecture in the vicinity.'[64]

Finally, on 16 February 1954 Wiebenga devised a plan that was found acceptable. **(Figure 16)** In this design, the mosque had lost most of Bashir's required building elements, appearing as a 'New Construction' building instead. As such, it had more similarities with Wiebenga's existing oeuvre, as in his brickwork factory hall and chimney for the Société Céramique in Maastricht,[65] than with any building in Hindustan, Qadiani or not. Only the detached minaret with the onion-shaped domes that Wiebenga had started designing in November 1953, and the small minaret-poles at each side of the entrance as sole reminders of Bashir's early ideal, gave away its function. Three weeks later, Aesthetics approved.[66] In Wiebenga's own words: 'After several meetings we succeeded at the end of many trials in making a plan that might find favor in the eyes of the authorities and such with the kind- and helpful-ness of the city engineer who told us the directions in which the authorities were thinking in terms of the architecture wanted.'[67] The official permit for the design was granted on 21 June 1954.[68] According to one newspaper, while the land had already been bought in 1950 and the plans finished in 1952, the ensuing long delay was caused by silent opposition in Christian circles in the municipal government. Reportedly, one member of the Aesthetics Commission had suggested building a so-called shelter church, a house of prayer designed not to be recognizable as such on the outside, a feature 'once forced on Catholics and Remonstrants'.[69] Other articles blamed the municipality's invocation of the zoning plan: only after the design was sufficiently villa-like, with nothing too explicitly hinting at its inner function, did the authorities exempt the Ahmadi from the rule and permit the construction of a mosque.[70]

The next month the press reported that Rabwah had approved the design made by Wiebenga, that the necessary permit had been given by the Ministry of Reconstruction, and that, after long doubts, the The Hague Aesthetics Commission had agreed to the drawings as well. The architect was finishing the builder's estimates, and Bashir hoped to begin construction even before winter. The nine meter-high building, according to the architect, would have two levels, with office space and living quarters located on the first. A minaret would rise three meters above the building, 'non-ascendable by keeping its diameter restricted to 66 centimeters, with a loudspeaker calling for prayer only once a week, on Fridays'. The prayer room would be located on the second level, together with a lecture room, connected to the prayer room by loudspeakers, which could be used for religious events as well.[71] At the end of August, more details on the planned construction started appearing. The tender was planned in a few weeks, and if the commission had been allotted right away and construction saw no delays, it should have been ready in May the next year. The first level would contain an office, a reception-room, a library, a living room, two bedrooms, a kitchen and some smaller spaces. The second level, with the prayer room and the mission room, would be connected to the first by a grand hall, with open stairs emerging from one of the walls. The façades would be made of grayish-yellow bricks and concrete, materials often used in The Netherlands at that period.[72] After the tender, the architect counted eleven candidate-contractors. In October, the expectation was that the first stone could be laid in March 1955.[73]

However, at the end of November, the press reported that construction could not commence as the mission had supposedly found even the lowest contractor's offer too high.[74] In response, Wiebenga had managed to gain municipal permission for reducing the side-wing to only one level in order to save drastically on costs, convinced that this would solve the issue.[75] However, the patron was adamant about not continuing with Wiebenga and set his mind to finding another designer. As this meant having to pay his former architect a very substantial amount of money for nothing, the 'high construction costs' of Wiebenga's design were perhaps not as determinant as the architect presumed. From Wiebenga's archive it appears that the years after were characterized by legal procedures, plot seizures and financial claims by the architect, who repeatedly stated he could not understand why his patron would not continue with him in spite of his eagerness to make completely new drawings and cheaper constructions. From a representational viewpoint, it seems that what the community leader actually required was another design from another architect who would be able to better represent his patron's particular construction of Islam in architecture. Even while Wiebenga still maintained that the commission was his as they supposedly would reach a solution of the disagreement soon, Bashir decided to give it to the relatively unknown Voorburg architect Frits Beck.[76] The design Beck came up with on 11 November basically reintroduced Bashir's representation of the Qadiani façade scheme, with an arched, protruding center and two flanking wings. At the same time, however, it appeared even more like a villa than Wiebenga's alternative through the use of already approved grayish-yellow bricks and concrete, by scratching the entrance minarets, and by reducing the main minaret to a chimney-like structure on the back of the roof, incorporating a concrete extension with a small cut-out crescent moon and star. **(Figure 17)** According to the newspapers, the movement had resorted to a design that had been abandoned earlier.[77] Apparently, the community leader had presented Beck with his early sketch, Wahid's Rabwah plan and the municipally requested materials, thereby reducing the design process with Beck to one mostly successful attempt. And apparently, as far as he was concerned, the basic Qadiani building elements as transformed by him from his Founder's mosque represented Islam more than Wiebenga's layer of Hindustani-Islamic decoration over a design much admired in municipal circles. In other words, the 'Muslim identity in a non-Muslim society' as thought of by the municipality as well as the architect and as subsequently to be captured in a 'modern Dutch' type was of much less relevance to the patron than his particular construction of religion in opposition to contesting versions. This way, in later times the building could (and indeed would) be 'upgraded' in a more recognizable direction, completing the Qadiani representation in more detail. It still had to be submitted to the

Aesthetics Commission,[78] but the choice for what to observers seemed as a straight villa-design with already-approved materials and a non-conspicuous minaret led to a very quick approval indeed. Already a week after the design's production, Aesthetics decided to approve the plan and its accompanying model, on condition of the adjustment of some minor details.[79] One month after that, the plan was approved.[80]

Beck's plan was given an official permit on 29 January 1955,[81] and on 11 February Qadiani member Zafrullah Khan, former Pakistani Minister of Foreign Affairs and judge at the International Court of Justice in The Hague, was photographed cutting the first sod next to a wooden model of the future mosque.[82] The foundation stone was to have been laid by the Caliph on 20 May, but as he had to stay in Zürich for reasons of health, it was Zafrullah Khan again who was photographed doing the honors, after reading a message in name of the leader.[83] Some newspapers reported that the ceremony consisted of laying a piece of stone from the Mubarak mosque in Qadian, the first center of the Ahmadiyya mission,[84] while another wrongly thought it came from a mosque in Rabwah, the current center.[85] Clearly, the community leader wanted to establish a direct link with the Founder's mosque in Qadian, not only by transforming its façade scheme as he now had essentialized it, but also by conspicuously having his foundation stone come from the building, and by inviting the Caliph to formally place it. In this, the community leader effectively represented the Islamic Renaissance that his Promised Messiah had planned to spread around the world by establishing his Mubarak Mosque as a starting point. Although the mosque in The Hague at that time was merely called 'the mosque' in the Dutch press, since it was the only one around, sometime later the name Mobarak Mosque was publicly attached to it by the missionaries as another way of representing its namesake in Qadian.[86] Later, however, accompanying a photograph of the construction site, one newspaper described the new mosque as a building that, at first sight, did not recall 'the exotic eastern atmosphere that comes to mind when we think of a mosque': it was rather seen as 'modern-Western architecture'.[87] Notably, the transformed building elements that would have been meant to represent a specifically Qadiani-Ahmadiyya construction of Islam were not recognized as such in Dutch eyes.

On 9 December 1955, the mosque was officially opened, again by Zafrullah Khan. After Imam A. B. Ayyub from Sumatra had opened the ceremony with a Koran recital, Bashir thanked those present for their interest, saying that the mosque perhaps did not look like some Islamic countries' mosques, but that one had to take the municipality's demands into account.

After giving thanks for the cooperation on the city's side, he stated that 'a mosque does not have typical forms and that is why the mosque has been adjusted to its surroundings'.[88] Strikingly, although the community leader had tried to introduce recognizably Qadiani building elements, especially in the first phases of the design process and even leading to a shift of architects, the patron had learned from previous experiences and decided that the Dutch public was just not yet ready for too obviously an Islamic representation. He seemingly went along with the shelter church idea and even turned it for the best, nominally representing the 'modern-Dutch' building style as recognized by the public as a sign of the flexibility of Islam and the integration of the movement into the Dutch architectural texture. Meanwhile, however, the link with the Founder's Mubarak Mosque in Qadian must have been still very clear to him in the façade scheme and foundation stone, and, had it not been for his leader's illness, in the Caliph's placement of the latter.

In July 1962, at a press conference on the 15th anniversary of the mission in The Netherlands, Hafiz announced that the mission would extend its activities to the Dutch speaking areas of Belgium, that the first Koran translation would see a second printing, and that the mission had gained 300 believers since 1947. The 'crown on these achievements' were the plans for the addition of two small minaret-turrets, which had already been sent to Aesthetics for approval,[89] and which, again, would be financed by the movement's female members.[90] The turrets were to be made of concrete and copper, and would rise two meters above the building.[91] At the beginning of that month, Aesthetics had decided to 'hold' a plan by architect J.M. Straathoff on the 'placement of two minarets above the entrance',[92] meaning that it required more details. On 13 December the architect reapplied, **(Figure 18)** on 2 February 1963 his plan was approved,[93] and in July the minarets saw the light of day. When the two gold-plated turrets were officially in use, a reception was held.[94] Hafiz stated: 'Our minarets will complete the mosque. They were constructed in The Netherlands with Pakistani examples in mind. They will have a symbolical meaning. We are not that far yet that they can actually call to prayer, like in Muslim countries.'[95] 'We ourselves do not value them that much. But when the outside world hears the word mosque, it wants to see something.'[96] And: 'We are satisfied with what we have, but the symbolism of it is of importance to the outside world.'[97]

One newspaper reported that the minarets gave the building 'the appearance of a real mosque, with the unpretentious turrets perfecting the mosque's character'.[98] Another stated: 'Those who have walked along the

Oostduinlaan every now and then probably never noticed that the small building at the end of the path is a mosque. This may very well be the case because of the absence of minarets. But now they are here. On the protruding part of the simple façade stand two small, thin minarets, crowned by beautifully shining gold-plated copper domes that sparkle in the sunlight.'[99] One newspaper, although showing a photograph of the two new minarets with the old one still rising visibly above the building, signaled the fact that many outsiders, while not having been able to notice the mosque at first, could now do so with these new additions.[100] Another stated that the mission was giving 'their Western house an Eastern appearance',[101] and, again, another one found the mosque 'a modest, modern construction that, aside from the tiny minarets and the crescent moon on the chimney, appears to be an attractive villa'.[102] Apparently, Beck's old minaret was indeed, by most observers, perceived to be not much more than a chimney. One newspaper had even concluded some years earlier that it was 'a lovely house at the edge of the forest, in which everyone would want to live. It even lacks a minaret'.[103]

In light of these misunderstandings in public discourse, the community leadership's raising the representational requirements should come as no surprise. When the movement had grown more confident and the dust of the first mosque in The Netherlands had settled down a bit, the wish for a more recognizable representation returned – if it had ever left. Patron Hafiz apparently wanted to extend the Qadiani representation, in the form of two turrets flanking the arched entrance portal, as a 'crown on these achievements'. The community leader's suggestion that he was only responding to the outside world's need for confirmation of an image, is no more than saying that, in his opinion, every Muslim community is entitled to a recognizable architectural representation. That they had to look like this because 'they could not be used for the call to prayer' was in flagrant contradiction with Wiebenga's earlier design which had included an approved minaret to be used as such. And the fact that 'Pakistani' examples were supposedly chosen without much ado does not mean that a generalized regional minaret type had been selected – to be merely reduced in size for the above reason – in light of the community's 'culture area'. In fact, the produced forms were remarkably similar to, and in light of earlier representational requirements, arguably derived from, the mosques in Rabwah that had used elements from the Founder's Mubarak Mosque and his successor's Noor Mosque in Qadian. It is an indication that the Qadiani Renaissance was still very important for the patron's representation of Islam. That these were not referred to before the press as Qadiani but as a typically Pakistani version of a generally Islamic liturgical necessity is yet another example of the tendency to nominally represent a specific religious construction as uncontestedly Islamic with only notions like 'culture group' necessary to explain any architectural choices. Notably, most Hindustani Muslim community leaders in The Netherlands interviewed in the course of this research, whatever their Islamic denomination, talked about their 'Pakistani' origins even when their particular ancestors came from those parts of British-India that would currently fall clearly within the Indian borders. They apparently preferred the public association with a Muslim country and the buildings therein to the historical accuracy of their origins lying in what is now seen as a Hindu country.[104]

Already in 1964, Hafiz expected his mosque to be too small for the celebration of the end of Ramadan,[105] and a photograph of the celebration of Abraham's sacrifice in 1965 showed that tents had to be used to handle the growing numbers of followers.[106] However, the much-needed extension would have to wait more than twenty years. In the meantime, the Dutch movement was led primarily by Dutch converts: chairman or Emir Verhagen and secretary Van der Velden. In November 1965, Mahmud Ahmad's son Nasir Ahmad was elected third Caliph and in June 1982, Nasir Ahmad's younger brother, Tahir Ahmad, was elected fourth Caliph. Then, on the morning of 8 August 1987, the mosque was almost burnt down by someone who expressly presented himself as 'Sunni', claiming that the Mobarak Mosque did not preach true Islam and that he felt that something had to be done.[107] Because the Ahmadi were fervently fought as non-Muslims by Hindustani Brelwi or 'Sunni' groups in The Netherlands, the Mobarak Mosque was not considered a 'true' mosque and could theoretically be approached in whatever way without religious consequence. After the fire, the mosque of course had a dilapidated appearance and was clearly in need of renovation.[108]

For the needed renovation and extension, the community leaders decided to approach the main Ahmadiyya architect, Abdul Rashid from London. Rashid had been designing mosques for Qadiani missions all around the world without charge, gaining much experience in the process and the trust of the Caliph himself. He was carrying out a major renovation project of monuments in Qadian, publishing a study on the subject. Rashid's services formed a welcome and affordable option for the Mobarak Mosque's extension, and Verhagen and Van der Velden gave him much room in designing it. On 25 September 1987, Rashid made some provisional ground plan sketches, approved by the Caliph, for a local architect to work out.[109]

(Figure 19) He decided that it would be best if the existing volume were to be copied in an equal volume at the back of the current building. However, as municipal authorities kept asking for adjustments of plans in reaction to his volume drawings,[110] the extension was heavily delayed. The first official extension proposal by the movement was sent on 24 July 1989,[111] but it took several rounds of negotiations with the municipality before it could finally be evaluated by Aesthetics on 13 September 1990, and even then the latter still advised against the proposed enlargement with the aim of protecting the green zone at the back of the mosque.[112] On 9 October, the mission sent in a volume plan and a wooden model about 80% of the size of the initial proposal, thereby saving the trees in the back yard.[113] Three weeks later, the authorities stated that they would not disapprove of a plan based on this reduced volume, but that future extension would not be permitted.[114]

During the following two years, Rashid started drawing façade plans. In his first drawing, he took the Qadian representation in mind by extending Straathoff's portal turrets with corner turrets and a high minaret of the same form and materials at the right corner of the façade. **(Figure 20)** However, the corner turrets and redesigned windows created too great a change in the existing building and were not welcomed by the Aesthetics Commission. In his next drawing, therefore, Rashid had to keep the existing window scheme and remove the corner turrets. On 5 November 1992, a second plan was approved by Aesthetics,[115] and on 6 June 1993 it was worked into an application.[116] **(Figure 21)** Since Rashid explicitly thought of himself as a modern architect, having found the new Dutch community leaders in The Hague agreed with his ideas, he had drawn the minaret as a steel post with a sphere on top. After some adjustments of details on parking space and after several retries,[117] the municipality gave a permit on 22 February 1995.[118] The condition was that the same brick material be used for the extension as was used for the original parts.[119] The renovation was meant to transform the mosque into a multi-functional space: the first level would have class-rooms for religious lessons and prayer-spaces for men and women; the second would have guest rooms for visiting missionaries; and a basement would be constructed for necessary office space. Because the neighborhood did not have any Muslim inhabitants and the community did not want to disturb the neighbors, the minaret would not have a loudspeaker.[120] Since Rashid's ultimate design was a formal copy of the existing building, it would remain in harmony with its surroundings just as the original building had done. Moreover, available drawings and calculations could be used for the extension, reducing costs and effort.[121] To finance construction costs, all followers would donate one month's salary a year for the next three years.[122]

Nevertheless, when confronted with the high prices of local contractors, the mission decided to keep things in their own hands. Under supervision of a Dutch follower with extensive building experience, a group of volunteers started construction on 29 May 1996 when the foundation stone for the renovation and enlargement was laid by the fourth Caliph, Tahir Ahmad. 'The small old brick that the Caliph laid does not look like the new, white stones that his followers placed on the earth behind the mosque, but the yellowish stone does come from the Punjab, spiritual homeland of the Ahmadiyya movement, as the 69-year old "pope" of the Ahmadi declared later.'[123] Another newspaper reported the brick was 'red', from what was misunderstood as 'the first house of prayer in India, anno 889 (sic)'.[124] Again, despite the main extension and renovation having been steered by the municipality towards a design 'in style', the link with the Founder's Mubarak Mosque was made very clear to community members in the foundation stone that came from Qadian and in its ritual placement by their Caliph as Ahmad's successor. The representation of the Islamic Renaissance as started in Qadian in effect was continued, although the original sketch from 7 October 1951 seemed to have vanished, as it was buried in Wiebenga's archive, and as the mosque had come to be interpreted as a mere 'Dutch villa' by the public and the new Dutch community leaders.[125] In the history of mosque design in The Netherlands, shifts in interpretations like these seem often to occur as community leadership shifts over time. It shows all the more that to understand the meaning behind architectural design it is of the utmost importance to reconstruct the representational motivations of the parties who were actually involved in the design process, and not to base one's analysis merely on interviews with people who fell outside this 'circle of creation'.

Then, even though the modern steel post had already been approved by the municipality, part of the Mobarak community afterwards strongly expressed their wish for a 'more recognizable' minaret.[126] To Rashid, this was no surprise. During his career, many other Ahmadiyya community leaders had asked for more recognizably 'Islamic' or even 'Qadiani' forms. This was why he had prefabricated a number of minaret models as possible options for Qadiani missions around the world, including an exact copy of the Minaret of the Messiah as well as a somewhat less literal specimen he had devised after an extensive study of the Rabwah and Qadiani mosque turrets.[127] **(Figure 22)** According to head missionary Naeem Ahmad Warraich, taking the Qadiani and Rabwah mosques and minarets as design examples (as well as providing actual foundation stones) to be incorporated in newly built Qadiani missions was an ideal for many missionaries. However, in his experience, whenever local municipalities and architects strongly disagreed the missionaries would not see it as a big problem.[128] Subsequently, chairman Verhagen and Rashid agreed to the latter model, keeping things less conspicuous than patrons like those of the Basharat Mosque in Pedro Abad, but still increasing their building's religious recognizability to the Qadiani followers in The Hague.

However, as the foundation was made to support only a simple steel post with a sphere, the minaret had to consist of a relatively expensive large steel pipe with the decorations in plastics and the dome in fiberglass. On 10 October, the architect made preliminary façade sketches in which, among other adjusted elements, his new minaret was included. **(Figure 23)** In this drawing it was noted that the façades would be stuccoed white. A week later, the municipality preliminarily agreed to the minaret as proposed.[129] Sometime afterwards, Verhagen let the municipality know that they had not been able to find bricks for the extension similar enough to the existing ones, and requested permission to use other bricks and to stucco the whole structure white.[130] A year after, on 13 October 1997, Rashid made an official application drawing, including additional changes in façade elements, with the Qadiani minaret replacing the former post. **(Figure 24)** The next month, Verhagen let the municipality know that they had found the appropriate façade bricks and that the stucco would not be necessary.[131] On 23 January 1998, the mission was permitted to deviate from the initial permit according to the filed application.[132] From this part of the design process it appears that the eventual use of grayish-yellow bricks in the extension as well as in the minaret was apparently not the ever-present and unquestioned 'Dutch building tradition' on the side of the patrons that some observers later seemed to want to make of it, although in the end the community leaders did re-introduce them when given the opportunity.

After the extension was officially opened on 30 October 1998,[133] the mission came to realize that by using brickwork and concrete for the minaret, bringing it in style with the existing building and saving money at the same time, the foundation would be able to support it, the reverse of their previous assumption.[134] As the construction of the minaret could not be started before the obligatory date due to lack of funds, because of an ongoing investment in a conference-center in Nunspeet, on 28 January 2001, the municipality revoked that part of the permit.[135] So, on 21 June 2002, what might have been a difficulty was turned into an advantage by having to request another permit according to Rashid's exact last minaret design,[136] but now based on brickwork and concrete decorations. Meanwhile, in 2003, Masroor Ahmad, grandson of the Founder's youngest son, was elected fifth Caliph. In February that year, objections were filed by neighborhood inhabitants against the mission's new minaret stating that 'while having only symbolical and no functional meaning, [it] does not fit, as to height and form, into the architectural structure of the neighborhood'.[137] However, on 16 May the plan was approved by the authorities who rejected all objections from neighbors, stating that 'a minaret is characteristic for this function and fits in the extraordinary destination on this location', while following a positive advice from the Aesthetics Commission which said that 'we appreciate the care with which the minaret has been substantiated in materials, colors and details'.[138] Apparently, the municipality now enthusiastically supported the minaret because it would be kept materially 'in style'. In answer to a request of December 2004, on 24 March 2005 the community received official permission to execute the minaret's dome in gold-color and also to restore the eroded green turret-domes besides the entrance with gold-plating.[139] This way, the turrets as well as the minaret would be in line with Straathoff's original design as approved in 1963.

It is important to note that head-missionary Naeem Ahmad Warraich said: 'We want to have a minaret, because a minaret is a symbol for the spread of the light of Islam.'[140] It is also important to note that the minaret itself would not be lighted, but that its lantern would be supplied with a lamp to be lit in the evenings. In a direct way, the use of the light as seen in the Minaret of the Messiah represented the beacon of light that the community wanted to be, just as their Founder represented himself as light in the symbolical darkness of his religious surroundings, and his movement as a lighthouse lighting the four corners of the world with his own minaret as an everlasting, material reminder of his message. Construction of the minaret started early 2005 and it was officially opened on 9 December 2005. Although Wiebenga's earlier design, including a free-standing minaret as municipally-approved for construction as well as for use, had been voluntarily discarded by the original patron for a more Qadiani design without one, the current minaret was now seen and presented as a symbol of what Muslim communities in general had achieved, 'against all odds', in 50 years of mosque architecture in The Netherlands.[141] **(Figure 25)**

The First Taibah Mosque, Amsterdam

In 1973-1975, just before independence, many Hindustani Muslims from Surinam had moved to The Netherlands, mainly out of fear of Creole-Christian domination. At that time, most members of the Qadiani-Ahmadiyya communities naturally joined the Mobarak Mosque, while the Lahore-Ahmadiyya communities used existing buildings as prayer halls.[142] The Brelwi communities ended up scattered in municipalities like Zwolle, Eindhoven, Lelystad, Utrecht, The Hague, Rotterdam and Amsterdam. In an attempt to re-establish an encompassing organization, Noorani created the WIM-NL in 1975 in Amsterdam, where some of the main SMA leaders had moved.[143] Noorani prominently used the 'Nur of Mohammed' representation in order to enhance the unity of Brelwi communities under his enlightened leadership in the face of the Ahmadiyya and Wahhabi contestants. After his father's death, the deceased was imaged under a crescent moon and starry sky with the Prophet's mausoleum radiating light towards him. Subsequently, the Prophet's tomb, consisting of the green dome and its adjacent minaret, and often pictured as radiating light, was conspicuously pervasive in almost every publication that WIM-NL printed, as was the radiating image of the Koran. The green WIM flag – consistently called 'the Islamic flag' by the followers and therefore the unsuspecting Dutch press – consisted of the Prophet's dome and minaret next to a crescent moon and star, the latter also referring to the flag of Pakistan. Medina was frequently described as the City of Light and the Prophet's tomb as lightening the world. **(Figure 26)** The ideas behind these images express Sufi notions involving a cosmic relation between heaven and earth, with heavenly domes, the revolving moon and stars, the cosmic pillar, rays of light, Mohammed as a column of light, and cities of light as the main components.[144] In fact, the SMA's head imam, when fulminating against the Wahhabi and Ahmadiyya blasphemies in a Dutch publication, continuously and in various ways compared the Prophet with the moon and the sun, and his successor-saints with the heavenly stars.[145] This very specific construction of Islam resulted in the wish for a very specific architectural representation, although successive patrons would never express it as such towards their architects.

In 1975, the mosque organization Stichting Welzijn voor Moslims in Nederland or SWM was founded in Amsterdam, but as the name for this Foundation in the beginning was also translated as Ahle Sunnat Wal Jamaat, the link with the SMA and the Brelwi School was clear to all concerned.[146] Moreover, there were strong connections between the Foundation and Noorani's World Islamic Mission. Noorani was involved in the very foundation of the Stichting Welzijn voor Moslims in Nederland,[147] and the latter started organizing WIM-conferences from 1977. Consequently, the SWM embraced the specifically Brelwi, anti-Ahmadiyya and anti-Wahhabi construction of Islam of the WIM as well. In its statutes, the SWM declared to base itself on the same principles as did the WIM, and aimed at reaching its goals in close cooperation with them. It would 'honour and implement the values of Ahle Soennat wa Jamaat, like the celebration of Ied Milaad-un Nabie [the Prophet's birthday], Daroed-o-Salaam (in an upright position honouring the Holy Prophet), the commemoration of Holy Men in Islam (Urs), Miraadj celebration [the Prophet's heavenly ascension], etcetera'. 'The foundation is an Ahle Soennat Wa Jamaat organization and the board members can only be Sunni Muslims whose actions, words and convictions will not be opposed to the Sunnat and the teachings of Islam, and who believe that Prophet Muhammad is the Last Prophet of Allah, and who regard a pretender of prophethood as a non-Muslim, and who do not offend the Prophet.' All board members would be appointed by the Spiritual Leader, his Eminence Hazrat Maulana Shah Ahmad Noorani Siddiqui.[148]

The Foundation began its activities from the building of the Stichting Interim Beheer or SIB, the organization for the 'coloured' users of the multi-purpose neighbourhood center 'Ganzenhoef' in De Bijlmer. Apparently because of 'ethnic and cultural problems', the SIB began to lose its representative position, finally ending in 1981. In 1979 the Foundation moved to the 'Hindoestaans Cultureel Centrum' on the Bijlmerplein. The spaces made available for the Muslim community included a small prayer hall, a storage room for the administration, and a kitchen that also had to be used as an ablution space. Only some 300 members of the 2000 families could make use of the building at once, and there were no separate prayer- and washing facilities for women. The housing for the administration of the organization was much too small, and problems soon arose with other users of the building over the celebration of Ramadan.[149] So, from 1979, the Foundation actively looked to establish its own prayer hall. From that point, community leader M.I.R. (Roel) Lachman, Secretary General of the SWM, under the spiritual guidance of Noorani, negotiated with local authorities and possible financiers with the aim of constructing a purpose-built mosque. A problem was that, compared to Muslims from communities of foreign labourers like Turks and Moroccans, Surinam groups, being Dutch citizens, were not entitled to subsidies other than for socio-cultural activities. However, Lachman decided to postpone the problem of finances to go ahead with his planning and to start searching for an architect.

In the community's Ganzenhoef days, Lachman had come to know of the Dutch architect Paul Haffmans, who had been involved in designing the multi-functional center.[150] The architect had shown an interest in multi-cultural design and had experience in designing housing in Iran and Nigeria, and had gained much experience with local construction authorities during his designs for the Ganzenhoef. In the architect's memory, the patron's initial request in terms of forms, with negotiations starting in 1981, was merely that his mosque would have to be 'like the Kaaba Mosque in Mecca and the Prophet's mosque in Medina', of which he showed him two images that he had brought with him from Surinam. **(Figure 27)** According to Haffmans, it was particularly the Medina Mosque that was revered the most by the patron since the Prophet was buried there. In the community leader's representation to Haffmans, the two images were themselves holy. According to Haffmans, he gained the impression at the time that the community leader did not have much knowledge of Islamic architecture and that there were no real mosques in Surinam altogether, 'except for a wooden building'. All in all, in the patron's initial discussion of mosque architecture with the architect, the mosques in Medina and Mecca were the only ones emphasized, while Mohammed's own mosque was most important to the community leader in its aspect as the Prophet's tomb.

In answer to this rather vaguely formulated request, Haffmans understandably started to create his own ideas of Islamic architecture in relation to his commission, just like Wiebenga had done. Versed in the ideas of architectural functionalism, Haffmans placed himself in the school of Rietveld and Le Corbusier, wanting to make buildings that were clearly structured, open and connected to the outside. In opposition to earlier design schools, which in his view mainly made use of 'walls encompassing an inside', he wanted to create architecture without walls or limitations. And, just as Wiebenga, Haffmans looked to apply his particular ideas on architectural modernity to the subject of mosque design. For that, he resorted to a book in which the author, a Turkish architect, aimed to establish an interior spatial analysis of what she defined as the three major spatial types of mosques: the pillared, the four-Iwaned, and the domed. In this, she chose to leave out formerly much-studied 'non-spatial' elements like particular forms and decorations, and focused on the spatial functions of structural elements like columns, portals and domes.[151] Basically, she categorized the world's inconsistent varieties of mosque architecture from a clearly functionalist viewpoint, positioning herself against the approach of using only 'decoration' as an Islamic essence, since the importance of elements like columns in opening up spaces was, not coincidentally, greatly stressed by architects of the functionalist school. In fact, in contemporary functionalist thought, outward appearances were sometimes not only seen as irrelevant, but thought of as something that could be done away with altogether. In consequence, this book gave Haffmans the theoretical opportunity to relate his own design ideas to his mosque commission: he did what Wiebenga had done before him, although he deliberately used different literature and did not regard Islamic architecture merely as a decorative layer to be put over a 'modern Dutch' style. Instead, Haffmans started looking for certain functional elements of mosques that constituted an Islamic essence and therefore could be put in a contemporary Dutch idiom.

Since his patron had repeatedly mentioned the mosques of Mecca and Medina, the architect focused on his literature's treatment of the pillared type as what the Turkish author imagined to be characteristic for all 'early mosques in Arabia'. By referring to Arab Bedouin housing, trading and travelling practices, she had explained the 'development' of the Arab mosque from a conspicuously functionalist perspective. From this, Haffmans extracted what he presented as the basic characteristics of Islamic architecture in the beginning years of Islam, to be translated into his Taibah design. In his own words: 'The origins of Arabian mosque architecture lie – generally speaking – in the stopovers for caravans in the desert: the caravanserai. This is a walled, open inner court with to one or more sides simple sleeping spaces for people and animals, a principle that is comparable to our current motels. Preaching and reading of the Koran later found place in similar walled spaces in open air. The believers sought protection against the burning sun by mats of palm leafs, spread on wooden poles just like we would do now with tents and parasols. These wooden poles were later replaced by pillars from Greek and Roman ruins, which then were often attached to each other by a grid of iron bars. This is how the "pillared mosque" developed, one of the most original forms of mosque construction. The roofing is small and walls are merely meant as a climatologic protection, the height of the space is limited, upper lighting adds to the immaterial atmosphere. The pillars stand in endless rows, sometimes 25 aisles broad, as a consequence of which, as opposed to Christian architecture, any form of hierarchical structure of elements, directions and spaces is absent. […] All believers orient themselves to Mecca by orienting themselves to [the Kiblah]. In this, there is no hierarchy, on the contrary, every Muslim is equal to his brother. Therefore, one situates oneself in tight rows as broad as possible starting from the front wall to the back, for prayer. The architect has to find a balance between a row as broad as possible and its limitation by sight and sound. The [imam], standing or sitting in the niche at the front (closest to Mecca) should be seen and heard during prayer.'[152]

In his first section sketch, we see that Haffmans creatively translated the functional-typological findings from his literature into a design that included a forecourt, covered as protection against the Dutch climate, with a domed fountain in the center. The prayer hall consisted of barrel-vaulted naves, supported by columns, running parallel to the Kiblah. **(Figure 28)** In effect, the Umayyad or Arabian mosque-type, as it was referred to in his literature, was taken as an ideal by Haffmans in representing his ideas on architecture in general and on mosque design in particular, in answer to his patron's request for a mosque 'similar to the Prophet's holy mosques' in Arabia. However, as the whole quarter was planned on a strict grid oriented towards the cardinal directions, Haffmans knew that the main building would have to be as well. As a consequence of the prescribed southeast direction of prayer and its future location in the Bijlmer, the mosque could not be set up with an ideal, straight ground plan.

In a second section sketch, we see that Haffmans placed the covered court beside the prayer hall instead of in front of it. He now introduced a dome and a minaret, as these features appeared to form important parts of the patron's formal preferences. The shapes of the minaret and of the dome were meant to recall the Persian examples which Haffmans had seen on his Iranian journey and which could also be found in his literature. **(Figure 29)** However, after this sketch, it became apparent that Lachman specifically wanted four corner minarets. Interestingly, in the architect's recollection the leader explained his desire by particularly referring to the Prophet's Mosque in Medina, as this was, in his mind, also supposed to have four minarets around Mohammed's centrally located tomb.

Although the mental foundation by patrons of a purpose-built prayer hall on what they see as the Primeval Mosque is common usage, in this case the relevant tradition was not a usual, but vaguely referred-to, principle of 'an arcaded courtyard' or 'a pillared prayer hall', but instead was the actual construction which stands on the very spot of what is often thought of as Mohammed's former house and mosque. In fact, the site has always been visited and worshipped by pilgrims, not so much because of some 'original mosque' idea, but mainly because of the actual presence of Mohammed's tomb, although the Saudis have been doing everything they can to reverse this – in their eyes, blasphemous – cult of the grave. The building on that spot had been founded by the Umayyad Caliph Al-Walid, and added to by later Abbasid, Mamluk and Ottoman rulers. As a consequence, the structure as it was largely visible before the major Saudi extensions consisted primarily of a Mamluk-built mausoleum with a dome and one accompanying minaret on the spot of the Prophet's grave, and with three differently shaped minarets on the corners of a rectangular complex around an open court, that had been built and rebuilt in succeeding periods.

Nowadays, of course, the oldest dome does not form the center of the court at all, since the Saudis started renovating the whole structure in the 1950s, adding a huge complex with multiple minarets in the 1980s. However, although the WIM-NL seemed to prefer the pre-Saudi part of the structure as much as possible in its images, Lachman's quincunx around the Prophet's grave was never clearly visible in the original building either. Like the WIM-NL imagery referring to the Light of Mohammed, it can be connected to Sufi cosmological ideas, with a central point surrounded by four arches or pillars representing the celestial garden on earth.[153] In effect, the community leader's quincunx formed a representation of an ideal Sufi shrine scheme. As mentioned, Hindustan had come into contact with Islam mainly through Sufi teachers, and their shrines had become focal points for powerful, estate-owning Pirs. These mausoleums, often consisting of a hemispherical dome on a square substructure with arches on all four sides and with non-ascendable turrets marking its four corners, had taken their basic structure and signification from their religious predecessors, the Hindu Quincunxial Shrines or Pañcayatana.[154] They invariably had an orientation to the direction of Mecca, the larger ones almost always featured a Kiblah niche in the appropriate wall, and they were effectively used as houses of prayer.[155] In fact, for many Hindustani Muslims, worshipping at a holy shrine, seeking the mediation of the Pir lying buried there and partly continuing existing Hindu religious notions and rituals, was the main means of coming into contact with God before reformist movements began their attempts to further Islamize the practices.[156] In the Brelwi vision of Islam, mosque- and shrine-based worship were even integrated in such a way that the whole dichotomy between 'shrine' and 'mosque' was effectively denied.[157] As a result, whenever, in the course of this research, Brelwi patrons from Surinam were asked to describe their commonly mentioned architectural reference point of 'mosques in India and Pakistan', they mainly proved to come up with admired mausoleums like the Taj Mahal. The latter, with its cosmic garden scheme and pools, is a perfect and quite literal example of the Sufi concept of the tomb as a celestial garden on earth.[158] As we will see later, its pools were even used, together with the Prophet's holy places, as a direct reference for the construction of Noorani's SMA mosque in Paramaribo. In fact, there is no trace of the triple-domed and court-yarded Mogul mosque type – confidently associated by Dutch typologists with the Hindustani-Islamic culture group – having been used in Surinam at all.[159]

Similarly, once in The Netherlands, Brelwi publications and images rarely ever referred to Mogul mosques, whereas they frequently referred to the radiating shrines of Sufi saints and Mohammed. Reza Khan, the initiator of the Brelwi school of Islam and reviver of Mohammed's sanctity, was especially mentioned. At the yearly celebration of his Urs, he was represented as a radiating light and a sweet-smelling rose from the garden of the Prophet, with his domed mausoleum in Bareilly prominently printed as an illustration to his wondrous life story.[160] Importantly, adjacent to the saintly tomb in Bareilly, a mosque had been built that conspicuously used the pre-Saudi dome and minaret of the Prophet's grave.[161] **(Figure 30)** Noorani actually presented the Prophet as the spiritual ancestor of a line of almost 40 generations of holy men, culminating in the Siddiquis.[162] For his new mosque in Amsterdam, Noorani explicitly chose the name 'Taibah',[163] not in its mere linguistic meaning of 'good, pure, clean' but in order to represent the immaculate location in Medina where Mohammed was buried.[164] As will be treated in the next case study, after Noorani had died in the course of the construction of the second Taibah Mosque, its patron not only associated it with the Prophet's tomb but also with the shrine of Reza Khan. Moreover, the Brelwi patrons of the WIM-associated Noeroel Islam Mosque in The Hague even requested their architect Oppier to insert a stone from their spiritual leader's grave into their own Mihrab.[165] All in all, although it seems correct to say that Brelwi centers in The Netherlands liturgically have more in common with an ordinary mosque than with a Sufi center or convent, the subsequent conclusion that 'the tombs of their founders and deceased leaders cannot play a role as a center of the organization, as they are too far away (in India or Pakistan)',[166] is too constricted in an architecture-representational sense. It seems that sanctity and the spiritual presence of a holy man, with Mohammed as the ultimate, sanctifying ancestor, formed a very important value for Dutch Brelwi community leaders. Consequently, the production of their religious constructions architecturally culminated, not in a generalized 'Indian building style', but in a Sufi shrine quincunx as the ultimate representation of Islam as it was meant to be.

Importantly, though, this particularly Brelwi representation, as it was projected onto the Medina empirical field by Lachman, was not an outspoken one. At that time in Amsterdam, the Prophet's Mosque, and nothing

Hindustani, was explicitly mentioned by the patron as the most important building and example for his future prayer hall. In Haffmans' memory, Lachman merely represented the Medina dome as Mohammed, while the four corner minarets were said to symbolize the companions of the Prophet. It seemed as if his representation was nominally meant to transcend all 'cultural' building styles. In fact, this was in line with Noorani's outspoken aim at a universal Islam, with Muslims identifying themselves as Muslims and not as citizens of some arbitrary nation or culture.[167] Noorani's WIM actually saw itself as the real patron and the Taibah as the first in a long line of WIM mosques.[168] However, despite this nominal universalism, the WIM still stood for a very particular Islamic construction. The transformation of specific building elements from the ultimate Saint's tomb, combined with the transformation of specific building elements from venerated shrines associated with Sufi sanctity, was a way of representing Brelwi Islam, spreading the Nur of Mohammed throughout the world in opposition to Wahhabi and Ahmadiyya reformist tendencies.[169] In that sense, it is important to recall that the earlier, Qadiani patron in The Hague had chosen to represent Ahmad's domeless prayer hall in Qadian, in effect avoiding any associations with the saintly cults and holy men's powers that the Qadiani-Ahmadi meant to be replaced by their own Prophet. The choice for the quincunx in Amsterdam and especially the later – as we will see – enhancement of that representation, through even more direct and detailed references to the Tomb in Medina can only be fully understood with the meaningful, contesting varieties of Islam and architecture among Hindustani-Islamic communities in mind.

All this was not something that the patron ever clearly communicated to the architect, with both parties basically working from – and attempting to represent – different realities. In reaction to Lachman's outward generalization, Haffmans had started looking for a way to represent the first mosques of Islam as they had been built by Mohammed and his successors in Arabia insofar they conformed to his own ideas on modern Dutch design principles. In accommodating his patron's wish to represent the Prophet's Mosque, Haffmans took a functionalist view of constructional and liturgical reasons behind pillared shades and broad rows of believers as a starting point, while it was the Sufi shrine scheme that mattered most to the community leader himself. In Haffmans' memory, as a matter of fact, when confronted with the pillars in his future prayer room, the imam found they would be 'in the way of visibility' and subsequently suggested getting rid of them by rethinking roofing structure and form, to which the architect answered that, in his view, 'any roofing needs the support of columns'. As it seems, what was presented by both architect and patron as a purely functional element to be included or rejected for purely functional reasons was really a representational element to be included or rejected for representational reasons.

In his third sketch, Haffmans included the four minarets that the community leader had required, although he located the main dome, as in the Arabian pillared type described in his literature, at the Mihrab. **(Figure 31)** When confronted with this scheme, Lachman, in line with the Sufi quincunx ideal, stated that the dome should be in center of the building, just like in Medina. Haffmans, realizing that in Medina the dome was not centrally located at all, translated his patron's wish in terms of the characteristics of Islamic architecture as he was studying it. 'As an image of the world-encompassing reach of Islam, the center, the stomach, the center of gravity, the dome has an important meaning for the image of the mosque. It is supposed to be in the center, in harmony with the whole, as also the whole architecture needs to be at peace, in harmony and without hierarchy in directions. The minarets in the first place serve as beacons to indicate the location of the mosque and the direction towards Mecca.'[170] In this explanation, Haffmans creatively incorporated his functionalist ideas of architecture in general and the origins of mosque architecture in particular, with practice, liturgy and now also proportionality as motivations behind mosque design. There are, however, many mosques that do not have four minarets, a central dome or even a centralized ground plan, whereas a centrally planned mosque with four equal corner turrets in itself does not indicate the direction of Mecca. It more and more seemed that the community leader really required the architect to represent the Prophet's Tomb in his drawings, projecting onto that structure, and identifying it with, the scheme of a generalized Sufi shrine. The Medina building had essentially to be lifted out of the empirical field and combined with other meaningful building elements in order for it to become usable in his specific reality representation.

Then, in a fourth sketch and the first drawing to be dated, from 16 August 1981, Haffmans located the dome at the center of the prayer hall. Moreover, he placed transparent domes on the roof over the columns, and he devised transparent, spared-out corners at the four minarets so the building would give an impression of being suspended in the air instead of being heavy and enclosed. Transparent abstractions of his earlier Persian domes were drawn over the minarets. **(Figure 32)** In Lachman's particular construction of Islam, the notion of light as the all-pervading 'Nur of Mohammed' played an important role and the community leader specifically wanted it to be incorporated in his future mosque.[171] Haffmans subsequently translated the notion into the functionalist idea of openness as a basic characteristic of architecture in general and mosque architecture in particular. The latter was contrasted with the much darker church architecture as perceived by the architect, not unlike his earlier view that Arabian mosques did not have the hierarchy of churches. In Haffmans' explanation, 'light coming from everywhere around' was a basic characteristic of mosques and therefore incorporated in the Taibah design. The omission of a minaret balcony at this stage was, as he recalled, carried out because of cost control. However, in Hindustani Sufi shrines the corner minarets are merely ringed turrets instead of ascendable towers with balconies to be used for the actual call to prayer, so a minaret balcony would not have been of great importance to the community leader to begin with. Cost control in itself does not necessarily explain particular choices for or against certain building elements, since relevant forms can always be – and have often been – included for lower costs when deemed necessary by patrons in mentally constructing their architectural representations. If anything, a tight budget will only enhance the importance of priorities.

On 20 August, Haffmans further developed his plan. In this sketch, he planned the walls of the court to be partly made of transparent materials, and in the walls of the prayer hall he inserted a window in the same form and materials as in the minaret corners, essentially coming down to a 'cubic' arch. He now also included a ring halfway up the minaret shafts as a representation of the balcony. **(Figure 33)** In Haffmans own words, he aimed at a minimum of symbolism to make the building recognizable as a mosque without being a copy of one and without drifting too far from the ideals of contemporary design, which had not much use for decoration. Whenever Lachman asked for building elements – like a central dome, corner minarets, light, arches and turret-rings – that formed indispensable components of his particular representation, Haffmans consistently and successfully reacted by adjusting, including and interpreting these according to his own ideas on functional design while keeping them recognizable for his patron.

After that, on 24 August, Haffmans decided to open up the building even more by adding more windows to the main hall. He now inverted their arch form to column shapes, extending his pillared mosque idea to the outside. Moreover, he worked out the suspension concept by drawing the corners partly around the minarets themselves, adding to the image of a 'hanging' mosque. **(Figure 34)** Clearly, the idea of 'walllessness' was growing in the development of the design. That the patron was content with Haffmans' latest drawing was shown in the fact that he used it in his subsequent negotiations with the municipality. To obtain subsidies, he presented his building to be destined 'for all Muslims in the Bijlmer', as at the time the municipality offered a small financial start-up for appropriate accommodations of 'the Hindus' and 'the Muslims' in the area. Larger amounts were only eligible for non-religious, socio-cultural activities.[172] Since other Muslim organizations had also requested a prayer space, Lachman tried to convince the municipality that all Muslim organizations in the Bijlmer should be referred to the SWM and that the SWM should be designated as the official Muslim conversation partner.[173] By now we start to recognize the apparently less-than-incidental pattern of community leaders keeping religious specificity on the inside and generality on the outside. In this case, the SWM had the explicitly outspoken intent to transcend any particular notions of culture, while it actually based itself on a particularly Brelwi belief system set up to oppose contesting Islamic constructions produced by other Hindustani-Islamic community leaders.

As the Bijlmer at that time was seen by the municipality as an ideal result of town planning, the zoning plan strictly prescribed that everything had to be placed underneath existing parking garages and flyovers. However, the patron thought it important that the mosque be realized in a central location and, even more important, that it would have to be clearly visible. Also Haffmans strongly pushed towards an open-air location. In his eyes, the Ganzenhoef experiment of shared facilities, a typical 1970s concept, had not altogether succeeded, partly because the confined and dark spaces underneath the parking garage had not invited people to take responsibility or even make proper use of them.[174] So, when the municipality finally offered the SWM an open plot directly adjacent to the Kraaiennest metro station, both Lachman and architect agreed. Haffmans would continue his design development on the basis of the chosen location.[175] In light of the limited spatial situation of 850 m2 municipally approved floor space,[176] Haffmans had to relocate the non-prayer-related functions from a forecourt to a first layer, with the prayer hall on a second, since the patron was adamant about praying under a dome. As in other aspects, the difference with the Mobarak Mosque is striking, as the latter's patron had his prayer hall built on the first layer and did not need to pray under a central dome at all. The dome, provoking associations with saintly shrines and a powerful representation of Sufi sanctity, apparently formed an indispensable element in the architectural representation of Islam as embraced by the Brelwi patron.

On 19 November, Haffmans presented the plan he had worked out, together with a model, which were positively received by the patron.[177] **(Figure 35)** Haffmans explained his final design. 'Here, the minarets are supplied with lanterns in a form that is similar to the minaret silhouette as it is prevalent in India, Pakistan and Iran. Next to the entrance, at one minaret a balcony has been placed which can be used for the call to prayer. [...] Of course, in the spatially and financially restricted situation of the Bijlmer, [some] things could be realized only symbolically. Still, in our opinion all features mentioned can be discerned. Foremost was establishing only the essential "foreign" elements with special forms, while the rest had to be in line with locally common building materials and contemporary forms. Thus to restrict or structure the estranging or strange impression this building provokes in our surroundings. [...] In colour scheme and choice of material similarity has been looked for with the original colours in the East: the mud colour comes back in the greyish-yellow concrete stones; the whitewashed walls come back in the white plates of steel.'[178]

On 7 January 1983, Haffmans made more detailed drawings, which were subsequently used for a permit application.[179] Some practical objections were filed which were subsequently rejected by the municipality.[180] The provincial authorities approved the project, as did Aesthetics, and on 2 December, the permit was granted.[181] Meanwhile, although Lachman had introduced a representative of the Pakistani Welfare Association in support of his claim that the initiative was supported by 'all Muslims in the quarter', the municipality hesitated on the continuation of funding in 1983 and later years.[182] After a shift of 'ethnic affairs' to a new municipal department and a change of aldermen, Lachman found less motivation to assist the initiative than under the former regime.[183] From that time on, the community leader started speaking of 'a meeting space' instead of 'a mosque', in order to be able to apply for subsidies for socio-cultural activities.[184] However, the municipality decided not to give him any, explaining that the Dutch government explicitly wanted to stand aside when it came to religious spaces. Even an interest-free loan was impossible.[185] As it also resisted all requests to acquit the ground rent[186] and to provide a bank loan guarantee,[187] it had become clear that the main part of the mosque's budget would have to come out of the community's own pockets, and Lachman started approaching potential donors in the Middle East. As the chosen contractor was interested in gaining contacts in the Middle East himself, he agreed to be paid in full only at the end of construction, when Lachman expected to be able to raise sufficient funds from invited parties.

In the meantime, Haffmans worked out the details of the design. The patron indicated that he would like the Islamic pinnacle, which Haffmans had planned on the dome, also to be placed on the minarets.[188] Moreover,

Haffmans had been thinking about how to materialize the central dome in a cost-effective way while reducing weight and not losing insulation. One option was a spiral tube, for which he had several companies make offers. However, the patron had his Brelwi contacts come up with a drawing of an onion-shaped, vertically segmented dome 'as Coventry' in the UK, where such a dome had apparently been devised. As with the quincunx scheme, corner turrets, balcony rings and arches, the onion-shaped dome formed one of the main ingredients of Hindustani shrine architecture. Haffmans subsequently took the drawing as an example and approached a constructor of polyester boats who was willing to construct a mould for the 16 segments, each containing a window at the base; an idea which Haffmans said he had based on the Ottoman mosques he had seen in Yugoslavia and in his literature. The dome's colour would be green, a feature which Lachman presented as generally Islamic, but which to the patron himself particularly represented the green dome of the Prophet's Tomb in Medina.[189] On 24 January 1984, the minaret pinnacles and the new dome were added in revised construction drawings, and sometime later Haffmans included them in a 3D image. **(Figure 36)**

On 11 December 1983, the first pole ceremony was held. It was Noorani himself who blessed the plot and, in concordance with ex-alderman Kuijpers, pressed the button with which to put the pole into the ground. In a speech, Member of Parliament Van Ooyen (PvdA) stated that the government had done little to make the mosque possible. He explained that church and state were officially separated and that, unfortunately, in policy concerning minorities virtually no attention was paid to their religious aspects. Ex-alderman Kuijpers called the (apparently technical) problems in placing the first pole symbolic of the problems the Amsterdam Muslim community had had in executing its plans for the mosque.[190] Apparently it was mainly the lack of financial cooperation that they spoke of (only about 10% of the construction costs came out of the municipality's pockets), as the permit approval had gone rather smoothly when compared to the Taibah's Hindustani predecessor in The Hague.

Construction went smoothly as well. On 6 September 1984, the celebration of the Feast of Sacrifice was held together with the celebration of reaching the highest point of construction. Visitors were encouraged to donate money for the mosque. On 11 January 1985, after Friday prayers in the building led by Noorani himself, the official opening of the mosque was announced to the Dutch press. It was said that the mosque was to be used by all Muslims in Amsterdam, and that the existing prayer halls in old Amsterdam buildings would be of secondary importance. Lachman spoke of a 'victory of the Muslim community in The Netherlands'. Then he explained that the actual prayer space was only meant for men, and that women had to follow the prayers in the library or other secondary spaces. Within a short time, however, they would 'get their own mosque'. In the current building, the prayer space was placed on the second level, including an ablution space. On the first level there was a space for education, the meeting room and the kitchen. The latter would be much used 'as it is customary in a mosque that lunch is had in the afternoon'; a custom which actually is not generally shared by all other Muslims in The Netherlands but which seems to be a specifically Hindustani practice. An imam who had arrived from Pakistan that week stated that everybody who believed in God would be welcome. The reporter noted that about 300 people attended the service that day, with Javanese, Surinamese, Turks, Moroccans and Africans present. He also stated that this piece of Amsterdam gained 'an Arabian atmosphere' when the call to prayer sounded. Moreover, he presented Noorani, underneath his picture, as an 'Arabian Muslim leader'.[191] In a later interview, 'the leader of the Arab speaking Muslims in the world' elaborated on the idea for a women's mosque. As women and men were not allowed to follow prayers in the same room, he wanted to give them their own mosque. To the reporter's question as to whether that meant the coming about of emancipation of women, Noorani as well as Lachman answered negatively.[192] Importantly, the over-all impression the community leaders had apparently chosen to give the press was one of general, Sunni Muslimness, and not one of a particularly Brelwi belief system.

At the opening on 18 January, Noorani inaugurated the mosque with a prayer and a speech. Other speeches were given by Junior Minister De Graaf, Member of Parliament Krajenbrink (CDA), ex-alderman Kuijpers, Surinam ambassador Heidweiler, Pakistani Maulana Abdul Satarkhan Niazi, the contractor, and Lachman.[193] The press reported on the occasion by calling Noorani 'the spiritual leader of all Sunni Muslims in the world'. Noorani expressed his content with the opening of the mosque 'in this part of the world', together with his wish for every Dutch town to have its own mosque in the end – which remark, of course, immediately made it to the headlines of several newspapers. According to Lachman, Muslims from all over the world had been approached for funds, although donations by governments, like the one from Libya, had been warded off, 'because one did not want to become involved in politics'. The Saudi Prince Abdul Aziz, however, and Yusuf Islam, a.k.a. Cat Stevens, one of the guests of honour and speakers, had given 'an inappropriately high amount'. Bishop Bomers had also been invited to speak, and he said that 'thanks to the Christians, the Muslims can practise their faith here'. However, he regretted the fact that 'there is such a small Christian community in Saudi-Arabia'. The deputy mayor said he had come despite the fact that, according to him, the presence of the state during a religious conference was unusual in light of the separation between church and state, but that the opening would prove to be a memorable event in the history of the city. In contrast, the other speeches spoke about the lack of subsidy for prayer spaces due to 'problems of separation between church and state'. Especially Krajenbrink of the (Christian) CDA called for Liberals and Socialists to accept that 'some groups' were lagging behind in religious facilities and that it was unreasonable that these groups had to carry their financial burdens themselves.[194] Junior Minister of Social Affairs De Graaf spoke of 'post-Christian society'. The pattern in The Netherlands had changed over the last quarter of a century by the introduction of foreigners. That had sometimes led to short-term tensions, but Dutch society had proven, according to De Graaf, to be able to process such an input of foreigners without disturbances in the end. Reverend Slomp, who specialized in contacts between Christians and Muslims, gave the community an old Koran and some translated bibles for their library on behalf of the Reformed Churches.[195] The next day, the 4th World Islamic Mission Conference in The Netherlands was held in the new mosque. **(Figure 37)**

After the opening, an interesting new development occurred. Whereas the Mobarak Mosque had been aesthetically evaluated by municipal officials and journalists, in the Taibah's case the architectural critiques were written by professional architects themselves. Here, we can discern the first public attempts at architecturally essentializing the 'modern Dutch' and the 'traditionally Islamic', simultaneously introducing the need for dichotomizing them and bringing the two together again. Maarten Kloos, who established ARCAM (the Amsterdam Center for Architecture) the next year, noted that in the Taibah Mosque the ablutions found place inside the building, while 'in the Middle East' one washed oneself 'out in the open'. He thought that to be one of the thought-provoking differences between mosques 'there' and 'here'. 'Islam has elsewhere, under completely different circumstances than the Dutch, already been materialized in many buildings. Does a mosque in Amsterdam have to refer to *those* mosques, or is there space for thought about what a mosque could mean in the *Dutch* environment? [...] A number of matters are intriguing. If the mosque is the place for a Muslim to find his place in Dutch society without becoming estranged from his own culture, then looking at the position of women is unavoidable. It is hoped to soon construct a women's mosque beside the Taibah Mosque, but in the meantime – and it is startling to the non-Muslim – women may only slip in through a side-door and through the storage room to the still unused library which is their temporary prayer room. It is the Islamic conviction that the man is "the supervisor" of the woman, but the question remains how long women are going to accept that here. The architect has stated in an explanation that he only wanted to give a special form to foreign elements, but he did not fully live up to that promise. The structuring of side- and back-façades in a number of planes is an unnecessary decorative element, the convex balustrades of balcony and fire stairs demand too much attention and the arched windows seem a little childish. That is a pity, because these details together take much away from what seems very essential: the simplicity of the building. Islam is based on religious concentration, purification and meditation. The mosque is a sheltered place where the direction towards Mecca can be found and where peace and harmony rule. An inconspicuous white volume without any fringe would essentially form the best answer to the question.'[196]

Stephen Goth and C. Cantrijn presented their view: 'Building a mosque is building within a centuries-old tradition in a culture which differs from the Dutch. A great problem in that can be finding a balance between the recognizable, typical mosque and the Dutch building tradition. Architects who dare accept this design task, will collide with the strict tradition of Islam and its specific building typology. Paul Haffmans, who designed the mosque in De Bijlmer, has solved this problem well. [...] The first impression of the mosque is a cliché image of a mosque, a basically cubic mass with a minaret at each corner and a dome in the center. It is, in abstraction, that which one imagines to be a mosque. The dark turquoise dome and the four minarets rather give it an *Efteling*-like impression than one of thought and culture. [...] The minarets have been used correctly to accentuate the corners of the main building. Two external balconies have been nicely detailed. Further detailing and use of materials have been well-applied [...] The Mohammedan will wash his feet, hands and head ritually before prayer. The space designed to that end more recalls a toilet space than of a place where a ritual event is being performed. [...] Inside the prayer hall, Haffmans does an excellent job of integrating his sensibility as a Western architect with the Eastern examples from which he drew his inspiration [...] The Mihrab has been very simply tiled. The upper part of the niche is covered in two concrete slabs in a stylized Eastern motif. With a solution like the one for the Mihrab, we are confronted anew with the tension between the Islamic tradition and contemporary Western architecture. Looking at the whole of the Taibah Mosque, one can conclude that architect Paul Haffmans has succeeded in finding a good balance between the diverging demands of his commission. The exterior is perhaps a little too extravagant. On the inside, it is a building with its very own character, the result of a combination of tradition, contemporary construction techniques and architectural ingeniousness.[197]

With these critiques, the concepts of 'typology', 'contemporaneity' and 'design task', – common usage in the world of architectural education and applied in design and evaluation – entered the world of Islamic architecture in The Netherlands. In this usage, there was no room for interest in the design process as an ongoing series of intensive negotiations between an architect and his influential patron. The grade of brilliance of the artist and his creative search for a solution to a program of practical requirements within a specific urban context was the main aspect in interpretation. Interestingly, 'modern Dutchness' was introduced on the Islamic scene as if it were an unambiguous concept instead of a body of divergent design preferences, while any outwardly Islamic aspects were confirmed as un-Dutch and un-contemporary. The categorization, constructed a century before within technical faculties, of Islamic architecture as a system of overly decorative style-characteristics placed over non-Islamic structures, was now combined with the contemporary belief that outer appearances could be merely derived from practicalities with no deeper meaning than function. This combination led to the regret that a mosque in the developed world, where things had presumably been reduced to their bare essence, should have to look like anything more than a white box. At the same time, the 'Efteling Type' was established as an unwanted category of modern Islamic design. Effectively, these first evaluations linked any 'Oriental' recognizability to the irrationality of the 'childish' mind, establishing extant Islamic architecture as a type different from – and not suited for – the real, grown-up, educated and modern world. Basically, it was not the architect who used an 'Efteling' perspective but the criticizing proponents of modern Dutchness themselves, confidently but uninformedly projecting their own Orientalist view of Islamic architecture onto the object of interpretation and evaluation.[198]

The Second Taibah Mosque, Amsterdam

As might have been expected, the building soon felt too small, especially during religious festivities. According to Lachman, the community had been growing rapidly and during Ramadan in 1987 they had 'some 1000' believers attending the mosque each day. Extension plans were deliberated with Haffmans along with plans for a women's mosque, and Haffmans even made a preliminary sketch for the extension.[199] **(Figure 38)** However, as some community members believed there was a rule that a mosque could only stand on bought land (for which some find the basis in Koran and Hadith), the rent for the plot was paid off for 100 years as soon as the municipality made it possible and the mosque could raise enough money by collection and a mortgage.[200] As a consequence, the motivation for donating money for the extension began to wane.

That is, until the arrival of Mohammed Junus Gaffar, who had been chairman of the SMA in Surinam between 1980 and 1990. He had come to The Netherlands at the age of 18 to follow a technical education, after which he returned to Paramaribo and accepted a chemical engineering job at mining company Suralco. During one of Noorani's lectures in Paramaribo he had been inspired by the WIM religious philosophy, subsequently become active in the mission, and eventually was elected and several times re-elected chairman of the SMA. As leader of the Sunni community and as an engineer with a side interest in construction, he had been the driving force behind several SMA mosques in Surinam, raising awareness, motivation and funds for their construction. In fact, it had been Noorani himself who had commissioned Gaffar with the rebuilding of the old SMA mosque from 1957, in an apparent attempt to re-unite the dispersed SMA communities. In 1985, after its construction, he visited Mecca and Medina, after which he resigned his job at Suralco and decided to put his attention completely to Noorani's mission. In 1990, he moved to The Netherlands to join his family, who had moved there five years before, and became active in the SWM and WIM-NL. In The Netherlands, Brelwi communities in The Hague, Rotterdam, Zwolle, Utrecht, Lelystad and Eindhoven had loosened themselves from the old SMA structure even more than in Surinam. Gaffar, under the guidance of his Pir, continued the quest of re-assembling the communities under Noorani's leadership, stressing the Wahhabi and Ahmadi as a common enemy to be opposed. Not all community leaders seemed willing to immediately give up their acquired independence, so Gaffar, in his own account, had to use all means available, from friendly persuasion and financial support to legal procedures.[201]

In Eindhoven, the Brelwi Anwar-e-Medina had encountered financial shortages in the middle of construction, leaving the foundations unfinished. In answer to this, the municipality threatened to appropriate the plot and demolish what had been built so far. After the Eindhoven community eventually turned to Gaffar to help them out, he managed to get them to become an SWM department under Noorani's WIM-NL. After that, he raised enough funds to get construction restarted, and the mosque was completed in 1997. Since the drawings had already been completed and approved before his entrance on the scene, Gaffar was only able to control interior decoration. Subsequently, he concentrated on renewing the Taibah Mosque in the Bijlmer as his new project, effectively meant to architecturally stimulate the unity of all Dutch Brelwi communities under Noorani's guidance. Because experiences with the designers of the Anwar-e-Medina, the Eindhoven-based Frank Domburg and Peter Scipio of the architectural bureau Ruimte 68,[202] had been so good, he decided to approach them for the Amsterdam commission as well.

In the ensuing talks with Taibah community leaders, several ideas were discussed. Some, mainly those who had been involved in the development of Haffmans' mosque, wanted to keep the old building and merely have Haffmans add an extension.[203] In their opinion, Islam forbade the demolition of mosques. Gaffar, however, argued against the process of 'gluing', as he said, instead opting for complete demolition of the old mosque and the construction of a new one. Although this was brought as a necessary process of practical improvement mainly in terms of size, he actually considered the old building as 'an ugly white box with fake-minarets and too many columns impeding the view'. As far as he was concerned, the community required a completely different architectural representation, and he did not think Haffmans suited for what he had in mind. As a compromise, some parts of the old mosque would have to be kept, in particular the characteristic stairway, the prayer hall floor and some of its columns. Gaffar, wishing to improve on his experiences in Paramaribo and Eindhoven, would have preferred the mosque to have a compound with separate functional spaces instead of the placement of these on a first floor underneath the prayer hall: that way, the domed prayer space, itself possibly spread over two levels, would have given the impression of greater height and 'exaltedness' ('*verhevenheid*'). As we recall, the domed hall rising from ground level had been a preference of his predecessor as well, although he had been restricted by spatial limitations. For that same reason, although the pillars had to go, the two-level concept of Haffmans was maintained in the second Taibah

Mosque, in addition to the appeasement of the older community members. Dome and minarets would have to be relocated and re-designed.

Gaffar showed the architects a picture of his 1985 SMA mosque in Paramaribo, which had also used the two-layered quincunx scheme. In the façades, the community leader had explicitly used arcaded galleries that referred to the Taj Mahal, although he did not tell that to his designers. He had even enhanced the Taj Mahal representation by designing a basin underneath the stairway to the second level, explicitly referring to its meaning as a celestial garden on earth, and by incorporating its monumental entrance portal as well. **(Figure 39)** As appeared from our last case study, one of the major diacritical features for expressing a Brelwi vision of Islam had been the idealized Sufi shrine scheme, signifying the mosque as an earthly paradise. In fact, Gaffar never tired of referring to paradisical traditions in Koran and Hadith, suggesting that only a community of true Muslims would be allowed into paradise; that a builder of a mosque would automatically attain a place in paradise; and that on Judgment Day only mosques would rise to heaven. However, since Taj Mahal-like structures formed an admired reference among some Lahori-Ahmadiyya communities as well, in this case Gaffar had placed the main mutual contrasting aspect in the transformation of completely different building elements than were usual in Paramaribo. The minarets he had designed were based on the minarets of the Kaaba Mosque in Mecca, although the contractor had abstracted these more than Gaffar had preferred. Moreover, where other Paramaribo mosques had chosen the conspicuous Taj Mahal-like onion-form, the dome had been based on that of the Prophet's mausoleum in Medina – its materials were even planned to turn green. Here, we see that Gaffar began to represent an even more specifically Brelwi construction of Islam, composed by the transformation of chosen forms from the Prophet's mosques, transcending the shrine-quincunx and onion-domes. In The Netherlands, in his ongoing attempt to gather the different Brelwi communities under Noorani's leadership, this ongoing representational process was even more visible in mosque design.

On 15 April 1997, Scipio and Domburg made a drawing partly based on Gaffar's Paramaribo picture and partly on their own study of what they saw as the culmination of Hindustani-Islamic architecture, the Taj Mahal, although Gaffar had not himself specifically mentioned that building.[204] **(Figure 40)** Apparently, the structure forms an image of Hindustani Islamicness to divergent groups, although each represents it from different motivations and interpretations, with divergent results in particular design choices.

As opposed to Wiebenga and Haffmans, the architects did not choose to work in a pre-determined school, aiming merely to react creatively to individual patrons and local contexts. However, they did have a vision of 'typological progress', since during their Eindhoven commission, they had started out with a stylized Ottoman dome as derived from the local Turkish Fatih mosque in a conscious attempt to create a proper 'Eindhoven mosque type'. The designers had subsequently been requested by their patron to change it into an onion-dome instead. As a matter of course, they assumed that the current community, 'culturally linked' to Eindhoven, would prefer a 'Hindustani' dome as well, as they also – correctly – identified elements of the Taj Mahal in the Paramaribo façade scheme and plan. In their first sketch, they based the minarets on the SMA mosque while they based façade schemes partly on Paramaribo and partly on the Taj Mahal, and the multiple domes on the Taj Mahal's. This first mosque design had two minarets, as the architects argued that a symmetrical fourfold scheme would have been impossible due to the cut-off west corner. This corner could not be demolished as it had been agreed that this side of the old design would be kept to appease those members of the community who had not wanted to say goodbye to Haffmans' design.

However, it appeared that Gaffar did not merely have the Paramaribo mosque or the Taj Mahal in mind at all, and his preference for building elements from the Prophet's Mosque in Medina came increasingly to the fore. During a meeting with the architects, Gaffar requested three, 'simpler' minarets, and higher minarets altogether.[205] At this time he also thought a fourth minaret would be impossible due to the cut-off west corner. Domburg and Scipio made a crude drawing of what he had in mind: a three-stepped, octagonally planned minaret, similar to the one next to the Prophet's Tomb as he had seen it in Medina and as he showed them on a poster he had brought with him. **(Figure 41)** Importantly, the other minarets around the Prophet's Mausoleum in Medina had divergent forms, but Gaffar imagined his multiple Amsterdam minarets to be based on that single, oldest, Mamluk-built specimen which he associated with Mohammed's grave and the Prophet himself. Whereas the Saudi – or Wahhabi as Gaffar consistently referred to them – had replaced several other minarets with their own 'Arabian' version, the Amsterdam community leader conspicuously reverted to the pre-Saudi original. That it is generally referred to as 'Mamluk' or that it still was built long after the Prophet's burial was of no relevance to the patron whatsoever and therefore it is not relevant to us: it is his own selection, association and subsequent transformation which we need to understand in order to understand the meaning of his eventual mosque in Amsterdam. On 5 June the architects drew their newly designed, threefold minarets into a second plan. **(Figure 42)** When handed the drawings two weeks later, the municipality found the general project to fit very well into a new municipal development plan for the particular Kraaiennest area to provide central and social functions for the whole neighbourhood. As a result, the required extension of the plot was possible.[206]

However, it then set the urban delimitations of the extendable plot in terms of sight lines.[207] **(Figure 43)** In effect, the municipality required the mosque to completely – one could even say extremely – adjust itself to its physical environment. It seemed that the basic square plan which the patron had in mind would have to be reduced on almost every side. In order for the mosque not to be reduced again to Haffmans' plan size, the extension would have to follow the very limitations that the municipality had set, making the plan multi-faceted and completely destroying the rectangular concept. On 17 January 1998, the architects made a new plan. **(Figure 44)** Here, we see the introduction of an octagonal prayer hall in answer to the uneven reduction of usable space, just as the architects had designed an octagonal prayer hall in Eindhoven since the Kiblah could not be aligned with the extant streets. The main dome was placed over the center of the octagon, while two smaller domes were kept, one over each of the two main arches that marked the entrances of an under-passage. However, according to the municipality, the established sight lines were different than those suggested by the architects, and it found two minarets and two columns in the under-passage too much. Eventually, it only agreed to one minaret on that spot and one at the back façade.[208]

On 14 April, the architects made a new plan based on these suggestions, together with a model of the mosque's under-passage. **(Figure 45)** On 16 April, 3D images of the mosque plan were produced, showing a white building with green domes, colours specifically meant by Gaffar to provoke associations with Mohammed's tomb in Medina. **(Figure 46)** In a poster-series one of these 3D drawings was shown, together with the Anwar-e-Medina as a new WIM member in Gaffar's quest for the assembly of Brelwi communities, underneath three images of Mohammed's mausoleum-mosque in Medina, mentioning Noorani as the spiritual leader of the world's Sunni community. **(Figure 47)** Gaffar then put forward his wish for a fourth minaret,[209] subsequently requesting the forms of the dome as well as the four minarets to be 'more like those of Medina', in support of which he again brought with him the poster of Mohammed's Tomb.[210] Clearly, the association with Mohammed's holy places, especially his tomb in Medina, was growing more and more explicit.

In reaction, on 2 May the architects sketched a fourth minaret in their last plan, and worked out a more detailed minaret based on Gaffar's poster. **(Figure 48)** On 12 May, they worked out Gaffar's wish in a ground plan, with façades following on 26 May. **(Figure 49)** On 29 May, a new 3D image was produced for a visit by Noorani himself. **(Figure 50)** When the leader was presented with the drawing, he expressed his content with its forms, although in the architects' memory he did request them not to include any people in their next production as the imaging of live creatures in mosques was something that was, in his opinion, forbidden by Islam.[211] However, the municipality was still not satisfied with the physical adaptation of the new plan's mosque, as it still did not 'connect' to its surroundings. It found that on the south side the design still crossed the sight lines; that the building was too high on the metro side, preventing light from entering under the railway; and that the part underneath the under-passage did not form a real part of the square. It suggested one large arch over the passage instead of several small ones, and the inset of the second level away from the metro-side.[212]

In reaction, the architects made a new ground plan and façade sketches on 7 October. **(Figure 51)** The fourth minaret was moved inward, as was the whole second level on the metro side. However, in municipal eyes, the particular proposal for a larger arch was unsatisfactory, whereas the south side still crossed set delimitations.[213] Strikingly, in March 1999 these municipal delimitations melted away in light of a new state policy program on large cities and social integration, providing municipalities with funds for restructuring problematic urban areas while stressing the participation of local communities. In the framework of this program, De Bijlmer had been classified as a socially problematic and unsafe neighbourhood. It was subsequently concluded that a pleasant and safe Kraaiennest-square was essential and that in the current situation and in the existing plans these aspects were not accounted for. Instead, the municipality, now provided with state funds, thought of levelling the fly-over on the square and of a new shopping mall – in short, of rearranging the whole situation. In these plans, the mosque extension delimitations and suggestions as had been put forward earlier were no longer valid.[214] The new delimitations that were set the next month basically reintroduced the rectangular plan that had been the architects' and patron's very first proposal. **(Figure 52)** It was specifically stated that 'the recognizability of the mosque [...] is of importance, independently of the development of a new Kraaiennest-square'.[215] In effect, the consistency and recognizability of the plan to its community, as opposed to earlier municipal requirements of physical adaptation, was now seen as an indispensable and stimulating factor in the search for harmonious cultural cohabitation.

So, the architects went back to their first ideas. On 19 April, they presented their new plan. **(Figure 53)** The next day, the municipality was very positive about the design, especially since Gaffar had stated that the mosque would have 'a modern appearance'.[216] On 31 August, the choice was made to maintain the floors of the first and second levels, and the columns of the first level, as much as possible for reasons of costs, next to the fact that this would also be the reminder of Haffmans' design that some members of the community had wished for. On the first level, Gaffar's view that the pillars were in the way of visibility of the old podium underneath the Mihrab would be solved by turning the direction 90 degrees by reusing part of the old stairway into a new podium on the west wall. Gaffar also thought Haffmans' conspicuous columns in the prayer hall on the second level were in the way of visibility of the Mihrab and openness in general, and therefore a solution for reducing the number of pillars would be studied.[217] Later, a light roof construction was created which could be supported by walls alone, so columns on this level could be significantly reduced. The concept of the 'pillared mosque' that Haffmans had devised in answer to his patron's latent wish for a representation of the Prophet's mosque, in the process translated as an Arabian type, was now left for a more open, widely domed prayer hall expressing the notion of 'exaltedness', in accordance with the new patron's more manifestly Brelwi representational requirements.

Subsequently, the architects together with Gaffar and Noorani presented their latest plans to the municipality,[218] and on 21 October it approved of the design.[219] On 8 February 2000, Aesthetics also reacted positively to the Taibah project, noting its appreciation of the plan as a whole.[220] Strikingly, Gaffar used the occasion of meeting the commission members to express his wish for a larger dome.[221] In his eyes, the Medina representation would be enhanced by including a windowed dome-drum similar to the one over the Prophet's grave. However, he did not explicitly mention that to his architects or to the municipality, explaining his preference mainly by stating that a higher dome would be more visible from the street level. Whereas the drum of the actual structure in Medina only contained a number of small holes, in this case the shape of the windows was to be modelled on the silhouette of the dome of the Prophet's mausoleum. On 21 March, the final plans were drawn, including the new drum, and a model and an axonometry of the interior were made. **(Figure 54)** An official permit application was filed including these drawings.[222] On 30 March, a 3D image was created as well. **(Figure 55)** Aesthetics then advised positively on the adjusted dome.[223] Since no valid objections were filed, the provincial authorities approved of the plan and on 8 November, the construction permit was given.[224]

On 6 May 2001, the foundation stone was placed by Noorani. The first pole was placed on 20 February 2002, also in the presence of the Spiritual Leader. Despite the regret of some community members at the demolition of their cherished mosque, a new phase in the life of the Taibah Mosque was begun. Gaffar eventually managed to develop enthusiasm by holding the community's celebrations around the Prophet partly on the construction site. Moreover, he gave his community members the opportunity to contribute financially to their new mosque by donations and loans, or by adopting a pillar or a Musallah – a prayer space within the mosque. The latter could be done 'in the name of your dear, departed ancestors'.[225] Importantly, during construction, Gaffar also came up with the idea of extra windows in the back façade at each side of the Mihrab. In this case as well, the shape of the windows was to be modelled on the silhouette of the Prophet's dome. On 18 February 2003, the architects worked out his idea in a drawing. **(Figure 56)** By introducing these extra windows and those in the dome drum, Gaffar aimed to provide more light in the building. Light was a particularly important aspect for the community leader, as he appeared also to have been the one who steered towards glass-windowed arches as large as possible in the façades of his mosque. He wanted to keep the building 'as transparent as possible', since to him light represented the Nur of Mohammed, and it stood for the Prophet's spiritual presence in the mosque. This brings to mind the spiritual presence of the Prophet believed to exist during the standing prayers at the yearly celebration of his birthday, a feature typical of the Brelwi communities.[226] Gaffar stated: 'We believe that on Judgment Day everything will disappear from the earth; the mosques, however, will rise to heaven. The light of heaven that falls from the windows on the inside of the mosque and fills everything, symbolizes the fact that our prophet Mohammed to us is a Light.'[227] Also, but secondarily, Gaffar presented the transparency of his mosque's outer walls as a way to show the community's modernity and willingness to be open to Dutch society, having 'nothing to hide'. In the end, Aesthetics advised positively for the extra windows.[228] Unfortunately, however, the contractor went bankrupt and the community could not reach their money, which had been frozen by the bankruptcy curator, for some time. After legal procedures the situation was resolved, but construction was very much slowed down. Gaffar managed to get permission to use the mosque prematurely for celebrations providing the necessary safety measures were taken.[229]

Construction was continued by a new contractor, but a shortage of funds threatened the construction of the minarets. After several options were suggested by Noorani and some other community members, from no minaret at all to only one or two at the front façade, Gaffar managed to cut a deal with his suppliers. They would still build four minarets, but the ones at the back façade would have two layers instead of three, making them shorter but still recognizably Medina-like. Where other Brelwi community leaders in The Netherlands sometimes had had to reduce their ideal of four minarets to only one or two in the face of too-heavy pressure by municipalities and/or architects, in Gaffar's mind this was simply not an option since it would have meant the total destruction of his representation of the Prophet's Tomb. Importantly, the fact that it was he who had insisted on keeping the ideal quincunx means that it was not a 'fundamentalist' influence from outside that had pushed for a 'traditionalist' design in the face of an 'obedient' Dutch Muslim patron. Severing the financial ties with foreign sponsors may therefore not have the effect on mosque design in The Netherlands that some expect it to have, as it proves to be Dutch Muslim patrons themselves who construct these architectural representations and as there is, in a representational sense, nothing traditionalist about their designs in the first place.

Then, on 11 December, Noorani suddenly died. In a memorial publication by WIM-NL, he was described to have radiated light during a lecture just before his death. He was buried in Karachi 'at the foot of his mother's grave', which brings to mind a much-quoted Hadith saying that 'paradise lies at the feet of the mother', and which therefore seems to form part of an ongoing, literal construction of Brelwi Islam.[230] There, he was 'surrounded by Wali's [saints]', in the graveyard at the domed shrine of the saint Wali Hazrat Shah Abdullah Ghazi. The description of the burial procession said that 'it looked like the day of Eid Milaadoen Nabie [the Prophet's birthday]'.[231] The cover of this publication showed an image of Noorani with a halo and a sun rising above him, next to the illuminated Tomb of the Prophet in Medina, and in another memorial publication he was depicted looking at a bright light radiating towards him from Mohammed's mausoleum-dome.[232] Strikingly, on the back of the latter publication, the image of the Taibah mosque was printed underneath, and therefore likened to, a cut-out of the central, domed part of Reza Khan's saintly shrine in Bareilly.[233] **(Figure 57)** To his mourning followers, the much-revered Brelwi Pir, already holy during his lifetime, had effectively attained an even greater sanctity at death, as would his son and successor Maulana Shah Anas Noorani at some time in the future.

The crude construction was completed at the end of 2004, after which a period of interior construction was started by community members themselves. In the detailing of the Taibah's interior decoration, Gaffar represented the Brelwi construction of Islam against lesser versions even further by providing the inner dome with a multitude of sparkling lights in reference to, in his own account, Mohammed's Nur. In effect, they remind of the Sufi cosmological notions of the radiating dome and revolving stars, as they were depicted in the memorial image of Aleem Siddiqui.[234] As shown earlier, in Brelwi verbal representations of Islam the saint-successors to Mohammed were sometimes compared to sparkling stars, channeling His light from the heavens to the earth. However, Gaffar told his architects and the press that his lights were merely meant to remind people of 'the starry skies over Surinam'.[235] **(Figure 58)** As before, this is yet another example of patrons representing themselves verbally as generally Islamic with only cultural or other non-religious characteristics responsible for any divergences with other mosque designs. In the end, even in the specifically chosen marble plating for his mosque's interior Gaffar stated to refer to the Prophet's shrine as he had seen it during Haj. At the time of writing, the mosque's dome materials were yet to – as planned – turn green and the building still remained to be officially opened as interior construction had not yet been completely finished. **(Figure 59)**

2. Moluccan-Commissioned Mosque Design in The Netherlands

After The Netherlands' first mosque was opened in 1955 by a Hindustani-Islamic community in The Hague, it did not take long for another important Muslim group to establish their own designed prayer hall. In 1956, the second mosque in The Netherlands was constructed in the Moluccan camp of Wyldemerck, near Balk in Friesland. Unfortunately, as the whole camp was demolished in the 1960s, the building itself or what is left of it no longer functions as a mosque. This, plus its seclusion in the woods of Friesland and the fact that it was considered as non-specific barracks architecture, has led to the virtual absence of attention to it within Dutch architectural discourse, although it has sometimes been mentioned in non-architectural studies that the building had an 'Oriental' image. However, when studied in depth, the mosque underwent an interesting design process. While it started out as a plain barracks, it ended up using a number of 'cultural' building elements not merely associated with some consistent Southeast-Asian type but representing a specific construction of Islam as opposed to contesting views held by other Moluccan-Islamic community leaders.

After a split within the Wyldemerck community and the subsequent move to the municipalities of Ridderkerk and Waalwijk, two new mosques were built for the two new Moluccan-Islamic communities, the Bait Ar-Rahman Mosque and the An-Nur Mosque. Since their openings in 1984 and 1990, their designs have been subject to architectural evaluation much more than Wyldemerck's. As the architect for both, who was strongly oriented towards universal spiritual principles of design, publicly imagined the preferences of the specific initiators to be of minor importance in the creative processes, the designs were mainly seen in terms of the architect's esoteric intentions. However, when studied in depth, the clear divergence between the initiators' religious constructions also appears in the design processes. In both cases, 'cultural' building elements from the country of origin were used but their interpretation, transformation and the motivations underlying their introduction differed to such an extent that it is impossible to put them under a single building style without losing sight of the contesting representations of Islam that they were meant to be.

Varieties of Islam among Moluccan Communities

Since their Christian counterparts tended to assume their home region was mainly and proudly Protestant, the small number of Moluccan Muslims in The Netherlands has never been very well-known, despite the fact that about half the population in the Moluccas was Muslim at the time of immigration. An important aspect of Islam in the Moluccan parts of Indonesia was its early introduction and subsequent relative isolation from the rest of the Islamic world until the second half of the 19th century, caused by the VOC's monopolization of trade and its concurrent rejection of outside Muslim traders.[1] While the process of syncretization with Adat or local custom had already begun at the initial acceptance of Islam, during its isolation by the Dutch it became much more a local and Moluccan religion.[2] In fact, compared with Islam in some other Muslim parts of Indonesia and to Christianity in Christian Moluccan villages, where there seems to have been tension between Adat and religion, and between state and religion, Islam on the Moluccan islands was almost completely integrated with local religious beliefs and politics.[3] This led to the syncretization of Islam and Adat at all levels of social interaction.[4] As Adat tended to be a heterogeneous collection of differing customs and beliefs, each Moluccan village or kampong basically had its own version of Islam as well. There was no encompassing Ulama, and in each village the religious leader, the Imam, came from one clan while the political leader, the Raja, came from another. Tombs of local holy men and prophets were worshipped and each clan constructed its own extensive genealogy of Arab, Indian or Wali ancestry.[5] The Prophet Mohammed was sometimes seen as the ultimate ancestor, having come to the Moluccas where he was buried, and there was even a replica of the Kaaba which served as a replacement for the original in Mecca.[6]

However, when the Dutch changed their Indonesian trade-policy, with all its benefits to the local aristocracy, to the outright colonial oppression of the 19th and 20th centuries, Islam came to be used in the organization of resistance throughout the region. In this process, some community leaders left the old syncretistic and localized versions of Islam for a more 'orthodox' alternative, based on increased contacts with the Middle East. In the Moluccas, the rise of this divergence between 'traditionalists' and 'modernists' or 'reformists' is generally placed in the 1930s.[7]

To support their colonial aspirations militarily in the face of Islamic uprisings, the Dutch empire in the Indonesian archipelago used its Royal Netherlands Indies Army (Koninklijk Nederlands Indisch Leger or KNIL). This army, led by Dutch officers, consisted mainly of European and native soldiers. Because of the Dutch preference for fellow-Christians in these military matters, the native compartment largely consisted of Moluccans, as during the Dutch occupation about half the Moluccan inhabitants had converted to Protestantism. The Moluccan Christian KNIL soldiers did not regard themselves mercenaries, but showed a certain loyalty to The Netherlands and were used as advance troops into resurgent Muslim areas such as Aceh and Java. Eventually, some even referred to themselves as 'black Dutchmen'. During World War II, some rebelled against the Japanese, afterwards fighting with British troops against Indonesian nationalists. As soon as the Dutch returned, most of them rejoined the KNIL, their numbers strengthened by many more new Moluccan recruits.[8] Strikingly, a small number of Moluccan Muslims also joined, apparently for economic reasons and for adventure.[9] However, as Muslims had always been discriminated against by the Dutch colonial government, most of them only joined when the Japanese invaded Indonesia, and generally they did not refer to themselves as black Dutchmen or feel the Dutch associations as did their Christian fellow-islanders.[10]

According to the literature, within the KNIL the Moluccans tended to distinguish themselves only along regional or ethnic lines.[11] As a consequence, it is assumed that the Islamic dispute between traditionalists and reformists had not filtered through to the KNIL regiments and that the rise of the same dispute among the later Moluccan Muslim immigrants in The Netherlands was merely instigated directly from the home region. However, like the Surinamese presumption of outside Pakistani influences on a formerly 'simple' Muslim community in Paramaribo, this was a simplification, especially since most Muslim Moluccans only joined the KNIL after the Japanese invasion and would have been unavoidably confronted with divergences in Islamic constructions before their recruitment. The fact that in the military context religion was not made an identifying factor per se does not mean that the Muslim parts of the KNIL would have remained untouched by any religious developments in the Moluccas themselves. Moreover, as we will see later, in the Moluccan case regional and ethnic alliances have been much intertwined with religious preferences.

After the formal transfer of sovereignty in 1949 to the Indonesian nationalist leaders, some Ambonese leaders, Christian and Muslim both, saw their political interests threatened by the future dominance of Java[12] and in 1950, they declared the Republik Maluku Selatan (RMS), the Republic of the South Moluccas. Former KNIL soldiers, stationed elsewhere, demanded that their demobilization, proclaimed after the colonial army had been dissolved, had to take place on Ambon or in Dutch-controlled New Guinea. Sukarno, fearing reinforcement of the RMS, refused. Having been granted the status of militaries in the Koninklijke Landmacht or Royal Dutch Army, the former KNIL soldiers won a legal case in the Netherlands, preventing the Dutch government from demobilizing them against their will on Indonesian-controlled territory.[13] The only solution left, and the 'worst possible solution' in the eyes of government,[14] was to grant them the right to be demobilized in the Netherlands. When given the option, most chose to be transferred, expecting to be treated as military personnel, living in military camps during their stay. Their sense of betrayal was great when they heard that they had been discharged from the army by the Dutch state while in transport.

The Wyldemerck Mosque, Balk

Once in The Netherlands, the soldiers and their families were put into camps all across the country. For this, former labor camps for the unemployed, monasteries, country manors, military barracks and even German concentration camps like Westerbork (now Schattenberg) and Vught (now Lunetten) were selected and renovated. Individual offers to house the immigrants with Dutch families were denied: the Moluccans were intended to be in The Netherlands only temporarily and not to be assimilated into Dutch society.[15] Initially, the camps were controlled by several ministries simultaneously, but as of 1952, this complicated situation was resolved with the establishment of the Commission for the Ambonese (Commissariaat van Ambonezenzorg or CAZ), with Van Ringen as the first Commissioner, to take care of the Moluccans from the cradle to the grave.[16]

The distribution of the former soldiers in the camps was arbitrary, and persons from different clans, villages and religions were often put together in one camp. Among the 12.500 Moluccans transported to The Netherlands were some 70 Muslim families, spread over a total of 20 camps. Schattenberg served as their center, with 33 Muslim families among a total of 595 Christian households. The Muslims prayed together on Fridays in a provisional prayer-room but at first they generally did not organize themselves or distinguish themselves from their Christian neighbors. They hoped for a return to a free Ambon in the near future, and since families from unrelated Muslim clans and villages had been arbitrarily put together, organization was initially problematic and unattractive.[17] However, as Muslims had always occupied the lower ranks in the former KNIL army, they were not represented in the internal camp council and that, unavoidably, came to be resented. This political exclusion, together with the fact that they were extremely outnumbered by Christians, resulted in a situation ripe for the appearance of a unifying Muslim leader.

Most of the Moluccan Muslims in Schattenberg had only taken lessons in reading the Koran in their kampong schools. However Achmad Tan, a Moluccan relative-in-law of rich Chinese Muslim textile merchants in Ambon, had received Dutch higher education. In addition, he had taken religious classes at one of Ambon's madrasas, and one of his relatives is thought to have been the Qhadi, or magistrate, of Ambon.[18] His parents had changed the family name from Mulud to Tan with an eye on the easier acceptance of non-Muslims in the Dutch colonial school system, and he appears to have been a known figure on Ambon. In Schattenberg, in spite of the official sub-commission installed by the Contact in Government Affairs (Contact in Overheidszaken or CIO),[19] he increasingly presented himself to the government as the one and only representative of Muslim Moluccans, demanding the undisturbed practice of the Muslim faith, special food restrictions, marriage rights, and education.[20] He also asked for a proper camp with a proper mosque.[21] At this time however, the CAZ would not consent. Tan became a political threat to the camp's council, who still denied Muslims and the lower military ranks their own representative to the Dutch government.[22] In addition, the Christian majority sometimes suspected Muslims to be pro-Indonesian.[23] After an incident between Muslims and Christians over Islamic food restrictions in December 1953, Tan was identified as the instigator and exiled to Camp Duinoord, near Groede in Zeeland, by the CAZ.[24] Since in Schattenberg, the potential religious division did not on its own result in a shared need for separate action,[25] it seems that Tan had to stir things up a bit to make a proper camp and a proper mosque indispensable. In June 1954, during the celebration of the end of Ramadan in Schattenberg, an event at which most Muslim Moluccans in The Netherlands were present, Tan was elected as their official political and religious leader.[26] Because of this representative function, and because of his 'positive behavior' in Duinoord, his exile was rescinded in October 1954.[27]

It was during his banishment in Duinoord that Tan began to work out ideas for a mosque as the center of a future Muslim camp. He had conversations on the subject with his friend, Sufyan Ollong, who was following an education in Vlissingen, also in Zeeland.[28] Importantly, in Moluccan Muslim villages, the positions of Imam and Raja, the religious and political leaders, were considered hereditary, along fixed, separated clan lines. In Tan's future camp, non-related clans and villages would be cast together, and the functions could no longer simply be chosen or appointed in customary ways.[29] Tan, by virtue of his education, background and charisma, had the opportunity to fill the gap, naturally combining the two positions in one person. His respect and influence in the community were large, and he was generally regarded as their representative by the government as well. Tan realized that he had to overcome potential conflict and internal divergence by constructing a unified group, at the same time legitimizing his essentially non-customary political and religious leadership.[30] Tan required the concentration into one Muslim kampong to construct this group under his own person, and, importantly, he explicitly made an anti-Indonesian stance, the RMS and the return to a free Ambon, sticking to a traditional kampong-Islamic organization and not introducing any innovative theological ideas, his primary themes.[31] This particular choice from the varieties of Islam among Moluccan communities would have to be represented by a particular selection and transformation of building elements. According to the literature, Tan merely wanted a building in 'Oriental style',[32] but there is much more to it than that, since, according to Ollong, 'Oriental' should be read as 'like with us on Ambon'. As Ollong remembers, Tan's provisional sketch, now lost, was specifically intended to represent a traditional Ambonese kampong mosque.

The Dutch government could no longer afford to neglect the Moluccan Muslim cause. In December 1954, the CAZ decided to establish a special Muslim Moluccan camp in Wyldemerck, near Balk in the province of Friesland. This was a former camp of the Dutch Labor Department (Nederlandse Arbeidsdienst or NAD), built by the National Buildings Department (Rijksgebouwendienst or RGD) in 1941-42, consisting originally of some 17 barracks. As one of four Moluccan camps in Friesland, it was already in use, but not adequate for the 40 additional families expected in 1955.[33] The remaining 10 barracks had to be renovated, sub-divided into smaller living quarters, and the number increased. A Mr. Gaasterland was appointed controller by the CAZ, and he and Tan prepared for the first Moluccan families who were to arrive in December 1954. Renovation design and interior decoration followed government-prescribed lines for standard barracks.[34] More important, the camp would not be administered internally by a quasi-military council like that in Schattenberg, but would be set up along the lines of a Moluccan Muslim kampong, led by Raja and Imam. Tan was, as a matter of course, made both, and he served as the main intermediary between community and government. In practice, he and Gaasterland formed the everyday-administration of Wyldemerck.

With the arrival of the first families, Friday prayers were held in the canteen-barracks, and Tan soon began negotiations with the CAZ for a mosque. The CAZ, having already financed several churches in Christian Moluccan camps, could not refuse. Apparently, as early as January 1955, Tan was invited by telephone to attend a meeting with the RGD district's architect Postma of the RGD in Leeuwarden on the design of the mosque, but he declined the invitation 'because that day will be a Friday and therefore I will not be able to leave the camp'. If this seems an arbitrary and unproductive decision from a constructional-bureaucratic viewpoint, in Tan's reality his absence from the mosque at that stage would probably have undermined his personal leadership and the specifically non-reformist-Moluccan construction of Islam he wanted to uphold among his imagined community. He wrote only that the RGD had to take the orientation towards Mecca into account.[35] On another occasion he specified that the plan should be large enough for the whole congregation and have separate ablution spaces and entrances for men and women,[36] seemingly the only formal criteria that Tan mentioned to distinguish his prayer house from any other barracks as they were being built or renovated at that time in the camp. **(Figure 60)** By 18 February, newspapers reported on the CAZ's plans for a mosque adequate for 150 people.[37] According to Tan, the CAZ had stated that the building would be constructed before 23 May of that year, the celebration of the end of Ramadan.[38] On 24 February, newspapers reported that Ghulam Ahmad Bashir and Abu Bakr Ayyub, missionaries of the recently designed Ahmadiyya Mosque in The Hague, had visited the camp the day before to inform themselves about the plans for the Wyldemerck mosque. Mohammed Zafrullah Khan had been detained, but Tan expected him to be present 'at the beginning of next month, when the construction of the mosque will be started'.[39] Three weeks later, a newspaper reported that Zafrullah Khan, who was to leave for Pakistan in a few days, had indeed expressed the wish to cut the first sod for The Netherlands' second mosque in Wyldemerck. More important, this article also stated that 'the whole will be constructed in Oriental style. According to the drawing there will even be some kind of minaret'.[40]

On 27 March, Khan, Bashir and Ayyub were, indeed, invited to cut the first sod. After deliberating on the exact location and orientation of the future construction, Zafrullah Khan put the first spade into the ground, facing towards Mecca with the community in a semi-circle behind him. Then followed Ayyub, then Tan, and then Bashir.[41] Here, we see that Tan already included a specific building ritual, as the half circle oriented towards Mecca around the village imam placing the first pole was, according to Ollong, seen to be a part of a standard Moluccan kampong ceremony of blessing a future mosque construction.[42] In this first pole ritual which, according to Ollong, was used in the construction of all Moluccan kampong communal buildings, the first sod is normally not the focus but only used to enable the imam to plant the first pole itself. It is not known if Khan's first spade in Wyldemerck was actually followed by a pole ritual. It could be that here the first sod, an important event in Ahmadiyya ceremony,[43] was given priority, which would be in line with the fact that Tan consciously made use of their status to let Khan and Ayyub take precedence in the actual cutting. He then stated that his mosque was not only meant for Moluccan Muslims but for other Muslims in The Netherlands as well.[44] Tan apparently wanted to place his community in a broader context, choosing the Ahmadi perhaps because of Zafrullah Khan's high position or because the only other important Muslim organization of that time, the Perkumpulan Ummat Islam, was mainly Javanese and strongly linked to the Indonesian embassy, which would not have fit particularly well with Tan's preference for the RMS and Moluccan kampong Islam. But perhaps even more important, the Ahmadiyya plans for the first mosque in The Netherlands had already been approved, and that must have formed a great stimulus to Tan. The two mosques could well have been planned to be opened simultaneously at the end of Ramadan in 1955: Khan and Tan may well have imagined it that way, with Khan cutting the first sod for both buildings within a period of two months.

The expectation on the day of the ceremony was that the Wyldemerck mosque construction would now start in several weeks' time, with 'the drawing having delayed things for a bit'.[45] However, a month later Tan disappointedly stated that the end of Ramadan would have to be celebrated without a proper mosque, as nothing had yet been done. According to him, the drawings were ready, but there was no money forthcoming from the Ministry of Finance. He asked himself if 'a group of Christians' would have been made to wait for an equally long time.[46] Subsequently, the service that Tan held in the canteen during the festivities on 15 May 1955 contained a strong message of Muslim brotherhood versus 'those who follow other religions, with self-invented celebrations that consist of parties, loudness and several sorts of food, drinks and pleasure'.[47] Nominally, it was aimed at unifying all Muslims in the world in the face of non-Muslimness or, arguably, Christianity. From a more contextual, representational perspective, however, Tan's particular selection and interpretation of Islamic texts aimed at unifying the contesting Moluccan-Islamic community leaders present by creating a shared opponent.[48] Four months after his sermon, Tan again expressed his irritation over the delays, with 'the mills in The Hague turning agonizingly slow'. Still, as the money had been made available, he expected the construction to start soon, although 'the mosque will be a little smaller than expected'.[49] However, over two months later, Tan found that the CAZ seemed not to be in much of a hurry 'because of the rumors that the Ambonese are planning on returning to Ambon'.[50]

All this disappointment was the result of Tan's apparent hurry to get the job done before another important Muslim celebration was to be held in Wyldemerck. His irritation with the CAZ clearly came from an over-optimistic expectation of Dutch construction-bureaucracy, taking informal drawings, meetings and approving nods for facts, and repeatedly saying so to the press. It was not until 4 July 1955 that Van Ringen officially commissioned Postma to build a mosque according to 'his previously submitted plan for a building with a capacity of some 150 persons, costing 50.000 guilders'.[51] Although it appears from this that Postma might already have sent in some sketches to the CAZ, the first evidence of a mosque in official RGD drawings stems only from 15 October. **(Figure 61)** For the first time, an RGD plan of the camp showed a mosque with the required orientation, but a plan for the mosque itself from December 1955 proved that all the architect had in mind was largely just another barracks. **(Figure 62)** The proposed structure had the standard pitched roof and façades of thin wooden planks, with no outer Islamic representation other than a crescent moon and star above the covered front entrance, obviously sketched in later with a different color of ink. It did, however, have separate washing troughs on both sides of a single fountain or foot-washing basin in the front hall, a feature which, in Ollong's recollection, Tan had specifically requested. Apparently, Postma had defined the mosque as a mere liturgical building type with some minor outer symbolism, just as Wiebenga had done at first instance, possibly assuming that the requested basin was a standard feature of any mosque and sketching in, where there was still room left so as not to deviate from a standard façade plan, what he assumed to be the general Islamic symbol as he had seen it during a travel to Turkey.[52]

However, the sketched-in crescent moon and star above the entrance do not normally form part of Moluccan kampong mosques, as these mostly seem to carry, if at all, the symbol as a roof-finial. Moreover, in Ollong's memory, Tan had meant the basin as a representation of the tanks ideally located in front of Moluccan kampong mosques, where separate washing troughs had been added in later times for Islamic hand and face ablution.[53] According to Ollong, on Ambon these basins ideally consisted of pre-existing natural reservoirs but people also created artificial tanks.[54] In his account, they would normally have been out in the open but Tan decided that in the Dutch climate the basin would have to be part of a covered hall. It appears that early mentions in newspapers' articles and literature that the drawing had been 'finished' or 'approved', had been not much more than a combination of Tan's own sketch and his wishful thinking. Apparently, especially since Tan had not attended the special meeting in January 1955, Postma had produced a type that represented the architect's personal view on the essentials of mosque architecture but not the specific construction of Islam as chosen by the Moluccan Muslim leader. As in other cases, the initiator would have nominally presented his representational requirements as generally Islamic, leaving his designer to think that he could construct his own typology. After the first official drawing in December 1955, there must have been more intensive contact between them, for it was only afterwards that the design obviously started to show more of the selected Moluccan-Islamic building elements that Tan seems to have had in mind from the beginning.

In his second plan of 25 January 1956, approved by the municipality on 26 February, Postma introduced some of the features that Tan had obviously missed in the first. **(Figure 63)** Now, the mosque showed a hipped roof instead of the former pitched roof. As it seemed, in the experience of Ollong, referring to his own traditional Ambonese kampong of Hila, the pitched roof in Moluccan villages was used mainly for sheds while the hipped roof was ideally used for houses if the owner could afford it. **(Figure 64)** In effect, Tan had managed to change the low-status pitched roof of Postma's first barracks design into a higher-status version.[55] Importantly, whereas he knew this would not have been a financially realistic option, Tan would have preferred a multiple-layered hipped roof instead of a one-layered version. An important example that had been discussed had apparently been the Wapaue mosque in Ollong's kampong Hila. **(Figure 65)** Kampong mosques like these were heavily surrounded by Islamized Adat beliefs.[56] Throughout Indonesia, the column-supported multiple-layered roofs on square ground plans as used in Hindu temples had come to be used for mosques as well.

These were still generally called 'Meru'-roofs, referring to the Hindu cosmic mountain of the same name. Occasionally, as in the case of the Wapaue, the mountain representation was enhanced by a myth whereby the mosque had once been situated on a holy mountain peak and later had been magically moved down with the peak included.[57] Also, sultans' mosques in the Moluccas, as well as the kampong mosques of their subjects, had square ground plans and a Meru-roof, with five layers for the sultan and two or three for villages.[58] However, throughout Indonesia, the tendency towards reform and delocalization was mainly represented by 'pan-Islamic' or Indo-Moorish building elements.[59] Some Moluccan prayer halls conspicuously used these Mogulesque domes and minarets as well.[60] **(Figure 66)**

Within this meaningful variety of architecture, Tan's selective preference for a layered roof instead of a dome, even if neither was budgetarily realistic, was one of the ways that he wanted to represent the Islam of an idealized, traditional Moluccan kampong community. Although he had had to change the number of hipped layers to one in Wyldemerck instead of the two in kampongs like Hila, now, at least, he had a more appropriate representation of a Moluccan kampong mosque than with a mere pitched shed. Further, whereas he felt that mosques in the Moluccas would generally be accompanied by a village Baileo, a building for communal activities,[61] the canteen could now be used for that function instead of being combined with prayers.

In addition, the design now showed different façades. While the other barracks were made of wood, notably including those designed and constructed in the same period as the mosque and after, the mosque's walls were to be made of white-painted asbestos sheets. This abrupt change of material together with the abrupt change of design is meaningful. Since Tan, as appears from his conversations with Ollong, wanted his mosque to stand out from its non-religious surroundings in order to fulfill its representational role, it is likely that he had a different material than wood in mind. According to Ollong, on Ambon, when a kampong community had enough means, the walls of their mosque as well as their high-status houses were built or at least partly built of materials more durable than wood, preferably white-plastered brick. In Wyldemerck, this would have been costly, and it is unlikely that Postma could have built his mosque out of bricks within the available budget. However, asbestos was a cheap, easy-to-work-with material that could be made to look more like white plastering than could wooden planks. As one journalist noted, the asbestos system-construction was chosen 'so as to incorporate a smaller amount of stone'.[62] This conclusion, strange when keeping in mind that the surrounding architecture was made of wood, would suggest that asbestos was indeed used to provoke an association with the durable materials of a kampong mosque on Ambon itself.

In April 1956, Tan placed the mosque's foundation stone, after which followed the relatively easy construction. According to Tan, the building was also to have four 'Kaaba-poles'.[63] And indeed, an RGD-plan of 26 April showed sketches of four inner columns. **(Figure 67)** Here as well, we see the conscious inclusion of a selected building element. The idea of four principal posts is a feature that can be found in many parts of the Indonesian archipelago, although their interpretation varies greatly. Very generally speaking, within the house as cosmological order, the posts serve as intermediaries between heaven and earth, representing the ancestors and the shared ancestral origins of the inhabitants. They are sometimes recipients of ritual attention, and they are frequently personified, named, and on occasion, even dressed. Sometimes, one of them (often the forward right) is seen as the most sacred, symbolically but sometimes also practically, serving as stairs to the attic or heaven.[64] With the advent of Islam and the foundation of mosques, they, together with many other pre-Islamic elements, were incorporated into Islamic practice and referred to as Islamic symbols.[65] From that time, the semi-mythological Muslim ancestors or Walis have often been associated with the four columns. Importantly, the four posts were also included in the kampong mosque of Ollong's village Hila, which seemed to form an example for Tan.[66] However, in light of the varieties of Islam and mosque architecture throughout the Moluccas in the 1950s, not all community leaders would have automatically opted for the inclusion of this building element. Tan's specific choice of the columns was another way of representing the Islam of an ideal kampong community, especially since they were designed only after the main structure and served no practical purpose whatsoever. It is no longer known if Tan had requested his pillars to be designed with a specific form in mind, and it is possible that Postma himself chose a classically fluted column shape in an attempt to make the (apparently very important) elements stand out more than mere wooden beams.

According to Tan when he laid the foundation stone, the mosque was eventually to have a minaret, but that part was still under discussion: 'In The Hague, one does things step by step.'[67] And indeed, only on 9 May a plan was drawn showing sketches of a minaret to be built next to the mosque, prominently placed away from the main building, and attached to it by a V-shaped steel band for support. **(Figure 68)** Initially, Meru-mosques in Southeast Asia did not as a rule include a minaret, and the first purpose-built minarets for the most part appeared only in the 19th and 20th centuries with the introduction of Mogulesque building elements.[68] This was the period when older mosques in Indonesia acquired minarets, primarily structures built next to, but, importantly, detached from, the main buildings themselves.[69] In the Moluccas, villages were generally either Muslim or Christian, so kampong mosques, in Ollong's account, did not need a minaret as a standard feature. However, the Dutch context was a different situation. Tan had initially managed to unite the competing Moluccan Muslims by distinguishing them from Moluccan Christians in Schattenberg. Since the main building alone, by lack of a Meru-roof, would have appeared merely as a Moluccan house, he needed a minaret for a general Islamic marker. Apparently, however, he did not have much interest in its specific form, since it is the only element that Ollong as well as Gaasterland distinctively remember being claimed, at several instances and with Tan's silent consent, by Postma as his own design. The architect, as mentioned before, had visited Turkey once and 'knew what a minaret looked like'. Perhaps the fact that Postma had sketched in the crescent moon and star on his first façade design and now also on the minaret, was evidence of his claim. The minaret itself was an asbestos pole, as they were used, according to Gaasterland, for contemporary lampposts. In this case, its lower half was widened with thin planks. The wooden balcony was not actually accessible but only housed the loudspeaker, and the dome, with its crescent moon and star, was made of gold-painted zinc.[70] In a plan of 22 May Postma drew his finial in closer detail. **(Figure 69)**

In the meantime, relations with the Ahmadi in The Hague had apparently cooled down. Although Tan had received some literature and even a sermon translated into Indonesian from Ayyub who had preached in Batavia earlier,[71] when Ayyub offered to come and preach for three days in the week, Tan declined, preferring to keep things in his own hands.[72] In the end, although there seemed to have been much thankfulness for the initial Ahmadiyya psychological support, no Qadiani influence on the Moluccan-Islamic community, dogmatic or architectural, was visible in the Wyldemerck Mosque.[73] At its official opening on 16 July, one year after its official commission but in time to be used for the celebration of sacrifice of 19 July, the Ahmadiyya Movement's leaders excused themselves.[74] From a representational viewpoint, the severance of Ahmadiyya ties was necessary for Tan to keep a firm grip on the traditional kampong Islam that he needed represented by his mosque in specific opposition to more reformist Islamic constructions. During the opening ceremony, Tan's four columns were described to the press as 'pillars of Faith, having their own names, symbolizing the sound basis on which the mosque stands'. In his opening speech, Tan declared that 'we are grateful that all this has been made possible, despite the fact that we are living in exile, thousands of miles away from our fatherland. We also wish to return, but it is Allah's will that we are here now. Our mission is to spread Islam, in our words as well as in our deeds. Only if we fulfil that mission, will Allah deem us worthy to return to our country'.[75] **(Figure 70)**

Tan died after a short illness on 21 March 1957, not long after the opening of his mosque. With the re-housing of Moluccan groups from Wyldemerck to assigned quarters in the municipalities of Waalwijk and Ridderkerk in the 1960s, his prayer hall was no longer needed. While most Wyldemerck barracks, including 'a mosque plus one tower', were put up for sale as sheds,[76] it was believed until recently that dismantling of the mosque was difficult because of the materials used, and that the building had been destroyed in 1969 and burnt on the spot, while the minaret was thrown out with the trash.[77] A memorial was placed near its old location within the former camp, a place whose trees, shrubs and sources had been left mainly untouched. However, recently it was discovered that the mosque had been sold to a farm in Haskerhorne, Friesland, to be reassembled and used for storage. The minaret and interior parts of the main building are apparently still missing. **(Figure 71)**

After the death of leader Achmad Tan, the Moluccan Muslim community in Wyldemerck quickly fell apart. Without his unifying influence, latent inter-clan and inter-village loyalties and religious divergences once again surfaced. Where the impossibility of customary selection procedures for community leaders had not formed a real problem in Tan's idealized kampong, now a much more complicated situation developed.[78] With the decision of the Dutch government in April 1959 to relocate the Moluccans from their temporary camps to regular quarters in other municipalities, the Wyldemerck inhabitants moved mainly to Ridderkerk and Waalwijk during the 1960s. Some repatriated to Indonesia and others chose to move to other Dutch towns.[79] For the most part, pro-RMS village clans went to Waalwijk in 1964, while pro-Indonesia village clans largely ended up in Ridderkerk from 1966.[80] And, while in Waalwijk most chose to become Dutch or to remain stateless, in Ridderkerk most Moluccan Muslims opted for Indonesian nationality.[81] Moreover, while the Waalwijk community seemed to tend to stick to Tan's kampong version of Islam, the Ridderkerk community showed a tendency towards a less 'local' and more 'progressive' version.[82] So even though the respective mosque organizations did not profile themselves as particularly pro-RMS or pro-Indonesia on the surface,[83] it would be naïve for us to assume that the overall religious divergence between the Waalwijk and Ridderkerk communities would not have had an effect on the architectural representations of Islam that relevant community leaders developed in processes of mutual contrasting.

As the former Wyldemerck community was split up into factions that contained fewer families than the thirty required for government-subsidized 'church-buildings' – 18 families in Waalwijk and 26 in Ridderkerk,[84] both parties had to make do with provisionally-appointed town houses for weekly prayer. In fact, the move to other locations meant that in both cases the struggle for a proper mosque had to start again from scratch, although the Moluccan communities in The Netherlands were the only ones who could still expect heavy government funding for religious facilities after the official severance of financial ties between state and church in 1975 aimed at 'normalization of relations'. They were exempted from the rule, thanks to the special 'Debt of Honor' that the authorities recognized towards their old Moluccan allies.[85]

The Bait Ar-Rahman Mosque, Ridderkerk

As the number of Ridderkerk families was less than the officially required 30 in the first years after the move, it was only on 7 May 1976, that imam Abdussabar Oppier could send a letter to the Ministry of Culture, Recreation and Social Work (Ministerie van Cultuur, Recreatie en Maatschappelijk Werk or CRM[86]) with an official request for a purpose-built Moluccan mosque.[87] When asked for a sketch, Oppier instructed his son (Abdul) Hamid, at that time following a technical education in Rotterdam, to make one.[88] Importantly, the imam required Islam to shift from the 'traditionalist' kampong construction as expressed in Wyldemerck and Waalwijk towards the more 'progressive' Islamic version that the Ridderkerk clans located in the general Indonesian area instead of in an isolated Moluccan village. Consequently, the imam required Islam to be represented by a mosque that incorporated general Indonesian building elements instead of those which he associated with a traditional Ambonese kampong. As Hamid remembered, his father did ask him to base his sketch partly on the Wyldemerck Mosque, in the sense that the four columns, regarded by the imam as a general characteristic of Indonesian mosques, should be included as symbols of 'the four schools of law in Islam'. Now, the mosque had to have an 'Indonesian dome' as well as an 'Indonesian minaret'. Moreover, the kampong custom of separation between prayer hall and Baileo, much-valued by Tan as a traditional

Moluccan kampong characteristic, was dismissed. Instead, Hamid came up with the idea of a split-level for the creation of integrated communal and office spaces, with an extra level below ground. In Hamid's recollection, the forms as used in his preliminary sketch and as asked for by his father had been largely based on the Mogulesque domes and minarets visible in mosques on Java as well as on Ambon and, for that matter, throughout Indonesia.

Understandably, as Hamid, later one of the leading mosque architects in The Netherlands, was only in his second year, the technical specifications of the design he sent in were not deemed adequate by the municipality. However, because the community insisted on a Muslim designer because he would 'know what a mosque looks like', imam Oppier was asked if he could suggest an official architect himself, instead of one being proposed by the RGD. Through contacts between community member Ibrahim Spalburg and Muslim convert Abdul Wahid van Bommel – who, as chairman of the Muslim Information Center in The Hague had quite a network among Muslims in The Netherlands at that time – the architect Latief Perotti was approached.[89] To be able to apply for government funding, a foundation was created under Dutch law that was officially aimed at a purpose-built mosque. On 26 July 1978, imam Oppier was instituted as its first chairman. Three years later, after his unexpected death during a stay on Ambon, he was followed by Hamid Samaniri. Ibrahim Spalburg was instituted as the mosque's secretary, a position he held under several successive mosque councils.

Perotti was an architect with a deep interest in spiritual matters. In an interview for a Masonic magazine, he explained that he had become a Freemason in 1968. This had given him a new point of view for the architecture of the spirit, defining it as his task to develop a higher consciousness in this life, steered by the Great Architect of the Universe. From that time, when he designed a sacral building, he kept the vision of Solomon's Temple [the example for every Masonic Lodge[90]] in mind. He also developed a strong interest in the anthroposophical building philosophy of Rudolf Steiner after a visit to the Goetheaneum in Dornach. Perotti then expanded his interest in the built environment as an expression of the spirit by studying the world's religious architectures, aiming to extract universal principles. Subsequently, he also found those principles to be present in Islam and Islamic architecture, which seemed to have incorporated the important elements of all the important religions from earlier times and he came to regard Islam as the final, closing religion.[91] Subsequently, he changed his name to Latief at the instigation of his Islamic teacher, the Indonesian imam Bapak Muhammad.[92]

In 1977, he established himself in Alphen a/d Rijn as an independent architect, with the architectural bureau Archyplan.

Perotti never seems to have mentioned his specifically Masonic view of religious architecture in non-Masonic contexts. At first, he apparently presented himself as a convert to Islam towards interviewers and towards his future Muslim patrons, who had approached him precisely for that reason.[93] In an article he wrote for a Dutch-Islamic magazine, he said he had performed Umrah at Mecca and Medina. He further stated that to him, a building worked as a filter between man and the cosmos. Because of his strong interest in the more spiritual and socio-psychological aspects of the built environment, he focused on the value of the symbol, on archetypes and their meaning for mankind. He pointed out the symbolic aspects of the Koran, cosmology and cosmography, forces of heat and nature, astronomy and astrology, mathematics, numbers, geometry, physics, medicine, pharmacology, mineralogy, calligraphy, decoration, color, light and transformation. In his eyes, architecture could be called 'Islamic' when these aspects had been given attention in the creative process leading to a building.[94] After his mosque commissions, however, he publicly preferred to refer to himself not as a Muslim, but as a Universalist who could 'just as well pray in a Catholic church'.[95] He stressed that he felt he had to transform 'the spiritual into matter'. According to him, this was not a generally accepted task, but since he had become conscious of the spiritual, he had not been able to do anything else. In his view, 'spiritual building' was giving a spiritual dimension to construction, so as to make sure a building began to live. The architect found that he was not taken altogether seriously by potential patrons and colleagues. Apparently, he felt himself to be in a rather isolated position since companies did not easily give commissions to him. However, he did not think of that as a bad thing, because in this way he got the more interesting commissions like the Greek temple in Archeon, the archeological theme park in his hometown.[96]

Importantly, according to Perotti, many Muslims 'only wanted to imitate, aiming for their mosque to be a version of what they knew from back home'. Perotti himself strongly opposed that. 'Building mosques can appease the identity problems of the second and third generations. But to call on the experience of Islamic youth, Islam has to be put forward in a new way. We have to go back to the source of Islam, the surrender to Allah.'[97] 'Why should a contemporary mosque look like the ones that were built centuries ago? […] Shouldn't there be some sort of progress in it? You have to be able to tell by looking at a mosque that Islam keeps up with the times, that it is not a static faith but full of change. I am a great proponent of that.'[98] The architect specifically wanted to create his own building type instead of copying the architecture from the Islamic world.[99] In fact, Perotti found that Islamic architecture was not to be established by 'cultural' building elements at all, but mainly by geometrical and proportional symbolism.[100]

On 18 February 1978, Perotti made a first sketch of the Ridderkerk mosque for the community.[101] This design strongly reflected his personal ideas on sacred architecture and religious symbolism. In the recollection of Hamid Oppier, who states to have been present during conversations on the matter, the architect explained, among other things, the sequence of spaces (symbolizing the transition from the profane to the sacral), the combination of square and circular forms (symbolizing the earthly and the static against the spiritual and the dynamic), the minaret (the letter 'Alif' and a heavenly marker), the five columns behind the mihrab (the five pillars of Islam), and a water-filled basin just behind the mihrab (the origin of life). When confronted with this design, imam Oppier took notice of all Perotti's symbolist intentions but, according to his son, he also had some critical remarks, which at this stage came down to the facts that there were no four central columns and that the minaret was placed right in front of the entrance, both of which the imam rejected as being 'non-Indonesian'. Although Oppier had apparently rejected the kampong construction of Islam and although he was searching for a more encompassing version as much as Perotti, he still required his religious construction to be defined in specific opposition to contesting views among other Moluccan-Islamic community leaders. As a consequence, he required Islam to be represented with very specific 'cultural' building elements – in this case the Mogulesque forms as associated with reform as opposed to the Meru forms as associated with traditionalism.

In the meantime, Perotti had been asked by the Foundation Islamic Center Rotterdam (Stichting Islamitisch Centrum Rotterdam) to design a mosque suitable for 3000 believers of all nationalities. The Center had been established by Muslim community leaders from different culture groups – including Spalburg – and wanted to make use of the municipal ideal, formulated in July 1976, of a two large, ethnically-shared purpose-built mosques, one in the center and one in the south of the city. This particular mosque was apparently to be placed on the site where the Netherlands Architecture Institute (NAi) is now located, across the street from the Boymans van Beuningen Museum.[102] The resulting drawing, published and explicated by the Islamic Center in the undated 'Brochure Moskee Rotterdam', was similar to Perotti's Ridderkerk design, showing the universal character of Perotti's design ideals. **(Figure 72)** Where the architect had not specified the Ridderkerk mosque's size, he had in this case, and now the numerology of the measurements he used came fully to the fore: everything was either divisible by 3 or 4. Of course, if any architect was suited for the job of creating a 'universal mosque', it was Perotti, but his ideas were not to be. Where Oppier had already expressly wanted more specifically 'cultural' building elements, here the generality of the idea was also one of the reasons, along with financial problems, the building was never executed. Apparently the municipality had learned that the Rotterdam Muslim ethnic groups each required their own prayer hall, using their own group's language and religious customs.[103] The idea of the 'shared-ethnic' prayer hall, including a planned exhibition center on Islam in general, was abandoned, and the municipality then developed the idea of a limited number of 'singular-ethnic' mosques.[104] From a governmental-administrative perspective, such an ideal of control was perfectly understandable, but from a representational viewpoint it was doomed to fail since the whole point of the architectural representation of Islam to Muslim patrons in The Netherlands appeared to be the definition of one's religious construction against contesting constructions produced by other community leaders within their own culture group. The generalization of Islamic architecture by the municipality as well as the architect came from their own specific realities and representational motivations. However, Perotti did receive an invitation to present a paper on his unexecuted design and his general design ideas at an international conference on Islamic Architecture and Urban Planning at the King Faisal University in Dammam in January 1980, titled 'Modern Architecture and Planning on Basis of Old Islamic Principles. A Case Study'.[105]

On 3 March 1980, Perotti made a second sketch for his Ridderkerk commission.[106] Here he included the four columns, relocated the minaret to the back of the mihrab and placed the basin, containing an 'aqua pillar',[107] in the middle of the hall with a washing space on either side. The sketch also re-introduced Hamid Oppier's lower ground level and included a calculation of the Kiblah direction with the help of the Indian Circle, a medieval method of finding the orientation towards Mecca. 'After some local opposition', he had to reduce his ideal minaret height from 33 to 21,60 meters.[108] This reduction had been initiated by Alderman Lagendijk, who genuinely wanted to facilitate a mosque and expected serious problems arising in the meeting of the – partly confessional – municipal council that would be necessary for any deviation from the zoning plan and for the sale of the plot.

However, even after that, the mayor granted his cooperation only on the condition that they produce a more modest design, as he expected resistance by council members if the mosque were too 'demonstratively Islamic'.[109] Also the RGD had some suggestions which included eliminating the parking spaces below ground as this would make the mosque too expensive, in addition to practical remarks and technical requirements concerning insulation and materials.[110] Finally, in his son's recollection, Imam Oppier found the minaret forms too 'Turkish', requesting Perotti to come up with a more 'Indonesian' minaret. As it seems, the numerical and geometrical symbolism that Perotti had wanted to incorporate had made use of building elements with unintended cultural associations, in this case, with a culture group non-representative for Indonesia, and so unusable for Oppier's required religious distinction from the contesting Islamic constructions produced by other Moluccan-Islamic community leaders.

In October 1980, Perotti made a third plan.[111] The minaret was reduced to 12 meters. The central dome was omitted altogether, a circular space for classes and day care was placed at the entrance, the 'aqua pillar' was raised above the roof, and the ground plan was divided into multiple spaces by walls and folding walls. Moreover, the façades were more or less given the image of a row of contemporary town houses. Finally, the minaret was drawn as a combination of geometrical shapes without recognizable references to any existing culture areas, completely in line with Perotti's ideas. In Hamid's memory, Oppier found the minaret, as might have been expected, not Indonesian enough. In addition, the circular forms and 'aqua pillar' were not seen as Indonesian either, while he found the lack of a dome completely unacceptable. Clearly, the specific construction of Islam that the community leader wanted represented in Ridderkerk clashed with the municipality's vision of 'integrated' design, and with some of Perotti's own ideas on sacred architecture. As appears from his design philosophy, the architect wanted to create a 'Dutch', but still 'recognizably Islamic', building, while trying to avoid – what he saw as – copies of existing homeland forms, explaining the religion mainly in symbolic terms and working towards some sort of an Islamic formal essence without any preexisting cultural associations. Understandably, when looking at the Ridderkerk design process, it was not easy for the architect to represent the realities of initiators, RGD and municipality as well as his own.

On 12 January 1981, Perotti sent Spalburg a letter with a fourth plan, summing up the adaptations he had introduced after his discussions about his former sketch.[112] According to Perotti, the prayer hall and space for the imam were enlarged, a storage room added, the roof construction simplified, the dome flattened (instead of omitted), the circular forms in the ground plan replaced by square ones, the meeting space and prayer space combined into one, the number of folding walls reduced, the 'aqua pillar' omitted, draught doors added at the women's and men's entrances, the design of the minaret and its attachment to the main building adjusted, the insulation improved, and the design of the façades further studied 'so as to create a larger identity with the inside and a better compliance with the surrounding buildings'. In the drawing, we see that the square and open ground plan of the prayer hall, considered to be a basic Indonesian mosque feature by Oppier, had returned without the folding-walls, and that the 'aqua-pillar' was erased. The circular classroom had become octagonal and the minaret given a different image, although again incorporating forms apparently not to be directly associated with any specific culture area. As far as mayor and aldermen were concerned, this design was acceptable. They requested the RGD to work the sketch into a definitive plan, later to be scrutinized by the Aesthetics Commission, with the added remark that for the adjustment of the zoning plan and the sale of the plot the cooperation of the municipal council would still be necessary.[113]

However, the designer's combination of the contrasting realities of opposing parties with his own could not, understandably, satisfy everyone. In subsequent negotiations between RGD and architect, parts of the plan had to be heavily adjusted. According to Hamid Oppier, the main entrance had to be relocated to the street side, eating away at the community's wish for separate entrances for both sexes. The dome had to be raised again to make the design more 'coherent'. The façade forms had to become more 'sober' and 'simple', and the minaret also had to be relocated to the street side to make it more 'visible' and the plan more 'exciting'. The initiators, after imam Oppier's death in January 1981 consisting of the mosque board and Hamid Oppier himself, also had had suggestions for the design. They found its current form too 'restless' and too different from the last. They also objected to the minaret's location directly behind and against the mihrab, as they found that 'in Indonesia' it would ideally be placed at one of the corners or to the side, detached from the main building. Further, the mosque still did not have what they thought of as recognizably Indonesian forms.[114] In June 1981, at the request of Perotti, Hamid Oppier made sketches of possible minaret constructions. Apparently, the RGD had also made some remarks about the minaret design in Perotti's plan.[115] Oppier sketched four or five different minaret types related to the general Muslim culture areas, based on literature on the world's Islamic architecture. He then proposed one of them to Perotti as typically Indonesian, in contrast to what he had seen as the 'Turkish pencil-minarets' from Perotti's initial mosque designs and the 'non-existent forms' of his subsequent proposals. For his alternative, 'really Indonesian', minaret design, Oppier had mainly used images of Mogulesque minarets on Java.

In July 1981, a new Perotti design that had met with the RGD's approval was discussed within the mosque administration, and was generally approved by the administrators as well.[116] **(Figure 73)** The dome's form was changed to a hemisphere; the minaret was, in Hamid Oppier's account, 'Indonesian' as proposed by Oppier, and it was moved away from the longitudinal axis to the street side, detached from the main building but connected to it by a covered passageway; and instead of the main entrance along the longitudinal axis it was moved to the street side with a fountain at its former location, against a monumental wall as proposed by a Moluccan-Islamic community member and executed by a Dutch artist.

On 13 August, Perotti's final plan was presented at a meeting of the relevant sub-council of the Ridderkerk general municipal council. Although this first presentation was only meant to be voted on in terms of formal accessibility, with a more extensive treatment during a following meeting, SGP member M. Veldhoen announced himself against the building.[117] 'Something like this belongs in Baghdad, not in Slikkerveer,' he was reported to have exclaimed when shown Perotti's design. He apparently thought its forms deviated too much from the rest of the buildings in Slikkerveer. CDA member P. Visser doubted that the 10-to-12 parking spaces planned would be enough for all the Muslims in the wider region who, he feared, would be coming in from all over. However, G.A. Verhaaf, secretary of the Commission and Chief of Urban Development, contested this fear as it was known that car ownership among Moluccan Muslims, for whom the mosque was specifically intended, was below Dutch average. The newspaper also said that it was not yet certain whether the mosque would be built, due to its height: either the design or the zoning plan would have to be changed.[118]

On 10 September, the sub-council held another meeting, during which it was to decide whether the proposal would be referred to the general municipal council. At the start, Visser felt the need to say that, although the sub-council had approved of the formal presentation of the design, it had not yet established a general viewpoint. Veldhoen decided to nuance his opinion as stated in the minutes of the earlier meeting and declared that he was not against the establishment of the mosque itself, but against its planned location in the center of Slikkerveer. Further, Visser requested that the minaret be omitted from the design with a view to aesthetics ('*welstand*,' or aesthetics in the sense of the Aesthetics Commission). In return, G.A. Verhaaf explained that a number of other locations had been proposed but that most community members lived in Slikkerveer. He added that the minaret had already been reduced from '20 meters' in the first plan to '12 meters' in this one, and that the community would probably stick to this as a desired minimum. M.T. Lagendijk, PVDA member, alderman of the relevant department and chairman of the Commission, declared his willingness to discuss this height once again with the community. However, together with Visser, CDA member A.C. Van Nes requested a design without a minaret, and asked for an alternative location. Veldhoen also confirmed his rejection of the planned location, as did Visser using the argument of aesthetics. The two members also spoke against the sale of the plot in light of the objections they had mentioned. As it was, the majority of the sub-council decided in favor of presenting the plan to the general municipal council.[119] One newspaper, covering the meeting, suggested that SGP and CDA, by opposing the mosque and the sale of the plot, were starting a new war of religions, the consequences of which would be difficult to estimate.[120]

On 28 September, the municipal council held a meeting in which this proposal formed one of the main items on the agenda, although the onlookers from the Moluccan-Islamic community had to first sit through a discussion on energy as the mosque was the last issue to be voted on.[121] The minutes of this last part of the meeting are too interesting not to cite at some length, as they form a revealing condensation of the arguments that have been generally used in discussions among politicians for and against 'visibly Islamic' design in the Dutch context.[122] PVDA member J. Kaptein fired away. 'Firstly, the mosque should preferably be built in Slikkerveer, as this neighbourhood harbours the largest concentration of Moluccans. Secondly, it is necessary that a mosque's longitudinal axis be parallel to the direction of prayer, that is to the South-East. The proposed plot completely answers to this requirement. From an architectural point of view, our party finds this to be important. [...] There will be few other plots in town that can offer a comparable location and size. We find it to be architecturally incorrect to place a building diagonally on a building plot. [...] We are of the opinion that the proposed plot is the only one suited for the construction of a mosque. Also architecturally, the mosque will be an enrichment of the totality of buildings in the street. Compared to the existing architecture, the mosque appears to have a somewhat deviant design, but that doesn't necessarily mean that such a building would not fit into its surroundings.'

CDA member J. Wendrich responded. 'Jesus said: love your enemies, treat well those who hate you. He also said: everything you want people to do to you, you should do to them. [...] If we were Turkish Christians in Turkey, we would like very much to be permitted to build a house of prayer, and to be allowed to serve God and honour him in the way that was put before us in the Bible. However, we would not get it into our heads to try and build on a conspicuous spot and in a building style that totally deviates from the locally used style. Now, if we project that onto the situation in Ridderkerk, then we understand the need of the Muslims to have their own building that can serve as a house of prayer and place of gathering, a place where they can serve God in their own way. But at the same time we ask ourselves why they want to defy us ('*voor het hoofd stoten*'), by wanting to build on such a central spot in such a challenging way, using a building style which in itself might be attractive, perhaps even more than we are used to, but completely deviates from what has been built around the construction site. [...] Let no one ever again come up with roof-extensions that supposedly don't fit into the streetscape. If this building fits into those surroundings, then you can build anything on any location and the Aesthetics Commission will have made itself superfluous. The need to build in an Eastern style eludes us. Just like the Bible doesn't have any rules on what a church should look like, the Koran doesn't either. I have here an English translation of the Koran [...]. I can assure you that in this book there are no indications for the construction of a mosque. Therefore, building in an adapted style doesn't seem to me as contrary to faith. [...] We are prepared to allow for the construction of a mosque, even on that particular spot, as long as one adjusts oneself to the local building style, then adaptation of the zoning plan to change the maximum height will not be necessary. [...] We have put our objections to Islam aside to enable the Muslims in our town to build a mosque and in particular to experience their Muslim-ness there, but we cannot agree with the establishment of an architecturally non-fitting building in the heart of Slikkerveer.'

SGP member Veldhoen cut in. 'No one, not even the constitution, can force us to sell a plot of land. In other words, the freedom that the constitution offers does not automatically read as an obligation to sell. Do we start or steer towards a religious war? Not at all. History clearly shows who has always been persecuted. [...] Islam is, according to our faith, a heathen religion. We cannot serve two masters. [...] Lastly, [...] one of the evaluation standards has always been that one evaluates the building in itself and in its relation with its surroundings. On the building itself I won't express a value-judgment, that is subjective, what one person likes, the other finds ugly, however, in relation with its surroundings it does not fit. This is a strange ('*wezensvreemd*') element in our culture pattern and in our architecture.'

Alderman Lagendijk reacted. 'As the alderman, responsible for this case, and I'm not hiding from it, I architecturally haven't got a single realistic argument, contrary to what the chairman has said, not to build this prayer hall on that particular spot. It just isn't there. Situated on the main routes of Ridderkerk there are at this moment six prayer halls of a different religion. I therefore fail to see why this space should not be built on the proposed street. [...] I have spoken with a delegate of the Aesthetics Commission on this case and he did not speak negatively about it. [...] Mr. Wendrich suggests to the Moluccan community that they want to defy us by building in such a conspicuous place. That has been a matter of meetings with CRM and of course also with the Moluccans themselves, and then a choice was made in favor of this spot, all the more because there was enough space. We are talking about a building of 42 x 24,5 m2. As for content this would be 3500 m3, comparable to half a Church of the Good Lord ('*Goede Herderkerk*'). What sort of objections should still exist on that spot, architecturally speaking, really eludes me. [...] I will not go into the religious considerations of Mr. Veldhoen. From their point of view it might be realistic to bring these things up. Not from mine. What I have to do is evaluate this plan on its architectural aspects.'

Member Kaptein concurred. 'It is very remarkable that it is exactly the confessional parties who are opposed to the construction. They formulate it cleverly: we do not oppose the plan for religious reasons – especially the CDA – but for architectural reasons. Now I would like to remind the CDA of their own election program [...], in which it states that city policy should establish foreign workers as full members of our life- and culture patterns and that they should be able to practice their religion according to their own norms. Well, we could ask ourselves what they mean by that. But to the culture pattern of Islamic faith belongs a mosque and to that mosque obviously belongs a minaret. There's no way around it, that's just the way it is.'

Member Wendrich defended. 'As I already pleaded, we are not against the construction of a mosque, but where do I get the necessity of doing that in an Eastern style. I don't see that, and the CDA doesn't see that. That is why we think that it can be done in a different style. That it should be in a certain direction, alright, that is why we don't object to its currently planned location. But why should it be done in an Eastern style with a minaret?' (Then Kaptein cut in with the question of what Wendrich regarded as a culture pattern. Wendrich: 'That is not a matter of some building, Mr. Kaptein.' Kaptein: 'A building is also a piece of culture.' Wendrich: 'No it isn't.')

D'66 member J.J. Kroeze added his view. 'I cannot understand the CDA. I keep having the feeling that they are looking for a stick to hit the dog with. All that talk about an Eastern style that supposedly doesn't fit. I find it an enrichment of our culture. In Rotterdam we have a Norwegian church, built in a Norwegian style. No-one had any objections against that.'

Alderman Lagendijk tried to appease Wendrich. 'The height of the minaret has already been reduced, to the disappointment of the Moluccan community itself. They see the thing as a symbolic expression of their faith. I have had two conversations, both of them a real pleasure, and I talked to them about the problems in the council concerning a number of cases that were put forward by you and Mr. Veldhoen. I became convinced that I should not sit here and plead for the removal of a minaret. Their conviction is that it is indispensable, and that is why I haven't made a proposal to you not to include it. The minaret hardly extends, perhaps 1 meter, above the Christian school next to it. It is no longer some piece-of-work of 21 meters. In the meantime, it has been reduced to 11 meters. That means that, at this time, it extends 2 meters above the permitted construction height on that location. Then I say, what are we talking about?'

When the chairman put the proposal to vote, it was accepted by 18 to 9. Immediately after, an application was filed. After some minor, practical adjustments requested by Aesthetics, another application was filed on 5 April 1982, and positive assent was received three weeks later.[123] The plan was made publicly accessible on 3 May.[124] On 15 December, some minor adjustments were incorporated in the builder's estimates. Aesthetics responded positively the next week and the municipality gave an official permit on 15 March 1983.[125]

Achmad Oppier, member of the religious council and relative of the former imam, replaced the late Abdussabar Oppier in conducting the actual 'ground breaking' ceremony, consisting of placing the first pole and performing the accompanying prayers.[126] Although this ceremony had already been partly performed during the first sod in Wyldemerck, it now focused not on the first sod but on the quintessential pole. Whereas in Wyldemeck it was felt to be a Moluccan ceremony, here, to the patrons, in Hamid Oppier's account, the ritual had strong Indonesian connotations.[127] In addition to this, a more 'Dutch' first pole ceremony was requested by the mosque administration, for which the Ministry of WVC (formerly CRM) was willing to give instructions to the RGD and to participate in the ceremony itself.[128] On 14 October 1983, this second, concrete, first pole was officially driven into the ground.[129] Present for the ceremony were representatives from the municipality, the RGD and, notably, the Indonesian embassy.[130] To be sure, the community had requested the RGD to make an exact calculation of the direction towards Mecca in addition to Perotti's medieval method,[131] as the latter, according to Hamid Oppier, mainly represented an important 'Islamic tradition' to the architect himself and not to the community. Similarly, the architect bestowed a much more esoteric meaning on the ground breaking rituals than the community members present, as he seemed to be the only one who observed how angels assisted in driving the first poles into the ground.[132] Construction went as planned and without major difficulties. Besides the first pole, there was also a ceremony for the placement of the dome on the main structure. The 'closing of the roof' or 'closing of the dome' was felt to be a crucial moment in construction, one needing extensive prayers. Here, too, in Hamid Oppier's recollection, this was thought of as a ceremony generally observed throughout the Indonesian archipelago, where the roofing of a house would often involve some form of celebration.[133]

On 1 October 1984, the mosque was officially opened. Mr. Gijsbers, director-general of WVC, tried to make amends for the mixed reception in Ridderkerk: 'That a space like this mosque, in a country where Christianity's presence is dominant, can be realized, has everything to do with the opinion that each has the right to practice his or her religion, individually or in communion with others. An opinion that is cast in our constitution. Unfortunately, within our society there are forces, luckily on a limited scale, that express intolerance and discrimination towards members of minority groups living in our country. That is, I think, an unfortunate matter. I am of the opinion that we have to make sure that equality of people is not made dependent on race, sex or religion. What's important is that we give each other, in everyday practice, the space to live with one another equally. We have to accept that we have a multicultural society in The Netherlands.'[134] **(Figure 74)**

In several interviews after the opening, Perotti gave a public explanation of his design in Ridderkerk in terms of general symbolism, apparently preferring to avoid any reference to the specifically 'cultural' building elements that the initiators had required in their representation of Islam. 'The essential characteristics of Islam and the traditional mosque were used as the philosophical basis and put into a design.'[135] 'In constructing the Ridderkerk mosque, I attached a strong role to oppositions: between men and women (separate spaces), light and dark, heaven and earth. In the prayer hall there are four columns: these symbolize earthliness. This transforms into the dome, which represents heaven.' To the question of whether he had a certain example in mind from the history of Islam, he answered: 'I have made a fairly intensive study of Islamic culture, but I was also led by the Western surroundings in which this mosque was built. In the various countries of the Middle-East and of the rest of the world, by the way, mosque construction differs totally. We now have added our own "type" to it.' When asked if there were any typically Moluccan elements, he said: 'Yes, we tried to do so. The building is transparent and light. This agrees with the nature of the target group.'[136] 'In all kinds of measurements and proportions, the Fibonacci sequences (thus the Golden Section as well) are visible, in addition to every possible numerical symbol. The number four stands for the four lower forces: the material, the vegetal, the animal, and the human. The four columns in the prayer hall refer to that. The square plan of this space stands for the earthly. The octagonal tambour, carried by the four columns, is a combination of two squares and symbolizes the transformation from the earthly to the higher or the dome which, together with the minaret, also represents the vertical axis to the heavenly.'[137] Moreover, the architect apparently preferred to explain the shifts in design that, as appeared from the design process, had been instigated by practical limitations or objections by government or initiators, in terms of general archetypes and universal symbolism as well. The entry was now placed beside the longitudinal-axis because of the aim to stress the independent importance of that axis: after entering, you had to 'consciously turn in the direction of Mecca'. Furthermore, the detached minaret at the corner of the main building now carried the symbolical meaning of a 'corner stone'.[138] As a consequence of this nominal, 'deculturalized' representation by the architect, the reality that the initiators themselves produced by means of their building was never picked up by observers, and its meaning of a very specific representation of Islam as opposed to contesting Islamic views held by other Moluccan-Islamic community leaders was completely lost in architectural discourse.

The An-Nur Mosque, Waalwijk

In 1969, the authorities in Waalwijk tried to get Christian and Muslim Moluccans to accept a proposal for a shared, multi-religious building that would serve as a church as well as a mosque.[139] This proposal met with disapproval on both sides, and by the time the Moluccan Muslim population fulfilled the requirement of a minimum of 30 families in itself, it was time to take action. However, whereas most families in Waalwijk, as said, had chosen to stick to traditional kampong Islam in the process of mutual contrasting with Ridderkerk's more 'progressive' or 'Indonesian' version, there certainly were also those community members who desired a shift away from the Moluccan and Indonesian perspectives towards a more reformist version.[140] While the Ridderkerk community's orientation towards Indonesia and a less 'local' Islamic construction had been something of a general sense within the group, the sharper distinction of religious views between members in Waalwijk could not remain without serious repercussions for the architectural ambitions that helped shape The Netherlands' third Moluccan mosque.

As a consequence, some members of the community decided to start their own negotiations with CRM independently from the established Moluccan-Islamic organization in Waalwijk. In 1978, a group called Organisatie Nurul Islam (ONI), aimed at building a mosque in Waalwijk, was created by a group of young adults under chairmanship of Arsad Ohorella, a community member with a technical education. Ohorella came up with a preliminary sketch, which is now no longer available but which, in the memory of several community members, did not have any specific Indonesian or Moluccan features, although it was recognizably 'general-Islamic' through 'dome and minaret'.[141] Strikingly, the kampong-associated building elements so valued by Tan in Wyldemerck as well as the Indonesia-associated building elements that were found to be of such great importance by Oppier in Ridderkerk in this case seemed to play only a negative part. This is not to say that this particular Waalwijk community leader did not value his Moluccan cultural background, but it did mean that he found that Islam was not to be asserted with any specifically Moluccan or Indonesian characteristics, as in his reality Islam ideally was the same for all Muslims.

However, just as the Ridderkerk community needed a recognized Dutch architect, so did ONI. On 22 November 1978, Arsad Ohorella and two other ONI members had a talk with Perotti,[142] a logical choice since he had started designing plans for the Ridderkerk mosque in February of that year and since he was the only architect at that time who conspicuously aimed at finding a general Islamic design. Three weeks later, ONI officially commissioned Perotti with the construction of a mosque in Waalwijk.[143] Secretary Astorias Ohorella, Arsad's brother, invited community member Boy Barajanan, who was working as a consultant in construction technology, to take part in a building commission. For this commission, ONI wanted people with architectural expertise under supervision of the hired architect.[144] Ibrahim Lessy, whose name was to reappear after a temporary shutdown of the commission, came second when a new chairman was voted.[145] Arsad Ohorella filled Boy Barajanan in on the state of matters of subsidy and the allotment of a suitable plot for which he had been negotiating with municipal authorities and CRM.[146]

In January 1979, Boy Barajanan offered a preliminary program for the construction of the mosque. In this program, the first thing mentioned under the paragraph 'preparation' was 'presenting own ideas on design', followed by 'having design checked by community making use of it, currently and in the near future'. The latter part would prove a particularly important pointer towards the initiators' design preferences. Next, Barajanan's points would be worked out in a proposal, with existing Moluccan prayer spaces in The Netherlands as possible sources of influence. Barajanan's program was discussed by the building commission, and it was decided that the municipality would be approached for a plot allotment. Furthermore, the number of families would be counted and signatures assembled. Barajanan was asked to contact I.H. Matulessy, a Moluccan architect working for CRM, and organizations involved in the construction of Moluccan churches. The ONI administration would be asked to obtain information on how to apply for funds from the relevant organizations. As for Perotti, he would only be asked to make the drawings at first, as long as there was a satisfactory financial arrangement: at that point the commission apparently did not intend to hand over the supervision of the whole project yet.[147]

The municipality subsequently proposed three alternative locations: one plot in the city center, bought in 1970 by the state for the specific purpose of a Moluccan house of prayer;[148] another plot on the Noordstraat next to the state highway, to be exchanged for the former one, and another just west of the second. As that on the Noordstraat was located very near to a concentration of Moluccan Muslims and to the existing house of prayer, the choice was easy for the community as well as for the municipality. As for Matulessy, he explained to Barajanan that he was the head of the Building Bureau Moluccan Churches (Bouwburo Molukse Kerkgebouwen) in Utrecht, a department of CRM especially created to advise on Moluccan churches but not to construct them. He explained that CRM had first to approve the financial and programmatic aspects of a proposal, after which the RGD would hire an architect. Of course, as he also had a design bureau experienced in designing Christian-Moluccan church buildings, Barajanan could propose him as an architect to the RGD.[149] However, after talks with Matulessy, in

Barajanan's account, ONI expressly decided to go through with Perotti's commission as they apparently expected him, as a supposed Muslim convert, to be much more suited to create an Islamic prayer hall. Unfortunately, because of a controversial shift in the imamate directly related to the split between the adherents of kampong-Islam and those of reform mentioned above, religious differences of opinion within the Waalwijk community prevented further actions on a new mosque.[150] Apparently the reformists, no longer content with the kampong-Islam taught in the old mosque, decided unilaterally to institute a Moluccan imam who had lived and studied Koran and Sunna in Saudi Arabia. As this manoeuvre was heavily contested by the established kampong organization and the Waalwijk community took a long time to recover, the building commission was out of action for a long time.

On 22 November 1983 Ibrahim Lessy took up where Arsad Ohorella had left. Having been, as we saw earlier, an important member of ONI, the reformist tendency appeared, for now, to have risen victorious from the polemics around the imamate and the form of Islam to be taught. Lessy was appointed chairman of a newly created foundation with the aim of constructing a mosque in Waalwijk, the Foundation Moluccan Mosque An-Nur. In a proposal for the program of requirements of 23 February 1984, the Foundation was said to have been created to continue the activities of the former ONI, which had been involved in negotiations on a new mosque with municipality and CRM in 1978 but which had been forced to stop 'due to re-organizational circumstances'. An-Nur continued these negotiations and assembled a program of requirements clearly based on the points of departure that Boy Barajanan had proposed in his January 1979 program of construction, including spatial functions and the required 1 square meter for each worshipper, although by now the congregation had grown from 50 families to 80. As for location, the Foundation decided to stick to the plot on the Noordstraat already approved by the municipality.[151]

Accompanying these requirements we find an undated and undetailed ground plan by Perotti.[152] In this preliminary plan, according to Lessy, Perotti had taken into account the width of the plot, the traffic noise on the north-side, and the orientation towards Mecca (impractical in relation to the street orientation) by placing the entrance at the street side, the communal spaces separated from the highway through a corridor, and the women's and men's prayer halls as turned squares side by side and in line with the Kiblah rather than the street. The four columns were not indicated as such in the drawing, but that was merely because not all internal elements were included: this preliminary version was not meant for scrutiny by RGD or municipal authorities. It later appeared that Perotti had planned to include them from the very beginning, although Lessy had never asked him to.[153]

Lessy reacted to Perotti's plan with the remark that the women's prayer room should not be beside the men's, since 'in Islam' women were not supposed to have equal space. Although, according to Lessy, women on Ambon either had their own mosques or their own prayer space behind the men's, separated by curtains, that was not the way that Islam was ideally practiced: they should preferably be situated 'on a balcony'. And, instead of one minaret, he had hoped for 'as many minarets as the Kaaba Mosque', as this mosque to him was 'the culmination of Islamic architecture'. At that time an image of it had been hanging conspicuously in the old prayer room's mihrab.[154] Apparently, although the community leader required his reformist construction of Islam to be represented by building elements that were 'deculturalized' as much as Perotti had required them to be in his own reality, Lessy's preferred alternative consisted of building elements specifically associated with Islamic orthodoxy and the Kaaba as the ultimate, 'non-cultural' center of the Islamic world, and not with some form of universalist spirituality. His representational motivation came from the desire to directly oppose his ideal version of Islam to contesting Islamic constructions produced by other Moluccan-Islamic community leaders. As can be expected, however, Perotti chose not to accept Lessy's requirements, stating that they could not be executed within the budget. Therefore, Lessy chose to position the women behind – instead of above – the men as second best,[155] and accepted the fact that there would only be money for one minaret. Notably, from this part in the design process it appears that the supposed 'equalization of the sexes' in the Waalwijk prayer space arrangement as it was later publicly stressed by the architect, was not in fact the patron's conscious choice that observers later assumed it to be. Lessy's tendency towards Islamic reform was aimed not at a modernization in 'modern-societal' terms but in terms of a radical shift away from kampong Islam towards a more purist version.

Meanwhile, the community leaders did have contact with Spalburg and Samaniri from the Ridderkerk mosque, wanting to learn from their experiences even though not having the same representational requirements. Naturally, they were informed about the Ridderkerk mosque's financing by the government. They then decided to continue with Perotti, making use of CRM as financier and RGD as patron instead of hiring him themselves, and presented Perotti as their preferred architect. The RGD had no problems with that, as Perotti had designed the Ridderkerk Mosque to their satisfaction. After an internal procedure that took about one year, in April 1986 the

RGD Coordinator Moluccan Churches requested the relevant provincial RGD director to start construction as soon as possible and to keep preparation time short.[156] On 21 November, the latter asked Perotti if he was still interested in building the Waalwijk mosque, to which the architect responded positively, and on 29 December the director officially commissioned Perotti to make a study of the possibilities of construction on the Noordstraat plot.[157] Boy Barajanan was the obvious choice for an intermediary between community and architect, and was made chairman of the mosque's building commission. Whenever Perotti made a plan, Barajanan would examine it with the mosque administration and give the architect his and their suggestions for adjustment.

As Perotti learned, the municipality had its own plans for the area. It intended to continue the provincial road (Taxandriaweg) between the mosque plot and the state highway further west, and now wished to change the route to bend around the future mosque. Based on this information, in April 1987 Perotti made a ground plan for scrutiny by the RGD.[158] Because of the nearby highway, he included a soundproof fence around the plot. Also, Perotti planned for a raised earthen platform of about 1,5 meters high because of the low situation of the plot in relation to its surroundings. The municipality apparently preferred people to look up to the building from the raised provincial road instead of down on it, and additionally, 'the liturgical aspect', according to the architect, made a higher situation necessary. Next, Perotti argued that the plan was more complicated [read: triangular] than usual because of noise protection, width of the plot, and orientation towards Mecca. Finally, he included a fountain as a 'symbolical element of liturgy', a conspicuous decoration of the entrance portal to make it stand out from the rest, a minaret with crowning and finial, a dome, and a covered passageway between minaret and mosque.[159]

A week later, the Foundation was given the opportunity to discuss façade drawings with the architect. Perotti said he had chosen the triangular ground plan for acoustic reasons, which was also why he had placed the prayer halls on the south, away from the highway. On the other hand, this way the number of façades would be restricted to three, creating more budgetary space. There would be a vertical symmetry along the axis and the orientation towards Mecca would be safe if he designed the mosque as a triangle. Because of the low ground, the mosque would be placed on a platform. Perotti also had hired a Waalwijk dowser to check the terrain on magnetic fields with a divining-rod, as the architect apparently believed that any 'negative radiation' would have to be neutralized for a religious building to have its transcendent effect. In fact, this was the architect's personal belief: neither the RGD nor Lessy saw any relevance in the ritual.[160] The combined platform and soundproof fence would be 2,60 meters high. To involve the minaret – intended to be detached from the main building but connected by a covered passageway as in Ridderkerk – in the mosque itself, transparent walls were to be used on that side. Finally, Perotti suggested making a model of the plan.[161]

To this last suggestion, Barajanan and the board members of the Foundation reacted positively. However, they also had some suggestions of their own, mostly about durability of materials, floor and heating, but they also asked for the cross-shape that was apparently visible in the minaret (just underneath the dome), to be erased. According to the architect, that particular element should be seen only as a detail in a larger context ('*momentopname*'), but he did remove it. In an addition to the report of the meeting, the foundation board noted its preference that the minaret be attached to the main building instead of separate,[162] thereby effectively distancing itself from the Moluccan way of building detached minarets. Perotti's façade design proposals were not made available by the architect, but according to Barajanan they already had all the elements seen in the final plan. Discussions and adjustments largely concerned the ground plan design of the overall plot. Apparently, the architect had taken most of his – and his initiators' – Ridderkerk design ideas with him to Waalwijk, although the initiators in Waalwijk had never asked for them. Also, having learned from the Ridderkerk commission, Perotti had decided to incorporate an 'Indonesian' minaret in Waalwijk, to be mainly proposed by an Indonesian, in this case an intern working at his office. According to Barajanan and to Oppier, who worked on the Waalwijk project as well, the intern had taken Javanese-Islamic architecture as an example.

Of course WVC, as the official financier, also had a say in the matter. It stressed that cost control was very important in the transmission of 'Moluccan churches' to the communities, and that costs had to be cut here. The raising of the terrain did not fit with their striving for soberness and functionality. Moreover, the sound-proof wall was no longer necessary since the municipality had included a soundproof fence between the highway and the apartment buildings beside the plot. Finally, the exchange of plots with the municipality meant that the planned size of the terrain would have to be cut in half as the plot in the city center was relatively small. Perotti said his plan could no longer be used and that he would make a new one.[163] In the meantime, as mentioned, Perotti also had a dowser check the terrain for radiation. As that appeared to be negative, he considered it necessary to include a carbon-based floor with copper pipes and bricks instead of concrete which, in his belief, would not be able to withstand any radiation.[164] In a later account, the architect also claimed that the municipality spent 'a few million' on moving the mosque plan to its current spot from an earlier one because of this radiation.[165]

Subsequently, Perotti made a new ground plan proposal, projected into a situation plan, on 17 July 1987.[166] This third plan met with the approval of all parties concerned. On 1 December, his proposal culminated in a more detailed plan that included façades. Together with a model and an axonometry, he and the Foundation demonstrated these in a public presentation.[167] **(Figure 75)** The RGD subsequently used these drawings in their application for a building permit.[168] One month later, the Aesthetics Commission gave their approval.[169] Subsequently, the municipal council's sub-commission approved the proposal with no further comments on the mosque plans,[170] and after that, the municipal council did the same.[171] Four months later, it also officially agreed to the exchange of plots.[172] Clearly, the mosque in Waalwijk met with less adversity in political circles than had its counterpart in Ridderkerk. On 6 December, the permit was granted.[173]

On 4 March 1989, imam Mohammed Kasim Ohorella performed the ground-breaking ceremony by ritually cleansing the ground with water and driving in a wooden pole on the spot where later on the forward right column underneath the dome would be placed, 'because it is closest to Mecca'.[174] However, as the forward right column, as mentioned, is considered the most sacred throughout the Indonesian archipelago, Muslim or not, and as it is logically not closest to Mecca at all, this interpretation should be seen as a conspicuous transformation of a 'cultural' building element with the aim of making it more 'generally Islamic', wholly in the line of reformist preferences. Likewise, at the closing of the roof on 14 August 1989,[175] when imam Ohorella symbolically controlled the crane, he found that this was the most important moment during construction, not because it was a typically Moluccan or even Indonesian custom but 'because the dome symbolizes the unity ('*saamhorigheid*') in Islam'.[176] Here as well, a 'cultural' building element was ostentatiously generalized. And similarly, in an interview just before the opening, Boy Barajanan declared: 'The mosque An-Nur in Waalwijk is only a Moluccan mosque as far as the Ministry of WVC is concerned. To us, the mosque remains the house of Allah. All mosques belong to Allah. And so every Muslim is welcome. […] The light, the cheerful and the amiable have everything to do with the nature of the Moluccans and their culture. […]

The four columns symbolize the natural elements of water, wind, fire and sand. [...] Symbolism, that the Muslim [...] is made to internalize from the age of four.'[177] Also here, building elements that to other Moluccan-Islamic community leaders were laden with Moluccan or Indonesian content were conspicuously deculturalized and refilled with general Islamic meaning. The only supposedly non-religious, 'Moluccan' building elements were established in the 'light and cheerful colors' of the mosque, a turn that would render its cultural content completely harmless given the specifically non-cultural representation that the initiators had required.

On 13 January 1990, Minister d'Ancona officially opened the mosque.[178] She handed over the keys to imam Ohorella, who then opened the doors. According to d'Ancona, with the opening of the mosque in Ridderkerk in 1984 and now the mosque in Waalwijk, 'the relations between the State and the Moluccan Muslim community in the Netherlands, in the religious domain, have now been normalized. [...] You now have the space to practice your religion on this spot. But also, in a metaphorical way, you now have the space, independent from anyone and under your own responsibility, to give this mosque the particular place in your community and Dutch society that you wish it to have'.[179] According to Perotti, when the mosque was opened by prayer, he saw angels occupying all corners of the building and he knew that the building was born.[180] **(Figure 76)**

After the opening, Perotti declared that, through his earlier experiences in Ridderkerk, this time he had been much more prepared for the spiritual aspect of building and for the question of how potentially present sacred values could be preserved and activated.[181] The triangular shape was an expression of the spiritual.[182] Moreover, the number three kept appearing in all kinds of measurements.[183] His Waalwijk interpretations of the square, the octagonal, the circle, the minaret and the four columns were already present in the Bait Ar-Rahman Mosque,[184] but now he had introduced 'the element of the feminine as a counterweight to the presence of the male energy'. In this, he wanted 'to express the co-dependence of the male and female aspect in nature as the most obvious example of the principle of polarity'.[185] It seems that the designer still preferred to explain publicly any specifically 'cultural' building elements in his design in terms of universalist symbolism, although, paradoxically, neither ONI or An-Nur had ever specifically asked for the four columns, an Indonesian minaret, or for any other Indonesian or Moluccan formal features. It was Perotti who had introduced them in the Waalwijk scene, having 'learned' from the Ridderkerk design process and having incorporated them in his Universalist ideas on sacred architecture. Importantly, Lessy still described the design as 'beautiful, artistic architecture and a subtle manifestation *of the own identity of our community* within Dutch society'.[186] However, he also described the four columns as 'the four corners of the Kaaba', since, according to him, they had not so much formed part of pre-Islamic Southeast-Asian culture as they had been introduced, at a very early stage, directly from the originating center of Islam, carrying only a general Islamic meaning.[187] Related to that, Lessy often wore Arab clothing when attending religious occasions, and he even claimed to have traced back his own descent to 33 generations ago from Yemen.[188]

All in all, Waalwijk responded much better to Perotti than did Ridderkerk. Waalwijk's design process was much less complicated and community leaders here generally tended, and still tend, to explain their mosque's features in terms of Perotti's symbolism much more than did the leaders in Ridderkerk.[189] It should come as no surprise that Perotti himself, in a comparison of his Ridderkerk and Waalwijk commissions, described the first as having had 'a stricter program of requirements', while speaking of the time in between the first and the latter in terms of 'the societal developments and trends that can be since observed'.[190] What remains is a fundamental, seemingly unbridgeable divergence between the realities of the architect and the initiators in both cases. On the one hand, where the initiators of the Bait Ar-Rahman Mosque said they had particularly thought of Indonesian building elements for their materialization of Islam, the architect claims that nothing Indonesian was – or had to be – incorporated at all, and that everything in the design sprang from his own spiritual creativity. On the other hand, where the initiators of the An-Nur Mosque said they had particularly thought of building elements that had no Moluccan or Indonesian associations in order to substantiate a completely different construction of Islam, the architect claims that he himself, and not some intern, officially designed the Indonesian minaret, thereby missing the point that it should not have been Indonesian in the first place.[191] Where in other cases the patrons supplied their own finances and, in that sense, were genuine patrons with a great deal of power towards their designers, in this case the sponsor was the Dutch government in the form of the RGD. After having themselves chosen Perotti in light of his presumed Muslimness, the Moluccan initiators no longer had as much discretion to steer, let alone dismiss, their architect as the Hindustani mosque patrons were earlier shown to have had. Still, even though the designer apparently preferred not to focus on it, they did have an important and meaningful influence on their eventual mosques. Moluccan mosque design in The Netherlands is an extreme example of how unintended miscommunications, deliberate misrepresentations, strategic self-attributions, and contextual shifts in explanations can lead to a complexity that defies straight, unambiguous interpretation. Moreover, it goes to show that it can be very difficult for parties involved in mosque design to think – or to let observers think – outside their own reality, even when later confronted with the actual reality of the party who sat at the other end of the designing table. Obviously, a Muslim-commissioned mosque design in The Netherlands is, by definition, a simultaneous representation of differing realities. As a consequence, the analyst cannot be confined to only one party, and should always regard the design process itself as the most objective source of information.

3. Turkish-Commissioned Mosque Design in The Netherlands

After the Hindustani-commissioned Mobarak Mosque in The Hague from 1955 and the Moluccan-commissioned Wyldemerck Mosque in Balk from 1956, things were quiet on the Islamic architectural front in The Netherlands for nearly 20 years, except for the 1963 addition of two minaret-turrets on the Oostduinlaan in The Hague. Not until 1975 was the third purpose-built mosque in The Netherlands completed, by a group of Turkish employees from the textile manufacturer Nijverdal-ten Cate in Almelo. The building, currently called the Yunus Emre Mosque, has often been referred to as The Netherlands' first real mosque, which has everything to do with the facts that the Mobarak Mosque was never recognized as a true Islamic building by mainstream Muslims, and that the Wyldemerck Mosque, demolished in 1969, was either little known or regarded as just another barracks.[1] The Yunus Emre was generally thought of by observers as a simple and traditional Turkish-Islamic building, perhaps not as 'Ottoman' as later Dutch-Turkish specimens, but still with recognizable building elements from the general Turkish culture area. When studied in depth, however, the design appears intended to represent not a mere and undivided culture group but a specific construction of Islam as produced by the patron in opposition to contesting views held by other Turkish-Islamic community leaders. Moreover, where in its first phase it did not yet have all the particular Turkish-Islamic building elements that would ideally have been included, the numerous later additions can be seen as intended to make up for those omissions.

Although a number of interesting prayer halls were built by Turkish patrons after the Yunus Emre, an example was opened in Zaanstad in 1994 that merits attention in being the self-appointed main materialization of The Netherlands' largest Turkish mosque association. Despite the fact that observers tended to regard the Sultan Ahmet Mosque as a failed copy of the traditional Ottoman building style, its design process shows that the mosque, by the careful selection and transformation of particular 'cultural' building elements, actually represented a specific construction of Islam meant to diverge from the alternative as formulated by competing Turkish-Islamic community leaders. On the other hand, a design for another Turkish-commissioned mosque was recently approved in Amsterdam that could be seen as an important materialization of another large Turkish mosque association in The Netherlands, whose adherents the Sultan Ahmet was intended to oppose. The Wester Mosque, although now in jeopardy as a result of much political turmoil, was regarded by many observers as a successful attempt to meld the Ottoman building style with the Dutch building style, a modernization in itself and a first step on the path towards a genuine Dutch Islam and a corresponding Dutch-Islamic building style. However, from an in-depth study of its design process it appears that this mosque can be seen to represent, through the careful selection and transformation of yet some other 'cultural' building elements, a construction of Islam that was to particularly contest the version as represented in Zaanstad.

Varieties of Islam among Turkish Communities

The first Turkish Muslims in The Netherlands were recruited in 1964 as workforce in the large industries then being developed.[2] When numbers grew, they started to organize themselves in groups corresponding to religious divisions in Turkey. The first Turkish-Islamic organization in The Netherlands was the Foundation Islamic Center (SIC), founded in Utrecht in 1972 by the Dutch Muslim convert Van Bommel.[3] The Center formed part of the movement of the Süleymanci or – as they preferred to refer to themselves – Süleymanli, followers of a Sufi teacher who had tried to counterbalance Atatürk's secularization and nationalization of what was left of the old Ottoman empire in the 1920s. In 1924, Atatürk founded the Directorate of Religious Affairs, or Diyanet Işleri Başkanliği, in his new capital of Ankara to prevent mosque organizations from becoming too politically active, threatening his secular-republican ideal. Importantly, the version of Islam that Diyanet propagated was 'liberally Sunni' but at the same time strongly based on 'Turkish culture', specifically opposed to 'Arab Islam' which was regarded as divergent and backward.[4] In reaction to Diyanet's secularization and nationalization of mosque organizations, the Süleymanli then founded their own Koranic schools. When the state put all Koranic schools under control of Diyanet in 1971, the Süleymanli shifted their attention to Turkish migrants abroad. In The Netherlands, the relations between the 1972 SIC and its provincial spin-offs was formalized in 1978 in the Foundation Islamic Center Netherlands (SICN) which controlled several organizations and mosques.[5] Until the end of the 1970s, the Süleymanli, highly organized in the industrial areas in the east, presented themselves to the government as representatives of the whole Turkish-Islamic community in the Netherlands.[6]

However, from the 1980s, Diyanet reacted to the foreign shift of the Süleymanli by orienting itself with the intent of keeping its modern, secular ideals high among the Turkish diaspora. In 1979, the Turkish-Islamic Cultural Federation (TICF) was created by several Süleymanli-opposed groups in The Netherlands, replacing them as the largest co-ordinating organization and the most important mouthpiece of Dutch Turks. In the following years, Diyanet gradually came to control the TICF.[7] It was subsequently seen as the Dutch counterpart of Diyanet in Ankara and was called Diyanet by the members themselves. Just as in Turkey, Diyanet in The Netherlands aimed to keep affairs of state and religion separated by providing mosque organizations with imams who had followed a theological education at a Turkish state university – seen by some as something of a paradox. Importantly, direct property rights in The Netherlands were not in the hands of the Turkish state, but in those of the 1982 Hollanda Diyanet Vakfi (HDV) or Islamitische Stichting Nederland (ISN), a foundation that covers the more material matters for the TICF. In Turkey as well, property rights over mosques are exercised in name of Diyanet by a foundation, the 1975 Türkiye Diyanet Vakfi.[8] In the end, Diyanet came to control most Turkish mosques in The Netherlands and was seen by the Dutch government as the most important representative of the Turkish-Islamic community instead of the Süleymanli.[9]

Another important Turkish group was formed by the Milli Görüş movement, represented in The Netherlands by the Netherlands Islamic Federation (NIF). The movement originated in Turkey in the Milli Selamet Partisi (MSP), the political party that strove for a larger role for religion in Turkish politics in the 1970s. Its successor, the Refah Partisi (RP) or Welfare Party, was banned and replaced by the Fazilet Partisi (FP) or Party of Virtue. Until the end of the 1970s, followers of the movement in The Netherlands went to existing Turkish mosques, but when Diyanet started to control more and more of these, the need arose for their own mosque association. In some places, there were confrontations between Milli Görüş and Diyanet over the administration of mosques.[10] After the Turkish military coup in 1980, important leaders of the MSP came to The Netherlands with the aim of mobilizing their supporters in the Dutch diaspora, resulting in the foundation of the

Müslüman Cemiyetler ve Cemaatler Federasyonu (MCCF) or Federation of Associations and Congregations of Muslims. At first, the Dutch Milli Görüş movement was oriented towards propaganda against the secularism of the Turkish state and against integration into Dutch society. From the second half of the 1980s, however, it became apparent that very few young Turks were drawn to this ideology, and to make the movement more attractive to the target group, a change of course was introduced, characterized by more openness, flexibility, and co-operation with Dutch organizations. Realizing that Turkish youngsters were no longer charmed by the thought of returning to the motherland, symposiums were organized on issues of minorities and integration, in which the great leader Erbakan himself was the main attraction. The new policy was formalized in 1987 in a new name, the Netherlands Islamic Federation (NIF).[11] Importantly, because it consciously chose to stress religion over republican or nationalist rhetoric, the movement attracted many Kurdish followers.[12] Still, it is distinctively Turkish in the sence that its leaders are Turks, it expresses itself in the Turkish language, and its orientations are shaped by modern Turkish society. In speeches the history of the Turkish people, especially in the period of the Ottoman empire, is often referred to with pride; however, the emphasis on the Turkish national identity is clearly subordinate to the religious one. Adherents tend to refer to themselves as Muslims of Turkish origin, rather than as Turks.[13] Ten years ago, Milli Görüş was rated to be the fastest growing Islamic movement in The Netherlands, with a great many young supporters.[14]

The Yunus Emre Mosque, Almelo

From the second half of the 1960s, textile manufacturer Nijverdalten Cate, based in Almelo, Twente, saw an opportunity to expand in the growing world market for textiles. At the outskirts of Almelo it had a large conglomeration of weaving and spinning factories built for its production section 'Indië' by its company architect, Gerrit Pelgrum. On the north side of this industrial terrain, Pelgrum had planned a complex of barracks called 'Casa Cortina' to house the growing number of foreign employees from Spain and Italy that the company was forced to hire due to the lack of laborers in the region.[15] More and more, however, these employees were recruited from Turkey, where villages with few opportunities contained an enormous pool of cheap labor eager to migrate temporarily to Europe.[16] Soon, Casa Cortina consisted almost entirely of Turks, with facilities for a Turkish kitchen, canteen, library and prayer room. Inhabitants came from several regions in Turkey, but the main recruitment centers were Izmir and Denizli, as in the latter there was a local textile producer that Nijverdal-ten Cate wanted to use in giving potential candidates from surrounding villages a crash course in machine handling.[17] Selection was carried out during regular recruitment trips to Turkey under Chief of Personnel Dirk Slettenhaar in concert with company interpreter Türker Atabek, who had originally been sent to The Netherlands in 1963 by an Istanbul establishment of the Dutch company Grasso for a technical course. Atabek had decided to stay and was subsequently one of only three interpreters in the region of Twente, having worked as such for several companies with Turkish employees.[18]

In spring 1972, discontent developed among the growing number of Turkish employees of Nijverdal-ten Cate over the shortage of prayer space in Casa Cortina. Representatives communicated this complaint to their Chief of Personnel Derk Slettenhaar whom they asked for an enlargement of their prayer room. The company directors gave their permission for the needed extension, but in conversations between Slettenhaar and the Turkish employees, the latter expressed the wish for a whole new prayer hall, a genuine purpose-built mosque.[19] To work out this idea, the initiators formed a construction committee, which consisted of 3 Turkish and 2 Dutch members. The main Dutch member was Slettenhaar who heavily supported the Turks' demand from a Christian-humanitarian conviction,[20] and the main Turkish member was Atabek. As the only Dutch-speaking Turk and the main communicator between workers and officials, Atabek was the most important community leader, patrons' representative, and the key to understanding the construction of Islam that was to be represented in The Netherlands' third mosque. He and Slettenhaar decided to spread the word on their project and to get more people to join their committee.[21] One week later, there were 6 Turks and 3 Dutch members, all employees at Nijverdal ten Cate.[22] In effect, Slettenhaar and Atabek had defined the future mosque as a shared Turkish-Dutch effort. It was decided that company architect Gerrit Pelgrum would be asked to design a building.

Slettenhaar put the first drawing on paper in a conversation with Atabek, who explained him about mosque basics. It was a provisional sketch of a ground plan with notes on the functions and history of imam, kiblah, salaat, decoration, minaret, dome, muezzin, and the call to prayer. **(Figure 77)** Inside the front hall, separated from the prayer room by a sketched wall with a single door, he noted that the mosque space should not be entered with shoes on. In the center of the back wall was a semi-circular mihrab, and to the right of the façade a minaret circle attached to the main building.

The plan was rectangular, and deeper than it was wide. The sketch was, as stated in a note, ideally based on the idea of the Primeval Mosque, specifically referring to the house that Mohammed built in Medina after his move from Mecca in 622. From a representational viewpoint, however, it used specific 'cultural' building elements, representing a standardized Turkish village mosque as thought of by the community leader. Whereas Atabek associated the classical Ottoman domed mosques with the larger cities and bygone times, he connected the village life of his constituency with the smaller and simpler versions that still abounded in the countryside, coming down to small longitudinal buildings with a front hall and a rectangular prayer hall covered by a hipped roof.[23] By choosing what he saw as a standard village mosque's building elements, the patron effectively represented his group as a traditional-Anatolian village community.

However, this sketch had insufficient information for company architect Gerrit Pelgrum to come up with an actual design for the exterior. In a later interview for a local newspaper, Pelgrum admitted to having designed weaving- and spinning-mills, halls and technical installations, but a mosque was apparently quite something else. 'I found it a bit strange. The Turks sketched something on paper, but I couldn't make anything of it. The interpreter Atabek offered to get drawings from Turkey.'[24] And indeed, Atabek and Slettenhaar approached Diyanet in Ankara for a design through company channels, three weeks later receiving a letter from Diyanet official Tayyar Altıkulaç with a formal answer referring to an enclosure.[25] Slettenhaar personally archived this letter as 'request drawing Turkish mosque' and its enclosure must have included the drawing, but the latter unfortunately is no longer found in the company archives or in those of the architect's heirs, and is no longer recalled by Atabek. Importantly however, although the Süleymanli were very much present in Twente and even in his own community, Atabek showed a clear preference for the involvement of the official Turkish Diyanet. Atabek, former Turkish Airforce officer, correspondent in The Netherlands for Turkey's main republican newspaper Hürriyet and main initiator (in 1982) of the Almelo Atatürk Society, considered himself a typical sprout of the secular-Islamic upbringing in the consciously liberal atmosphere that characterized many officials' families. He felt he continuously had to counter existing stereotypes of Turkey among the Dutch, who, in his perception, seemed to think of his country only in images of 'the Arabian Nights' combined with 'a scorched and backward countryside'. Instead, he preferred to focus on what he presented as a shift from the badly dressed, poor Turks arriving at the airport in the 1960s to their well dressed, sophisticated successors of the 1970s. 'Progress in Turkey is coming along very rapidly. The experiences of the first Turkish arrivals have been communicated to the new ones, as a result of which the Turks now know what awaits them and what is expected of them.'[26] On the other hand, according to Atabek, the language difference, the lack of personal contacts with the Dutch and the fact that the Turks still felt like strangers in The Netherlands had led many Turks in The Netherlands to become more fanatical followers of Islam than they probably would have been had they remained in Turkey.[27] From his point of view, contemporary Turks were basically a modern, secular-republican people, with any overly religious expressions being unfortunate answers to socio-economical problems. He recalled that the 'Islamists' forcefully tried to gain dominance in his mosque initiative and had to be warded off. The construction of Islam that he required to be represented in Almelo was to be explicitly based on modern, secular and liberal values and not on some traditionalist or orthodox version embraced by contesting Turkish-Islamic community leaders. He wanted his community to have intensive contacts with local Almelo society, just as he regarded a traditional Turkish village mosque to have been rooted in local society,[28] and he specifically did not want his community to become an isolated bastion of religion.

    Here we begin to see the rationality behind certain choices for particular building elements with certain associations. In Turkey, the secular state had a preference for what can be called 'modern-republican design', using either building elements from pre-Ottoman times and from the West, or using Ottoman building elements transformed into what were seen as modernized or stylized versions.[29] Importantly, uncut classical Ottoman design was until the 1980s thought of, at least in the higher, secular circles of which Atabek was a member of, as old-fashioned and associated with traditionalism and non-secularism.[30] Generally though, the design of mosques was not regarded by the professional elite as very interesting and consequently was left largely to local community leaders.[31] In the Turkish-republican system, all mosques were transferred to Diyanet only after completion, after which it provided state-educated imams and muezzins.[32] Apparently there was no stringent control over the architecture itself. However, when an international design competition was held for the Grand National Assembly building in Ankara in 1937, the only entry that chose to make allusions to a mosque – with a domed assembly hall and two minaret-like towers – was wholeheartedly rejected by the jury. The incorporation of dome and minaret forms was considered 'inappropriate for the secular nationalism of the republic'.[33] Moreover, when a governmental mosque in Ankara, the Kocatepe, was to be designed in 1954 as part of a complex which would include Diyanet headquarters, the democrat party opted for a heavily stylized modernization of an Ottoman central dome with four surrounding minarets. It was only after great pressure from the Justice Party that in 1967 – the foundations already laid and then conspicuously demolished with dynamite – the design was changed to a more classical Ottoman representation. **(Figure 78)** The result incorporated a selected number of building elements from several classical Ottoman buildings at once, with its main volume referring to the Blue Mosque as the culmination of Ottoman-Islamic grandeur. However, its minarets were disproportionately high and thin by any existing classical Ottoman standards, and higher than any others in Turkey. Their increased height even exceeded what was proportionally 'necessary' to accommodate the also increased height of the dome, with height and slenderness effectively representing the increased role of Islam in the public sphere that its patrons stood for. It took 20 years to be built due to the fact that only from 1980 did the Justice Party have sufficient power in Ankara to move the construction along.[34] On the other hand, when the Turkish armed forces – self-proclaimed guardians of the secular state – commissioned a mosque in Etimesgut in 1967, to be placed amidst barracks and garrison buildings of an armored brigade, they opted for a design that conspicuously dismissed any Ottoman references.[35] In light of the apparent varieties of Islamic architecture in Turkey and all their diverging connotations, chances are that the Diyanet design that Atabek had received from Ankara would not have been what would have been seen as a traditional Turkish mosque. Rather, it would have included Western and abstracted or stylized Ottoman building elements specifically meant to represent the modern Republic in the diaspora. Perhaps it had even been based on the original Kocatepe design itself, since the structure had come to be seen as the icon of Turkish-Islamic modernism.[36] As such, it is still very well-known among Diyanet community leaders in The Netherlands. In any case, according to Pelgrum, the official Turkish design met with resistance. 'I got the drawings from Atabek, but a committee found them too modern.'[37] According to Atabek, the Dutch members, from their 'traditionalist' perspective of Turkey, probably objected to the design because it did not correspond to their idea of what a typical Turkish mosque should look like. Rejecting any overly religious statement, Atabek returned to his village-rooted idea of an Anatolian mosque. In his view, a classical Ottoman mosque would have been fitting and admirable in its own time, but in contemporary society it was no longer appropriate and too reminiscent of a too obvious role of Islam in the public sphere.

Still preferring the Turkish government's official role in the matter, he subsequently requested his father, then Director of the Özel Idare ('*Special Office*') headquarters in the provincial capital of Yozgat, to send him an architect's sketch of a Turkish village mosque. The Özel Idare are administrative service organizations set up by the state in its provincial capitals to support the villages in their districts, mainly through technical projects but apparently also by providing standard drawings for communal village buildings. According to Atabek, this sketch, which itself is also no longer to be found, was a prayer hall design which his father had chosen as representative of the sketches provided to Yozgat villages. It had been based on the standardized Anatolian village mosque's building elements as already treated and as visible in several older village mosques in the Yozgat region, with their rectangular ground plan, front hall, women's balcony, hipped roof, and single minaret to the right of the front façade.[38] **(Figure 79)** According to Atabek, the plan as it came from Yozgat was similar to the one that Pelgrum and the committee eventually presented to the municipality, although after some deliberation with his constituency a low dome was introduced on the back of the hipped roof to make the prayer hall more recognizable as a Turkish mosque without being classical Ottoman. Although not all Yozgat village mosques had such a dome – the copper would have been too expensive for many – in Atabek's experience, those who could afford it did. This drawing was apparently much more to the committee's liking, and Atabek and Slettenhaar asked Pelgrum to translate it into a design for the Dutch construction bureaucracy.

Pelgrum had decided to acquaint himself with mosque architecture as well. 'In the meantime, I looked up a few things in the library.'[39] Although several newspapers reported that the architect used images from books on Islamic architecture, Pelgrum himself admitted that he had only consulted W. Speiser's very general 'Baukunst des Ostens'.[40] This volume has few pictures of Turkish mosques, only the exterior of the Mirimah Mosque and the interior of the Blue Mosque in Istanbul are shown.[41] In fact, according to Atabek, Pelgrum copied the characteristics from the Yozgat example as much as possible in a drawing and a model in September 1972, with the exception that he had added a low dome, and drawn the minaret as if it were a chimney. **(Figure 80)** Instead of a protruding heavy base with a slender straight column, it was more like a thick, conical, low tower with a low balcony. The minaret being the first ascendable one in The Netherlands, Atabek remembers that the architect was afraid of making it too high or slender. When asked by a journalist, Pelgrum unfolded what seems to be the original

Yozgat drawing. 'Look, this tower is 29 meters high and it stands on a little foot of 2,60 meters. A tower like that can be blown down by the wind. Our tower measures 20 meters and has a foot of 3 meters.' According to Pelgrum, calculations for the tower hadn't posed many problems, as 'you start from a factory chimney'.[42] The mosque was planned for an empty field in the Casa Cortina complex, where the building could be oriented towards the southeast and at the same time along existing street lines and barracks.

To continue with the idea of village mosque communality, Slettenhaar and Atabek subsequently developed the idea of a shared village effort almost to the extreme, as we will see. On 15 September, representatives of the Foundation Foreign Employees (Stichting Buitenlandse Werknemers), the Almelo citizens and employers, municipal authorities and the Council of Churches (Raad van Kerken), were invited to join a new, more general committee. Atabek, who had been secretary of the first committee, continued this position in the second. The administration was to consist of two Dutch chairmen, one Turkish (Atabek) and one Dutch secretary, and one Turkish and one Dutch accountant. Strikingly, although most positions were not yet filled, the ethnic distribution was an important factor to the initiators, who tried to get the widest possible village support for the mosque. To raise the needed 100.000 guilders, they counted on gifts from Turks (especially at the end of Ramadan), on collectors who would go door-to-door, and on an employer donation.[43] Importantly, although Slettenhaar's and Atabek's direct, pragmatic aim was to create the necessary financial and political support for construction, the underlying rationale for Atabek was that Islam would ideally be intertwined with the liberal values of modern society.

The day after these parties met, local newspapers started reporting on the project, showing Pelgrum's design for the front façade. One stated that the 600 Turkish employees of Nijverdal-ten Cate were planning on raising the money largely from among themselves, and that they had full confidence that most of their 3500 'fellow nationals' in the province of Twente would be willing to give money for the construction. They even hoped for support from outside the region by planning to call on a weekly Sunday Turkish radio program for help. The architect Pelgrum had succeeded 'in creating an appropriate design with the help of several Turks, books and photographs, answering to the architectural and religious demands'. Construction costs would be kept as low as possible by Turkish masons and painters working in their spare time.[44] Other local newspapers began describing the design to their curious and eager readers: 'The Turkish interpreter Atabek made sure that drawings and prints of mosques came to Almelo. Mr. Pelgrum borrowed books from the library and started studying images of mosques. Eventually, a design left the drawing table that fulfilled the demands of the Muslims, and that could be executed in agreement with the Koran. The mosque will measure 9x13 meters with an upper structure of 9x3 meters. The prayer space will be 9x9 meters. In front of the mosque a square will be built that, for example on important days when there is no room left, can be used for prayer as well. Moreover, the mosque will get a 19 meters high minaret that will be made of white stones. The minaret will also get a balcony from which the imam will call the believers to prayer five times a day.'[45] 'There will be a balcony for female visitors, and at the entrance there will be foot washing faucets and shoe closets. The mosque will have a copper dome, the edge of which will have lights. The minaret will have colored lights, so there will surely be created an exotic image in the evening. With this mosque, Almelo will be getting another Turkish first, the third one after the Turkish doctor and the Turkish-Dutch school.'[46] 'The building will have white plastered walls with a green roof and a stone base. On the dome, the sign will be attached that adorns every mosque's dome in Turkey. Moreover, the mosque will be accessible to Mohammedans from all countries, even for non-Mohammedans as long as they will take off their shoes.'[47] 'The copper dome will shine, just like the hundreds of mosques in Turkey. Almost 300 Mohammedans will be able to find a place in the prayer room, furnished with Oriental carpets that will create an atmosphere which will bring into mind the Aya Sofia and especially the Blue Mosque of Istanbul. Almelo will now have The Netherlands' first mosque: there is a mosque in The Hague, but that is Pakistani.' According to this last newspaper, it was definitely not intended that Nijverdal-ten Cate lead the construction program, and attempts were made to include the other employers in the support of the project. Furthermore, the Turks were apparently convinced that a proper prayer space was also necessary for education by the imam. 'Nothing else than a proper mosque will fulfill that demand, a place where the large chandelier, the tens of colored lights and the presence of the appropriate washing faucets will give the interior an Oriental look. In short, their own place for prayer, a piece of religious Turkey in The Netherlands.'[48] Mainly through Slettenhaar's and Atabek's efforts at finding a communal political and religious basis, in local public discourse this third architectural representation of Islam in The Netherlands was approved and even enthusiastically supported, although few observers seemed to realize that the great classical Ottoman mosques and their concurrent connotations of religious fervour were exactly what the Almelo mosque was not meant to bring to mind.

It seemed the initiators planned on raising money from governmental sources as well. On 28 September, Slettenhaar and Atabek went to the Ministry of VROM (handling affairs of public space) where they were advised to create a foundation as soon as possible.[49] The subsidies for prayer halls would then amount, until 1 March the next year, to 25% of construction costs. After that, financing would be 20%. The plot and any work by the Turks would be included, even if the plot were donated and the Turks worked for free. On the same day, the Turkish Consulate General in Rotterdam was visited. The Turkish consul, Ilhan Akant, and the official imam were interested and positive. They also stressed the importance of a foundation, as they would not be able to do anything before that. Subsequently it was decided that, a foundation would be created, with Slettenhaar as main chairman, Atabek as main secretary, and a certain Dutch teacher at the local technical school as main accountant. With their secondary positions still to be assigned, the total of the daily board would ideally consist of 3 Dutchmen and 3 Turks. For the government commission for church construction that would have to decide on the request, this would notably be the first for a mosque.[50]

During discussion of the foundation statutes two weeks later, it was decided to include a requirement to always keep the overall mosque administration equally divided between Dutchmen and Turks as well. The Council of Churches had apparently much criticized the over-representation of the Dutch and the corporate world in the statutes as initially proposed. Too many Dutch would raise a suspicion of paternalism, and too many company representatives would be only the result of 'the Eastern mentality of cringing inferiority and of never refusing directly'.[51] In fact, the situation seemed to have been less 'colonial' than suggested, since the choice to include Dutch local citizens and corporations was a conscious attempt by the Turkish-Islamic ommunity leader to establish political, financial and religious roots in what he saw as modern society. As for the official name of the Foundation, the board itself initially suggested 'Foundation Turkish Mosque Almelo' (Stichting Turkse Moskee Almelo),[52] after which Nijverdal-ten Cate expressed a preference for 'Twente Mosque Foundation' (Stichting Moskee Twente),[53] probably to eliminate any too-direct association with the Almelo company since that was the express intent of its management.[54] Also VROM, with an eye on possible subsidies, had advised them to include the word Twente in the foundation's name, so as to give the whole a more general character.[55] Finally, three weeks after that, the name 'Stichting Turkse Moskee Twente te Almelo' was agreed upon. Importantly, when one of the Dutch board members suggested omitting the word 'Turkish', it was decided to keep it in the text. Apparently, notwithstanding a repeatedly expressed, idealized accessibility of the future mosque to all Muslims, the idea of Turkishness itself was greatly valued by the Turkish board members. At the same time, a purely Turkish name for the building would not be recognizable enough to the village community in which the main initiator clearly wanted to be deeply rooted.[56] Meanwhile, new members were added to the board on each possible occasion, in the attempt to create a large social, political and religious base. By the time the Foundation was officially created, the board had the astonishing number of 15 Dutchmen and 15 Turks.[57]

On 27 November, the Foundation sent the municipality Pelgrum's drawings from September and pictures of his model. Moreover, it mentioned the expected 'costs' for the plot and the expected subsidies from the Ministry. Apparently, only part of the proposed location was the property of Nijverdal ten Cate while the rest was owned by the municipality, so they proposed a debt acknowledgement with the condition that the land would not be sold to anyone else and would be handed back to the municipality in case the Foundation was abolished.[58] The municipality itself, however, impressed by the initiative, had something else in mind and was adamant in its opinion that this mosque did not belong on the Kolthofsingel. They preferred instead, a plot much closer to the city center where there was still open space. The price mentioned for the original company plot and the subsidies by VROM created the positive expectation with the municipality that they would be able to sell the center plot to the Foundation without a problem. However, where the money that was allocated for the original plot was actually expected to be re-donated by Nijverdal-ten Cate, in this new scenario the municipality had to be paid in full. Although it would transfer the plot for a good price, the new situation would lead to the necessity of requesting financial support from more companies.[59]

On 19 February 1973, Pelgrum made a new drawing, based on his former sketches but now projected onto the new situation. Apparently Pelgrum had proposed, to no avail, to include some of his own ideas and ideals in this sketch. 'Originally, I had drawn the minaret to the left side of the entrance, on the Wierdensestraat that is. But for religious reasons it had to stand on the right side. I preferred it to be on the left side, so you would be able to see it from the street. I tried to have it my way with the imam but he didn't accept it.'[60] The minaret being placed to the right was clearly regarded as Turkish 'tradition', and although the empirical field shows that there are many exceptions if the situation so dictates, it seems to be the ideal.[61] Moreover, Pelgrum had planned on orienting the mosque more eastwards to extant street lines. 'The imam came to me with a compass in his pocket. It pointed towards the southeast. To be honest, I would have preferred to turn it a bit, but I think you should accept that. Alignment or no alignment. It now stands in a pure direction to Mecca, and that is sacred to those people.'[62] The municipality found the plan acceptable and requested an opinion from the Aesthetics Commission.[63]

Aesthetics rejected the design with harsh words. 'The Commission utterly regrets that a piece of "postcard-architecture" has been drawn in such a conspicuous situation in the Almelo cityscape. It is of the opinion that the aesthetics of Almelo as well as of the religious community which will be using the building will benefit more from a good design by a Dutch architect, than by a bad construction which in (lack of) design ('*vormgeving*') tries to recall a Turkish cultural and physical environment.'[64] Apparently, the commission knew that the design was based on the drawing of a Turkish architect, while they preferred a less Turkish design, which they considered would be more likely produced by a Dutch designer. As a consequence of the heavily subjective character of the 'postcard-architecture' critique having been lost somewhere along the line, some later observers actually came to think that the Almelo mosque was based on a postcard.[65]

Strikingly, the commission then translated their wishes into their own design proposal. Pelgrum described the events as follows: 'The plan was completely dismissed. When they came with a plan themselves, Atabek was appalled. "That is not a Turkish mosque, but an Arab mosque," he shouted in anger. "We don't want this one." Nor did the Aesthetics Commission find the location appropriate either [...].'[66] In Atabek's memory, the commission had used general books on Islamic architecture to come up with their own sketch, 'an Arab creation with a square minaret'. Unfortunately, this sketch is no longer to be found, or at least not made available by the current commission, but in all probability would have been meant as a Dutch translation incorporating what the commission took to be 'general' characteristics of mosque design. However, hardly any 'general' formal elements or principles can be distilled from the varieties of Dutch or Islamic architecture without provoking specific associations. In this case, the patron connected the design with 'Arab culture' while he required certain 'Turkish' building elements to particularly represent a modern, secular and liberal construction of Islam in opposition to contesting versions embraced by other Turkish-Islamic community leaders.

Meanwhile, municipal authorities themselves went on as planned. Mayor and aldermen stated that they had recommended the municipal council's cooperation on adjustment of the zoning plan.[67] At the beginning of July, the alderman established that the location would definitely be the corner Wierdensestraat/Alidastraat, conditional on the province's agreement to the adjustment of the zoning plan.[68] Contrary to the Aesthetics Commission, the municipality did not seem unwilling to find a solution for the aesthetics controversy. So, when Slettenhaar went to Izmir on a recruitment trip on 8 August, he suggested taking along Pelgrum, so the latter would be able to acquaint himself with 'the Turkish building style'. Some municipal officials would come to explicate the aesthetics commission's objections, so the architect could focus his attention especially on these details.[69]

Subsequently, Slettenhaar and Atabek, who regularly made these trips to hire new employees, took along the architect with them to Istanbul and Izmir, where they were able to purchase the prefabricated copper crescent moons for the Almelo dome and minaret. A Turkish chandelier was not necessary as that of an Almelo church to be demolished was bought by the municipality and donated to the mosque.[70] They visited big-city as well as smaller-villages mosques, talking to Turkish builders and imams along the way. **(Figure 81)** Pelgrum said he had seen dozens of mosques, from 'the giant Blue Mosque' in Istanbul to 'insignificant little prayer houses' in the villages. 'I saw the smallest mosque in Turkey; a lot smaller still than this one. I also saw monstrosities. Sometimes very bad constructions.' 'By the way, a lot of small mosques in Turkey don't have a dome. A Turkish imam told me that this is a matter of money.' According to Pelgrum, a very specific problem had been the orientation, as mosques are ideally supposed to be directed towards Mecca. 'I had a difference of opinion on that. In Turkey they told me: "You have to place it in a southern direction." I had planned it southeastwardly. I couldn't convince them that I was right.'[71] What is important for us to realize is that this miscommunication was not necessarily caused by Turkish ignorance on the location of The Netherlands in relation to Mecca, as seems to be implied here. Turks were very much aware of European countries and their distance from Turkey. Instead, it shows how the representation of a specific Turkish habitat in the diaspora formed the dominant idea, for those who stayed behind, over a decontextualized Islamic orientation. In fact, the orientation towards Mecca as merely an ideal and not a consistent practice can be discerned in many more instances in the world of Islamic architecture, as it seems to be only one of many elements to be selected from the built environment in the representation of contrasting constructions of Islam. Still, during his trip and despite the orientation miscommunication, Pelgrum had gained more insight into Turkish mosque architecture, or at least into individual views on it. For example, the muezzin's balcony would have to be raised to a higher point, according to advice from one Turkish builder.[72] In fact, there is no one standard for Turkish mosque design, and the empirical field shows many diverging measurements and proportions. However, just as anywhere else, each Turkish builder may imagine his own typological abstractions and construction ideals to be generally applicable.

After they had come back, Slettenhaar reported on the situation. He thought that Pelgrum, in a subsequent conversation with officials from the municipality and Aesthetics, would be able to evaluate the construction with more insight. This conversation was planned for 23 August,[73] and during the meeting slides of mosques would be presented, on the inside as well as on the outside. During the exhibition 'Almelo 73' of 7-12 September, the model would be presented and part of 5000 picture postcards featuring the model sold.[74] One newspaper signaled that if for a while it had seemed as if the mosque project had been delayed indefinitely, nothing could be further from the truth. 'Now,' the reporter stated, 'the initiators even want to commence construction in a few weeks, if only to prevent Almelo – the first city to have such a plan – from lagging behind other cities where mosque projects are planned. Architect Pelgrum, after he had visited mosques, taken pictures, and talked to architects in Turkey, expects the Aesthetics Commission to put aside their objections during a presentation of the drawings and slides of Turkish mosques he will bring with him.'[75] Apparently, the expectation was that the Aesthetics Commission would have to be, and would now be, convinced of the Turkish factuality of the design – with hindsight, a naïve thought as its members were supposed to occupy themselves with aesthetics in a specifically 'Dutch' environment.

Pelgrum presented his slides and his new plan on 23 August. These drawings are no longer available, but in Pelgrum's builder's estimates of 22 November, we clearly see the main adjustments he had made after his trip. **(Figure 82)** The balcony was indeed placed higher, supported by a layered console of muqarnas, and it had gained a higher balustrade. The minaret had gained a base and was no longer depicted with brickwork but with white plastering like the main building. The plinth was no longer depicted as rustic stones but also of plastering. The finials no longer consisted of two balls and a crescent moon but of the exact prefabricated forms he had brought back from Turkey. The only thing Pelgrum had left intact was the relative bulk of the minaret, as, according to Atabek, he still feared collapse if the structure were made as slender as those he had seen in Turkey.

However, a newspaper then reported that the construction of the mosque was again made uncertain by a new rejection by Aesthetics. After it had seen the slides it had reconsidered the location and the new design, but neither met with approval. Whereas the commission only had an advisory role, the municipality would not be able to put aside such a negative judgment. The alderman said that further talks between parties were necessary. In his opinion, this should not be an issue under which the Turks would suffer. The reporting journalist feared that the foreign laborers were going to be the victims of a difference of opinion between Aesthetics and the municipality, unless Turkish interests were valued higher than all sorts of constructional irregularities. As for the objections to the location, according to him the municipality would have to solve that one themselves, as they had allocated the plot in the first place.[76] A week after that, the Foundation reminded the alderman of his initial approval of the mosque and its location, and urged him to reach a decision as they had not heard from the municipality since the commission's negative advice. The Turks, who had donated relatively large sums of money, were apparently becoming impatient.[77]

An internal memo from the office of mayor and aldermen expressed the huge dilemma they felt they were in. 'This advice condemns the plan in itself, in relation to its design – one speaks of "postcard architecture" – as well as in relation to its location. This means that the plan will be affected in its most principal aspects. Moreover, the initiators – from their viewpoint, by the way, perhaps not totally unexplainably – feel attached to it to a degree that for now they are not inclined to make an adjusted plan. Recently they organized a meeting during which the plans were further explicated, amongst other things, by slides of similar buildings in Turkey. For this meeting, the complete Aesthetics Commission had been invited. As was stated to me by the head of Construction Control, who was also present, this explication did not influence the view of the Aesthetics Commission. One admits [..] that the building in the environment in which it is rooted would perhaps be very much in place, but one sticks to the view that, if the design wants to be realized here, the building should be placed on a less conspicuous spot than on the Wierdensestraat, and that it should be placed in a "more spacious" environment, possibly on a raised terrain. Under these circumstances, the creation of an opening from which can be worked towards a solution, in which the accomplishments of the work for which the initiators have troubled themselves on the one hand, and the threatened aesthetic interests on the other, will both be honored as much as possible, is a difficult if not impossible case. In this situation the question arises which interests weigh the most. In other words, if we shouldn't deviate from the Aesthetics Commission's advice. That the interests of the religious community concerned, also with an eye on its social position in this country, should weigh heavily in this case, is a statement which nobody will want to deny. That everybody in the community in which it is planted will have their peace with a statement to its benefit, is doubtful at the very least. In our view, mayor and aldermen should reach a decision in the matter anyway.'[78]

Subsequently, a newspaper reported that the construction of the mosque could be started soon since mayor and aldermen approved of its construction. However, the municipality had apparently expressed a wish to exchange thoughts with the Foundation on the objections of the Aesthetics Commission to particular elements of the exterior. Although it was an advice which the municipality would not officially have to follow, its intent was to adjust the mosque as much as possible to the wishes of the Commission.[79] On 20 November, the Foundation officially applied for a building permit,[80] on 25 January 1974 the provincial authorities approved,[81] and on 22 March the permit was granted.[82]

The Foundation informed the board members that construction would start on 1 April. Although the attention was focused on the later placement of the foundation stone, the Foundation wished to invite the members to the cutting of the first sod.[83] The day after, the media reported on the event. According to them, the situation of the mosque had led to 'quite a few difficulties', as there had been 'objections to the placement of the entrance on the South-East', and a 'standard placement on the Wierdensestraat had been requested'. However, eventually the building was situated 'according to Mohammedan faith'.[84] Here, they seemed to have mainly talked to Pelgrum as it was most likely his initial but rejected preference for aligning the mosque to the extant streets that was referred to.

On 3 May, the foundation stone ceremony was held. Between speeches of the mayor, the Turkish ambassador, Slettenhaar and a Turkish-Islamic community member (translated by Atabek), the actual foundation stone was placed by the ambassador, and the day was concluded in Atabek's Turkish restaurant Lokanta.[85] In his speech, Mayor Schneiders stated that the municipality had expressly looked for a spot as close as possible to the city center: 'Because, just like in your country, religion has a very important function in life and in culture. Everyone entering Almelo passes your mosque, which will be a sign that you live and work among us.' Ambassador Oktay Cankardes stated that the building had great value: 'It is an example of how different beliefs and nations can live and build together.' Slettenhaar found that now the encounter between the Christian world and 'Mohammedanism' could really take place: 'That will often not be easy. But the dialogue can begin in Almelo. Now, we have to start thinking what should happen next, as our Turkish friends will remain in need of our help.'[86]

Construction was swift, and the dome and minaret-spire were soon put into place. Strikingly, the minaret was built according to Pelgrum's early chimney-like drawings and not according to the adjusted design that he had made after his trip to Turkey. Apparently the negotiations between municipality and Aesthetics, held after the latter's negative advice, had resulted in the removal of any added building elements that were deemed even more 'postcard-like'. On 17 October, although the building did not yet have its white plastering, lights, or inventory, and had not been officially opened, the mosque was taken into use with the celebration of the end of Ramadan.[87] The service was broadcast live on Radio Wereldomroep.[88] The mosque was officially opened by Minister Boersma of Social Affairs, in the presence of delegates from the Turkish Consulate in Rotterdam and Embassy in The Hague, among whom the Turkish ambassador himself, on 27 January 1975. First it was ceremonially inaugurated by a recitation from the Koran performed by imam Turan,[89] a Diyanet-educated imam who had worked in the Turkish Embassy in The Hague, and was currently working in Enschede. He had been requested by the Foundation as official imam to the mosque in Almelo,[90] which again serves to show the important role of Diyanet as preferred by community leader Atabek over any rivalling religious groups. The opening itself, with interviews with Atabek, Slettenhaar and Pelgrum, was broadcast on Dutch television. Slettenhaar ended his welcoming speech with a wish. 'May this slender minaret, which in Turkey itself calls the believers to prayer on a daily basis, form a non-diminishing call to hospitality and tolerance to all present.'[91] Boersma, admired for giving his speech partly in Turkish, said that it came down to much more than only employees. It came down to a piece of Turkey which existed in Almelo and which wanted to be grateful to its God. 'The call from the minaret will sound daily over Almelo besides the customary bell chimes. That is proof of the fact that we do not live next to each other but with each other.'[92] According to the Minister, the Almelo mosque was not only a sign of respect to God, but also 'a piece of homeland for the Turkish community and a confirmation of its own identity'.[93] Mayor Schneider, knowing that the Minister was to travel to Turkey soon, gave him a document in which Almelo named Denizli as its sister city, with the request to hand it to his counterpart in the Turkish government as a symbol of unity.[94] Denizli had been suggested by Atabek, as it was one of the centers where he and Slettenhaar had recruited many employees from the surrounding countryside. Ambassador Cancardes thanked everyone who had helped to raise the mosque. 'Unfortunately, it does not happen that often in this world that people take such a tolerant stance towards a different conviction, towards a different belief, as in this case.' He expressed his hope that the mosque would form a symbol of friendship and cooperation between the two nations.[95] **(Figure 83)**

Then, on 14 December, the mosque administration stood down to be replaced by a new one. With Atabek as the chairman until 1989, Slettenhaar would remain available for advice and support, and the mosque would from now on be a wholly Turkish affair.[96] Unfortunately, however, the demise of the Dutch textile industry resulting from the oil crisis, competition by low-salary countries in the Far East and by artificial fiber production, led to a drastic reduction of employment opportunities in Twente. In 1976, Nijverdal-ten Cate had to reduce its employees by 700, from 5.500 to 4.800, because of the loss of 28 million guilders in 1975, and the loss of 30 million in 1976 meant a further planned reduction of 1200 employees in the following two years, as stated by Alberdink Thijm on 15 December 1976.[97] The Turkish-Islamic community was hit hard. However, the number of Turkish Muslims in Almelo still kept growing through family reunification and natural growth, and in the eyes of the mosque board, the building needed to be expanded with space for office, meeting, ablution, kitchen and educational facilities. In essence, a formerly simple group of male migrant laborers was to be transformed into an organized diaspora community of families.

Although the need for expansion was mainly presented in terms of numbers, there was more to it than that. It had come to be felt that the existing mosque, although based on a standardized and idealized Anatolian village model, had only consisted of a mere prayer hall. In the community leaders' experience, in their Anatolian villages this hall would have been used for prayer only, with auxiliary structures serving as school, library, ablution space, shop, kitchen and canteen. While on the village level the architecture-historical terms 'Imaret' or 'Külliye' are generally not used and while a mosque may sometimes merely consist of a prayer hall with some sheds, a fountain and a canteen corner with chairs, coffee and minor retail, the idea of a complex of communal buildings itself is apparently indeed regarded by some as a Turkish village ideal.[98] In light of the varieties of architecture in any culture area, this would not have consistently been the case in all villages in all of Turkish Anatolia. However, it apparently formed an ideal village 'tradition' to the patrons and that is what is relevant in representational analysis. In The Netherlands, as much as in Turkey, it served a strong social function on the one hand, while on the other hand the (small) income from the present facilities could be used for maintenance of the mosque itself. In the community leaders' home villages, a new prayer hall could be built according to a provincial design provided like the one in Almelo, whereas auxiliary buildings would be constructed according to local custom as regular sheds. The front hall would be an open or (mainly) glass-covered arcaded portico used for the removal of shoes, while ablutions would be performed in a separate fountain outside the main building. In Casa Cortina, separate functions had been distributed over different barracks, but in the new location all functions had to be performed in that single prayer hall which had originally never been meant as such. Especially after family-reunification, the situation came to be seen as undesirable.

Although some members of the community found the idea of a new financial burden unattractive in light of massive Turkish unemployment (the costs were later estimated by the architect to be even higher than the original prayer hall[99]), it was decided that the extra space was necessary in light of expanding communal needs.[100] On 19 November 1979, the Foundation sent a letter to the municipality in which it stated the need for an auxiliary building for 'meetings, Koranic lessons to children and office space'. It requested permission to place a white painted, ready-to-use unit on the rented plot next to the existing mosque. According to the Foundation, such a unit would provide a quick solution to the problem of space. The request was accompanied by a page from a commercial brochure of a container-unit or 'portakabin', commonly used for temporary office- or canteen-space at building sites.[101] **(Figure 84)** As in the Anatolian context as thought of by the community leaders, the auxiliary buildings in a mosque complex would have been constructed as no more then simple sheds, the portakabin would be a great way to save costs on construction. However, on 18 February 1980, municipal officials advised mayor and aldermen not to grant permission for the container-unit. 'The image added to the Foundation Mosque's letter is a container-unit. These are ready-to-use dwellings which are specifically designed to be easily moveable. As a result, the temporality of the placement of these dwellings is prominently visible in their design and structure. A permanent placement is clearly contrary to the nature and the character of the dwelling. The Aesthetics Commission will find this dwelling unacceptable: a greater conflict of nature, character and form between mosque and unit than this one is unthinkable. Sender should be made to consider discussing the nature and design of a more definitive construction with the [municipality].'[102]

After this rejection, the board withdrew the idea of a temporary unit. Atabek hired the Almelo architect Haverkamp to design a building 'in style', meaning a white plastered brickwork construction with a hipped roof of about the same size as the existing prayer hall, except for the dome and the second layer. According to Atabek, the similarity in style was chosen so as to stand a better chance before the authorities, not because it was a Turkish tradition. On 28 April, the mosque filed an application for a construction permit for an auxiliary building with the destination of 'library etc.'. Outer covering of walls and roof would be 'as existing mosque'.[103] **(Figure 85)** From that moment on, all parties would speak of a 'library'. On 17 June, Aesthetics approved the plan.[104] On 23 June, in answer to some questions about possible parking problems, the municipality was informed that the mosque and the library would not be used at the same time and that the latter would not attract as many people as the first.[105] Consequently, municipal officials, mayor and aldermen, the relevant municipal council's sub-commission, the municipal council itself, and the provincial authorities all approved without further comments.[106] On 11 June, the permit was granted.[107]

The architect, Atabek and the contractor agreed that, because finances had not yet been fully arranged, construction would follow actual terms of payments.[108] Construction started in June 1981, and on 30 January 1982 it was 'nearly finished', according to the municipal construction inspector.[109] Apparently, construction had halted due to lack of funds. Nevertheless, it was used, together with the extant prayer hall, for communal Friday prayers as of January 1982.[110] Meanwhile, on 25 January, the Ministry of WVC (Wellbeing, Public Health and Culture) had installed the Temporary Arrangement Subsidizing Prayer Spaces Muslims (Tijdelijke Regeling Subsidiering Gebedsruimten Moslims) as a renewal of the General Arrangement Subsiziding Prayer Spaces (Globale Regeling inzake Subsidiering Gebedsruimten) from 1976, which had also been temporary and had expired on 16 March 1981. It granted Muslim communities the opportunity to apply for mosque building subsidies with a maximum of 30% or 30.000 guilders, as a temporary compensation until 1 January 1984 for the fact that, until the Normalization, church construction had been heavily subsidized.[111] On 2 March 1982, Haverkamp started negotiations with WVC on subsidizing the extension using this possibility, with the argument that construction was already nearly finished, but that because of the lack of funds construction activities had come to a halt.[112] As a result, WVC granted the maximum of 30.000 guilders to the mosque.[113] Construction was officially completed on 3 November 1982.[114] **(Figure 86)**

In light of ongoing attempts by religiously orthodox Turks in the region to influence the mosque Foundation, Atabek and the rest of the board decided in 1983 to become an official member of the ISN, the Dutch Diyanet. The name was changed from Stichting Turkse Moskee Twente to Islamitische Stichting Nederland Moskee Almelo. Meanwhile, the Turkish-Islamic community in Almelo kept growing. Although the library was at times used as a prayer room as well, the mosque soon needed more space for religious celebrations. With the end of Ramadan in April 1988 in mind, Atabek requested Turkish architect Mehmet Bedri Sevinçsoy, who ran the Utrecht based architectural firm Mabeg, to design a second extension. He was chosen because he was the first Turkish architect recognized under Dutch law and because community members could communicate with him more easily. But much more important, was the fact that he had just begun working on a large Diyanet mosque project, the Fatih Mosque in Eindhoven. Until he moved back to Turkey, he was to be the preferred architect for several Diyanet mosques in The Netherlands.

So, Sevinçsoy was commissioned with the second extension, also 'in style'. On 20 October 1987, he filed a permit application. **(Figure 87)** This time, the building would be constructed not of plastered brickwork but of white Inkalite plates.[115] The first extension and the mosque itself would be connected by an enlargement of the main prayer hall and a special building for toilets and ablution facilities surrounding the – still freestanding – minaret. The existing faucets in the front hall would be removed. Next to that, a detached building for communal activities would be erected, which would hold the canteen or coffeehouse and a space for the small-scale sale of Turkish goods. The latter was later noticed by municipal authorities and considered a breach of the permit, but it was tolerated because only 'Islamic products' would be sold.[116] In the Turkish custom mentioned before, the income from these functions would be used to pay for maintenance. Combined with the first extension, this building now created a proper courtyard in front of the main entrance. The 'hall' from the former 'library' was used as a space for women while their children were being taught from the Koran, and it was now designated as such on the drawing. Aesthetics, after some minor practical adjustments,[117] advised positively on 22 January 1988.[118] Six months later, the provincial authorities also approved.[119] Meanwhile, the mosque had decided that buying the plot, in the end, would be cheaper than renting it.[120] After an amount had been agreed on, the municipal council approved the sale on 21 July,[121] and on 26 July the permit was granted.[122] Construction started in December 1988 and ended in February 1989.[123] **(Figure 88)**

In the meantime, all member-mosques of Diyanet had been given Turkish names, just like their counterparts in Turkey. Mosque names were largely derived from famous Turkish mosques and from chosen figures of national history and culture. In Almelo, although Atabek had now retired as chairman, the newly named Yunus Emre Mosque continued on its path of transcending the singular prayer hall from the early years into the ideal Anatolian village 'tradition' of the architectural complex with communal functions. In this case, the patrons no longer thought it necessary to hire the services of a recognized, expensive architect, so the designer was a contractor from Rijssen, Ter Steege. On 16 September 1992, he sent an application for a building permit to extend the Almelo mosque with a 'Mosque entry/toilet/ablution space', using external materials and colors 'as existing'.[124] **(Figure 89)** A week later, the municipality let the mosque know that they would start the Article 19 procedure.[125] On 13 October, Aesthetics approved the design.[126] However, the planned extension led, for the first time, to serious objections on the part of neighborhood inhabitants in light of perceived practical inconveniences.[127] Apparently, a newspaper article on the subject had resulted in worries about 'how far the mosque would be allowed to extend before the line between mosque and inhabitants was crossed'.[128] Therefore, the municipality decided to first change the zoning plan in the right direction and to only afterwards start up an Article 19 procedure for the mosque, meanwhile holding its construction application.[129] Not until two years later, on 23 March 1995, could the contractor send his designs from September 1992 to the municipality again.[130] Apparently no valid objections were filed. The provincial authorities approved,[131] and the permit was granted on 18 July.[132]

At this point, the former ablution space had been converted into part of the prayer hall, surrounding the minaret base and provided with its own entrance for women. A completely independent ablution space had been erected next to this entrance. As a result of the extension, the entry of the mosque's main prayer hall would consist of a courtyard surrounded by auxiliary buildings. The idea of a covered forecourt, as a representation of the open or glass-covered portico from Anatolian village mosques, was just a step away. In fact, this idea seemed to have already been developed by Atabek during his (former) chairmanship, in light of the fact that during celebrations, in Turkish custom, this part was used for prayers by the overflow of believers. So, two weeks after having sent in his designs for the second time, on 6 April Ter Steege also sent in a provisional plan for a transparent shed over the forecourt. Although the main plans had already been approved by Aesthetics, the shed had to be scrutinized. On 26 April, the municipality let the contractor know that Aesthetics had no objections to a transparent shed, if adjusted, and 'fitting', for the mosque. The quality of this preliminary drawing was apparently deemed below standard, and they advised the hiring of 'a capable architect'.[133] Four months later, Ter Steege had a supplier of sheds send him an offer for an arched screen for the entry of the mosque.[134] On 9 November, the contractor applied for a permit for a shed,[135] and on the same date the municipality agreed.[136] **(Figure 90)** On 21 November, Aesthetics approved of the design,[137] and on 23 April 1996 the permit was granted.[138] After construction, a low, wooden separation was installed under the covered portico and in front of the main façade, so the space could be used for removal and storage of shoes, just as under the (half)open porticoes of the represented Anatolian village mosques.

Although most auxiliary functions of the mosque had now been moved into auxiliary buildings, the problem of space for actual prayer for the ever growing community was not yet solved. On 9 October 1997, the mosque and its contractor applied for permission to extend the main prayer hall, breaking through the south wall and extending the hall in that direction.[139] **(Figure 91)** This time, the idea of the hipped roof was abandoned, keeping the construction in style as far as materials and colors were concerned but not as for form. This serves as a reminder that auxiliary buildings in Turkish village mosque complexes as perceived by the Almelo patrons did not necessarily have to be consistent with the main prayer hall or even with each other: they merely consisted of inconspicuous sheds and shaded corners, although they were ideally always there. The low priority of the outer appearances would have been reason for not hiring a recognized architect after Sevinçsoy, which, in its turn, had provoked the irritation of the Aesthetics Commission. Subsequently, the municipality informed the mosque that the planned extension would come too close to the streets, and that this made the design contradict the zoning plan. Therefore, it had not yet been sent to Aesthetics. Moreover, the mosque had to indicate on the drawings how it was planning to solve the expected parking problems that would result from the extension.[140] On 25 November, an adjusted plan was sent.[141] **(Figure 92)** Aesthetics approved with the remark that the roof had to be better adjusted to the roof of the existing prayer space. The commission had sketched in a possibility in red.[142] **(Figure 93)** Essentially, their suggestion came down to a southward extension of the roof by extending its southern slope, maintaining the singular roof form of the main building and keeping its overall appearance 'in style.'

On 3 April 1998, the mosque applied for a construction permit for the enlargement of the main hall according to the new roof design as sketched by Aesthetics.[143] **(Figure 94)** However, the municipality still needed more information on solving the expected parking problems.[144] As the mosque took too long to come up with the information, the municipality declared the application inadmissible.[145] Subsequently, the mosque board explained the situation to the authorities. The extension plans concerned a hall which was meant for celebrations, mainly during Ramadan. On busy days like these, people had to stand outside and pray, while the planned extension would provide shelter. This would not effectively increase traffic to the mosque.[146] In response, the municipality informed the mosque that they still had to include seven parking spots in their plans.[147] On 17 November 1998, the mosque applied for a permit once again, using the same plan as before only now with extra parking spaces.[148] The municipality[149] and Aesthetics approved the plan.[150] Since no further objections were deemed valid,[151] on 6 April the permit was granted.[152] On 16 April 1999, construction began, and on 13 April 2000, it was completed.[153] **(Figure 95)**

The Sultan Ahmet Mosque, Zaanstad

Until 1977, the Turkish-Islamic communities of labourers in and around Zaanstad, working in different factories in the conglomeration of villages on the outskirts of Amsterdam, had had to make use of individual rooms in scattered company barracks for prayers. Then, the municipality appointed an abandoned school building in Kogerveld for the purpose, and, with a space in which to meet, some members decided on 15 June 1978 to create the Turkish Islamic Center (Turks Islamitisch Centrum). They requested an imam from the Department of Religious Affairs of the Turkish consulate, and were assigned one for the duration of Ramadan that year. As there were also Süleymanci imams available and as, in the 1970s, there were conflicts on whether they or Diyanet would provide imams during Ramadan, the community leaders' choice of the state option was an early sign of their affiliation. After the official institution of Diyanet in The Netherlands in 1979, the Zaanstad community received their first Turkish imam in October 1979 for a term of 4 years.[154] They moved from the old building in Kogerveld to former school barracks in Poelenburg which the municipality was willing to rent and near which most community members lived. In 1989, the community bought the property and the plot on which the buildings were located, and the mosque was then officially transferred to the ISN. A plan for a new building could now be developed, as property rights had been established and the ISN was able to facilitate the necessary bank guarantee.

Mosque secretary Ahmet Altikulaç was a former ISN secretary and – not unimportant – a nephew of Diyanet official Tayyar Altikulaç, who, as we recall, had sent the assumed 'modern-republican' mosque design to Almelo. Whereas in the latter case the Dutch board members declined in the face of too much modernity, it seems that since Almelo many Diyanet mosque community leaders had developed a preference for modernized (in the sense of stylized but still recognizably Turkish) features. Some patrons chose to look at modern mosques in Turkey: the Mevlana in Rotterdam, for instance, refers to contemporary mosque design in Izmir. Others created their own modern-republican forms: the Süleymaniye in Tilburg uses the crescent moon and star in its ground plan as an explicit reference to the Turkish national flag.[155] The real flagship of the ISN, however, would be built in Zaanstad, as this mosque was intended to be the largest in The Netherlands, and as such would host the Diyanet conferences.[156] Moreover, after construction it would be chosen to be on the cover of an important Turkish Diyanet album about member mosques in Western Europe. Finally, it would use the services of architect Bedri Sevinçsoy, who had become the ISN's favoured architect,[157] effectively representing the Turkish 'modern-republican' design school in The Netherlands. In fact, when Perotti had wanted to design a mosque for the Turkish-Islamic community in Enschede, the ISN – 'aided by lawyers' – rejected his participation in the project.[158] Instead, as we will see later, Sevinçsoy was invited to design the new prayer hall, although his alternative was eventually built not in Enschede but in Zaanstad.

Sevinçsoy, born and raised in the European quarter of Taksim in Istanbul, had been exposed to architectural design philosophy from a very early age as his father was a Turkish architect. The latter was inspired more by Western architecture than Ottoman forms and had as such worked on the Opera at Taksim, a modernist structure without any recognizable Ottoman elements.[159] Bedri himself was educated in an Italian school and brought up in elite, professional surroundings which wanted nothing to do with religious fervour. He planned on following in his father's footsteps with an architectural education in Istanbul. In 1979, he decided to come to The Netherlands, where he studied architecture at the Academie voor Bouwkunst in Arnhem in order to be recognized as an architect in The Netherlands.[160]

In Almelo, Sevinçsoy had been asked to expand the existing prayer hall with auxiliary buildings to complete the image of an ideal Anatolian village's socio-religious complex. For that commission, it had not been necessary to include fundamental ideas on the modernization of Islamic design, since the patrons put no value on the outer appearance of the auxiliary sheds and since the municipality had simply requested the extension to be 'in style', although he did use 'modern' Inkalite materials. However, when asked to design a prayer hall in Eindhoven, it was a completely different matter. Sevinçsoy never meant to become a specialist in religious architecture, but he found the commission interesting as the ISN patrons specifically required a modern, though still recognizably Turkish, mosque. Sevinçsoy had the Turkish Historical Society in Ankara send him a package of architectural studies of buildings by Sinan, the admired 16th century architect who worked for powerful patrons under the Sultans in the Ottoman glory days. **(Figure 96)** From these drawings and from his experience in Turkey, he looked to extract what he saw as essential characteristics of Turkish mosque design, to be transformed into modern buildings by stylization.

To some observers, Sevincsoy's eventual Eindhoven Fatih design stood for a mere copy. **(Figure 97)** Perotti, in between his Ridderkerk and Waalwijk designs, found it to be '[...] architecture from the year zero. You have to oppose that. You should not establish any Aya Sofias in The Netherlands, I think'. 'One wants a copy of important mosques in the homeland. But Muslim groups in The Netherlands were not there when the newest developments occurred in these countries.'[161] However, as we have already seen, design preferences of mosque community leaders in The Netherlands have much less to do, despite current architectural beliefs, with 'backwardness' against 'innovativeness' than with the architectural representation of contesting constructions of Islam. Moreover, to classify the design as an 'Aya Sofia' is missing its main point, since the Aya Sofia was exactly the projected materialization of religious values that Diyanet as well as the Eindhoven patrons and architect did not wish to support, as we will explore further in the last Turkish case study. Finally, Sevinçsoy's design actually did follow design preferences that in Turkey were seen as a modernization of classical-religious architecture, although, of course, it did not go as far in its stylization of Ottoman building elements as the first Kocatepe design. It is important to note that the Eindhoven mosque was not a backward copy but a transformation of a particular selection of building elements. For its patrons, it perfectly represented the Turkish-republican ideal of a modern religion without the overt religious grandeur of past Ottoman times. In an interview, chairman I. Top exclaimed: 'Look, now this is an example of modern Turkish architecture. It makes a very tasteful impression on the Dutch.'[162]

After Almelo, according to Sevinçsoy, Turkish mosque patrons had wanted their buildings to be set up as a whole complex under one roof. There would be religious and secular tutoring, a shop and a library, coffee would be served, hair would be cut, and meetings could be held. In other words, the mosque itself had gained an entertainment function and was much more than just a house of prayer. Of course, in Turkey, community mosques had strong social functions, but these were normally distributed over a larger complex. According to Sevinçsoy, they would not be included in the designed prayer hall building itself. When Sevinçsoy was invited to design a purpose built mosque in The Netherlands however, he was presented with an extensive program of requirements going far beyond the prayer function. Of course, the prayer hall would have to be large, but the space for social traffic would have to be even larger.[163] That minarets in The Netherlands were restricted in height so as not to infringe on the cityscape, he found to be understandable. 'A mosque should fit into its surroundings, that is logical.' Importantly, however, that did not mean to him 'a mosque with Dutch stepped gables': Dutch architecture, in Sevinçsoy's words, had hardly any influence on his designs, save perhaps for climate and available materials. A true Turkish mosque, for him would have a hemispherical dome, not supported by columns – that would obstruct a clear view – and that would cover as large an area as possible. It would also have a minaret with a round or 12-sided shaft, and an inner court with an ablution fountain.[164] These appeared to be the main building elements that the architect had selected from his Sinan drawings in order for a design to at least remain recognizably Turkish in a subsequent process of stylization.

On 12 February 1990, Sevinçsoy made a design for a very large ISN mosque in Enschede, which remained unexecuted for lack of funds. **(Figure 98)** In this design, Sevinçsoy used the square prayer hall, dome and minaret forms as he had extracted them from Sinan's work, and as already included in his project in Eindhoven. In addition, besides a second level and minaret, he introduced arched windows, four protruding corner extensions and an entrance portal with conspicuous roof edges. Derived from what were seen as 'traditionally Turkish' buildings, with protruding balconies, porticoes and galleries with overhanging, sometimes lead-plated, roof edges, elements like these had come to be unofficially defined as the most typical Turkish traits in the search for national design. They were subsequently translated into several (semi-)governmental commissions for secular, 'modern-republican' buildings.[165] **(Figure 99)** Sevinçsoy admittedly looked towards these buildings in finding appropriate architectural elements with which to represent a modern-republican construction of Islam in The Netherlands, and the cornice was certainly not a 'failed representation of Dutch slant roofs painted red', as some observers speculated.[166] His expressed aim at architectural integration was substantiated not with any typically Dutch forms but with the modernization of selected Turkish building characteristics. Another good example was his proposed design for a mosque and apartment complex for a square in Lombok, a quarter of Utrecht with a high concentration of Turkish Muslims. An undated drawing shows a square planned mosque with protruding corners on a square with apartment blocks and shops, including the recognizably Turkish cornice and protruding balconies. **(Figure 100)** In the end, the project did not see the light of day because of the lack of funds on the part of the ISN patrons.[167]

It was after his unexecuted Enschede and Utrecht mosque plans that Sevinçsoy developed the idea of extending his services to Turkish-Islamic community leaders so that these would be able to make use of standardized, customizable, and thus cheaper, construction elements which could be varied according to budget and municipal limits. In 1991, in the course of developing two plans for ISN mosques in Etten Leur and Lelystad, he created prefab-constructible concrete rings for minarets and minaret balconies based on his Utrecht design, so the patrons could decide on how much money and municipal effort they wanted to spend on height. **(Figure 101)** He also commissioned a plastics firm to come up with a re-usable mould for a dome. Although the plans were not executed in those two municipalities, his customizable design elements were indeed used in Zaanstad, Gorinchem, Delft and Helmond. Moreover, his Zaanstad window scheme was repeated in his later commissions. Through his 'modern-republican' design preferences and customizations he had effectively become the main Diyanet architect, and had he not left for Turkey it is probable that there would have been more Turkish purpose-built mosques than there are, as he would have provided small communities with expanded opportunities by drastically cutting costs.[168]

With all of his former designs in mind, Sevinçsoy deliberated with Altikulaç on the main Diyanet mosque in Zaanstad. Like many other ISN community leaders before him, the patron agreed to the designer's preference for Turkish modern-republican architecture and to his rejection of the traditionalist character of classical Ottoman forms. While Altikulaç, and many other ISN mosque administrators, had images of Istanbul's classical Ottoman mosques hanging in his board room next to the ever-present picture of Atatürk, he found these buildings beautiful but not of this time and certainly not appropriate for the modern-Dutch context. The patron embraced the official Diyanet construction of Islam, not any 'Islamist' alternatives circulating among contesting Turkish-Islamic community leaders in The Netherlands, and he required this construction to be represented in a modern-Turkish mosque design, not in a conspicuous copy of the Blue Mosque in Istanbul. Subsequently, Sevinçsoy came up with a plan, a model and an axonometry on 20 September 1991. **(Figure 102)** The proposal effectively consisted of a combination of the building elements he had used and created so far, and in his eyes, it was the most beautiful of all his designs. 'It is large, it is located amidst green shrubs, and it has everything in it,' he said.[169] It had the square scheme, protruding front corner extensions, entrance portal and cornices of Enschede, together with the customized dome and minaret elements of Utrecht, Etten Leur and Lelystad. As in these try-outs, the dome and minarets clearly referred to Ottoman, lead-plated examples, while he had added a basin in the hall representing the Ottoman inner courts' ablution fountain, although the real ablution spaces in Zaanstad were placed to the sides.[170] The Ottoman külliye had been integrated into a single building, covering all needed functions. To be sure, although the 'traditional-Anatolian' forms from Almelo had been left for more 'Ottoman' building elements, importantly, the latter had not been copied just like that. The central dome was not designed to rise high above its square base, and there were no supporting half-domes or curtain walls – building elements normally very much associated with classical Ottoman architecture, and used as such in our third case study. Moreover, Sevinçsoy and Altikulaç had decided to keep the minarets relatively low, expecting municipal opposition but also because, according to the architect, modern sound installations made overly high minarets superfluous[171] and, in addition, an unwanted 'pyramidal' effect would arise.[172] Notably, height and slenderness, outward signs which have earlier been shown to represent an Islam with a much larger role in the Turkish public sphere than propagated by the state, were seen as too old-fashioned to substantiate a modern-republican Islamic construction. In our third case study, we will see that these values, including the rejected 'pyramidality', would be re-invoked and exaggerated precisely because of their connotations with religious grandeur.

The municipality expressed its desire to approve of the plan, as the new building would 'improve the mosque's current function'.[173] Two weeks later, Aesthetics also approved.[174] As this first plan was a preliminary application, more detailed drawings were needed, with indications of facilities for fire safety, handicapped visitors and parking space,[175] but the overall design apparently needed no major changes as far as authorities were concerned. Although the municipality had no official policy on Islam, the general approach to the mosque was that it would positively add to the city's cultural diversity and to the emancipation of its Turkish Muslims.[176] However, the municipality did establish that the number of visitors to the largest mosque of The Netherlands was to be translated into a minimum of 80 parking spaces,[177] and for that reason the mosque had to buy an extra plot opposite the planned entrance.[178]

Next, Altıkulaç and imam Abdul Kadir Topuz presented Sevinsçoy's plan to the public. According to Altıkulaç, the old building was much too small, while more and more people had to pray outside on the parking lot, especially on Fridays and during Ramadan. The new building would be able to hold, instead of 700, 1700. In his opinion, the mosque would be the largest in Europe with the exceptions of one in France and one in Rome. According to Topuz, the first level would contain space for socio-cultural and sports activities, the second would have a prayer hall, a library, a canteen and two small meeting spaces, while the third level would have a classroom for religious lessons, a meeting space for youngsters, a conference space, a guestroom, and a board room.[179]

On 2 April, the final application forms and construction plans were sent to the municipality.[180] **(Figure 103)** The latter approved,[181] and since a number of non-design-related objections were declared unfounded by the municipality as well as the Province, the permit was granted on 26 April.[182] On 28 May, the Turkish ambassador, Zeki Çelikkol, and a representative from the ISN, Fahri Demir, together performed the first pole celebration. As of 21 October, however, mayor and aldermen had to propose another Article 19 start-up, since the permit had not been settled because of an ongoing legal procedure and the first had apparently expired. The Municipal Council agreed on the same date.[183] Construction continued, carried out with the voluntary help of community members – a suggestion made by Sevinsçoy to cut down on construction costs,[184] and took a relatively short 1,5 years.[185] Although construction was not yet finished, the first level or basement hall could be used during Ramadan in 1994.[186] On 27 November, the mosque was opened by Minister of Domestic Affairs Hans Dijkstal and representatives of the Turkish embassy. That the prayer hall was seen as Diyanet's main representation in The Netherlands was shown by an extensive and explicitly ISN-related campaign around the opening, and by the fact that it was chosen to be on the cover of the Turkish Diyanet's album on its mosques in Western Europe.[187] **(Figure 104)** The large basement's hall would be used for ISN meetings and other kinds of conferences, and the multifunctional spaces under the mosque's roof would be used for all kinds of socio-cultural activities. The mosque presented itself as transparent, open to visitors, excursions and conferences, developing intensive contacts with local and national politics and politicians, and pro-active in its stance towards social integration into Dutch society. Recently, in response to the growing interest of Dutch media in the subject of Muslim architectural integration, Altikulaç, by now Chairman, claimed that his mosque fitted into its immediate physical surroundings by way of the materials used and the low height of the minarets. He suggested that the design had been devised to result in an 'inviting' image, as specifically opposed to 'exaggerated' designs as seen in our next case study, the Wester Mosque in Amsterdam.[188] **(Figure 105)**

The Wester Mosque, Amsterdam

Before our account of the Wester Mosque on its currently planned location begins, the mosque already had a history of problematic relations between the patron, Üzeyir Kabaktepe of the Milli Görüs community Aya Sofia, and the municipal district's office De Baarsjes.[189] Much of this seemed to have been motivated by a latent fear of Turkish domination of the neighbourhood: the MG movement, as described earlier, had always been depicted as a religiously orthodox, 'Islamist' organization. But Kabaktepe never showed himself to be a religious fanatic. What he did constantly stress, however, was his adherence to the idea that religion should have an important and meaningful place in society, and he never tried to hide his antipathy towards forced secularity in Turkey. After Kabaktepe, at the age of 8, had come with his mother to join his father in The Netherlands, his parents warned him against nationalism. For them, Islam formed the central value.[190] In Kabaktepe's own words, 'I am a Muslim in The Netherlands and The Netherlands are a much more Islamic country than Turkey. [...] Expressions of faith, whether they come from Jews, Christians, Muslims or Hindus, are allowed in the public sphere as well. A Muslim girl may, if she wants, carry a headscarf at university, at school or when she works for the government.' As opposed to that, he found that 'Diyanet is a Turkish-Islamic movement in

The Netherlands that is directly connected to the Turkish Republic. The Turkish Republic determines which sermons will be held by which imams from which pulpits in which mosques'.[191]

When he was eighteen, Kabaktepe became involved with the Milli Görüs movement. To them, instead of modern-republican Turkish nationhood, it was the larger Ottoman Empire as a group of people united by faith, with a specific Turkish character, that formed the main identifying value. In 1987, he moved to Amsterdam to organize Turkish youth there: stray Turkish youngsters formed easy victims for petty crime, especially in Amsterdam-West. In 1989, he began a travel agency in De Baarsjes, and in this district MG became the most active. A plan soon evolved for a common center in which Turks of all ages could meet for social activities and prayer. De Baarsjes formed the most logical choice. In his subsequent contacts with the municipality, Kabaktepe stressed his aim of keeping Turkish youngsters away from street life, and elderly Turks out of coffee houses, by emancipating them and bringing them into contact with Dutch society. 'Emancipation [...] will come sooner through accentuating the own identity than through the erosion of the own cultural background by forced assimilation.' On 23 February 1993, the Milli Görüs Sociale en Kulturele Vereniging Amsterdam-West was founded, and at that time the name Aya Sofia was first mentioned as an informal name for the mosque association and for a future complex. Kabaktepe was very conscious of the meaning of this name: it was not without significance in contemporary Turkey, as MG was propagating, against the republican state's wish, the re-conversion of the Aya Sofia in Istanbul from a museum to a genuine mosque.[192]

However, an array of proposals involving several possible locations and architectural plans was then rejected by alternating parties, and tension slowly built up. On 11 February 1994, Kabaktepe decided to start using an abandoned garage, on what was generally called the Riva-terrain, as a mosque, mainly for Ramadan celebration. Sometime later, as director of the MG-related investment company Manderen BV, he managed to buy the property. The religious use of this building led to a series of conflicts involving demonstrations, near-evictions, heavy media attention, and rapidly worsening relations with the municipality, as the latter was preparing a new zoning plan for the area, mainly involving housing and companies. In a breakthrough, on 10 March it offered to allow 1000 m2 for socio-cultural activities, in this case a mosque. Although this ended that conflict, the main problem now centered on the maximum of 1000 m2, because Kabaktepe needed much more than that to give substance to his plans for a prayer house with accompanying socio-cultural activities. The District, under chairman Freek Salm (PvdA), however, feared the coming of a 'Turkish fortification' in a neighbourhood specifically meant for multi-cultural housing. Again, an array of proposals was rejected, leading to, again, a series of conflicts involving a near-eviction and now also a legal procedure. In the end, on 11 December 1996, the Raad van State (the Dutch Supreme Court) decided in favour of the District, supporting the municipal wish to keep religious facilities in this housing area small in scale. In May 1997, the District invited Aya Sofia to come up with a plan that would fit into the area's new zoning plan.[193]

The mosque requested project developer Volker Stevin to design a proposal. After having produced initial drawings with office- and apartment blocks harbouring an unrecognizable prayer hall within their walls, former state-architect Kees Rijnboutt was asked instead to design a fully recognizable mosque – which he did on 14 February 1999. **(Figure 106)** According to Rijnboutt, he had, in light of the problematic relations between MG, the municipality, and the inhabitants, explicitly meant it to be composed ('*beheerst*') and modest ('*ingetogen*'). He had consulted some general literature with a range of mosque images, and had eventually come up with a generalized, low-rise, and modern design that was not supposed to have a traditionally Turkish outlook.[194] This design was fervently rejected by Kabaktepe as being 'an exotic sugar cake, a little block with a little cap and a rocket-minaret', and 'a Disney-like office box with a cigar sticking out'.[195] Instead, he wanted his building to have the characteristics of a classical Ottoman mosque, which, in Kabaktepe's account, should have an array of half-domes cascading down from a main dome in the center, specific proportions between height and volume, slender, pencil-shaped minarets, arcaded galleries, and a stepped base or plinth. All this would give the building an important 'pyramidal image'. In his travels to Istanbul, visiting many Ottoman mosques, Kabaktepe had developed a great admiration for the – what he called – 'Sinan-style'. In his own account, he had gathered quite a collection of books on the subject, specifically referring to the well-known study of Ottoman architecture by Goodwin.[196] The community leader especially admired the Blue Mosque, which he had always considered as the ideal Ottoman design, although he realized, of course, it had been created only after Sinan's death. **(Figure 107)**

Kabaktepe seemed to share this ideal representation of Ottoman architecture with other religious groups in Turkey, who had managed, as we recall, to change the modern-republican – and partly built – design for the Kocatepe Mosque in Ankara 180 degrees to a construction they repeatedly likened to the Blue Mosque.[197] As the Blue Mosque was placed conspicuously facing the former Byzantine church of Aya Sofia, some authors recognized the religious content of the Kocatepe as conspicuously facing the modern-republican content of Atatürk's memorial.[198] In that sense, both mosques were meant as political statements, as victories of Ottoman Islam. In the preference for the Blue Mosque's building elements and the accompanying dislike, in Ankara and Amsterdam, of modern-republican architecture – often formulated in quasi-objective terms of function or aesthetics – a pride in Ottoman-religious grandeur can be discerned, much deeper in significance than practicality or taste alone. From a representational viewpoint, Kabaktepe stood for a much more 'sacral' construction of Islam than the secularized version embraced by contesting Turkish-Islamic community leaders, and he required this construction to be represented by building elements associated with religious values and not with secular ones. In Kabaktepe's view, Turkish mosques in The Netherlands, specifically like the one in Zaanstad, for which he used the words 'Efteling' and 'Walt Disney', lacked the 'mystery of Ottoman construction, the transcendence of the visitor to heaven with the transcendence of the pyramid of domes'. Strikingly, this exact 'pyramidal' trait had been mentioned by Sevinsçoy as something to be avoided at all cost: it stood for overly religious values and a lack of modernity and appropriateness to the building's modern-Western surroundings.

In fact, Rijnboutt's sketch could well have had a good chance as a first proposal for an ISN community but he had unknowingly been confronted with a patron who, in his desired representation of Islam, wanted to oppose the modern-republican mosque approach as he recognized it in the architect's drawing, even if the architect had never meant it as such. At the beginning of 1998, however, Aya Sofia had also come into contact with the housing corporation Het Oosten under director Frank Bijdendijk, who thought he could see possibilities for developing the terrain in a way that all parties would be satisfied. One of the options presented was a plan that would transcend the delimitations of the zoning plan, but which also would be so evocative that the District, now under chairman Henk van Waveren (also PvdA), would gladly set an Article 19 procedure in motion to allow for more than the strictly-adhered-to maximum of 1000 m2 social functions.[199] An agreement was reached by Kabaktepe, Van Waveren and Bijdendijk. A building permit would be provided by the District for the plan made by Het Oosten as project developer for MG, as it would not only include a mosque but also involve housing, office facilities, retail and parking opportunities for the whole neighbourhood. Bijdendijk's corporation would sell or rent out the apartments, and Kabaktepe and his holding would own some of the shops in order to use their profits for maintenance of the mosque.[200]

For his plan, Bijdendijk hired Marc Breitman, a French-Jewish architect based in Paris. Bijdendijk explained his choice of Breitman. 'I had some good experiences with Marc Breitman on a housing project in [...] Amsterdam. Besides, he has worked in Baghdad and Tunis and is familiar with mosques.'[201] However, more importantly than Breitman's exposure to Islamic architecture, Bijdendijk appeared to have a strong preference for the particular architectural design style of architects like Krier and Breitman, who, in Bijdendijk's view, aimed at 'designing housing in which real people can feel safe, instead of creating monuments for themselves'.[202] Breitman is usually regarded to work within the Post-Modernist school, formulated as an answer to the Modernist trend and using classical building elements in contemporary design. Classical building elements, of course, have been used in cyclical movements literally for thousands of years, each time transformed and vested with new meanings in new socio-political contexts, used in processes of mutual contrasting between patrons as well as architects. In this case, they were defined against the perceived, unnatural character of modernist architecture, and seen as forming part of the naturally developed character of urban settlements.[203] Notably, the dominant trend among Dutch architects still seems to regard classical building elements as overly decorative and a step beneath the development as started by designers of the Rationalist school a hundred years ago.

In September 1998, Breitman came up with a first drawing, to be presented to the MG community, Het Oosten and the district. According to the architect, no talks had been held yet with Kabaktepe, and all that Bijdendijk had asked at that time was that he design a single-domed mosque for the Amsterdam Turkish-Islamic community, and that it be 'the most beautiful mosque in The Netherlands'. Breitman had meant this preliminary sketch to represent – what he called – a general Turkish mosque typology, incorporating elements from different classical Ottoman prayer halls in one building, adjusting it to the Dutch urban context by positioning it at the center of a square.[204] **(Figure 108)** However, to Kabaktepe, it looked like an 'Arabian model', with a dome on a square box and a short minaret. In the patron's view, this design had been based on Breitman's study of mosques in the Arab countries where he had worked, while Kabaktepe wanted a classical Ottoman mosque, 'like the Blue Mosque', instead. Apparently, what constitutes 'a typical classical Ottoman mosque' is not as straightforward as one would assume, and intra-type differences can be very important. Breitman came up with a revised plan on 25 November 1998. **(Figure 109)** In this sketch, we see a mosque with auxiliary spaces attached to the main building. The Kiblah was aligned with the canal, although it was slightly off and the building as a whole was turned a degree or so, but an attached gallery at the canal side compensated for that fact. The ground plan was square, the central dome was circular and rested on a square base supported on all four sides by semi-domes and with smaller domes on its four corners. According to the architect, he had not meant the drawing as a mere copy of the Blue Mosque, although the latter did form, to him, a major image of the Ottoman mosque typology. Still, even though there was only one minaret here with only one balcony, located to the left of the entrance façade, and even though on top of the dome Breitman had drawn a lantern, in Kabaktepe's reality the new drawing obviously consisted of a transformation of his admired Blue Mosque's building elements.

In consquence, this design was much more to the community leader's liking, and on 24 March 1999 Breitman was able to submit a proposal to the municipality in which he offered three possible options as a solution to the problem of the Riva-terrain. The first two options would remain within the frame of the old plan established by the municipality for height and for functional and spatial distribution. One plan would be to renovate the existing prayer hall, and another to keep the original prayer hall building intact. According to Breitman, both had the disadvantage of the difficulty of orientation towards Mecca, and he didn't quite work them out in detail as he did with the last option, a completely new plan for the terrain. **(Figure 110)** In this plan, Breitman put a new mosque at the center of the complex, 'creating a better distribution of activities and enhancing the quality of public space through the creation of new squares and the removal of parking to underground levels'. This plan would be in line with what he defined as the Dutch architectural tradition of a central religious building surrounded by a square and housing. The orientation of the mosque would be solved effortlessly and the height of housing still be within the established frame.[205]

The District also took to Breitman's preferred option. In October 2000, it announced it would use the article 19 procedure.[206] Architect Piet Vernooy of the bureau 4DEE Architect was asked to devise some professional 3D images for a public presentation in November 2000. He was requested to detail Breitman's plan in line with the surrounding Amsterdam School buildings as a way to bridge the gap between Aya Sofia, the municipality, the district and the neighbourhood inhabitants, which he did as much as he could.[207] **(Figure 111)** After seeing the presentation, the District unanimously supported the plan, confirming the three parties-agreement[208] and approving the start-up of an article 19 procedure.[209] On 18 January 2001, Aesthetics decided that the programmatic requirements had first to be scrutinized by the commission, and that only after these had been approved, a permit for the project could be applied for.[210]

One week later, project leader Van der Ven explicated the plans for 'a mosque with annexes, apartments and company spaces for the Turkish community by the hand of Breitman'. The main goal for the programmatic requirements was 'to create an open situation in which all forms of Islam could find a place'. The programmatic approach of the plan was characterized by a mixture of different urban functions. In the program, 3000 m2 was available to the Turkish-Islamic community and 9000 m2 for housing. The 3000 m2 for the Turkish-Islamic community would be subdivided into 1000 m2 for the mosque, 1000 m2 for socio-cultural use, including sports facilities, a youth center, a gym and a language center, and 1000 m2 for companies and offices. For security, the aim was a 'transparent' plan with maximum openness, creating sufficient social control which should prevent possible criminal activities. Parking would be underground. Aesthetics, however, saw several problems. For a gate between mosque square and hinterlying street (the De Witte de Withstraat), in order to create a passage to the mosque and, importantly, a space for the necessary shops, two historically valuable properties would have to be demolished. Moreover, according to the commission, the mosque gave the impression of being insulated by the annexes, which would disturb the geometric plan of the prayer hall itself. The argument that most mosques in Turkey actually did have such surrounding buildings was not seen as realistic. 'From a historical point of view, this would have been the result of a process taking years,' the commission thought it knew. However, the commission at least approved of the positioning of the mosque. More important, it stated that it wanted to see the suggested grandeur realized.[211]

In May 2001, Breitman presented Kabaktepe with a drawing in which the mosque façades showed more details. Notably, he had not used Vernooy's generally admired proposal or even his own preliminary sketches. In fact, although he had planned on using bricks from the beginning, he did not wish to merely copy a classical Ottoman mosque as required by Kabaktepe, and neither did he wish to merely conform to an Amsterdam School as required by the District. Instead, he wanted to create a Dutch mosque type according to his own ideas on urban context, ideally incorporating the classical elements that he typically used. **(Figure 112)** However, as creative and culturally blended as this design was and as much as it fitted perfectly into the architect's own design philosophy, Breitman's detailed follow-up on his last proposal appeared unacceptable to his patron, who thought he recognized a neo-classic church.'Man, that's not a mosque!,' Kabaktepe exclaimed to his designer.[212] Apparently, the community leader would not compromise his preferred architectural representation of Islam outside the realm of materials. According to Kabaktepe, the architect, in what was supposed to be merely a phase of material detailing, had resorted once again to his previous formal ideas on religious architecture. Whereas during his very first sketch, in Kabaktepe's account, he had used his experience in Arab countries, he now had based himself, in the patron's view, on churches instead of mosques. As a reaction to this drawing, Kabaktepe took Breitman to the Sultan Ahmet Mosque in Zaanstad and to the Mevlana Mosque in Rotterdam, both prominent Diyanet prayer halls. The architect and the community leader agreed that prayer spaces were too low and exterior forms, colours and materials were much too 'modern', giving the impression of a 'cinema'. In short, the building elements as incorporated in these Diyanet mosques were the complete reverse from any which classical Ottoman standard.

At the request of Kabaktepe, Breitman reintroduced some of the earlier Blue Mosque-associated building elements in a more detailed plan for the official application of the whole project to be filed on 7 December 2001. **(Figure 113)** The new apartment block adjacent to the existing buildings on the left was drawn in line with the Amsterdam School, while the rest of the project, starting with the building on that corner, predominantly made use of Breitman's classical elements. In answer to the Aesthetics Commission's remarks about unwanted insulation of the mosque, the northern annexes had been removed although the south-Western annex, which was to be a library, was kept. More details were shown, and heights for dome and minaret were now set at 25 and 42 meters. Dolf Dazert, senior project leader of Het Oosten (also referred to as Het Oosten/Kristal, as the latter was used as main project developer), presented the design for the Riva-terrain to the District. The mosque would remain the nucleus of the plan. For its design, 'classical-Turkish forms' had been looked at. It was a preliminary design, but according to Dazert this was also how they meant it to be definitively executed. Importantly, C. Hollack, senior project leader of the District, mentioned that the plan had been discussed in the Aesthetics Commission the week before. The interior area had been found to be 'a little too rich' and the mosque 'very dominant'. However, in Hollack's words, a choice had been made of this architect, and he did have this kind of design as basis. Hollack was adamant that they honour his particular style.[213] In Dazert's recollection, commission members had objected to the neo-classical features of the design and had asked for forms completely in line with the Amsterdam School surroundings, which he and Hollack knew the architect would not likely accept.[214] Six weeks later, the design as presented was made publicly accessible.[215] Some objections against the plan were filed by inhabitants,[216] but on 16 April, the District decided to approve, explicitly mentioning the 2000 m2 social facilities and the planned cupola and minaret heights of 25 and 42 meters.[217] From that time on, the architect was bound by those numbers.[218]

Although Kabaktepe was at first content that an official application had finally been filed, he was, on second thought, not so sure about the design itself anymore. The minaret looked heavy and bulky to him, and there was no stepped plinth. In the patron's eyes – especially since Breitman had, in what was supposed to be a phase of mere material detailing, come up with building elements that were a far cry from what he apparently had had in mind himself – it was time to introduce the artist to classical Ottoman design and -designers in the flesh. Kabaktepe proposed to Bijdendijk that the three of them travel to Istanbul in the spring of 2002 to acquaint Breitman with 'genuine' mosque architecture and architects. Although Breitman, with all his experience in Muslim countries, was sure he could design a mosque without actually visiting Turkey or Turkish architects, he did relish the thought of going.[219] Eventually, according to Dazert, Kabaktepe, Bijdendijk, Breitman and Dazert went to Istanbul for 14-17 March 2002. In Bijdendijk's words: 'The three parties went on a study-trip to Istanbul, and there we discovered some interesting things.' According to him, it was the domed mosques of 16th century architect Sinan that especially provided necessary inspiration. Kabaktepe specified: 'Then we took a journey to Istanbul and Edirne. And in the end, it was the Selim Mosque in Edirne that was taken as the model for the final design of the Wester Mosque.'[220]

In fact, according to Kabaktepe, Breitman and Dazert in later interviews, Edirne was not actually visited on that particular journey, but the Edirne mosque had come into the picture when the parties visited a Turkish architect in order for him to explain the finesses of Ottoman architecture to Breitman. Kabaktepe had chosen him because he had designed what the community leader saw as 'the last great Ottoman mosque in Turkey', the Sabanci Mosque in Adana. Notably, the latter's main volume showed similarities to the elevation and ground plan of the Edirne Selimiye while the number of minarets showed a possible association with the Blue Mosque. **(Figure 114)** However, whatever the actual design process between patron and architect, and whatever the 'inside' representation contained in the Sabanci mosque itself, Kabaktepe only chose to contact the architect and therefore it is only the latter's account which mattered to the design process in Amsterdam. The architect's advice was not to take the Blue Mosque as a model for contemporary Ottoman design, as the relatively closed semi-domes made the actual construction 'too dark and too bulky'. In Kabaktepe's recollection, the designer pointed out that it was better to use the great architect Sinan's example as a source of inspiration instead, especially his Edirne octagonal dome-base and arched curtain walls alternating with semi-domes.

Importantly, his view seemed related to Turkish architecture-historical literature, in which the Selimiye Mosque, as Sinan's ultimate masterpiece, seems to have come to overrule the Blue Mosque as one of the main representations of 'Ottomanness'. An important role in this re-evaluation of the Selimiye was played by authorities like Aptullah Kuran and Godfrey Goodwin, who, in 1987 and 1993 respectively, began to compare Sinan with Alberti, Bramante and Palladio.[221] In their views, Sinan was a true artistic genius at the end of a line of architectural development, without whom the famous Ottoman grandeur would never have been created. Goodwin especially presented Sinan's creation in Edirne as the latter's personal artistic masterpiece, much like Rembrandt who to some art historians has come to represent Dutch artistic genius separated from any worldly contexts of patrons' representational requirements or target groups. To Goodwin, no later building could ever begin to equal the wonderful achievements in Edirne,[222] and the Blue Mosque, formerly a very important symbol of Ottoman grandeur in the eyes of Western and Eastern beholders alike, was reduced to an exaggeration of the sublime, a fake, a resort to the supporting semi-domes which Sinan himself had already brilliantly surpassed.[223] As a result, the Selimiye came to be commonly thought to transcend and perfect older notions of proportion, space, roof-span, slenderness, lightness and beauty. In current Turkish architecture studies, Sinan's comparability to Western European architects and architectural treatises has been developed even further, and Sinan has been fully restored to his former status of Divine Maestro.[224]

After the trip to Istanbul and the imported ideas on sublime classical Ottoman architecture, the patron decided to withdraw the plan for the mosque from his permit application and to come up with a more appropriate design with his architect. Although Breitman admittedly rejected the Turkish architect's attempts to tell him how to design a genuinely classical Ottoman mosque or to copy the Selimiye, on 2 July 2002 he devised a new sketch. The mosque now had a high-rising central dome, a low plinth with corners steps, a slender minaret with two balconies, an octagonal dome-base, and arched curtain walls alternating with semi-domes. Notably, whereas the architect experienced this shift as merely an answer to the patron's newly expressed need for more space, in Kabaktepe's reality the current design was an obvious transformation of the Selimiye's main building elements.[225] **(Figure 115)** In Dazert's memory, the patron's request for a raised, stepped platform that would cover a large part of the square, which he deemed a classical Ottoman characteristic, had not been found realistic by the District as it would exceed all set delimitations. In Breitman's next mosque plan on 17-4-2003, he reduced the number of windows in the dome drums and the arched curtain walls, making the mosque, in his view, proportionally more correct. **(Figure 116)** On 30 December, Het Oosten re-applied for a building permit for the complex, still without the mosque and mainly based on a requested simplification of façades.[226] After the Aesthetics Commission approved the plan, a permit was granted for the complex – except for the mosque – on 21 March 2003.[227]

The year 2003 would also prove to be the year of introduction of the new Milli Görüs mosque to the public in the national media by spokesman Haci Karacaer, although the latter does not appear to have been deeply involved in the actual design process between Kabaktepe and Breitman. Karacaer had come to The Netherlands when he was 19, in 1982. 'I believed in Turkish nationalism, and this being Kurdish myself. That something wasn't right became clear to me when the right-wing Center Party arose in The Netherlands. Suddenly, I saw that their slogans and thinking was not a far cry from ours. […] Then I decided: from now on, I determine my own identity. These days, I call out that I'm Dutch and that I'm proud of it. […] I went looking for an organization that did have the religious component, but without the nationality issue. That is how I ended up with Milli Görüs, the only Turkish organization in which nationality does not play a part. These people find religion much more important than being Turkish. That is why they're criticized so often by other Turks. […] Our leading notions are integration, participation, emancipation and achievement. […] With the Wester Mosque, I really have dreams. The renewal of Islam won't come from the East, but from the West. That is the torch with which I will light up in Amsterdam.'[228] 'The Wester Mosque will be the most beautiful mosque in The Netherlands, which is the explicit ambition of Frank Bijdendijk. A monumental building which, with domes and minaret, will show the historic, architectural splendour of the Oriental mosque. That is the image that we're going to create, and with it, we will step out of the oppressive shade of the shelter-church. [...] It's going to be a city-project that fits harmoniously into its surroundings, also regarding the use of materials. That means light and darker red bricks and façade details which are akin to the Amsterdam School of the neighbouring architecture. An adult, richly materialized mosque it should be, and not a cheap white box in between housing blocks, with a few thin minarets, as most newly built mosques look like. That's why we haven't hired any of the recently graduated Moroccan, Turkish or Pakistani architects. They are [...] still inexperienced.'[229] 'That [Breitman] is Jewish, is only a detail. He's a great architect and his designs were simply the best.'[230] 'We want to be part of the neighbourhood. We don't want to be, as is often the case with mosques these days, an island in the city. Isolated, seemingly inaccessible to strangers. That has to be, and can be, different, for example, by taking the neighbourhood into account while designing. [...] The new accommodation should not stick out too much. When you ride your bike past it, you have to get the idea that the building has been there for a long time.' According to Karacaer, its new name, the Wester Mosque, analogous to the nearby Wester Church or Westerkerk, instead of the Aya Sofia, had something to do with that. Anything not to give the impression that here lay some sort of a big, closed and somewhat threatening Turkish fortification, the District's main fear. 'The Essalaam Mosque, for example, made its plans in splendid isolation. Instead, we laid our cards on the table, thereby avoiding all sorts of discussion after the event.'[231] Karacaer was not very much taken to the architecture of other purpose-built Dutch mosques. That neighbours felt threatened by the presence of such buildings was understandable to him. 'Ali Baba's castles,' he called them. 'But that is a purely architectural consideration.'[232]

Apparently, there was a strong need on the part of the community leaders to represent their future mosque as a physically integrated design, one that was 'Dutch' in the specific context of its planned location, as contrasted with other mosques in The Netherlands. It was stressed that the design included certain material details as a typical feature of the 'Amsterdam School'. However, in Dazert's recollection, until that moment it had been obvious to any one involved that the complex as a whole was essentially a neo-classic design using many of the formal elements – like classical frontons – which the architect had used in other commissions and against which the original Amsterdam School had meant to be a reaction.[233] In fact, Breitman himself strongly denied that any Amsterdam School elements had been incorporated into his mosque design. In his view, the mere use of brick would not by itself make the building specifically Amsterdam School, since most of Amsterdam was built with bricks, including the projects he had earlier executed for Bijdendijk and which had not been associated with the Amsterdam School at all. Besides, to his knowledge many mosques in Turkey were also made of bricks. Keeping this in mind, any of the Amsterdam School's material and especially formal characteristics ascribed to the Wester Mosque were projections of the community leaders to make their design seem even more physically integrated, rather than a reference to the architect's own ideas on modern design and urban context. In effect, their interpretations also diverted public attention away from the specific religious content of the future mosque's classical Ottoman forms.

Moreover, the fact that Breitman had been hired seemed to have more to do with Bijdendijk's preference for his designs than with any perceived 'inexperience' on the part of Dutch mosque architects or with his Jewish background as a conscious choice on the part of MG to demonstrate social integration. The stress on his qualities and on other architects' lack of them should be seen as resulting from the community leaders' view that 'modernist' architects would not be suited to appropriately materialize the representation of their particular construction of Islam – not an unrealistic expectation. Similar to Kabaktepe, Karacaer found the public call for 'modernist' mosque alternatives a forced return to the 'shelter-church'. To him, a real mosque had a genuine stratification of domes, culminating in a large one on top. Next to that, when asked about existing Turkish mosques, he tended to find them proportionally incorrect and badly coloured in pastels. And, finally, when asked about religious differences, he found that the Islam of Diyanet was more about formal obligations like praying on Fridays, while his own movement was about a real, pure, religious way of life. Specifically, he stated that where other Dutch mosques included things like cafés and stores, in the Wester Mosque they had been banned from the building itself. 'A real mosque doesn't have these things.'[234] It seems that the community leaders had formed an idea of the archetypical Ottoman Külliye consisting of a prayer-hall surrounded by social and shopping spaces. Retail, however necessary for a mosque's viability, would have to be banned from the main prayer building. Whereas some classical Ottoman Külliyes actually did have shops underneath the main prayer hall, even some built by Sinan, the concept of separation between sacred and profane spaces as in some way to be derived from these structures had come to form one of the main aspects that would distinguish the Wester Mosque's patron's construction of Islam against the more secular version circulating among other Turkish groups in The Netherlands. Where Sevinçsoy had come to the conclusion that the mixing of social and religious functions in one building would be no problem in the Western context as it was simply a modern requirement, Karacaer and Kabaktepe took this mixing as contrary to classical Ottoman mosque architecture, which should be upheld in the host-country as much as in the motherland.[235]

Since costs were rising in light of delays caused by objections and legal procedures, a simplification of the plan was needed.[236] On top of that, in May 2004 a judge decided that the exemption procedure had not been legitimate, to begin with, so a new application would have to be started again. Breitman made adjustments to his mosque plan in September 2004, mainly consisting of reducing the gutter height of the mosque and of removing the library-annex from the ground plan. **(Figure 117)** Kabaktepe stressed the facts that, on the one hand the design would now stand a better chance of acceptance within a new application procedure, and, on the other, would cost less. On 29 October, a revised, preliminary mosque plan, lowering the gutter height and removing the library, was filed.[237] **(Figure 118)** The former zoning plan exemption application had entailed 2000 m2 for social facilities and 1000 m2 for business, but in the current plan the patrons had returned to the concept of a mere 1000 m2 for social facilities (just the mosque) and 2000 m2 for business. In the interest of construction, Kabaktepe had put his need for 2000 m2 for social facilities aside, hoping that a quick exemption procedure would be possible. Prices were rising to the point that the costs for construction would be too high to even start, which, according to Van Waveren, was probably the exact goal of opposition in the first place.[238]

After that, in the winter of 2004/2005, Kabaktepe had the Turkish architect of the Sabanci Mosque come from Istanbul to assist Breitman with designing a less expensive building whilst enhancing his preferred classical Ottoman building elements. The Turkish architect had apparently claimed that he could design a more appropriate mosque for less money: since architects in Turkey were contractors at the same time, he had had much experience with this kind of design and construction. As such he would be able to import the necessary materials directly from Turkey. Where Breitman had planned on using a supporting construction of steel and wood on top of a 9m high layer of concrete, the Turkish architect claimed that a 'genuine' Turkish mosque would have to be built with thick concrete walls all the way to, and including, the dome, with attention to acoustics and effects of mass. Moreover, according to him, there were strict proportional rules to be applied to the main volume, dome and minaret, which would essentially have to be redesigned from scratch. He brought drawings to support his case. **(Figure 119)** However, Breitman reacted that these Turkish construction methods and measurements could not possibly be upheld within construction regulations in The Netherlands, that acoustics could be solved in other ways than with concrete, and that the image of mass would also be reached by the first layer of massive concrete followed by stucco on higher levels. The necessary concrete slabs for the dome would be far too expensive for construction and transportation to The Netherlands, and would leave visible seams. Besides, the project had come too far in terms of energy and costs to change it now in such an extreme way: the whole plan and permit application would have to be revised. In the end, he managed to turn his patron's attention back to his own design.[239] Although Breitman was not unwilling to make a mosque type that would be recognizably Turkish and even Ottoman, this alternative, in his own words, was too much of a stereotype, and too removed from the Dutch urban context. In his account, this particular episode was just another sign that any 'Dutchness' of the Wester Mosque project had been a prerequisite on his and on Bijdendijk's side, where the community leader actually preferred a purely traditional, classical Ottoman model.

On 4 May 2005, the builder's estimates' construction drawings for the mosque were filed, to be scrutinized by Aesthetics.[240] One week later, the commission showed itself positive about the development of materials and details of the mosque.[241] The next month, Van Waveren presented a model of the mosque as 'the result of five years of consultation'.[242] **(Figure 120)** Importantly, the former objectors to the plans now had to admit that the latest permit application was advantageous to them since it had abandoned the idea of extra social facilities besides the mosque.[243] An informal agreement was apparently reached the next day, and a week later the District agreed to start an exemption procedure.[244] As a result of these negotiations, Breitman made a new ground plan on 27 October. **(Figure 121)** On 10 December, when the agreement was put to paper, the construction adjustments contained in this new drawing were explained. In exchange for the objectors retracting their opposition to the zoning plan exemption and the permit for the Wester Mosque, the minaret would be relocated to the main building and its corner, away from the nearest apartments. The gallery would also be placed closer to the main building. The height of the main building, excluding pinnacle, would be 25 meters. The number of square meters for the mosque would be 1000, excluding gallery and electricity building. The difference of opinion over the height of the minaret (the 42 meters of the first actual application in 2001 against the 35 meters of the 3-party agreement in 2000) would be put to the judgment of an Arbitration Committee. The agreement was signed by the District, Manderen BV, Het Oosten, and objectors.[245]

In February 2006, the Arbitration Committee judged that 'according to their research' Ottoman minarets were 'almost always' built at an angle of 45 degrees or more between the top of the minaret and the tangential of the dome. In their opinion, this formed an essential part of the architecture of mosques ('proportional concepts being an important part of the aesthetic evaluation of buildings'). The commission had looked at what would happen if an angle of fewer degrees would be used, and had subsequently come to the conclusion that in that case the composition of the whole would be seriously compromised.[246] Apparently, although the empirical field of Turkish mosque design is infinitely varied in Turkey as well as in the diaspora, they had taken a specific representation of reality for standard practice, having been pointed in that direction by Kabaktepe and Breitman. The latter had held a presentation for the committee, during which he showed them a selection of mosques from Istanbul with a dome-minaret angle of at least 45 degrees, although, in his recollection, he did mention that not all Ottoman mosques answered to that rule. At the same time, he argued that the composition of his own plan would be seriously compromised when a lower angle would be introduced. **(Figure 122)**

On 28 February 2006, Minister of Justice Piet Hein Donner (CDA) performed the plot inauguration ceremony, in the presence of a Turkish imam, a rabbi, a Catholic preacher and a Protestant minister, who each blessed the plot in his own way.[247] It is important to note that no official representative of the Turkish embassy or the Turkish Directorate of Religious Affairs seems to have been present. As compared with the Diyanet mosques treated above, the ceremony was not presented as a Turkish state affair but as a purely religious occasion. Donner stated that 'a palm tree grows by placing a stone on top, because by growing against its weight it will be strong enough to carry fruit. The project for the mosque that is going to be built here, has grown against a similar weight. There has been a battle over every square centimetre of the terrain, over every stone in the buildings, every tree and every property. In this process, the plan has been adjusted, expanded and restricted. But the result is that now construction can start of the most beautiful mosque in The Netherlands. A mosque, moreover, that is a symbol for the mixing of many cultures. A mosque for Turkish Dutchmen, in Amsterdam School clothing. […] I regard it to be an honour to be able to be here at the beginning of the construction of a mosque that has added so much to the integration by growing against the pressure. […] To ban faith and religion from the public sphere is [...] dangerous and senseless. Without faith, harmonious living is impossible, and without religion it won't thrive. [...] One thing is certain, the freedom of religion entails the right to build houses for god, whether they are called church, mosque or temple. [...] The times that we tolerated other religions only if their buildings were invisible, are behind us, not in front of us'.[248] The ceremony ended after a plaque, to be inserted as a future foundation stone, was signed by all parties.[249] Notably, the Amsterdam School fiction had now established itself as a fact in public discourse, up to the point that sometime later, as we recall, the members of MemarDutch even condemned the Wester Mosque's supposed 'Amsterdam School' as 'outdated.' On top of that, they referred to its design as 'Efteling' and 'Disney', using the MG patron's very own means in having set himself and his mosque off against community leaders with contesting constructions of Islam and Islamic architecture.[250]

On 7 March 2007 the permit was granted.[251] Shortly after, however, Kabaktepe was fired as the director of MG's investment company Manderen BV by German headquarters, to be replaced by Aya Sofia chairman Fatih Dag.[252] Since Het Oosten as well as the District found it difficult to believe that what they saw as a liberal Islamic course and social integration would still be the Wester Mosque's main concerns, especially in light of MG headquarters' supposedly radical-Islamic beliefs, Bijdendijk withdrew his cooperation.[253] On 16 October 2008 Dag held a symbolic first pole ceremony, but the wooden stick had to be removed straight away since he had not been given the necessary municipal permission.[254] At the time of writing, whether the costly project would still be executed by Aya Sofia was unclear.

4. Moroccan-Commissioned Mosque Design in The Netherlands

After Hindustani, Moluccan and Turkish Muslim patrons had established their first purpose-built mosques in 1955, 1956 and 1975, it is striking to see that Moroccan patrons built their designed prayer-halls only beginning in 1990. Moreover, the first two mosques that were opened by Moroccan patrons in Huizen and in Eindhoven that year did not include recognizably Moroccan building elements. The patrons of the An-Nasr Mosque in Huizen had explicitly requested their architect not to use the Moroccan forms that he had encountered during a work-visit to Morocco.[1] The Al Fourkaan in Eindhoven is a particularly interesting case for analysis since, because of its rather sober use of Islamic imagery, it should have obvious potential as a 'modern Dutch' example as a reference for the recent discussion on physical integration. Instead, this mosque has been conspicuously absent from architectural evaluation from the beginning. This could have something to do with the fact that the patron's Islamic stance has generally been classified by the AIVD, the Dutch security service, as radically Salafist and therefore non-integrated,[2] which would make the assumed connection between 'integrated Islamic design' and 'integrated Muslims' somewhat problematic. When studied in-depth, the building's lack of 'cultural' building elements can be recognized as a representation of a particular construction of Islam specifically intended to oppose contesting Islamic constructions produced by other Moroccan-Islamic community leaders.

In comparison, the El Islam Mosque built in The Hague in 1997 was, especially through its mix of Moroccan-associated window forms and Dutch-associated materials, visibly consistent with the surrounding block, identified as a successful blend between the North-African and the Dutch building styles. As such, it was seen as another step on the path towards an integrated Dutch Islam and an integrated Dutch-Islamic prayer hall. However, a study of its design process indicates that the Dutch content was actually more the result of municipal requirements translated by the architect, whereas the patrons themselves rejected too much Dutchness and stressed the North-African building style. Although it was presented as a determined, automatic choice in light of culture area, it too was a representation of a specific construction of Islam in opposition to contesting versions within the patrons' own culture group, with Eindhoven as a good example.

Finally, to the great surprise of the Rotterdam municipality, the design of the Essalaam Mosque currently being constructed there by a Moroccan patron does not incorporate any North-African style characteristics. It does, however, include very visible Islamic imagery, the answer to which has been sought in the background of the financier, the almost proverbial 'Sheikh from Dubai'. Since the designer himself explained the mosque in part as derived from a particular mosque in Dubai as well, the 'Arab' or 'Mamluk' building style seemed to be a satisfying and logical enough explanation. Subsequently, the Essalaam came to be seen as the culmination of emancipation or segregation, according to the 'integrative' preferences of the observer involved. However, from the design process a completely different motivation arises on the patron's side, with nothing to do with Dubai. His mosque was to be the representation of an Islam that was to be diametrically opposed to the versions as upheld in both The Hague and Eindhoven.

Varieties of Islam among Moroccan Communities

Morocco, like Turkey, has constituted an important source of cheap labour for expanding Dutch industry. Notably, about two-thirds of the Moroccan migrants in The Netherlands have come from the Rif Mountains. This region in northern Morocco was largely inhabited by Berber-speaking communities which had cultivated their autonomy from central authorities for centuries. Since 1912, in contrast to the rest of Morocco, the Rif had been a Spanish protectorate, which added little to the region's development. Seasonal migration was the main solution to the problem of high population density with scarce means of survival. After Moroccan independence in 1956 under Sultan Mohammed V (King from 1957), discontent developed among the Riffians over their place within the new state. A rebellion in 1958 was crushed by the king's son, crown prince Mulay Hassan (King Hassan II from 1961), but the hostile attitude towards the regime remained.[3] The young state subsequently instituted and upheld a precise mixture of religion, nationalism and royalism: Maliki Islam, the local school of religious interpretation, and the Makhzen, the feudal system revolving around the Moroccan king, were blended into the new constitution with the aim of holding all ethnic and religious communities together. Hassan II knew how to enhance the position of the throne in political and religious matters by strategic alliances with, and rejections of, certain groups, to which purpose he fully made use of the historical notions of the Moroccan king as Sharif, or physical successor to Mohammed, and as Amir al-Muminin, or commander of all believers, a title used by the first Caliphs after the death of the Prophet. The yearly Bay'a, or pledge of loyalty, to the king was meant to revoke the pledge of Mohammed's disciples. In this ritual, the most important religious, political and military leaders were expected to renew their loyalty to the throne. By this and by other ceremonies Islam was linked to the position of the king and the sacrality of his person was constantly confirmed.[4]

However, to some Moroccan-Islamic community leaders, including many in the Rif Mountains, the all-pervading role of the king and his state formed an unwanted intrusion of politico-religious autonomy, and subsequently a number of Islamic movements gained in importance in the organization of opposition to the royal nationalization attempt.[5] The Ministry of Pious Foundations and Islamic Affairs was purposefully established to supervise mosques, preachers and imams so as to prevent dissident groups such as these organizing themselves under the flags of Islamic movements separate from the official version.[6] When European countries needed cheap labour, the Moroccan government steered recruitment towards the Rif with the aim of releasing both the economic misery and the politico-religious pressure in the region. From 1965, each year about 3000 Moroccan men, mainly from the Riffian country-side, migrated to The Netherlands. Not surprisingly, the affiliation of most Moroccans in The Netherlands with Morocco itself mainly followed the lines of kinship and village, and less that of national pride or a sense of affiliation with the Moroccan state. On the contrary, Morocco as a state was often associated with corruption and a lack of social justice. Positive connotations were largely in the field of visits to friends and family. As a consequence, any attempts in The Netherlands at organizing Moroccans in their own religious and political associations were severely hindered by multiple internal oppositions along the lines of imported conflicts at the level of family, village, region or national politics.[7]

The growth of politico-religious opposition in Morocco and abroad soon inspired Moroccan authorities to strengthen their bonds with migrants in the diaspora. In 1973, the Federation of Amicales of Moroccan Labourers and Traders was founded in Rabat, with one of King Hassan's sons as honorary chairman.[8] In 1975, the Federation of Moroccan Amicales Netherlands was founded, together with a number of local departments in the municipalities with the largest concentrations of Moroccans.[9] The foundation of mosque organizations, next to dispatching preachers, became the most important way of exerting influence over the Moroccan subjects in The Netherlands, and at the end of the 1970s, most mosques fell under Amicales control. Subsequently, however, the organization came to be seen as 'the spying eyes of King Hassan II', and most mosque community leaders gradually dissociated themselves from it. Within Morocco itself, however, the Ministry did manage to tighten its grip on the foundation of mosques, which henceforward needed the prior written permission of the governors of provinces and towns, who were obliged to consult the Ministry first. In addition, Imams were appointed by the Ministry in conjunction with the governor and the regional council of religious scholars. Private initiative was restricted to the application for authorization to build the mosque and to providing the money for construction and for the foundation that would sustain the mosque and personnel. Both appointment of personnel and administration of the mosque and its day-to-day functioning were relegated to the authorities, and after prayer hours, the mosque was kept shut.[10]

In 2006, Hassan II's son-successor Mohamed VI even established a special television network that was specifically meant to disseminate the official, 'tolerant version of Islam, as practiced according to the Moroccan traditions, against the encroaching radical Islam'. The broadcasts were to be viewed in the Moroccan mosques under the supervision of the Ministry of Islamic Affairs. Besides the important Friday prayers having already been subjected to prior authorization of the Ministry, a 10-minute sermon was now to be broadcast preceding the daily evening prayers in which members of the highest Council of Moroccan religious specialists would explain a verse from the Koran. Additionally, longer programs were meant to educate imams. According to the Minister, 'The aim is to spread the good word among the believers and to protect the mosques against weak and deviant sermons.' Especially in the hard-to-reach mosques 'in the countryside', both visitors and imams would often be 'illiterate' and Koranic texts would often be interpreted in a very 'univocal' way, playing into the hands of 'radical' preachers.[11]

In The Netherlands, an alternative was found in the Union of Moroccan Muslim Organizations Netherlands (UMMON), founded in 1977 by the chairmen of the most important Moroccan organizations in The Netherlands to solve some confusion over the correct timing of Ramadan. In 1982, the sleeping institution was given legal status, and the UMMON soon came to be regarded as the main representative of Moroccans in The Netherlands by the government, with some 80% of the Moroccan mosque organizations under association. While the UMMON did not formally represent a Moroccan religious or political institution, the intensive contacts between UMMON and diplomatic representatives of Morocco showed that there was a tight connection with, and a loyal attitude to, the Moroccan state and the king in particular. However, it was not simply a matter of all associated mosques having as much inclination towards the official Moroccan Islam as their association's board itself, as especially the stance on the king's role seems to vary among the different UMMON members.[12] When the organization was accused by Mohammed Rabbae, political refugee from Morocco and politician for the Dutch 'Green Left' party, of being directly associated with the Moroccan authorities in 1993,[13] several mosque boards pulled away again.[14] Still, as the Dutch government was recently told by the Moroccan authorities 'in name of the Moroccan king', giving up the Moroccan nationality would remain impossible for all Moroccan-Dutch citizens 'due to the lifelong loyalty of all Moroccans to His Majesty the King, Commander of the Faithful'.[15] At the same time, the king himself decided to send 167 'moderate' imams to Europe and Canada – seven of whom would go The Netherlands – for the month of Ramadan, in order to 'protect' Moroccan Muslims against 'Islamic radicalization', stimulating them 'to abide by their Moroccan roots and traditions'.[16] Even more recently, forty Moroccan-Dutch imams were called back to a conference in Rabat on Islam in Europe. The latter, according to a Moroccan-Dutch commentator, could be related to increased efforts he had noticed while visiting mosques in Morocco, to standardize the nationally propagated Maliki version of Islam against any Salafi tendencies and imams.[17]

On the other side of the spectrum, on arrival in The Netherlands some anti-nationalist Moroccan-Islamic community leaders managed to establish their own mosques, opposing the official construction of Islam in Morocco by embracing what they saw as more general Islamic beliefs. Although these Moroccan-Dutch mosque community leaders have varying backgrounds, they basically share an 'Islamist' dislike of the royalist inclination of Moroccan Islam.[18] In fact, this rejection of the role of the Moroccan state and its concurrent national-Islamic values are what attracts them to more general, non-Moroccan Islam and Islamic organizations in the first place. Much more frequently than other Muslim groups in The Netherlands, Moroccan-Islamic community leaders seem to be looking to associate themselves with international Islamic organizations that do not spring from their home country.

Moreover, the majority of young Dutch Muslims rejecting any cultural influences in Islam and embracing some form of religious purity, whether they call themselves Salafi or not, seems to consist of Moroccans.[19]

The Al Fourkaan Mosque, Eindhoven

Where many other Moroccan labourers had come to the Netherlands in the early 1970s mainly for its economic advantages, Ahmed Cheppih considered himself a refugee from persecution for his Islamic activism in the Moroccan Rif. After taking early retirement in Eindhoven in 1986, Cheppih chose to make Islamic affairs his next profession. In order to establish The Netherlands's first Islamic primary school and a center for the spread of Islam, he and fellow community leader Mohammed (el) Bakkiouli connected with a supporting organization, Al Waqf Al Islami.[20] The Waqf was a Saudi-based international charity fund sponsoring educational facilities mainly in countries with a Muslim population or Muslim minorities and basically aimed at spreading a purified version of Islam through the principle of 'Dawah'. The latter, in a very general way, meant 'invitation [to Islam]' but was, in the context of Saudi charity funds, largely used in its sense of mission along the lines of Salafism, the brand of Islam thought to have been practised by the Prophet and his Companions. This Sunna-based, authentic purity apparently connected well with Cheppih's own religious stance.

On 18 May 1987, Bakkiouli and Cheppih established the first Islamic primary school in The Netherlands, the Tariq Ibn Ziyad in Eindhoven, named after a well-known Berber military leader who invaded Spain in the beginning of the 8th century. Fellow board member of the school and the community's main imam was the Sudanese Imadeldin Ismail Bakri. Whereas Bakkiouli was to be chairman from the very start, Cheppih was to function as a secretary only from the next year, as Cheppih's main project was the creation of a new building for their mosque organization, Al Fourkaan. The latter is one of the names of the Koran, taken to mean as much as 'criterion for/ distinguisher between right or wrong', 'the way out of difficulty' or 'salvation'. In that same month of May 1987, Cheppih asked a construction engineer, active in development cooperation and charity within church circles, if he could help them out with programmatic requirements. In the latter's account, the community meant to renew and expand their present location in an old tire-factory in a commercial/industrial area.[21] After he had advised against a plan for four floors, he came up with a plan for two separate buildings of two floors each. The programmatic requirements he made showed that the community leader intended to create a complete 'cultural center with prayer hall' which would include classrooms, a gym, two stores, offices and desks, a conference room, a library, a book shop, a large dining room for 250 people, 8 in-house bedrooms and a parking lot with 50 parking spaces.[22] As for formal requirements, Cheppih took the engineer to see the Great Mosque of Brussels, run by a Saudi organization he had contacts with. This structure was actually a standard rotunda made for a Cairo panorama at the 1897 world exhibition in the Jubelpark, then provided with an Orientalist entrance portal and minaret to make it look more like a 'Mamluk' building. Later, the building having lost the portal and left only with the 'Mamluk' minaret, the Belgian government had sold the dilapidated rotunda to the Saudi-based Muslim World League in 1978. Since then, as shown on the engineer's photographs, the building had been provided with a straight, non-Mamluk minaret and a simple, arched fence as the main markers of its function as a mosque. **(Figure 123)** It is notable that this early visit to Brussels already showed Cheppih's disinterest in Moroccan mosque design or, for that matter, in any extant mosque design in The Netherlands itself.

In the meantime, it appeared that a plot near the Islamic primary school in Eindhoven, an empty terrain at the corner Otterstraat/Wezelstraat where temporary classrooms of the adjacent technical school had been demolished, could be made available by the municipality. This plot would not be large enough for Cheppih's original plans, but its advantage was that the zoning plan already mentioned the possibility of special buildings and no exemption procedure would be necessary for a mosque. In order to start negotiations, the Foundation Islamic Cultural Center Al Fourkaan (Stichting Islamitisch Cultureel Centrum Al Fourkaan) was established on 8 June 1988, with Cheppih as one of the chairmen and Bakkiouli as secretary.[23] To create an actual design, their engineer advised them to hire his contacts, Boon & Slagter Architects. David Boon then established the new programmatic requirements for the new location in January 1989, together with Cheppih. Space requirements were considerably downsized in light of the available plot, and rooms were fewer and smaller, while gym, dining hall and conference hall were erased altogether. Importantly, it stated: 'The prayer room must be oriented towards the east (Mecca) with a niche for the imam (Mihrab) at that side. The prayer room for women should be connected to the men's but a separation should be installed between the two and the space should be separately accessible from the staircase. From the women's prayer space a direct view of the Mihrab should be made possible. There should be separate entrances for men and women with separate locker rooms, toilets and washing facilities.' As for looks, it had to be a 'simple, purposeful ('*doelmatig*') building, without exuberant ('*overdadig*') forms or decoration', although 'the recognizability of the mosque should be taken care of'.[24]

In the architect's recollection, Cheppih conveyed the message that the building had to be recognizable as a mosque mainly on the inside, and that while the essential elements of mihrab, dome and minaret had to be there, these should not be stressed.[25] As the request for formal soberness and essentialism was made even before a first sketch, austerity apparently represented an important value to the patron. From a representational viewpoint, Cheppih had translated his preference for authentic Sunna purity to architectural simplicity, meaning to represent in the design of his future mosque that no specific architectural culture represented his ideal Islam. In fact, in the patron's perspective, it was the culturalization of the authentic Islam of Mohammed and his Companions that had disturbed the purity of the message. In his eyes, in a true mosque there was no place for any building elements forming a possible distraction from true Islam.[26] Notably, as his anti-cultural alternative was arguably created by the community leader's negative stance towards the Moroccan nationalist version of Islam, he specifically had Moroccan architecture in mind when thinking about too 'cultural' and too 'distracting' building elements.

As it happened, the Moroccan state controlled mosque design as much as it controlled Islamic practice and administration. Morocco was never ruled by Ottoman emperors or Mamluk sultans and this independence has been played out by Moroccan royalty in their aims at unification and nation-building. In royal mosques and mausoleums, Ottoman and Mamluk building elements were largely rejected in favour of those defined as typically Moroccan, like brickwork, hipped roofs and the single, square-planned minaret. This representation of Moroccanness has been promulgated as the official style of architecture for all new mosques in Morocco as well as outside the country. The matter of design was important to King Hassan II and, as an advocate of 'authentic Moroccan architecture' he let it be known at a colloquium on construction in December 1979 that the historical precedents of the Almohad building style were the 'correct' ones. At the same time, the king championed the continuation and revival of indigenous handicrafts and building craftsmanship, and initiated the publication of an authoritative two-volume study on the matter by André Paccard. The modern use of 'Moroccan' building elements, commonly referred to as the Hassanian style, became the norm in almost every major architectural project, governmental and institutional.[27]

Of course, the most conspicuously Hassanian representation was built under commission of the king in Casablanca between 1986 and 1993. This mosque, simply called the Hassan II, made use of all the building elements that had been defined as Moroccan and was forcefully presented as a nationally supported project. The anti-nationalist Moroccan-Islamic community leaders in The Netherlands who were interviewed during this research, however, specifically recall family members being coerced to contribute to it financially, and to them the project has come to be the culmination of a narrow-minded, culturally perverted Islam. Interestingly, where mosques are generally imagined to diverge from church architecture in an anti-hierarchical, broad-structured ground plan, the Hassan II was built with the longitudinal focus of the basilica to facilitate processions confirming the power of the king and the unity of the country.[28] **(Figure 124)** Its inauguration ceremony was explicitly held on the eve of the Prophet's birthday and exactly 400 years after the great Al-Mansur inaugurated his Baadi Palace in Marrakech.[29] Furthermore, it was explicitly intended to be the largest mosque on earth except for the ones in Mecca and Medina, and it even included a powerful laser beam aimed at the first from its minaret. The particular combination of these selected and transformed building elements represented, through their expected connotations, the role of the king as the only rightful successor to the prophet and as the commander of all believers. It certainly seems to have held that meaning to those community leaders with a diverging view of what constituted true Islam and Islamic leadership. Although the Hassan II and its counterparts in royal cities and country-side villages have successfully settled in the Dutch observer's mind as a harmonious, 'cultural' building style, in 2003 a staggering 37% of the 30.000 prayer halls in the country were 'store front' mosques. Not being able to control the sort of Islam – and the sort of architecture – used when out in the open, they were set up in existing buildings in popular neighbourhoods and urban shanty towns by a variety of self styled cultural and educational associations as part of a loose umbrella network of nationwide Islamic associations.[30] Once outside the Moroccan state's architectural reach, community leaders affiliated with these organizations were no longer obliged – or likely – to abide by the royal rules of building.

However, Cheppih did not express any of these religious contestations and architectural connotations to his architect in so many words, keeping his representational – and concurrently formal – requirements seemingly general. According to the architect, the patron still wanted his 'simple' and 'purposeful' prayer hall to be 'a real mosque'. For that, austerity had to find a materialization that would entail adequate Islamic recognizability while still being a negation of overt splendour. In short, the community leader had to search for the purified essentials of Islamic architecture, incorporated in a design that, in other things, was no different from any other contemporary Dutch cultural center. Consequently, confronted with the vaguely formulated commission of designing a recognizable mosque without using too many recognizable Islamic building elements, the architect was faced with the task of finding out for himself what would define such a mosque design. For that, he resorted to his own preferences, which lay mainly in the Bossche School. The latter was a design system created by architect and priest Dom Hans van der Laan, largely based on austere geometry and proportions with the purpose of rebuilding and replacing Catholic churches in Brabant and Limburg damaged during the war. Next to his attraction to this school, Boon had had experience in the renovation of some of the 19th and 20th century neo-Gothic churches in the area. All in all, the architect's orientation towards the church and towards church architecture was of importance in his proposals for the Fourkaan Mosque, starting with the first sketch. He established the outline of the building on the back of the program by creating a perfect square ground plan within the plot as delimited by the municipality, using a largely west-east orientation from the entrance to the mihrab, an idea that, besides following extant street lines, he had taken from the neo-Gothic Catholic church across the street. **(Figure 125)** Importantly, although this meant a deviation from the exact direction towards Mecca, according to the architect Cheppih had had no problems with this at that time.

Subsequently, Boon filled in Cheppih's main practical requirements in his latest ground plan outline. **(Figure 126)** In translating functions to forms, Boon resorted to centrality, which he considered a major characteristic of church architecture, since churches in his experience had their domes placed mainly at the center of the crossing. In addition, the architect had descriptions of existing mosques in The Netherlands in his archive: Haffmans' Taibah, Perotti's Bait Ar-Rahman and Sevincsoy's Fatih, all carrying the octagonal dome drum as well as the main hemispherical dome and the semi-circular mihrab protruding from the kiblah. In Boon's sketch, the prayer hall seemed to rise as an independent building from a two-layered annex attached to its front. The first layer of both annex and main volume would harbour the different functions, while the second level had a women's prayer space in the annex and a men's prayer space in the main volume. To emphasize centrality, Boon had created an octagonal plan in annex and main volume, with two cut corners as separate entrances. Through this levelling,

Boon also made sure that the future dome would not be an ostentatious feature on the outside as it would hardly be visible from the street level, since both his patron's as well as his own ideas on religious architecture contained the idea of simplicity. After some minor practical adjustments, this plan was largely accepted by Cheppih and worked out in some more detail by the architect. A pole, consistently called a 'mast' by the architect since it was never supposed to be a real, ascendable minaret or even to have a supporting function, was placed underneath the main or men's entrance as the most visible side from the public street. He agreed with his patron that it would eventually have to be higher than the surrounding buildings in order to be effective as a marker. Subsequently, this plan was sketched in a municipal situation plan, in which we see the Eastern orientation as well as the plan's adjustment to extant street lines. **(Figure 127)** It seems that, as far as Cheppih was concerned, following 'modern Dutch' ideas of architecture was perfectly acceptable as long as his Islamic purity would be represented. According to Boon, other board members wanted more stress on Islamic recognizability than Cheppih, but the architect as well as Cheppih had the argument of the budget to keep things simple and, in their eyes, essential.

In response to a first cost estimation,[31] Cheppih asked the architect to reduce the height of the first level by 20 cm. and of the second by 80 cm. The architect advised against this, since it would result in saving only a very small amount of money while his carefully established proportions and – what he saw as the minimum height of – a public, religious space would be disturbed. Moreover, the dome budget was lowered to half the original amount.[32] Apparently, the community leader did not consider the height or a possible grandeur of the prayer space important enough to justify higher costs. Whereas Boon's preference for simplicity suited this particular patron perfectly, the underlying Bossche School design philosophy on proportions was not considered relevant. Furthermore, the dome was important in its presence but apparently not so much in the quality of its appearance. Still, for the community leader there was apparently enough compatibility between him and the architect to continue the commission. It even became clear that the patron planned on letting the architect coordinate the whole project, including exterior and interior decoration,[33] something that many other mosques preferred to do under their own supervision in saving costs and, even more important, in the application of specific 'cultural' building elements of decoration and craftsmanship. Here, Cheppih had no such value, and his dislike of too distractive or 'cultural' building elements would result in a planned absence of conspicuous decorations altogether.

In the meantime, the architect started thinking about elevations. For that, he decided to study some literature on the architectural background of his patrons. As they were from Morocco, Boon mainly looked at books containing chapters which focused on Moroccan architecture.[34] He found out that what strongly characterized Moroccan architecture in the face of other culture areas was the pyramid shaped roof, and he subsequently made copies of those objects that incorporated this feature. **(Figure 128)** He decided that, in light of the lower budget, a transparent roof light would be most feasible. On 10 May 1989, in the first detailed plan to be presented to Cheppih, Boon combined the Moroccan pyramid roof with a substructure that had incorporated his own ideas and preferences on proportions, measurements and geometry as he had looked for them in the Bossche School church architecture. **(Figure 129)** In his account, it was the church as built by Dom Van der Laan in extension to the St. Benedict Abbey in Oirschot that had inspired him as to window forms, floor proportions and interior doorways.[35] The minaret was, for now, drawn as a simple mast without any decoration.

Once confronted with this proposal, Cheppih required major adjustments in the line of the recognizability of his mosque as a representation of a culturally purified Islam. Although the overall façade and ground plan design were deemed appropriate, his interest lay in the elements used in roof, interior doorways and minaret. He wanted interior doorways designed with arches instead of rectangular openings, he wanted the mast to have the appearance – although symbolic – of a minaret, and he wanted a dome instead of a pyramidal roof. All this, of course, as later repeatedly stressed by the architect, for the lowest price possible, but as these adjustments did not actually save money but cost more in total, this was another sign that budgetary constraints themselves only led to sharper priorities and never actually determined the design per se. When looked at from a representational viewpoint, Cheppih classified particular building elements as carriers of the general Islamic recognizability he required, separate from any specific culture, a representational necessity in the face of an impure Islam astray from the true path. Subsequently, the architect made a further study of Moroccan architecture in a search for the required forms. He found many examples of horseshoe arches and slender minarets with pointed finials and circular balconies in his North-African literature. **(Figure 130)** The minaret forms were the result of Ottoman presence in the regions east of Morocco: the architect was still searching for inspiration in the general culture area of his patron, although he did not distinguish between the Maghrebian countries and although the patron had not asked for Moroccan building elements. On

7 June, the architect translated Cheppih's comments into sketches roughly based on his literature examples. Here we see horseshoe arches, a mast with a ring as an abstracted balcony and with a crescent moon, and an adjusted circular base for a future circular dome-drum. **(Figure 131)**

However, a pole with a mere ring instead of a balcony, even if abstracted and only symbolically Islamic, was not as recognizable as the patron wanted, so the architect had to look further in his literature for minaret forms and decoration patterns easily suited to a simple cylindrical mast. Boon found that geometry, as an important component of Bossche School church architecture, was also applicable to Islamic decoration design, next to being a major interest of his in his painting, and Cheppih agreed. Both architect and patron preferred abstraction and geometry as an expression of religion over too 'cultural' building elements, although, of course, from a completely different representational motivation. The architect then found what to him seemed to be a North African minaret feature suited for abstraction into a mast decoration, present in Ottoman-built structures with arcade-consoled balconies and pencil finials. Boon expressly never meant to look into the varieties of Islamic architecture too deeply: he wanted to study the subject in the context of what he took as his patron's culture area only in order to understand him a little better while he basically looked for suitable Islamic markers appropriate to represent Islam as a general religion, in line with his and his patron's views. Next to the particular minaret forms, he found a geometrical pattern of zigzag lines to be appropriate. **(Figure 132)** Subsequently, he made a sketch of a minaret in his notes, coming down to a pencil-shaped mast with an abstracted, arcade-supported balcony. **(Figure 133)** Strikingly, next to it he had sketched what he regarded as a basic neo-Gothic church tower with corner turrets, a double-arched window and a crescent moon instead of a rooster or cross. According to him, it was an example to be abstracted into the upper part of the mast as well. As it turned out, Boon was inspired by church architecture in more than just a few ways. Furthermore, the ring was apparently there to stay, separately from the sketched balcony, since the architect made an attempt at drawing a decoration of the zigzag pattern on it based on his literature reference.

On 7 July, Cheppih filed an application for an 'Islamic Cultural Center' in the name of 'the owner Stichting "El Ouaqf"'. In the accompanying designs, we see that the architect planned on using a multi-segmented main dome, which, in his recollection, he had done in keeping some kind of proportion and measurement, since a non-segmented dome would have been too Modernistic in his view, and not conform to the design school he adhered to. In line with budget and simplicity, both main dome and mihrab cupola were to be transparent. The minaret had the abstracted arcade-supported balcony, next to a pair of rings like a double-balconied Ottoman example in the North African literature he had used and which, according to the architect, had been introduced mainly for reasons of proportion and visibility. Entrance doors and minaret balcony and -rings had been supplied with the zigzag lined decoration pattern, and the rectangular doorways between the prayer spaces had been changed into an arcade with horseshoe arches. **(Figure 134)** A month later, Aesthetics approved,[36] and the next week the municipality let Cheppih know that they found his plan acceptable.[37] On 25 September, The Netherlands' branch of Al Waqf was officially founded, with Abdullah Osman Abdulrahman Al Hussaini from Jeddah, one of Al Waqf's leading men, as chairman, Bakkiouli as secretary and Bakri Ismail as fellow board member.[38]

On 9 October, the construction permit was given by the municipality to the Fourkaan foundation,[39] although the construction commission was given by the community to a contractor in the name of Al Waqf.[40] It seemed that to the community leader the difference between the Fourkaan, the Dutch Al Waqf and the Saudi Al Waqf was only nominal and a Dutch-bureaucratic necessity, whilst the international organization was meant to be the main patron. That Cheppih specifically wanted to be part of something bigger than his own culture would also continue to be expressed in design. He decided that the planned yellow bricks in the outer walls would have to be changed into white as far as the annex was concerned. Boon had earlier introduced the coloured bricks as he thought them to be more appropriate, size-wise, for a public building than the cheaper-looking white version, but also as a reference to what he had found to be typically North-African building materials. However, Cheppih did not put any value whatsoever on the associated Morocanness of the bricks, although in the end the architect managed to convince him in using them partly on the interior and on the exterior of the main volume because of their perceived public quality and warmth.[41] Apparently, like what Perotti had accomplished in Waalwijk, Boon had shifted the cultural content of a building element towards generality, although here it was aesthetics while in Waalwijk it had been symbolism that was used as a supporting argument.

It is notable that the facts that the mosque would have an 'integrated' and 'modern-Dutch' design with only marginal outer Islamic recognizability and that it had been received with enthusiasm by Aesthetics as well as municipal architectural departments proved to be of no relevance to the neighbourhood inhabitants whatsoever during any part of the permit application or construction. Besides the usual complaints of expected traffic problems and noise, the construction site was repeatedly damaged and set on fire.[42] One neighbourhood organization referred to the fact that the Islamic primary school had also been established without consulting the inhabitants 'whilst in the middle of the incidents around Rushdie and the Iran-Iraq war'. Furthermore, 'One sees the rise of Islam among Turkish and Moroccan minorities as an expression of resignation ('*resignatie*'): whereas the political, cultural and social integration of minorities has failed for the most part, a withdrawal can be observed in a national-religious isolation. As a result, inhabitants are left feeling that they should open themselves for a population that right now is turning away from *their* culture.'[43] Although they clearly mistook the community's purist Islamic stance for a traditionalist Moroccan version, the local CDA seemed to support the inhabitants in their concerns, asking mayor and aldermen to reconsider the permit.[44] Apparently, the relatively non-conspicuous design, which in effect largely confirmed the physical integration which the Dutch public had called for at several occasions during other mosques' conceptions and which many current architects and municipal officials are still calling for, did not mean that the community involved would be regarded as socially integrated or even that the public would accept the presence of a Muslim prayer hall per se. The assumed and ideal connection between physical and social integration as a fact and/or a panacea to all problems proved an illusion and a representation in itself.

To be sure, Cheppih would not have specifically meant his mosque design to be 'integrative towards Dutch society' but as a representation of a purist construction of Islam towards those Moroccan-Islamic community leaders embracing a contesting version. As a consequence, the negative stance of surrounding Dutch communities towards his future prayer hall was not translated into a different representational requirement. Continuing his path towards architectural austerity and essentialism, the patron requested his architect to design the interior doorways as simple arches without the horseshoe shapes introduced in answer to Cheppih's earlier comments on the rectangular 'Bossche School' doorways. On 13 November, Boon made a new sketch, showing a standard arch with a raised keystone instead of the horseshoe shape of its predecessor. **(Figure 135)** Apparently, here too it was a purified, non-cultural Islamic recognizability that was valued, and not some formal 'Moroccanness'. After that, Cheppih decided that the cupola over the mihrab should be erased.[45] In the search for 'budgetary space', this invention of the architect, largely based on his extant Dutch mosque references, was deemed superfluous: actually, Cheppih had only asked, in reaction to the first drawings and as an essentialization of Islamic architecture, for a main dome, a minaret post and arched interior doorways. On the other hand, not much later Cheppih requested the architect to extend his geometrical patterns to the entrance doors.[46] Subsequently, Cheppih decided that the arcade between the men's and women's prayer space should have low walls since, as had already been stated in the programmatic requirements, spaces had to be connected as for visibility of the Mihrab but there had to be some kind of separation. Moreover, coated glass would have to be applied between all spaces on the second level.[47] As all these adjustments had everything to do with a purist construction of Islam while not leading to any cost reduction at all, it must be concluded, once again, that budgetary constraints were for the most part only put forward for those building elements that had not been defined as relevant in the required representation. Apparently, form follows representation more than mere function, aesthetics or budget.

The architect next looked for suitable decorations for the entrance doors and minaret rings, which he found in a book on Islamic architectural decoration.[48] He made copies of the Turkish Eşrefoglu Mosque's window shutter and the tiling of the Bayazid Bastami, the mausoleum of a Persian Sufi. **(Figure 136)** He then used the first in a sketch – which is now lost – for the Fourkaan's future entrance doors, and the latter in a sketch for its minaret rings, dated January 1990. **(Figure 137)** As said, Boon was expressly little interested in the varieties of Islamic architecture and contexts, looking for suitable forms only insofar they could be appropriately adjusted into general, abstracted Islamic motifs and, of course, insofar they lived up to his own design preferences. Then, the architect found an alternative to his proposed pattern for the minaret rings in a book specifically devoted to Islamic geometrics which claimed that 'the vastness of the desert developed in these people a cosmic sense of scale and distance in relation to topography and the heavens, combined with a minute order and geometry in their observation of natural forms'.[49] It treated geometrics in Islamic art and architecture as a typifying feature, which perfectly suited the architect's search for a generally Islamic pattern. Both designer and his chosen literature regarded geometry in religious buildings as representing an essence that transcended diverging contexts and opposing meanings. Boon took a triangular shape, from the Chihil Dukhteran minaret in Isfahan,[50] which he found to be more appropriate then the latest version. **(Figure 138)** On 3 April, the new minaret decorations were worked out into a detailed drawing. At Cheppih's request, the mast now had a hilal with three balls as a finial. An axonometry was made and the building seemed ready to go. **(Figure 139)**

Then, however, an imam from Al Waqf came to visit the construction site and concluded that the orientation was not directed exactly towards Mecca. Whereas Cheppih had apparently formerly agreed to the eastward orientation, he was now expected to request an adjustment of the plan, but since the permit had been given on the basis of the former orientation and the foundations were already placed, he had to settle for an interior adjustment. Subsequently, the architect sketched in the correct orientation in an old ground plan. Here, he creatively tried to solve the situation by adjusting the mihrab with an added protrusion and an extra opening in such a way that the niche would give the illusion of the correct direction. **(Figure 140)** However, the patron preferred to shift the kiblah to the southeast corner, which coincidentally provided a more accurate orientation. It was subsequently decided that folding doors would be installed in the old mihrab, and that a wooden mihrab would be placed in the southeast corner of the prayer space, for which the architect would make a sketch.[51] The presence of two mihrabs in two different directions would have disturbed the representation of Islamic purity, so the niche originally planned, though built according to the permit, had to be removed from view on the inside. Importantly, the exact orientation of the kiblah, although often represented as an essential and universal rule by its adherents, is much less consistent in Islamic architecture than is thought.[52] As a consequence, the choice for or against this building element can form a conscious representation itself, deriving its meaning from context and not from some supposedly fixed principle. On 25 April, the Fourkaan's new inner orientation was shown in a plan for an angled floor pattern, a feature normally only visible in existing buildings-turned-mosque and not in newly built prayer halls. The architect also sketched in an additional, semi-circular mihrab in the southeast corner of an old ground plan, followed by a more detailed drawing of the structure. Notably, in order to avoid the disturbance of visibility by a planned column in front of that corner, the mihrab would have to be built just off-center. **(Figure 141)** On 28 May, construction was completed,[53] and on 2 June, the mosque was officially opened. **(Figure 142)**

The El Islam Mosque, The Hague

As part of a reconstruction scheme for Schilderswijk, a neighbourhood with a large number of Muslims, the municipality of The Hague designated an empty plot at the corner Segherstraat/Van der Vennestraat, also called 'Vennemax Kop 5' or 'Blok 5', to be provided with a block of affordable rental apartments above a ground floor of shops. Architect Bert Dirrix, of Dirrix van Wylick Architects in Geldrop and professor at the architectural faculty of Eindhoven, was approached by representatives of municipality and housing corporation "s Gravenhage' to design the project. However, as the mosque community El Islam, located in a building at nearby Vaillantlaan, expressed its wish for a purpose-built mosque in the immediate vicinity, an idea was developed within the municipality in which the plot would be divided between social housing and a new Muslim prayer hall that would be consistent with each other as well as with the surrounding architecture.

As Ali Belhaj, chairman of El Islam, was publicly thought of as a socially integrated community leader with a healthy dislike of Islamic fundamentalism, this was not expected to be a problem. He was also the secretary of UMMON, and the El Islam Mosque was one of the central actors within the UMMON organization. Where, as said earlier, UMMON-associated mosque community leaders can differ greatly in their adherence to the official Moroccan Islam, Belhaj was one of the sterner ones. He immediately warned the media and the police when a group of Moroccan youngsters in his mosque started to show signs of preference for 'radical' literature.[54] In a rejection of Salafism, he stated: 'As Moroccans we did not use to have a second or third school. There was only the Maliki school: that was Morocco. But because of immigration of Moroccans to other countries, because of contacts with people from the Middle East and the regions there, there are now Moroccans who have switched from Maliki to a different school. Or no school at all. They say: "No, I go straight to the Koran, straight to the Hadith." Yes, you can do that, but not everyone can. It is possible, but the question then becomes: how can you exactly read the Koran?'[55] Also the imam that Belhaj had hired rooted his sermons in the traditional Maliki school of Islamic interpretation, at the same time transmitting a clear rooting in Moroccan tradition. He had been particularly displeased when a visitor had openly tried to correct his Maliki way of praying, with the exact positioning of the hands during prayer being one of several issues of Moroccan-Salafi self-distinction against any form of Maliki embedment.[56]

For their building, chairman Belhaj and secretary Arabi initially wrote down a short program of requirements. In this, they said that they did not want any apartments above the mosque. Furthermore, they preferred to be on the corner at Van der Vennestraat/Seghersstraat, and wanted two separate entrances with large doors, one for men and one for women. On the first level they requested a shoe closet, washing space and prayer room for 350 men; on the second, a shoe closet and a prayer room for another 350 men; on the third, a shoe closet, washing space and prayer room for 150 women and a library; on the fourth, class rooms, a toilet, a kitchen, an office and a meeting room. They required attention to insulation and parking facilities, and wanted to speak as soon as possible to the architect of the building in order to further explicate their wishes.[57]

After talks with the municipality and the housing corporation, Belhaj and Arabi agreed to commission a feasibility study in order to find out if the budget and requirements would be suitable for that particular location.[58] Both municipality and corporation still envisioned the two functions as one project led by one architect so as to keep matters coordinated and architecturally consistent, and in their minds Bert Dirrix would logically be the overall designer as he was already involved in the project.[59] Dirrix, the corporation and Belhaj then decided that the mosque and the apartment block would be vertically separated so no apartments would be situated above or below the mosque, and that the corner of the block would be the obvious location for the mosque so as to create separate entrances for men and women on the two intersecting streets. The adjacent blocks had four floors and so would the mosque. On the first floor would be an ablution space and a men's prayer room; on the second, an ablution space and an auxiliary men's prayer room for special occasions; on the third, an ablution space and a women's prayer room and library which could be used as an overflow in case the number of women grew; and on the fourth, space for an office and class rooms. There were no requests on the part of the patron for specific materials, but the building should be 'sober' and spaces 'simply structured'. Only much-used parts like entrance doors should be made from sound materials. Importantly, although Dirrix' report mentioned the 'specific suitability to the extant and newly planned streetscape' as a factor, it also stated that 'the formal expression of religious signs is necessary; an "Oriental image" is preferable in the sense of the demarcation of its content, and the orientation towards Mecca is of great importance'.[60]

The Foundation agreed to Dirrix' role, but arranged to be represented by Abdelmajjid Khairoun, now the chairman of the Netherlands' Muslim Council (Nederlandse Moslim Raad). At the time, he ran the Alfomin Foundation ('Algemeen Fonds voor Moslim Instellingen' or General Fund for Muslim

Institutions), with which he managed insurances, taxes, travel, and construction projects for Muslims in general and Moroccans in particular. Apparently, he had been a contact of Belhaj, and was already known among Moroccan-Islamic communities.

Subsequently, Dirrix started to develop his ideas on mosque design. His main reference was a book describing mosque architecture from an art-psychological view, in which architectural forms were essentially connected to religious experiences. The author, a Jewish-Dutch sculptor and psychologist, had developed what he called an 'art-phenomenological' (as opposed to art-historical) approach to architecture which was based on the architectural-analytical concept of 'frontality'. He had first applied it to the works of the much-admired Dutch architect De Bazel, and had then used it in an analysis of mosques. That is, Ottoman mosques, as he considered these to be much more 'context-transcending' than any others.[61] Another important source for Dirrix was an article by Paolo Portoghesi on his modern mosque in Rome, in which he referred primarily to the principles underlying his choices and not to prescribed forms.[62] The fact that Dirrix chose this literature instead of the usual picture books is important, as it indicates an aim to design a prayer hall for the most part according to general principles and not according to specifically 'cultural' building elements, as he was expected by the corporation as well as the municipality to create something consistent with his own apartment block as well as the architectural surroundings.

For over a week, Dirrix progressively translated the findings from his literature into his own ideas. He concluded that, in light of the needed functional spaces of the mosque and the fact that it had to share the location with housing, a narrow, rectangular mosque would be best. The different functions of removing shoes, ablution and praying could then be separated from each other by the placement of pillars, a basic idea extracted from Portoghesi. The compartments would then be a consistent space, covering 'a total ritual'. Furthermore, he concluded that a strict Mecca-oriented kiblah would be impractical in light of the spatial consequences for the relationship with streets and adjacent housing, and he decided to stay with the slightly-off orientation of the community's old mosque.[63]

In the meantime, Arabi and Belhaj had concluded that four layers would result in relatively low prayer spaces, which they found to be impractical (as there would be too many people crowded up under a low ceiling) but also culturally inappropriate: in their experience, Moroccan mosques ideally had relatively high prayer rooms.[64] Where Cheppih in Eindhoven had rejected height as a valuable building element in his architectural purification process, here it was deemed a Moroccan characteristic and a necessity. The municipality, in turn, proposed to leave the part of the block at the edge of the corner partly open in order to create a transition space, and to mark that edge with 'a tower-shaped element (minaret)'. This space would then be separated from the public street by a fence.[65]

On 25 October, Dirrix sent a ground plan sketch to the parties concerned.[66] The architect had essentially translated De Miranda's main feature of 'frontality,' associated by the author with a broad kiblah, and Portoghesi's forest of columns, accentuating the 'horizontality' of mosques, into the El Islam's new context, combining them with the municipal request for a transition area and the patrons' wish for higher spaces. **(Figure 143)** Subsequently, the architect devised the façade sketches, and once he had received the Aesthetics Commission's reaction based on these drawings, he presented the whole package to his patrons at the end of November. **(Figure 144)** To the community leaders, he explained his design as follows: 'The mosque ("where one kneels"), recognizable by minaret and formal Oriental references, is a house where believers gather for communal prayer. The internal character is established by a rectangular substructure, in which the Mecca-oriented rear wall (the kiblah) determines the direction of prayer and the whole floor is covered with carpets. The strongly axial orientation of the central axis through the mihrab (wall-niche) automatically gets its counterweight in the strong frontality (width) of the kiblah. To get a correct orientation of the kiblah towards Mecca (almost southeast), the rectangular form has been slightly turned in the sharply cut town planning lay-out. The spatial outline that is subsequently created has been filled in as circulation-, washing- and entrance space. A four-floored structure of the program as established in the programmatic wishes was asked for, four construction layers related to the adjacent existing and planned housing layers […]. The different (piled up) prayer spaces […] need a bigger height by their status, use and size […]. The sum of three heightened layers […] presents a disconnection from the housing layers and can amply harbour the requested program. In that way the four-levelled program of requirements has been translated into three construction layers. […] The main point of the men's entrance consists of the recessed façade on the Van der Vennestraat as a transition space/ forecourt.'[67] The Aesthetics Commission evaluation was largely positive in relation to the appearance and the 'fitting-in' of the mosque. However, they preferred a higher fence at the forecourt in order to improve the continuity with the adjacent block, and a less conspicuous 'border-motif' between mosque and housing at the Van der Vennestraat, as the emergency stairwell and the 'rolled-over block' at the third layer 'provoked an ostentatious attention that would be more befitting to a main entrance'.[68]

In his proposal, Dirrix had not included a dome while he had drawn the minaret using forms which his patrons identified as 'Turkish', even if translated into a square plan with a square balcony. Ottoman mosques had been the sole focus of De Miranda's book on general mosque design, and Dirrix had clearly meant his minaret as a general sign of Islam instead of as a Turkish representation. However, where Boon had fully abstracted an Ottoman – mistaken for Moroccan – form into something 'purely Islamic' for Cheppih, here the cultural association was still there for Belhaj and Arabi. Furthermore, where the main structure was concerned, the architect had translated his authors' abstract visions of Islam and Islamic architecture instead of using 'cultural' building elements. For the municipality and housing corporation, the building first of all had to fit into its architectural surroundings, a feature to which Dirrix' patrons had agreed in the programmatic requirements. His 'Islamic' explanation of the design in the vision of his literature, however, did not convince his patrons. As it was, Dirrix' preliminary sketch for the mosque, although by no means meant as a final proposal, was deemed by his patrons too divergent from what they had in mind for them to be able to continue with him for the design part of the commission. Although they had mentioned that their mosque should fit its surroundings, a total surrender to it, as they perceived the current proposal, was not what they wanted. In effect, the patrons required a clearly Moroccan construction of Islam to be represented in their mosque, in opposition to the contesting Islamic constructions embraced by other Moroccan-Islamic community leaders as in, for instance, Eindhoven. In the process of mutual contrasting as defined in this context, whereas Cheppih explicitly rejected any Moroccan building elements, Belhaj and Arabi could not do without. It was the specifically North African building style that the latter had had in mind all along, but in Eindhoven as well as in The Hague it appeared that presenting the own construction of Islam – and the forms to be particularly associated with it – towards a designer as a mere *contested* version was not an option.[69]

Khairoun thanked the architect for his survey and stated that the patrons regarded his commission as completed. 'In light of the fact that designing mosques requires specific knowledge, it is in the patron's interest that a Muslim architect make the design for the mosque. During the meeting we, the Alfomin Foundation and the El Islam Foundation, have put forward our positions and decided to use our own architects, who will assume responsibility for the realization and construction of the mosque.' He further stated that Dirrix from now on would only have an advisory role, and that 'our architect' Abdul Hamid Oppier would contact him.[70] Oppier, after having played his part in the creation of the Ridderkerk Mosque, had now designed two mosques for Moroccan groups in Zaltbommel and Woerden, as partner in Kaman Architects in Rotterdam. In contrast to the first Moroccan mosque in Eindhoven, the patrons who had hired Oppier had favoured Moroccan building elements. In Zaltbommel, Oppier had tried to combine a Moroccan dome with a Turkish minaret and Dutch materials in his search for innovative combinations of architectural 'traditions', but the patrons, as well as Oppier himself, in the end preferred a Moroccan minaret instead.[71] In Woerden, he had corrected this by using, in answer to his patrons' wishes, specifically Moroccan building elements in both minaret and dome. After Arabi and Belhaj had rejected Dirrix' design because they wanted their mosque to look distinctively Moroccan, Khairoun naturally thought of Oppier.

At the request of El Islam, Oppier then proposed to execute the design of the El Islam mosque. He concluded that a new alternative would have to be developed that would take a truer orientation to Mecca into account while not leading to negative consequences for either project. The housing project by Dirrix and the mosque would have to be aligned for urban delimitations and mass but the 'recognizability' of the mosque would also have to be a factor. The plan would be reviewed by Dirrix, but because of Oppier's 'experience and shorter communication lines with the users', as he described it, the design proposal could better be made by Oppier himself.[72] Clearly, the community wanted the mosque and the adjacent housing to be separate projects so they could control the design of their prayer hall as their own chosen architectural representation. On the other side, the municipality restated its wish for a consistent architecture in which the first layer would consist of commercial activities and the upper layers of housing so as to create a 'walking promenade' character for the whole block. In their view, this could not be accomplished if the plot were divided into separate projects with separate project leaders.[73] Clearly, the municipality preferred the mosque to be a liturgical element in an integrated mixture of neighbourhood functions and spaces, with an accompanying stress on the continuity of forms in the whole block and a strong preference for Dirrix. It would be up to the two architects to find a solution and merge what seemed to be two irreconcilable realities.

Subsequently, Oppier established his patrons' new programmatic requirements, formulating their formal demands as a prayer hall with a kiblah towards Mecca, that would fit into the urban context, but one recognizable 'as a mosque'.[74] Notably, the required Moroccanness of the architecture was still not specifically mentioned either to the municipality or Dirrix, although it had constituted a 'sine qua non' to the patrons from the very beginning, as was clear to Oppier. Dirrix and Oppier then created a solution for their respective patrons' opposition by agreeing that Oppier would be the project architect for the mosque, while Dirrix would be the project architect for the housing block, and the supervisor/coordinator of the construction plan as a whole.[75]

On 24 March, Oppier made a preliminary ground plan with a rectangular prayer hall as it would be ideally oriented towards Mecca. This served as the basis for his later designs, as he often drew a protruding women's entrance portal and a protruding minaret at the corners of this extruding rectangular, providing an exterior marker for the inner prayer hall's orientation. On 14 April, he sketched it into a situation plan for the municipality. **(Figure 145)** The municipality then set the urban delimitations largely based on Oppier's ideal, but it also stated that the mosque was to have a covered forecourt of 200 m2 at the first layer as a transitional area between street and building, that protruding elements on the first layer at the street side were to be avoided, and that the heights of the three layers of the mosque were to be aligned as much as possible to those of the adjacent housing, with a recessed top layer at the Seghersstraat..[76] Obviously, the municipality still embraced the idea of a continuous architectural style throughout the whole block, especially at the first layer, with a transition area in order to avoid any disturbance to passers-by and inhabitants.

In reaction, Oppier objected that the proposed forecourt would take almost half of the plot and therefore should be reduced to 50 m2. In his eyes, the heights of the inner layers should be allowed to diverge from those of the adjacent housing, as long as in the outer façades a certain continuity was maintained. Moreover, a protrusion to mark the women's entrance – serving to indicate the building's true orientation towards Mecca – should be allowed.[77] Dirrix, as project coordinator, incorporated Oppier's requests in his advice to the municipality.[78] The next day, Oppier made his first façade sketches. **(Figure 146)** Here we see that the architect had taken the idea of a spaced-out, fenced corner, but that he had drawn a 'Moroccan' minaret on the Van der Vennestraat, with its base starting from the second layer so as not to disturb the alignment of the building's plinth. He designed arched windows to mark the main prayer hall at the second layer, and placed an open pavilion as a 'Moroccan' pyramid roof on top. At the edge of the corner he had planned a large see-through window scheme with the intent to make this hardly usable space the marker of the mosque's entrance. At the upper layer at the Segherstraat he had drawn a balcony, intended to create a place where visitors could go outside.

In a subsequent drawing of ground plans, façades, and section that Oppier made on 18 May, the minaret was aligned to the Segherstraat, whereas the pyramid roof, the roof for the women's entrance and the kiblah wall adjacent to Dirrix' housing block indicated the orientation towards Mecca.[79] **(Figure 147)** The windows were now drawn with horseshoe arches as the recognizably Moroccan feature Oppier had seen during his visits to Morocco and the Hassan II Mosque. The circular windows were an experiment of his own. However, Arabi reacted to the plan with the remark that a minaret should always start at street level, firmly based on the ground. He saw this as a 'Moroccan tradition', as in his idea only in other culture areas would minarets rest on the main structure itself. In the design process he would repeatedly refer to the recently completed Hassan II mosque in Casablanca, with all Moroccan building 'traditions' it had used, as a perfect example. However, although he greatly valued the minaret as a primary marker, he did not need it to be large enough for an actual staircase. In effect, he could not do without a minaret, not because it was a 'functional place for the muezzin', a 'cultural reminder of home', or a 'social marker of emancipation', but because it was a material means to represent his particular construction of Islam as opposed to contesting versions among other Morocccan-Islamic community leaders.

Subsequently, Oppier's requests were largely incorporated by the municipality in a new proposal for the urban delimitations.[80] On 9 June, Oppier made more detailed sketches for Dirrix, on which the latter wrote comments. **(Figure 148)** Dirrix, pressing for appropriateness to the surrounding architecture and his own design for the adjacent housing block, wanted the plinth to be consistent and materials to consist of orange bricks in Waal-size. Although these conditions were later thought by some observers to have been conspicuously preferred by the patrons in their socially integrating stance, they were essentially specified by the municipality in its goal to keep the project in line with surrounding architecture. On 12 July, Oppier presented his plans with a provisional model to Aesthetics. **(Figure 149)** The commission was relatively positive about the design, although it did ask for more continuity in the façade scheme by proposing to omit the minaret's protruding base and put it at the far end so as to make it a border marker between mosque and housing block, while marking the direction of Mecca at the same time.[81]

Between 3 and 8 August, Oppier made some new ground plan sketches. He indeed had relocated the minaret to the far end of the mosque, directly adjacent to Dirrix' housing block. He had turned the minaret's ground plan parallel to the kiblah towards Mecca together with part of the first layer to create an opportunity for a door at the Vennestreetside to a space that could be rented to third parties. It would be occupied by a Moroccan-Islamic community member who had donated a substantial amount of money and who would sell Moroccan articles in a store he planned to establish in the mosque. This would fulfil the municipality's need for a first layer of enterprise and, at the same time, provide the mosque with future income. At the second layer, only the minaret would maintain its alignment, so the door would be covered by the floor of the second layer itself. He had planned the pyramid roof as an open pavilion on poles starting from the third layer's floor, creating a patio surrounded by partly transparent walls so the space would be opened up and the women on the third layer would be able to look down to the imam praying in the second layer's main prayer room and mihrab. Oppier's alignment of the ideal rectangular prayer hall was visible in the minaret, in the partition wall with Dirrix' project, in the protruding women's entrance, and now in the pyramid roof as well. **(Figure 150)** However, the connection between the prayer rooms was rejected by Arabi, who thought the void a waste of space and who held the separation between men's and women's spaces in high value as a typical 'Moroccan-Islamic tradition'. He also requested that the entrances and their spaces be as far apart as possible.

Oppier noted that whereas the Aesthetics Commission had requested the minaret to be placed on the border of the two projects, Dirrix wanted it to be moved away from his housing project so the two would appear as a continuous block.[82] Oppier then made a new provisional model of his mosque. Now the minaret was relocated away from Dirrix' housing block and was given a protruding plinth from the street level. **(Figure 151)** Since no part of the pavement was included in the plot this would lead to higher property costs, in addition to the fact that the existing underground cables would have to be diverted by the municipality at higher costs for the patrons. That Arabi in spite of budgetary constraints decided that his minaret should have a protruding base at ground level is another indication of its importance as a chosen element of his architectural representation of a specifically Moroccan Islam.[83] According to Arabi, the patrons then had a meeting focused on the subject of 'what is Moroccan architecture', making use of tourist brochures on Morocco that Khairoun had brought in. It was decided that the double arched window was typically Moroccan. On 5 September, Oppier applied this, together with other building elements as he had studied them from the Moroccan section in his volume on Islamic architecture, in a new façade sketch.[84] **(Figure 152)** The minaret was now to be executed in prefab concrete with a variety of 'Moroccan' window motifs, and the façade was provided with a 'Moroccan' window scheme as well. Only a motif with three circles, which he meant as an upside-down Hilal, had come from his own formal experiments. Furthermore, he had erased the fence around the forecourt as he wanted to open up that section to prevent the image of a 'prison'. The rectangular window over the entrance had been given a horse-shoe shape to make it more consistent with the rest of the Moroccan imagery. In the model, the entrance door to the rentable space had already gone, and here we see that he meant to relocate the door to the minaret base. The patrons still required a separate entrance to the store, and this way the first layer's façade would not be disturbed more than necessary.

The next time Aesthetics evaluated Oppier's design, the full commission was apparently assembled instead of just a few members. As a consequence, they could find no internal agreement on the location of the minaret. Suggested were the location adjacent to the housing block, at the main entrance, on the roof, starting from the ground and starting from the second layer. One member even suggested two minarets instead of just one, which would not have been a Moroccan building element as El Islam would have seen it: in the 'Hassanian style', a singular minaret is defined as a basic element of Moroccan architecture. The only thing the assembled members agreed on was a dislike of the fence around the forecourt and, notably, on their preference for the mosque to be designed as an autonomous project and not to conform to the adjacent housing block.[85] Apparently, the municipal wish for a single consistent architectural image was not shared by the Aesthetics Commission.

On 19 October, Oppier made new façade drawings for Dirrix.[86] **(Figure 153)** We see here that he had used Aesthetics' outspoken dislike of a fence and drawn a series of doorways and windows at the fence's former location, to be opened up to the streets with decorated grilles. Although Arabi still found the inner court a waste of good space, the mosque apparently had to keep a transitional area for the municipality which feared that without it the assembled believers would create a disturbance to passing traffic. Furthermore, since the future user of the store had required separate installational facilities, the base of the minaret now contained an installation while the entrance had been relocated to its left. Oppier had also sketched a turret at the corner-point to further mark the entrance of the building next to the large window scheme. The latter had now been changed to double windows, to be more consistent with the other rows of double windows in the façade, having been defined by Oppier and his patrons as a Moroccan 'tradition', as well as making them easier to produce and insure. Moreover, Oppier had introduced 8-pointed star-shaped windows at the Segherstraat façade, a form that he and Arabi thought more 'Islamic' than circular ones. And finally, he had closed up part of the balcony since in Arabi's opinion this was also a waste of usable space. The architect had used panels as a solution to the divergent height of the adjacent apartment block.

Besides some minor adjustment preferences and an overall positive evaluation, Aesthetics rejected the proposed 'relation between floor and void with large windows and sharp corner [...] (also think of night image!)', meaning Oppier's large see-through window scheme at the edge of the corner.[87] On 1 December, Oppier filed for a permit.[88] In his drawings, we see that the architect had changed the window scheme at the corner on the Segherstraat in answer to the Commission's final request: now, the marked see-through element at the edge had gone. **(Figure 154)** Moreover, the window at the upper layer to the minaret's right had been erased: this was the only window, apart from the transparent roof pavilion, to the women's space, but Arabi had requested Oppier to prevent outsiders from being able to look inside. Aesthetics approved,[89] as did the municipality and the Province,[90] and on 11 August, the permit was given.[91]

On 6 October 1995, Oppier made the construction drawings.[92] **(Figure 155)** Now, we see a change in the decoration pattern of the minaret, as Oppier had introduced the 8-pointed star in the minaret's base and had lowered the minaret's double window to be more in line with the adjacent row of double windows. Moreover, he had added a structure on the roof for technical installations. Notably, he had reintroduced the window in the women's space to the right of the minaret, as he found the absence of one too disturbing in the pattern of the façade: he had solved the issue by providing the window with partly opaque glass. In Oppier's recollection, his was a constant search for forms which would be 'Moroccan' enough but also internally and externally consistent.

On 17 November, the first pole ceremony was held. At the same time, an agreement was signed by El Islam and a neighbourhood organization in relation to mutual obligations and continuing discussions.[93] However, during construction, on 14 June 1996, Oppier had to make a sketch for new wooden doors for the main entrance. Apparently, Arabi was of the opinion that even a semi-open covered area was a waste of usable space, in addition to providing opportunities for vandalism. In fact, the patrons wanted the doors to be made of cedar, which they regarded as a 'Moroccan tradition' since in the Hassan II Mosque, which had conspicuously made use of Moroccan building elements as for handicrafts, materials and forms as defined by the king, the doors had also been made of cedar wood. They would be decorated in Moroccan style by a community member who was a carpenter. Moreover, on 19 June, the architect had to make a rough sketch of a new minaret without the formerly planned prefab concrete elements, now with a shaft of bricks and a dome with decorative tiling over a concrete underlayer.[94] The change to bricks was not aimed at the physical – and therefore social – integration that some observers later thought to recognize in the overall building, but had been requested by the contractor.[95] He had miscalculated costs and could not provide the prefab concrete materials for the agreed price. **(Figure 156)**

On 15 July, Oppier made a new sketch and a final model. **(Figure 157)** Now the decorative fence at the forecourt had been changed into the closed doors as requested by Arabi. The minaret was drawn with the new window shapes, although its materials as sketched still indicated prefab concrete; the change to bricks, since this had been the main material as requested by the municipality in the first place, was felt not to require an official re-application. The women's entrance had been aligned with the façade, answering to a municipal social safety advice stating that the recessed women's entrance would create a place for urination. Also, the minaret, because of its protrusion and its conspicuous windows 'running the risk to be selected as a target for vandalism,' should preferably be aligned with the rest of the façade at the first layer.[96] Apparently, the orientation marker in the form of a recessed door and a shed above the women's entrance had not been regarded by the patrons as an essential element of the representation of a specifically Moroccan Islam. That it was more of a priority matter in a process of representation than of conformation to municipal worries, however, was shown in the fact that the protruding minaret base was firmly retained. Lastly, at Arabi's request, Oppier had completely closed the balcony with panels.

As the contractor eventually pulled out of the construction process because of his miscalculations, Oppier and Arabi together completed the coordination of construction and decoration. The latter was done by a team specializing in 'typically Moroccan' wood and stucco handicrafts, similar to those used in the Hassan II. On 5 December 1997, the mosque was officially opened by the Moroccan consul and PVDA Alderman P. Noordanus. The fact that an official Moroccan representative was present at this celebration, as opposed to the openings of Moroccan mosques that fervently rejected the official Moroccan Islam, is meaningful. Just as in the case of the official Turkish representation during the opening of the Sultan Ahmet Mosque, it denotes at least a certain degree of affiliation of the board members with the current state's view of Islam, and it therefore should form an important consideration in the representational analysis of their chosen mosque design. Noordanus called the El Islam 'one of the most beautiful buildings that have recently been built in the Schilderswijk' and expressed his admiration for the initiative and the architect, who he thought of as 'a magician'. The building, in light of its use of Dutch bricks and its continuity within the block, was generally regarded as a perfect architectural example of the social integration of a Muslim community into the Dutch environment. Moreover, the mosque was even included in the first The Hague Architecture Calendar, as one of 12 remarkable buildings in the municipality. **(Figure 158)**

The Essalaam Mosque, Rotterdam

On 12 September 1991, the municipality of Rotterdam established the zoning plan Kop van Zuid for the area just south of the city center, to be developed as an important, architecturally representative showcase. Next to an Aesthetics Commission, a special 'Quality Team' was instituted, consisting of both municipal representatives and internationally renowned architects. This Q-team was to make sure that all proposed architectural projects would be in line with the municipal ambition to become The Netherlands' capital of modern architecture. Within the zoning plan, along an extant major road and railway line, a new park was planned, to consist of raised terrains, grass and trees within a walled, linear zone or 'strip' that would be at an angle with the already existing Varkenoordse Park to its southeast.

In 1994, the Moroccan mosque community Essalaam let the municipality know that their building, a former bakery, was getting too small. They requested the municipality for a location on which to construct a new prayer hall. At about the same time, however, the Moroccan mosque community El-Mohcinine suffered from the same problem. Subsequently, the regional mosques association SPIOR recommended that they work together as regards the local government and start a shared Foundation.[97] As mentioned earlier, Rotterdam had, after a failed attempt at establishing two 'shared-ethnic' mosques, developed the idea of establishing a limited number of 'singular-ethnic' mosques. The shared Essalaam/El-Mohcinine project would be appropriate to the municipal ideal of creating one large Moroccan prayer hall for several Moroccan-Islamic communities at once. Subsequently, it proposed to incorporate this future mosque in the 'strip' along the major road and railway line, making it a municipal Moroccan-Dutch-Islamic showcase. The inhabitants of the adjacent apartment building protested against the coming of the mosque in a series of letters and meetings in 1995,[98] but in 1996 the municipality turned down their objections, which were mainly practical, and decided to go ahead with the plan.[99]

In December 1997, the municipality established that the building had to be adapted to the formal elements of the strip. It would mark the point where the strip bent into the Varkenoordse Park, the paths aligning the strip's walls would form the outer limits, and the plot itself could not exceed 800m2. The maximum height, 'excluding minaret and possible dome' would be 12 meters and would be divided into three construction layers. The building would have to have a 'representative image' towards its surroundings, especially the northwest façade towards the strip, and the main entrance would be located at that side. The upper two layers could be turned towards Mecca.[100] The municipality then presented a number of alternative volumes to the Q-team together with 'reference images with different typologies for mosques', and subsequently 'the Q-team was informed as to the main elements that could be determinant in mosque design'. Eventually, the Q-team chose a construction with its upper part turned in the direction of the Varkenoordse Park, which happened also to be the direction towards Mecca. **(Figure 159)** The team stressed that the mosque should have 'a high quality design according to presented references'.[101] Read between the lines, both Q-team and municipality expected the Moroccans to welcome the opportunity to show their cultural background, in line with what was generally thought of as a multi-cultural emancipation process. In the mean time, the communities had joined forces in the Foundation Essalaam Mosque, with Abdurrazaq Boutaher as chairman and Ahmed Ajdid as project manager.[102]

Ajdid had been requested by Boutaher to arrange for funds as well as construction. Although he was never to have any official position on the board, he may count as the community's main patron and representative towards architect, municipality and sponsor.[103] To the Dutch public – and even to part of the Essalaam community itself – it seemed as if he, having that much power over such an important matter as a new building, had come out of nowhere. However, he and chairman Boutaher were in fact connected by the Dutch security service as well as Dutch journalists with a number of organizations in The Netherlands allegedly related to the Muslim Brotherhood.[104] Although Ajdid himself never wished to deny or admit any such connections, his particular construction of Islam and architecture did show some obvious similarities to the explicitly pan-Islamic ideals of the Movement as opposed to the purification tendencies of Salafism.[105] Born and raised in the Moroccan Rif, Ajdid did not want his community to become involved in any form of official Moroccan funding or support, as he was against the whole idea of any form of national or nationalist Islam altogether. To him, Islam was 'less narrow-minded' than that, 'surpassing nations', 'world-encompassing' and 'with roots lying in the Middle East and not in Morocco'. Although he explicitly saw himself as a Moroccan, he traced his family down a line of ten generations to 'Middle Eastern' descent. Ajdid found Moroccan Islam to be a blatant corruption of the much more powerful Islam begun in Medina by Mohammed, with the latter as the real commander of all believers instead of 'some suppressing Moroccan king'. However, although he detested the Moroccan version as much as did Cheppih in Eindhoven, his own religious stance was not connected to any precultural purism. On the contrary, he wanted to be connected to a 'dignified' Islam, supported by a 'dignified' Islamic organization, and represented by a 'dignified' Islamic building. Architecturally, although he nominally regarded certain Moroccan skills as contributing to what he saw as the wonderful array of Muslim building styles, he disliked 'the typical Moroccan, narrow-minded, small-scale tendency towards the overkill of forms and colours'. From a representational viewpoint, Ajdid embraced a specifically pan-Islamic religious construction in direct opposition to the official-Moroccan version as visible in, for instance, The Hague. Like Cheppih in Eindhoven, he rejected any nationalization of Islam, but instead of resorting to a cultural purification or 'deculturalization' of Islamic architecture he aimed at a cultural culmination in which all of the Islamic world's architectural splendours would be proudly united. Of course, as with Cheppih, since his underlying motivation was an explicit opposition to the official-Moroccan version, Moroccan building elements were to be particularly shunned in practice. When some community members had proposed a Moroccan design, he had refused his cooperation by suggesting that, in that case, they should 'go to the Moroccan king'.

After he found an alternative sponsor in the Al-Maktoum Foundation in Dubai represented by chairman Mirza Al-Sayegh, he set out to also find an architect there. With the municipal delimitations in mind, Ajdid visited a Dubai conference in January 1998, where he met an architect from

Abu Dhabi, Abdallah Nabeel A. Nazeer. He gave Nazeer the details on the Q-team's preferences and the architect was to send him a preliminary proposal to show the municipality. Ajdid also used his stay to travel around the emirates taking photographs of different buildings that contained particular architectural elements that attracted him and that he could use as references. Among these, there were pictures of religious as well as secular buildings, a seemingly arbitrary selection of objects and details. **(Figure 160)** The main object was a mosque in Sharjah, of which he took several photographs. This structure largely answered to Ajdid's practical requirements and to the municipal outline of main mass and front extension. It is important to note that Ajdid chose these buildings himself, and that his sponsor had not communicated any wishes on design. Several observers later thought they knew that his financier would have determined the supposed 'Mamluk' style of the Essalaam Mosque over an assumedly more logical Dutch-Moroccan alternative, but Moroccan or Dutch building elements were simply not what the community leader had in mind to begin with. Nor did his sponsor, as we will see later, have preconceived ideas on the need for 'Arabicness' or any interest in the design's formal features altogether.

On 19 February 1998, Nazeer made a sketch for Ajdid. **(Figure 161)** It was later assumed by some that the architect had been introduced by Al Maktoum and that the design had been a decontextualized 'moonlander' from another world,[106] but neither assumption was correct. Nazeer, noting that one municipal criterion was for the main entrance to face the strip, but also wanting to keep true to the kiblah direction, had meant to align the volume as a whole with the Varkenoordse Park – in line with Mecca – without sacrificing the orientational consistency of the building. However, the main façade would then be at an angle with the strip, which he subsequently solved by incorporating the main – or men's – entrance in the base of the right minaret and by placing a fountain in front of it, aligned with the strip. As can be seen in his drawings, he then called the – obviously – main façade the 'left side', and the – obviously – right side the 'front elevation', which might be illogical from a decontextualized point of view but not in its specific context. Ajdid took this design as an example – not as a definite design proposal as he would want to see it actually built – to the municipality, which apparently was not particularly charmed by the plan. Ajdid concurred that the Abu Dhabi proposal in its current form was unfit for his project, and since his sponsor strongly advised him to hire a Dutch architect to make things easier within the municipality, it was agreed that the latter would come up with some names of Dutch architects.

Of the five suggested architects, not all were expected by the patron to be flexible enough, and he rejected most of them.[107] However, Delft architect Wilfried van Winden (Molenaar & Van Winden Architects) had the communication skills, openness, interest and flexibility that made Ajdid think that this architect could be perfect to materialize his representational requirements. Importantly, Van Winden himself assumed that it had been his creative designs, represented in brochures incorporating the bureau's non-Modernist architectural objects constructed with a rich use of brick materials and decorative detailing, which had attracted Ajdid.[108] Also, the architect had bought a Dutch-language publication on Islamic architecture for the occasion and brought it with him. It was a much-used typological overview of style periods and culture areas exemplified by their most famous buildings and art objects.[109] This, in the designer's experience, struck a final cord on the side of the patron.[110] As a consequence, the architect thought that he was expected to come up with a creative design around practical requirements, whereas Ajdid assumed that the architect would tightly follow the patron's own formal preferences.

In answer to a requested enlargement of the mosque's plot – the new Foundation included two former communities – the municipality was willing to allow for a column-supported upper level extension.[111] Subsequently, the designer started to study Islamic architecture from his book. At that time, Ajdid had not mentioned any specific building elements or given any references as an important part of his representation. As in other cases, the patron initially presented himself, his Islam, and his formal requirements in vague terms, leaving his architect with the assumption that he should work out his own classification of architecture to be used in design. So Van Winden made copies of a wide selection of buildings that he himself found to incorporate certain building elements that could be appropriately and creatively combined with his own design preferences. **(Figure 162)** In his own words, he concentrated on buildings and building elements with certain patterns of bricks and tiling as providing opportunities for what he saw as the combination of architectural characteristics that were both Dutch and Moroccan. On 26 June 2001, he came up with a first sketch. **(Figure 163)** It consisted of ground plans and elevations for a mosque that had round forms and asymmetrically placed minarets so as to creatively smooth over the municipally- required bend in the building. Moreover, the upper layers extended beyond the first layer. The design's building elements had been taken and transformed from his selected array of examples, copies of which he included in his design proposal.

Ajdid, however, found the architect's round forms, introduced as a solution to the orientation problem, 'not as usual'. It was 'too modern', as 'in The Netherlands people would rather have nothing new'. What he wanted was a rectangular building with its main structure directed towards Mecca. In support, he brought his selection of photographs from the emirates to the architect as examples of what he had in mind. Furthermore, he wanted a 'very chic' multifunctional space, not for daily use but for special occasions like celebrations, lectures and exhibitions, also for 'non-believers' so as to make the distance between them and religious Muslims smaller. No other functions should be combined with this room as it was, again, 'too chic'. The dome did not need to join the men's prayer room, as the community needed all the floor space they could get. Apparently, like the Moroccan patrons in The Hague, Ajdid did not attach much value to praying underneath a dome, although in this case his architect was later able to convince him to introduce the spatial connection between dome and prayer rooms anyway. Furthermore, next to finding the sketches too modern, the reference images that the architect had used, including bricks and tiling, were deemed 'too old (year zero)'. It appeared that the community leader did not put any value on material Moroccanness, Dutchness or any combination of the two as expected by municipality and architect. Ajdid simply advised Van Winden to look up images of mosques on the internet by typing the word 'mosque' in some search engines.[112] The patron kept his formal wishes down to a negation of the proposed and to a generalization of the required, leaving his architect, as the latter understandably experienced it, with very little to go on.

On 5 July, Van Winden came up with a new sketch, now showing a more rectangular plan with different minarets and a domed portico, roughly as in Ajdid's Sjarjah example, although here the portico was turned towards the strip as requested by the municipality. **(Figure 164)** He had vaulted the entrance portal along the lines of Moorish – as well as classical – architecture, still searching for a combination of Islamic and Western building elements. The architect apparently also made a provisional model of the proposal, meant as a volume study and so without exact details. According to the designer, Ajdid did not react very positively to it, as he claimed it looked more like a 'swimming pool with a garage' than a mosque. The white plastic material of the model provoked an association in the patron's mind that was far from his dignified and splendid idea of a mosque. Moreover, Ajdid stated that the minarets should be symmetrically beside the entrance and that the form was still not correct. According to him, 'for people in The

Netherlands, a mosque should be as traditional as possible'. He found all this to be a waste of time as the architect supposedly had not done enough research on the subject.[113] This rather baffled Van Winden, who later blamed Moroccan politeness in that his Moroccan patron would have felt obliged to assume that the designer was the specialist. However, previous case studies indicate that, much more than a concern for politeness, patrons generally tend initially to uphold the generality of Islam while avoiding the specifics of their particular Islamic construction and the building elements to be associated with it. In this case, Ajdid's confusing variety of reference pictures and his ambiguous requirement of 'chic', 'traditionalism' and 'modernity' was too inconsistent to make for a coherent representation of what the patron did want. A planned meeting between municipal representatives and architect had to be cancelled because 'architect and patron [were] still discussing the first sketches'.[114]

In the account of both parties, this is when they almost went their separate ways again, and Ajdid almost decided to go and look out for another architect instead of Van Winden. However, as a last resort, they agreed to separately come up with mosque references containing elements that each wanted to see included in design. Notably, Ajdid now gave the architect more keywords meant for an internet search: 'Medina', 'Lahore' and 'Casablanca'.[115] It is important to note here that it was Medina that was mentioned as the main keyword, although it was not as yet given prominence by Ajdid in so many words. Where Gaffar in De Bijlmer had specifically taken the older elements of the Prophet's tomb as an example, Ajdid thought of the modern Saudi construction around it. As for Lahore and Casablanca, according to Ajdid he had meant these, in some details, as parts of the encompassing Islamic splendour as he wanted to see represented in Rotterdam, not as inspirational sources per se. However, all these important motivations were not mentioned to the architect at that time.

Consequently, connecting Ajdid's nominal Casablanca reference to his Moroccan background and therefore understandably assuming that that was the most important factor in his comments, the architect started to collect images of Moorish buildings in Granada, Casablanca, Rabat and Amsterdam. However, he also included three images of the Dubai Al-Jumairah Mosque, which he had found in his search on the internet to be particularly attractive in its coherent use of colours and materials. **(Figure 165)** Ajdid in turn sent the architect a multitude of images of mosques from around the world which, again, did not seem to have any consistency. **(Figure 166)** Of course, to him all these buildings did have something very important in common: all together they represented the idea of the international, encompassing and splendid Islam to which he was so attracted. Here as well, the order of his references is important to note: the series began, again, with the Medina mosque, followed by a variety of buildings from around the world, with Ajdid focusing attention on specific details that particularly attracted him. In the end, amidst his and his patron's still widely divergent references, Van Winden identified the Jumairah and what he saw as its Mamluk building elements as an important common reference point since Ajdid had, when asked, also expressed admiration for it.

On 18 July, the architect came up with another plan in which he had incorporated his own Jumairah and Moorish building elements as well as some from Ajdid's array of references. **(Figure 167)** There were now two symmetrical minarets beside the entrance, as requested by the patron and as visible in the Jumairah. Like the designer's Moorish references, there was a two-level portico extension and a bottom layer of arches and columns on the back façade, while side and back façades incorporated diamond-shaped niches and openings as devised by the designer. Both the main dome and the two rear corner cupolas used the netted stucco patterns of the Jumairah. A crenellated roof edge served, according to Van Winden, not as a reference to any building in particular but as a distinctive, home-designed marker. Notably, the front cupola was erased. In reaction, Ajdid stated that he found this sketch to be beautiful, although the front cupola had to return, the minarets would have to be about 42 m. high, and exits needed to be large.[116] The height of the minarets had been derived from the Rotterdam Mevlana Mosque, as at that point Ajdid reasoned that if it had been allowed for the Mevlana it would be allowed for the Essalaam.

In the next model, and in the next sketch of 25 July, the architect reintroduced the front cupola, while the mihrab was extended along the first layer and given a second band of diamond-shapes. **(Figure 168)** However, the patron now wanted the two rear domes to go, while the façade was to be less white and more 'beige stucco' and the main dome less hemispherical – the latter in his mind a feature from 'India'.[117] To the Moroccan patron, 'India' represented the wrong culture area, although he had classified 'Moroccan' as old-fashioned and 'Dutch' as too modern. Moreover, his earlier array of references, including 'Hindustani' domes, had not been put to a scale of culture area at all, another sign that it was exactly their number that had been important and not the individual form. Importantly, in regard to specific 'cultural' building elements, it was not the Jumairah that Ajdid had in mind as an ideal, since the rejected corner cupolas were a clear and characteristic element of the latter. That same day, however, Ajdid sent the architect a picture of the Jumairah from the Internet.[118] In the patron's later account, this was only done as an example, by using the designer's own introduced reference, of what he saw as a better dome shape and scheme of proportions. The architect, understandably from his point of view, took it as a confirmation of the importance of the Jumairah's building elements per se. From now on, the Jumairah formed a firm reference for Van Winden. On 31 July, he made a new sketch, incorporating a translation of the Jumairah's minaret and dome forms. **(Figure 169)**

The next day, however, Ajdid gave the architect three unspecified mosque images as reference images, two of them with the dome form as he desired, but one of them the Prophet's Mosque in Medina which does not carry a central dome. **(Figure 170)** He did not explain his choice of the latter, and all three represented quite divergent formal types from where the architect was standing. However, in the continuously changing series of patron's references, the Prophet's mosque in Medina seemed to have become a constant factor, appearing more and more as an architectural ideal of the patron's required representation of Islam. In his rejection of Moroccan-nationalist Islam and the associated Moroccan building elements, and in his subsequent search for a pan-Islamic version, Ajdid had effectively come to see Medina as the utter, transcending, pan-Islamic center incorporating the entire Islamic world's cultural splendour. He time and again enumerated the 'national styles' incorporated in it and the number of nationalities that worked on it. Ajdid had projected his ideal of an encompassing Islam, symbolized by the Prophet and the building where it all began, instead of a building by a self-proclaimed Moroccan Caliph enforcing his 'Hassanian style', onto the current Medina complex. Whether the latter's patrons had actually meant it like that or not is of no relevance to this analysis. The important thing is that Ajdid found that Medina incorporated and encompassed all known Muslim culture areas. Where Gaffar in De Bijlmer had conspicuously chosen the pre-Saudi dome and minaret from Mamluk times, referring to an image mainly of these alone, Ajdid focused precisely on the Saudi extension, referring to images of the modern complex as a whole. And, where Gaffar had transformed his selected Medina building elements into an ideal Brelwi quincunx, Ajdid had to transform his into a rectangular scheme with a turned portico as expected by municipality and Q–team. Where, in his account, he would have preferred to represent the Medina mosque in its broad-structured ground plan, the Rotterdam plot necessitated a 'folding' of the Medina façades around the municipally-required depth-structure and the required multiple levels. As Medina itself was a huge complex with many more domes than could be introduced in Rotterdam, Ajdid decided that above his own entrance portal one cupola would have to represent one of the cupolas over the Medina entrance. His mihrab cupola would have to represent the Dome of the Prophet as it was located at the back façade of Medina complex, and his required central dome – since Medina did not really have a central dome apart form the multitude of low, movable, non-descript sun-shades – would follow the form of the central dome type he had encountered 'throughout the Middle-East'. The latter incorporated, in his view, the Prophet's dome form but with an improved, deeper, vertically-segmented relief. In this way, the basic structure as well as the details of Medina's outer image would still be visible in the limited Rotterdam situation. With hindsight, the three latest reference images suggested a Medina substructure and minarets as in the one picture, combined with a dome as in the other two. However, at that point Ajdid did not mention these important facts, let alone the specific meaning Medina had for him, to his architect.

On the contrary, whenever the architect discussed a subsequent plan with Ajdid, the latter kept expressing his essentially representational requirements in quasi-objective terminology, as if his formal requests were aesthetically pleasing or practically necessary. In effect, however, all suggestions Ajdid made came directly from his many Medina books, posters and images as he studied them at home. Although he frequently mentioned the Medina mosque, he did so purely as if the latter coincidentally provided him with the formally or functionally appropriate building elements that his own future mosque required. Meanwhile, during the many meetings and telephone calls in response to a continuous stream of design proposals, Ajdid constantly had his architect make provisional sketches, on the latest drawings or as separate telephone notations, of the forms as described by him to be incorporated in a next, better design.

This procedure of the patron, slowly but firmly changing the Jumairah/Moorish design into a Medina-based representation, effectively began on 14 August. On that day, Van Winden presented his latest plan and a new model to Ajdid. **(Figure 171)** As we can see, the patron had the architect sketch all kinds of adjustments in the drawings. He wanted the minarets to have balcony balustrades and a different top, openly referring to Medina and its 'egg shape'. He also wanted the minaret bases to be higher, fewer windows in the back façade, a square door opening at the side façade and the slender circular columns supporting the sides of portico made more solid.[119] Furthermore, the portico should be more 'like Medina',[120] meaning that it was to be closed with doors instead of the open arcade that it was now, and that it had to be executed with arches and not with diamond shapes.[121] All the while and in every detail requested, whether it was mentioned 'as an example' or not, Ajdid admittedly had had his Medina images in mind.

After the municipality agreed to these plans,[122] the Q-team was next to evaluate the design. For this occasion, Ajdid's suggestions were incorporated into a new sketch on 12 September. **(Figure 172)** Moreover, the architect had included references to outer stucco patterns, possibly made of polyester-concrete, as he was under the impression that Ajdid wanted Moorish stucco on the outer walls. With hindsight, however, the patron had earlier proposed 'beige stucco' with an eye on representing Medina's natural stone walls instead of using bricks or tiling, whereas Moorish stucco would be much too narrowly Moroccan to him. Furthermore, Van Winden had sketched an Alhambra-derived fountain in front of the mosque, including a reference image in the presentation. Ajdid had agreed to that, but, again with hindsight: it did not mean that Moorish building elements per se were what he wanted for his mosque design itself. The reaction was positive: 'The Q-team considers the design for the mosque as promising. The Team is curious about the way in which the traditional appearance of the elevations will be translated into Dutch construction methods. The architect is requested at this early stage to see that measures are taken that prevent the elevations from becoming soiled with, for example, rainwater.'[123] According to Van Winden, the Q-team effectively expressed its hope that the mosque would not be executed in stucco but in a combination of bricks and tiling, seeing it as the architect's trademark and perfect for a building in which Dutch and Moroccan building elements, or West and East, would meet.

Notably, as much as Ajdid's anti-Moroccan-Islamic representation of Medina was never picked up by the municipality, it was never recognized in architectural discourse either, as observers always seemed to know that the Dubai sponsor must have determined the supposedly Dubai design, especially in light of the architect's focus on the Jumairah. As one journalist reported after a presentation: 'It is striking that the mosque [...] is not a typically Moroccan mosque, but that it has an obviously Arabic design. A request from the patron, according to the architect. "Apparently here applies: who pays the piper, calls the tune," says the municipal council member Abdel Salhi, targeting the Arabian sheikh. Salhi, himself of Moroccan descent, finds it unfortunate that Moroccan influences are totally absent in the architecture. "I find it important that now Moroccan elements should be visible in the interior at least. Otherwise it will be very strange for the visitors, for the greatest part Moroccans, and it will be as if they are in a rented mosque," says the PvdA member.'[124] He was not the only one who had expected the design to be Moroccan. 'When the Rotterdam ex-alderman Meijer of the Green-Left Political Party, who set up the municipal policy on mosques before the year 2002, when Fortuyn was killed, saw our design, he called us,' said Molenaar in an interview. 'He asked why the mosque was so little Moroccan, while it was largely meant for Moroccans. Moroccan mosques often have straight towers and no dome. But the Moroccan patrons were opposed to Moroccan references. They wanted an archetypical mosque.' The then alderman Herman Meijer indeed had thought that the Moroccan-Islamic community in South-Rotterdam would logically choose a Moroccan image, and he himself seemed to be attracted to the Hassan II Mosque in Casablanca.[125] On that same day, Ajdid was interviewed by Rijnmond Radio and Television, explaining that he found Moroccan architecture 'old-fashioned'. All this seemed completely arbitrary to observers, not being able to understand why a Moroccan-Islamic community wanted non-Moroccan architecture. Blaming the sponsor seemed, to them the only logical conclusion. However, as we have seen, the patron's preference for non-Moroccan building elements developed long before he found his financier who never expressed any preference for Medina whatsoever.

Over the following months, again, a series of seemingly straightforward aesthetic and functional requests were made by Ajdid on design adjustments which were actually meant to change Van Winden's design in the direction of his preferred Medina building elements. He wanted the arches in the upper parts of the minarets to be higher, he wanted the minarets 50 meters high in order to establish better proportions, the column-supported arches in the portico were no good and he rejected, once again, the diamond-shaped niches and windows, preferring arches instead. At the first layer, he wanted fewer windows, 'related to glass insurance'. Ajdid now found the roof edge with 'points' to be old-fashioned. There also had to be enough entrance doors, and large enough, 'to prevent traffic jams'.[126] He found that the form of the minaret top and the balustrade for the minaret balcony should be 'more like Medina', that the portico windows should be designed as niches, that the minaret base should have arched little windows and a frame, that the plinth should be darker 'against pollution', and that the roof edge should consist of a cornice rather than of crenellation. Finally, he wanted a roof sheltering the portico arches. In all this, Ajdid effectively ignored a series of suggestions made by Noah Al-Kaddo, the representative of the Maktoum supported Islamic Cultural Center in Dublin whom the sponsor As-Sayegh had suggested for advice, e.g. that the second minaret and front extension should be left out of the design because of their high costs and superfluity.[127] Once again, this goes to show that the sponsor was not concerned with any specific Dubai reference in Rotterdam, let alone the literal copy of the Jumairah that some observers later thought to recognize in it. Meanwhile, Ajdid was growing increasingly frustrated that his architect did not seem to want to incorporate his preferred Medina building elements exactly as he told him. On the other side, precisely because Ajdid tended to use functional and aesthetic reasons for his proposed adjustments, Van Winden thought he could, and was supposed to, improve on them from his own professional expertise and creativity.

On 9 November the architect made an English version of the explanatory texts to accompany his latest drawings, which he took to As-Sayegh in Dubai the following week. While he was there, he made a point of photographing the Jumairah Mosque, including those details that Ajdid had wanted him to remove, like the crenellated roof edge, the thin columns supporting the roofless, open portico, and the cupolas around the central dome. **(Figure 173)** When, in response, Ajdid blatantly referred to an image of the window and door schemes in the Medina façades, Van Winden protested that this example should not be taken too literally. Ajdid, however, then responded that 'we have to apply the basic elements of a mosque'.[128] Strikingly, the patron's Medina-derived building elements were now openly imagined as 'basic mosque elements', meaning that the Medina mosque was taken as the standard for Islamic architecture. Ajdid no longer covered his representationally preferred design merely by supposedly functional requirements or aesthetic preferences but also by absolute generalization. That the 'basic elements' that Ajdid presented had been constructed only recently and that the Prophet's house, whatever it looked like, certainly had never included them is not relevant to our analysis. Apparently, the notion of the Primeval Mosque can supply an unlimited number of building elements for design, whether consisting of some supposedly archetypical ground plan, arcaded gallery, rows of pillars, dome-and-minaret form or decoration pattern. Importantly, in understanding the architectural representations of patrons it is not enough to merely refer to Medina 'as a historical reference', for instance from some supposedly nostalgic old Muslim searching for a recognizable image of the good old days or from some supposedly proud young Muslim looking for an emancipating Islamic symbol in a hostile non-Islamic environment. The whole point is precisely which building elements are chosen, and why those, and how they are transformed and combined with other building elements with the intent of representing a particular construction of Islam. The community leaders of the Taibah and the Essalaam both focused on Medina, but their mosques can be grouped into one category only with the greatest typological abstraction. Where Gaffar wanted to rise above rejected Ahmadiyya and Wahhabi constructions by stressing the role of Mohammed's light and by mixing certain pre-Saudi Medina building elements with certain Hindustani ones, Ajdid wanted to rise above a specifically rejected Moroccan construction by focusing on an encompassing and splendid Islam and by mixing mainly recent Medina building elements with a building scheme as municipally required in the new context.

After the Article 19 procedure had been set in motion,[129] Ajdid travelled with a video-camera to Medina.[130] He zoomed in extensively on details of windows, domes, doors, mouldings, decorations, roof edges, columns and finials. From here on, Ajdid consistently expressed his requests to Van Winden by openly showing and mentioning his Medina video references. **(Figure 174)** He even preferred his façades to have stones the exact size of those of the Medina mosque, and for this he had brought a material sample. Moreover, he insisted on a green roof over the portico, combined with a rectangular niche in the minaret base, medallions in the façades, a dark plinth, window mouldings, repetitive decorations, thicker columns in the minaret lantern, and a zigzag-like decoration band in the minaret shaft he called 'Ottoman'. The latter, whether correct or not, was another sign that it was not any specific Arabic or Mamluk quality of the structure but a conceived pan-Islamic value which the patron projected onto the building. As for the dome, he wanted a band of alternating windows and decorations in the drum.[131] In his own account, he had taken this idea from the decorations above the Medina mosque's entrance. Furthermore, he wanted a thin band of repeating arched windows over the façade doors and windows.[132] In one of Van Winden's drawings, he had colored in some of the Medina building elements he wanted. According to Ajdid, during the design process he had a room full of his architect's successive plan proposals on which he had then repeatedly colored his own preferred Medina features. **(Figure 175)**

A little further down the road, Ajdid tried to get rid of the Jumairah netted dome profiles that the architect had drawn earlier. In a later interview, it came out that Ajdid imagined his own portico cupola would follow the cupolas over the Medina mosque's entrance portals, while his mihrab cupola would be based on the Prophet's dome. The latter's representation would be enhanced by the band of 'windows' that he wanted placed just underneath his mihrab cupola. As for his central dome, Ajdid still justified his desired adjustment with practical arguments. The vertical relief, in his explanation to Van Winden, would better dispose of the water from the many rains in the Dutch climate than would the Jumairah's.[133]

On 4 June, the architect came up with a new plan.[134] **(Figure 176)** In this, Van Winden had introduced the medallions and the window band in the Mihrab, as well as a series of façade arches instead of the former diamond-shapes, as required by his patron. He had also followed through on Ajdid's climatologic dome reasoning and drawn all domes with a new relief that would dispose of the rainwater even better than Ajdid's proposed alternative. Ajdid, as can be expected, stressed that he really wanted the doors and windows to be 'like Medina'. Moreover, he found that the minaret dome was not satisfactory while he still missed the thin band of windows in the façades. He also indicated that the upper window band in the mihrab should be placed higher and the lower should be erased. Overall, he found this particular drawing to have been 'a waste of time'.[135] In his own account, he expected to be able to shift the dome reliefs back to his Medina transformation later and let that part rest. Van Winden, in turn, made reference to a 'difficult' conversation on aesthetics, as he missed the reasoning in the patron's distinctions between what was 'beautiful' and not.[136] Importantly, in pressing for his Medina building elements, Ajdid used aesthetic as well as functional reasons, but where the architect thought he could relate to the latter, he did not always see the point of the first. Actually, of course, both reasonings were neither independent or objective. They had been adjusted to the Medina building elements Ajdid required for the architectural representation of his particular construction of Islam.

On 7 and 8 July, the architect made some new sketches of window schemes. **(Figure 177)** However, Ajdid wanted the piers between the windows completely erased and window openings less broad, essentially answering to the Medina mosque's façades. Moreover, because they would be 'hard to clean', he now wanted 'no real windows' under the dome of the Mihrab. Although he had earlier suggested a band of windows there, he had come to realize that the Prophet's dome had blind niches. Understandably, communication had now reached a low point.[137] Obviously, Ajdid measured his designer's quality not by the creativity or technical, problem-solving capacity of his design proposals but by his ability to translate the essentials of Ajdid's self-constructed representation into matter. On the other hand, the architect found Ajdid's innumerable interventions to be counter-productive, as if he wanted primarily to control the process and did not want to reach a design as a first priority, feeding inconsistent information, confusing requirements and little room for creativity. Ajdid even inquired whether the latest relief on the dome could be adjusted again, referring to video stills of 'the newest mosque in Dubai', which he had filmed on his way to Medina.[138] **(Figure 178)** From the images that Ajdid gave his architect it obviously appeared that what the patron really wanted was not some Dutch-climate adapted form but the deep vertical segmentation that he had identified in the central domes of 'the Middle-Eastern type' since he thought of these as large-scale improvements of the Prophet's dome in Medina.

On 26 July, the architect showed Ajdid a new plan in which he had incorporated most of the patron's remarks, except for the dome segmentation. **(Figure 179)** Despite that, Ajdid still had comments on minaret dome, windows and arches, steering towards the Medina mosque again.[139] On the same date, the designer applied for a building permit, making use of these drawings.[140] That did not stop Ajdid from continuing his Medina-derived comments on the drawings. He wanted the column bases, balconies, and window sizes to be adjusted, the plinth and façades to have a border and the minaret base door provided with an arch. He wanted an octagonal star-shaped motif in the balustrade,[141] the base of the minaret higher in relation to the main building, and the two outside back façade doors to have darkened glass like those closer to the Mihrab.[142] He wanted the plinth raised, and balcony muqarnas and medallions placed higher.[143] He requested that the arches of the main entrance rest on an extra layer of stone[144] and he wanted the arches of the windows to have 'the first two stripes erased'.[145] He wanted the entrance doors executed with the circular motif characterizing the Medina doors,[146] the octagonal part of the minaret smaller, the openings in the minaret's top a little higher and the medallions executed in alternating grey and white blocks. He wanted the roof edge to be 'like Medina', and the mihrab provided with cannelures instead of the old, Jumairah-derived netted pattern. These cannelures were, in Ajdid's later account, actually taken from the gallery at the back façade underneath the Prophet's dome in Medina, and were meant to emphasize the reference to the Prophet's dome in the Rotterdam mihrab. Also the band of blind windows, now to be changed into a row of circular decorations, just below the mihrab's dome were meant as such.[147] **(Figure 180)** He wanted the columns beside the windows to be 'smaller',[148] and he made a series of requests as to the adjustment or addition of decoration patterns, like a zigzag pattern in the minaret shafts instead of the old Jumairah-derived netted pattern, also to be applied to the window arches. He suggested an eight-pointed star decoration in the octagonal part of the minaret, the balcony and in the side and rear window arches, and a triangular pattern in the minaret mouldings.[149] Ajdid actually gave the architect a computer-drawn example of the triangular and octagonal patterns as he had devised it from his Medina images.[150] **(Figure 181)**

Van Winden's client's meticulous representational requirements especially showed when Ajdid insisted that the space between the colonnettes in the minaret lantern be closed up 'as a protection against wind and rain'. When the architect then proposed to place glass there, to keep things transparent – since in his view a lantern was supposed to provide light for its substructure in any architectural tradition, Ajdid did not agree because 'no windows [were] necessary' there. The patron showed no sensitivity towards his architect's functional argument. He wanted the lantern closed in a particular way because it would conform to his videotaped Medina minarets, with rectangular loudspeakers that reached midway in the lanterns in replacing the old saucer-shaped ones. When the architect found out, he protested, since in Rotterdam the loudspeakers were not going to be installed in similar ways, which he felt would make this feature merely an imitation. This argument had no effect, however, as Ajdid had known from the beginning they were loudspeakers and that his representation of them would not be actually used as such. The architect understandably again experienced these discussions with his patron as 'difficult'.[151] In the end, a door was drawn halfway up the colonnettes with the horizontal segmentation of the loudspeaker forms, while the upper half was closed by glass.[152] **(Figure 182)**

On 3 December, the architect incorporated Ajdid's comments in a new plan. **(Figure 183)** A few days after that, Ajdid gave Van Winden some computer drawings of octagonal decoration patterns for domes, blind arches and minarets.[153] Still, the patron wanted his central dome to have a different shape, one with a 'bend' and the vertical segmentation like the idealized 'Middle-Eastern type' that Ajdid had long been pressing for.[154] **(Figure 184)** The patron said he found the existing dome 'not acceptable'.[155] The architect, however, reacted that this would influence the municipal procedure, although he could propose to make the top a little more 'pointy', to which Ajdid agreed. Ajdid rejected a proposed similar change in the minaret top, as he basically wanted to cling to the existing one. Ajdid found, of course, that the aesthetic principle of consistency was not as important as his representational requirements. He furthermore wanted a real balustrade on the top balcony, a grille over the windows in the entrance door arches, a better proportion of white and grey in the zigzag decoration, a further adjustment of the roof edge, and the form of the minarets' lamps taken from his Medina example.[156]

The architect next made a new dome design, inquiring of the municipality whether the proposed change could be executed in the running exemption procedure without causing delay:[157] to this the municipality agreed.[158] **(Figure 185)** On 5 March, the architect incorporated the new form in all three domes, with Ajdid's other requests, in a new plan. **(Figure 186)** The commisioner, however, still wanted the arch scheme of the entrance doors to be corrected, and a small decoration placed in the upper part of the minaret base. Ajdid gave Van Winden a floppy disk containing another black-and-white, systematic overview of his Medina stills.[159]

On 25 March, a coloured plan, with most of Ajdid's requests included, was made to be sent to the municipality as a required further detailing of previously filed plans. **(Figure 187)** However, Ajdid first wanted the blue in the minaret a little more greyish, an adjustment of the mouldings underneath the domes, an adjustment of the dome finials 'according to photo references', and a correction of the stones underneath the arches of the portico.[160] Ajdid complained that not all of his Medina comments had been processed, like the zigzag lines, the window scheme and the arch scheme of the entrance doors. Furthermore, he wanted the door in the northeast façade now to be a window. The minaret's oval shaped dome and the latter's base needed a different proportional relation. And lastly, the balls in the minaret finial should be of unequal sizes.[161] Again, Ajdid provided Van Winden with a new CD with 'clearer pictures',[162] consisting of colour stills from his Medina video focusing on decoration patterns, portico, minaret domes, the muqarnas underneath the balustrades, medallions, metal rosters, octagonal stars, zigzag lines in minaret shafts and arches, the triangular motif in the mouldings, the doors, and the minaret columns above the first balcony. Importantly, he had inserted two particular stills from his video on 'Dubai's newest mosque', focusing on its vertical dome segmentation, into the Medina stills. Ajdid still wanted to get rid of the particular relief planned by the architect. **(Figure 188)**

On 1 April, Van Winden made a new color drawing to be sent to the municipality. **(Figure 189)** However, before that, Ajdid required some final adjustments along the lines of his Medina-derived representation. He wanted the minaret decorations drawn similar to the façade's, at the first minaret layer he wanted a railing where there was no door, the muqarnas underneath the balcony should have three layers instead of four, in the side façade windows the zigzag line should start from the bottom up instead of the other way around, and the portico's arch scheme still required corrections.[163] On 8 April, the architect included these lasts comments in a final color plan which he then sent the municipality.[164] **(Figure 190)** After the Province approved, the building permit was given on 7 May.[165]

Subsequently, on 14 August, representatives of the Emirates National Oil Company Ltd, the Embassy of the UAE The Hague, the Al Maktoum Islamic Center and the municipality met to sign the agreements for the plot trade and ground rent. However, the discussion was turned in a completely different direction because of a letter to As-Sayegh by Alderman Pastors dated 12 August, in which the latter proposed to use the meeting to discuss the mosque's design. He found that 'the mosque itself could also be a model of integration', and that 'also Muslim organizations are now very interested in building mosques to modern architectural design', apparently referring to the members of Memar.[166] In fact, their alternative design had been specifically devised as a theoretical replacement of Van Winden's Essalaam, and Pastors actually had met with them several times to talk about their plan, enthusiastically expressing his admiration for it.[167] For Pastors, this Muslim-initiated message of 'integration architecture' formed a welcome thought. He was a member of a right-wing party called Leefbaar Rotterdam, which had Muslim integration high on its agenda and whose members had protested strongly against the Essalaam Mosque. After the last polls the party came to be represented in office by the Aldermanship for Physical Infrastructure, staffed by Pastors who immediately tried to reverse the municipal stance on mosque architecture in Rotterdam. The permit for the Essalaam, of course, had already been given, but Pastors still took great pains to get the sponsor to adjust the design into something less conspicuous, or, as he said, something more 'modern' and 'Dutch'. The towering minarets, in particular, and the dome gave the mosque too 'Arabian' a look. He specifically wished the largest mosque in Europe to be 'a model of integration'.[168] Notably, like most observers, Pastors automatically – and incorrectly – assumed that it must have been the sponsor who had determined the design and that he was also the one to turn to for any adaptation.

During the meeting, Al-Sayegh, referred to as Director of the Emirates National Oil Company Ltd as well as Chairman of the Foundation Mosque Essalaam, expressed his willingness to talk about the interior, while Pastors indicated that it was the exterior of the mosque that should be discussed. Pastors explained his letter, and stated that the new municipal government had the task of realizing the further integration of minorities. In his account, Dutch families were moving out of town, integration was not going well, and at that moment people looked differently at the position of Islam in society. As an explanation Pastors mentioned the low degree of development of Islamic countries, the relatively high criminality among immigrants with an Islamic background – which also applied to the use of support, health care and other facilities of the state. From this perspective, he looked for a gesture by the Foundation towards the Rotterdam population. Pastors referred to the Mevlana Mosque and stated that now there was a need for a step in the right direction, that there was no need for an even more 'traditional' design but instead for a 'design of the future'. Al-Sayegh responded that the Foundation's intention was exactly to contribute to the integration of Moroccans in Rotterdam. He also said that they would, in concert with the municipality, study whether the design of the exterior could be adjusted to the satisfaction of both parties. He requested the municipality to take the initiative, and to regard the UAE Embassy and the Rotterdam mosque board as conversation partners. On 21 October he would return to Rotterdam and see if an agreement had been reached. To his question as to whether the first pole ceremony could still be held on the 21st, the municipality said that would not be possible because of upcoming efforts in relation to the design. Apparently, the municipality anticipated a complete change of the mosque's design, with the inevitable accompanying restarts of procedures. Also Al-Sayegh's intention to sign the exchange of plots and ground rent agreement provoked the municipal reaction that this would be useless since a change of design would entail different costs for the plot. Parties agreed to put their efforts into finding an agreement on an adjusted design before 21 October.[169]

The report of this meeting shows that nothing concrete had been settled, and read between the lines it clearly shows the diverging expectations of the parties. Two days later, Ajdid stated that the Sheikh would not put any extra money in the design and that changing it now would simply cost too much. Besides, according to him it would not be an 'Arabian Nights palace' at all. 'If there would be no dome and minarets on it, you would not even see that it is a mosque. It is a classic European style. It even looks a little bit like the Rotterdam city hall.'[170] Apparently, the community leader now chose to use the idea of physical integration in answer to municipal projections of socially segregating intentions on the community's side, missing the point of the design's particularly religious meaning to the patron himself. However, where that had been effective in the Wester Mosque's case, no-one seemed to follow the argument here, and other newspapers still reported that construction would have to be postponed and that the design would have to be made more 'contemporary'. In an interview, Pastors stressed that the existing design was too intimidating and too traditional, especially with its 50-meter high minarets and its sugary pastels. In addition, in his opinion, it would completely deviate from its surroundings, a labourers' quarter with the well-known Feyenoord soccer-stadium, where 'even' the light posts did not reach the height of the planned minarets. 'Formally we didn't have any means left to do something about it. Everything was done,' said Pastors, but 'the design is a wrong signal, a reference to the past. This, you find only in the outer provinces of Islamic countries. In Toronto and Rio de Janeiro there are more modern buildings: transparent, progressive. We need something like that, a signal that we want to move forward and that we are integrating'. According to Pastors, the Sheikh appeared to be receptive. 'He recognized it, didn't think of it as a problem. All sensitivities that rise so often in The Netherlands, the suspicion of discrimination for example, weren't there. [...] The original design had its roots in the idea that different communities were growing towards each other. Currently, we rather feel like we are growing apart. We want to turn this trend. That's why a gesture like this, such a serious concession, is so important. They, as well, feel that we have to do this together.'[171]

So, on 10 September, the municipality's architectural department wrote an advice for Van Winden in which it wanted the Essalaam design 'to stimulate integration between populations, to be accessible to all citizens, and to be future-oriented instead of traditional'. These basic notions were first translated into a number of questions on accessibility and incorporation. 'Is the strip in front of the building later optimally accessible to everyone, or will there be a forecourt, a semi-public area that does not invite a public use? Is it, now and in the future, going to be a building that forms part of the direct living area, or does the building stand in its own, somewhat distant zone? Is the building open, does it invite visits? Can women access the court and can they also go inside? Are there any other "public" functions, like a library, in the substructure, and are these recognizably and invitingly designed? Are these spaces also accessible, perhaps even rentable, at the times when the mosque itself is closed? Does the building fit into the surroundings, or is it, and will it remain, an out-of-place element ('*vreemde eend in de bijt*')? [...] Is the building a copy of a mosque from elsewhere and from the past, or does the building search for interpretations of existing typologies and does the design represent current society in The Netherlands? Will the building belong to Rotterdam's cultural heritage, as a series of public buildings adds to the cultural possession of this city? Will the building be more than the representative of emancipation or also a proof of communication with its surroundings and its city?'

'As for the building being open and inviting to be visited, much will, of course, depend on the eventual administration. Will the neighbourhood's school children be invited, can public meetings be held there, will there be sports and games on the forecourt for everyone? However, the board and the architects can look again, now critically, at the factual accessibility. The building is a church, a sacral space, but it also has meeting spaces. Are these spaces also appropriate for use by more non-churchly activities? Is the entrance a gesture of "be welcome" or does the stranger need to be assisted over the threshold? […] It is now a question in what measure the richly detailed building, in its imagery, attracts instead of rejects. The size and the number of forms can lead to a monumentality, preventing people from coming close. What you want to reach from an accessibility criterion is to directly, from the first glance, give an attractive, curious impression that invites to a closer study. The façades deserve a use of materials radiating tranquillity. It is a matter of choosing the material in such a way that a unity develops, a main form that induces "trust" and draws people near instead of pushing them away.'

'Will it be a contemporary building or a sad copy? […] The Zeitgeist aimed at the outcome of diversity in this city. Building according to one's own culture was a means to show the city's multiple colours. Architect, patron and also municipality subsequently […] didn't opt for "the Dutch mosque", or for the Western mosque of 2003. […] Aesthetics agreed to the main form […]. However, in our opinion, points for improvement can still be proposed from the viewpoint of the rejection of unwanted monumentality. As for the proportion between the height of the building and the height of the minarets, the minarets seem too high. We were not able to confirm the mentioned rule of proportion, and it is not applied in modern mosques anyway. We request the architect to re-inspect this proportion. […] As for the use of materials, there are question marks as to what degree minarets and mosque currently melt together into an architectural manifestation. […] The window openings, ornaments and decorations are not always firmly founded in the whole. Through simplification or more modesty a greater obviousness can be reached. [A further] conversation and the processing of its consequences can lead to an enrichment and thereby to the stimulation of acceptance of the building by the public, hopefully leading to a positive evaluation of this new cultural building in Rotterdam.'[172]

Here, we see how preconceived, long-existing ideas on the dysfunctional, ostentatious, irrational and oppressive characteristics of Islamic architecture rise to the surface, to be directly opposed to a supposedly functional, modest, tranquil and liberal Dutch design alternative. Strikingly, the latter is presented as 'progressive' without mentioning the phenomenon that there are many more 'progressive' alternatives in the empirical field. From a representational viewpoint, since a multitude of contemporary designs within the Dutch architectural variety are not 'accessible', do not have 'inviting' courtyards and 'sober' decorations and do not even boast the here much-admired 'transparent' façades, the request that these specific building elements be particularly applied to a mosque is a politico-religious choice, a subjective representation using quasi-objective evolutionary terminology. As the architects of Molenaar & Van Winden, who believed they had progressed beyond the fringeless modernism they saw propagated in this municipal advice, wholeheartedly rejected any of the arguments and problems presented in it, the subjectivity and internal divergence on the matter of what constitutes 'future-oriented' design proved itself. Moreover, as our Fourkaan case study already showed, even if a community leader were to embrace a design the architect or municipality regarded as physically integrated or progressive in some way, it still would not mean that the particular community would be socially integrated from the perspective of the Dutch public, the authorities or other Muslim community leaders. While 'modern-Dutch' architecture and 'social integration' in themselves are ambiguous notions open to divergent interpretations, the presumably straightforward and causal connection between the two has previously been shown to be a downright fallacy.

As can be expected, Ajdid also rejected any change of his precious and painfully achieved design, although not especially because he would have been against Pastor's idea of 'physical integration' or Memar's idea of 'Dutch-Islamic modernity'. The patron thought of his project as the representation of a 'culturally encompassing' construction of Islam specifically opposed to both the official-Moroccan and purist versions embraced by other Moroccan-Islamic community leaders. Consequently, Pastor's and Memar's 'deculturalized' design alternative would perhaps have been a good first sketch for Cheppih but it was simply out of the question as far as Ajdid was concerned. When the municipality responded to his refusal that then they would not sign their part of the plot exchange-agreement, the Foundation threatened to take them to court. The authorities chose not to go that way, and finally decided to sign the agreement. As to the design, it was agreed that there were going to be more talks, on condition that, should they not reach an agreement, the mosque could be built according to the original design.[173] That there was no agreement became very apparent when the foundation stone of the Al-Maktoum Islamic Center was placed on 21 October in the presence of representatives of the municipality and of the Moroccan-Islamic community, with Al-Sayegh as representative of the sponsor and chairman of the Foundation. That the patron had stuck to his choices could be distilled from Pastors' bitter statement that the mosque was 'a missed opportunity', and 'an example of the state of integration in 2003'. Following that, he spoke again of the 'relatively high criminality among citizens with an Islamic background'.[174] The speech of Mayor Ivo Opstelten was experienced by some as even more embarrassing, when he claimed to hope that visiting the mosque would become a nice outing for Rotterdam inhabitants. 'You have indicated that the mosque will be opened up for non-Muslims as well. So, it would be nice if neighbours could show the inside to their guests. These could be nice excursions: we don't always have to go to a museum or the Euromast.'[175] Moreover, the mayor concluded that the municipal request for adjustments had been legitimate, as 'integration sometimes gains more from modesty in the outer forms of faith, than from making it as explicit as possible'.[176] He found it to be a missed opportunity, as he had hoped for a shared entrance for men and women, for 'a gesture with which you would listen to our wish; the wish for acknowledgement of our culture'.[177]

But, on behalf of the mosque organization and the financier, Al-Sayegh wasted no negative words on the issue. His speech was a song of praise to the fine city of Rotterdam, in which he called for all Muslims to participate on all fronts and to become a real part of the society.[178] Directly afterwards, however, Pastors confronted him saying that he had not lived up to the agreement of an adjusted design. Al-Sayegh answered that the agreement had been that the municipality would come with proposals for adjustments itself, otherwise the current design would be maintained. The Foundation had only received some vague ideas, nothing with which the board could really *do* anything. Apparently, Pastors had deemed the 'integration architecture' advice concrete enough to provide Essalaam with tools for change, especially since Memar had already devised a ready-for-use design alternative. Combined with the general and incorrect assumption that the foreign sponsor had determined the design and that he would also be the one to change it, the general lack of insight into the religious motivations behind the architectural representations of Dutch Muslim patrons could only lead to municipal disappointment. However, district chairman Henderson tried to save the day by stating that all parties had put thought in the matter for nearly six years, resulting in the current design and in the completion of procedures. He expressed his happiness that 'the dream now becomes reality'. And lastly, Ibrahim Spalburg, representing SPIOR, the local association of mosques that had brought the two Rotterdam Moroccan-Islamic communities together in their search for a location, tried to appease the situation by arguing that looks were not the most important aspect of a mosque. 'Firstly it is about content and function.'[179] However, as we have come to see by now, any architectural object is actually all about looks, even if idealized not to be. The gratuitous remark, which often seems to start off discussions on the subject, that Muslims do not need a building to pray, 'just some grooves in the sand and the direction to Mecca', is, since it is always and everywhere followed by a heavy discussion on appearances, a representation itself. A mosque is not merely a boundary that marks a space or a place, it is a boundary that marks a reality.

A few days after this event, the architects for the first time gave an extensive interview to a local newspaper. It printed a small frame with the Essalaam's southern façade design next to a large photograph of the Jumairah taken from roughly the same side, both having been provided by the architects. Molenaar rejected the idea that their mosque was 'traditional'. In his words, although it was a stylistic development of a mosque in the Mamluk style, it was not a traditional Mamluk or Moroccan mosque. It was a mixture of different styles, and the new prayer house would be most like a contemporary prayer house in Dubai and the mosque in Medina. 'At first, we also had an idea of designing a Dutch version of a Moroccan mosque. But the mosque board didn't think much of that. It was rather a sort of presumptuousness on our part. Like: We will show you what kind of mosque should be placed there.' The architect told the interviewer that they subsequently looked at and studied different mosques from all over the world, resulting in the current design. Because of the limited plot, the mosque had to be layered and its minarets, in order for the right proportions to be maintained, this high. Otherwise 'you get an amputated mosque. We wanted to design a dignified and proud mosque. [...] And isn't it magnificent that at such a place you have a building that radiates the dignity of an important religious community in this city'. According to Molenaar, the use of Oriental and other foreign elements in Dutch architecture would be visible more often in the future. 'We see the rediscovery of ornament and dignity in the form of a building as very central to contemporary architecture. As a result of modernism, the meaning of expressive buildings has been lost. We, on the other hand, find it important to continue the lines of history in the future.' The architect compared things with the period around 1900, when architects like Berlage rose. Then as well, buildings were constructed with Oriental influences. 'The times that everything has to be modernistic, are over. There is no longer a dominant style. On the contrary, it is fantastic that there are influences from all sorts of exotic cultures on the originally Dutch culture.'[180]

Notably, from this moment, almost all media reports, architectural critiques and architectural theses on the subject would describe the Essalaam design as 'Mamluk' while evaluating it as largely derived from the Dubai Jumairah mosque – almost always completely missing the importance of the Medina reference despite the fact that the architects did mention it. However, only from a much-abstracted typological viewpoint can the Essalaam and the Jumairah be put, together with the Medina Mosque, into a 'Mamluk' box. On closer inspection, even just of the article and its two images, the differences between the Rotterdam design and the Dubai mosque are multiple, especially knowing that many of the Jumairah-derived building elements had once been included in the design process but were subsequently erased and substituted one by one for Medina-derived building elements by the patron. Moreover, as the design process also shows, although the overall scheme of the Essalaam might seem similar to the Jumairah's it had actually been largely set at a very early stage by municipality and Q-team, even before the Jumairah or 'the Sheikh from Dubai' had come into the picture. Furthermore, the 'dignity' and 'pride' mentioned several times in the article were values that the architects had picked up directly from the patron's representational requirements. The latter had been projected onto the most recent Medina mosque's extension as the supposed materialization of a transcending and world-encompassing Islam in opposition to the official-Moroccan and purist versions that the community leader had come to reject. The Jumairah had been introduced from the architect's side, and had seemed an excellent, shared representation after the patron had outspoken his admiration for the building, but it later appeared that it had only been one of many examples of Islamic architecture to the community leader. In fact, it was the Medina mosque that counted as the culmination of pan-Islamic splendour, incorporating all thinkable greatness of Islam to the patron, while any supposed and separated 'Mamlukness' was completely and utterly irrelevant to him.[181]

On 24 November, the first pole was placed into the ground and construction started.[182] However, even during construction – the coordination of which the architect was no longer involved in – Ajdid continued to influence the design. In the course of the next year, he wanted the triangular decoration mouldings, the balcony muqarnas and the portico's column shafts in the construction drawings to be more in line with his Medina references.[183]

Moreover, the designer enquired of Ajdid why he had chosen to close up the back façade openings beside the mihrab at the layer of the men's prayer space. As this, in the architect's opinion, would drastically decrease the amount of light in that room, he advised that the closures were substituted for glass windows.[184] In his own account, however, the patron had decided to close up the windows around the Mihrab precisely because there would be too much light there, 'disturbing the visibility of the imam'. Strikingly, whereas Gaffar in Amsterdam had decided to add openings in the back façade exactly beside the mihrab, seemingly to 'functionally' lighten the room but in fact to enhance his Brelwi representation of the Light of Mohammed, here the intruding daylight was given no meaning at all. The kind of light that did matter to Ajdid a lot was the outer lighting, in which, in his account, he also represented the Medina Mosque and for which he had a model made. After that, some 3D images were made as well. **(Figure 191)** In the end, the only important Medina building elements that Ajdid regretted not to have been able to convince his architect of were the green roof over the entrance, the white dome with blue mosaics over the portico, and the vertical relief in the central dome.

From 2005 onward, part of the Moroccan Essalaam community expressed their growing discontent with the fact that the financier had moved several 'non-Moroccan' connections into the board.[185] Led by Mohamed Ebraymi, chairman of an organization for older Moroccans in Feijenoord, they felt that Boutaher had frittered away their mosque – by now officially named 'Al-Maktoum Islamic Center Rotterdam' instead of Essalaam Mosque – to the Dubai Sheikh. In December 2006 they even established a Foundation, allegedly representing the interests of 95% of the community and explicitly meant to regain power.[186] A year later, the built-up tension almost resulted in violence.[187] And in June 2008, the board chose to use a court order in its attempt to deny the most adamant of its rival community leaders access to their prayer hall.[188] Although both parties accused each other of 'religious conservatism', in the media it was maintained that the conflict was not about Islam but about 'money and influence'.[189] However, as Boutaher had earlier exclaimed: 'What do they want to infuence? That the imam should preach something else? It costs 15000 euro a month to exploit the new mosque. Will the community pay that from its own income?'[190] The next month, Moroccan protesters physically attacked Ajdid and verbally threatened Boutaher.[191] Because of a financial conflict between the board and the general contractor,[192] at the time of writing the mosque still remained to be completed. **(Figure 192)**

Conclusion:
The Architectural Representation of Islam in The Netherlands

Design Interpretation and Diverging Realities

As a first conclusion to this study, it can be stated that the complex empirical field of Muslim-commissioned mosque design in The Netherlands lends itself only with great distortion to reduction to a single typological scheme. Only highly selective perception would allow the observer to see a progression from monolithic 'Indian', 'Indonesian', 'Turkish' and 'Moroccan' building styles towards a 'Dutch' building style, to conceptualize an evolution from 'traditionalist' designs via 'hybrid' or 'Efteling' and 'Disney' designs towards a 'modern' design, or to observe a shift from 'shelter' mosques, 'homesickness' mosques and 'emancipation' mosques towards 'integration' or 'liberal' mosques. If earlier observers have made such observations, they did so by focusing on exactly those architectural representations and representations of architecture that would seem to support such a scheme while unknowingly or pragmatically leaving out those that would confuse it. If typological labels such as these are upheld as analytical concepts, the Mobarak Mosque could be called 'an embarrassing shelter mosque for an oppressed Muslim community eventually leading to the Essalaam Mosque as the modern result of Dutch Muslim emancipation successfully completed', with as much right as it could be called 'a successfully adapted modern Dutch design eventually leading to the Essalaam Mosque as a traditionalist sign of Muslim homesickness in a failed process of social integration'. Any analyst of architecture who wishes to surpass a plain morphological exercise without interpretation has to realize that his possible focus and personal perspective on aspects of culture, modernity, nationality and/or integration might, but does not need to be, a reality as represented in the design. To make things even more complicated, different building elements within one object of research might very well have been introduced from different realities and therefore have to be analyzed as different reality representations. If not, the analyst will project the wrong intentions onto the wrong parties, in no small way assisted by the many pragmatic reinterpretations and strategic self-attributions of the parties involved.

First of all, municipalities, for all the divergences that they showed among each other but also among and even within their own departments, councils and commissions, mainly looked towards their future mosque as an opportunity for Muslims to show their stance on incorporation into Dutch society. Existing cultural building styles from the Muslim home countries were generally seen as un-Dutch, to be rejected, adjusted or stimulated according to the relevant municipal body's ideological position on a scale ranging from total assimilation to untouched cultural diversity. Not surprisingly, municipalities were basically concerned with relations between Muslims and non-Muslims as social groups within a shared political unit. They reacted to mosque applications by constructing ideas about the particular architectural forms to be seen as a suitable expression of these relations and subsequently used these ideas in location proposals, the interpretation of zoning plans, the setting of urban delimitations, the evaluation of aesthetic qualities, the reaction towards neighbourhood objections and in architectural advices. Before anything else, in the municipal reality a Dutch mosque was a representation of the manner in which 'non-Dutch' Muslims were to be socially integrated into 'The Netherlands'.

On the other hand, designers mainly looked towards their future mosque as an opportunity for Muslims to construct a new building style that would creatively overcome the assumed clash between Islamic architectural traditions and the Dutch physical context. It could be done by blending a Dutch-cultural building style with a Muslim-cultural building style, it could be done by reducing cultural forms to general functional or religious principles, and it could be done by somehow combining these actions. However, all involved heavily subjective abstraction since in the chaotic field of the built environment no such things as objective 'cultural' building styles or 'deculturalized' functional or religious principles were to be found except in the mental constructions of the designers in question. The rejection and selection of building elements from the Dutch and the Islamic architectural fields was primarily based on an architect's pre-existing design preferences in the face of contesting visions of architectural contemporaneity. During this creative process, a presumably shared Islamic liturgy was seen as the untouchable essential whereas the assumed cultural building styles were seen as the variable suppliants of outer imagery, to be rejected, adjusted or stimulated according to the architect's own stance on typological progress. Before anything else, in a designer's reality a mosque was the representation of the manner in which 'traditional' Muslims were to be incorporated into the diaspora 'modernity'.

Diverging from these issues of nationality and modernity as they were projected onto Dutch mosque designs by municipalities and architects, however, patrons themselves mainly looked towards their future mosque as an opportunity to define their religious vision towards opposing versions. By selecting particular building elements from the complex field of Islamic architectural history, elements whose contemporary associations had a certain meaning to them, they distinguished an individual construction of Islam. Patrons were not always imams or Islamic specialists versed in religious dogma, but they invariably took a specific interest in expressing their religious construction by strategically focusing on its diacritica, meaning, those of its elements that in their perception made it recognizable against contesting versions. It was a matter of focusing on the outer fringes of Islam, of producing boundaries between Muslimness and non-Muslimness, but what steered their design preferences was not any obvious divergence with the larger non-Islamic context but the intrinsic divergence of the own Islamic boundary definition with those upheld by other Muslim community leaders. In other words, self-definition through Islamic-architectural means did not revolve around being Muslims against non-Muslims, but around being good Muslims against bad Muslims. As a consequence, 'cultural' building elements were used but only to the degree and in the manner that patrons found them to suit the religious construction they had produced first, and this completely depended on the way that the 'cultural stuff' was used in the architectural representations of patrons embracing those views of Islam that were regarded to be particularly false. Before anything else, in a patron's reality a mosque was the representation of his specific construction of Islam as opposed to contesting versions circulating within his self-defined culture group.

However, where municipalities and architects were reasonably straightforward in the presentation of their architectural constructions of nationality and modernity towards each other and towards patrons, the latter were much less direct towards municipalities and architects in that the particularity of their religious construction was invariably completely downplayed. No patron seems to have ever started out by saying 'I am a Muslim who follows the such-and-such path of Islam and I need to recognize it in my mosque design', instead beginning with a list of practicalities, with a statement the equivalent of 'we are Muslims and therefore our design should be Islamic' and perhaps with some seemingly general and vague images without explication, forcefully upholding the claim to speak for Islam as one faith and leaving municipalities and architects with all kinds of expectations on the forms that were to follow. Only in the course of an often very long design process with an often very unsuspecting designer and municipality would it appear that the particularity of the Islamic construction led to a great particularity in design preferences on the patron's side. In fact, already by consciously selecting a certain architect with a certain design oeuvre, on the basis of his expected positive reaction to forms that had been in mind from the very beginning, patrons effectively managed to determine a great part of their eventual mosque. By strategically steering the designer, and, if necessary and feasible, dismissing him and replacing him with someone more likely to accept their formal preference and influence, they subsequently managed to determine a great part of the rest of the design as well. Strikingly, the particular building elements required were still mostly motivated not by a particular construction of religion but on a mixture of culture, function, practicalities, aesthetics, budget and/or integration, depending on the reality of the party at the other side of the table. This frequently led to much confusion since the particular way that the patron subsequently filled in these supposedly objective aspects in reaction to proposals from architect and municipality appeared to be arbitrary and unpredictable. This common characteristic, which seemed inefficient from the point of view of designers and municipalities in their assumption that patrons themselves would want to reach a design as good, as economical and therefore as direct as possible as well, beckons an explanation.

From a representational perspective, this explanation should be looked for in the very fact that the main purpose of a patron's building activities was to represent his own construction of Islam as the ultimate over other versions. Consequently, the 'constructional' aspects of his Islam could not be admitted. Barth's 'cosmologies in the making' could never be presented as actually having been 'made', since the whole purpose of a cosmology is to position a group in a meaningful, fixed and unchanging cosmos.[1] A religious construction as materialized in a religious building by definition is exclusive and excluding towards contesting versions of that religion and that building. If a temple's obvious 'making' is annoyingly requested by a researcher to be explained and motivated, its 'maker' will have to resort to 'non-cosmological' argumentation, made up on the spot along the lines of expected plausibility. Or, in terms of Schefold, Domenig and Nas, the enquiring researcher will by definition be led to believe by his informants that their version of a certain building type is objective, historically sound, and the one and only truth, leading, in the face of an inconsistent empirical field, only to confusion on his side if he would not relate that version to divergent ones in the same culture area as a meaningful transformation in a process of mutual contrasting. And lastly, in Mekking's terms of the representational cycles of architectural themes, a religious building such as a mosque should be seen as a cosmic center constituting the Axis Mundi or the very navel of the world. Either constructed to *subjugate* everything else or to *precede* everything else, it always uses a multitude of possible building elements cutting cleanly through imaginary boundaries of history and geography as long as it suited its cosmic meaning. Any explanation reducing that meaning would be deemed highly inappropriate, if not unthinkable, by its patron. Therefore, he would only explicate, when asked, the obviously 'constructional' aspects of his architectural representation in terms of objectified but very subjective and flexible variables like culture, style, aesthetics and function. To Mekking, as we recall, one of the most important characteristics of architecture as a representational medium was that it enabled a patron to make a profound statement towards particular target groups without resorting to rationalization or verbalization.

To put it more concretely, it simply could not be directly communicated towards the architect or the municipality why a Muslim mosque patron required some very particular building elements indeed. At the point of being asked, a patron would never say 'that dome from that building and that minaret from that area combined and transformed in that way represent this version of Islam against that one', but things like 'a mosque simply needs a dome', or 'that sort of dome is merely what all domes look like in our culture', or 'Islam does not need culture', or 'that sort of minaret gives a beautiful impression', or 'a real mosque does not include retail', or 'we want a proud and dignified building', or 'we simply do not have the money for anything else', generally confirming already critical observers in their evaluation that most Muslim-commissioned mosque designs in The Netherlands have been a matter of cheap nostalgia, misplaced pride, architecture-historical ignorance, incorrect functional choices, or plain bad taste. However, within the complex empirical field of mosque design in The Netherlands as it eludes consistent typologies, the patron's all-pervading drive to create the ultimate cosmic center actually is the only valid comparative criterion that can both consistently explain the stylistic inconsistencies of the architectural objects researched as well as the argumentational inconsistencies of their Muslim patrons.

In the case of the The Hague Mobarak Mosque, successive patrons insisted on the inclusion of foundation stones, façade, minaret forms, and name from the Qadiani Mubarak Mosque without ever clearly mentioning that, and especially why, they wanted them to be included. In their reality, the mosque was meant to be the representation of Qadiani Islam, a continuation of the world-wide Islamic Renaissance that had begun with the construction of their Promised Messiah's mosque and minaret in Qadian. As much as the latter, it was to be a genuine cosmic center, a blessed lighthouse lighting its dark surroundings of unbelief, specifically designed in reaction to contesting Islamic visions circulating within the own culture group. Towards the unsuspecting architects and municipal departments, however, the successive patrons merely claimed their choices for certain building elements to have been either generally Islamic, specifically Pakistani or aimed at blending in with Dutch society. In the case of the first Taibah Mosque in Amsterdam, the patron essentially projected a Sufi shrine quincunx with a central dome and four corner turrets over Mohammed's grave in Medina, with the Prophet forming the ultimate holy man, the source of all Sufi sanctity and the main identifying value for his Brelwi community. His mosque was to represent the ultimate, Brelwi Islam in opposition to particularly false versions like the one in The Hague. To the architect, however, the patron only spoke of the quincunx and Mohammed's holy places as carrying general Islamic meaning, whereas to the municipality the patron chose to present his prayer house as a general socio-cultural center in which all Muslims could participate. The patron of the second Amsterdam Taibah Mosque kept the old Sufi shrine quincunx but turned attention even more towards Medina, introducing particular building elements from the minaret and dome of Mohammed's grave and combining them with his own creations of lighting and transparency. The latter were a representation of the Holy Prophet's Light as the most important identifying and unifying characteristic of scattered Brelwi communities and as the only legitimate source of Islam. In his reality, the mosque was to be a cosmic center, the materialization of Mohammed in the face of those heretics denying the Prophet's unique and finalizing position in the cosmos. To his unsuspecting architects, however, he explained his combinations and transformations with arguments of Surinamese culture, general aesthetics and everyday practicalities of visibility, whereas towards the municipality he explained the more transparent of his building elements to be aimed at social adaptation.

The initiator of the Wyldemerck Mosque in Balk required the building elements of a layered roof, a basin and four pillars – the strongly localized Islamic features associated with the cosmic mountain supported by holy men – in setting off the Islam of an idealized kampong community against contesting versions in the Moluccas. To his architect and the government, he initially merely claimed his community to need some basic liturgical requirements of orientation, ablution and entrance separation, whereas subsequently he only claimed to require some more recognizable Ambonese mosque features since that is where his community came from and would eventually return to. The initiator of the Ridderkerk Bait Ar-Rahman Mosque, in his turn, specifically wished to embrace a less localized and traditional Islamic construction and prayer hall than his predecessor in Wyldemerck. His cosmic center was to be the representation of a wider and more modern Islam, explicitly incorporating the four pillars to be publicly associated with the four schools of Islam supporting a genuine hemispherical dome instead of a group of holy men supporting a layered mountain. Towards the architect, however, he never spoke of that important distinction, merely representing his required building elements as typically Indonesian. On the other hand, what the initiator of the Waalwijk An-Nur Mosque required was to represent a more orthodox Islam, shedding off any remaining localized and regionalized Islamic constructions and building elements as visible in both Wyldemerck and Ridderkerk, aiming for his mosque to conspicuously use building elements from the Kaaba Mosque as the very source of Islam, the absolute center of the Islamic world, with his own future prayer hall as a genuine cosmic center in its own right.

The patron of the Almelo Yunus Emre Mosque particularly required that his prayer hall not be associated with religious fervour but with secular values instead, selecting a standardized Anatolian village mosque's building elements as associated with a harmonious, pre-urban community, and subsequently stressing the mobilization of all political, economical and religious strata in the municipality in representing the non-exclusiveness, liberalism and tolerance of Islam. Towards the architect and municipality, however, he said he preferred a village mosque model since that is where his community members came from. In case of the Sultan Ahmet Mosque in Zaanstad, the patron fully supported the architect in his preference for this particular cosmic center to be the representation of a modern-republican Islam, with his designer selecting and combining stylized Ottoman and national-Turkish building elements associated with modernity and the separation of state and religion. However, he never mentioned any of these motivations towards the municipality, and to the media he merely stated that the design was made to fit its physical surroundings. The patron of the Wester Mosque in Amsterdam, in the creation of his own cosmic center, specifically preferred classical Ottoman building elements associated with strongly sacral values and a much greater role of religion in the public sphere than in the case of the contesting Islamic construction as embraced and represented in Zaanstad. Towards his architect, however, he consistently legitimized his choices with reasons of the superior cultural, aesthetic and functional characteristics of his preferred design, whereas to the municipality and the media he tended to stress reasons of emancipation in the sence of the design's visibility and of social adaptation in the sense of its materials.

In case of the Al Fourkaan Mosque in Eindhoven, the patron strongly rejected the official Moroccan construction of Islam and required his own prayer hall to be a marker of Islam in its most original and authentic state. He insisted on the incorporation of a small number of recognizably 'Islamic' building elements but, paradoxically, only for the reason and in the way that their main message was their abstraction from culture, positioning his religious view as pure and far removed from any worldly and profane temptations. In this, he regarded the supposed 'Dutchness' of the rest of the building as a necessary and neutral coating, not as yet another cultural influence on religion or a new local-Islamic building style. Towards his architect, however, he merely explained his cosmic design preferences with the argument of budget. The patrons of the El Islam Mosque in The Hague, in their turn, required their cosmic center to show a purely Moroccan Islam, using exactly those building elements that were to be associated with the Moroccan king as the rightful successor to the Prophet. Towards their architects, however, they initially never actually mentioned the Moroccan building elements as a necessary requirement, whereas only secondarily did they explain their Moroccan preferences purely for reasons of keeping up Moroccan culture. Meanwhile, towards the municipality, they confirmed any Dutch building elements incorporated from the side of the designer as an expression of social integration. Subsequently, the patron of the Rotterdam Essalaam Mosque required his religious construction to be associated with pan-Islamic values, represented by a prayer hall using specific building elements from the Medina Mosque as the encompassing center of the universe, with his ideal Islam surpassing all national versions and his ideal cosmic center including all Muslim cultural building styles. Towards his architect, however, he simply rejected things Moroccan as 'old-fashioned' and anything Dutch as 'too modern', subsequently preferring an avalanching multitude of 'cultural' building elements, only to gradually work his way towards his required representation of the Medina Mosque. All the while, he never bothered to explain its importance to either architect or municipality, only momentarily resorting to the argument of physical adaptation in a fruitless endeavour to get his design accepted by the public.

Overcoming the Clash of Classifications

By now it must be clear that any proposed 'solution' to the perceived 'problem' of mosque design in The Netherlands, negating the reality of Muslim patrons themselves and merely projecting issues of nationality and modernity onto their architectural preferences, might raise public admiration and expectations but is bound to miss the point and fail when actually confronted with the diverse field of religiously contesting community leaders. For one, Dutch Muslim mosque patrons do not seem to have been looking to express their stance on social integration into Dutch society in their designs as much as has been thought by municipalities or even as much as they themselves have claimed from time to time. On the one hand, a patron as in the case of the Al Fourkaan Mosque, who voluntarily steered his design away from building elements associated with his home country and towards austerity and a minimum of Islamic recognizability, showed no actual interest in physical integration per se and was regarded as socially non-integrated by the authorities altogether. On the other hand, patrons as in the case of the El Islam Mosque, who were regarded as socially integrated by their municipality and who confidently spoke of physical integration themselves, subsequently insisted on the inclusion of recognizable 'cultural' building elements even to the point of switching designers against the municipal will. Moreover, a patron as in the case of the Wester Mosque verbally and successfully associated a minor, material part of his design to social integration while leaving the religious implications of his overall design preference unmentioned, whereas a patron as in the case of the Essalaam Mosque unsuccessfully defended himself against allegations of social segregation by weakly using the physical adaptation argument without even the slightest tendency to actually correct the obvious misinterpretations of the 'cultural' building elements that he had introduced. All in all, it could be said that a patron's main representational motivation, his particular construction of Islam, was invariably imagined to be more general than it was, and variably imagined to be more socially integrating than it was meant to be, with Dutch society having been much less of an actual target group during the design process than those fellow Muslims who embraced contesting views of Islam. To be sure, this does not mean that he did not want his community to be truly integrated in some way. It merely means that the particular architectural forms he required cannot be deduced from his view on how to accomplish social integration, whereas they can be deduced from his particular version of Islam. The latently or at times even manifestly presumed causal connection between social and physical integration of Muslims in The Netherlands as upheld in the municipal reality quickly works out to be a downright fallacy.

Of course, a municipality may still aim for its view on ideal social relations between Muslims and non-Muslims to be expressed in the architectural forms of any mosque within its borders, but in order to reach it more efficiently, it would better not project that aim onto its Muslim patrons even should the latter claim to share it. A municipality should certainly not evaluate the end-result of a design process in terms of a successful or an unsuccessful social integration of the Muslim community involved. If there is a 'problem' with mosque design in The Netherlands, it is not one of clashing cultures, of Islam versus The Netherlands, but of clashing classifications, of a municipal reality versus a patron's reality. It therefore calls for a different kind of 'solution' other than trying to forcibly convince municipal Muslims that they should embrace a particular building style symbolizing anything from emancipation to adaptation. To begin with, a municipality should not attempt to directly enter a discussion on possible means of social or physical integration of 'the Muslims' behind mosque patrons, since the latter have been shown to easily find ways to translate their a priori representational choices in either 'emancipative' or 'adaptive' terms if they so desire. Instead, a municipality first needs to realize the existence of the multitude of Islamic varieties within The Netherlands as much as within any Muslim home country. Then, it needs to find out the particular constructions of Islam as produced by the patrons it has within its municipal borders. Finally, it needs to aim at reaching a basic understanding of the particular architectural representation that a patron has already had in mind before establishing first contact, even if he can be predicted to prefer steering the discussion towards non-religious aspects. Once the basic representational motivation behind the assembly of building elements, chosen by the patron in the creation of his ultimate cosmic center, is understood and accepted, only then should the municipality enter into a more efficient discussion on how this particular representation could be materialized by other means.

Moreover, Muslim patrons have also been shown to have been much less occupied with showing their stance on architectural incorporation into the diaspora modernity than previously assumed by architects, even if some patrons later claimed such. The New Construction style of the Mobarak Mosque, the Functionalist style of the first Taibah Mosque, the Universalist style of the Bait Ar-Rahman Mosque and An-Nur Mosque, the post-Modernist style of the Wester Mosque, the Bossche School style of the Al Fourkaan Mosque or the neo-Mamluk style of the Essalaam Mosque: all these 'styles' prove to have been as good as non-existent in the realities of patrons themselves. As long as their own religious construction was recognizably incorporated in the form of certain combinations and transformations of building elements, whatever their designers verbally made of them or physically added to them was of minor importance as long as it did not disturb the overall construction of Islam as produced in the face of contesting versions. However, before that basic layer of required building elements was reached, even the most phlegmatic architect could be condemned to a lengthy trial-and-error process if he did not grasp his patron's particular Islamic construction. Mostly, the tendency to start directly from a list of practical requirements, a budget, and some seemingly vague images towards a sketch proposal proved to be counterproductive. Forms invariably gained priority over costs and practicalities in the course of the design process, although the latter were often introduced as the most important factors during first contact. Even if the patron claimed to have only very general requirements of architectural imagery, he proved to think with a very particular religious construction in mind requiring a very particular architectural representation. And even if the architect thought he had more or less thoroughly studied Islamic architecture in its religious or cultural aspects, chances were that the patron 'had not read that book'. All books used were written from a very particular, selective stance, although each claimed to be general to its chosen subject or even to have found the ultimate definition of the truly Islamic. Moreover, within the variety of literature that resulted from the variety in stances, the particular choice by the architect in question and his particular choice for only particular parts of his literature only led him further away from his patron's representational requirements. His first sketch by definition was based not on some objective reality but on a subjective idea of a subjective idea of a reality, and the chances that his patron had constructed the same reality were very slim indeed.

Of course, architects may still aim at creating some sort of a 'culturally blended' or 'deculturalized' building style if they wish to do so, but, in order to reach that aim efficiently, what they better not do is project that aim onto their patrons beforehand. As shown, the patron who supposedly aimed at a certain new style in the architect's reality might have looked at the building elements involved from a completely different angle. In this case, if there is a 'problem' with mosque design in The Netherlands, it is not one of clashing cultures but, again, of clashing classifications, of an architect's reality versus a patron's reality. The 'solution' is, once again, not to forcibly convince Muslim communities that they should, at last, embrace a 'progressive' building style, and neither is it to connect to a Muslim patron who happens to share a preference for those building elements that are associated, in the architect's reality, with 'modernity' and then presenting that patron as a general example for other Muslim patrons. Chances are that the preferred building elements concerned might be embraced only by particular patrons who interpret and incorporate them with their particular religious constructions in mind. They would then use them in a process of religious contestation with community leaders embracing contesting views of Islam and architectural representations, making the assumedly general example a factually specific exception right from the start. For instance, a Moroccan patron rejecting the official Moroccan construction of Islam as in the case of the Al Fourkaan might readily include in his architectural representation what seem to be 'modern' building elements from the architect's perspective whereas in the patron's own reality these lead less to a new 'style' than to a representation of Sunna purity. Subsequently, he might stimulate other Moroccan patrons as in the case of the El Islam and the Essalaam to resort to what they would see as contesting Islamic constructions and designs. In fact, of course, in light of ongoing processes of religious construction, mutual contrasting and reality representation, the chance that there will ever be a Dutch Islam or Dutch-Islamic building style is about as realistic as the chances that there will ever be a Hindustani/ Moluccan/ Turkish/ Moroccan Islam or -Islamic building style, or, for that matter, a Dutch Christianity or Dutch-Christian building style. Recognizing any of these in the world's complex empirical field will only have meant abstracting the latter to a point of stonily negating the many diverging religious and architectural constructions unavoidably dotting the field. Instead, as in the case of a municipality, the architect would do better to aim at reaching a basic understanding of the particular architectural representation that a patron has already had in mind before establishing first contact, even if he can be predicted to prefer steering the discussion towards non-religious aspects. Again, only once the basic representational motivation behind the assembly of building elements, chosen by the patron in the creation of his ultimate cosmic center, is understood and accepted, can the architect enter into a more efficient discussion on how this particular representation could be materialized by other means.

Towards a Dutch Mosque Design?

If you will, the phenomenon of 'the Dutch mosque' already exists in all the extant purpose-built prayer halls that dot the Dutch urban landscapes, as these prove to be no simple 'copies' or 'pastiches' at all but complex transformations developed within contemporary Dutch contexts. Architectural critiques in newspapers, magazines, debates and exhibitions in The Netherlands have tended to compare only the most superficial and judgmental interpretations of these mosques with the publicly much-admired modern Dutch design alternatives created by architectural students. Besides leading to municipal expectations and ever so many municipal disappointments, they also raised social tensions since Muslim patrons who did not wish to use these popular alternatives were confronted with accusations of segregation and fundamentalism. The fact is, however, that as long as a first design proposal has not yet entered the design process, nothing definite can be said of its chances of survival. The preceding study has shown that it depends wholly on the construction of Islam as produced by the individual patron himself, and if and how the latter is willing to come to a compromise with a certain municipality and designer.

Although the procedure, generally followed by socially engaged designers when creating an alternative mosque typology, of researching the history of Islamic architecture and studying the new urban context and the programmatic requirements of a particular commission genuinely aims to be very contextual, from the patrons' perspective it could not be less so. As we have seen, an architect's pre-existing design philosophy will have ultimately determined how he looks at architectural history. Inevitably, from the inconsistent flux of 'Dutch' and 'Islamic' architecture, he will have had to extract a limited number of building elements, events, rules, values, principles, and developments. He may present these as having been objectively present in the empirical field and to have neutrally determined his proposed design alternative, but they will in fact have been subjectively selected and adapted to fit a stylistic preference already there. As a result, in practice there is a good chance that the particular Muslim patron will react by completely dismissing the proposal. To him, the architectural representation of Islam has nothing to do with seemingly detailed typologies or morphologies to be extrapolated from the built environment by a detached architectural researcher, but everything with the specific religious construction as he chose to oppose it to contesting versions, and with the associated building elements as he selected and transformed them in the mental creation of his ultimate cosmic center. The ubiquitous 'domes and minarets' will not disappear from the architectural requirements of Muslim patrons anytime soon, not because the latter lack the knowledge of new approaches to old functions, or need to be reminded of home, or search for a globalized Islamic identity, or want to defy Dutch society, or think in colonial stereotypes, or choose Orientalist architects, or live in paternalistic municipalities, or connect to fundamentalist sponsors, or because they have not been confronted with enough alternative typologies. Domes and minarets will continue to be built, because they will remain indispensable in providing the most obvious means for incorporating the very specific architectural diacritica needed to identify a patron's ultimate Islam against lesser versions.

Based on the preceding case studies, the preconceived 'Polder Mosque' design alternative as devised by Memar for the Essalaam Mosque would not have suited most of the Muslim patrons treated here, particularly not the Essalaam's, but it would arguably have stood a good chance as a first proposal for the Al Fourkaan. To be sure, that does not mean that the Al Fourkaan is to be connected to an integrated, liberal and transparent community and that the rest of them are not: all of these values – as well as the lack of them – are projected onto the objects from a specific architect's reality and do not constitute facts. Neither does it mean that designs like the Al Fourkaan's are to be connected to younger generations of Muslims and designs like the Essalaam's to older generations. The patrons of the Essalaam and the Wester Mosque had hardly reached the age of thirty when they started their projects, whereas the patron of the Al Fourkaan had already retired. Moreover, the actual initiator of the new Annasr design, which was planned to hurl the Dutch mosque into the 21st century as the culmination of social and physical integration of young Dutch Muslims, was Khalil El Moumni, a first generation Riffian-Moroccan imam who did not speak Dutch and who was not considered particularly liberal by the Dutch authorities. The age of patrons, with the physical integration of Muslims in The Netherlands having been confidently predicted by observers to take place after each next-generational hill, appears to play a much less determining role in the architectural representation of Islam than presumed.

In fact, when looked at some of the – allegedly – most architecturally adapted mosque designs in The Netherlands, the Al Fourkaan, the Polder

Mosque and the Annasr, interesting connections can be discerned that have less to do with age than with religious attitudes. Like in the case of the Al Fourkaan's patron Achmed Cheppih, El Moumni's Islamic stance had explicitly been unwelcome in Morocco, where it was seen as anti-royalist.[2] In his own words, 'Ordered by the Ministry of Islamic Affairs, I stopped preaching. […] The reason for the suspension, as far as I know, was that I promised my Lord, from the moment I ascended the pulpit, the pulpit of God's messenger, that I would never lie, feign, or flatter from this pulpit, and that I would never kneel or bow for anyone other than the One, the Only, who has created me. […] Our ancestors moved away from the Arabian Peninsula and spread over the earth to preach the eternal message of the messenger of the right guidance, our Lord Mohammed. They thereby saved humanity from digression and led men to the right path, from ignorance to the light. Thus were our fathers, when they lived on dates and water, and when they rode horses, camels, mules and donkeys, and when they sailed boats. But when God tested them with matter and wealth, they were tempted by the two. They then forgot their God-given task, and lost the cause that was bestowed upon them by the messenger of God when he said to them: "Let those among you who were witnesses inform those who were absent." Despite the temptation and misery that hit the community, however, one group among them will be saved thanks to God's guard, to accomplish its mission and fulfil its duty until Judgment Day. […] I hereby call upon the Islamic boys and girls abroad ['*in den vreemde*']. I say to them: "Your task in this land is big and important."'[3]

As a consequence of El Moumni's sermons, the Annasr attracted many young Moroccan followers of Salafism, as did the Al Fourkaan.[4] And on 28 December 2002, El Moumni let Mohammed Cheppih, the Al Fourkaan's patron's son, religiously educated in Saudi-Arabia, (then) Chairman of the Dutch chapter of the Muslim World League, and a key figure in the rise of Salafism in The Netherlands,[5] perform the Friday service in Dutch explicitly in order to attract more young Muslims.[6] Interestingly, Mohammed Cheppih subsequently attempted to establish a mosque building in Rotterdam which would specifically be designed for young Muslims.[7] For that, he contacted MemarDutch, aiming to hire the architects in order to materialize their Polder Mosque exactly as it had been designed on the drawing table. He established the foundation 'Stichting Poldermoskee in Oprichting' and, according to Erkoçu, managed to get enthusiastic approval within the municipality, which looked for a suitable location for it since it had been meant as a replacement of the Essalaam and would need a similarly open field.[8] Apparently, whereas the design had been especially and explicitly devised to fit its environment, it had now been intrinsically vested with such 'integrative' meaning that the environment had to fit the design.

When the initiative seemed to have stranded, it was effectively picked up by the Annasr in 2006, with El Moumni calling for a newly built prayer hall on the location of his current converted church. It would not only have to have a prayer room but also spaces for cultural and teaching facilities in order to attract more young followers.[9] According to Erkoçu, El Moumni's dream of establishing a mosque that would be particularly attractive to young Muslims would be carried out, not by the imam, but by the Annasr's Moroccan board members Brahim Bourzik, who was a friend of Mohammed Cheppih, and Bourzik's father, who was a friend of El Moumni. In the architect's account, the imam himself had come to be associated with fundamentalism and traditionalism among the municipality, and had to be kept out of the discourse around the new project and retire in order for the plan to be accepted as Dutch and progressive. Subsequently, to be able to present a plan for El Moumni's dreamed prayer hall at the 30th anniversary of the Annasr, the patrons approached Erkoçu two months before the actual date of the presentation. In effect, they thereby determined a great part of their prayer house's future design even before first contact with the architect, since the latter's design ideas were publicly very well-known. Since the patrons seemed to agree to most of Erkoçu's stylistic preferences and since they even explicitly stated that the mosque should not look 'too Islamic', the design process promised to be very swift. However, when confronted with the architect's first proposal, in the latter's recollection they did request him, to his surprise, to incorporate a 'more real' minaret instead of a merely symbolic point marking the structure's corner, and a separate side-entrance for women instead of a shared portal. In his second proposal, the designer therefore drew a larger, square tower on the corner and a separate women's entrance at the side, leading to a separate women's prayer space with its own mihrab and minaret. The subsequent presentation was, according to Erkoçu, well received by the municipality, with the patrons hoping to convince the mainly Saudi sponsors present to donate the necessary funds. The only change that the community leaders requested of their architect afterwards was to scratch the word 'liberal' from his description – in his recollection because of the term's association with 'right-wing' political liberalism – and to shift the building's colour to green.

So, although the Annasr's design process is still only in its very first phase and further research will be necessary as well as interesting, there are already some manifest similarities between the particular religious boundary constructions behind the Annasr and the Al Fourkaan, as well as some preliminary similarities between their actual design processes. Whereas the verbal discourse was attuned to the municipality's general search for architectural Dutchness and to the designer's general search for architectural progress, the patrons' specific architecture-representational requirements appeared to be steered by the production of a specific construction of Islam. That the latter might be connected to religious purism, as embraced by certain other Moroccan Muslim community leaders in The Netherlands with a dislike of official-Moroccan Islam, did not seem to form a consideration in the realities of the municipality and the designer. Consequently, as in all other cases, the patrons' essentially religious aim resulted in confusion among the party at the other side of the designing table as soon as a building element was requested that did not fit that party's particular interpretation of Dutchness or progress.

In the meantime, Mohammed Cheppih went to Amsterdam to see if his Polder Mosque would stand a better chance under that municipal regime than under the one in Rotterdam, where the initiative had come to a standstill, allegedly due to problems with finding a location. Together with MemarDutch, he presented the design in a closed meeting, again stressing the fact that it would be especially meant for young people. Only after two years of silence, however, could Cheppih enthusiastically state that it would finally be accomplished, although not as a newly built mosque. With the support of the Slotervaart Chairman Marcouch, he had been given the opportunity to use a vacated building. Apparently, MemarDutch was no longer involved.[10] Cheppih claimed that existing prayer halls were often closely associated with a particular cultural or ethnic group and country, calling them 'Homesickness Mosques' in imitation of his former architects. Dutch would be the language used in his mosque, also for sermons, and the form of Islam would be 'free of cultural influences from other countries', 'mainstream', a 'consensus Islam' that would emphasize similarities rather than differences. For that, he suggested that he would use alternating 'switch imams'. 'In our project we identify most with the vision of someone like Tariq Ramadan. But Ramadan agrees with us that within a mosque like this, a Salafist and a Muslim Brother will also be welcome.' Furthermore, in his mosque men and women would pray together, with men at the front and women at the back and no division between them. The usual practice of men and women praying in separate rooms, he asserted, was not based on anything in the Koran, but a typical example of cultural influence on religion.[11]

To the surprise of some observers, despite the fact that his building would not be a purpose-built prayer hall after all, Cheppih still claimed to have 'fallen in love' with it right away.[12] From a representational viewpoint this is not surprising. In light of his purist vision of Islam as described above, and despite the realities of modernity and nationality on the sides of the architects and municipal bodies involved as well as his own verbal representations towards them, it could be deduced that in his religious reality the design for the earlier Polder Mosque would not have represented a specifically modern-Dutch Islam at all, since Islam in Cheppih's eyes had in fact no cultural traits to begin with. Instead, it would have represented Islam as 'pre-cultural', as it had been meant from the start, before processes of culturalization had corrupted the true message. Explicating his theology as it would be preached in the Polder Mosque, he said: 'I don't know if we should speak of a Polder Islam. As far as I'm concerned, Islam is universal.'[13] In effect, the earlier Polder Mosque's signification to the patron had lain, not in the presence of building elements conveying a supposed 'Dutchness' or any other 'Western-ness', but in the absence of 'fake-Islamic' building elements associated with culture instead of religion.[14] For that message to be understood, an existing building without outer Islamic recognizability would be almost as suitable as a designed building without outer Islamic recognizability. He explicitly stated that a modern mosque had to look 'Dutch', which in his eyes, however, merely meant 'a mosque that on the outside would not look like a mosque'. 'Many people said, you are such a modern initiative. [...] But the thing is that people have so little knowledge that they forget that at the start of the historical development of the mosque there was no such thing as a curtain or wall separation between men and women. [...] a mosque was not only a prayer hall but already housed things like law courts and education. [...] It is a return to the roots.'[15] And: 'In the days of the Prophet men and women prayed in the same room. I wish to go back to those days.'[16]

In fact, purist visions of mosque design as produced by patrons like Cheppih, which are seemingly 'modern' and 'Western' but are actually meant to return to a supposed Islamic origin,[17] find a basis in some Salafi fatwas that run counter to the prescriptions of all established schools of jurisprudence. Al-Albani, for example, next to writing a book in which he redefined the proper gestures and formulae that constitute the Muslim prayer ritual 'according to the Prophet's practice', stated that mihrabs were a later innovation and that it is actually lawful to pray in a mosque with one's shoes.[18] As we have seen, the Primeval Mosque can be invoked as a blueprint for modern design in many divergent ways, depending completely on the specific Islamic lens through which it is seen. Through the purist lens, the Prophet's house did not harbour a prayer niche yet and He and his followers would have logically kept their shoes on out in the open courtyard. Given the intensifying search for constructions of Islamic purity, especially among young Dutch-Moroccan Muslims,[19] it can be predicted that it will be in these circles that 'the first purpose-built modern-Dutch mosque' will be located by observers. If and when it is built, however, it can also be predicted to call for architectural opposition by those patrons producing contesting visions of Islam while verbally claiming to be no less 'modern', 'Dutch' or 'youthful' in their own right.[20] Among the seemingly confusing multitude of Islamic forms that will continue to be developed in The Netherlands, no observer will be able to consistently explain why which patrons chose which forms if he does not break through the layers of socially- and physically-integrative rhetorics around what actually appear to be religious realities.

The general assumption that contemporary mosque design is experiencing a self-chosen standstill created by traditionalist patrons who have to be pushed forward by modernizing architects, proves to be based less on an empirical reality than on an architectural critical perspective that craves for 'future-oriented progression' instead of 'nostalgic copying'. It thereby misses the multitude of religiously meaningful varieties within today's 'domes and minarets' as much as the multitude of religious significations by those mosque patrons who purposefully rejected them. The fact that most mosque designs in the West still appear to reject a full assimilation into their new urban surroundings should no longer come as a surprise. In spite of extant architectural beliefs, mosques do not generally follow the 'characteristics of their region' or 'the spirit of their times', but the politico-religious alliances of their patrons. And the fact that 'traditionalist' mosque designs are still the most popular models even in predominantly Islamic countries, where every other kind of architecture seems to have been subject to what is seen as 'modernization', should no longer come as a surprise either. If cult buildings represent locally contesting visions of a religion, they will always and everywhere remain in need of specific transformations of religiously signifying building elements. In order for us to understand Muslim-commissioned mosque design without getting caught between a simplifying evolutionary discourse and the complexities of the empirical field, there is much to be gained from consistently and publicly uncovering what has generally been deemed uninteresting until now: the very first design proposals as they were actually put to real patrons, and the latter's subsequent reactions to these in the series of unfolding reality representations that constitute the design processes.

Notes

Introduction

1 E.H. Gugel, *Geschiedenis van de Bouwstijlen in de Hoofdtijdperken der Architectuur*, Arnhem: P. Gouda Quint, 1886 [1869]. p. 493.
2 W. Kromhout, Mahomedaansche Kunst, Tweede Lezing, in: *Zeven Voordrachten over Bouwkunst*, Amsterdam: Maatschappij voor Goede en Goedkope Lectuur, 1908, pp. 65-123; p. 71. All English quotations from Dutch sources in this dissertation are my translations.
3 H. Evers, *De Architectuur in Hare Hoofdtijdperken*, Amsterdam: Veen, 1916, pp. 417, 475.
4 J.H.W. Leliman, *Geschiedenis van de Bouwstijlen in de Hoofdtijdperken der Architectuur van Prof. E. Gugel. Vierde druk, geheel omgewerkt en belangrijk uitgebreid door J.H.W. Leliman*, Rotterdam: D. Bolle, 1918, p. 86.
5 J. Godefroy, *Geschiedenis van de Bouwkunst. De Ontwikkeling van de Bouwstijlen van af den Oorsprong tot het Hedendaagse Tijdperk. Deel I: Oudheid en Middeleeuwen*, Amsterdam: Ahrend, 1920, pp. 314-316.
6 H. Sutterland, *Geschiedenis der Bouwkunst*, Vol 2, Delft: Waltman, 1946.
7 W. Meulenkamp, "In de Turksche smaak…" De Turkse Tent, de Moorse Kiosk en het Oosters Paviljoen in Nederland 1700-1900, in: H. Theunissen, A. Abelmann and W. Meulenkamp (eds), *Topkapi & Turkomanie. Turks-Nederlandse Ontmoetingen sinds 1600*, Amsterdam: De Bataafsche Leeuw, 1989, pp. 118-129.
8 F. van der Maden, De Komst van de Film, in: K. Dibbets and F. van der Maden (eds), *Geschiedenis van de Nederlandse Film en Bioscoop tot 1940*, Weesp: Het Wereldvenster, 1986, pp. 11-52; p. 29 and Plates; J. de Hond, *Verlangen naar het Oosten. Oriëntalisme in de Nederlandse Cultuur, ca. 1800-1920*, Leiden: Primavera Pers, 2008, pp. 195-196.
9 See http://www.efteling.nl/Page.aspx?PageId=912&ParentName=Park&LanguageId=1. All internet sources in this dissertation were last checked on 30-11-2008.
10 'Dutch Christianity' consists of a multitude of contesting beliefs, interpretations, communities, and churches. Eg. see E.G. Hoekstra and M.H. Ipenburg, *Handboek Christelijk Nederland. Kerken, Gemeenten, Samenkomsten en Vergaderingen*, Kampen: Kok, 2008.
11 Eg. F. Lindo, *Heilige Wijsheid in Amsterdam. Ayasofia, Stadsdeel de Baarsjes en de Strijd om het Riva Terrein*, Amsterdam: Het Spinhuis, 1999; F. Buijs, *Een Moskee in de Wijk. De Vestiging van de Kocatepe Moskee in Rotterdam-Zuid*, Amsterdam: Het Spinhuis, 1998; R. Strijp, *Om de Moskee. Het Religieuze Leven van Marokkaanse Migranten in een Nederlandse Provinciestad*, Amsterdam: Thesis, 1998; H.L. Beck, A Hidden Agenda or Hidden Prejudices? Building a Turkish Mosque in Tilburg, in: W.A. Shadid and P.S. van Koningsveld (eds), *Intercultural Relations and Religious Authorities: Muslims in the European Union*, Leuven [etc]: Peeters, 2002, pp. 49-66; N. Landman and W. Wessels, The Visibility of Mosques in Dutch Towns, in: *Journal of Ethnic and Migration Studies*, 31 (6), 2005, pp. 1125-1140; T. Sunier, Constructing Islam. Places of Worship and the Politics of Space in The Netherlands, in: *Journal of Contemporary European Studies*, Vol 13, No 3 (December), 2005, pp. 317-334, and: The Western Mosque. Space in Physical Place, in: *ISIM Review*, No 18, Autumn 2006, pp. 22-23; M. de Rijk, *De Nieuwe Moskee. Politiek en Geloof in een Provinciestad*, Amsterdam [etc]: Atlas, 2006; M. Maussen,

Ruimte voor de Islam? Stedelijk Beleid, Voorzieningen, Organisaties, Apeldoorn [etc]: Het Spinhuis, 2006.
12. M. Frishman and H.-U. Khan (eds), *The Mosque. History, Architectural Development and Regional Diversity*, London: Thames and Hudson, 2002 [1994], pp. 11-14 (and the later chapters on separate regions).
13. B. Dijker, *Een Minaret in het Stadsgezicht. Nieuwbouw Moskeeën in Nederland, Registratie en Vormgeving*, Utrecht: Utrecht University, 1995.
14. W. Wessels, *Van Kerkstraat naar Moskeedreef? Over Nieuwbouwmoskeeën en Ruimtelijke Ordening in Utrecht en Driebergen-Rijsenburg*, Utrecht: Utrecht University, 2003.
15. Eg. see 'Minaret Blijft Uiterlijk Moskee Bepalen,' in: *Nederlands Dagblad*, 22-10-2007, p. 8.
16. See http://www.mucumo.tk and http://www.memardutch.nl.
17. 'Dit Moet de Laatste Traditionele Moskee zijn,' in: *De Volkskrant*, 16-01-2004, p. 16; B. Hulsman, Heimweemoskee of Poldermoskee. Jonge Moslims in Nederland zijn Uitgekeken op de Minaret, in: *NRC*, 1-5-2004, pp. 33-34.
18. R. van der Zee, Kathedralen voor Allah, in: *HP/De Tijd*, 28-11-2003, pp. 26-32.
19. *Moskee-Architectuur in Nederland*, exhibition traveling through The Netherlands from September 2004, see: www.museumarabesk.nl; *Moskeeën in NL*, exhibition in ABC Architectuurcentrum Haarlem, 2005, see: www.architectuurhaarlem.nl.
20. Eg. http://armandbos.nl/; http://www.lombox.nl/architectuur/moskee.html; http://www.ad.nl/denhaag/article856874.ece;http://www.ebbingekwartier.nl/content/view/92/59/.
21. E. Erkoçu, A. Hammiche and C. Bugdaci, Minaretten in de Polder, in: *De Architect*, 37 (6), 2006, pp. 30-39; pp. 30-33.
22. 'Nieuwbouw voor Annasrmoskee,' in: *Algemeen Dagblad, Rotterdam*, 19-11-2006. (http://www.ad.nl/rotterdam/stad/article822480.ece)
23. 'Ontwerp Annasr-moskee Strak en Duurzaam,' in: Architectenweb.nl, 22-11-2006. (http://www.architectenweb.nl/aweb/redactie/redactie_detail.asp?iNTypeID=56&iNID=8381)
24. See: http://reporter.kro.nl/uitzendingen/2007/0402_moskeeen/intro.aspx.
25. Invitation and introduction to the debate 'Baas in Eigen Moskee', organized by NAi & MemarDutch at the NAi in Rotterdam on 4-10-2007.
26. H-U Khan, An Overview of Contemporary Mosques, in: Frishman and Khan 2002, pp. 247-267; pp. 253-254.
27. R. Holod and H-U. Khan, *The Contemporary Mosque. Architects, Clients and Designs since the 1950s*, London: Thames and Hudson, 1997, pp. 227, 13-14.
28. J. Steele, Case Study VI: The West. Symbolism and Context: The New Dilemma, in: I. Serageldin and J. Steele (eds), *Architecture of the Contemporary Mosque*, London: Academy Editions, 1996, p. 145.
29. O. Khalidi, Approaches to Mosque Design in North America, in: Y.Y. Haddad and J.L. Esposito (eds), *Muslims on the Americanization Path?*, New York [etc]: Oxford University Press, 2000, pp. 317-334; pp. 318, 322, 332.
30. A.I. Kahera, *Deconstructing the American Mosque: Space, Gender and Aesthetics*, Austin: University of Texas Press, 2000, pp. 64-65.
31. I.D. Limon, *Islamische Kulstätten des 20. Jahrhunderts im europäischen Raum*, Kaiserslautern: Dissertation, 2000, pp. 63-68, 125.
32. N. Rabbat, Islamic Architecture as a Field of Historical Enquiry, in: *Architectural Design*, Vol. 74, nr. 6 (Nov-Dec) ['Islam + Architecture'], 2004, pp. 18-23.
33. N. Avcioglu, Identity-as-Form: The Mosque in the West, in: *Cultural Analysis*, Vol. 6, 2007, pp. 91-112; pp. 99, 101-105.

34 C. Welzbacher, *Euro Islam Architecture. New Mosques in the West*, Amsterdam: SUN, 2008, pp. 38-43.
35 C. Welzbacher, The Architecture of Euro-Islam, in: *A10, New European Architecture*, Nr. 19, Jan/Feb 2008, pp. 58-60.
36 S. Kraft, *Islamische Sakralarchitektur in Deutschland. Eine Untersuchung Ausgewählter Moschee-Neubauten*, Münster: Lit., 2002.
37 G. Haider, "Brother in Islam, Please Draw us a Mosque." Muslims in the West: A Personal Account, in: R. Powell (ed), *Expressions of Islam in Buildings*, Singapore: Concept Media; The Aga Khan Award for Architecture, 1990, pp. 155-166; p. 158.
38 G. Haider, Muslim Space and the Practice of Architecture. A Personal Odyssey, in: B.D. Metcalf (ed), *Making Muslim Space in North America and Europe*, Berkeley [etc]: University of California Press, 1996, pp. 31-45; p. 38.
39 Y. Tabbaa, *The Transformation of Islamic Art during the Sunni Revival*, Seattle and London: University of Washington Press, 2001; pp. 4-9, 162-164.
40 F. Barth: Introduction, in: F. Barth (ed), *Ethnic Groups and Boundaries. The Social Organization of Culture Difference*, Illinois: Waveland, 1998 [Oslo: Universitetsforlaget, 1969], pp. 9-38; *Cosmologies in the Making. A Generative Approach to Cultural Variation in Inner New Guinea*, Cambridge [etc]: Cambridge University Press, 1987; *Balinese Worlds*, Chicago [etc]: University of Chicago Press, 1993; Enduring and Emerging Issues in the Analysis of Ethnicity, in: H. Vermeulen and C. Govers (eds), *The Anthropology of Ethnicity. Beyond 'Ethnic Groups and Boundaries'*, Amsterdam: Het Spinhuis, 1994.
41 Barth 1998, pp. 14, 33; 1987, pp. 31, 54; 1993, pp. 335-336; 1994, p. 12.
42 Barth 1998, pp. 10-15, 33-34, 38; 1987, pp. 10, 31, 52-54; 1993, pp. 4-5, 335-336, 339; 1994, pp. 12-16, 30.
43 R. Schefold, G. Domenig and P. Nas (eds), *Indonesian Houses. Tradition and Transformation in Vernacular Architecture*, Leiden: KITLV Press, 2003.
44 Schefold, Domenig and Nas 2003, pp. 1, 5-6, 8, 16-17.
45 Barth 1987, p. 54.
46 Schefold, Domenig and Nas 2003, p. 5.
47 See A.J.J. Mekking and E. Roose (eds), *The Global Built Environment as a Representation of Realities*, Amsterdam: Amsterdam University Press, forthcoming 2009.
48 See the authoritative volume, and its references, by Nico Landman, *Van Mat tot Minaret. De Institutionalisering van de Islam in Nederland*, Amsterdam: VU Uitgeverij, 1992.
49 See http://www.bestemmingsplan.nl.

Chapter 1

1 B.D. Metcalf, *Islamic Revival in British India. Deoband, 1860-1900*, Princeton; Guildford: Princeton University Press, 1982, pp. 25-26.
2 M. Zafeerudin, *Mosque in Islam*, New Delhi: Qazi Publishers & Distributors, 1996 [Translation from Urdu, Nizam-e-Masajid, 1956], pp. 7-8. There are no Deobandi mosques in The Netherlands, but a Deobandi-associated prayer hall is the planned Abbey Mills Islamic Centre in London. It was commissioned by the puritanical missionary organization Tablighi Jamaat, and its blob-like design was consciously meant to reject historical examples with domes and minarets. Paradoxically, it

became controversial *precisely because* it would be financed by such a 'conservative' movement. See: http://arts.guardian.co.uk/features/story/ 0,,1934985,00.html#article_continue.

3 U. Sanyal, *Devotional Islam and Politics in British India. Ahmad Riza Khan Barelwi and His Movement, 1870-1920*, Oxford: Oxford University Press, 1999 [1996].

4 G.R. Al-Qadiri ('Hoofdimaam van de Surinaamse Moeslim Associatie'), *Het Wahabisme. De Pseudo-Islamitische Ondermijnende Beweging*, Amsterdam [etc]: Liefhebbers van de Heilige Profeet, 2004, pp. 203, 237-239.

5 Metcalf 1982, pp. 264-314.

6 Sanyal 1999, pp. 240-248; Landman 1992, p. 221.

7 I. Adamson, *Mirza Ghulam Ahmad of Qadian*, London: Elite, 1989, p. 62; A.M. Khan (ed), *Mosques Around the World. A Pictorial Presentation*, Ahmadiyya Muslim Association USA, 1994, p. 11; Since hardly any Surinamese Muslims in The Netherlands associate themselves with Wahhabism, objections to the worship of Sufi saints and Pirs are still mainly found among the Ahmadi. Landman 1992, p. 221.

8 R.A. Chaudhri, *Mosque. Its Importance in the Life of a Muslim*, London: The London Mosque, 1982, pp. 40, 55; Khan 1994, pp. iix, 20.

9 Y. Friedmann, *Prophecy Continuous. Aspects of Ahmadi Religious Thought and its Medieval Background*, Berkeley [etc]: University of California Press, 1987.

10 E.g. in Ahmad's speech for the Second Conference of Great Religions in Lahore, December 26th-28th 1896, as printed in M.G. Ahmad, *The Philosophy of the Teachings of Islam*, Tilford: Islam International Publications [Lahore 1896], 1996.

11 Adamson 1989, pp. 13-16; Friedmann 1987, pp. 2-3.

12 Khan 1994, p. 12.

13 *Noor Ul Haq*, vol 2, p. 42, cited in: http://www.alislam.org/library/articles/new/ building-mosques.html.

14 Adamson 1989, p. 4.

15 Adamson 1989, p. 79.

16 E.g. as used in the headers of public announcements of the early mission in The Netherlands.

17 Adamson 1989, pp. 152-153.

18 Friedmann 1987, p. 147-162.

19 See http://aaiil.org/text/articles/light/ qa_promisedmessiahmujaddidrevelationahmadismuslims.shtml.

20 Friedmann 1987, p. 23.

21 Adamson 1989, pp. 152-153.

22 Friedmann 1987, p. 32.

23 Friedmann 1987, p. 39.

24 See Khan 1994.

25 See http://www.alislam.org/spanish/ahmadiat%20espana/ index_ahmadiat_en_espana.html, and http://www.alislam.org/gallery/mosques. Notably, as in The Hague, the well-known Qadiani follower Mohammed Zafrullah Khan seems to have played a supporting role here.

26 C.J.M. de Klerk, *De Immigratie der Hindostanen in Suriname*, Amsterdam: Urbi et Orbi, 1953, pp. 41-45.

27 H. van de Kerke, De Taibah-Moskee te Amsterdam in de Geschiedenis van de Hindoestaans-Surinaamse Moslims, in: R. Kloppenburg and L. Pathmananoharan-Dronkers (eds), *Religieuze Minderheden in Nederland*, Utrecht: Stichting 350 Jaar Rijksuniversiteit Utrecht, 1986, pp. 33-45; pp. 33-34.

NOTES

28 Eg. N. Boedhoe, Hindostaanse Moslims, in: C. van der Burg, T. Damsteegt and K. Autar, *Hindostanen in Nederland*, Leuven; Apeldoorn: Garant, 1990, pp. 107-123; p. 107.
29 According to Landman, in the Hindustani region where most workers had been recruited, the Brelwi school would have been the most popular at that particular time, although he finds that in the literature on Islam in Surinam the Brelwi connection is only mentioned after 1950. Landman 1992, p. 221, footnote 73.
30 M.S.A. Nurmohammed, *Geschiedenis van de Islam in Suriname*, Paramaribo: Gedenkboek Surinaamse Moeslim Associatie, 1985, p. 15 and further.
31 *Noorani Memorial Editie 2004*, WIM Nederland, Amsterdam, 11-2004.
32 *The Message International*, Speciaal Nummer 2003, Noorani Editie, WIM Youth Circle, Amsterdam, pp. 11-16.
33 *The Message International*, Speciaal Nummer 2003, Noorani Editie, WIM Youth Circle, Amsterdam, pp. 4-8, 21-22.
34 Nurmohamed 1985, p. 21.
35 Landman 1992, p. 221.
36 Landman 1992, p. 223.
37 Handelingen van de Gemeenteraad 1950, 6 February, pp. 210-211, *Archive The Hague Municipality*.
38 Handelingen van de Gemeenteraad 1950, 6 February, p. 219, *Archive The Hague Municipality*.
39 *Haagsch Dagblad*, 07-02-1950.
40 *Het Parool*, 11-02-1950.
41 Q.U. Hafiz, press release of De Ahmadiyya Muslim Missie in Nederland, 07-07-1950, *Private Archive Kerkgenootschap De Ahmadiyya Beweging in de Islam*, The Hague, Mobarak Mosque; Henceforward abbreviated as '*Archive Mobarak Mosque*'. The focus on a more liberal position of women is one of the main diacritica for Ahmadiyya communities in distinguishing their construction of Islam from a Brelwi version. Eg. see Landman 1992, p. 198.
42 *Haagsche Courant*, 08-07-1950.
43 *Haagsch Dagblad*, 15-07-1950.
44 The sale was official on 02-10-1950, and the price was 25.376 guilders. Buyer's contract, 02-10-1955, *Archive Mobarak Mosque*.
45 *Leeuwarder Courant*, 11-08-1950; *Geldersch Dagblad*, 12-08-1950.
46 *De Telegraaf,/Nieuws van de Dag*, Amsterdam, 26-08-1950.
47 Letter from Dekker, Paats and De Vries to Hafiz, 30-05-1950, *Archive Mobarak Mosque*.
48 Buyer's contract, 02-10-1955, *Archive Mobarak Mosque*.
49 J. Molema and P. Bak (eds), *Jan.Gerko Wiebenga. De Apostel van het Nieuwe Bouwen*, Rotterdam: Uitgeverij 010, 1987.
50 Calendrical Overview, Wiebenga 1954, and sketch 07-10-1951, NAI.WIEB.204, *Archive Netherlands Architecture Institute*, henceforward abbreviated as *Archive NAI*.
51 At first Wiebenga used the assistance of architects J. Lipplaa and H.A. Van Oerle, but later continued the commission on his own. Letter from Van Oerle to Wiebenga, 06-11-1953, NAI.WIEB.204, *Archive NAI*.
52 Letter from Wiebenga to Bashir, 26-08-1952, NAI.WIEB.204, *Archive NAI*.
53 Calendrical Overview, Wiebenga 1954, NAI.WIEB.204, *Archive NAI*.
54 K.O. Hartmann, *De Ontwikkeling der Bouwkunst, Van de Oudste Tijden tot Heden. Eene Inleiding in de Kennis van Geschiedenis, Techniek en Stijl. Deel I: De Bouwkunst in de Oudheid en onder den Islam*, Amsterdam: Maatschappij voor Goede en Goedkope Lectuur, 1923 [Translation from German, Leipzig 1910-1911], p. 405.

55 There are picture postcards of non-Hindustani mosques in his files, together with a written description of 'Indian' and 'Persian' architectural forms, NAI.WIEB.204, *Archive NAI*.
56 P. Bak, De Laatste Werken, in: Molema and Bak 1987, pp. 128-137; p. 132.
57 Letter from Wiebenga to Bashir, 25-10-1951, NAI.WIEB.204, *Archive NAI*.
58 Letter from Wiebenga to Bashir, 07-11-1951, NAI.WIEB.204, *Archive NAI*.
59 Letter from Wiebenga to Bashir, 26-08-1952, NAI.WIEB.204, *Archive NAI*.
60 Calendrical Overview, Wiebenga/Bashir Litigation 1954, and Costs Overview, Wiebenga/Bashir Litigation 1954, NAI.WIEB.204, *Archive NAI*.
61 Letters from Wiebenga to Bashir, 05-11-1953, 07-11-1953 and 03-04-1954, NAI.WIEB.204, *Archive NAI*; Behandelstaten van de Commissievergaderingen (henceforward abbreviated as 'Behandelstaten') 1953/1954, bnr. 579, inventory Nr. 388, decisions nr. 774, and Notulen van Commissievergaderingen, Notulenboek (henceforward abbreviated as 'Notulen') 1947-Feb.1958, inventory nr. 360: 02-10-1953, 06-11-1953 and 26-02-1954, *Archive The Hague Aesthetics Commission 1948-1990*.
62 Letter from Z. de Lyon to Wiebenga, 25-11-1953, NAI.WIEB.204, *Archive NAI*.
63 Drawings of 18-11-1954, 23-11-1954 and 19-12-1954, NAI.WIEB.204, *Archive NAI*.
64 Letter from Wiebenga to Bashir, 03-04-1954, NAI.WIEB.204, *Archive NAI*.
65 J.B.Vercauteren, Fabrieksgebouwen voor de Société Ceramique te Maastricht, in: Molema and Bak 1987, pp. 30-35.
66 Behandelstaten 1954, bnr. 579, inventory Nr. 389, decision nr. 774'53, and Notulen 1947-Feb.1958, inventory nr. 360, *Archive The Hague Aesthetics Commission 1948-1990*.
67 Letter from Wiebenga to Bashir, 03-04-1954, NAI.WIEB.204, *Archive NAI*.
68 Letters from Wiebenga to Bashir, 03-04-1954 and 07-07-1954, NAI.WIEB.204, *Archive NAI*.
69 *Haagsch Dagblad*, 13-08-1954; *Nieuw Rotterdamsche Courant*, 16-08-1954.
70 *Haagsche Courant/Het Vaderland*, 14-08-1954.
71 *Haagsch Dagblad*, 13-08-1954; *Haagsche Courant*, 14-08-1950.
72 *Haagsche Courant*, 30-08-1954.
73 *Algemeen Dagblad*, 08-10-1954.
74 *Algemeen Dagblad*, 03-12-1954; *Nieuws van de Dag*, 15-12-1954.
75 Letter from Wiebenga to Bashir, 23-10-1954, and Letter from Wiebenga to the Municipal council of The Hague, 20-10-1954, NAI.WIEB.204, *Archive NAI*; Behandelstaten 1954, bnr. 579, inventory Nr. 389, decision nr. 1065, and Notulen 1947-Feb.1958, inventory nr. 360, *Archive The Hague Aesthetics Commission 1948-1990*; The one-levelled wing is the plan that is shown in Molema and Bak 1987, p. 134.
76 Letters from Bashir to Wiebenga, 27-09-1954 and 08-11-1954, NAI.WIEB.204, *Archive NAI*.
77 *Haagsch Dagblad*, 05-11-1954.
78 *Haagsch Dagblad*, 25-11-1954.
79 Behandelstaten 1954, bnr. 579, inventory Nr. 389, decision nr. 1159, and Notulen 1947-Feb.1958, inventory nr. 360, *Archive The Hague Aesthetics Commission 1948-1990*.
80 Behandelstaten 1954, bnr. 579, inventory Nr. 389, decision nr. 1159, and Notulen 1947-Feb.1958, inventory nr. 360, *Archive The Hague Aesthetics Commission 1948-1990*.
81 *Het Parool*, 10-02-1955; Beschikking 184/668/55, Dossier Oostduinlaan 79, Dienst Stedelijke Ontwikkeling, Gemeentelijk Bouw- en Woningtoezicht The Hague, henceforward abbreviated as *Archive DSO*.

NOTES

82 *Nieuw Rotterdamsche Courant/Het Vrije Volk/Het Binnenhof*, 12-02-1955, with a separate photograph of the wooden model itself in *Het Vaderland*, 12-02-1955.
83 *Het Vaderland*, 21-05-1955.
84 *Haagsch Dagblad/Het Parool*, 21-05-1955.
85 *Het Vrije Volk*, 21-05-1955.
86 Exactly when the name 'Mobarak' came to be used explicitly is no longer known by the current community leaders.
87 *Haagsche Courant,* 12-10-1955.
88 *Het Vaderland*, 10-12-1955.
89 *Het Vrije Volk/Haagsche Courant*, 14-07-1962.
90 *Leeuwarder Courant*, 19-07-1963.
91 *Algemeen Dagblad*, 14-07-1962.
92 Behandelstaten 1962, bnr. 579, inventory Nr. 396, decision nr. 825, and Notulen Nov.1961-Sept.1964, inventory nr. 362, *Archive The Hague Aesthetics Commission 1948-1990*.
93 Behandelstaten 1962, bnr. 579, inventory Nr. 396, decision nr. 825, and Notulen Nov.1961-Sept.1964, inventory nr. 362, *Archive The Hague Aesthetics Commission 1948-1990*.
94 *Haagsche Courant*, 29-07-1963: 'last Saturday.'
95 *Haagsche Courant*, 09-07-1963, with a photograph of one of the turrets.
96 *Algemeen Dagblad*, 14-07-1963.
97 *Haagsche Courant*, 14-07-1963.
98 *Het Vaderland*, 16-07-1963.
99 *De [unreadable]*, 17-07-1963; see partly burnt newspaper article-collection, *Archive Mobarak Mosque*.
100 *Haagsch Dagblad*, 23-07-1963.
101 *Algemeen Dagblad*, 14-07-1963.
102 *De Tijd-Maasbode*, 01-02-1964.
103 *Het Vaderland, Den Helder*, 06-02-1961.
104 Likewise, some Hindu scholars in India have been attempting to disprove an Islamic origin to buildings such as the Taj Mahal. Eg. P.N. Oak, *The Taj Mahal is a Hindu Palace*, Bombay: Pearl Publications; Bombay [etc]: India Book House, 1969 [New Delhi: P.N. Oak, 1965].
105 *De Tijd-Maasbode*, 01-02-1964.
106 *Haagsche Courant*, 13-04-1965.
107 *Haagsche Courant*, 11-08-1987.
108 *De Volkskrant*, 12-08-1987; Letter from Verhagen to the Caliph, 20-11-1987, *Archive Mobarak Mosque*; *Het Parool*, 30-05-1996; *Wijkblad Benoordenhout*, April 1996, p. 10.
109 Letter from Rashid to Verhagen, 29-09-1987, *Archive Mobarak Mosque*; The local architect hired to work out Rashid's drawings was The Hague-based Deurloo.
110 Letter from Van der Velden, secretary of the Movement in The Netherlands, to the Caliph, 30-03-1990, *Archive Mobarak Mosque*.
111 Letter from the Mission to DSO, 24-07-1989, *Archive Mobarak Mosque*; Dossier Oostduinlaan 79, *Archive DSO*.
112 Dossier Oostduinlaan 79, *Archive DSO*.
113 Volume plan dated 9-10-1990, and wooden model, *Archive Mobarak Mosque*.
114 Letter from Verhagen to the Caliph, 02-11-1990, *Archive Mobarak Mosque*.
115 Dossier Oostduinlaan 79, *Archive DSO*.
116 Bouwvergunningsaanvraag, 16-7-1993, *Achive Mobarak Mosque*.

117 Dossier Oostduinlaan 79, *Archive DSO*.
118 Letter from the municipality to the Ahmadiyya Community, 22-02-1995, *Archive Mobarak Mosque*.
119 Letter from Verhagen to DSO The Hague, 29-10-1996, *Archive Mobarak Mosque*.
120 *Wijkblad Benoordenhout*, April 1996, p. 11.
121 Letter from Verhagen to Kromhout Rijnsburg BV, 07-06-1995, *Archive Mobarak Mosque*.
122 *Haagsche Courant*, 30-05-1996.
123 *Het Parool*, 30-05-1996.
124 *Haagsche Courant*, 30-05-1996.
125 In a similar case of 'loss' of Qadiani meaning, chairman Verhagen had always assumed that the rays of light imaged in the Movement's logo as exuding from the Minaret of the Messiah had really been sound waves referring to the call to prayer.
126 Interview with K. Mahmood, financial specialist of the movement in The Netherlands, The Hague, 31-08-2005.
127 Interview with Rashid, London, 18-08-2005.
128 Interview with Warraich, The Hague, 19-06-2008.
129 Letter from Roeleveld, Hoofd Afdeling Bouwconstructie, on behalf of Mayor and Aldermen to Bogaards Bouwkundig Konstructieburo, Katwijk, 17-10-1996, *Archive Mobarak Mosque*.
130 Letter from Verhagen to Maatkamp, DSO, 29-10-1996, *Archive Mobarak Mosque*.
131 Letter from Verhagen to Maatkamp, 7-11-1997, *Archive Mobarak Mosque*.
132 Dossier Oostduinlaan 79, *Archive DSO*.
133 *Trouw*, 31-10-1998; Press release Ahmadiyya Gemeenschap, *Archive Mobarak Mosque*.
134 Interview with Verhagen, The Hague, 08-09-2005.
135 Letter from Stadsdeelkantoor Haagse Hout to the Ahmadiyya Gemeenschap, 28-01-2002, *Archive Mobarak Mosque*; Dossier Oostduinlaan 79, *Archive DSO*.
136 Letter from Verhagen to Stadsdeelkantoor Haagsche Hout, 21-06-2002, *Archive Mobarak Mosque*.
137 *Wijkblad Benoordenhout*, February 2003, p. 35; Several letters from neighbors to DSO, February 2005, *Archive Mobarak Mosque*.
138 Letter from DSO to the Ahmadiyya Gemeenschap, 16-05-2003, *Archive Mobarak Mosque*.
139 Letter from DSO to the Ahmadiyya Gemeenschap, 24-03-2005, *Archive Mobarak Mosque*.
140 *Haagsche Courant*, 23-06-2005.
141 *Reformatorisch Dagblad*, 30-9-2005.
142 As yet, they do not seem to own any purpose-built mosques themselves.
143 *The Message International*, Speciaal Nummer 2003, Noorani Editie, WIM Youth Circle, Amsterdam, p. 23.
144 Eg. see S. Akkach, *Cosmology and Architecture in Premodern Islam. An Architectural Reading of Mystical Ideas*, Albany: State University of New York Press, 2005, pp. 129-140, 177-179.
145 Al-Qadiri 2004, eg. pp. 51, 58-59, 95, 99-100, 162, 324.
146 Van de Kerke 1986, p. 41.
147 Landman 1992, p. 223.
148 Akte van Statutenwijziging, 21-11-1997.
149 Van de Kerke 1986, p. 42.
150 Since Lachman is dead, the following has largely been based on interviews with Haffmans, Amsterdam, 3/29-8-2006, current Taibah community leader Mohammed

NOTES

Junus Gaffar, Amsterdam, 16-8/14-9-2006, and Lachman's former WIM-NL colleague Roy Kasiem (telephonic), 26-11-2007.

151 U. Vogt-Göknil, *Die Moschee. Grundformen Sakraler Baukunst*, Zürich: Verlag für Architektur Artemis, 1978.
152 P. Haffmans, Een Nieuwe Moskee in de Bijlmermeer. Minaretten terzijde van de Metrohalte Kraaiennest, in: *Architectuur/Bouwen*, Jaargang 1 (3), March 1985, pp. 29-32; Moskee en Cultureel Centrum te Amsterdam, in: *Bouw*, Nr. 9, 27-4-1985, pp. 81-85; Moskee en Cultureel Centrum in Amsterdam, in: *Bouwen met Staal*, Jaargang 19-3, Nr. 73, September 1985, pp. 35-37; and the original notes for these articles, *Archive Haffmans*.
153 Akkach 2005, p. 95.
154 J. Pereira, *The Sacred Architecture of Islam*, New Delhi: Aryan Books International, 2004, p. 144.
155 C.W. Ernst, An Indo-Persian Guide to Sufi Shrine Pilgrimage, in: C.W. Ernst and G.M. Smith (eds), *Manifestations of Sainthood in Islam*, Istanbul: The Isis Press, 1993, pp. 43-67.
156 A.F. Buehler, *Sufi Heirs of the Prophet. The Indian Naqashbandiyya and the Rise of the Mediating Sufi Shaykh*, Columbia, SC: University of South California Press, 1998, p. 170.
157 Sunyal 1999, p. 6.
158 Eg. see C.B. Asher, *Architecture of Mughal India*, Cambridge: Cambridge University Press, 1992, pp. 209-215.
159 See the photographs in Nurmohammed 1985, pp. 33 and further, and the drawings in J.L. Volders, *Bouwkunst in Suriname. Driehonderd Jaren Nationale Architectuur*, Hilversum: Uitgeverij G. van Saane, Lectura Architectonica, 1966, pp. 82, 126-127. In the latter, images of an early mosque (p. 82) and an early Hindu temple (p. 126) both show the use of the Quincunxial Shrine structure.
160 Eg. see *The Message International*, Vol. 2, Nr. 5, 2001, pp. 23-29.
161 Similarly, the UK mausoleum for the Brelwi Pir Abdul Wahab Siddiqui of the International Muslims Organization or IMO also incorporated the form and color of the Prophet's dome. See: http://www.blessedsummit.com/photogalllery-meezar-shareef.html.
162 *The Message International*, Speciaal Nummer 2003, Noorani Editie, WIM Youth Circle, Amsterdam, pp. 8-10.
163 *Taibah News. Speciaal Nummer in verband met de Officiële Opening van Masdjid Taibah op 19 januari 1985, en de '4th World Islamic Mission Conference' op 20 januari 1985*, p. 6.
164 Interviews with Gaffar, Amsterdam, 16-8/14-9-2006, and Kasiem (telephonic), 26-11-2007. Other Dutch Brelwi mosques carry names that evoke similar connotations to Light, Medina, the Prophet's Dome, and/or Mohammed himself. Eg. see http://www.tangali.net/Moskeeen%20Ahle%20Sunnat.htm.
165 Telephone interview with Hamid Oppier, 28-11-2007. The architect declined their request.
166 N. Landman, Sufi Orders in The Netherlands. Their Role in the Institutionalization of Islam, in: W.A.R Shadid and P.S. van Koningsveld (eds), *Islam in Dutch Society. Current Developments and Future Prospects*, Kampen: Kok Pharos Publishing House, 1992b, pp. 26-39; p. 38.
167 See http://www.wimnet.org/articles/identity.htm.
168 See http://members.tripod.com/~wim_canada/wimintro.htm.
169 On several WIM websites, the logo of a sun rising above and lighting a dark globe is shown next to images of the prophet's tomb.

170 See his aforementioned articles on the subject.
171 Telephone interview with Kasiem, 26-11-2007.
172 'Kort verslag n.a.v. gesprek Wethouder L.J.Kuijpers met de Stichting Welzijn Moslims, in aanwezigheid van Afdeling Sociale Zaken d.d. 15-6-'82,' HdV/AB/nr.1205/18-6-1982, Archive Haffmans.
173 'Verslag Bouwteam Gebedsruimte Moslims Bijlmermeer d.d. 6 juli 1982,' HdV/AB/nr.1226/7-7-1982, Archive Haffmans.
174 'Het Sprookje van Ganzenhoef is Uit. "Sociaal-Cultureel Centrum" in Bijlmer werd Flop,' in: Het Parool, 15-1-1985.
175 'Afsprakenlijst Bouwteam Gebedsruimte Moslims Bijlmermeer d.d. 12-8-'82,' HdV/AB/nr.1254/6-9-1982, Archive Haffmans.
176 Letter from Gemeentelijk Grondbedrijf to SWM, 22-10-1982, Archive Haffmans.
177 'Besluitenlijst Bouwteam Ontmoetingsruimte Moslims Bijlmermeer d.d. 19-11-'82,' HdV/AB/nr.1372/23-11-1982, Archive Haffmans.
178 See his aforementioned articles on the subject.
179 Bouwaanvraag 1/3142 BWT 1983, dossier 69929, Archive Stadsdeel Amsterdam Zuid-Oost.
180 Letter from Ir. Oskam, Directeur Dienst Ruimtelijke Ordening, to the alderman of Ruimtelijke Ordening, 7-9-1983, Archive Haffmans.
181 Bouwvergunning 1/3142 BWT 1983, dossier 69929, Archive Stadsdeel Amsterdam Zuid-Oost.
182 'Vergadering Bouwteam Gebedsruimte Moslims Bijlmermeer d.d. 30-9-'82,' HdV/AB/nr.1302/11-10-1982, Archive Haffmans.
183 'Verslag Gesprek Coordinatieburo Etnische Groepen (CEG) met Stichting Welzijn Moslims (SWM) d.d. 19-10-'82,' HdV/AB/nr.1342/4-11-1982, Archive Haffmans.
184 Letter from De Vet to Jonker, 2-11-1982, Archive Haffmans.
185 'Samenvatting Gesprek Wethouder P. Jonker, Stichting Welzijn Moslims in aanwezigheid van Ambtenaren van de afd.AS/CMB d.d. 28 maart 1983,' CMB nr.1582, 25-4-1983, Archive Haffmans.
186 Letter from SWM to the Alderman, 24-5-1983, Archive Haffmans.
187 Letter from SWM to Jonker, 19-6-1983; Letter from the Alderman of Finances to the Alderman for the Coordination of Minority Policy, 30-8-1983, Archive Haffmans.
188 'Bespreking met Stichting Moslims op 03-06-83,' Archive Haffmans.
189 Telephone interview with Kasiem, 26-11-2007.
190 Het Parool, 12-12-1983.
191 'Een Overwinning voor de Moslims,' in: Het Parool, 12-1-1985.
192 'Eerste Vrouwenmoskee ter Wereld in De Bijlmer,' in: De Telegraaf/Nieuws van de Dag, 17-1-1985.
193 Program of Official Opening, Taibah News 1985, p. 17.
194 'Moslimleider pleit voor Bouw Moskeeën in heel Nederland. Nieuwe Gebedsruimte geopend in Amsterdam,' in: De Volkskrant, 20-1-1985; De Telegraaf, 21-1-1985.
195 Trouw, 21-1-1985.
196 M. Kloos, Reinheid in een Kuil van Beton, in: De Volkskrant, 8-3-1985.
197 S. Goth and C. Cantrijn, Taibah Moskee in De Bijlmer. Islamitische Traditie in Westerse Context, in: De Architect, Vol 16 (3), March 1985, pp. 64-67.
198 For other, more recent critiques of Dutch mosques by Maarten Kloos, see F. van Lier, "Zonder Minaret is het net een Planetarium," in: http://reporter.kro.nl/uitzendingen/2007/0402_moskeeen/moskeeen_in_nederland.aspx.
199 'Moskee Taibah is te klein geworden,' in: De Nieuwe Bijlmer, 4-6-1987.

NOTES

200 'Taibah Moskee na Jaren uit de Brand,' in: ?, 1990 (?), and 'Moskee verkeert weer in grote Geldnood, in: (?), 6-12-1990, *Archive Haffmans*; Before, the collection of money for the monthly payments had posed a huge problem in the community up to the point that the mosque was almost to the point of being publicly auctioned by the Afdeling Grondzaken. 'Moskee niet bezorgd over aflopen Ultimatum,' in: *De Nieuwe Bijlmer*, 17-8-1989.
201 Also see H. Müller's 'Zo'n Fundamentalist maakt alles Kapot,' in: *De Volkskrant*, 16-10-1998, p. 13. Note that parts of the content of Müller's article have been contested by Noorani in a legal procedure.
202 Ruimte 68 is currently run by Peter Scipio.
203 Eg. see the report of a meeting of Scipio and Domburg with Gaffar and Imandi, 31-5-1997, *Archive Ruimte 68*.
204 Interviews with Scipio and Domburg, Eindhoven, 22/30-8-2006.
205 Internal Memo, 31-5-1997, *Archive Ruimte 68*.
206 Internal Memo, 23-6-1997, and Letter from Ruimte 68 to the Stadsdeelraad Zuid-Oost, 22-7-1997, *Archive Ruimte 68*.
207 Fax from Stadsdeel Zuidoost to Ruimte 68, 11-11-1997, *Archive Ruimte 68*.
208 Internal Memo, 20-1-1998, and Fax from Stadsdeel Zuidoost to Ruimte 68, 30-1-1998, *Archive Ruimte 68*.
209 Internal Memo, 19-4-1998, *Archive Ruimte 68*.
210 Internal Memo, 21-4-1998, *Archive Ruimte 68*.
211 Internal Memo, 7-6-1998, *Archive Ruimte 68*.
212 Letter from Stadsdeel Zuidoost to Ruimte 68, 16-7-1998, *Archive Ruimte 68*.
213 Internal Memo, 8-10-1998, *Archive Ruimte 68*.
214 'Verslag Gesprek Moskee Taibah 3 Maart 1999,' Projectgroep Kraaiennest, and Internal Memos, 3/11-3-1999, *Archive Ruimte 68*.
215 Fax from Stadsdeel Zuidoost to Projectgroep Kraaiennest, 'Stedebouwkundige Randvoorwaarden Moskee,' 6-4-1999, *Archive Ruimte 68*.
216 Internal Memo, 28-4-1999, *Archive Ruimte 68*.
217 'Notulen Bouwvergadering d.d. 31-8-1999,' *Archive Ruimte 68*.
218 'Verslag Gesprek Moskee Taibah 15 Sept. 1999,' Projectgroep Kraaiennest, *Archive Ruimte 68*.
219 Internal Memo, 18-11-1999, *Archive Ruimte 68*.
220 Letter from the Aesthetics Commission to Ruimte 68, 1-3-2000, *Archive Ruimte 68*.
221 Internal Memo, 8-2-2000, *Archive Ruimte 68*.
222 Construction Permit Application, 27-3-2000, *Archive Ruimte 68*.
223 Letter from the Aesthetics Commission to Ruimte 68, 19-4-2000, *Archive Ruimte 68*.
224 Construction Permit Nr. 200000086, Dossier Nr. ZO69929, *Archive Stadsdeel Zuidoost*.
225 See http://www.taibah.nl/nieuwbouw/Forms/.
226 Sanyal 1999, p. 163.
227 ' Surinaamse Moslims willen openheid,' in: *Eindhovens Dagblad*, 19-11-1997.
228 Letter from the Aesthetics Commission to Ruimte 68, *Archive Ruimte 68*.
229 Letter from Stadsdeel Zuidoost to Gaffar, 10-2003, and Letter from Stadsdeel Zuidoost to Bestuur Moskee Taibah, 30-9-2004, *Archive Stadsdeel Zuidoost*.
230 Perhaps the earlier referred-to burial of Aleem 'near Aisha' in Medina had a similar function.
231 *The Message International*, Speciaal Nummer 2003, Noorani Editie, WIM Youth Circle, Amsterdam, pp. 17-20.
232 *Noorani Memorial Editie 2004*, WIM Nederland, Amsterdam.

233 Inside this publication it was also explicitly mentioned, again illustrated by an image of Reza Khan's shrine, that Noorani had continuously referred to the saint's name in his lectures and in his mission, and that he had always showed him much respect and love. *Noorani Memorial Editie 2004*, p. 8.
234 A similar example can be found in a Shia shrine in Aleppo, built shortly after the death of Nur al-Din, 'the sworn antagonist of Shi'ism in all its forms.' Here, a sculptured frieze of tiny lamps may be seen to represent the miraculous light of al-Husayn. Y. Tabbaa, *Constructions of Power and Piety in Medieval Aleppo*, Pennsylvania: The Pennsylvania State University Press, 1997, pp. 111, 115.
235 As he also did in Eindhoven, where he had installed similar lights. 'Eigen plek voor Eindhovense Surinaamse Moslims,' in: *Groot Eindhoven/Valkenswaards Weekblad*, 19-11-1997.

Chapter 2

1 R.H. Chauvel, *Nationalists, Soldiers and Separatists. The Ambonese Islands from Colonialism to Revolt, 1880-1950*, Leiden: KITLV Press, 1990, p. 161; A. van der Hoek, *Religie in Ballingschap. Institutionalisering en Leiderschap onder Christelijke en Islamitische Molukkers in Nederland*, Leiden: Leiden University; Amsterdam: VU Uitgeverij, 1994, pp. 52-53.
2 D. Bartels, *In de Schaduw van de Berg Nunusaku. Een Cultuur-Historische Verhandeling over de Bevolking van de Midden-Molukken*, Utrecht: Landelijk Steunpunt Edukatie Molukkers, 1994, p. 172.
3 For examples and references see Van der Hoek 1994, pp. 52-59.
4 D. Bartels, *Guarding the Invisible Mountain. Intervillage Alliances, Religious Syncretism and Ethnic Identity among Ambonese Christians and Moslems in the Moluccas*, New York: Cornell University, 1977, p. 307.
5 Some Moluccan Muslims wear Arab clothing when attending Friday prayers, and when interviewing Moluccan clan leaders in The Netherlands, whole genealogies were sometimes produced that were claimed to trace back descent to 33 or more generations ago from the Arabian Peninsula.
6 These examples, and many more interesting localizations of Islam, can be found in Bartels 1994, pp. 172-190, and in G.J. Knaap, *Kruidnagelen en Christenen. De Verenigde Oost-Indische Compagnie en de Bevolking van Ambon 1656-1696*, Leiden: KITLV Uitgeverij [Utrecht 1985], 2004, pp. 89-105.
7 See Chauvel 1990, pp. 160-169.
8 D. Bartels, *Moluccans in Exile. A Struggle for Ethnic Survival. Socialization, Identity Formation, and Emancipation Among an East-Indonesian Minority in the Netherlands*, Leiden: Center for the Study of Social Conflicts, University of Leiden; Utrecht: Moluccan Advisory Council, 1989, p. 10.
9 Van der Hoek 1994, pp. 69-79.
10 J.J. Sikkema, *Wyldemerck. Molukse Moslims in Nederland*, Amsterdam: University of Amsterdam, 1991, p. 24.
11 See Van der Hoek 1994, p. 204.
12 Van der Hoek 1994, p. 66.

NOTES

13 H. Smeets, De Plaats van Keuze, in: W. Manuhutu and H. Smeets (eds), *Tijdelijk Verblijf. De Opvang van Molukkers in Nederland, 1951*, Amsterdam: De Bataafsche Leeuw, 1991, pp. 7-16.
14 H. Smeets, De Organisatie van de Ambonezenzorg, in: Manuhutu and Smeets 1991, pp. 17-39; p. 17.
15 Smeets 1991, p. 18.
16 Smeets 1991, pp. 24-33.
17 T.W. Wittermans, *Social Organization among Ambonese Refugees in Holland*, Amsterdam: Het Spinhuis, 1991 [London 1955], p. 58.
18 For a more detailed study of Tan's background on Ambon, see A. van der Hoek, *De Islamitisch Molukse Gemeenschap en haar Leider Imam Achmad Tan*, Leiden: Leiden University, 1987.
19 ARA II, CIO nr.84, *National Archive*; Over the past decade and even during the course of this research, the relevant documents in the National Archive have undergone several shifts in inventory systems and the Archive stresses that they are still under scrutiny. However, all former denotations will be linked to any new ones.
20 Letter from Tan, Laupopuw and Tamasoa to CIO, 31-07-1952, ARA II, CIO nr.84, *National Archive*.
21 Van der Hoek 1994, p. 173;Letter from Tan to CIO., ARA II, CIO nr.84, *National Archive*.
22 Van der Hoek 1994, p. 174.
23 Bartels 1989, pp. 272-273.
24 Letter from the Commission's secretary, P.A. Lanting, to all parties concerned, 21-12-1953, CAZ, *National Archive*.
25 Wittermans 1991, p. 65.
26 Collection of signatures of most of the 69 Muslim heads of family present, 10-6-1954, CAZ, *National Archive*. In practice and unofficially, Tan started fulfilling this position a year earlier. Sikkema 1991, p. 29.
27 Letter from Van Ringen to all parties concerned, 9-10-1954, CAZ, *National Archive*; Letter from Lanting to Tan, 16-10-1954, CAZ, *National Archive*.
28 Interview with Ollong, Ridderkerk, 13-7-2005.
29 Van der Hoek 1994, p. 182.
30 Also see Van der Hoek 1987, pp. 29, 38-41.
31 'Ambon moet Vrij! Interview with Achmad Tan, Leider der Zuid-Molukse Islamieten in Nederland,' in: (?), nr.61, 10-11, 1954, pp. 6-7, Archive Ghani van den Bergh; *Leeuwarder Courant*, 19-03-1955; Van der Hoek 1987, pp. 40, 65
32 See Van der Hoek 1994, p. 176.
33 *Leeuwarder Courant*, 19-03-1955.
34 G. van den Bergh, *Wyldemerck. Kamp voor Islamitische Molukkers, 1954-1969*, Utrecht: Moluks Historisch Museum; Landelijk Steunpunt Edukatie Molukkers, 1996 [Ridderkerk 1994], p. 17.
35 Letter from Tan to Logeman, RGD Leeuwarden, 20-1-1955. *Archive Ghani van den Bergh*.
36 Van den Bergh 1996, p. 59.
37 *Leeuwarder Courant/Friese Koerier*, 18-02-1955.
38 *Friesche Koerier*, 24-02-1955.
39 *Balkster Courant*, 26-02-1955.
40 *Leeuwarder Courant*, 19-03-1955.
41 *Friesche Koerier/Leeuwarder Courant*, 28-03-1955; *Balkster Courant*, 02-04-1955.

42 Also see J. Dumarçay, Indonesian Methods of Building with Stone, in: G. Tjahjono (ed), *Architecture. Indonesian Heritage Series Vol. 6*, Singapore: Archipelago Press; Jakarta: Buku Antar Bangsa, 1998, pp. 56-57.
43 See Khan 1994.
44 *Friesche Koerier/Leeuwarder Courant*, 28-03-1955; *Balkster Courant*, 02-04-1955.
45 *Friesche Koerier/Leeuwarder Courant*, 28-03-1955; *Balkster Courant*, 02-04-1955.
46 *Leeuwarder Courant*, 02-05-1955.
47 Van der Hoek 1987, pp. 41-48.
48 Note that Van der Hoek's connection of this sermon of Muslim brotherhood with 19th century Egyptian modernism and reform is admittedly her own association (Van der Hoek 1987, p. 41). Moreover, the author also found that Tan had not introduced any innovative theological ideas and that he specifically chose 'to unify the Moluccans on the basis of Islam, with which the religiously homogenous organizational structure of a Moluccan kampong was maintained' (Van der Hoek 1987, pp. 40, 65).
49 *Balkster Courant*, 03-09-1955.
50 *Balkster Courant*, 17-12-1955.
51 Letter from Van Ringen to Postma, 4-7-1955, *Archive Ghani van den Bergh*.
52 Interview with D. Gaasterland, Groningen, 9-7-2005; Postma made his statement in the context of a discussion on the minaret design.
53 For possible explanations of the origins of water tanks in front of Indonesian mosques in general, see H.J. de Graaf, De Oorsprong der Javaansche Moskee, in: *Indonesië*, nr. 1, 1947-1948, pp. 289-307; pp. 299-300, and C. Guillot, La Symbolique de la Mosquée Javanaise. A Propos de la "Petite Mosquée" de Jationom, in: *Archipel*, nr. 30, 1985, pp. 3-20; pp. 11-14.
54 For a short treatment of the role of Moluccan mosque tanks see H. O'Neil, The Mosque as a Sacred Space, in: Tjahjono 1998, pp. 94-95.
55 For a general discussion of a hierarchy of Indonesian roof forms see G. Tjahjono, The Javanese house, in: Tjahjono 1998, pp. 34-35.
56 See Bartels 1994, pp. 175-176, 179.
57 Also see De Graaf 1947-1948, p. 298.
58 For the origins of the multiple-layered or Meru-roof in Indonesian mosques see H.J. de Graaf, The Origin of the Javanese Mosque, in: *Journal of Southeast Asian History*, Vol.4 (1), 1963, pp. 1-5; For a treatment of the phenomenon in the Moluccas see De Graaf 1947-1948, and H. O'Neill, Regional Mosques: Tradition and Eclecticism, in: Tjahjono 1998, pp. 96-97.
59 H. O'Neill, Islamic Architecture under the New Order, in: V. Matheson Hooker (ed), *Culture and Society in New Order Indonesia*, Kuala Lumpur [etc]: Oxford University Press, 1993, pp. 151-165; O'Neill 1998, p. 97.
60 After independence, the Meru versus pan-Islamic distinction remained important in Indonesia: whereas Sukarno preferred the latter as 'modern-Islamic', the Suharto regime, in search of a more 'national' architectural representation, made much use of the Meru-form. A. Kusno, *Behind the Postcolonial. Architecture, Urban Space and Political Cultures in Indonesia*, London [etc]: Routledge 2000 [New York 1997].
61 Also see Bartels 1994, eg. pp. 186-187.
62 *Balkster Courant*, 21-04-1956.
63 *Balkster Courant*, 21-04-1955.
64 See J. Davison, The House as a Ritually Ordered Space, in: Tjahjono 1998, pp. 18-19; and R. Waterson, Construction Rites, in: Tjahjono 1998, pp. 19-21.

65 See M.C. Ricklefs, Six Centuries of Islamization in Java, in: Levtzion, N. (ed), *Conversion to Islam*, New York [etc]: Holmes & Meier, 1979, pp. 100-128.
66 See L.C. Joseph, *Aspek Arsitektur Tradisional Daerah Maluku*, Ambon: Proyek Inventarisasi Dokumentasi Kebudayaan Daerah, Dep. P&K Propinsi Maluku, 1982, p. 81.
67 *Balkster Courant*, 21-04-1955.
68 G.F. Pijper, The Minaret in Java, in: *India Antiqua*, 1947, pp. 274-283.
69 O'Neil 1998, p. 97.
70 Interview with Gaasterland, Groningen, 09-07-2005.
71 Van der Hoek 1994, p. 178-181.
72 *Leeuwarder Courant*, 19-03-1955.
73 And there certainly is no indication whatsoever that 'with Pakistani money' 'a wooden building' was put down 'in Wildenberg', as one newspaper wrote down on the occasion of the opening of the Waalwijk Bait Ar-Rahman Mosque. *Brabants Dagblad*, 6-10-1990, p. 33.
74 Van der Hoek 1994, p. 179.
75 *Leeuwarder Courant/Friesche Koerier*, 16-07-1956; *Balkster Courant*, 21-07-1956.
76 Advertisement, by the Inspection of Domains in Leeuwarden, for the sale on 12-9-1968 of equipment and barracks, including 'a mosque with tower, made of double-walled asbestos-plates', Archive Ghani van den Bergh.
77 As noted down by Van den Bergh, 1996, p. 109.
78 As described in some detail by Van der Hoek, 1994, p. 184-185.
79 See Van der Hoek 1994, footnote 57, p. 190.
80 See Van der Hoek 1994, pp. 189-192, for a description of relevant, traditional inter-village loyalties; see E. Rinsampessy, *Saudara Bersaudara. Molukse Identiteit in Processen van Cultuurverandering*, Assen [etc]: Van Gorcum; Wychen: Pattimura, 1992, pp. 42-47, for a treatment of inter-village or *Pela*-bonds in The Netherlands in general.
81 Landman 1992, pp. 35-36.
82 Bartels 1989, p. 27.
83 Van der Hoek 1994, p. 197.
84 Van der Hoek 1994, footnote 55, p. 189.
85 Van der Hoek 1994, p. 186.
86 Its Moluccan Department had replaced the former CAZ.
87 Letter from Abdul Sabar Oppier to CRM, 7-5-1976, Archive Hamid Oppier.
88 Interview with Hamid Oppier, Krimpen a/d Lek, 24-01-2006.
89 Telephone Interview with Abdul Wahid van Bommel, 01-2006.
90 See W.J. Hamblin and D.R. Seely, *De Tempel van Salomo. Mythe en Geschiedenis*, Haarlem: Altamira-Becht, 2007 [London: Thames & Hudson, 2007], pp. 182-187.
91 W.G. Ket, Vrijmetselaar Perotti Bouwt Islamitische Godshuizen, in: *AMT (Algemeen Maçonniek Tijdschrift)*, Vol. 44, nr. 3, March 1990, pp. 73-76.
92 Ikram, Interview met Latief Perotti, in: *Salaam. Moslim Jongeren Blad*, Vol.1 (4), 1991, pp. 22-24; p. 22.
93 Interviews with Abdul Hamid Oppier, Krimpen a/d Lek, 24-01-2006, Hamid Samaniri, Ridderkerk, 28-12-2005, Boy Barajanan, Waalwijk, 1-2-2006, and Ibrahim Lessy, Waalwijk, 2-2-2006; During an interview in between the architect's mosque commissions, he also told Van der Hoek that he was 'a practising ('*belijdend*') Muslim'. A. van der Hoek, Interview with Perotti, in: A. van der Hoek and H. Obdeijn (eds), *De Islam. Godsdienst en Gemeenschap. De Moskee als Ontmoetingsplaats, Bouwstenen voor Intercultureel Onderwijs*, vol. 39, Leiden: Coördinaat Minderheden Studies, Leiden

University, 1989, pp. 32-34; p. 32; Van der Hoek 1994, p. 187; Email from Van der Hoek to Roose, 21-11-2007.
94 L. Perotti, Herontdekking van Islamitische Principes in de Moderne Architectuur, in: *Qiblah, Informatiebulletin Federatie Moslim Organisaties Nederland*, nr. 1, February/March 1981, pp. 11-14.
95 Ikram 1991, p. 22; B. Stigter, Islamitische Architectuur in Nederland. Waar de Kameel Knielde, in: *NRC Handelsblad*, 09-08-1991, CS, p. 2.
96 Ikram 1991, p. 22.
97 Van der Hoek 1989, pp. 33-34.
98 W. Wennekes, Hoe groter de Moskee, hoe dichter bij Allah. Islamitische Bouwkunst in Nederland, in: *Intermediair*, vol.29, nr.28, 16-7-1993, pp. 20-25; p. 25.
99 Stigter 1991.
100 Also see L. Perotti, Het Heiligdom. Kwartier Maken voor God, in: *De Heilige Plaats. Het Heiligdom en de Betekenis voor Vandaag, Nieuwe Soefi Reeks*, nr.12, October 1997, pp. 47-61.
101 Drawing by Perotti, *Archive Opaal Architecten*.
102 Buijs 1998, pp. 29-30.
103 Buijs 1998, p. 29.
104 Maussen 2006, p. 126.
105 Perotti's paper was not selected for publication in the conference's Proceedings, but a summary is presented in Perotti 1981.
106 Drawing by Perotti, *Archive Bait Ar-Rahman Mosque*.
107 See Letter from Perotti to Spalburg, 12-01-1981, *Archive Bait Ar-Rahman Mosque*.
108 As he stated in Van der Hoek 1989.
109 'Verslag van de op 19 april gehouden Algemene Vergadering van de Stichting Molukse Moskee Ridderkerk in het Wijkcentrum "Oosterhonk" te Ridderkerk,' *Archive Stichting Molukse Moskee Ridderkerk*, henceforward referred to as *Archive Bait Ar-Rahman Mosque*.
110 'Memorandum' from Perotti to Spalburg, 25-03-1980, *Archive Abdul Hamid Oppier*.
111 Drawing by Perotti, *Archive Opaal Architecten*.
112 Letter from Perotti to Spalburg, 12-01-1981, and drawing by Perotti, *Archive Bait Ar-Rahman Mosque*.
113 Letter from mayor and aldermen to the RGD, 31-03-1981, *Archive Abdul Hamid Oppier*.
114 Also see 'Verslag van door de Stichting Molukse Moskee Ridderkerk ontwikkelde Activiteiten in het Jaar 1981,' *Archive Bait Ar-Rahman Mosque*.
115 Also see 'Verslag van door de Stichting Molukse Moskee Ridderkerk ontwikkelde Activiteiten in het Jaar 1981,' *Archive Bait Ar-Rahman Mosque*;.
116 'Verslag van door de Stichting Molukse Moskee Ridderkerk ontwikkelde Activiteiten in het Jaar 1981,' *Archive Bait Ar-Rahman Mosque*.
117 10-09-1981-Report of Commission Meeting of 13-08-1981, Commissie voor Openbare Werken, Notulen der Vergaderingen 1981, Archiefdossier Bestuursdienst Gemeente Ridderkerk, Dossier nr. 10994, Volgnr. 8915, *Archive Municipality of Ridderkerk*.
118 *Oost-Ijsselmonde*, 18-08-1981.
119 08-10-1981-Report of Commission Meeting of 10-09-1981, Commissie voor Openbare Werken, Notulen der Vergaderingen 1981, Archiefdossier Bestuursdienst Gemeente Ridderkerk, Dossier nr. 10994, Volgnr. 8915, *Archive Municipality of Ridderkerk; Noord-en Waalbode*, 16-09-1981.
120 *De Combinatie*, 24-09-1981.
121 *Het Zuiden*, 01-10-1981.

NOTES

122 26-10-1981-Report of Council Meeting of 28-09-1981, Notulen van de Vergaderingen van de Gemeenteraad 1981-II, pp. 557-568, Archiefdossier Bestuursdienst Gemeente Ridderkerk, Dossier nr. 9283, Doos nr. 926, Volgnr. 7160, *Archive Municipality of Ridderkerk*.
123 Bouwdossier J.S.Bachstraat 2A, 'Moskee,' Dossier nr 166, Doosnr 21, Volgnr 167, Bouwvergunningendossier nr B83-004, *Archive Municipality of Ridderkerk*.
124 *De Combinatie*, 29-04-1982.
125 Bouwdossier J.S.Bachstraat 2A, 'Moskee,' Dossier nr 166, Doosnr 21, Volgnr 167, Bouwvergunningendossier nr B83-004, *Archive Municipality of Ridderkerk*.
126 Interview with Hamid Samaniri, Ridderkerk, 28-12-2005; 'Eerste Spa voor Moskee de Grond in,' in: (?), *Archive Bait Ar-Rahman Mosque*; The exact date of this ritual is not known, but it was probably during September 1983.
127 For a treatment of Indonesian pole rituals, see Waterson 1998, pp. 20-21.
128 Letter from WVC to the mosque administration, 14-10-1983, *Archive Bait Ar-Rahman Mosque*.
129 'Voor- en Nabeschouwing van de Eerste Paal voor onze Moskee,' *Archive Hamid Samaniri*.
130 'Programma bij het slaan van de eerste Paal van de te bouwen Moskee op Vrijdag 14 oktober 1983,' *Archive Bait Ar-Rahman Mosque*.
131 Also see Letter from the Ministry of Volkshuisvesting, Ruimtelijke Ordening en Milieubeheer (VROM), Dienst van het Kadaster en de Openbare Registers, to the RGD, 08-06-1983, *Archive Hamid Samaniri*.
132 K. van der Velde, Nederlandse Soefi's bespreken het heilige en het mystieke, in: *Trouw*, 27-11-1995; Perotti 1997, p. 51.
133 Also see Waterson 1998, p. 20.
134 *Waalpost*, 04-10-1984.
135 L. Perotti, Koepel en Minaret sieren Ridderkerkse Moskee. Integratie van Architectuur, Kunst en Techniek, in: *Bouwkunde en Civiele Techniek*, nr. 3, 1986, pp. 11-18.
136 Van der Hoek 1989.
137 T. Maas, Baith Al-Rahmaan Moskee te Ridderkerk. Geen Steen zonder Symbolische Bijbedoeling, in : *De Architect*, Vol. 16, May 1985, pp. 52-55; p. 55.
138 Maas 1985, p. 54.
139 Van der Hoek 1994, p. 187.
140 Van der Hoek 1994, pp. 198-199, 201.
141 Interview with Boy Barajanan, Waalwijk, 1-2-2006; Telephone Interview with Astorias Ohorella, 2-2006.
142 Letter from Perotti to ONI, 28-11-1978, *Archive Boy Barajanan*; Program of Construction, 8-1-1979, Boy Barajanan, *Archive Boy Barajanan*.
143 Letter from ONI to Perotti, 14-12-1978, *Archive Boy Barajanan*.
144 Letter from S.A. Ohorella to Boy Barajanan, 14-12-1978 ('Donderdag 19.00'), *Archive Boy Barajanan*.
145 Report of the ONI Meeting of 17-12-1978, Astorias Ohorella, *Archive Boy Barajanan*.
146 Program of Construction, 8-1-1979, Boy Barajanan, *Archive Boy Barajanan*.
147 Report Meeting Building Commission 11-1-1979, *Archive Boy Barajanan*.
148 Also see Notulen van de Openbare Vergadering van de Raad der Gemeente Waalwijk gehouden op 31-10-1988, Agenda' s en Notulen Raadsvergaderingen Waalwijk 1988, Dossier 1517, *Archive Municipality of Waalwijk*.
149 Letter from Matulessy to Barajanan, 28-02-1979, *Archive Boy Barajanan*.
150 As described in some detail in Van der Hoek 1994, pp. 198-201.

151 Concept Program of Requirements, Foundation Moluccan Mosque An-Nur Waalwijk, 23-02-1984, *Archive Boy Barajanan*.
152 Drawing by Perotti, *Archive Barajanan*. As the patron is already indicated as Foundation Moluccan Mosque An-Nur, it should be dated between 22 November 1983 and 23 February 1984.
153 Interview with Ibrahim Lessy, waalwijk, 2-2-2006.
154 Also see *Brabants Dagblad*, 6-1-1990.
155 Also see J. Huisman, *Mooi Gebouwd Nederland*, The Hague: SDU Uitgeverij, 1992, pp. 98-99.
156 Letter from RGD Coordinator Moluccan Churches to RGD Director Noord-Brabant and Limburg, 25-4-1986, SSA nr. RGDDAO9800253, *Archive RGD*.
157 As referred to in a letter from RGD Director Noord-Brabant and Limburg to Perotti, SSA nr. RGDDAO0900549, *Archive RGD*.
158 Drawing by Perotti, *Archive RGD*.
159 Proposal for Establishment of Budget by G.A. Nijrolder (RGD), 16-4-1987 and Reaction of W. Treffers (RGD), 19-5-1987, SSA nr. RGDDAO0900549, *Archive RGD*.
160 Interviews with Boy Barajanan, Waalwijk, 1-2-2006, and with Ibrahim Lessy, Waalwijk, 2-2-2006.
161 Report Meeting Foundation An-Nur with Perotti, 21-4-1987, *Archive Boy Barajanan*.
162 Report Meeting Foundation An-Nur with Perotti, 21-4-1987, *Archive Boy Barajanan*.
163 Summary Report Meeting of 18-5-1987, 2-6-1987, RGDDAO0900549, *Archive RGD*.
164 Concept Budget, 12-2-1988, RGDDAO0900549, *Archive RGD*.
165 Perotti 1997, p. 54.
166 Drawing by Perotti, *Archive Barajanan*.
167 Held in socio-cultural center 'De Leest' on 8-1-1988, *Maasroute*, 14-1-1988, p. 3. Photograph of model by Perotti in *Archive Barajanan*.
168 Construction Permit Application, 19-1-1988, Bouwdossier Noordstraat 79, *Archive Municipality of Waalwijk*.
169 Advice Aesthetics Commission Waalwijk, 17-2-1988, and letter from Waalwijk Aesthetics Commission to RGD, 22-2-1988, Bouwdossier Noordstraat 79, *Archive Municipality of Waalwijk*.
170 Report Meeting of Commissie Ruimtelijke Ordening en Volkshuisvesting of 14-6-1988, Gemeentebestuur Waalwijk (1877)1922-1996(2001), Dossier 1633, *Archive Municipality of Waalwijk*.
171 Notulen van de Openbare Vergadering van de Raad der Gemeente Waalwijk, gehouden op 30-6-1988, as established on 29-8-1988, Agenda's en Notulen Raadsvergaderingen Waalwijk 1988, Dossier 1518, *Archive Municipality of Waalwijk*; *De Waalwijker*, 30-6-1988.
172 Notulen van de Openbare Vergadering van de Raad der Gemeente Waalwijk, gehouden op 31-10-1988, as established on 24-11-1988, Agenda's en Notulen Raadsvergaderingen Waalwijk 1988, Dossier 1518, *Archive Municipality of Waalwijk*.
173 Construction Permit nr. 9920, 6-12-1988, Bouwdossier Noordstraat 79, *Archive Municipality of Waalwijk*.
174 *Brabants Dagblad*, 4-3-1989; *De Waalwijker*, 9-3-1989.
175 *Brabants Dagblad*, 22-8-1989, p. 2
176 *Brabants Dagblad*, 25-8-1989.
177 *Brabants Dagblad*, 13-1-1990, p. 31.
178 *Maasroute*, 13-1-1990; *De Telegraaf*, 15-1-1990; *Maasroute*, 20-1-1990.
179 *Brabants Dagblad*, 15-1-1990, p. 9.

180 Van der Velde 1995; Perotti 1997, p. 58.
181 Perotti 1997, p. 51.
182 L. Perotti, Nieuwe Moskee in Waalwijk, in: *Qiblah, Informatiebulletin Federatie Moslim Organisaties Nederland*, Spring 1990, pp. 17-25; p. 19.
183 Huisman 1992, pp. 98-99; Perotti 1990, p. 19; *Het Weekjournaal*, 18-1-1990; 'Project: Moskee An-Nur, Waalwijk,' in: *Bouwwereld*, 86, nr. 17a, 24-8-1990, pp. 16-20.
184 P. Onvlee, RGD bouwt zijn laatste Moskee, in: *Open Huis, Ministerie van VROM*, Vol. 13, nr. 10 (October), 1989, pp. 15-18, p. 18; J.H. Kohne, Symboliek in Beton, in: *Cement, Vakblad voor de Betonwereld*, Vol. 42, nr. 10 (October), 1990, pp. 20-21.
185 Perotti 1990, p. 18.
186 Onvlee 1989, p. 17.
187 Lessy's view is actually in line with some Moluccan oral traditions, saying that Islam was introduced by Wali from the Middle-East. Bartels 1994, pp. 172-173.
188 See http://www.nrc.nl/W2/Lab/Profiel/Molukken/moslims.html; Interview with Ibrahim Lessy, Waalwijk, 2-2-2006.
189 See P. Vreuls, De Moskee van Waalwijk, in: *ANWB Kampioen*, Vol. 113, nr. 12 (December), 1998, pp. 80-82.
190 Onvlee 1989, p. 17.
191 Letter from Perotti to Roose, 25-8-2007, *Author's Collection*.

Chapter 3

1 'Nederlands Eerste en Enige Moskee,' in: *Qiblah. Informatiebulletin Federatie Moslim Organisaties Nederland*, Vol. 2, nr. 1 (January/February), 1978; D. Deniz, *De Ontstaansgeschiedenis van de Witte Moskee in Almelo, 1972-1975*, Zwolle: Windesheim School, 2005.
2 K. Canatan., *Turkse Islam. Perspectieven op Organisatievorming en Leiderschap in Nederland*, Rotterdam: Erasmus Universiteit, 2001, pp. 81-83.
3 Canatan 2001, p. 86.
4 Canatan 2001, p. 90.
5 Landman 1992, footnote 38, p. 88.
6 Canatan 2001, p. 87.
7 Landman 1992, pp. 101-102.
8 Canatan 2001, pp. 48-49.
9 Landman 1992, p. 98; During the selection of case studies in 2004, there were no purpose-built Süleymanli mosques in The Netherlands. At the time of writing, there were three (Almelo, Amersfoort, Delfzijl). Email from H. van de Schoor, Leiden University, to Roose, 20-8-2008.
10 Canatan 2001, p. 92.
11 Landman 1992, pp. 120-127.
12 Landman 1992, p. 117.
13 N. Landman, Sustaining Turkish-Islamic Loyalties: The Diyanet in Western Europe, in: H. Poulton and S. Taji-Farouki (eds), *Muslim Identity and the Balkan State*, London: Hurst & Company, 1997, pp. 214-231; p. 219.
14 T. Sunier, *Islam in Beweging. Turkse Jongeren en Islamitische Organisaties*, Amsterdam: Het Spinhuis, 1996, p. 68.
15 'Afdeling Indië slaat nieuwe wegen in,' in: *Twentsche Courant*, 27-6-1969, p. 7.

16 Tubantia, 12-9-1972; 'Minister Boersma motiveert toestemming werving buitenlanders. Te weinig werknemers beschikbaar om vacatures bij NtC te vervullen,' in: *Dagblad v/h Oosten/ Tubantia/ Twentsche Courant*, 21-9-1972.
17 Company Report 'Opleiding Buitenlandse Werknemers' by D. Slettenhaar, 12-1970, Inv. Nr. 1137, *Archive Ten Cate*.
18 "Tercüman Atabek: Turkije geen verschroeid en achterlijk land!," in (?), Stad en Streek, 14-1-1970, p. 11, *Archive Türker Atabek*.
19 M. Klomp, *Samen een gebedshuis bouwen, maar geen woord over het gebed. Een onderzoek, in het kader van de dialoog, naar de houding van Turkse Moslims en Nederlandse Almeloërs, waaronder Christenen, voor, tijdens en na de bouw van de Almelose moskee*, Kampen: Theological University Kampen, 1987.
20 Since Slettenhaar has died, this statement was based on an interview with his son, Henk Slettenhaar, 18-5-2006, Almelo.
21 Minutes of the Construction Mosque Committee, 20-6-1972, Dossier Moskee Almelo, p. 8, *Archive Slettenhaar* (a copy of which is kept at the library of the Theological University Kampen); Klomp 1987, p. 7.
22 Minutes of the Construction Mosque Committee, 27-6-1972, Dossier Moskee Almelo, p. 9, *Archive Slettenhaar*; Klomp 1987, p. 7.
23 Interviews with Atabek, 10-4-2006, Almelo, and 26-11-2007, telephonic. Also see A. Kiziltan, Anadolu Beyliklerinde Cami ve Mescitler (XIV yüzyil sonuna kadar), Istanbul: Istanbul Teknik Üniversitesi, 1958, pp. 47-68.
24 *Dagblad v/h Oosten*, 31-8-1974. Pelgrum himself has passed away.
25 Letter from Diyanet Isleri Baskanligi to Nijverdal ten Cate, sent 21-7-1972/received 7-8-1972, Dossier Moskee Almelo, p. 10, *Archive Slettenhaar*.
26 "Tercüman Atabek: Turkije geen verschroeid en achterlijk land!," in (?), Stad en Streek, 14-1-1970, p. 11, *Archive Türker Atabek*.
27 Klomp 1987, p. 25.
28 As also thought by A. Özdemir and K. Frank, *Visible Islam in Modern Turkey*, Basingstoke [etc]: Macmillan; New York: St. Martin's Press, 2000, p. 183.
29 S. Bozdoğan, *Modernism and Nation Building. Turkish Architectural Culture in the Early Republic*, Seattle, Washington [etc]: University of Washington Press, 2001, pp. 47-54, 240-293.
30 Bozdoğan 2001, pp. 300-303.
31 S. Bozdoğan, The Predicament of Modernism in Turkish Architectural Culture. An Overview, in: S. Bozdoğan and R. Kasaba (eds), *Rethinking Modernity and National Identity in Turkey*, Washington [etc]: University of Washington Press, 1997, pp. 133-156; p. 148.
32 Özdemir and Frank 2000, pp. 182-183, 195-203.
33 Bozdoğan 2001, pp. 279-282. Notably, when a prayer hall was added to the complex in 1990, its design purposefully and conspicuously lacked any classical Ottoman recognizability. J. Erzen and A. Balamir, The Parliament Mosque, Ankara, in: Serageldin and Steele 1996, pp. 105-107.
34 M.E. Meeker, Once There Was, Once There Wasn't. National Monuments and Interpersonal Exchange, in: Bozdoğan and Kasaba 1997, pp. 157-191; pp. 175-178, 183, 191; G. Ersan, Secularism, Islamism, Emblemata: The Visual Discourse of Progress in Turkey, in: *Design Issues*, Vol. 23, nr.2 (Spring), 2007, pp. 66-82; pp. 72-76.
35 See http://www.archnet.org/library/sites/one-site.jsp?site_id=243.

36 In fact, it seems to have played a prominent role in the design for a recent mosque in Istanbul. See: http://news.bbc.co.uk/2/hi/europe/7636142.stm; http://wowturkey.com/forum/viewtopic.php?t=52770.
37 *Dagblad v/h Oosten*, 31-8-1974.
38 See H. Acun, *Bozok Sancağı (Yozgat ili) 'nda Türk Mimarisi*, Ankara: Türk Tarih Kurumu, 2005.
39 *Dagblad v/h Oosten*, 31-8-1974.
40 *Dagblad v/h Oosten*, 31-8-1974.
41 W. Speiser, *Baukunst des Ostens: von der Zeitenwende bis zum 19. Jahrhundert*, Essen: Burkhard-Verlag Ernst Heyer, 1964.
42 *Dagblad v/h Oosten*, 31-8-1974..
43 'Bijeenkomst oprichting commissie bouw Moskee op vrijdagmiddag 15 september 1972,' Dossier Moskee Almelo, p. 11-12, *Archive Slettenhaar*; Extra Bulletin for the Turkish employees of Nijverdal ten Cate, 9-1972, Dossier Moskee Almelo, pp. 15-17, *Archive Slettenhaar*; Klomp 1987, p. 8.
44 *Tubantia*, 16-9-1972; Dossier Moskee Almelo, p. 13, *Archive Slettenhaar*.
45 *De Koppeling*, 10-11-1972/*NRC handelsblad* 14-11-1972, Dossier Moskee Almelo, p. 50, *Archive Slettenhaar*.
46 *Tubantia*, 16-9-1972; Dossier Moskee Almelo, p. 13, *Archive Slettenhaar*.
47 *Dagblad van het Oosten* (?), 24-11-1972, Dossier Moskee Almelo, pp. 64-65, *Archive Slettenhaar*.
48 *Dagblad van het Oosten*, 16(?)-9-1972; Dossier Moskee Almelo, p. 22, *Archive Slettenhaar*.
49 Letter from Slettenhaar to Mr. J.J.C. Alberdingk Thijm, 5-10-1972, Dossier Moskee Almelo, p. 25, *Archive Slettenhaar*.
50 'Verslag van de tweede vergadering van de C.O.M. op vrijdag 29 september 1972,' Dossier Moskee Almelo, pp. 18-21, *Archive Slettenhaar* and Inv.Nr. 1370, *Archive Ten Cate*; *Dagblad van het Oosten/Tubantia*, 3-10-1972; Persbericht 3-10-1972, Inv.Nr. 1370, *Archive Ten Cate*.
51 See Letter from Smelt to C.O.M., Dossier Moskee Almelo, pp. 28-30, *Archive Slettenhaar*.
52 'Notulen van de vergadering Comité Oprichting Moskee,' 11-10-1972, Inv.Nr. 1370, *Archive Ten Cate*.
53 Internal company memo from Van der Noordaa to Slettenhaar, 20-10-1972, Dossier Moskee Almelo, p. 37, *Archive Slettenhaar*.
54 See letter from Van der Noordaa to Alberdingk Thijm, 19-9-1972, Afd. RbV-A, Inv. Nr.1137, Map R113, *Archive Ten Cate*.
55 Letter from Notary De Haan to Slettenhaar, 25-10-1972, Dossier Moskee Almelo, p. 40, *Archive Slettenhaar*.
56 'Notulen van de vergadering Algemeen Bestuur Stichting Turkse Moskee Twente te Almelo d.d. 2 november 1972,' Dossier Moskee Almelo, pp. 42-43, *Archive Slettenhaar*.
57 Letter from De Haan to Slettenhaar, 14-11-1972 and Foundation Statutes, 13-11-1972, Dossier Moskee Almelo, pp. 52, 54-57, *Archive Slettenhaar*.
58 Letter from Loning to mayor and aldermen of Almelo, 27-11-1972, Dossier Moskee Almelo, pp. 66-67, *Archive Slettenhaar,* and Bouwdossier Bellavistastraat 30, *Archive Municipality of Almelo,* and Afd. RvB-A, Inv.Nr.1137, Map R101, *Archive Ten Cate*.
59 Letter from Le Poole to Alberdink Thijm, 30-11-1972, Dossier Moskee Almelo, p. 72, *Archive Slettenhaar*, and Afd. RvB-A, Inv.Nr.1137, Map R101, *Archive Ten Cate*.
60 'Turkse moskee bekroond met minaret en koepel,' in: *Twentse Courant*, 4-9-1974, Dossier Moskee Almelo, p. 172, *Archive Slettenhaar*.
61 Also see Özdemir and Frank 2000, p. 240.

62 *Dagblad v/h Oosten*, 31-8-1974.
63 Request Form from Bouw- en Woningtoezicht to Aesthetics Commission, 5-4-1973, Bouwdossier Bellavistastraat 30, *Archive Municipality of Almelo*.
64 Answering Form from Aesthetics Commission to Bouw- en Woningtoezicht, 12-4-1973, Bouwdossier Bellavistastraat 30, *Archive Municipality of Almelo*.
(http://www.nicis.nl/kenniscentrum/binaries/nicis/bulk/producten/city8binnenw3.pdf)
65 Eg. see M. Maussen, Gemeente en Moskee. Een Halve Eeuw Schuivende verantwoordelijkheden, in: *City Journal, Wetenschappelijk Tijdschrift voor de Steden*, nr. 8 (June), 2007, pp. 30-35; p. 31.
66 *Tubantia*, 31-8-1974.
67 Letter from mayor and aldermen to the Foundation, 25-6-1973, Bouwdossier Bellavistastraat 30, *Archive Municipality of Almelo*.
68 Letter from Slettenhaar to the mosque administration, 13-8-1973, Dossier Moskee Almelo, pp. 104-105, *Archive Slettenhaar*.
69 Letter from Slettenhaar to the mosque administration, 13-8-1973, Dossier Moskee Almelo, pp. 104-105, *Archive Slettenhaar*, and Inv.Nr.1370, *Archive Ten Cate*.
70 *Dagblad van het Oosten* (?)/*Tubantia*, (?)-8-1973, Dossier Moskee Almelo, pp. 108, 110, *Archive Slettenhaar*.
71 'Turkse moskee bekroond met minaret en koepel,' in: *Twentse Courant*, 4-9-1974, Dossier Moskee Almelo, p. 172, *Archive Slettenhaar*.
72 *Dagblad van het Oosten* (?)/*Tubantia*, (?)-8-1973, Dossier Moskee Almelo, pp. 108, 110, *Archive Slettenhaar*.
73 Also see the letter from the director of Public Works and Building Inspection (Gemeentewerken en Bouw- en Woiningtoezicht), inviting Pelgrum to attend the treatment on 23-8-1973 of the construction plans for a mosque on the Alidastraat, 15-8-1973, Dossier Moskee Almelo, p. 107, *Archive Slettenhaar*, and Bouwdossier Bellavistastraat 30, *Archive Municipality of Almelo*.
74 Letter from Slettenhaar to the mosque administration, 13-8-1973, Dossier Moskee Almelo, pp. 104-105, *Archive Slettenhaar*.
75 *Tubantia*, 15-8-1973, Dossier Moskee Almelo, p. 109, *Archive Slettenhaar*.
76 *Dagblad van het Oosten*, 17-9-1973, Dossier Moskee Almelo, p. 113, *Archive Slettenhaar*.
77 Letter from the Foundation to Holsbrink, 26-9-1973, Dossier Moskee Almelo, p. 114, *Archive Slettenhaar*, and Bouwdossier Bellavistastraat 30, *Archive Municipality of Almelo*, and Inv.Nr. 1370, *Archive Ten Cate*; Letter from Slettenhaar to the mosque administration, 26-9-1973, Dossier Moskee Almelo, p. 116, *Archive Slettenhaar*.
78 'Nota aan de Secretaris,' 18-10-1973, Bouwdossier Bellavistastraat 30, *Archive Municipality of Almelo*.
79 *Tubantia/Twentsche Courant*, 1-11-1973, Dossier Moskee Almelo, p. 118, *Archive Slettenhaar*.
80 Construction Permit Application, 20-11-1973, Bouwdossier Bellavistastraat 30, *Archive Municipality of Almelo*.
81 Positive Advice from the Director of Bouw- en Woningtoezicht, 18-3-1974, Bouwdossier Bellavistastraat 30, *Archive Municipality of Almelo*.
82 Construction Permit B73-1569, Bouwdossier Bellavistastraat 30, *Archive Municipality of Almelo*.
83 Letter from Loning to the mosque administration, 26-3-1974, Dossier Moskee Almelo, p. 146, *Archive Slettenhaar*.
84 Dagblad van het Oosten, 2-4-1974, Dossier Moskee Almelo, p. 149, *Archive Slettenhaar*.

85 'Programma Eerste steenlegging Turkse moskee Wierdensestraat,' Dossier Moskee Almelo, p. 151, *Archive Slettenhaar*.
86 *Dagblad van het Oosten*, 3-5-1974, *Twentse Courant/Trouw/Tubantia* 4-5-1974, Dossier Moskee Almelo, p. 157, 158, 160, *Archive Slettenhaar*.
87 *Dagblad van het Oosten*, 11-10-1974, *Trouw*, 16-10-1974, Dossier Moskee Almelo, p. 181, *Archive Slettenhaar*.
88 *Dagblad van het Oosten*, 18-10-1974, Dossier Moskee Almelo, p. 183, *Archive Slettenhaar*.
89 *Dagblad van het Oosten*, 8-1-1975, Dossier Moskee Almelo, p. 199, *Archive Slettenhaar*; Program for the opening, Dossier Moskee Almelo, pp. 212-213, *Archive Slettenhaar*.
90 Letter from Slettenhaar and Atabek to CRM, 2-1975, Dossier Moskee Almelo, p. 245, *Archive Slettenhaar*; In response to the Foundation's request in this letter to subsidize costs for imam and maintenance according to the Regeringsnota Buitenlandse Werknemers, CRM declined the imam-part. Letter from CRM to the Foundation, 16-4-1975, Dossier Moskee Almelo, p. 251, *Archive Slettenhaar*.
91 'Eerste Turkse moskee in oosten open,' in: (?), 27-1-1975, Dossier Moskee Almelo, p. 241, *Archive Slettenhaar*; Chairman's speech, Dossier Moskee Almelo, pp. 222-225, *Archive Slettenhaar*
92 'Klanken van de minaret samen met het beieren van de klokken,' in: *Dagblad van het Oosten*, 28-1-1975, Dossier Moskee Almelo, pp. 237-238, *Archive Slettenhaar*..
93 *Tubantia*, 28-1-1975, Dossier Moskee Almelo, p. 239, *Archive Slettenhaar*; *Twentsche Courant*, 28-1-1975, Dossier Moskee Almelo, pp. 242-243, *Archive Slettenhaar*.
94 *Tubantia*, 28-1-1975, Dossier Moskee Almelo, pp. 239, *Archive Slettenhaar*; Mayor's speech, Dossier Moskee Almelo, pp. 227-231, *Archive Slettenhaar*.
95 *Twentsche Courant*, 28-1-1975, Dossier Moskee Almelo, pp. 242-243, *Archive Slettenhaar*.
96 'Verslag van de vergadering van het algemeen bestuur op 14 december 1976,' 16-1-1977, Dossier Moskee Almelo, p. 256, *Archive Slettenhaar*.
97 *Dagblad van het Oosten*, 15-12-1976, Klomp 1987, Bijlage 5, p. 85.
98 Özdemir and Frank 2000, p. 191.
99 'Prijsopgave Uitbreiding Turkse Moskee Almelo,' Architectural Bureau Haverkamp, 2-7-1980, *Archive Yunus Emre Mosque*.
100 Untitled newspaper article, in: (?), 4-5-1981, *Archive Yunus Emre Mosque*.
101 Letter from Atabek to the Almelo City Hall, stadsbouwcommissie, 19-11-1979, Bouwdossier Bellavistastraat 30, *Archive Municipality of Almelo*.
102 Letter from the Director of Gemeentewerken en Bouw- en Woningtoezicht to mayor and aldermen, 18-2-1980, Bouwdossier Bellavistastraat 30, *Archive Municipality of Almelo*.
103 Construction Permit Application B80-6681, Bouwdossier Bellavistastraat 30, *Archive Municipality of Almelo*.
104 Advice from the Overijsselse Welstandscommissie B80-6681, 17-6-1980, Bouwdossier Bellavistastraat 30, *Archive Municipality of Almelo*.
105 Internal memo Bouw- en Woningtoezicht, 23-6-1980, Bouwdossier Bellavistastraat 30, *Archive Municipality of Almelo*.
106 Advice from the Director of Bouw- en Woningtoezicht to mayor and aldermen, 31-7-1980; Letter from mayor and aldermen to the Foundation, 26-11-1980; 'Circulaire voor de leden der Commissie voor de Ruimtelijke Ordening,' 1-12-1980; Public Announcement from the Mayor, 14-1-1981; Decision on the 'Verklaring van geen Bezwaar,' Gedeputeerde Staten van Overijssel, 22-5-1981, Bouwdossier Bellavistastraat 30, *Archive Municipality of Almelo*.

107 Letter from mayor and alderme to the Foundation and accompanying Construction Permit B80-6681, 11-6-1981, Bouwdossier Bellavistastraat 30, *Archive Municipality of Almelo*.
108 '1e Bouwvergadering Uitbreiding Turkse Moskee d.d. 20-6-1981, Restaurant Lokanta, Notulen Haverkamp 23-6-1981,' *Archive Yunus Emre Mosque*.
109 Control Overview Bouw- en Woningtoezicht, Bouwdossier Bellavistastraat 30, *Archive Municipality of Almelo*.
110 '9e Bouwvergadering Uitbreiding Turkse Moskee d.d. 5-1-1982, Restaurant Lokanta, Notulen Haverkamp 7-1-1982,' *Archive Yunus Emre Mosque*.
111 Letter from WVC to 'The Adressed,' 2 (?)-1-1982, with accompanying explication of the Regeling, *Archive Yunus Emre Mosque*.
112 Letter from Haverkamp to WVC, 2-3-1982, *Archive Yunus Emre Mosque*.
113 Letter from WVC to the Foundation, 5-9-1983, *Archive Yunus Emre Mosque*.
114 Control Overview Bouw- en Woningtoezicht, Bouwdossier Bellavistastraat 30, *Archive Municipality of Almelo*.
115 Construction Permit Application B87-964, 20-10-1987, Bouwdossier Bellavistastraat 30, *Archive Municipality of Almelo*.
116 'Gespreksnotitie,' and Groundplan with location of shop crossed in, 22-2-2000, Bouwdossier Bellavistastraat 30, *Archive Municipality of Almelo*.
117 Letter from Het Oversticht to Dienst Gemeentwerken, 7-12-1987, Letter from the Director of Bouw- en Woningtoezicht to the Foundation and Mabeg van Hasselt, 10-12-1987, Letter from Het Oversticht to Dienst Gemeentewerken, 18-12-1987; Bouwdossier Bellavistastraat 30, *Archive Municipality of Almelo*.
118 Advice (positive) from the Overijsselse Welstandscommissie Het Oversticht B87-964, 22-12-1987, Bouwdossier Bellavistastraat 30, *Archive Municipality of Almelo*.
119 Decision of GS of Overijssel on the 'Aanvraag Verklaring van geen Bezwaar,' 12-7-1988, Bouwdossier Bellavistastraat 30, *Archive Municipality of Almelo*.
120 Letter from mayor and aldermen to the Foundation, 18-5-1988, *Archive Yunus Emre Mosque*.
121 Raadsbesluit Gemeente Almelo 2097R/162, *Archive Yunus Emre Mosque*.
122 Letter from mayor and aldermen to Islamitische Stichting Nederland Moskee Almelo and accompanying permit B87-964, 26-7-1988, Bouwdossier Bellavistastraat 30, *Archive Municipality of Almelo*.
123 Control Overview Bouw- en Woningtoezicht, Bouwdossier Bellavistastraat 30, *Archive Municipality of Almelo*.
124 Construction Permit Application B92-422, 16-9-1992, Bouwdossier Bellavistastraat 30, *Archive Municipality of Almelo*.
125 Letter from Dienst Ruimtelijke en Economische Ontwikkeling to Yunus Emre, 23-9-1992, Bouwdossier Bellavistastraat 30, *Archive Municipality of Almelo*.
126 Advice (positive) nr. 9208126 of Het Oversticht, 13-10-1992, Bouwdossier Bellavistastraat 30, *Archive Municipality of Almelo*.
127 Internal memo from Ruimtelijke Ontwikkeling to the Almelo Police, 3-11-1992, Bouwdossier Bellavistastraat 30, *Archive Municipality of Almelo*.
128 Yellow memo, before 18-11-1992, attached to internal memo Ruimtelijke Ontwikkeling, 17-5-1995, Bouwdossier Bellavistastraat 30, *Archive Municipality of Almelo*.
129 Advice from Ruimtelijke Ontwikkeling, 21-12-1992, Bouwdossier Bellavistastraat 30, *Archive Municipality of Almelo*.

NOTES

130 Letter from Ter Steege to Bouwtoezicht, 23-3-1995, Bouwdossier Bellavistastraat 30, *Archive Municipality of Almelo*.
131 Letter from mayor and aldermen to the Municipal council, nr 42, 6-4-1995; Municipal council decision nr. 42, 13-4-1995; Internal memo Ruimtelijke Ordening, 26-4-1995; Request Declaration of No-Objection GS Overijssel, 7-6-1995; Letter from GS Overijssel to mayor and aldermen of Almelo, 20-6-1995; Nota aan B&W, Aanvraag Bouwvergunning, 10-7-1995, Bouwdossier Bellavistastraat 30, *Archive Municipality of Almelo*.
132 Letter from mayor and aldermen to Yunus Emre, 18-7-1995, Bouwdossier Bellavistastraat 30, *Archive Municipality of Almelo*.
133 Letter from Ruimtelijke Ontwikkeling to Ter Steege, 26-4-1995, Bouwdossier Bellavistastraat 30, *Archive Municipality of Almelo*.
134 Fax from Voskamp to Ter Steege, 28-8-1995, Bouwdossier Bellavistastraat 30, *Archive Municipality of Almelo*.
135 Aanvraagformulier Schetsplan P95-779, and confirmation letter from Ruimtelijke Ontwikkeling to Yunus Emre, 9-11-1995, Bouwdossier Bellavistastraat 30, *Archive Municipality of Almelo*.
136 Forms nr 1-2, accompanying the above confirmation letter, 9-11-1995, Bouwdossier Bellavistastraat 30, *Archive Municipality of Almelo*.
137 Advice nr. P95-779, Het Oversticht, 21-11-1995, and Schetsplan/Voorlopig Advies P95-779 containg a 'Verklaring van geen Bezwaar', 23-11-1995, Bouwdossier Bellavistastraat 30, *Archive Municipality of Almelo*.
138 Letter from mayor and aldermen to Yunus Emre, 23-4-1996, Bouwdossier Bellavistastraat 30, *Archive Municipality of Almelo*.
139 Aanvraagformulier Schetsplan, P97-885, 9-10-1997, Bouwdossier Bellavistastraat 30, *Archive Municipality of Almelo*.
140 Letter from Bouwtoezicht to Yunus Emre, 4-11-1997, Bouwdossier Bellavistastraat 30, *Archive Municipality of Almelo*.
141 Letter from Bouwtoezicht to Yunus Emre, 9-12-1997, Bouwdossier Bellavistastraat 30, *Archive Municipality of Almelo*.
142 Advice nr. P97-885, Het Oversticht, and Schetsplan/Voorlopig Advies, 4-12-1997; Letter from Bouwtoezicht to Yunus Emre, 9-12-1997, Bouwdossier Bellavistastraat 30, *Archive Municipality of Almelo*.
143 Aanvraagformulier Bouwvergunning, B98-316, 3-4-1998, and confirmation letter from Bouwtoezicht to Yunus Emre, 6-4-1998, Bouwdossier Bellavistastraat 30, *Archive Municipality of Almelo*.
144 Bouwvergunning Rapportage, and letter drom Bouwtoezicht to Yunus Emre, 24-4-1998, Bouwdossier Bellavistastraat 30, *Archive Municipality of Almelo*.
145 Letter from mayor and aldermen to Yunus Emre, 25-5-1998, Bouwdossier Bellavistastraat 30, *Archive Municipality of Almelo*.
146 Internal memo Stadswerk/Stadsontwerp, 9-6-1998, Bouwdossier Bellavistastraat 30, *Archive Municipality of Almelo*.
147 Letter from Bouwtoezicht to Yunus Emre, 16-10-1998, Bouwdossier Bellavistastraat 30, *Archive Municipality of Almelo*.
148 Aanvraagformulier Bouwvergunning, B98-992, and confirmation letter of Bouwtoezicht to Yunus Emre, 17-11-1998, Bouwdossier Bellavistastraat 30, *Archive Municipality of Almelo*.
149 Letter from Bouwtoezicht to Yunus Emre, 27-11-1998, Bouwdossier Bellavistastraat 30, *Archive Municipality of Almelo*.

150 Advice nr. B98-992, Het Overstricht, 30-11-1998, Bouwdossier Bellavistastraat 30, *Archive Municipality of Almelo*.
151 Proposal nr. 16, letter from mayor and aldermen to the municipal council, 21-1-1999; Almelo Municipal council decision nr. 167, 28-1-1999; Declaration Stadswerk (undated); Aanvraag Vergunning/ Vrijstelling 99/1627, 26-2-1999; Letter from GS Overijssel to mayor and aldermen, 12-3-1999, Bouwdossier Bellavistastraat 30, *Archive Municipality of Almelo*.
152 Letter from mayor and aldermen to Yunus Emre, 6-4-1999, Bouwdossier Bellavistastraat 30, *Archive Municipality of Almelo*.
153 Construction Report, Bouwdossier Bellavistastraat 30, *Archive Municipality of Almelo*.
154 Also see J. den Exter, *Diyanet. Een reis door de keuken van de officiële Turkse islam*, Beverwijk: CBP, 1990, pp. 52-55.
155 Interviews with the secretaries of the Mevlana Mosque, Rotterdam, 8-12-2004, and the Süleymaniye Mosque, Tilburg, 12-1-2005.
156 Interview with Ahmet Altikulaç, secretary of the Sultan Ahmet Mosque from the first ISN membership year. This was also stated by the architect to municipal representatives, see the 'Notitie inzake de bouw van een moskee te Zaandam, D. Schilp, Afdeling Verkeer, 15-10-1991,' Bouwdossier Poelenburg 156, *Archive Municipality of Zaanstad*.
157 Stigter 1991.
158 Wennekes 1993, p. 25; Another example of the Dutch Diyanet's control over its member mosques as well as their designs is given in De Rijk 2006, pp. 81-82, 218-230, 251-252, 260, 326, 329, 333.
159 In Sevinçsoy's father's book collection, kept by Sevinçsoy's former Mabeg-colleague Wim Vugs in Den Bosch, are a number of books on German architecture. In his father's time, German architects were much admired and hired at architectural institutes and by the Turkish elite. See R. Holod and A. Evin, *Modern Turkish Architecture*, Philadelphia, Pa: University of Pennsylvania Press, 1984; and A. Batur, *A Concise History. Architecture in Turkey during the 20th Century*, Istanbul: Chamber of Architects of Turkey, 2005.
160 'Eindhovense Moskee is de Grootste van Nederland,' in: *Huizen en Wonen*, Vol. 2, Nr. 6, 25-2-1989, pp. 1-2; p. 2.
161 Van der Hoek 1989.
162 'Turkse Gemeenschap in en rond Eindhoven blij met Fatih Moskee,' in: *Eindhovens Dagblad*, special edition, pp. 15-21; p. 16.
163 L. Veerman, Moskee Centrum van Allochtone Cultuur. 'Marmer is gewoon te duur,' in: *Trouw*, 14-9-1993.
164 Veerman 1993.
165 See Bozdoğan 2001, p. 34 and further, and Holod and Evin 1984, p. 51 and further.
166 'Oosters Licht en Rode Dakpannen,' in: *De Volkskrant*, 8-12-1994. A similar case seems to be the Sehitlik Mosque in Berlin, Germany. Connected to the German branch of Diyanet, the patrons purposefully chose what they saw as a 'profane' cornice, an element that in their eyes would not have been built as part of a classical Ottoman mosque but that would consciously show its function as a 'cultural center'. Also, in all other kinds of architectural innovation they located a modernization of the classical Ottoman type. To them, it was 'recognizably Turkish but not a repetition or copy'. See: http://www.sehitlik-moschee.de/sehitlik_moschee.php.
167 Interview with Wim Vugs, Sevinçsoy's former Mabeg colleague, 19-7-2006, Den Bosch; Wessels 2003, p. 49. The final building appears to incorporate elements from

NOTES

Sevinçsoy's project as well as from the icon of Turkish-republican modernism, the first Kocatepe design in Ankara. See: http://www.ad.nl/utrecht/stad/2134362/ Moskee_wordt_pronkstuk_Lombok.html.
168 Recently, Diyanet seems to have bestowed a similar role on the Turkish-Dutch designer Erdal Önder (eNa architecten, Bergen op Zoom, http://www.enaarchitecten.nl). See Welzbacher 2008, pp. 93-95.
169 Veerman 1993.
170 'In Nederland is het te koud om je buiten te wassen,' in: *Trouw*, 2-12-1994.
171 Veerman 1993.
172 'Nieuwe moskee wordt op twee na grootste van West-Europa,' in: *Noord-Hollands Dagblad*, 23-11-1991.
173 Dienst Stadsontwikkeling en Openbare Werken (DSOW) Zaanstad, Afdeling Stedebouw, Intern Stedebouwkundig Advies voor het Buro Beginselbehandeling, 26-9-1991, Bouwdossier Poelenburg 156, *Archive Municipality of Zaanstad*.
174 DSOW Zaanstad, Afdeling Bouw- en Woningtoezicht, 'Informatie over Bouwplan aan de Stichting Noordhollandse Welstandscommissie, Commissie voor Zaanstad,' 27-9-1991, and Procedure List 'Afdeling Bouw- en Woningtoezicht Advies mbt Aanvraag Bouwvergunning 7867;' Bouwdossier Poelenburg 156, *Archive Municipality of Zaanstad*.
175 Several letters between DSOW and Sevinçsoy, and Procedure List 'Afdeling Bouw- en Woningtoezicht Advies mbt Aanvraag Bouwvergunning 7867'; Bouwdossier Poelenburg 156, *Archive Municipality of Zaanstad*.
176 Maussen 2006, pp. 172-178.
177 'Notitie inzake de bouw van een moskee te Zaandam, D. Schilp, Afdeling Verkeer, 15-10-1991,' Bouwdossier Poelenburg 156, *Archive Municipality of Zaanstad*.
178 'Nieuwe Toestand,' 18-10-1991, Bouwdossier Poelenburg 156, *Archive Municipality of Zaanstad*.
179 'Turkse Moslims sparen voor Supermoskee,' in: *De Zaanse Gezinsbode*, 17-3-1992, p. 3.
180 Application Form ISN Zaandam to mayor and alderman of Zaanstad, 2-4-1992, Bouwdossier Poelenburg 156, *Archive Municipality of Zaanstad*.
181 'Voorstel B&W aan gemeenteraad, vergadering d.d. 3-9-1992,' 'voorstel 240/ agendapunt 7.1,' and 'Raadsbesluit d.d. 3 september 1992, voorstel 240;' Bouwdossier Poelenburg 156, *Archive Municipality of Zaanstad*.
182 Gedeputeerde Staten Noord-Holland, Decision nr. 93.710713, 13-4-1992; Construction Permit Decision BV.91000903, mayor and aldermen of Zaanstad, 26-4-1993, Bouwdossier Poelenburg 156, *Archive Municipality of Zaanstad*.
183 'Voorstel B&W aan gemeenteraad, vergadering d.d. 21-10-1993,' 'voorstel 319/ agendapunt 8.6,' and 'Raadsbesluit d.d. 21 oktober 1992, voorstel 319;' Bouwdossier Poelenburg 156, *Archive Municipality of Zaanstad*.
184 'Besprekingsverslag dd. 23-6-1993,' Mabeg Architectuur BV, *Archive Sultan Ahmet Mosque*; *Noord-Hollands Dagblad*, 26-11-1994.
185 See 'Besprekingsverslagen and Bouwvergaderingen' from 14-5-1993 to 28-10-1994, Mabeg Architectuur BV, *Archive Sultan Ahmet Mosque*.
186 'Bouwvergadering nr. 10, 11-2-1994,' Mabeg Architectuur BV, *Archive Sultan Ahmet Mosque*.
187 See the invitations and public announcements around the opening of the mosque, *Archive Sultan Ahmet Mosque*; *Yurtdişi Camiler Albümü*, Ankara: Türkiye Diyanet Vakfi Yayinlari, 1997.
188 Hopman 2007.

189 This history, running from 1989-1996, is described in great detail in Lindo 1999.
190 Lindo 1999, p. 15.
191 F. Bolkestein, *Moslim in de Polder. Frits Bolkestein in Gesprek met Nederlandse Moslims*, Amsterdam: Contact, 1997, pp. 74, 81-82.
192 Lindo 1999, pp. 5, 13, 15-17, 20-21.
193 Lindo 1999, pp. 41-55, 58-97, 158.
194 Interview with Rijnboutt, Amsterdam, 22-05-2008.
195 Interview with Kabaktepe, Amsterdam, 3-7-2006; also see: http://reporter.kro.nl/uitzendingen/2007/0402_moskeeen/intro.aspx.
196 G. Goodwin, *A History of Ottoman Architecture*, London: Thames and Hudson, 1971.
197 Ersan 2007, p. 76.
198 See Meeker 1997, p. 157. Atatürk's mausoleum had consciously used building elements referring to pre-Islamic civilizations instead of provoking associations with 'the tomb of a sultan or a Saint'. Bozdoğan 2001, p. 289; A. Çinar, *Modernity, Islam, and Secularism in Turkey. Bodies, Places, and Time*, Minneapolis: University of Minnesota Press, 2005, pp. 108-109.
199 Lindo 1999, p. 159.
200 'Riva-terrein wordt Vernieuwd', in: *Het Parool*, 13-12-2003, Regio Amsterdam, p. 5.
201 Max van Rooy, Een Minaret van Baksteen. Amsterdam-West Bouwt Moskee in Amsterdamse Schoolstijl, in: *NRC*, 14-02-2003, p. 21.
202 Interview with Bijdendijk, 1-9-2004, Amsterdam.
203 See http://www.breitman-breitman.com/intro-e.html.
204 Interview with Marc Breitman, 7-12-2007, Paris.
205 Proposal for the Riva Terrain, 24-3-19989, *Archive Wester Mosque*; Interview with Mohamed El Bouk, Het Oosten/Kristal, 19-7-2006, Amsterdam.
206 'Verslag Vergadering Stadsdeelraad dd 17 december 2002,' 18-2-2003, *Archive Stadsdeel De Baarsjes*.
207 Telephone interview with Piet Vernooy, and email from Vernooy to Roose, 11-12-2007.
208 'Verslag dd 3 december 2001 Commissie van Advies Wonen, Grotestedenbeleid, Bestuurszaken en Veiligheid,' 8-1-2002, *Archive Stadsdeel De Baarsjes*.
209 'Verslag Vergadering Stadsdeelraad dd 17 december 2002,' 18-2-2003, *Archive Stadsdeel De Baarsjes*.
210 Meeting List of Aesthetics Commission, 006-02, *Archive Stadsdeel De Baarsjes*.
211 'Welstandadvies Stedebouwkundig Programma van Eisen, Aanvraag 29399,' 24-1-2001, *Archive Commissie voor Welstand en Monumenten Amsterdam*.
212 Van Rooy 2003.
213 'Verslag dd 3 december 2001 Commissie van Advies Wonen, Grotestedenbeleid, Bestuurszaken en Veiligheid,' 8-1-2002, *Archive Stadsdeel De Baarsjes*.
214 Interview with former Project Leader at Het Oosten/Kristal Dolf Dazert, 26-7-2006, Doorn.
215 24-01-2002; Ontwerp Besluitnummer 01/WW184, *Archive Stadsdeel De Baarsjes*.
216 Letter from Dazert to Breitman, 7-10-2003, *Archive Kristal*.
217 Besluitnummer 02/WW030, *Archive Stadsdeel De Baarsjes* and *Archive Kristal*.
218 Letter from Dazert to Breitman, 7-10-2003, *Archive Kristal*.
219 Letter from Breitman to Dazert, 18-9-2001, *Archive Kristal*.
220 Van Rooy 2003.
221 A. Kuran, *Sinan. The Grand Old Master of Ottoman Architecture*, Washington D.C. [etc]: Institute of Turkish Studies [etc], 1987; G. Goodwin, *Sinan. Ottoman Architecture and its Values Today*, London: Saqi Books, 1993. Already in his early standard work,

Goodwin treated the Selimiye as 'the climax of the work of Sinan and therefore of all Ottoman architecture'. Goodwin 1971, p. 261.
222 Goodwin 1993, pp. 65, 109.
223 Goodwin 1993, pp. 64, 74, 76, 109.
224 G. Necipoğlu, *The Age of Sinan. Architectural Culture in the Ottoman Empire*, London: Reaction Books, 2005, p. 127.
225 The much-heared assumptions that the Wester Mosque was based on the Blue Mosque or the – also famous – Süleymaniye Mosque in Istanbul are therefore not correct. Eg. R. Stiphout and O. van der Wal, De Mooiste Islamitische Bouwwerken. Nederlandse Moskeeën steeds vaker gebaseerd op Buitenlandse Voorbeelden, in: *Elsevier, Speciale Editie: Islam*, 2006, pp. 18-25; pp. 24-25.
226 Letter from Construction Control to Het Oosten, 21-3-2002, Bouwdossier Baarsjesweg 199, *Archive Stadsdeel De Baarsjes*.
227 Letter from Construction Control to Het Oosten, 21-3-2002, Bouwdossier Baarsjesweg 199, *Archive Stadsdeel De Baarsjes*.
228 'Haci Karacaer. Ik Probeer een Olifant te laten Dansen,' in: *De Volkskrant*, 18-01-2003, Magazine, p. 12.
229 Van Rooy 2003.
230 'Building Bridges. Mosque Adopts Dutch Design', in: Holland Insight Online, 11-04-2003. (http://paypernews.datawire.nl/HollandInsight/daily/2003/4/11/HI/HI_00_20030411_19/articles/artikel_HI_00_20030411_19_153.php)
231 'Meer Minaretten,' in: *Het Parool*, 18-10-2003, PS van de Week, pp. 6-12; p. 9.
232 Van der Zee 2003.
233 In fact, on 11 May 2005 the Aesthetics Commission still objected to the architect not having designed certain elements of the complex in line with its Amsterdam School surroundings. 'Verslag Commissie II, dd 11 mei 2005, volgnr. 29399 (2e behandeling),' *Archive Stadsdeel De Baarsjes*.
234 Interview with Karacaer, Amsterdam, 27-6-2006.
235 Actually, many Ottoman-derived, newly-built mosques in Turkey do include a 'hypermarket' in their design. See K.K. Eyüpgiller, 20th Century Mosque Architecture in Turkey, in: *EJOS, Electronic Journal for Oriental Studies*, IX (6), 2006, pp. 1-37. (http://www2.let.uu.nl/solis/anpt/ejos/pdf9/Eyupgiller-fin2006-01.pdf)
236 'Verslag Vergadering Raadscommissie Wonen, dd 17 februari 2004,' 20-4-2004, *Archive Stadsdeel De Baarsjes*.
237 Construction permit application J04/6469 BWT 2004, 29-10-2004, Bouwdossier Baarsjesweg 199, *Archive Stadsdeel De Baarsjes*.
238 'Verslag Vergadering Raadscommissie Wonen, dd 21 juni 2005,' 20-9-2005, *Archive Stadsdeel De Baarsjes*.
239 Interview with Mohamed El Bouk, Het Oosten/Kristal, 19-7-2006, Amsterdam.
240 Letter from Bouwstart Project management to Stadsdeel De Baarsjes, 4-5-2005, Bouwdossier Baarsjesweg 199, *Archive Stadsdeel De Baarsjes*.
241 'Verslag Vergadering Welstandscommissie II, dd 11 mei 2005, 36-29399,' *Archive Stadsdeel De Baarsjes*.
242 'Verslag Vergadering Raadscommissie Wonen, dd 21 juni 2005,' 20-9-2005, *Archive Stadsdeel De Baarsjes*.
243 'Notulen vergadering Raadscommissie Wonen, dd 20 september 2005,' 12-10-2005, *Archive Stadsdeel De Baarsjes*.
244 'Besluitenlijst Vergadering Stadsdeelraad 27 september 2005,' *Archive Stadsdeel De Baarsjes*.

245 'Overeenkomst Westermoskee,' 10-12-2005, *Archive Stadsdeel De Baarsjes*; *Nieuwsbrief Chassébuurt*, December 2005.
246 Letter from the arbitration commission to the Stuurgroep Westermoskee, 2-2006, *Archive Stadsdeel De Baarsjes*.
247 *NRC/Volkskrant*, 1-3-2006.
248 Speech for Minister Donner, 28-2-2006, *Archive Stadsdeel De Baarsjes*.
249 See http://www.wijblijvenhier.nl/index.php?/archives/407-Start-bouw-Westermoskee.html.
250 Erkoçu, Hammiche and Bugdaci, 2006, pp. 32, 37.
251 See http://www.baarsjes.amsterdam.nl/?ActItmIdt=39309.
252 'Machtswisseling Milli Görüs voedt vrees voor radicalisering onder Turken,' in: *De Volkskrant*, 15-5-2006, p. 1.
253 'Gejuich over bouw Westermoskee is verstomd,' in: *De Volkskrant*, 11-10-2006, p. 2; Also see: http://www.ikonrtv.nl/ikondocumentaire/documentaire.asp?old=2512.
254 'Eerste paal Westermoskee de grond in en meteen er weer uit,' in: *Parool.nl*, 16-10-2008.

Chapter 4

1 Dijker 1995, pp. 70-73.
2 'Saudi influences in The Netherlands. Links between the Salafist mission, radicalisation processes amd Islamic terrorism,' (translation from the Dutch paper 'Saoedische invloeden in Nederland,' 4-2004), AIVD Publications, 6-1-2005. (http://www.aivd.nl/contents/pages/10887/saudiinfluencesinthenetherlands.pdf)
3 F. Buijs and C. Nelissen, Tussen Continuïteit en Verandering. Marokkanen in Nederland, in: H. Vermeulen and R. Penninx (eds), *Het Democratisch Ongeduld. De Emancipatie en Integratie van Zes Doelgroepen van het Minderhedenbeleid*, Amsterdam: Het Spinhuis, 1994, pp. 177-206; pp. 177-178.
4 Landman 1992, pp. 149-150; J. Waterbury, *The Commander of the Faithful. The Moroccan Political Elite, a Study in Segmented Politics*, London: Weidenfeld and Nicolson, 1970; M. Tozy, *Monarchie et Islam Politique au Maroc*, Paris: Presses de Sciences Po, 1999.
5 A. Ahalli, Marokko en zijn Islamisten: Reformisten, Rebellen en Jihadisten, in: E. van de Bovenkamp and H. el Kaddouri (eds), *Marokko uit de Schaduw. De Onbelichte Kanten van Vierhonderd Jaar Betrekkingen Nederland-Marokko*, Amsterdam: Aksant; Utrecht: SMT, 2006, pp. 99-112.
6 For references see Landman 1992, p. 156.
7 Buijs and Nelissen 1994, pp. 177-178, 180, 187, 202-203.
8 R. Strijp, *Om de Moskee. Het Religieuze Leven van Marokkaanse Migranten in een Nederlandse Provinciestad*, Amsterdam 1998, p. 60.
9 O. Bouadi et.al.(eds), *De Vele Gezichten van Marokkaans Nederland. Een Wie is Wie*, Amsterdam 2001.
10 Holod and Khan 1997, p. 18.
11 'In moskee Marokko officiële Islam op tv,' in: *NRC*, 20-6-2006.
12 Landman 1992, pp. 167-168.
13 M. Rabbae, *Naast de Amicales nu de UMMON. De Mantelorganisaties van de Marokkaanse Autoriteiten in Nederland*, Utrecht: Nederlands Centrum Buitenlanders, 1993.

14 K. Canatan, M. Popovic and R. Edinga, *Maatschappelijk actief in moskeeverband. Een verkennend onderzoek naar de maatschappelijke activiteiten van en het vrijwilligerswerk binnen moskeeorganisaties en het gemeentelijk beleid ten aanzien van moskeeorganisaties*, Den Bosch: Ihsan, 2005, p. 21.
15 *De Volkskrant*, 9-7-2008.
16 *Elsevier*, 16-7-2008; *De Volkskrant*, 18-7-2008.
17 See http://www.wijblijvenhier.nl/index.php?/archives/1770-Neo-malikisme.html#extended.
18 Landman 1992, pp. 174-180.
19 E. Bartels and M. de Koning, For Allah and Myself. Religion and Moroccan Youth in The Netherlands, in: P. Bos and W. Fritschy (eds), *Morocco and The Netherlands. Society, Economy, Culture,* Amsterdam: VU University Press, 2006, pp. 146-154.
20 I. Johnson and D. Crawford, A Saudi Group Spreads Extremism in "Law" Seminars, Taught in Dutch, in: *The Wall Street Journal*, 15-4-2003; S. Abbos, *De Moslim Bestaat Niet. Een zoektocht naar de Islam*, Amsterdam: Bakker, 2005, pp. 57-59. These references contain interviews with Cheppih's son Mohammed. Ahmed Cheppih himself was, in light of heavy, negative media attention around the Fourkaan Mosque, no longer available for interviews.
21 Statements of the engineer (who prefers to remain anonymous) were based on a series of telephone interviews in 2/3-2007.
22 'Bouwplan Islamitisch Cultureel Centrum met Gebedsruimte,' 30-5-1987, *Archive Boon & Slagter Architects*.
23 Kamer van Koophandel Eindhoven, Historie Handelsregister, nr. 1741090956.
24 'Bouwplan Islamitisch Cultureel Centrum Al Fourqaan,' Boon & Slagter, 30-1-1989, *Archive Boon & Slagter Architects*.
25 Interview with David Boon, Eindhoven, 21-3-2007.
26 According to Amar Nejjar, current chairman of Al Waqf in The Netherlands. Interview with Nejjar, Eindhoven, 4-4-2007.
27 Holod and Khan 1997, pp. 51-52; A. Paccard, *Le Maroc et l'Artisanat Traditionnel Islamique dans l'Architecture*, Annecy 1979.
28 A.J.J. Mekking, Houses of Prayer, Houses of Preaching. A Structural Comparison of Islamic and Calvinist-Rooted Religious Architecture, in: *Het Kerkgebouw in het Postindustriële Landschap/ The Church in the Post-Industrial Landscape*, Zoetermeer, pp. 79-90.
29 H.-U. Khan, Identity, Authenticity and Power: the Mosque of Hassan II, in: *ISIM Newsletter*, 3/99, July 1999, p. 8. (http://www.isim.nl/files/newsl_3.pdf)
30 See A. Lotfi, Managing Religious Affairs in Morocco, in: Bos and Fritschy 2006, pp. 33-43; p. 40.
31 'Bouwplan islamitisch Cultureel Centrum Al Fourquaan, Overzicht Stichtingskosten,' Boon & Slagter, 16-3-1989, *Archive Boon & Slagter Architects*.
32 'Bouwplan islamitisch Cultureel Centrum Al Fourquaan, Overzicht Stichtingskosten,' Boon & Slagter, 6-4-1989, *Archive Boon & Slagter Architects*.
33 Letter from Boon & Slagter to Cheppih, 17-4-1989, *Archive Boon & Slagter Architects*.
34 A. Hutt, *Islamic Architecture. North Africa*, London: Scorpion, 1977; J. Hoag, *Islamische Architektur. Weltgeschichte der Architektur 4*, Stuttgart: Belser; Mailand: Electa, 1976 [Translation from Italian, Mailand 1975].
35 See http://www.architectuur.org/laan01.php.

36 Aesthetic advice construction plan 622/89, Welstandscommissie Eindhoven, 4-8-1989, Bouwdossier 622/89, Islamitisch Cultureel Centrum, Otterstraat 2/Wezelstraat, *Archive Municipality of Eindhoven*.
37 Letter from Dienst Bouw- en Woningtoezicht to Stichting Islamitisch Cultureel Centrum, 10-8-1989, Bouwdossier 622/89, Islamitisch Cultureel Centrum, Otterstraat 2/Wezelstraat, *Archive Municipality of Eindhoven*.
38 Kamer van Koophandel Eindhoven, Uittreksel Handelsregister, nr. 41091392.
39 Construction permit nr. 89Q021826-AR(622/890,BB, 9-10-1989, *Archive Boon & Slagter Architects*.
40 Concept-letter to Copplemans Bouwbedrijven, 10-1989, *Archive Boon & Slagter Architects*.
41 'Islamitisch Cultureel Centrum Eindhoven. Verslag van de 1ste bouwvergadering, 11-10-1989,' 12-10-1989, *Archive Boon & Slagter Architects*.
42 'Islamitisch Cultureel Centrum Eindhoven. Verslag van de 2de bouwvergadering, 1-11-1989,' 3-11-1989; 'Islamitisch Cultureel Centrum Eindhoven. Verslag van de 3de bouwvergadering, 22-11-1989,' 30-11-1989, *Archive Boon & Slagter Architects*.
43 'Latent racisme of politiek simplisme? (De komst van een moskee in een woonwijk en de reaktie van wijkbewoners daarop),' Eindhoven 21-11-1989, Bouwdossier 622/89, Islamitisch Cultureel Centrum, Otterstraat 2/Wezelstraat, *Archive Municipality of Eindhoven*.
44 'Raadsvragen aan het College van B. en W, voor de CDA fractie, J. Zijlstra,' 12-12-1989, Bouwdossier 622/89, Islamitisch Cultureel Centrum, Otterstraat 2/Wezelstraat, *Archive Municipality of Eindhoven*.
45 'Islamitisch Cultureel Centrum Eindhoven. Verslag van de 3de bouwvergadering, 22-11-1989,' 30-11-1989, *Archive Boon & Slagter Architects*.
46 'Islamitisch Cultureel Centrum Eindhoven. Verslag van de 4de bouwvergadering, 13-12-1989,' 20-12-1989, A*rchive Boon & Slagter Architects*.
47 'Islamitisch Cultureel Centrum Eindhoven. Verslag van de 6de bouwvergadering, 14-2-1990,' 21-2-1990, *Archive Boon & Slagter Architects*.
48 O. Grabar and D. Hill, *Islamic Architecture and its Decoration: A.D. 800-1500*, London: Faber and Faber, 1967 [London 1964], Plates 451 and 187.
49 K. Albarn et al, *The Language of Pattern: An Enquiry Inspired by Islamic Decoration*, London: Thames and Hudson, 1974.
50 Albarn 1974, p. 41.
51 'Islamitisch Cultureel Centrum Eindhoven. Verslag van de 9de bouwvergadering, 24-4-1990,' 7-5-1990, *Archive Boon & Slagter Architects*.
52 Eg see M.E. Bonine, The Sacred Direction and City Structure. A Preliminary Analysis of the Islamic Cities of Morocco, in: *Muqarnas*, vol. VII, 1990, pp. 50-72; Y. Saliya, Hariadi and G. Tjahjono, The Indonesian Experience, in: Powell 1990, pp. 188-195.
53 'Islamitisch Cultureel Centrum Eindhoven. Verslag van de bouwkundige oplevering van bovengenoemd gebouw, gehouden 28 mei 1990 te 13.30 uur,' 28-5-1990, *Archive Boon & Slagter Architects*.
54 'Manoeuvreren in een mijnenveld. Radicalisering moslimjeugd doet appèl op welzijnswerk,' in: *Zorg + Welzijn*, Nr. 4, 23-2-2005.
55 W. Boender, *Imam in Nederland. Opvattingen over zijn Religieuze Rol in de Samenleving*, Amsterdam: Bert Bakker, 2007, p. 178.
56 Boender 2007, pp. 180, 190, 194-195, 215, 219.
57 'Marokkaanse Moskee Vaillantlaan,' program of requirements, *Archive diederendirrix*.

NOTES

58 'Notitie aan planteam Koppen van der Vennemax, P/93/1932/PV/E,' Peter Vrijaldenhoven (Woningbouwvereniging 's Gravenhage), 28-6-1993, *Archive diederendirrix*.
59 Letter from Vrijaldenhoven to Dirrix, P/93/1949/PV/EV, 1-7-1993, *Archive diederendirrix*.
60 'Marokkaanse Moskee Vaillantlaan, Stichting Al Islam, Moskee lokatie Segherstraat/ Van der Vennestraat, Bespreking Programma van Wensen,' Dirrix van Wylick Architecten, 2-7-1993, *Archive diederendirrix*.
61 F. de Miranda, *De Moskee als Kunstwerk en als Huis van Gebed*, Wassenaar: Miranda, 1977 [Also translated to English as 'The Mosque as Work of Art and as House of Prayer', Wassenaar 1977].
62 P. Portoghesi, Moschee und Islamisches Kulturzentrum in Rom, in: *Deutsche Bauzeitschrift*, nr. 7, 1992, pp. 983-985.
63 'Marokkaanse Moskee, Van der Vennestraat, Den Haag,' 12-7-1993/21-7-1993, *Archive diederendirrix*.
64 Interview with Belhaj and Arabi, The Hague, 14-2-2007.
65 Letter from Henk v/d Weerd, Dienst Ruimtelijke en Economische Ontwikkeling, to Dirrix, 4-8-1993, *Archive diederendirrix*.
66 Letter from J. van de Ven to Al Islam, municipality and housing corporation, 25-10-1993, *Archive diederendirrix*.
67 'Marokkaanse Moskee, Van der Vennestraat, Den Haag, Stichting Al Islam, Korte Toelichting op Schetsontwerp,' in: Presentation Brochure 'Moskee Al Islam,' *Archive diederendirrix*.
68 'Adviezen Gemeentelijke Instanties,' in: Presentation Brochure 'Moskee Al Islam,' *Archive diederendirrix*.
69 A similar case seems to be the Granada Mosque, Spain. Behind its 'Andalusian' – or, rather, *Moorish* – design and 'European' Islam was an imam explicitly founding himself in traditional Maliki Islam, claiming that his teachings were based on Moroccan views 'that have remained free of any of the modernist and extremist tendencies of the last 150 years in the Arab world'. See: http://www.cislamica.org/islam/cienciasdeldin/sobreeldhikrdeallah.html, and http://www.mezquitadegranada.com/materialonline/biografias/muhammadkassbi.html.
70 Letter from Alfomin to Dirrix van Wylick Architects, 10-1-1994, *Archive Opaal Architecten*.
71 Interview with Oppier, Krimpen a/d lek, 7-2-2007; J. van der Bliek, De ideale moskee bestaat niet, in: *Onze Wereld*, April 2000, pp. 28-31; p. 29.
72 'Concept Werkafspraken Moskee Al Islam,' Kaman. Oppier Architecten, Rotterdam, 11-2-1994, *Archive Opaal Architecten*.
73 'Kort besprekingsverslag voorbespreking bouwteam Koppen Vennemax Blok 5 dd. 15 februari 1994,' 15-2-1994, *Archive Opaal Architecten*.
74 'Programma van eisen voor nieuwbouw moskee aan de Vennestraat/Segherstraat te Den Haag,' 1-3-1994, *Archive Opaal Architecten*.
75 Fax from Dirrix to Oppier, 9-3-1994, *Archive Opaal Architecten*.
76 'Stedebouwkundige randvoorwaarden lokatie Seghersstraat/ Van der Vennestraat/ Snijdersstraat (H1H190 – "VenneMax blok 5"),' 16-04-1994, *Archive Opaal Architecten*.
77 'Reactie op concept Stedebouwkundige Randvoorwaarden Segherstraat/ Van der Vennestraat/ Snijderstraat,' Kaman Oppier Architecten, 3-5-1994, *Archive Opaal Architecten*.

78 'Reactie op concept Stedebouwkundige Randvoorwaarden Segherstraat/ Van der Vennestraat/ Snijderstraat,' Dirrix van Wylick Architecten, 15-5-1994, *Archive Opaal Architecten*.
79 Letter from Oppier to Dirrix, 18-5-1994, *Archive Opaal Architecten*.
80 '2^e Concept dd. 8/6/1994,' *Archive Opaal Architecten*.
81 'Welstandscommissie, Aantekeningen Collegiaal Vooroverleg 12/7/94,' and 'Reactie Welstand, Rotterdam dd. 120794,' 12-7-1994, *Archive Opaal Architecten*.
82 'Kort besprekingsverslag bouwteam Koppen Vennemax blok 5, dd. 25 augustus jl,' 25-8-1994, *Archive Opaal Architecten*.
83 In the model the minaret seems to be aligned with the street, but this was not intended. It had been devised like that so as to be able to shift it up and down the street along the façade in showing the effects of relocation.
84 U. Scerrato, *Monumenten van Grote Culturen. Islam*, Alphen a/d Rijn: ICOB, 1980 [Translation from Italian, Milan 1972].
85 'Verslag bespreking Welstandscommissie 8 september 1994 te Den Haag betreffende moskee aan de vd. Vennestraat,' Rotterdam 18-10-1994, and 'Verslag besproken punten Welstand 8 september 1994 grote commissie,' *Archive Opaal Architecten*.
86 Fax from Oppier to Dirrix, 19-10-1994, *Archive Opaal Architecten*.
87 'Concept bijeenkomst collegiaal overleg Welstand Den Haag,' Bert Dirrix, 23-11-1994, *Archive Opaal Architecten*.
88 Letter from Oppier to Dienst Bouwen en Wonen, 01-12-1994, *Archive Opaal Architecten*.
89 'Notulen van de vergadering van de Welstandscommissie gehouden op donderdag 29 december 1994,' Gemeente Den Haag, Dienst Bouwen en Wonen, 16Wcie291294, Ste01941367, *Archive Opaal Architecten*.
90 Letters from Gedeputeerde Staten Provincie Zuid Holland, Dienst Ruimte en Groen, to B&W 's Gravenhage, Al Islam and Buurtbelang 86, 18-7-1995, DRG/ARB/107045A,B,C, *Archive Opaal Architecten*.
91 Bouwvergunning Seghersstraat ongd. Tpv. 108 t/m 114 / Van der Vennestraat ongd tpv. 6 t/m 20, 11-8-1995, *Archive Opaal Architecten*.
92 'Tekeningenlijst, Al Islam Moskee te Den Haag,' 11-5/3-10/6-10-1995, *Archive Opaal Architecten*.
93 'Een nieuwe moskee,' in: *Gemeente Den Haag, Dienst Stedelijke Ontwikkeling, Archive Opaal Architecten*.
94 'Moskee El Islam, 24/05/96 en 19/06/96, Bouwvergadering 5 en 6,' including handwritten notes and drawings, *Archive Opaal Architecten*.
95 'Moskee El Islam, 07-05-1996, Bouwvergadering 4,' 13-5-1996, *Archive Opaal Architecten*.
96 'Advies Sociale Veiligheid Nieuwbouw Moskee Van der Vennestraat/Segherstraat te Den Haag,' Politiecorps Haaglanden, 20-2-1995, *Archive Opaal Architecten*.
97 H. van de Kaa, *De Essalaam-Moskee: Van Slagroomtaart tot Scudraket. Een Discoursanalyse van het Proces rond de Vormgeving van de Rotterdamse Essalam-Moskee*, Amsterdam: University of Amsterdam, 2003, p. 2.
98 Van de Kaa 2003, pp. 36, 49-50.
99 Van de Kaa 2003, p. 3.
100 'Stedebouwkundige Randvoorwaarden Moskee Es Salam,' December 1997, *Archive M&vW Architects*.
101 'Verslag Voorbespreking Commissie voor Welstand en Monumenten Rotterdam,' 12-12-1997, chairman I.E.B. Wittermans, *Archive M&vW Architects*.

NOTES

102 'Agendapost Vergadering Commissie RO/SR, 25 februari 1998,' *Archive M&vW Architects*.
103 Interview with Ajdid, Rotterdam, 1-4-2007.
104 'Rotterdamse handlangers willen "terreurtheoloog" Al-Qaradawi naar Nederland halen,' in: *De Telegraaf*, 24-3-2007; 'The Radical Dawa in Transition. The Rise of Islamic Neo-Radicalism in The Netherlands,' AIVD Publications, 9-10-2007, p. 52.
105 'From Dawah to Jihad. The Various Threats of Radical Islam to the Democratic Legal Order,' AIVD Publications, 30-5-2005, p. 24.
106 See Hulsman 2004.
107 One of the contestants seems to have been Kas Oosterhuis with 'a blob-like design'. 'Weg met de cliché-moskee,' in: *Trouw*, 11-11-2008.
108 Interview with Van Winden, Delft, 29-3-2007.
109 M. Hattstein and P. Delius, *Islam. Kunst en Architectuur*, Cologne: Könemann, 2000 [Translation from German, Cologne 2000].
110 'Architect Wifried van Winden versiert gebouwen,' in: *De Leunstoel*, 2004. (http://deleunstoel.nl/archief_artikelen.php?subrubriek_id=2&artikel_id=166)
111 Fax from M&vW to Boutaher and Ajdid, 30-5-2001, *Archive M&vW Architects*.
112 Minutes of meeting of 26-6-2001, *Archive M&vW Architects*.
113 Minutes of meeting of 5-7-2001, *Archive M&vW Architects*.
114 Email from dS+V to plan team members, 5-7-2001, *Archive M&vW Architects*.
115 Telephone notation, 5-7-2001, *Archive M&vW Architects*.
116 Report meeting 18-7-2001, *Archive M&vW Architects*.
117 Report meeting 25-7-2001, *Archive M&vW Architects*.
118 Email from Ajdid to M&vW, 25-7-2001, *Archive M&vW Architects*.
119 Report meeting 14-8-2001, *Archive M&vW Architects*.
120 Telephone notations, 18-9-2001, *Archive M&vW Architects*.
121 Report meeting 11-10-2001, *Archive M&vW Architects*.
122 Letter from dS+V to Stuurgroep Parkstad, 13-9-2001, *Archive M&vW Architects*.
123 'From the Minutes of the meeting of the Quality Team Kop van Zuid, Date 14 September 2001,' Email from dS+V to M&vW, 26-11-2001, *Archive M&vW Architects*.
124 'Nieuwe moskee wordt "de grootste en mooiste,"' in: *Rotterdams Dagblad*, 17-10-2001.
125 'Dit Moet de Laatste Traditionele Moskee zijn,' in: *De Volkskrant*, 16-01-2004, p. 16.
126 Reports of Communications 29-10-2001, *Archive M&vW Architects*.
127 Reports meetings 16-10-2001 & 4-11-2001, *Archive M&vW Architects*. For Al-Maktoum's role in the Dublin Mosque, see http://www.redbrick.dcu.ie/~isoc/mosques.html.
128 'Verslag bespreking gehouden op 22 november 2001,' *Archive M&vW Architects*.
129 'Bekendmaking Gelegenheid tot Inspraak [29-11-2001] op Voornemen Vrijstelling te verlenen,' Deelgemeente Feijenoord, *Archive M&vW Architects*.
130 Mail from M&vW to Ajdid, 3-5-2002, *Archive M&vW Architects*.
131 Reports meeting 14-5-2002, *Archive M&vW Architects*.
132 Report meeting 21-5-2002, *Archive M&vW Architects*.
133 Report meeting 30-5-2002, *Archive M&vW Architects*.
134 Letter from M&vW to dS+V, 4-6-2002, *Archive M&vW Architects*.
135 Report meeting 4-6-2002, *Archive M&vW Architects*.
136 Report meeting 18-6-2002, *Archive M&vW Architects*.
137 See report meeting 9-7-2002, *Archive M&vW Architects*.
138 Report meeting 11-7-2002, *Archive M&vW Architects*.
139 Report meeting 26-7-2002, *Archive M&vW Architects*.

140 Construction Permit Application, 26-7-2002, and Letter from M&vW to Ajdid, 29-7-2002, *Archive M&vW Architects*.
141 Report meeting 28-8-2002, *Archive M&vW Architects*.
142 Reports meeting 7-9-2002, *Archive M&vW Architects*.
143 Report meeting 19-9-2002, *Archive M&vW Architects*.
144 Telephone notation, 20-9-2002, *Archive M&vW Architects*.
145 Telephone notation, 23-9-2002, *Archive M&vW Architects*.
146 Telephone notation, 27-9-2002, *Archive M&vW Architects*.
147 Report communication 3-10-2002, *Archive M&vW Architects*.
148 Report meeting 25-10-2002, *Archive M&vW Architects*.
149 Report meeting 1-11-2002, *Archive M&vW Architects*.
150 Fax from Ajdid to M&vW, 3-11-2002, *Archive M&vW Architects*.
151 Report meeting 26-6-2002, *Archive M&vW Architects*.
152 Report Meeting 28-8-2002, *Archive M&vW Architects*.
153 Fax from Ajdid to M&vW, 8-12-2002, *Archive M&vW Architects*.
154 Telephone notation, 3-2-2003, *Archive M&vW Architects*.
155 Report meeting 7-2-2003, *Archive M&vW Architects*.
156 Reports meeting 12-2-2003, *Archive M&vW Architects*.
157 Fax from M&vW to Gemeente Rotterdam, Bowoto, 25-2-2003, *Archive M&vW Architects*.
158 Telephone notation, 3-3-2003, *Archive M&vW Architects*.
159 Report meeting 5-3-2003, *Archive M&vW Architects*.
160 Report meeting 26-3-2003, *Archive M&vW Architects*.
161 Telephone notation, 27-3-2003, *Archive M&vW Architects*.
162 Internal memo, 27-3-2003, *M&vW Architects*.
163 Report meeting 2-4-2003, *Archive M&vW Architects*.
164 Letters from M&vW to Ajdid, 9-4-2003, *Archive M&vW Architects*.
165 Letter from dS+V to Foundation Essalaam Mosque, 7-5-2003, *Archive M&vW Architects*.
166 Letter from Pastors to As-Sayegh, 12-8-2003, attached to 'Overlegdocument tbv. Raad en Commissie 2003-1098,' 23-10-2003. (http://www.bds.rotterdam.nl/content.jsp?objectid=117968)
167 Interview with Ergün Erkoçu, 28-11-2007, The Hague.
168 *Telegraaf*, 16-08-2003, ANP Archive doc.nr. 1251192.
169 Letter from Ontwikkelingsbedrijf Rotterdam to Al-Sayegh, and Concept report meeting 14-8-2003, *Archive M&vW Architects*.
170 'Rotterdam wil nieuw ontwerp moskee,' in: *Trouw*, 16-6-2003.
171 'Moskee in Rotterdam Eigentijdser,' in: *De Volkskrant*, 16-08-2003.
172 'Overwegingen en voorstellen voor de inpassing van de Essalam Moskee,' Notitie dS+V Rotterdam [author not specified], 10-9-2003, *Archive M&vW Architects*.
173 *Algemeen Dagblad*, 27-09-2003.
174 *NRC*, 23-10-2003.
175 *Telegraaf*, 22-10-2003.
176 *NRC*, 24-10-2003.
177 'Eerste Steen een Mengeling van Trots en Gekrenktheid,' in: *Rotterdams Dagblad*, 22-10-2003.
178 'Essalam-moskee moet ook Attractie zijn', in: *De Volkskrant*, 22-10-2003, p. 3.
179 'Eerste Steen een Mengeling van Trots en Gekrenktheid,' in: *Rotterdams Dagblad*, 22-10-2003.
180 'Gebruik van oriëntaalse invloeden iets van deze tijd,' in: *Rotterdams Dagblad*, 25-10-2003.

181 Another example of the role that the Medina mosque can play to Dutch-Moroccan patrons seems to be the An Nour Mosque in Gouda. Its original plan showed a large building with a prominent minaret on a clearly visible location, 'looking more like the Prophet's Mosque in Medina than anything Moroccan'. At the same time, as they had come to be connected to the Moroccan Amicales, the board members had required a shift towards a more 'universal Islam' (which they located 'in Saudi-Arabia') and a new Moroccan imam (who later turned out to be Salafi). It was only due to municipal resistance, pushing towards construction on the spot of an old garage in a row of town houses, that the design became less conspicuous. M. de Koning, *Zoeken naar een 'Zuivere' Islam. Geloofsbeleving en Identiteitsvorming van Jonge Marokkaans-Nederlandse Moslims*, Amsterdam: Bert Bakker, 2008, p. 327, and personal statements and emails to Roose, Spring/Summer 2008.
182 Telephone notation, undated, *Archive M&vW Architects*.
183 Email, containing report meeting 25-8-2004, from M&vW to Ajdid, 27-8-2004, *Archive M&vW Architects*.
184 Email from M&vW to Ajdid, 18-8-2004, *Archive M&vW Architects*.
185 *Algemeen Dagblad*, 23-10-2005
186 *Algemeen Dagblad*, 15-12-2006.
187 *Algemeen Dagblad*, 7-10-2007.
188 *Algemeen Dagblad*, 10-06-2008.
189 *De Volkskrant*, 25-6-2008.
190 *Algemeen Dagblad*, 8-10-2007.
191 *De Volkskrant*, 5-7-2008; *Algemeen Dagblad*, 6-7-2008.
192 *Algemeen Dagblad*, 2-7-2008.

Conclusion

1 As concluded by Ipenburg, one of the researchers behind the recent Handboek Christelijk Nederland (Hoekstra and Ipenburg 2008): 'Nobody calls himself a member of a sect. As a matter of course, a sect is always someone else.' 'Achtenzestig maal gereformeerd,' in: *Nederlands Dagblad*, 14-3-2008.
2 Abbos 2005, pp. 73-81.
3 K. El Moumni, *Waarom ben ik Moslim?*, Rotterdam: El Moumni, 2001 [Translation from Arabic, Casablanca: El Moumni, 2000], pp. 3, 40-41.
4 'Saudi Influences in The Netherlands. Links between the Salafist Mission, Radicalization Processes and Islamic Terrorism,' AIVD Publications, 6-1-2005, p. 4. (http://www.aivd.nl/contents/pages/10887/saudiinfluencesinthenetherlands.pdf)
5 'De aantrekkelijke antwoorden van de zuivere Islam. Ultra-orthodoxe Islamvariant Salafisme wint snel terrein onder zoekende Nederlandse Moslimjongeren,' in: *NRC*, 16-10-2007, p. 7.
6 'Arabisch wijkt voor Nederlands in Moskee,' in: *Rotterdams Dagblad*, 28-12-2002.
7 'Plan voor Jongerenmoskee in Rotterdam,' in: *De Telegraaf*, 5-10-2004.
8 Interview with Ergün Erkoçu, 28-11-2007, The Hague.
9 'Imam El Moumni stopt met Preken,' in: *Algemeen Dagblad*, 27-6-2006.
10 'Poldermoskee: Het Mekka van de Polder,' 17-04-2008, in: http://www.wijblijvenhier.nl/index.php?/archives/1545-Poldermoskee-Het-Mekka-van-de-Polder.html.

11 '"Polder Mosque" for young Dutch Muslims,' 26-05-2008, in: http://www.radionetherlands.nl/currentaffairs/region/netherlands/080526-polder-mosque.
12 'Jongeren Krijgen Poldermoskee,' in: *De Volkskrant*, 14-04-2008.
13 Podcast 'Het Andere Geluid,' 22-04-2008, in: http://www.nioweb.nl/2008/04/22/het-andere-geluid-dinsdag-22-april/.
14 Compare the planned – and approved – enlargement of the Salafi As Soennah Mosque in The Hague, currently housed in a former factory and considered dangerously 'radical' by the authorities. According to the community leaders, the new mosque will not have a minaret since it is not in the Koran and since a true Muslim, like Mohammed, does not care about 'luxury' or 'symbolism'. P. Pouw, *Salaam! Een Jaar onder Orthodoxe Moslims*, Amsterdam: Nieuw Amsterdam, 2008, pp. 219-220.
15 Podcast 'Poldermoskee,' 18-04-2008, in: http://www.nrc.nl/podcast/article1056894.ece/Poldermoskee.
16 'Jonge Moslima's sceptisch over Nieuwe Moskee,' in: *Contrast*, Nr. 15, June 2008, pp. 14-16; p. 15.
17 A similar case is the Islamic Forum in Penzberg, Germany. Behind its 'modern design' and 'European Islam' seemed to be an imam searching for 'Islamic purity.' *Stuttgarter Zeitung*, 07-12-2007.
18 S. Lacroix, Al-Albani's Revolutionary Approach to Hadith, in: *ISIM Review*, Nr. 21, Spring 2008, pp. 6-7.
19 See De Koning 2008.
20 Perhaps a good example is the recent Assalaam Mosque in Helden. Despite the obvious inclusion of Moroccan building elements, in all speeches of (young) Moroccan community leaders on the importance of 'a tolerant Islam' and on the use of 'Dutch bricks', the words 'Moroccan architecture' were never even mentioned. (http://odin.informatiefabriek.nl:8080/roller/page/redactiestreekbode?entry=moskee_assalaam_symbool_van_vrede) According to the architect, however, the Moroccan recognizability had been a strong prerequisite for his patrons, whereas he had wanted to 'integrate' it. See the image and listen to the interview on http://www.l1.nl/L1NWS/_rp_links4_elementId/1_1719212.
Another example is the new design for the Hindustani-commissioned Miesbahoel Islam ('Light of Islam') Mosque in Zwolle. In confrontation with the media, a young community leader stressed that Miesbahoel Islam was a Dutch-based organization, rejecting any attachment to foreign Islamic sponsors who would determine what kind of Islam should be preached. Construction itself would be carried out by a Dutch contractor, while the design would be handled by a Dutch architect. Since their building had to 'fit', the architect had supposedly been given *carte blanche*. (http://groups.yahoo.com/group/moslimnieuws/message/2406) When looking at the forms of the actual design, however, it combines the segmented onion-dome, the arched substructure, and the three-stepped (unascendable) minaret earlier shown to have been used in representations of Brelwi Islam. (http://jouweb.windesheim.nl/portal/page?_pageid=534,1716468&_dad=portal&_schema=PORTAL&p_news_item_id=31446).

Selected Bibliography

Abbos, S. (2005) *De Moslim Bestaat Niet. Een zoektocht naar de Islam*, Amsterdam: Bakker.

Acun, H. (2005) *Bozok Sancaği (Yozgat ili) 'nda Türk Mimarisi*, Ankara: Türk Tarih Kurumu.

Adamson, I. (1989) *Mirza Ghulam Ahmad of Qadian*, London: Elite.

Ahalli, A. (2006) Marokko en zijn Islamisten: Reformisten, Rebellen en Jihadisten, in: E. van de Bovenkamp and H. el Kaddouri (eds), *Marokko uit de Schaduw. De Onbelichte Kanten van Vierhonderd Jaar Betrekkingen Nederland-Marokko*, Amsterdam: Aksant; Utrecht: SMT, pp. 99-112.

Ahmad, M.G. (1996) *The Philosophy of the Teachings of Islam*, Tilford: Islam International Publications [Lahore 1896].

Akkach, S. (2005) *Cosmology and Architecture in Premodern Islam. An Architectural Reading of Mystical Ideas*, Albany: State University of New York Press.

Albarn, K. et al (1974) *The Language of Pattern. An Enquiry Inspired by Islamic Decoration*, London: Thames and Hudson.

Al-Qadiri, G.R. (2004) *Het Wahabisme. De Pseudo-Islamitische Ondermijnende Beweging*, Amsterdam [etc]: Liefhebbers van de Heilige Profeet.

Asher, C.B. (1992) *Architecture of Mughal India*, Cambridge [etc]: Cambridge University Press.

Bak, P. (1987) De Laatste Werken, in: J. Molema and P. Bak (eds), *Jan Gerko Wiebenga. De Apostel van het Nieuwe Bouwen*, Rotterdam: Uitgeverij 010, pp. 128-137.

Bartels, D. (1977) *Guarding the Invisible Mountain. Intervillage Alliances, Religious Syncretism and Ethnic Identity among Ambonese Christians and Moslems in the Moluccas*, New York: Cornell University.

— (1989) *Moluccans in Exile. A Struggle for Ethnic Survival. Socialization, Identity Formation, and Emancipation Among an East-Indonesian Minority in the Netherlands*, Leiden: Center for the Study of Social Conflicts, University of Leiden; Utrecht: Moluccan Advisory Council.

— (1994) *In de Schaduw van de Berg Nunusaku. Een Cultuur-Historische Verhandeling over de Bevolking van de Midden-Molukken*, Utrecht: Landelijk Steunpunt Edukatie Molukkers.

Bartels, E. and M. de Koning (2006) For Allah and Myself. Religion and Moroccan Youth in The Netherlands, in: P. Bos and W. Fritschy (eds),

Morocco and The Netherlands. Society, Economy, Culture, Amsterdam: VU University Press, pp. 146-154.

Barth, F. (ed) (1998) *Ethnic Groups and Boundaries. The Social Organization of Culture Difference*, Illinois: Waveland [Oslo: Universitetsforlaget, 1969].

— (1998) Introduction, in: F. Barth (ed), *Ethnic Groups and Boundaries. The Social Organization of Culture Difference*, Illinois: Waveland [Oslo: Universitetsforlaget, 1969], pp. 9-38.

— (1987) *Cosmologies in the Making. A Generative Approach to Cultural Variation in Inner New Guinea*, Cambridge [etc]: Cambridge University Press.

— (1993) *Balinese Worlds*, Chicago [etc]: University of Chicago Press.

— (1994) Enduring and Emerging Issues in the Analysis of Ethnicity, in: H. Vermeulen and C. Govers (eds), *The Anthropology of Ethnicity. Beyond 'Ethnic Groups and Boundaries'*, Amsterdam: Het Spinhuis.

Batur, A. (2005) *A Concise History. Architecture in Turkey during the 20th Century*, Istanbul: Chamber of Architects of Turkey.

Beck, H.L. (2002) A Hidden Agenda or Hidden Prejudices? Building a Turkish Mosque in Tilburg, in: W.A. Shadid and P.S. van Koningsveld (eds) *Intercultural Relations and Religious Authorities: Muslims in the European Union*, Leuven [etc]: Peeters, pp. 49-66.

Bergh, G. van den (1996) *Wyldemerck. Kamp voor Islamitische Molukkers, 1954-1969*, Utrecht: Moluks Historisch Museum; Landelijk Steunpunt Educatie Molukkers [Ridderkerk 1994].

Bliek, J. van der (2000) 'De ideale moskee bestaat niet,' in: *Onze Wereld*, April 2000, pp. 28-31.

Bovenkamp, E. van de and H. el Kaddouri (eds) (2006) *Marokko uit de Schaduw. De Onbelichte Kanten van Vierhonderd Jaar Betrekkingen Nederland-Marokko*, Amsterdam: Aksant; Utrecht: SMT.

Boedhoe, N. (1990) Hindostaanse Moslims, in: C. van der Burg, T. Damsteegt and K. Autar, *Hindostanen in Nederland*, Leuven; Apeldoorn: Garant, pp. 107-123.

Boender, W. (2007) *Imam in Nederland. Opvattingen over zijn Religieuze Rol in de Samenleving*, Amsterdam: Bert Bakker.

Bolkestein, F. (1997) *Moslim in de Polder. Frits Bolkestein in Gesprek met Nederlandse Moslims*, Amsterdam: Contact.

Bonine, M.E. (1990) The Sacred Direction and City Structure. A Preliminary Analysis of the Islamic Cities of Morocco, in: *Muqarnas*, vol. VII, 1990, pp. 50-72.

Bos, P. and W. Fritschy (eds) (2006) *Morocco and The Netherlands. Society, Economy, Culture,* Amsterdam: VU University Press.

Bouadi, O. et.al (eds) (2001) *De Vele Gezichten van Marokkaans Nederland. Een Wie is Wie*, Amsterdam: Hilversum: NPS; Amsterdam: Mets & Schilt.

Bozdoğan, S. (1997) The Predicament of Modernism in Turkish Architectural Culture. An Overview, in: S. Bozdoğan and R. Kasaba (eds), *Rethinking Modernity and National Identity in Turkey*, Seattle, Washington [etc]: University of Washington Press, pp. 133-156.

— and R. Kasaba (eds) (1997) *Rethinking Modernity and National Identity in Turkey*, Seattle, Washington [etc]: University of Washington Press.

— (2001) *Modernism and Nation Building. Turkish Architectural Culture in the Early Republic*, Seattle, Washington [etc]: University of Washington Press.

Buehler, A.F. (1998) *Sufi Heirs of the Prophet. The Indian Naqashbandiyya and the Rise of the Mediating Sufi Shaykh*, Columbia, SC: University of Souh California Press.

Burg, C. van der, T. Damsteegt and K. Autar (1990) *Hindostanen in Nederland*, Leuven; Apeldoorn: Garant.

Buijs, F. and C. Nelissen (1994) Tussen Continuïteit en Verandering. Marokkanen in Nederland, in: H. Vermeulen and R. Penninx (eds), *Het Democratisch Ongeduld. De Emancipatie en Integratie van Zes Doelgroepen van het Minderhedenbeleid*, Amsterdam: Het Spinhuis, pp. 177-206.

— (1998) *Een Moskee in de Wijk. De Vestiging van de Kocatepe Moskee in Rotterdam-Zuid*, Amsterdam: Het Spinhuis.

Canatan, K. (2001) *Turkse Islam. Perspectieven op Organisatievorming en Leiderschap in Nederland*, Rotterdam: Erasmus Universiteit.

—, M. Popovic and R. Edinga (2005) *Maatschappelijk actief in moskeeverband. Een verkennend onderzoek naar de maatschappelijke activiteiten van en het vrijwilligerswerk binnen moskeeorganisaties en het gemeentelijk beleid ten aanzien van moskeeorganisaties*, Den Bosch: Ihsan.

Chaudhri, R.A. (1982) *Mosque. Its Importance in the Life of a Muslim*, London: The London Mosque.

Chauvel, R.H. (1990) *Nationalists, Soldiers and Separatists. The Ambonese Islands from Colonialism to Revolt, 1880-1950*, Leiden: KITLV Press.

Çinar, A. (2005) *Modernity, Islam, and Secularism in Turkey. Bodies, Places, and Time*, Minneapolis: University of Minnesota Press.

Damluji, S.S. (ed) (1998) *The Architecture of the Prophet's Holy Mosque Al Madina*, London: Hazar.

Davison, J. (1998) The House as a Ritually Ordered Space, in: G. Tjahjono (ed), *Architecture. Indonesian Heritage Series Vol. 6*, Singapore: Archipelago Press; Jakarta: Buku Antar Bangsa, pp. 18-19.

Deniz, D. (2005) *De Ontstaansgeschiedenis van de Witte Moskee in Almelo, 1972-1975*, Zwolle: Windesheim School.

Dibbets, K. and F. van der Maden (eds) (1986) *Geschiedenis van de Nederlandse Film en Bioscoop tot 1940*, Weesp: Het Wereldvenster.

Dumarçay, J. (1998) Indonesian Methods of Building with Stone, in: G. Tjahjono (ed), *Architecture. Indonesian Heritage Series Vol. 6*, Singapore: Archipelago Press; Jakarta: Buku Antar Bangsa, pp. 56-57.

Dijker, B. (1995) *Een Minaret in het Stadsgezicht. Nieuwbouw Moskeeën in Nederland, Registratie en Vormgeving*, Utrecht: Utrecht University.

El Moumni, K. (2001) *Waarom ben ik Moslim?*, Rotterdam: El Moumni [Translation from Arabic, Casablanca: El Moumni, 2000].

Erkoçu, E., A. Hammiche and C. Bugdaci (2006) Minaretten in de Polder, in: *De Architect*, 37 (6), pp. 30-39.

Ernst, C.W. (1993) An Indo-Persian Guide to Sufi Shrine Pilgrimage, in: C.W. Ernst and G.M. Smith (eds), *Manifestations of Sainthood in Islam*, Istanbul: The Isis Press, pp. 43-67.

— and G.M. Smith (eds) (1993) *Manifestations of Sainthood in Islam*, Istanbul: The Isis Press.

Ersan, G. (2007) Secularism, Islamism, Emblemata: The Visual Discourse of Progress in Turkey, in: *Design Issues*, Vol. 23 (2), pp. 66-82.

Erzen, J. and A. Balamir (1996) The Parliament Mosque, Ankara, in: I. Serageldin and J. Steele (eds), *Architecture of the Contemporary Mosque*, London: Academy Editions, pp. 105-107.

Evers, H. (1916-1918) *De Architectuur in Hare Hoofdtijdperken*, Amsterdam: Veen.

Exter, J. den (1990) *Diyanet. Een reis door de keuken van de officiële Turkse islam*, Beverwijk: CBP.

Eyüpgiller, K.K. (2006) 20th Century Mosque Architecture in Turkey, in: *EJOS, Electronic Journal for Oriental Studies*, IX (6), pp. 1-37.

Friedmann, Y. (1987) *Prophecy Continuous. Aspects of Ahmadi Religious Thought and its Medieval Background*, Berkeley [etc]: University of California Press.

Frishman, M. and H.-U. Khan (eds) (2002) *The Mosque. History, Architectural Development and Regional Diversity*, London: Thames and Hudson [London: Thames and Hudson, 1994].

Godefroy, J. (1920) *Geschiedenis van de Bouwkunst. De Ontwikkeling van de Bouwstijlen van af den Oorsprong tot het Hedendaagse Tijdperk. Deel I: Oudheid en Middeleeuwen*, Amsterdam: Ahrend.

Goth, S. and C. Cantrijn (1985) Taibah Moskee in De Bijlmer. Islamitische Traditie in Westerse Context, in: *De Architect*, Vol 16, (3), pp. 64-67.

Goodwin, G. (1971) *A History of Ottoman Architecture*, London: Thames and Hudson.

— (1993) *Sinan. Ottoman Architecture and its Values Today*, London: Saqi Books.

Graaf, H.J. de (1947-1948) De Oorsprong der Javaansche Moskee, in: *Indonesië*, nr. 1, pp. 289-307.

— (1963) The Origin of the Javanese Mosque, in: *Journal of Southeast Asian History*, Vol.4, (1), pp. 1-5.

Grabar, O. and D. Hill (1967), *Islamic Architecture and its Decoration: A.D. 800-1500*, London: Faber and Faber [London 1964].

Gugel, E.H. (1886) *Geschiedenis van de Bouwstijlen in de Hoofdtijdperken der Architectuur*, Arnhem: P. Gouda Quint [1869].

Guillot, C. (1985) La Symbolique de la Mosquée Javanaise. A Propos de la "Petite Mosquée" de Jationom, in: *Archipel*, nr. 30, pp. 3-20.

Haddad, Y.Y. and J.L. Esposito (eds) (2000), *Muslims on the Americanization Path?*, New York [etc]: Oxford University Press.

Haffmans, P. (1985) Een Nieuwe Moskee in de Bijlmermeer. Minaretten terzijde van de Metrohalte Kraaiennest, in: *Architectuur/Bouwen*, Jaargang 1 (3), pp. 29-32.

— (1985) Moskee en Cultureel Centrum te Amsterdam, in: *Bouw*, Nr. 9 (27 April), pp. 81-85.

— (1985) Moskee en Cultureel Centrum in Amsterdam, in: *Bouwen met Staal*, Jaargang 19-3, nr. 73 (September), pp. 35-37.

Haider, G. (1990) "Brother in Islam, Please Draw us a Mosque." Muslims in the West: A Personal Account, in: R. Powell (ed), *Expressions of Islam in Buildings*, Singapore: Concept Media; The Aga Khan Award for Architecture, pp. 155-166.

— (1996) Muslim Space and the Practice of Architecture. A Personal Odyssey, in: B.D. Metcalf (ed), *Making Muslim Space in North America and Europe*, Berkeley [etc]: University of California Press, pp. 31-45.

Hamblin, W.J. and D.R. Seely (2007) *De Tempel van Salomo. Mythe en Geschiedenis*, Haarlem: Altamira-Becht, 2007 [London: Thames & Hudson, 2007].

Hartmann, K.O. (1923) *De Ontwikkeling der Bouwkunst van de Oudste Tijden tot Heden. Eene Inleiding in de Kennis van Geschiedenis, Techniek en Stijl. Deel I: De Bouwkunst in de Oudheid en onder den Islam*, Amsterdam: Maatschappij voor Goede en Goedkope Lectuur [Leipzig: Carl Scholtze, 1910-1911].

Hattstein, M. and P. Delius (2000) *Islam. Kunst en Architectuur*, Cologne: Könemann [Cologne: Könemann, 2000].

Hoag, J. (1976) *Islamische Architektur. Weltgeschichte der Architektur 4*, Stuttgart: Belser; Mailand: Electa [Mailand: Electa, 1975].

Hoek, A. van der (1987) *De Islamitisch Molukse Gemeenschap en haar Leider Imam Achmad Tan*, Leiden: Leiden University.

— (1989) Interview with Perotti, in: A. van der Hoek and H. Obdeijn (eds) *De Islam. Godsdienst en Gemeenschap. De Moskee als Ontmoetingsplaats. Bouwstenen voor Intercultureel Onderwijs*, vol. 39, Leiden: Coördinaat Minderheden Studies, Leiden University, pp. 32-34.

— (1994) *Religie in Ballingschap. Institutionalisering en Leiderschap onder Christelijke en Islamitische Molukkers in Nederland*, Leiden: Leiden University; Amsterdam: VU Uitgeverij.

Hoekstra, E.G. and M.H. Ipenburg (2008) *Handboek Christelijk Nederland. Kerken, Gemeenten, Samenkomsten en Vergaderingen*, Kampen: Kok.

Holod, R. and A. Evin (eds) (1984) *Modern Turkish Architecture*, Philadelphia, Pa: University of Pennsylvania Press.

— and H-U. Khan (1997) *The Contemporary Mosque. Architects, Clients and Designs since the 1950s*, London: Thames and Hudson.

Hond, J. de (2008) *Verlangen naar het Oosten. Oriëntalisme in de Nederlandse Cultuur, ca. 1800-1920*, Leiden: Primavera Pers.

Huisman, J. (1992) *Mooi Gebouwd Nederland*, The Hague: SDU Uitgeverij.

Hulsman, B. (2004) Heimweemoskee of Poldermoskee. Jonge Moslims in Nederland zijn Uitgekeken op de Minaret, in: *NRC,* 1-5-2004, pp. 33-34.

Hutt, A. (1977) *Islamic Architecture. North Africa*, London: Scorpion.

Ikram (1991) Interview met Latief Perotti, in: *Salaam. Moslim Jongeren Blad*, Vol. 1 (4), pp. 22-24.

Johnson, I. and D. Crawford (2003) A Saudi Group Spreads Extremism in 'Law' Seminars, Taught in Dutch, in: *The Wall Street Journal*, 15-4-2003.

Joseph, C. (1982) *Aspek Arsitektur Tradisional Daerah Maluku*, Ambon: Proyek Inventarisasi Dokumentasi Kebudayaan Daerah, Dep. P&K Propinsi Maluku.

Kaa, H. van de (2003) *De Essalaam-Moskee: Van Slagroomtaart tot Scudraket. Een Discoursanalyse van het Proces rond de Vormgeving van de Rotterdamse Essalam-Moskee,* Amsterdam: University of Amsterdam.

Kahera, A.I. (2000) *Deconstructing the American Mosque: Space, Gender and Aesthetics*, Austin: University of Texas Press.

Kerke, H. van de (1986) De Taibah-Moskee te Amsterdam in de Geschiedenis van de Hindoestaans-Surinaamse Moslims, in: R. Kloppenburg and L. Pathmananoharan-Dronkers (eds), *Religieuze Minderheden in Nederland*, Utrecht: Stichting 350 Jaar Rijksuniversiteit Utrecht, pp. 33-45.

Ket, W.G. (1990) Vrijmetselaar Perotti Bouwt Islamitische Godshuizen, in: *AMT (Algemeen Maçonniek Tijdschrift)*, Vol. 44, nr. 3 (March), pp. 73-76.

Khalidi, O. (2000) Approaches to Mosque Design in North America, in: Y.Y. Haddad and J.L. Esposito (eds), *Muslims on the Americanization Path?*, New York [etc]: Oxford University Press, pp. 317-334.

Khan, A.M. (ed) (1994) *Mosques Around the World. A Pictorial Presentation*, Ahmadiyya Muslim Association USA.

Khan, H.-U. (1999) Identity, Authenticity and Power: the Mosque of Hassan II, in: *ISIM Newsletter*, 3/99 (July), p. 8.

— (2002) An Overview of Contemporary Mosques, in: M. Frishman and H.-U. Khan (eds), *The Mosque. History, Architectural Development and Regional Diversity*, London: Thames and Hudson, 2002 [London 1994], pp. 247-267.

Kiziltan, A. (1985) *Anadolu Beyliklerinde Cami ve Mescitler (XIV yüzyil sonuna kadar),* Istanbul: Istanbul Teknik Üniversitesi, pp. 47-68.

Klerk, C.J.M. de (1953) *De Immigratie der Hindostanen in Suriname*, Amsterdam: Urbi et Orbi.

Klomp, M. (1987) *Samen een gebedshuis bouwen, maar geen woord over het gebed. Een onderzoek, in het kader van de dialoog, naar de houding van Turkse Moslims en Nederlandse Almeloërs, waaronder Christenen, voor, tijdens en na de bouw van de Almelose moskee*, Kampen: Theological University Kampen.

Kloos, M. (1985) Reinheid in een Kuil van Beton, in: *De Volkskrant*, 8-3-1985.

Kloppenburg, R. and L. Pathmananoharan-Dronkers (eds) (1986) *Religieuze Minderheden in Nederland*, Utrecht: Stichting 350 Jaar Rijksuniversiteit Utrecht.

Knaap, G.J. (2004) *Kruidnagelen en Christenen. De Verenigde Oost-Indische Compagnie en de Bevolking van Ambon 1656-1696*, Leiden: KITLV Uitgeverij [Utrecht 1985].

Kohne, J.H. (1990) Symboliek in Beton, in: *Cement, Vakblad voor de Betonwereld*, Vol. 42, nr. 10 (October), pp. 20-21.

Koning, M. de (2008) *Zoeken naar een 'Zuivere' Islam. Geloofsbeleving en Identiteitsvorming van Jonge Marokkaans-Nederlandse Moslims*, Amsterdam: Bert Bakker.

Kraft, S. (2002) *Islamische Sakralarchitektur in Deutschland. Eine Untersuchung Ausgewählter Moschee-Neubauten*, Münster: Lit.

Kromhout, W. (1908) Mahomedaansche Kunst, in: *Zeven Voordrachten over Bouwkunst,* Amsterdam: Maatschappij voor Goede en Goedkope Lectuur, pp. 65-123.

Kuran, A. (1987) *Sinan. The Grand Old Master of Ottoman Architecture*, Washington D.C. (etc): Institute of Turkish Studies (etc).

Kusno, A. (2000) *Behind the Postcolonial. Architecture, Urban Space and Political Cultures in Indonesia*, London (etc): Routledge [New York 1997].

Lacroix, S. (2008) Al-Albani's Revolutionary Approach to Hadith, in: *ISIM Review*, Nr. 21, Spring 2008, pp. 6-7.

Landman, N. (1992) *Van Mat tot Minaret. De Institutionalisering van de Islam in Nederland*, Amsterdam: VU Uitgeverij.

— (1992b) Sufi Orders in The Netherlands. Their Role in the Institutionalization of Islam, in: W.A.R Shadid and P.S. van Koningsveld (eds), *Islam in Dutch Society. Current Developments and Future Prospects*, Kampen: Kok Pharos Publishing House, pp. 26-39.

— (1997) Sustaining Turkish-Islamic Loyalties: The Diyanet in Western Europe, in: H. Poulton and S. Taji-Farouki (eds), *Muslim Identity and the Balkan State*, London: Hurst & Company, pp. 214-231.

— and W. Wessels (2005) The Visibility of Mosques in Dutch Towns, in: *Journal of Ethnic and Migration Studies*, 31 (6), pp. 1125-1140.

Leliman, J.H.W. (1918) *Geschiedenis van de Bouwstijlen in de Hoofdtijdperken der Architectuur van Prof. E. Gugel. Vierde druk, geheel omgewerkt en belangrijk uitgebreid door J.H.W. Leliman*, Rotterdam: D. Bolle.

Levtzion, N. (ed) (1979) *Conversion to Islam*, New York (etc): Holmes & Meier.

Limon, I.D. (2000) *Islamische Kulstätten des 20. Jahrhunderts im europäischen Raum*, Kaiserslautern: Dissertation, pp. 63-68, 125.

Lindo, F. (1999) *Heilige Wijsheid in Amsterdam. Ayasofia, Stadsdeel De Baarsjes en de Strijd om het Riva-Terrein*, Amsterdam: Het Spinhuis.

Lotfi, A. (2006) Managing Religious Affairs in Morocco, in: P. Bos and W. Fritschy (eds) *Morocco and The Netherlands. Society, Economy, Culture*, Amsterdam: VU University Press, pp. 33-43.

Maas, T. (1985) Baith Al-Rahmaan Moskee te Ridderkerk. Geen Steen zonder Symbolische Bijbedoeling, in : *De Architect*, Vol. 16 (May), pp. 52-55.

Maden, F. van der (1986) De Komst van de Film, in: K. Dibbets and F. van der Maden (eds), *Geschiedenis van de Nederlandse Film en Bioscoop tot 1940*, Weesp: Het Wereldvenster, 1986, pp. 11-52.

Manuhutu, W. and H. Smeets (eds) (1991) *Tijdelijk Verblijf. De Opvang van Molukkers in Nederland, 1951*, Amsterdam: De Bataafsche Leeuw.

Matheson Hooker, V. (ed) (1993) *Culture and Society in New Order Indonesia*, Kuala Lumpur (etc): Oxford University Press.

Maussen, M. (2006) *Ruimte voor de Islam? Stedelijk Beleid, Voorzieningen, Organisaties*, Apeldoorn (etc): Het Spinhuis.

— (2007) Gemeente en Moskee. Een Halve Eeuw Schuivende verantwoordelijkheden, in: *City Journal, Wetenschappelijk Tijdschrift voor de Steden*, nr. 8 (June), pp.30-35; p. 31.

Meeker, M.E. (1997) Once There Was, Once There Wasn't. National Monuments and Interpersonal Exchange, in: S. Bozdoğan and R. Kasaba (eds), *Rethinking Modernity and National Identity in Turkey*, Washington (etc): University of Washington Press, pp. 157-191.

Mekking, A.J.J. (2004) Houses of Prayer, Houses of Preaching. A Structural Comparison of Islamic and Calvinist-Rooted Religious Architecture, in: *Het Kerkgebouw in het Postindustriële Landschap/The Church in the Post-Industrial Landscape*, Zoetermeer, pp. 79-90.

— and E. Roose (eds) (forthcoming 2009) *The Global Built Environment as a Representation of Realities,* Amsterdam: Amsterdam University Press.

Metcalf, B.D. (1982) *Islamic Revival in British India. Deoband, 1860-1900*, Princeton; Guildford: Princeton University Press.

— (ed) (1996) *Making Muslim Space in North America and Europe*, Berkeley (etc): University of California Press.

Miranda, F. de (1977) *De Moskee als Kunstwerk en als Huis van Gebed*, Wassenaar: Miranda.

Molema, J. and P. Bak (eds) (1987) *Jan Gerko Wiebenga. De Apostel van het Nieuwe Bouwen*, Rotterdam: Uitgeverij 010.
Müller, H. (1998) Zo'n Fundamentalist maakt alles Kapot, in: *De Volkskrant*, 16-10-1998, p. 13.

Necipoğlu, G. (2005) *The Age of Sinan. Architectural Culture in the Ottoman Empire*, London: Reaction Books.
Nurmohammed, M.S.A. (1985) *Geschiedenis van de Islam in Suriname*, Paramaribo: Gedenkboek Surinaamse Moeslim Associatie.

O'Neill, H. (1993) Islamic Architecture under the New Order, in: V. Matheson Hooker (ed), *Culture and Society in New Order Indonesia*, Kuala Lumpur (etc): Oxford University Press, pp. 150-165.
— (1998) The Mosque as a Sacred Space, in: G. Tjahjono (ed), *Architecture. Indonesian Heritage Series Vol. 6*, Singapore: Archipelago Press; Jakarta: Buku Antar Bangsa, pp. 94-95.
— (1998) Regional Mosques: Tradition and Eclecticism, in: G. Tjahjono (ed), *Architecture. Indonesian Heritage Series Vol. 6*, Singapore: Archipelago Press; Jakarta: Buku Antar Bangsa, pp. 96-97.
Onvlee, P. (1989) RGD bouwt zijn laatste Moskee, in: *Open Huis, Ministerie van VROM*, Vol. 13, nr. 10 (October), pp. 15-18.
Özdemir, A. and K. Frank (2000) *Visible Islam in Modern Turkey*, Basingstoke (etc): Macmillan; New York: St. Martin's Press.

Paccard, A. (1980) *Le Maroc et l'Artisanat Traditionnel Islamique dans l'Architecture*, Saint-Jorioz: Editions Atelier 74.
Pereira, J. (2004) *The Sacred Architecture of Islam*, New Delhi: Aryan Books International.
Perotti, L. (1981) Herontdekking van Islamitische Principes in de Moderne Architectuur, in: *Qiblah, Informatiebulletin Federatie Moslim Organisaties Nederland*, nr. 1 (February/March), pp. 11-14.
— (1986) Koepel en Minaret sieren Ridderkerkse Moskee. Integratie van Architectuur, Kunst en Techniek, in: *Bouwkunde en Civiele Techniek*, nr. 3, pp. 11-18.
— (1990) Nieuwe Moskee in Waalwijk, in: *Qiblah, Informatiebulletin Federatie Moslim Organisaties Nederland*, Spring, pp. 17-25.
— (1997) Het Heiligdom. Kwartier Maken voor God, in: *De Heilige Plaats. Het Heiligdom en de Betekenis voor Vandaag. Nieuwe Soefi Reeks*, nr.12 (October), pp. 47-61.

Portoghesi, P. (1992) Moschee und Islamisches Kulturzentrum in Rom, in: *Deutsche Bauzeitschrift*, nr. 7, pp. 983-985.

Poulton, H. and S. Taji-Farouki (eds) (1997), *Muslim Identity and the Balkan State*, London: Hurst & Company.

Pouw, P. (2008) *Salaam! Een Jaar onder Orthodoxe Moslims*, Amsterdam: Nieuw Amsterdam.

Powell, R. (ed) (1990) *Expressions of Islam in Buildings*, Singapore: Concept Media; The Aga Khan Award for Architecture.

Pijper, G.F. (1947) The Minaret in Java, in: *India Antiqua*, pp. 274-283.

Rabbae, M. (1993) *Naast de Amicales nu de UMMON. De Mantelorganisaties van de Marokkaanse Autoriteiten in Nederland*, Utrecht: Nederlands Centrum Buitenlanders.

Rabbat, N. (2004) Islamic Architecture as a Field of Historical Enquiry, in: *Architectural Design*, Vol. 74, nr. 6 (Nov-Dec) ['Islam + Architecture'], pp. 18-23.

Ricklefs, M.C. (1979) Six Centuries of Islamization in Java, in: N. Levtzion (ed), *Conversion to Islam*, New York (etc): Holmes & Meier, pp. 100-128.

Rinsampessy, E. (1992) *Saudara Bersaudara. Molukse Identiteit in Processen van Cultuurverandering*, Assen (etc): Van Gorcum; Wychen: Pattimura, pp. 42-47.

Rooy, M. van (2003) Een Minaret van Baksteen. Amsterdam-West Bouwt Moskee in Amsterdamse Schoolstijl, in: *NRC*, 14-02-2003, p. 21.

Rijk, M. de (2006) *De Nieuwe Moskee. Politiek en Geloof in een Provinciestad*, Amsterdam (etc): Atlas.

Saliya, Y., Hariadi and G. Tjahjono (1990) The Indonesian Experience, in: R. Powell (ed), *Expressions of Islam in Buildings*, Singapore: Concept Media; The Aga Khan Award for Architecture, pp. 188-195.

Sanyal, U. (1999) *Devotional Islam and Politics in British India. Ahmad Riza Khan Barelwi and His Movement, 1870-1920*, Oxford: Oxford University Press [1996].

Scerrato, U. (1980) *Islam. Monumenten van Grote Culturen*, Alphen a/d Rijn: ICOB [Milan: Mondadori, 1972].

Schefold, R., G. Domenig and P. Nas (eds) (2003), *Indonesian Houses. Tradition and Transformation in Vernacular Architecture*, Leiden: KITLV Press.

Serageldin, I. and J. Steele (eds) (1996) *Architecture of the Contemporary Mosque*, London: Academy Editions.

Shadid, W.A.R. and P.S. van Koningsveld (eds) (1992) *Islam in Dutch Society. Current Developments and Future Prospects*, Kampen: Kok Pharos Publishing House.

— and P.S. van Koningsveld (eds) (2002), *Intercultural Relations and Religious Authorities: Muslims in the European Union*, Leuven (etc): Peeters.

Sikkema, J.J. (1991) *Wyldemerck. Molukse Moslims in Nederland*, Amsterdam: University of Amsterdam.

Sinaceur, M.-A. (1996) *La Mosquée Hassan II*, Drémil-Lafage: Éditions Daniel Briand.

Smeets, H. (1991) De Plaats van Keuze, in: W. Manuhutu and H. Smeets (eds), *Tijdelijk Verblijf. De Opvang van Molukkers in Nederland, 1951*, Amsterdam: De Bataafsche Leeuw, pp. 7-16.

— (1991) De Organisatie van de Ambonezenzorg, in: W. Manuhutu and H. Smeets (eds), *Tijdelijk Verblijf. De Opvang van Molukkers in Nederland, 1951*, Amsterdam: De Bataafsche Leeuw, pp. 17-39.

Speiser, W. (1964) *Baukunst des Ostens: von der Zeitenwende bis zum 19. Jahrhundert*, Essen: Burkhard-Verlag Ernst Heyer.

Steele, J. (1996) Case Study VI: The West. Symbolism and Context: The New Dilemma, in: I. Serageldin and J. Steele (eds), *Architecture of the Contemporary Mosque*, London: Academy Editions, p. 145.

Stierlin, H. (2002) *Islam. Van Bagdad tot Córdoba. Vroege Architectuur van de 7e tot de 13e Eeuw*, Cologne: Taschen.

Stigter, B. (1991) Islamitische Architectuur in Nederland. Waar de Kameel Knielde, in: *NRC Handelsblad*, 09-08-1991, CS, p. 2.

Stiphout, R. and O. van der Wal (2006) De Mooiste Islamitische Bouwwerken. Nederlandse Moskeeën steeds vaker gebaseerd op Buitenlandse Voorbeelden, in: *Elsevier, Speciale Editie: Islam*, pp. 18-25.

Strijp, R. (1998) *Om de Moskee. Het Religieuze Leven van Marokkaanse Migranten in een Nederlandse Provinciestad*, Amsterdam: Thesis.

Sunier, T. (1996) *Islam in Beweging. Turkse Jongeren en Islamitische Organisaties*, Amsterdam: Het Spinhuis.

— (2005) Constructing Islam. Places of Worship and the Politics of Space in The Netherlands, in: *Journal of Contemporary European Studies*, Vol. 13, nr. 3 (December), pp. 317-334.

Sutterland, H. (1946) *Geschiedenis der Bouwkunst. Vol 2*, Delft: Waltman.

Tabbaa, Y (1997) *Constructions of Power and Piety in Medieval Aleppo*, Pennsylvania: The Pennsylvania State University Press.

— (2001) *The Transformation of Islamic Art during the Sunni Revival*, Seattle and London: University of Washington Press.

Tjahjono, G. (1998) The Javanese house, in: G. Tjahjono (ed), *Architecture. Indonesian Heritage Series Vol. 6*, Singapore: Archipelago Press; Jakarta: Buku Antar Bangsa, pp. 34-35.

— (ed) (1998) *Architecture. Indonesian Heritage Series Vol. 6*, Singapore: Archipelago Press; Jakarta: Buku Antar Bangsa.

Tozy, M. (1999) *Monarchie et Islam Politique au Maroc*, Paris: Presses de Sciences Po.

Veerman, L. (1993) Moskee Centrum van Allochtone Cultuur.'Marmer is gewoon te duur,' in: *Trouw,* 14-9-1993.

Velde, K. van der (1995) Nederlandse Soefi's bespreken het heilige en het mystieke, in: *Trouw,* 27-11-1995.

Vercauteren, J.B. (1987) Fabrieksgebouwen voor de Société Ceramique te Maastricht, in: J. Molema and P. Bak (eds), *Jan Gerko Wiebenga. De Apostel van het Nieuwe Bouwen*, Rotterdam: Uitgeverij 010, pp. 30-35.

Vermeulen, H. and C. Govers (eds) (1994) *The Anthropology of Ethnicity. Beyond 'Ethnic Groups and Boundaries'*, Amsterdam: Het Spinhuis.

— and R. Penninx (eds) (1994) *Het Democratisch Ongeduld. De Emancipatie en Integratie van Zes Doelgroepen van het Minderhedenbeleid*, Amsterdam: Het Spinhuis.

Vogt-Göknil, U. (1978) *Die Moschee. Grundformen Sakraler Baukunst*, Zürich: Verlag für Architektur Artemis.

Volders, J.L. (1966) *Bouwkunst in Suriname. Driehonderd Jaren Nationale Architectuur*, Hilversum: Uitgeverij G. van Saane, Lectura Architectonica.

Vreuls, P. (1998) De Moskee van Waalwijk, in: *ANWB Kampioen*, Vol. 113, nr. 12 (December), pp. 80-82.

Waterbury, J. (1970) *The Commander of the Faithful. The Moroccan Political Elite, a Study in Segmented Politics*, London: Weidenfeld and Nicolson.

Waterson, R. (1998) Construction Rites, in: G. Tjahjono (ed), *Architecture. Indonesian Heritage Series Vol. 6*, Singapore: Archipelago Press; Jakarta: Buku Antar Bangsa, pp. 19-21.

Welzbacher, C. (2008) *Euro Islam Architecture. New Mosques in the West*, Amsterdam: SUN, 2008.

— (2008) The Architecture of Euro-Islam, in: *A10, New European Architecture*, Nr. 19 (Jan/Feb), pp. 58-60.

Wennekes, W. (1993) Hoe groter de Moskee, hoe dichter bij Allah. Islamitische Bouwkunst in Nederland, in: *Intermediair*, vol.29, nr.28, 16-7-1993, pp. 20-25.

Wessels, W. (2003) *Van Kerkstraat naar Moskeedreef? Over Nieuwbouwmoskeeën en Ruimtelijke Ordening in Utrecht en Driebergen-Rijsenburg*, Utrecht: Utrecht University.

Wittermans, T.W. (1991) *Social Organization among Ambonese Refugees in Holland*, Amsterdam: Het Spinhuis [London, 1955].

Zafeerudin, M. (1996) *Mosque in Islam*, New Delhi: Qazi Publishers & Distributors [Translation from Urdu, *Nizam-e-Masajid*, 1956].

Zee, R. van der (2003) Kathedralen voor Allah, in: *HP/De Tijd*, 28-11-2003, pp. 26-32.

Samenvatting in het Nederlands

De teneur van de respectievelijke internationale publicaties over de architectuur van hedendaagse moskeeën in het Westen is opvallend uniform en kan als volgt worden samengevat: '*De islam heeft eigenlijk helemaal geen gebouw nodig, en moslims kunnen in feite overal in de openlucht bidden als het maar in de richting van Mekka is. De weinige vormvereisten die er zijn voor een islamitische gebedshal laten zich destilleren uit de eerste moskee, het huis dat de Profeet Mohammed in 622 na Christus in Medina bouwde. Het bestond uit een aantal basale bouwelementen die zich simpelweg naar de nieuwe islamitische liturgie voegden. De grote onderlinge verschillen in de uiterlijke vormgeving van latere moskeegebouwen hadden dus niets te maken met de religie op zich, maar met het simpele feit dat, automatisch, de regionale architectuurkarakteristieken werden overgenomen van de culturen die werden geïslamiseerd. Na een eerste periode van pure kopieën van lokale gebedshallen kwamen de herkenbare islamitische regionale stijlen en de bijbehorende vormtypen op, zoals zichtbaar in de Mogul moskee met drie uivormige koepels in de Hindoestaanse regio, de Zuidoost-Aziatische moskee met gelaagd schilddak in Indonesië, de Ottomaanse moskee met centrale koepel in Turkije, en de Moorse moskee met tentdak in Marokko. Toen de islam zich eenmaal naar het moderne Westen ging verspreiden, gebruikten de eerste immigranten nog nostalgische kopieën van de moskeeën zoals zij die kenden uit de thuislanden, vanwege de heimwee die zij ervoeren in een vreemde culturele omgeving. Vervolgens gingen zij met één cultureel been in de westerse samenleving staan en verlieten ze de historiserende stijl voor een meer eclectische, Disney-achtige stijl, een hybride mengelmoes van allerlei moskeestijlen uit de islamitische oorsprongslanden met de westerse stijlen en materialen uit hun nieuwe omgeving. In de huidige tijd zien we dat moslims al meer integreren in de westerse samenleving en voorzichtig de eigentijdse moskee beginnen te omhelzen.*' De laatste wordt ook wel Amerikaanse moskee, Euromoskee, westerse moskee of gewoon moskee-van-de-toekomst genoemd, afhankelijk van het geloof van de betreffende schrijver in het nationale, continentale of mondiale karakter van 'moderniteit'.

De denkwijze zoals geproduceerd in de voorgaande parafrase lijkt intuïtief logisch, maar blijkt echter bij nadere beschouwing van de vormgeving van moskeeën in ons eigen land niet houdbaar. In Nederland kunnen sommige Hindoestaanse moskeeën alleen met heel veel fantasie als Mogul vormtype geclassificeerd worden, en de oudste lijkt überhaupt geen islamitische kenmerken te hebben meegekregen. De weinige Molukse moskeeën lijken meer op elkaar, maar toch verschillen de initiatiefnemers hemelsbreed in hun verbale verwijzingen naar Zuidoost-Azië. In Turkse moskeeën kan men meestal wel een Ottomaans voorbeeld herkennen, maar de onderlinge afwijkingen in de mate van stilering daarvan zijn soms enorm. En waar in een aantal Marokkaanse moskeeën wel herkenbaar Moorse vormen zijn gebruikt, is dat in andere gevallen zo ostentatief niet gedaan dat ook hier geenszins sprake is van een consistent vormtypologisch schema. Om de 'verwarring' nog groter te maken zijn er oudere moslims die 'modernistisch', en jongere moslims die juist 'historiserend' lijken te hebben gebouwd. Ondertussen weet elk van hen zijn eigen moskee wel op de een of andere manier als 'Nederlands' te omschrijven en die van een ander als 'on-Nederlands'. Kortom, iedere keer dat we de gedachte hanteren dat moslims met Hindoestaanse, Molukse, Turkse en Marokkaanse banden gebruikmaken van hun eigen Mogul, Zuidoost-Aziatische, Ottomaanse en Moorse 'stijlkenmerken', en dat moslims die deze banden minder en minder ervaren zich meer en meer op modern-Nederlandse vormgeving richten, stuiten we op vele afwijkingen van deze ideaaltypische verdeling naar tijd en ruimte. Sterker nog, als we er op deze manier naar proberen te kijken zonder allerlei ontwerpen op pragmatische gronden weg te laten of juist om strategische redenen voor het voetlicht te halen, raken we onherroepelijk in de knoop. Wat is er toch aan de hand met moskeeontwerp in Nederland?

In deze dissertatie wordt beargumenteerd dat er helemaal niets aan de hand is met moskeeontwerp in Nederland, maar alles met de manier waarop wij tot nu toe naar moskeeën in het algemeen hebben gekeken. Daarvoor gaan we eerst terug naar de negentiende eeuw, de eeuw waarin de architectuurgeschiedschrijving zoals wij die kennen, grotendeels is uitgevonden. Het is namelijk daar dat de wortels liggen van de huidige misverstanden rondom de betekenis van de vormgeving van islamitische gebedsruimtes. In deze tijd ontstond de gedachte dat, vergelijkbaar met de evolutionaire wetenschappen, de architectuur van de wereld ook vorm-conform te categoriseren ofwel te 'typologiseren' zou zijn naar ruimte en tijd. Wat wij nu zien als werkelijk bestaande 'regionale stijlen' en 'stijlperioden' is grotendeels toen als principe geformuleerd, en als een statisch gegeven op de complexe geografische en historische praktijk geprojecteerd. Innig verbonden met deze projectie van zich-uit-elkaar-ontwikkelende 'stijlen' was de stellige overtuiging dat architectuur zich wereldwijd naar een hoger plan bewoog, met het Westen als eindput van het beschavingsproces. De islamitische architectuur moest natuurlijk ook een plekje krijgen in dit wereldomvattende evolutionaire schema, en werd daarom geografisch onderverdeeld in de Arabische, de Turkse en de Perzische regionale stijlen, en historisch geplaatst tussen de klassieke en middeleeuwse stijlperioden. Deze plaatsing was volledig logisch vanuit de heersende gedachte dat moslims, omschreven als een bende woeste tentnomaden op kamelen die natuurlijk geen eigen architectuurtraditie kenden, door hun dweepzieke hang naar overdrijving slechts decoratief konden voortborduren op bestaande 'klassieke' gebouwen in de door hen veroverde cultuurgebieden. Dat kon prachtige ornamentiek opleveren, die vanwege de oriëntalistische associatie met sprookjesachtigheid in de loop der tijd in het Westen wel werd verwerkt in gebouwen als sigarettenfabrieken en bioscopen, maar als zodanig werd het verschijnsel geen constructieve rol toebedacht in de architectonische voorstuwing van de vaart der volkeren. Het is vanuit dit vooruitgangsgeloof dat ook moskeeën in de diaspora chronologisch 'herkend' gingen worden als 'nog steeds' gebaseerd op de oude regionale stijlen uit de islamitische oorsprongslanden, of als 'al enigszins' gebruik makend van de 'moderne' bouwkunst, of als 'reeds volledig' daaraan aangepast.

Vormtypologische indelingen naar tijd en ruimte voldoen echter wel aan de behoefte om *grip* te krijgen op de werkelijkheid, met name voor hen die een bouwkundige 'progressie' willen herkennen of op gang brengen, maar vormen in feite een obstakel om te komen tot *begrip* van de werkelijkheid, met name voor hen die de gebouwen in al hun complexiteit willen analyseren en verklaren. Zelfs de veronderstelde vormtypologieën van historische moskeeën blijken steeds weer gebaseerd te zijn op de opportunistische selectie van een aantal iconische 'hoogtepunten' uit de islamitische architectuur, en ook zij komen geenszins overeen met de veel ingewikkeldere historische praktijk van tegenstellingen binnen, en overeenkomsten tussen, zogenaamd verschillende 'periodes' en 'regio's'. Recente studies naar transformaties in de islamitische en christelijke architectuurgeschiedenis tonen aan dat de periodieke en regionale stijlcategorieën lang niet zo reëel zijn als in de negentiende eeuw geformuleerd, en dat het religieuze aspect van zowel een islamitisch als een christelijk gebedshuis bij lange na niet in slechts enkele 'door de liturgie' voorgeschreven bouwelementen ligt. Architectonische vormen blijken niet geëvolueerd te zijn uit eerdere vormen, alsof ze onderdeel waren van een natuurlijk proces. Ook waren het geen uitingen van cultuurgebieden, alsof alles in een regio automatisch een nationaal karakter kreeg. In plaats van dit alles blijkt zowel de islamitische als de christelijke architectuur transformaties te hebben ondergaan die werden veroorzaakt door continue wederzijdse uitdagingen van elkaar beconcurrerende heersers. Het gebruiken óf verwerpen van specifieke bouwelementen uit eerdere en andere contexten gaf hen, door de nieuwe betekenissen die zich er inmiddels aan hadden gehecht, de mogelijkheid om zich strategisch tegenover elkaar te positioneren in termen van het geloof. De vormgeving van een moskee of een kerk werd dus niet *in abstracto* bepaald door een 'natuurlijke ontwikkeling' naar iets eigentijds of door een 'automatische aanpassing' aan iets regionaals, maar *in concreto* door een calculerende opdrachtgever die doelbewust bestaande bouwelementen naar een nieuwe context transformeerde omdat zij voor hem de passende politiek-religieuze betekenis droegen in het aanschijn van zijn directe rivalen.

Opdrachtgevers blijken dus vele malen belangrijker te zijn voor het begrijpen van de betekenis van religieuze gebouwen dan we gewend zijn te denken. Maar als we kijken naar hoe in de literatuur over opdrachtgevers van hedendaagse moskeeën in het Westen wordt gesproken, komt er bepaald geen positief beeld naar voren. Zij worden zonder blikken of blozen omschreven als non-communicatief, non-integratief, achterlijk, ouderwets, kinderlijk, leurend met goedkope kalenderplaatjes, niet wetend wat ze echt willen, ongehinderd door smaak of door kennis van architectuurgeschiedenis, lijdend aan een teveel aan heimwee, misplaatste trots of zelf-oriëntalisme, en geen respect tonend voor de autonome positie van de hedendaagse architect als kunstenaar. Een enkeling omschrijft hen zelfs als 'alzheimerpatiënten'. In feite doet men het voorkomen alsof opdrachtgevers van moskeeën in het Westen buiten de geschiedenis en de samenleving staan, alsof ze slechts gestuurd zouden worden door de emotionele behoefte aan een herkenbare islamitische identiteit in een vervreemdende, niet-islamitische omgeving, en zo onwetend of zelfs moedwillig de verdere 'evolutie' van de islamitische architectuur zouden tegenhouden. In dit licht worden ze vooral gezien als een factor waaraan tegenwicht moet worden geboden en die moet worden bijgestuurd en opgevoed. De negentiende-eeuwse projectie van de dweepzieke traditionele moslim die alleen maar decoratief kan voortborduren op het bestaande, het latere geloof dat architectuurcitaten verwerpelijk zouden zijn en dat het mogelijk is om puur vanuit de functie een vorm te ontwerpen, en het huidige ideaal van de autonome kunstenaar die vanuit zijn individuele creativiteit reageert op slechts een praktisch programma van eisen en een specifieke urbane omgeving, zijn samengesmolten tot een architectuur*kritische* manier van kijken die elke serieuze toenadering van hedendaagse moskeeopdrachtgevers blokkeert. Juist zij vormen echter de onmisbare sleutels tot een juist begrip van de architectuur van hun gebedshuizen. Om ons te kunnen verplaatsen in hun motivaties, zullen we hen dus moeten accepteren als volwassen sociale actoren, en niet als alzheimerpatiënten met een ongeneeslijke vorm van heimwee.

In deze dissertatie wordt daarom een methode geïntroduceerd waarmee een gebedshuis niet langer als een onderdeel van een zogenaamde 'objectieve' werkelijkheid wordt gezien, maar als niets meer en niets minder dan de materialisatie van een mentale constructie. Wij zullen een architectonisch ontwerp gaan beschouwen als *de representatie van een of meerdere werkelijkheden*, afhankelijk van hoeveel mensen een daadwerkelijke rol hebben gespeeld in het creatieve proces. Zij richten zich daarbij eerst op een door hen op dat moment ervaren of mentaal geconstrueerde werkelijkheid, en daarna doen zij hun gedachten uitgaan naar het vinden van geschikte bouwelementen uit eerdere representaties met de juiste betekenis voor hun eigen context. Gebaseerd op de genoemde studies naar transformaties in de islamitische en christelijke architectuurgeschiedenis, zal voor ons een centraal uitgangspunt zijn dat een cultusgebouw met name bestaat uit bouwelementen die bewust door rivaliserende religieuze leiders zijn geselecteerd om daarmee hun uiteenlopende geloofsconstructies te representeren. We schuiven de gebruikelijke standaardwerken over islamitische architectuur dan ook terzijde en slaan niet-architectonische studies van de islam in Nederland open, om tot de ontdekking te komen dat elk van onze moslimcultuurgroepen, als ware het Nederlandse christenen, intern verdeeld wordt door gemeenschapsleiders die elkaar heftig religieus betwisten. Vervolgens zullen we de specifieke selectie van bouwelementen door Nederlandse moskeeopdrachtgevers in het licht gaan plaatsen van de specifieke versies van de islam die zij wilden representeren. Overigens kunnen de bouwelementen die zij expliciet *verwierpen* eveneens zeer belangrijk zijn, aangezien deze mogelijkerwijs associaties oproepen met de religieuze versies die werden betwist. Daarom is voor ons de studie van het ontwerp*proces*, en niet van slechts het eindproduct, een belangrijke ingang tot de werkelijkheid van een opdrachtgever. We zullen hier dus de hele schetshistorie van een ontwerp, inclusief de schetsen met bouwelementen die het niet gehaald hebben of die eerdere bouwelementen hebben vervangen, zoveel mogelijk trachten te reconstrueren.

De toepassing van deze methodiek op de ontwerpprocessen van een twaalftal Nederlandse moskeeën laat zien dat ook hedendaagse opdrachtgevers, door hun architect bewust te selecteren, aantoonbaar te sturen en zonodig te vervangen, een zeer grote invloed weten uit te oefenen op de vormgeving van hun gebedshuizen. De frequent georganiseerde debatten tussen architectuurcritici, over de oorzaak en de wenselijkheid van het zichtbare gebruik van 'islamitische' bouwelementen in het Nederlandse stadsbeeld, lijken daarmee een aanzienlijk deel van hun publieke relevantie te verliezen. Vervolgens wordt duidelijk gemaakt dat het obligate ideaal dat islamitische gebedshallen alleen wat basale liturgische vormvereisten kennen, zodat hun onderlinge vormafwijkingen vooral te maken zouden hebben met de respectievelijke culturele banden van hun gebruikers, ook ten aanzien van hedendaagse moskeeën een ernstige denkfout is. De huidige 'verwarring' over het fenomeen dat, volledig onafhankelijk van leeftijd of generatie, de ene Hindoestaanse, Molukse, Turkse of Marokkaanse opdrachtgever in Nederland successievelijk geen Mogul, Zuidoost-Aziatische, Ottomaanse of Moorse bouwelementen toegepast wil zien en de andere wel, kan daarmee naar het rijk der fabelen worden verwezen. In de werkelijkheid van de moskeeopdrachtgevers zelf zijn hun gebedshuizen geen representaties van een regio of periode, maar van hun specifieke interpretaties van de islam, afgezet tegen andere, concurrerende interpretaties, met name diegene die circuleren binnen hun eigen culturele 'referentiekader'. Al met al blijken hedendaagse moskeeopdrachtgevers net zo goed onderdeel van de geschiedenis te zijn als hun historische voorgangers. De bouwelementen die zij uitkiezen zijn niet bedoeld ter markering van wat het betekent om een moslim te zijn te midden van niet-moslims, zeg maar als materialisatie van 'de islam' tegenover 'de niet-islamitische samenleving', maar van wat het betekent om een 'goede' moslim te zijn te midden van 'slechte' moslims, als materialisatie van 'de ware islam' tegenover 'valse varianten'.

    Wanneer opdrachtgevers van nieuw te bouwen moskeeën echter in het openbaar wordt gevraagd waarom zij in de ontwerpfase toch zo hardnekkig aan constellaties van bepaalde bouwelementen vasthielden, verwijzen zij steevast naar de in Nederland gewenste werkelijkheden van 'sociale integratie' en 'architectonische vooruitgang' in plaats van naar de eigen werkelijkheid waarop het ontwerp werd gebaseerd. In deze dissertatie wordt beargumenteerd dat het voor hen, juist omdat ze allen de ultieme, ware islam willen vertegenwoordigen in plaats van slechts een omstreden versie ervan, niet wenselijk is om de verschillen tussen hun inmiddels gerealiseerde gebouwen te verklaren uit de verschillen tussen hun voorafgaande geloofsconstructies. Dit betekent overigens niet dat de bewuste opdrachtgevers niet oprecht zouden streven naar een bepaalde manier van integratie of vooruitgang. Het betekent echter wel dat de zeer specifieke bouwelementen die zij tijdens het ontwerpproces selecteerden alleen herleid kunnen worden op hun zeer specifieke beleving van de islam. Dat er in Nederland 'nog steeds' koepels en minaretten worden gebouwd is bij nader inzien dan ook niet omdat moslim*gemeenschappen* nostalgisch aan thuis herinnerd willen worden of beklagenswaardige slachtoffers zijn van zelf-oriëntalisme, en zelfs niet omdat zij als trotse burgers in de multiculturele samenleving willen staan. De bevindingen van dit proefschrift wijzen erop dat, zowel in de diaspora als in de islamitische wereld, koepels en minaretten steeds weer opnieuw worden toegepast omdat ze voor rivaliserende gemeenschaps*leiders* onmisbaar zijn ter mobilisatie van potentiële gemeenschaps*leden*. 'Islamitische' bouwelementen, oneindig te variëren en te transformeren als deze zijn, geven hen de mogelijkheid om hun uiteenlopende en veranderende religieuze constructies architectonisch te definiëren tegenover toekomstige gebruikers. Ook de opdrachtgevers die het ostentatieve gebruik van deze bouwelementen verwerpen blijken, ondanks ook hún rationalisaties in termen van sociale en fysieke aanpassing, specifiek religieuze werkelijkheden te representeren, met name voortspruitend uit secularistische of puristische visies op de islam. Zij roepen daarom op tot architectonische reacties van concurrerende religieuze leiders, die hun afwijkende geloofsbeleving en hun afkeer van secularisme of purisme wederom representeren met 'islamitische' bouwelementen. De internationale obsessie om deze categorieën steeds weer te interpreteren als parameters voor de mate van 'integratie' en 'moderniteit' van hele gemeenschappen, en niet als uitdrukkinsmiddelen van de specifieke islamitische constructies van concrete opdrachtgevers, ontneemt ons letterlijk het zicht op de werkelijkheid.

Curriculum Vitae

Eric Roose was born in Middelburg on 18 June 1967. After completing grammar school at the Christelijke Scholengemeenschap Walcheren (CSW), he studied Law at Utrecht University in 1985. After receiving his BA, he decided to continue his studies at Leiden University, combining an MA program in Public International Law with an MA program in Cultural Anthropology. He specialized in State and Law in Africa, and in Cognitive and Structural Anthropology, completing both studies in 1991. After a career in a large Dutch aviation company and a growing interest in non-Western art, he began studying Art History at Leiden University in 2001. He graduated cum laude with an MA in Comparative World Architecture Studies in 2004, and subsequently started his PhD research at that same university. Between 2005 and 2008 he was also an Affiliated Fellow at the International Institute for the Study of Islam in the Modern World (ISIM). He is currently a Postdoctoral Fellow at the Amsterdam School for Social Science Research (ASSR) of the University of Amsterdam.

Figures

FIGURES

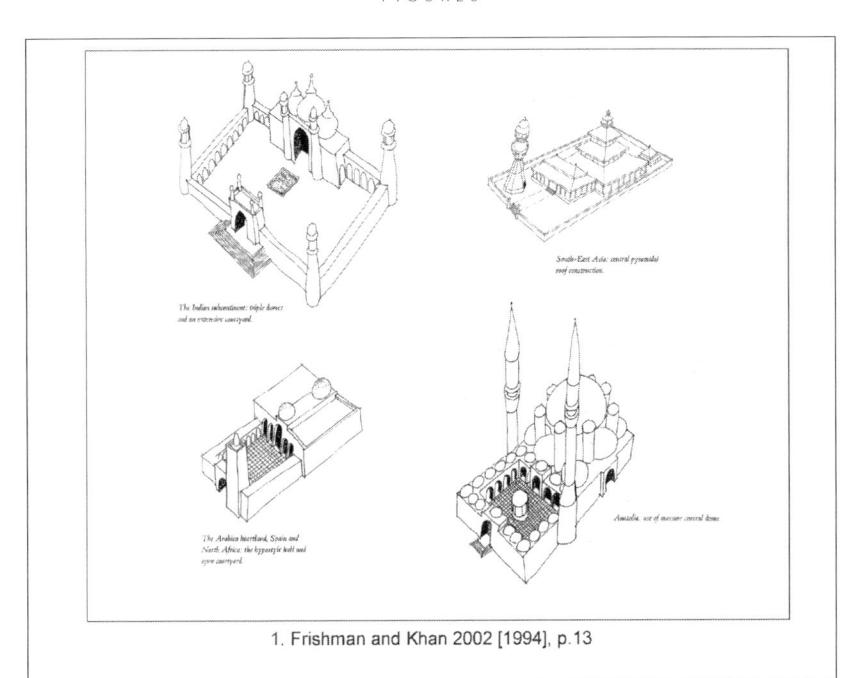

1. Frishman and Khan 2002 [1994], p.13

2. Memar, 1-2003, Archive MemarDutch

THE ARCHITECTURAL REPRESENTATION OF ISLAM

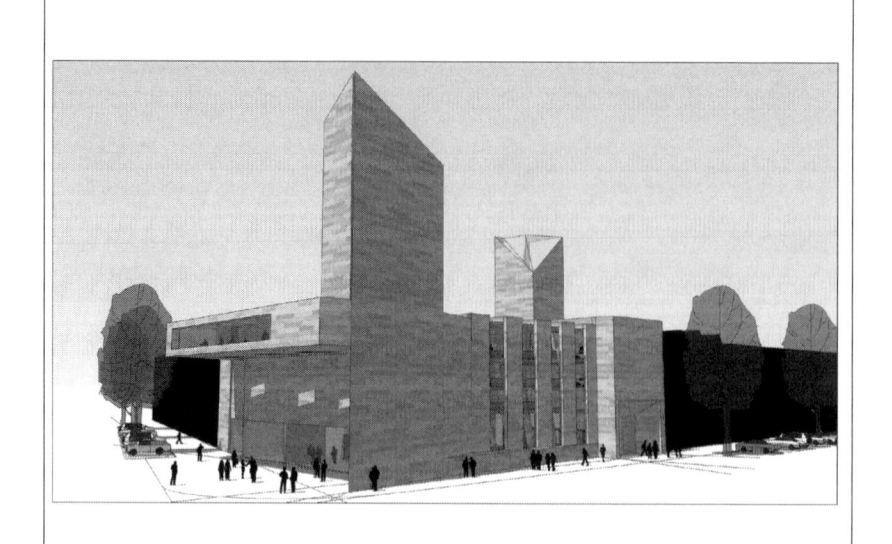

3. Erkoçu, 11-2006, Archive Concept0031

The Aqsa Mosque in Qadian, India

The Mubarak Mosque in Qadian, India

4. Khan 1994, pp. 12, 40; www.alislam.org/gallery/qadian

FIGURES

The Noor Mosque in Qadian, India

5. Khan 1994, p. 14

6. www.alislam.org/gallery/qadian; Khan 1994, p. 40; Archive Mobarak Mosque

THE ARCHITECTURAL REPRESENTATION OF ISLAM

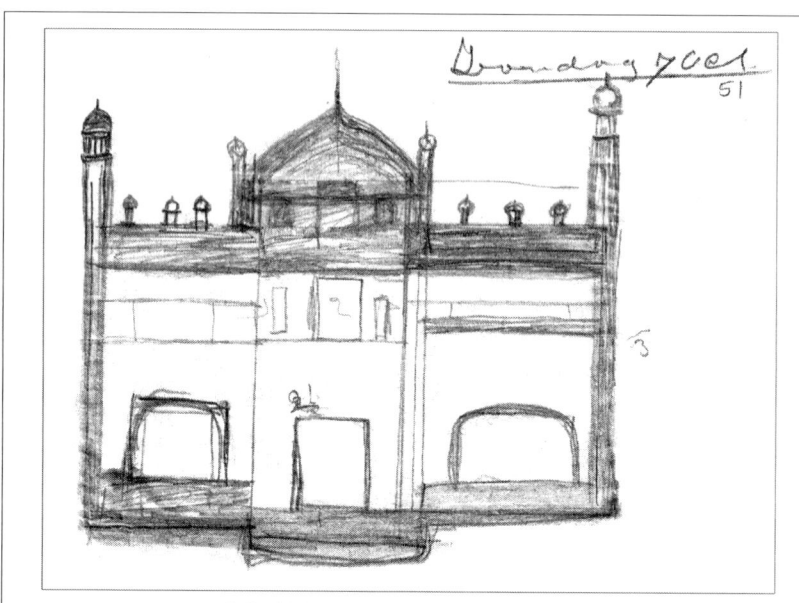

7. Khan 1994, pp. 41, 90, 92, 106

8. Bashir/Wiebenga, 7-10-1951, Archive NAi

324

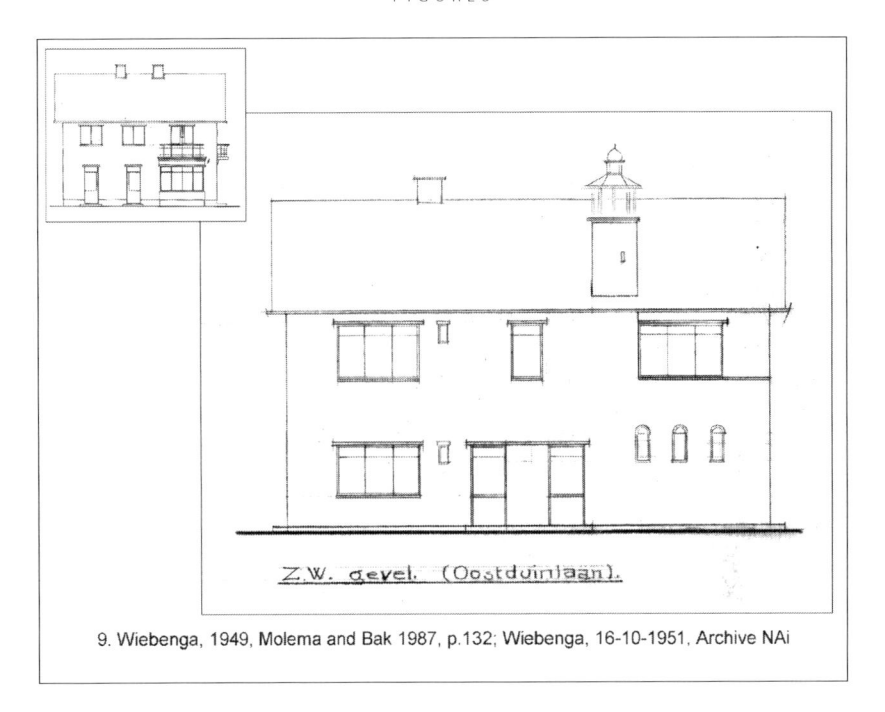

FIGURES

9. Wiebenga, 1949, Molema and Bak 1987, p.132; Wiebenga, 16-10-1951, Archive NAi

10. Wiebenga, 20-10/22-10-1951, Archive NAi

THE ARCHITECTURAL REPRESENTATION OF ISLAM

11. Wahid, 12-8-1952, Archive NAi

12. Wiebenga, 12-10/13-10-1952, Archive NAi

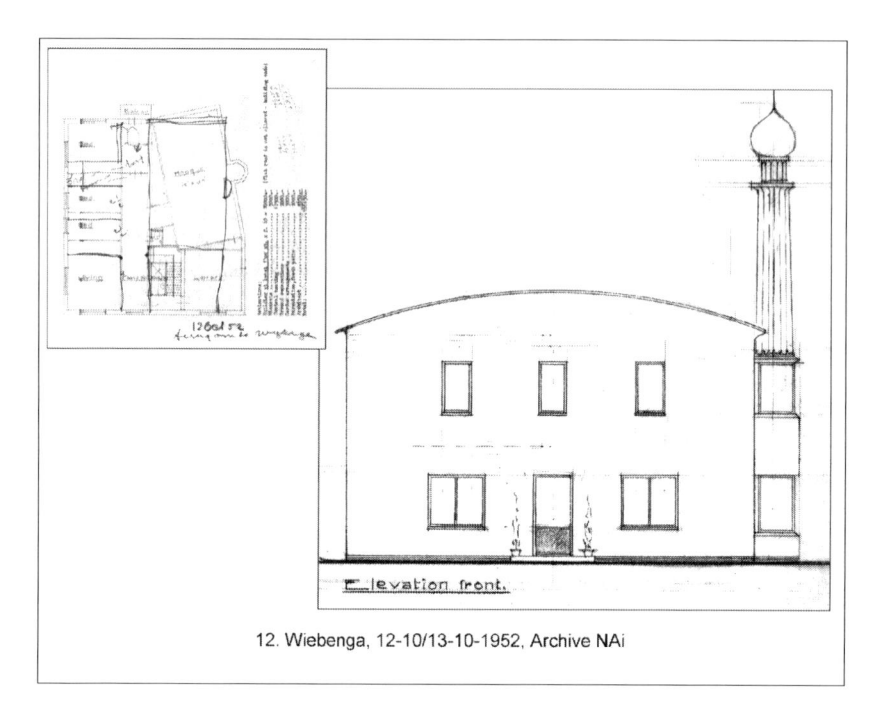

326

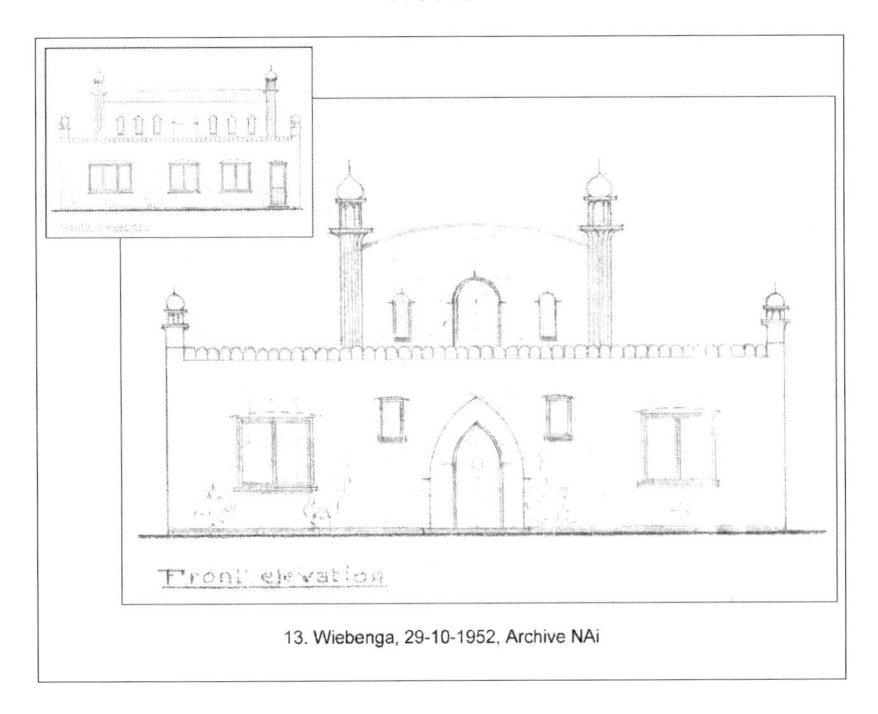

FIGURES

13. Wiebenga, 29-10-1952, Archive NAi

14. Wiebenga, 25-7-1953, Archive NAi

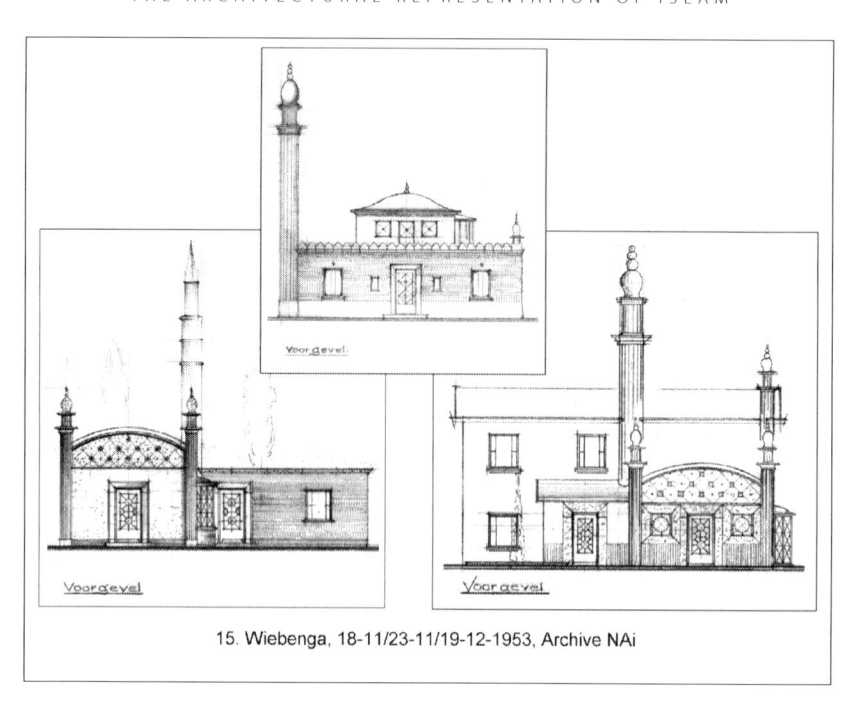

THE ARCHITECTURAL REPRESENTATION OF ISLAM

15. Wiebenga, 18-11/23-11/19-12-1953, Archive NAi

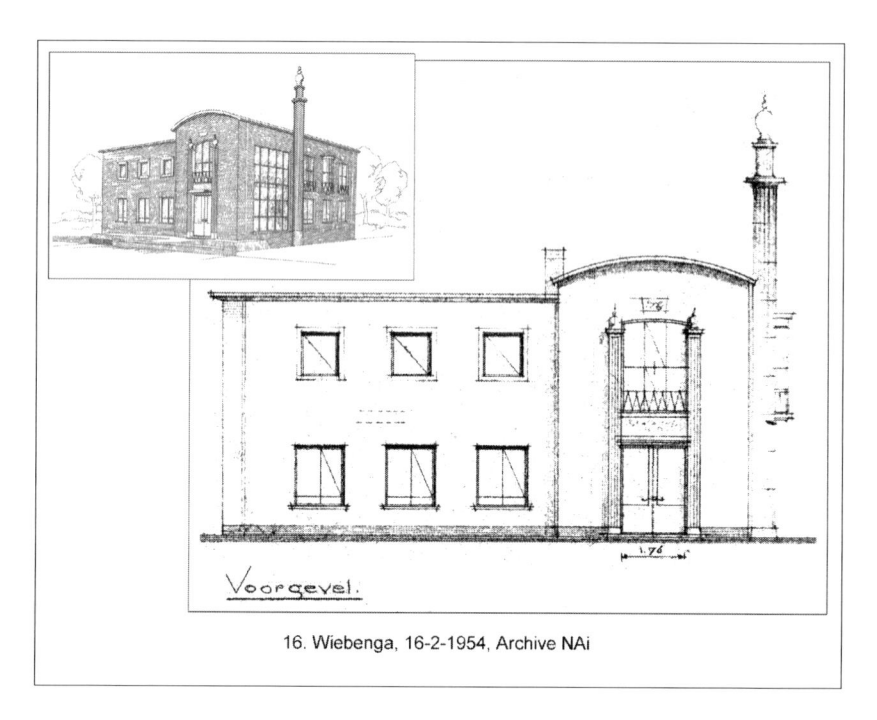

16. Wiebenga, 16-2-1954, Archive NAi

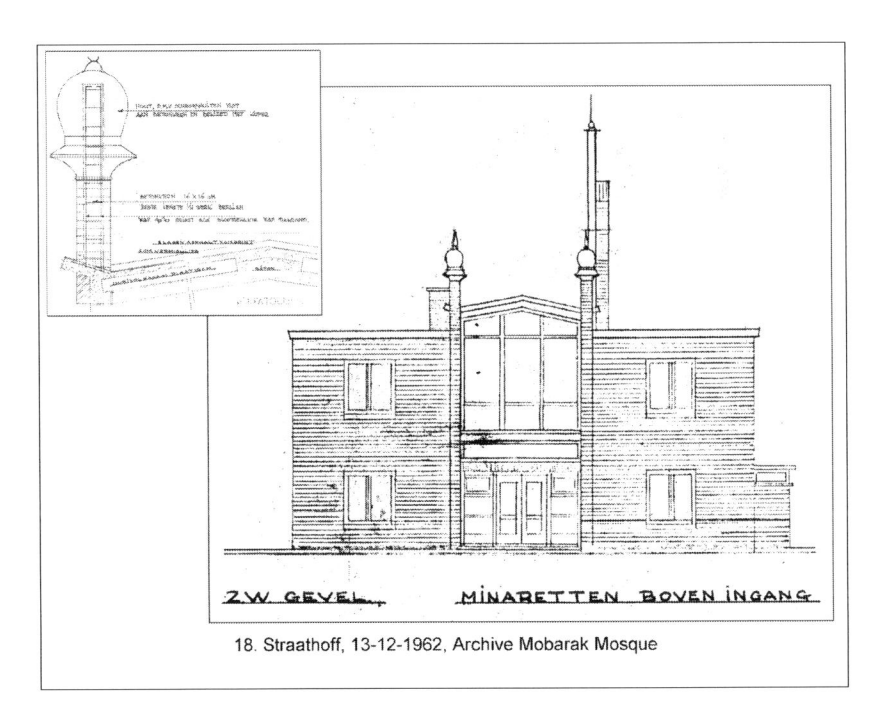

FIGURES

17. Beck, 11-11-1954, Archive Mobarak Mosque

18. Straathoff, 13-12-1962, Archive Mobarak Mosque

THE ARCHITECTURAL REPRESENTATION OF ISLAM

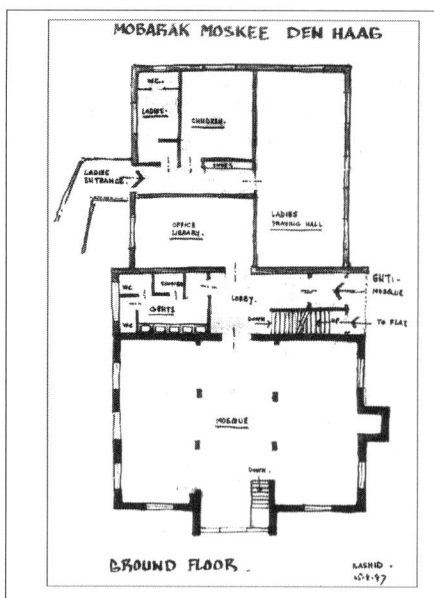

19. Rashid, 25-9-1987, Archive Mobarak Mosque

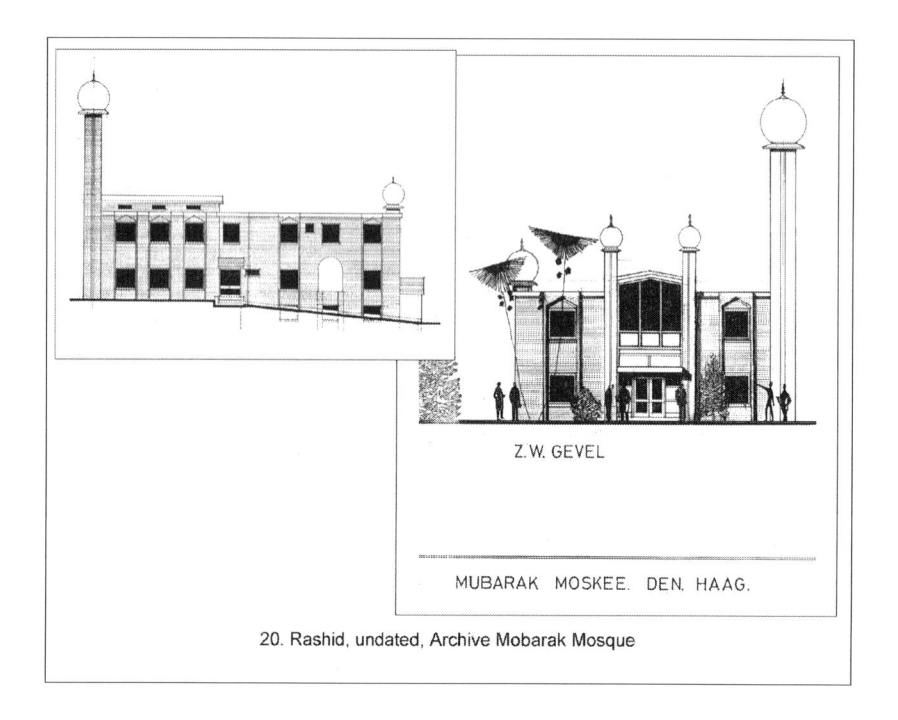

20. Rashid, undated, Archive Mobarak Mosque

FIGURES

21. Rashid, 6-6-1993, Archive Mobarak Mosque

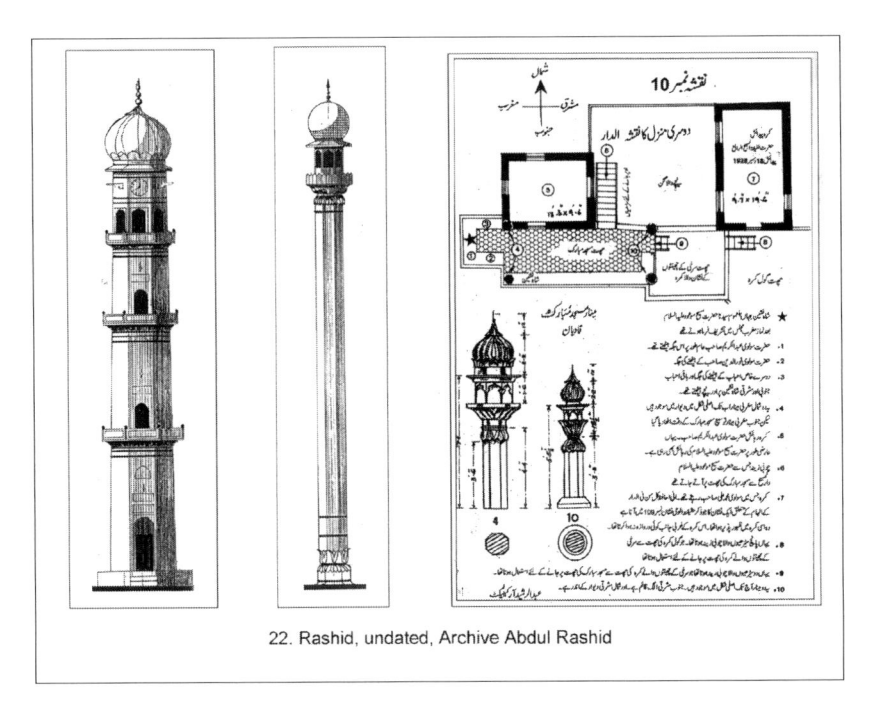

22. Rashid, undated, Archive Abdul Rashid

THE ARCHITECTURAL REPRESENTATION OF ISLAM

23. Rashid, 10-10-1996, Archive Mobarak Mosque

24. Rashid, 13-10-1997, Archive Mobarak Mosque

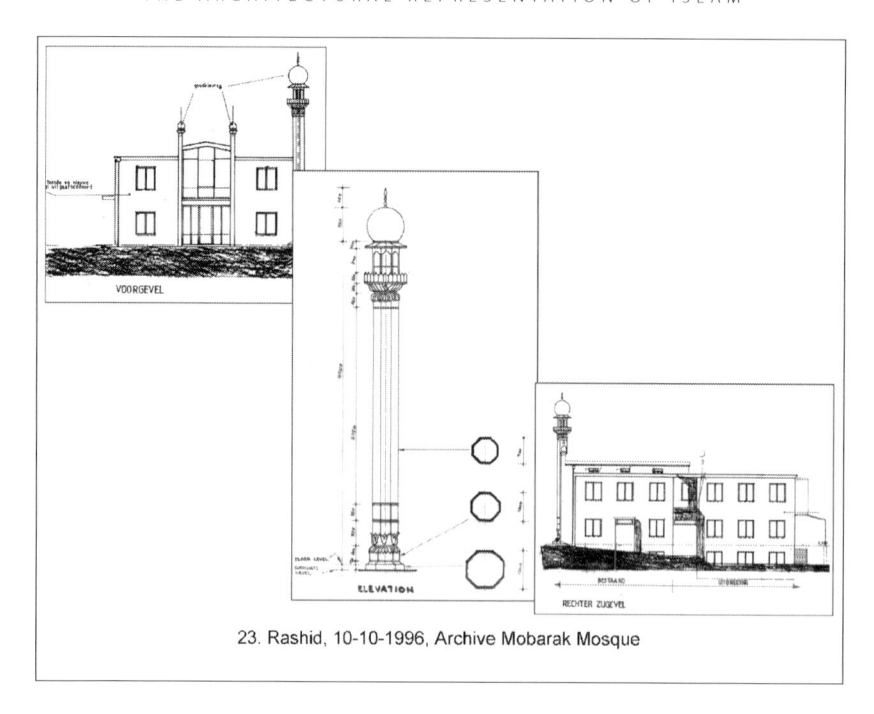

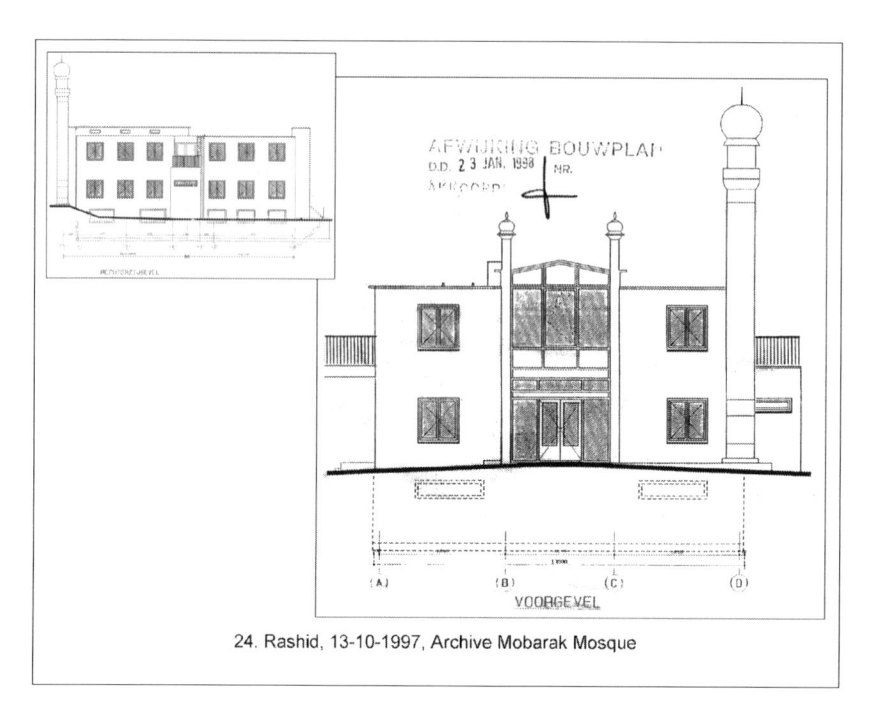

FIGURES

25. 2005, Author's Collection

26. The Message International, Vols. 2000-2005

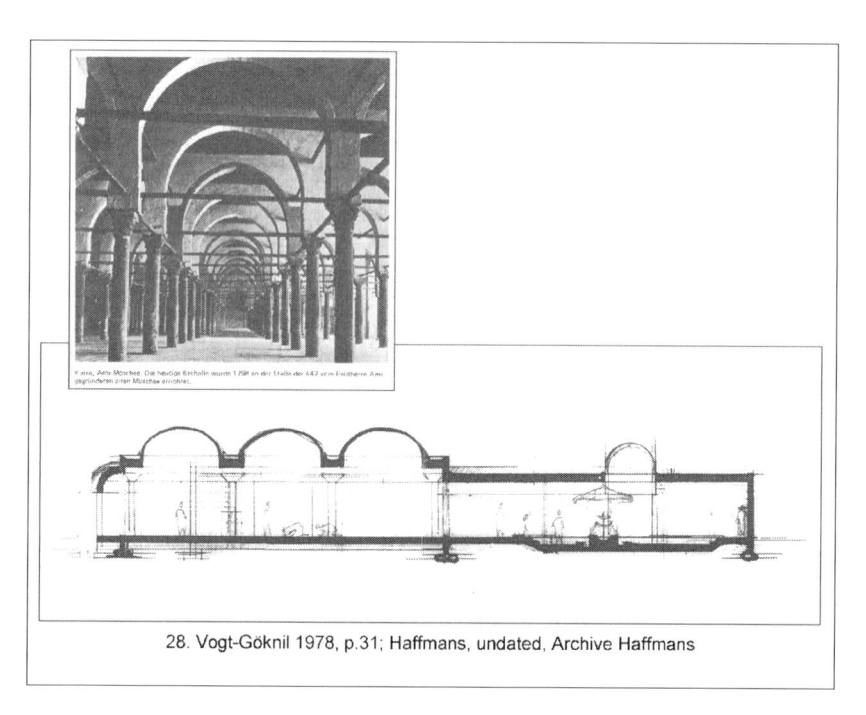

THE ARCHITECTURAL REPRESENTATION OF ISLAM

27. Haffmans, undated, Archive Haffmans

28. Vogt-Göknil 1978, p.31; Haffmans, undated, Archive Haffmans

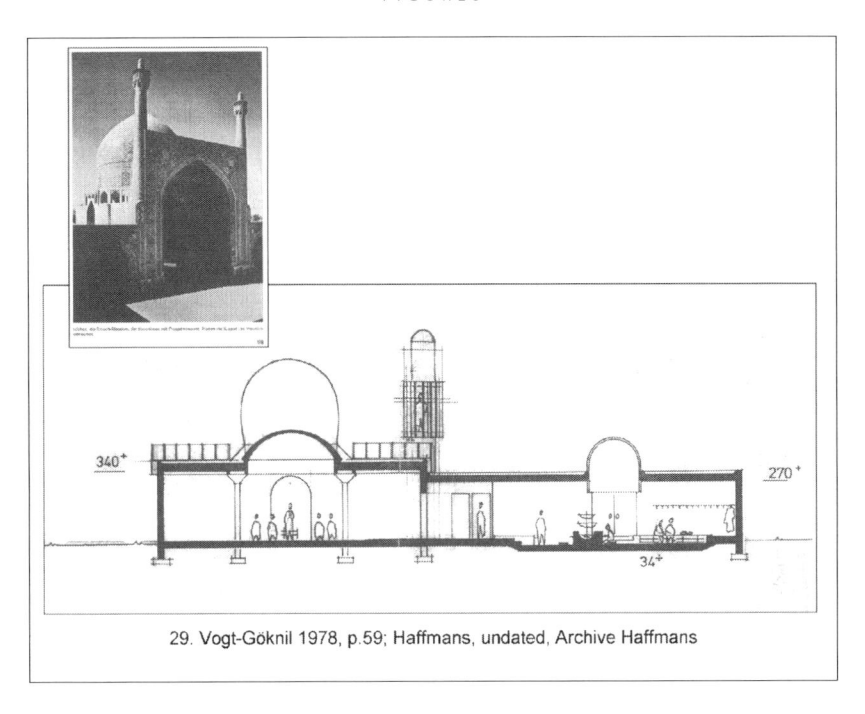

FIGURES

29. Vogt-Göknil 1978, p.59; Haffmans, undated, Archive Haffmans

30. Archive Taibah Mosque; www.ala-hazrat.org/photog.htm

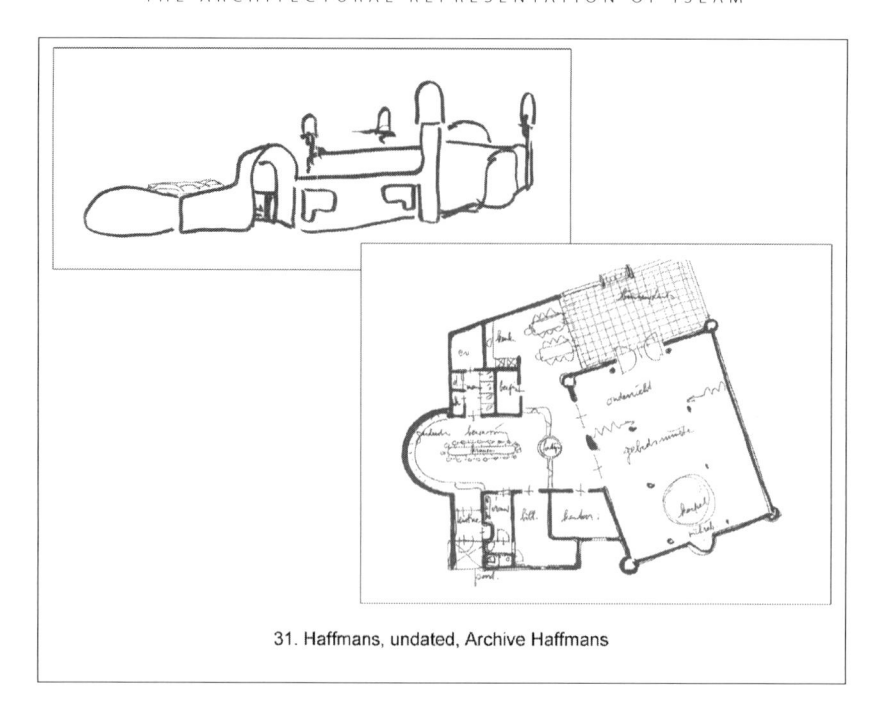

THE ARCHITECTURAL REPRESENTATION OF ISLAM

31. Haffmans, undated, Archive Haffmans

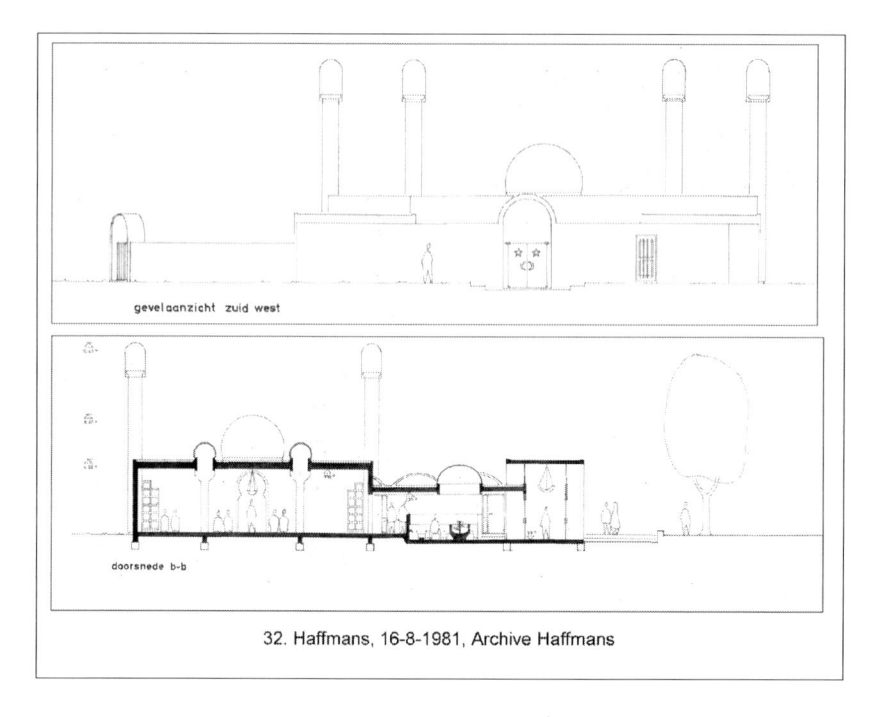

gevelaanzicht zuid west

doorsnede b-b

32. Haffmans, 16-8-1981, Archive Haffmans

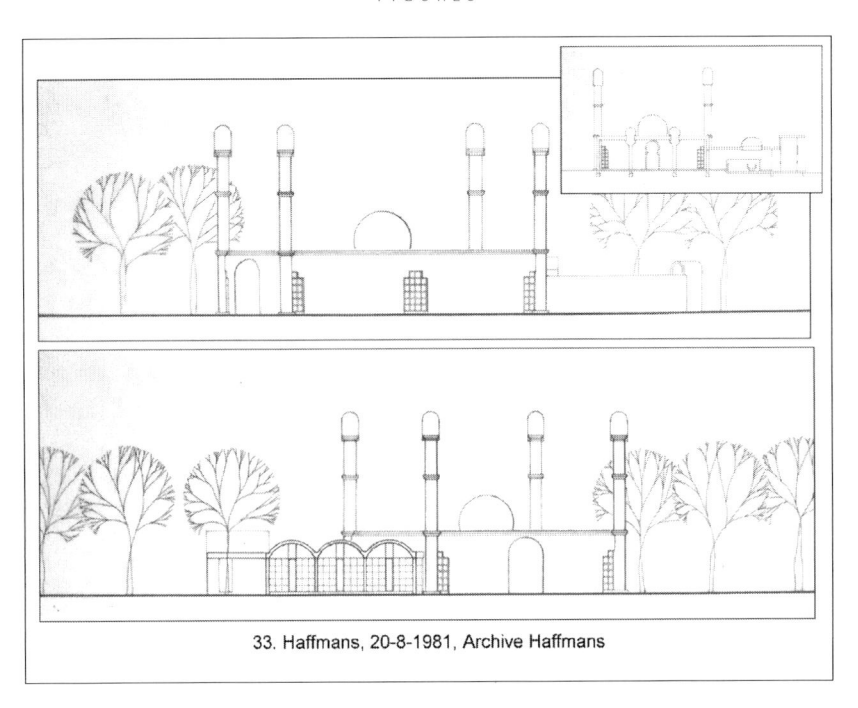

FIGURES

33. Haffmans, 20-8-1981, Archive Haffmans

gevelaanzicht n.o.

gevelaanzicht z.o.

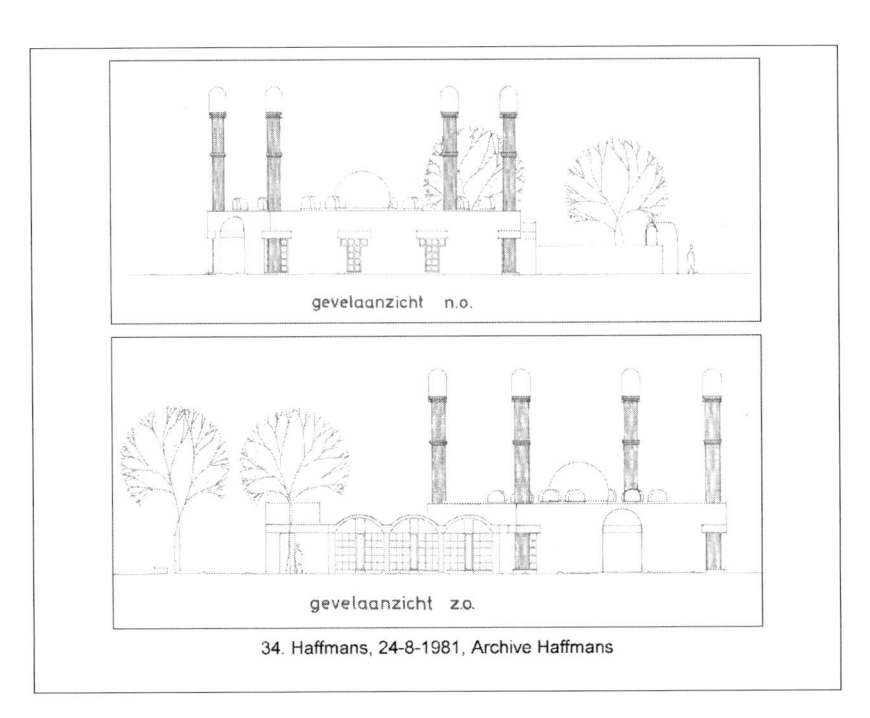

34. Haffmans, 24-8-1981, Archive Haffmans

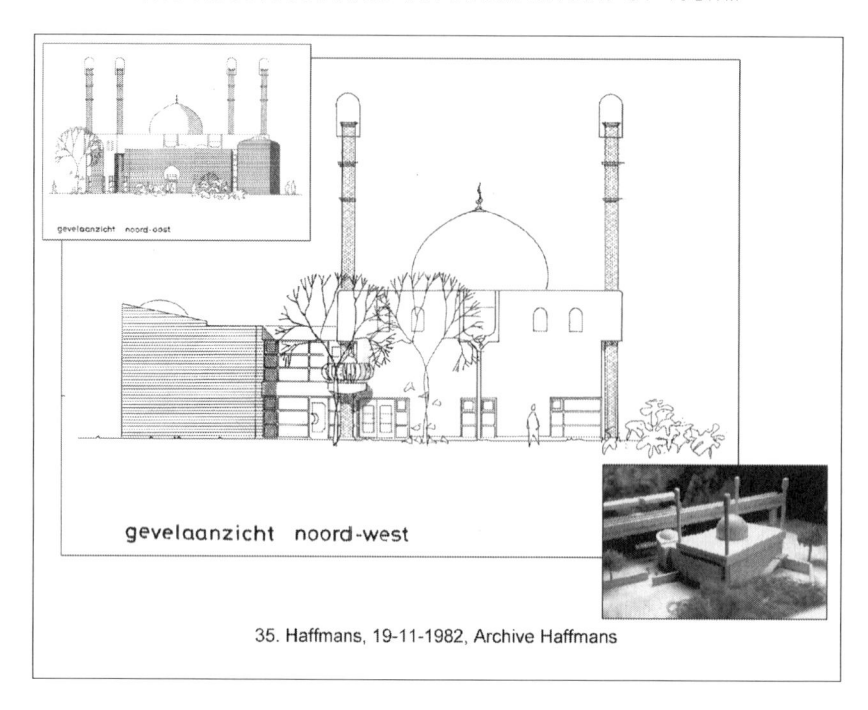

THE ARCHITECTURAL REPRESENTATION OF ISLAM

35. Haffmans, 19-11-1982, Archive Haffmans

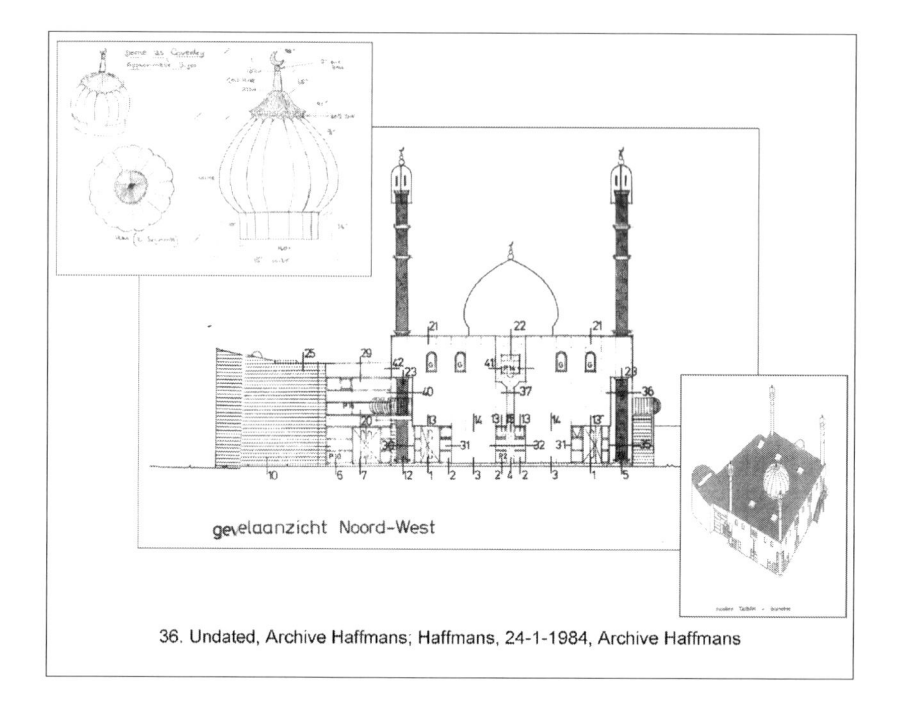

36. Undated, Archive Haffmans; Haffmans, 24-1-1984, Archive Haffmans

338

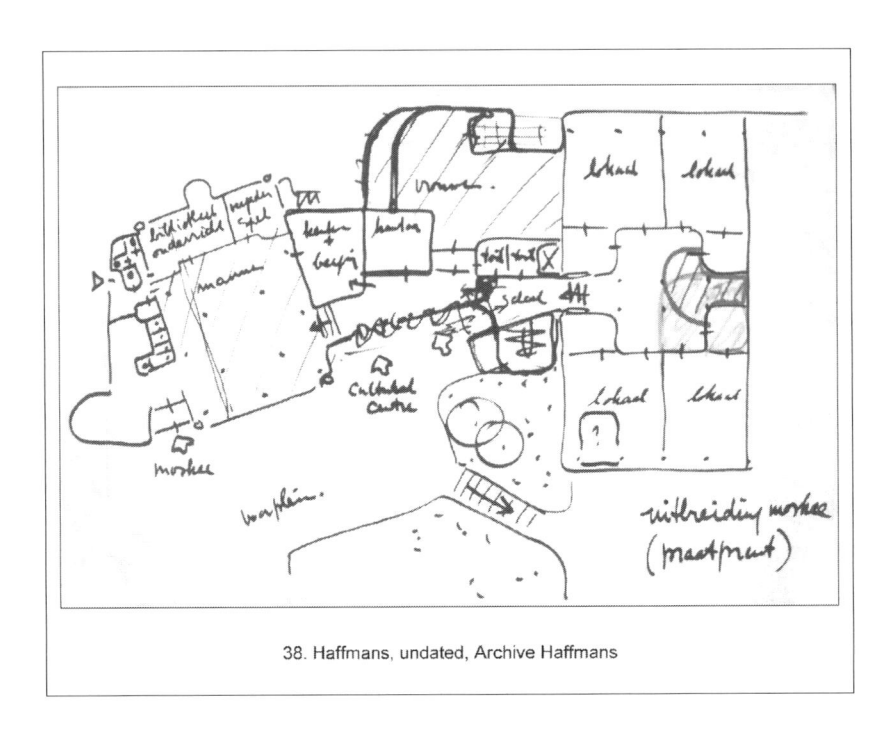

FIGURES

37. 1985, Archive Haffmans

38. Haffmans, undated, Archive Haffmans

THE ARCHITECTURAL REPRESENTATION OF ISLAM

39. Archive Ruimte 68

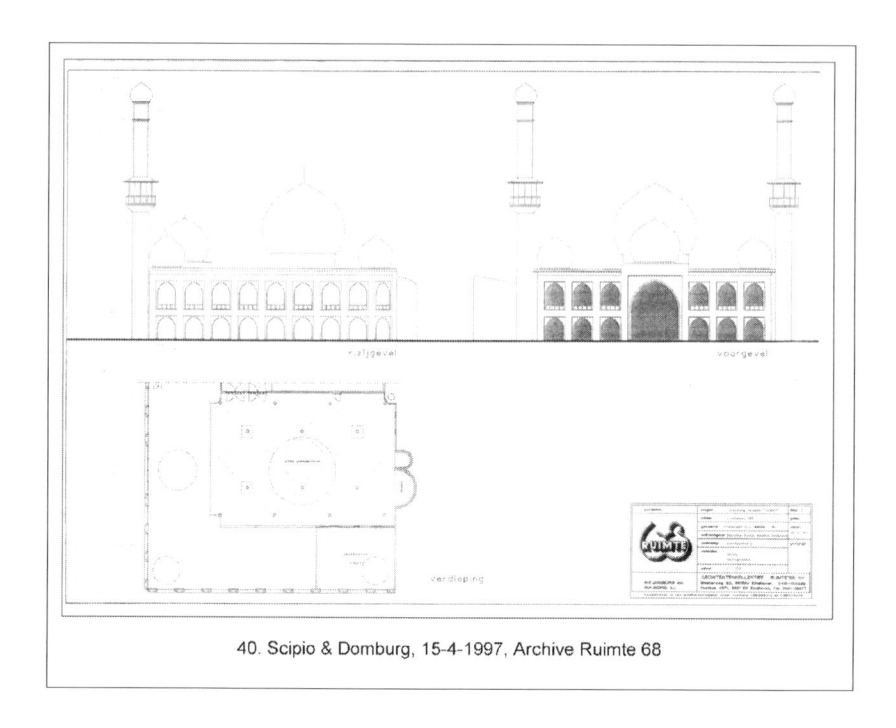

40. Scipio & Domburg, 15-4-1997, Archive Ruimte 68

FIGURES

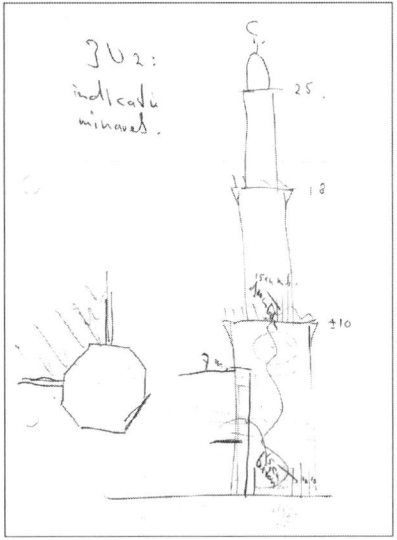

41. Archive Ruimte 68; Scipio & Domburg, 31-5-1997, Archive Ruimte 68

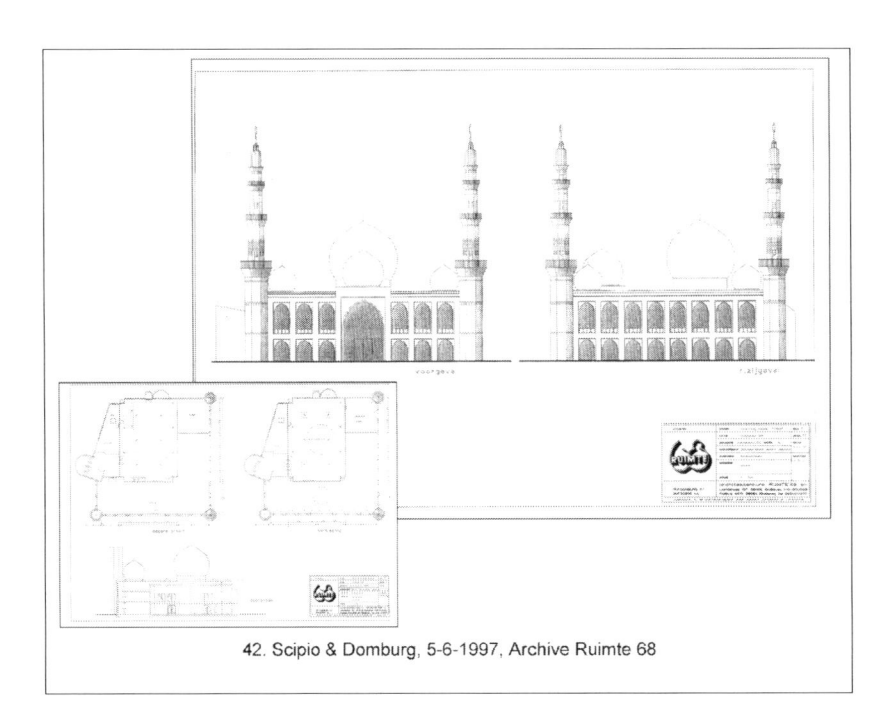

42. Scipio & Domburg, 5-6-1997, Archive Ruimte 68

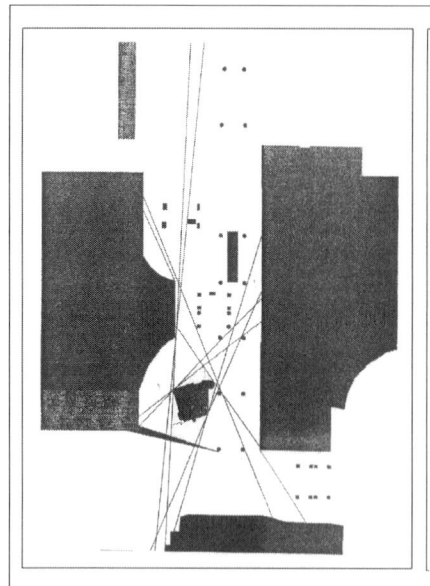

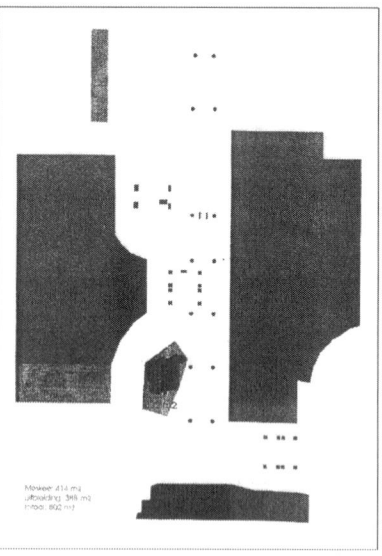

43. Municipality of Amsterdam, 11-11-1997, Archive Ruimte 68

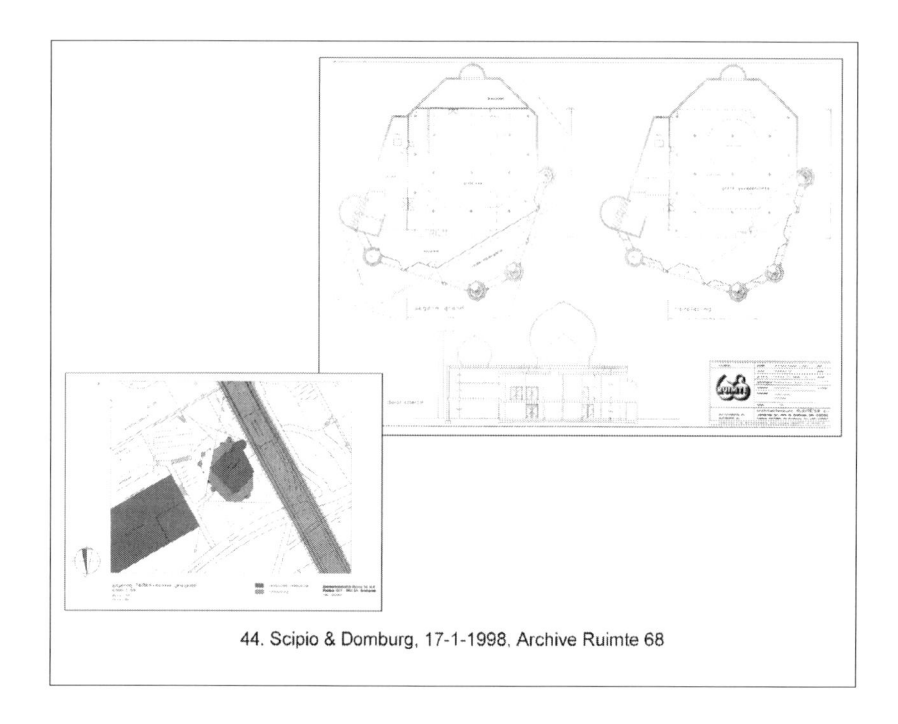

44. Scipio & Domburg, 17-1-1998, Archive Ruimte 68

FIGURES

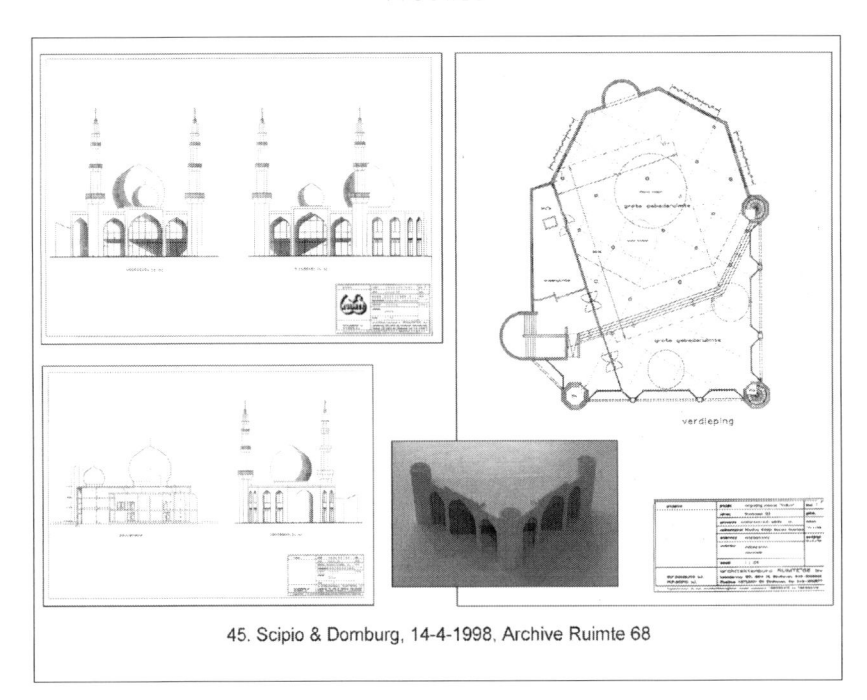

45. Scipio & Domburg, 14-4-1998, Archive Ruimte 68

46. Scipio & Domburg, 16-4-1998, Archive Ruimte 68

THE ARCHITECTURAL REPRESENTATION OF ISLAM

47. SWM, 4-1998, Archive Ruimte 68

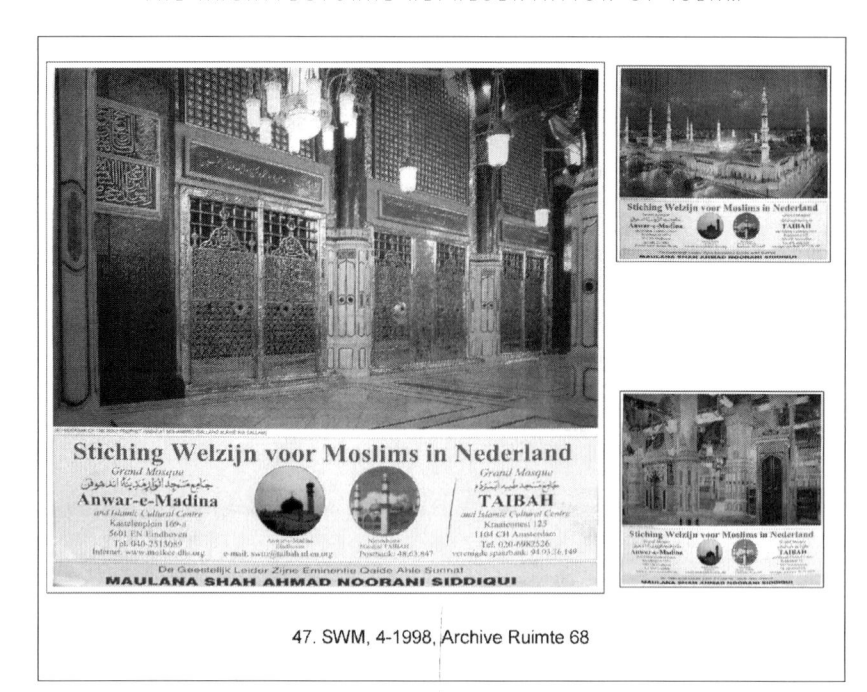

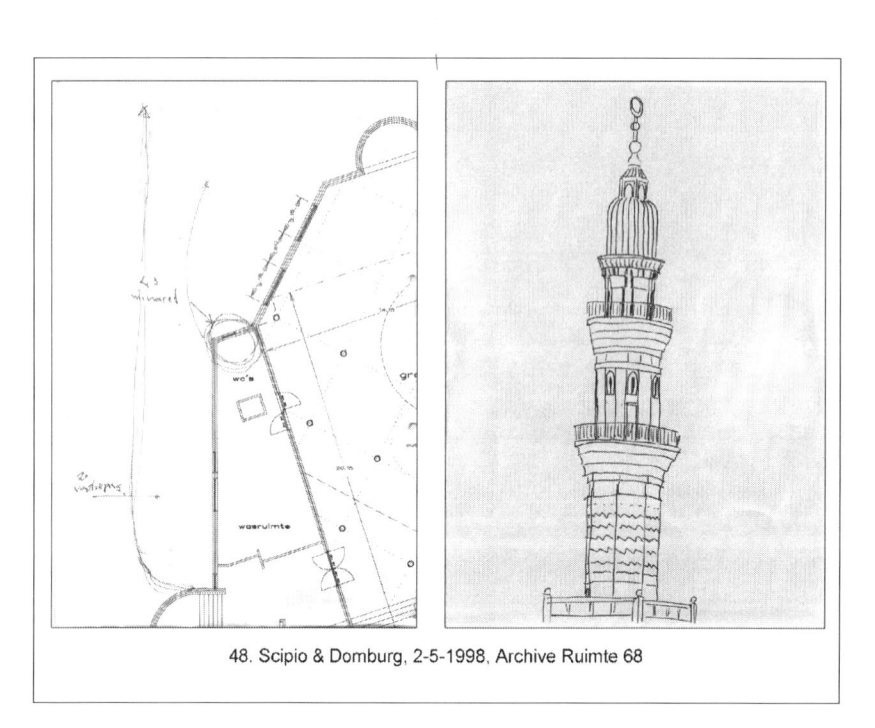

48. Scipio & Domburg, 2-5-1998, Archive Ruimte 68

FIGURES

49. Scipio & Domburg, 12-5/26-5-1998, Archive Ruimte 68

50. Scipio & Domburg, 29-5-1998, Archive Ruimte 68

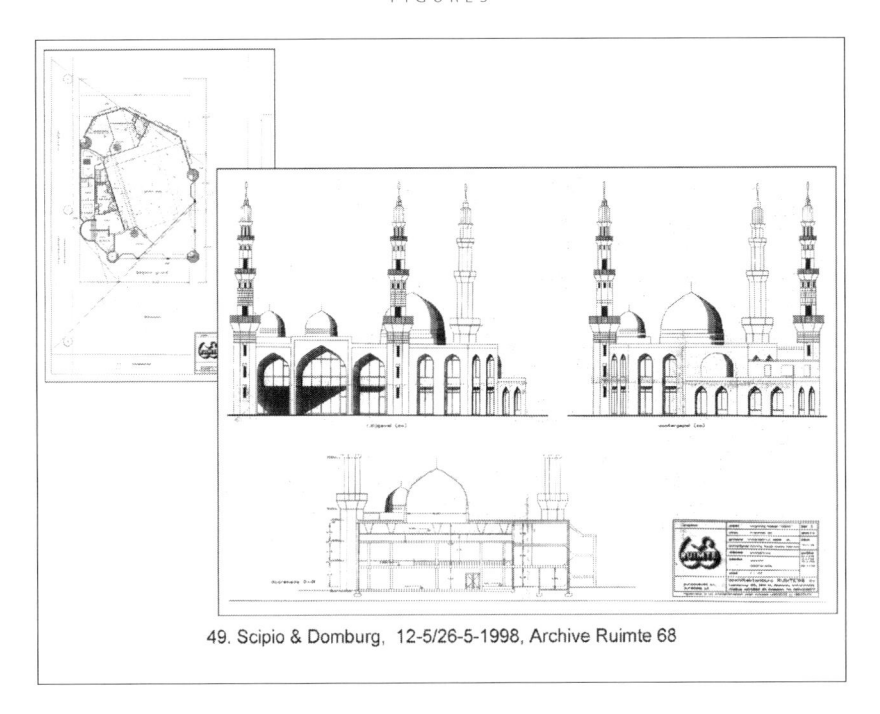

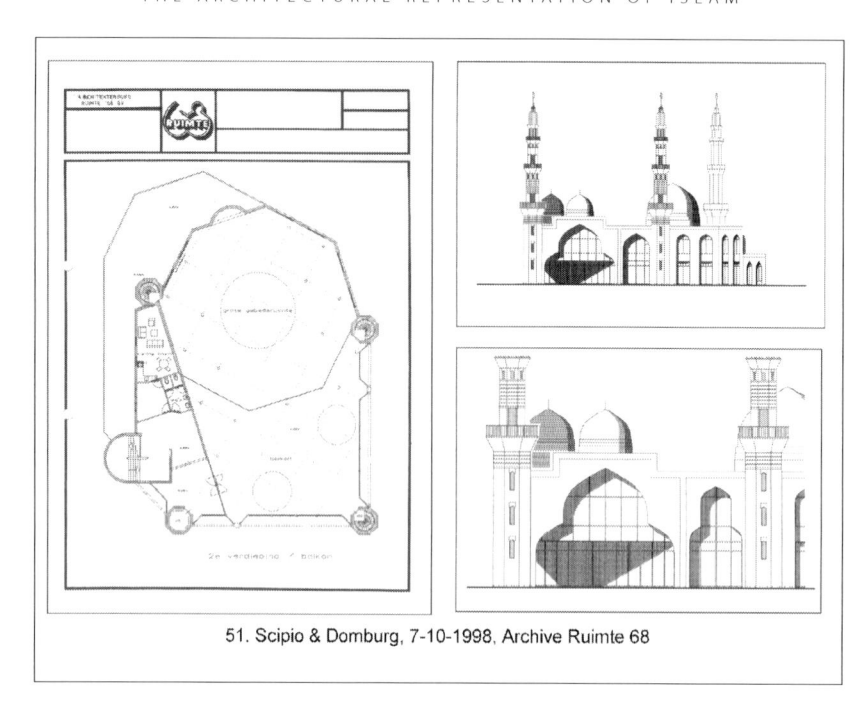

THE ARCHITECTURAL REPRESENTATION OF ISLAM

51. Scipio & Domburg, 7-10-1998, Archive Ruimte 68

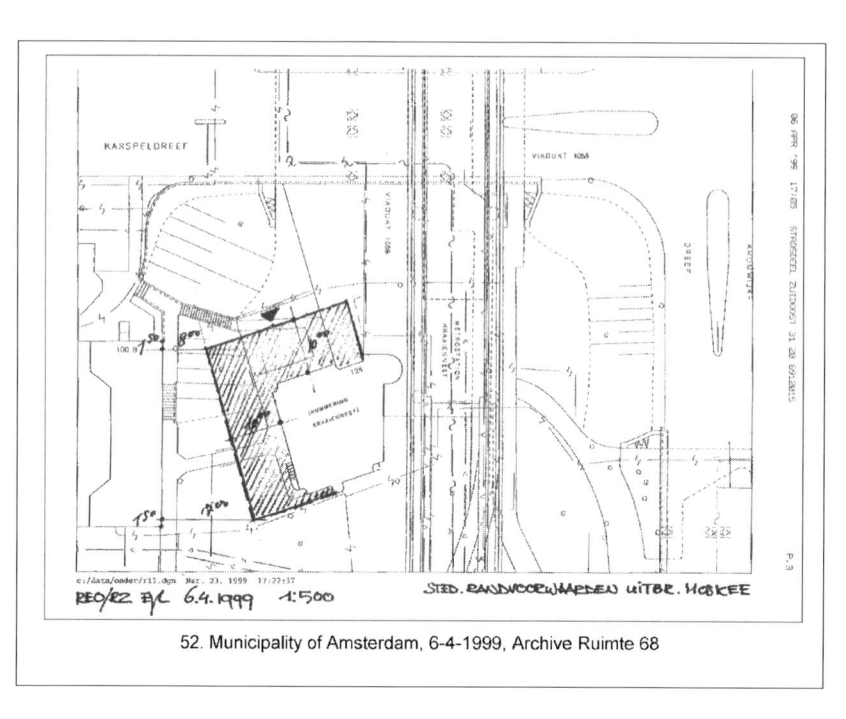

52. Municipality of Amsterdam, 6-4-1999, Archive Ruimte 68

FIGURES

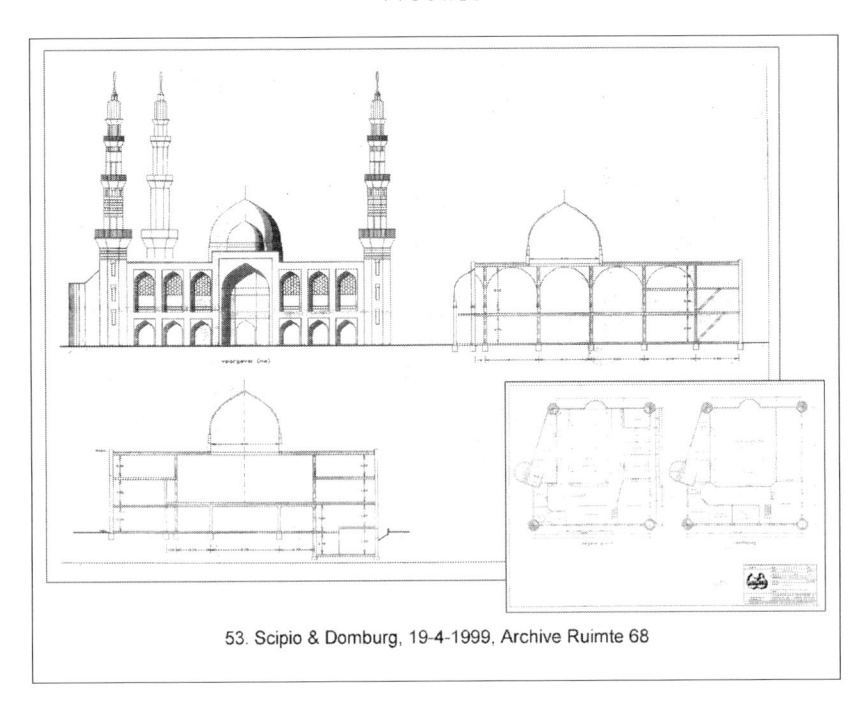

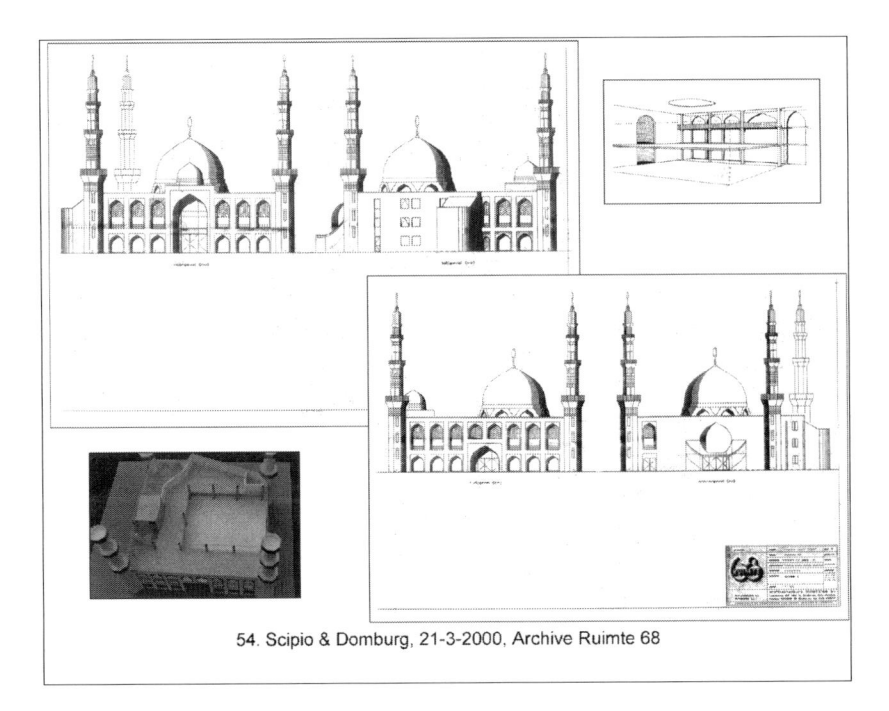

53. Scipio & Domburg, 19-4-1999, Archive Ruimte 68

54. Scipio & Domburg, 21-3-2000, Archive Ruimte 68

THE ARCHITECTURAL REPRESENTATION OF ISLAM

55. Scipio & Domburg, 30-3-2000, Archive Ruimte 68

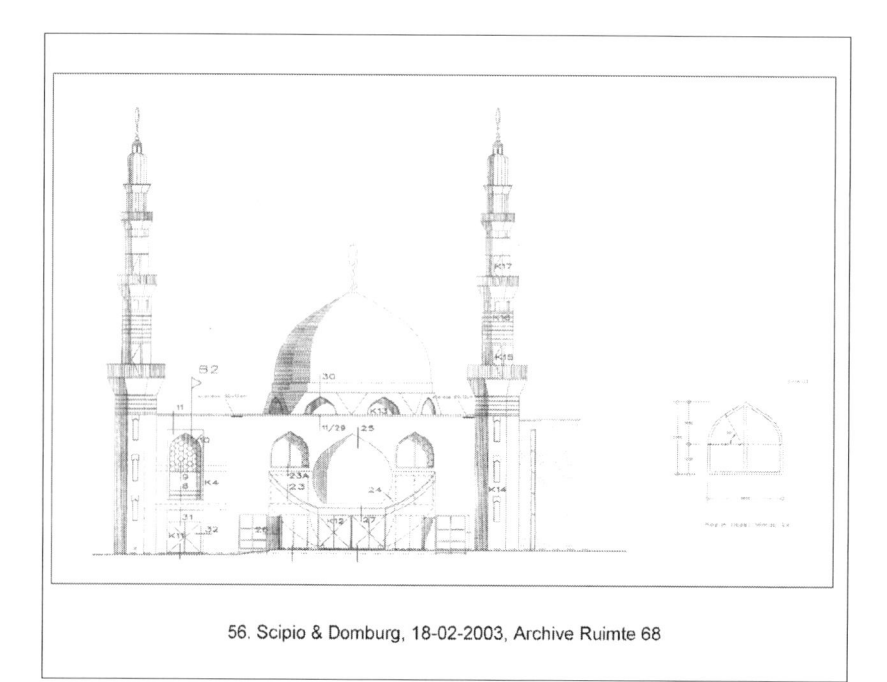

56. Scipio & Domburg, 18-02-2003, Archive Ruimte 68

FIGURES

57. The Message International, Special Editions 2003/2004

58. 2007, Author's Collection

THE ARCHITECTURAL REPRESENTATION OF ISLAM

59. 2007, Author's Collection

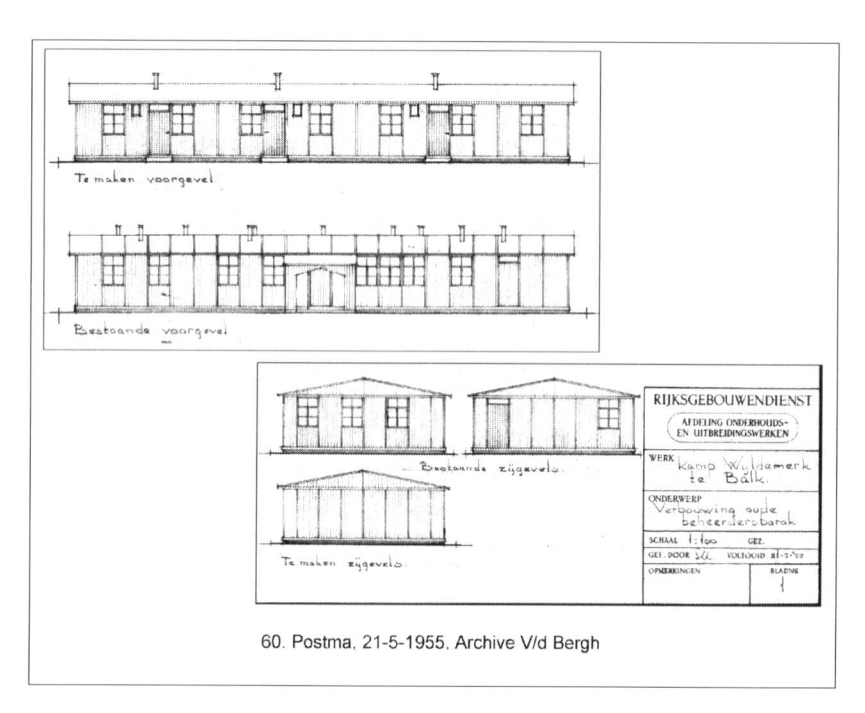

60. Postma, 21-5-1955, Archive V/d Bergh

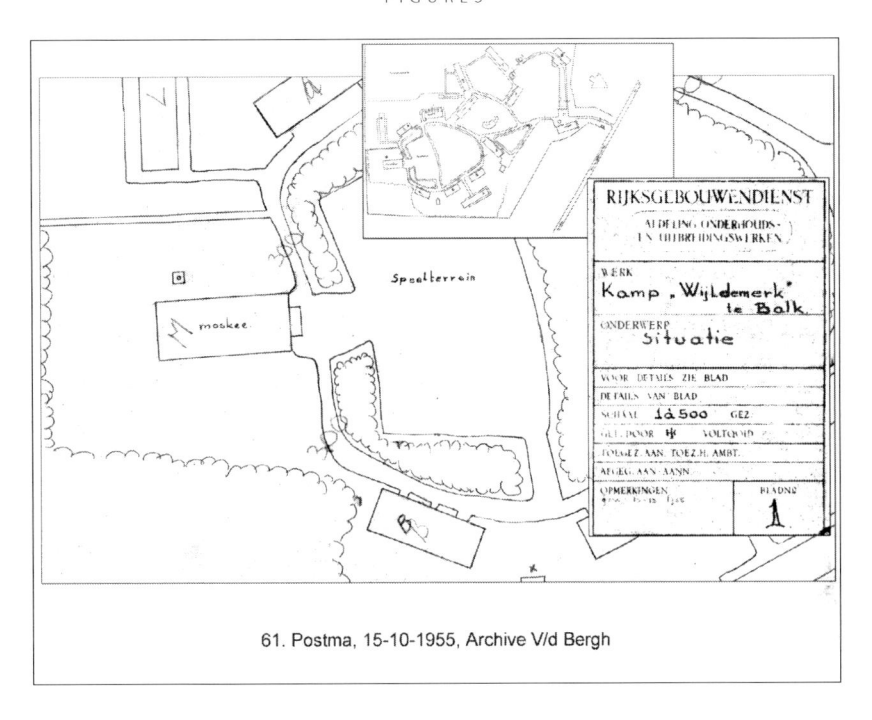

FIGURES

61. Postma, 15-10-1955, Archive V/d Bergh

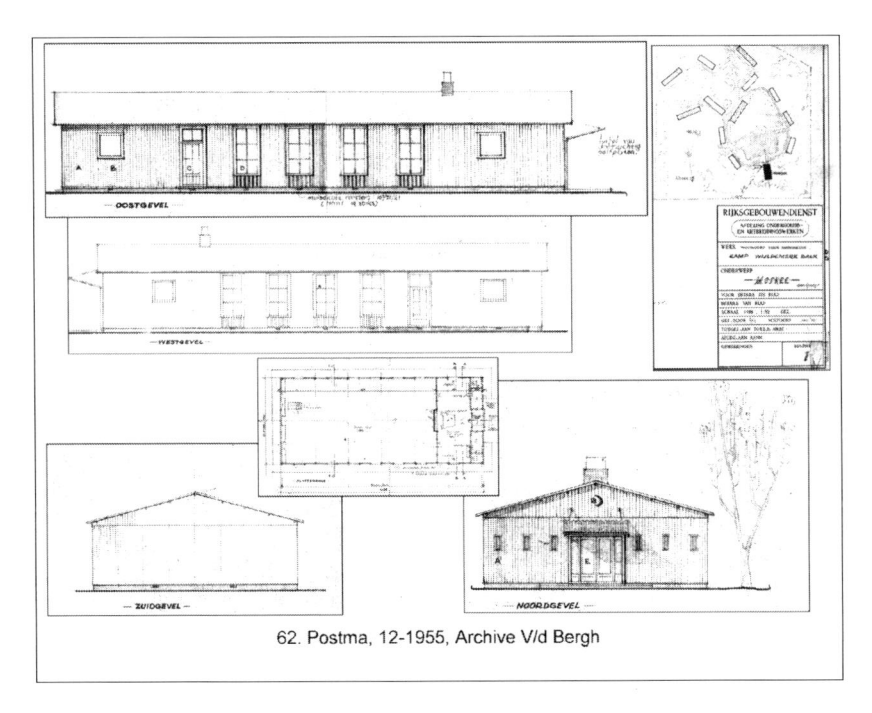

62. Postma, 12-1955, Archive V/d Bergh

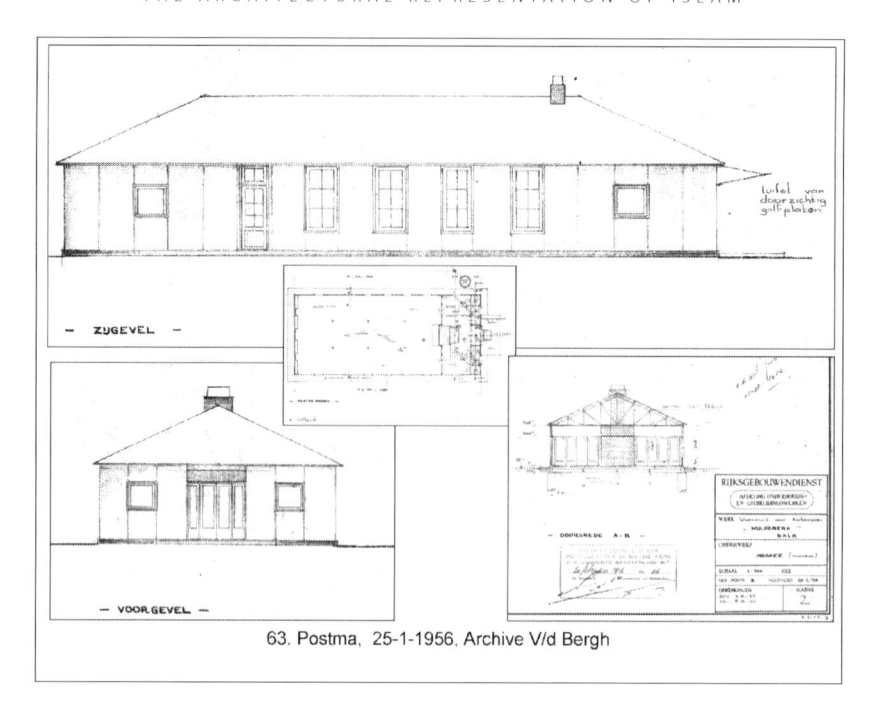

THE ARCHITECTURAL REPRESENTATION OF ISLAM

63. Postma, 25-1-1956, Archive V/d Bergh

64. Collection Ollong

FIGURES

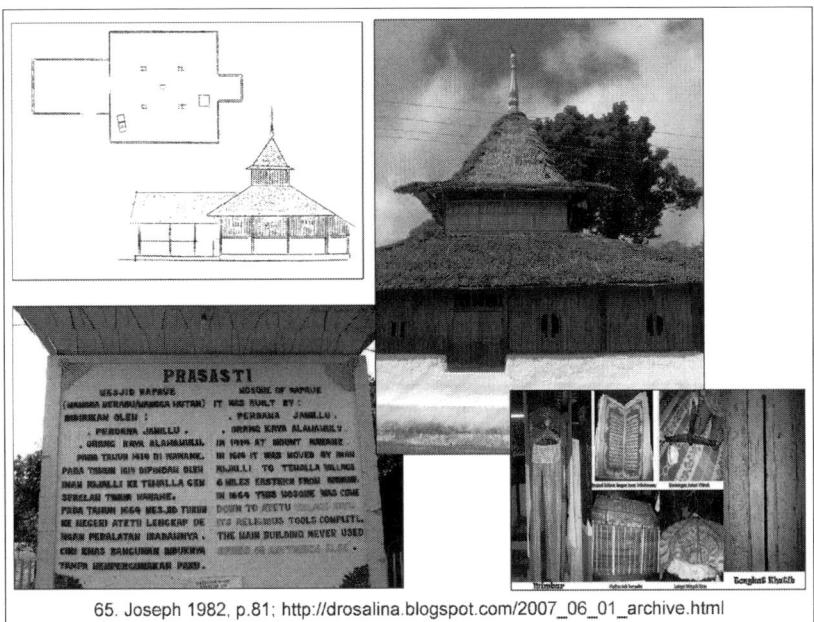

65. Joseph 1982, p.81; http://drosalina.blogspot.com/2007_06_01_archive.html

66. Chauvel 1990, p.192

THE ARCHITECTURAL REPRESENTATION OF ISLAM

67. Postma, 26-4-1956, Archive V/d Bergh

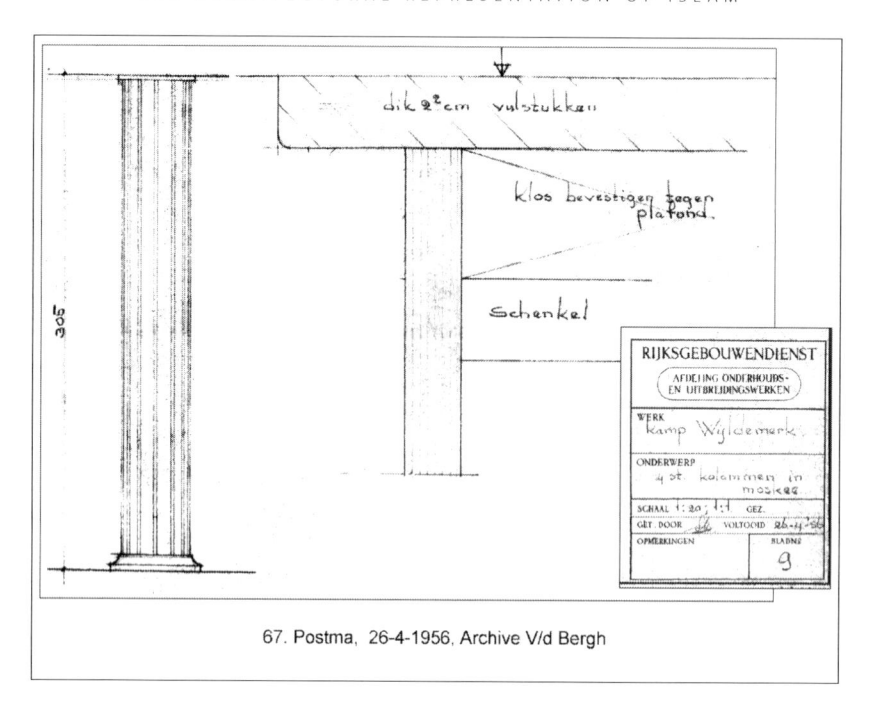

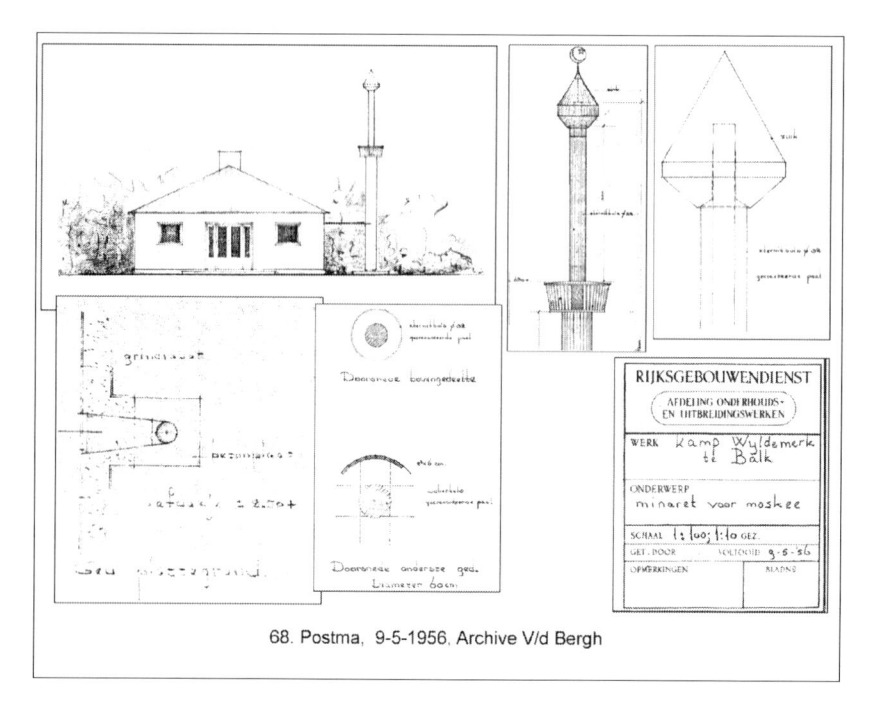

68. Postma, 9-5-1956, Archive V/d Bergh

FIGURES

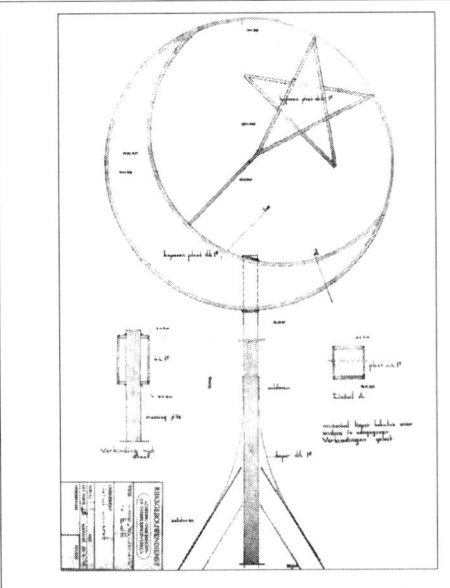

69. Postma, 22-5-1956, Archive V/d Bergh

70. 1955, Archive V/d Bergh

THE ARCHITECTURAL REPRESENTATION OF ISLAM

71. 2005, Archive V/d Bergh

72. Perotti, undated, Collection Maussen; Perotti 1981, pp.13-14

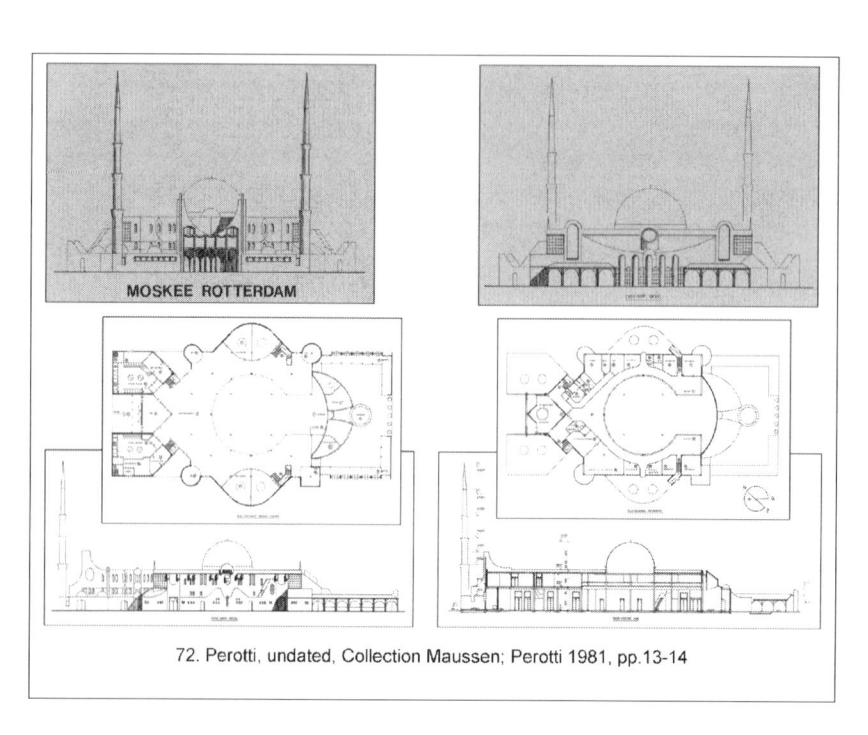

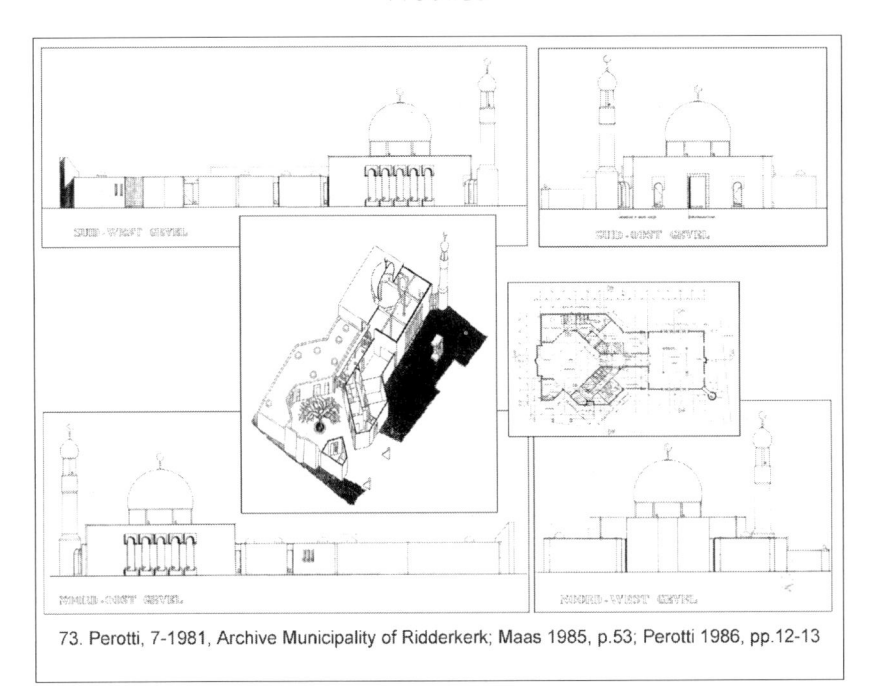

FIGURES

73. Perotti, 7-1981, Archive Municipality of Ridderkerk; Maas 1985, p.53; Perotti 1986, pp.12-13

74. 2006, Author's Collection

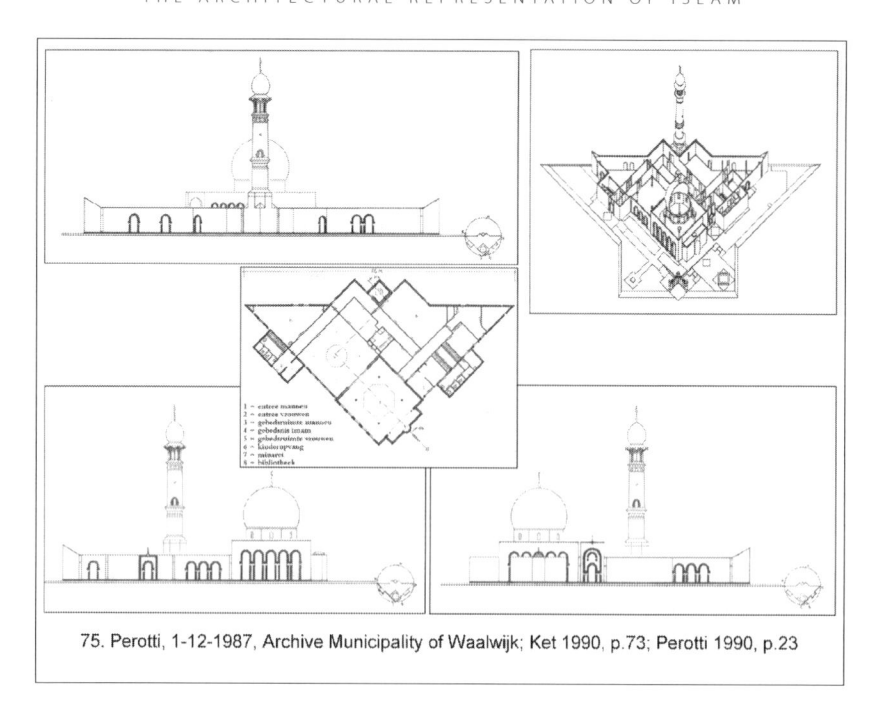

THE ARCHITECTURAL REPRESENTATION OF ISLAM

75. Perotti, 1-12-1987, Archive Municipality of Waalwijk; Ket 1990, p.73; Perotti 1990, p.23

76. 2006, Author's Collection

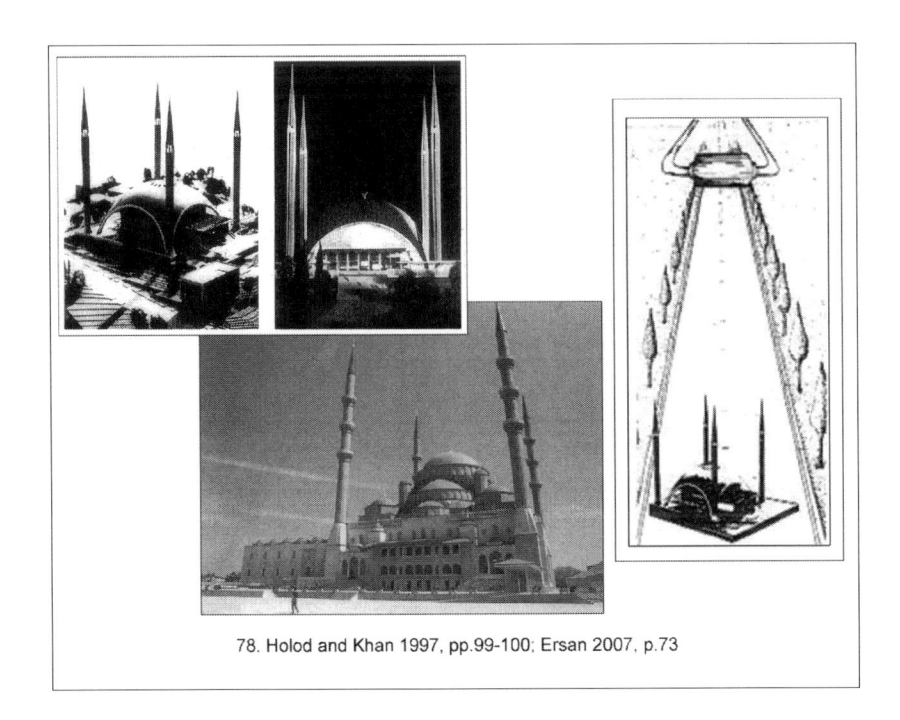

FIGURES

77. Slettenhaar, 6-1972, Archive Slettenhaar

78. Holod and Khan 1997, pp.99-100; Ersan 2007, p.73

359

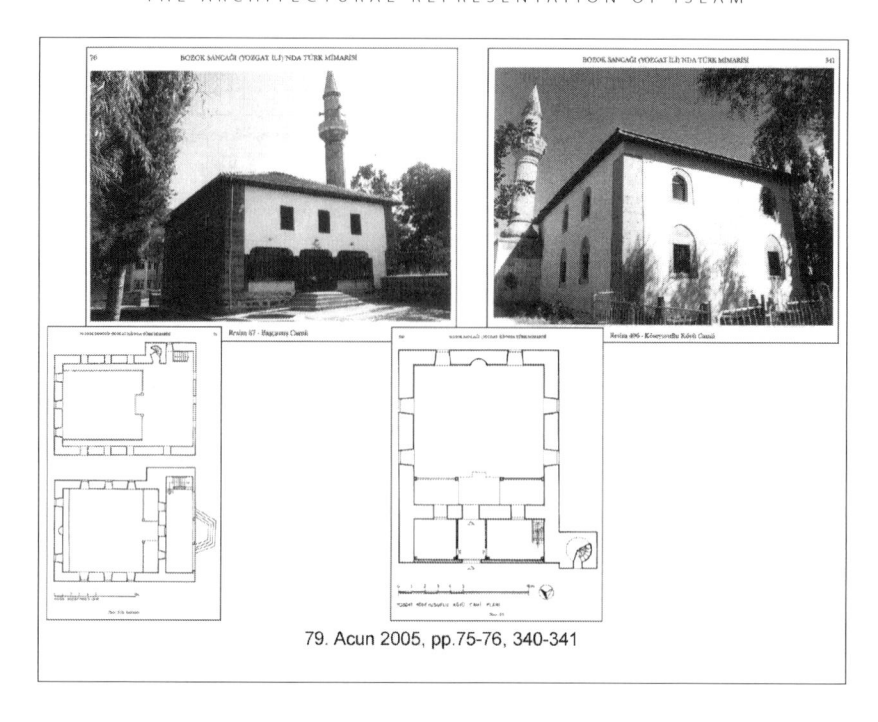

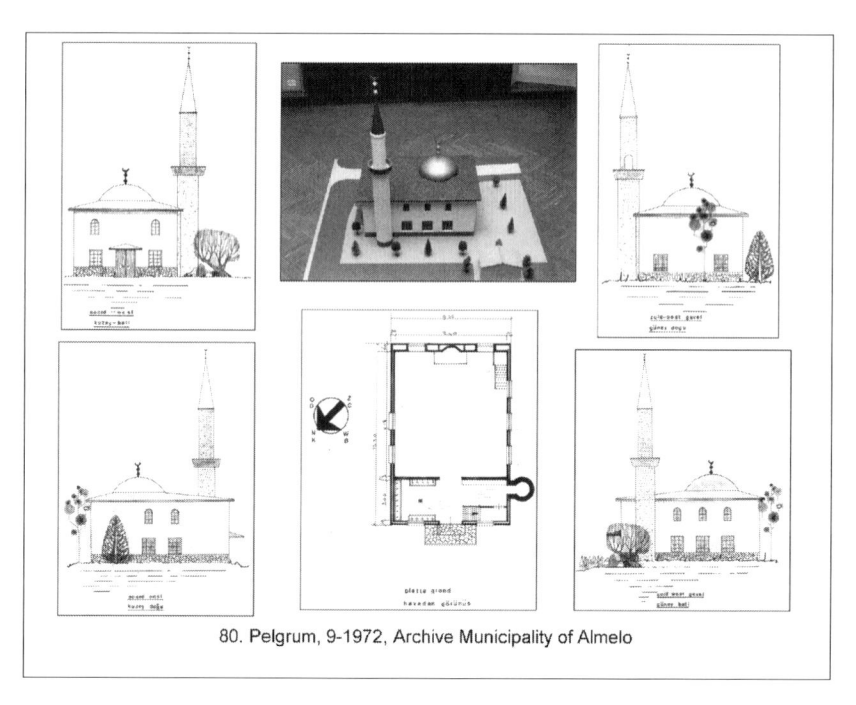

THE ARCHITECTURAL REPRESENTATION OF ISLAM

79. Acun 2005, pp.75-76, 340-341

80. Pelgrum, 9-1972, Archive Municipality of Almelo

FIGURES

81. 8-1973, Archives Pelgrum and Slettenhaar

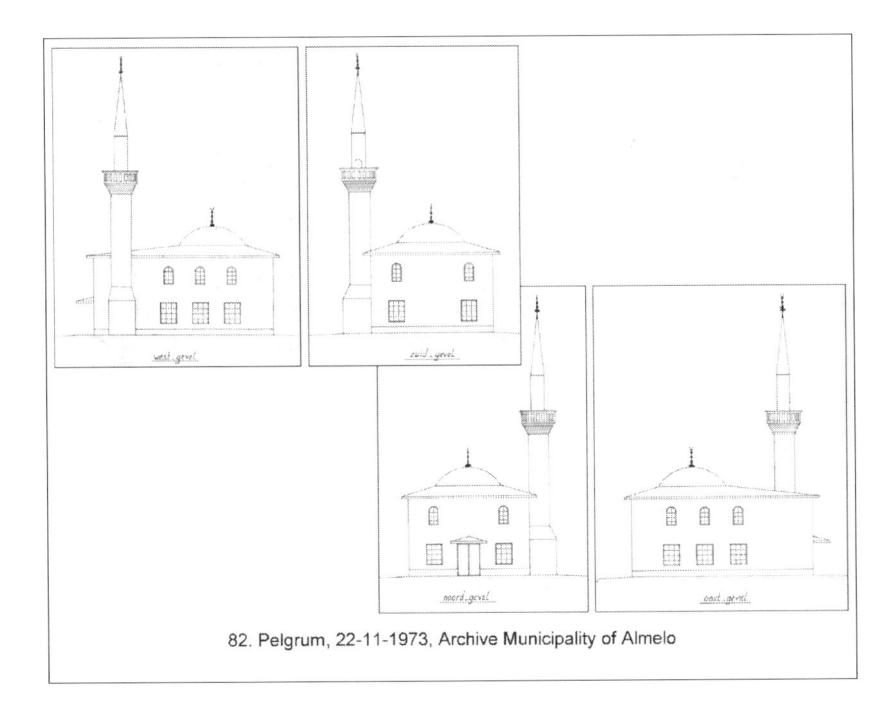

82. Pelgrum, 22-11-1973, Archive Municipality of Almelo

THE ARCHITECTURAL REPRESENTATION OF ISLAM

83. 1975, Archive Municipality of Almelo

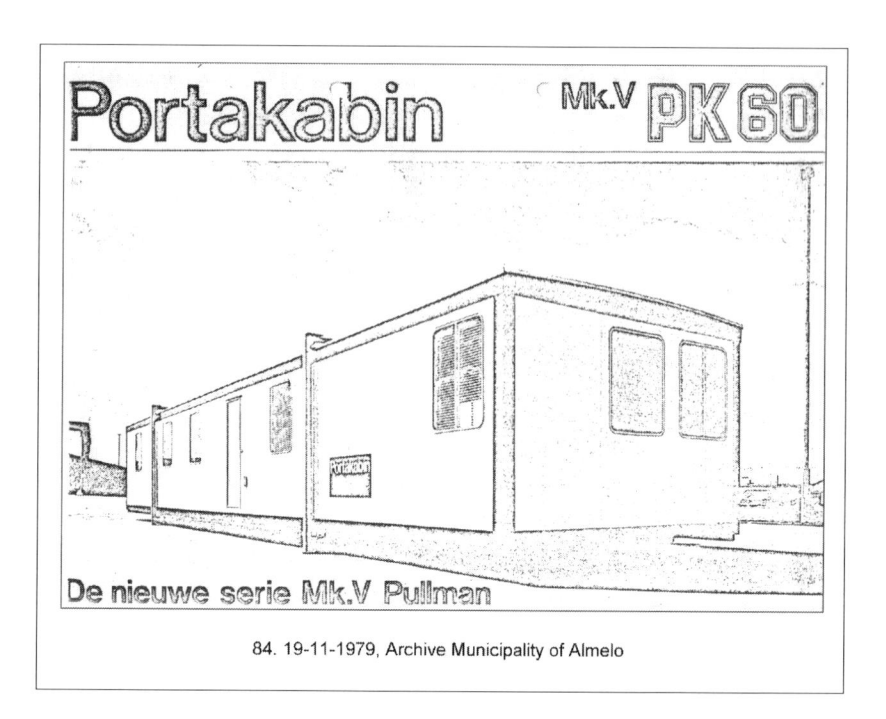

84. 19-11-1979, Archive Municipality of Almelo

FIGURES

85. Haverkamp, 28-4-1980, Archive Municipality of Almelo

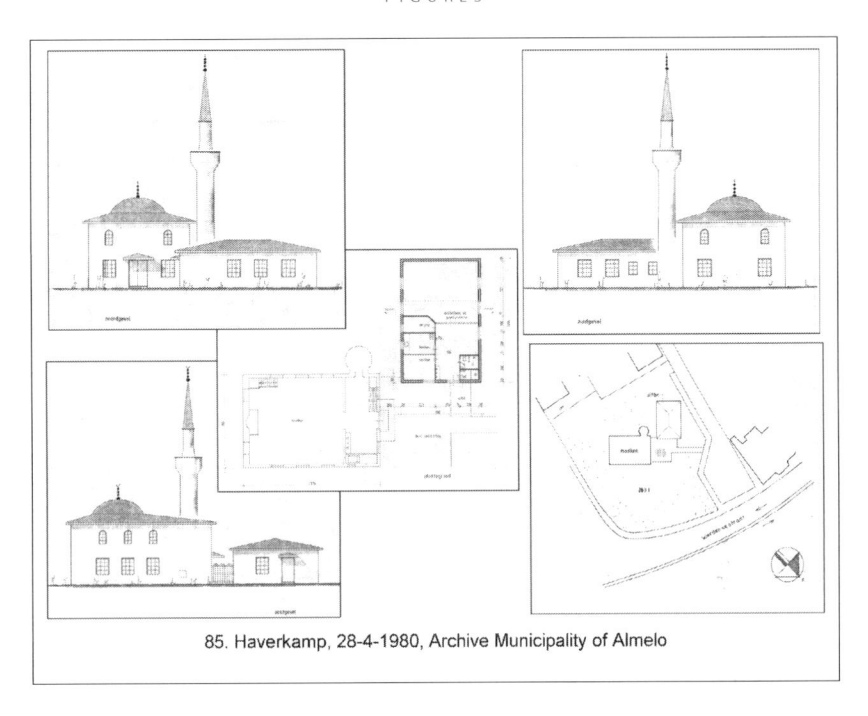

86. 1982, Collection Atabek

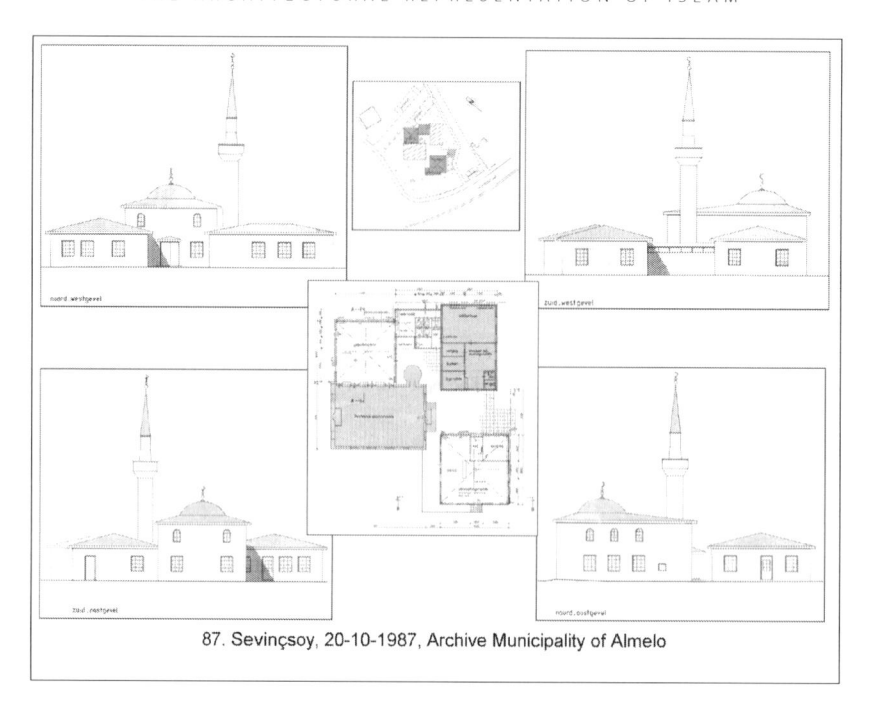

THE ARCHITECTURAL REPRESENTATION OF ISLAM

87. Sevinçsoy, 20-10-1987, Archive Municipality of Almelo

88. 1989, Archive Municipality of Almelo

FIGURES

89. Ter Steege, 16-9-1992, Archive Municipality of Almelo

90. Ter Steege, 6-4/9-11-1995, Archive Municipality of Almelo

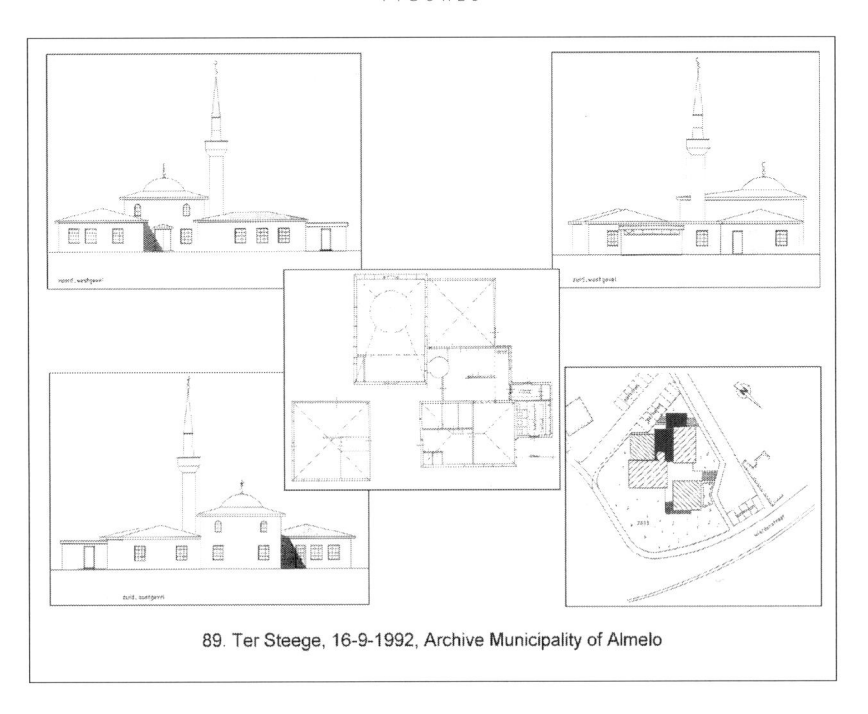

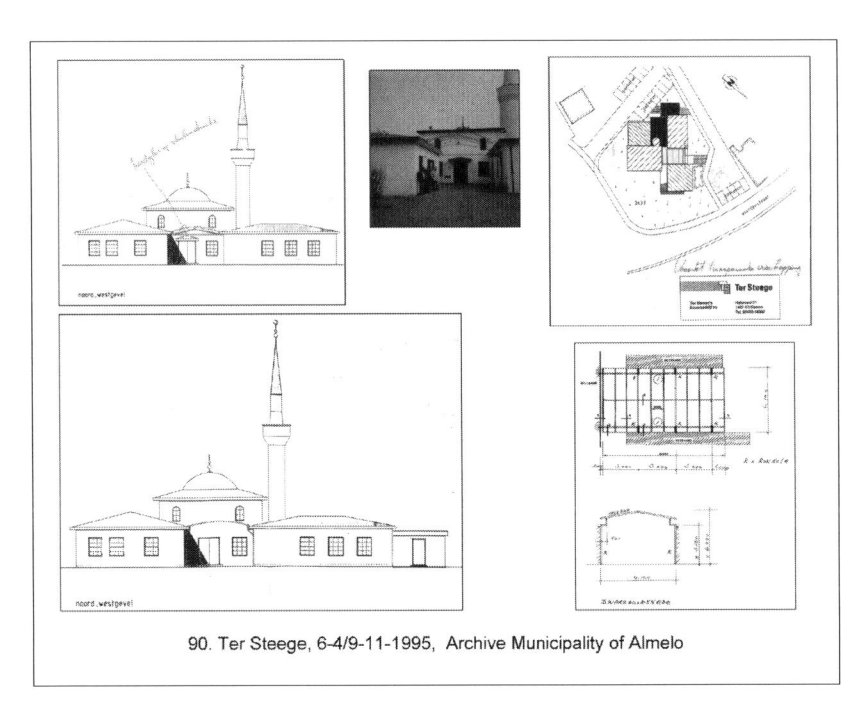

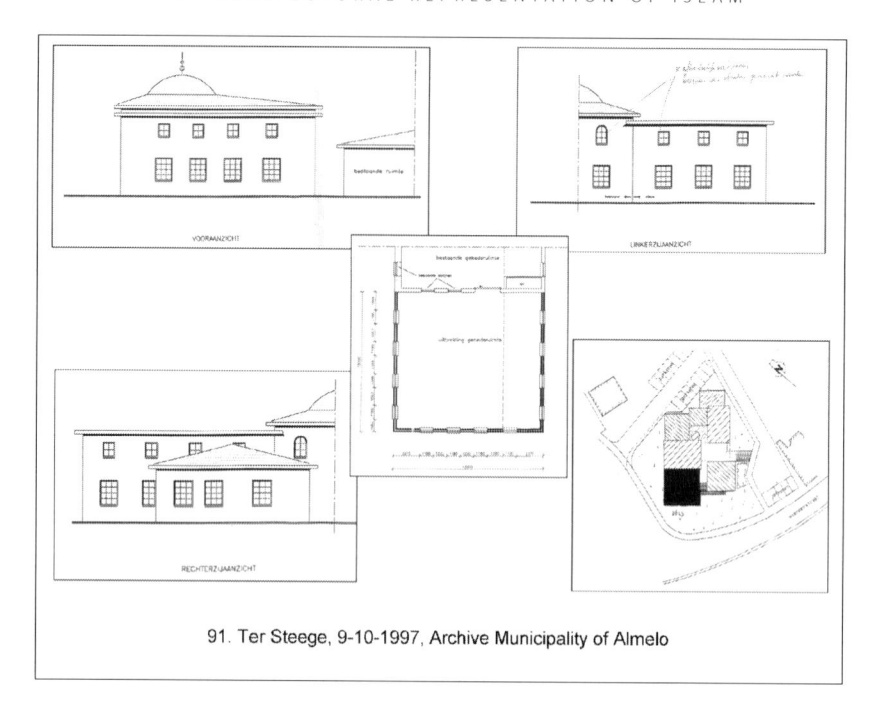

THE ARCHITECTURAL REPRESENTATION OF ISLAM

91. Ter Steege, 9-10-1997, Archive Municipality of Almelo

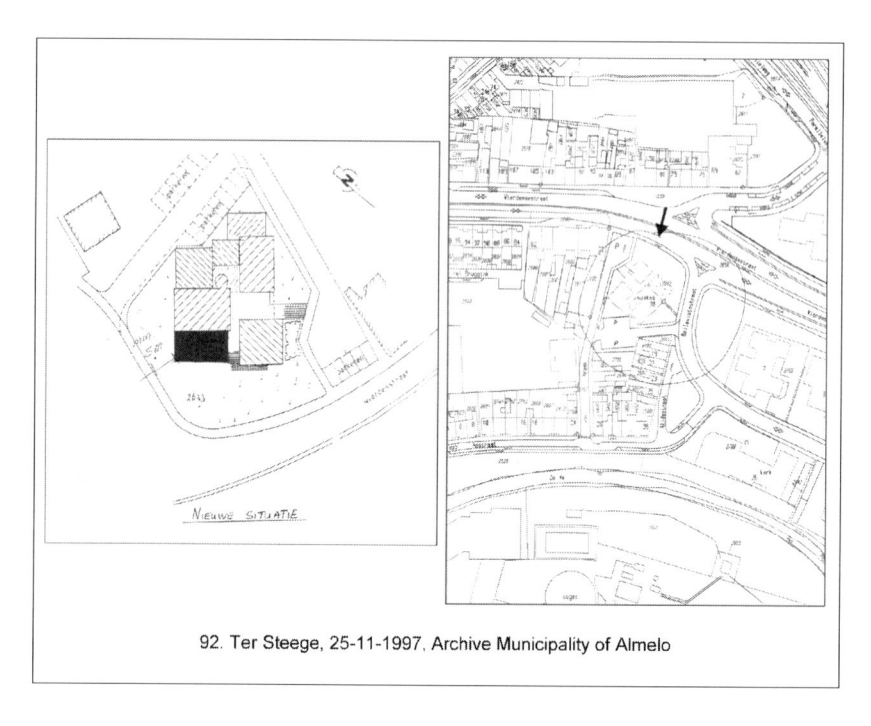

92. Ter Steege, 25-11-1997, Archive Municipality of Almelo

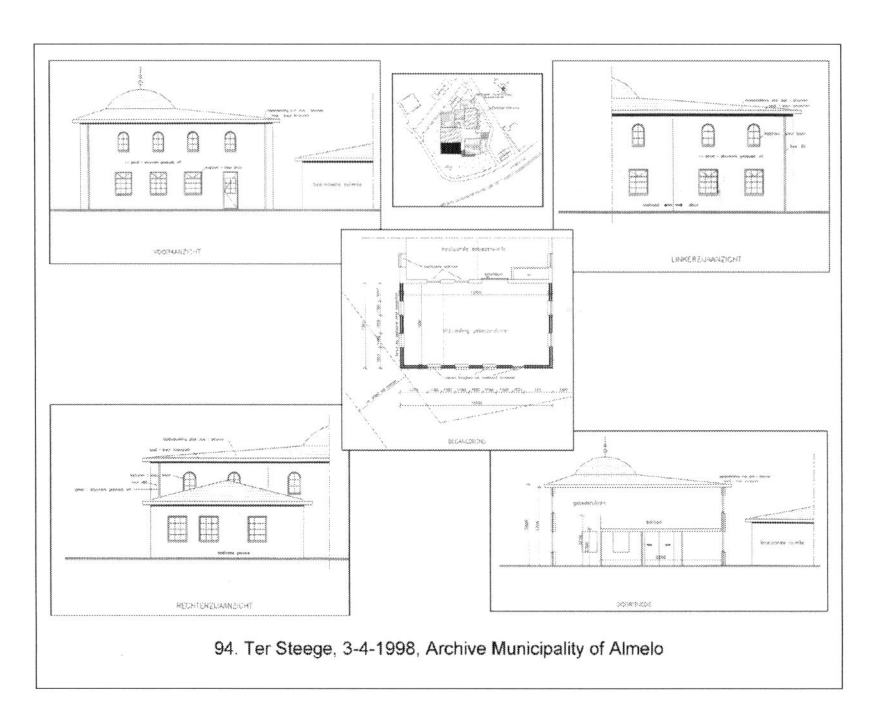

FIGURES

93. Het Oversticht, 4-12-1997, Archive Municipality of Almelo

94. Ter Steege, 3-4-1998, Archive Municipality of Almelo

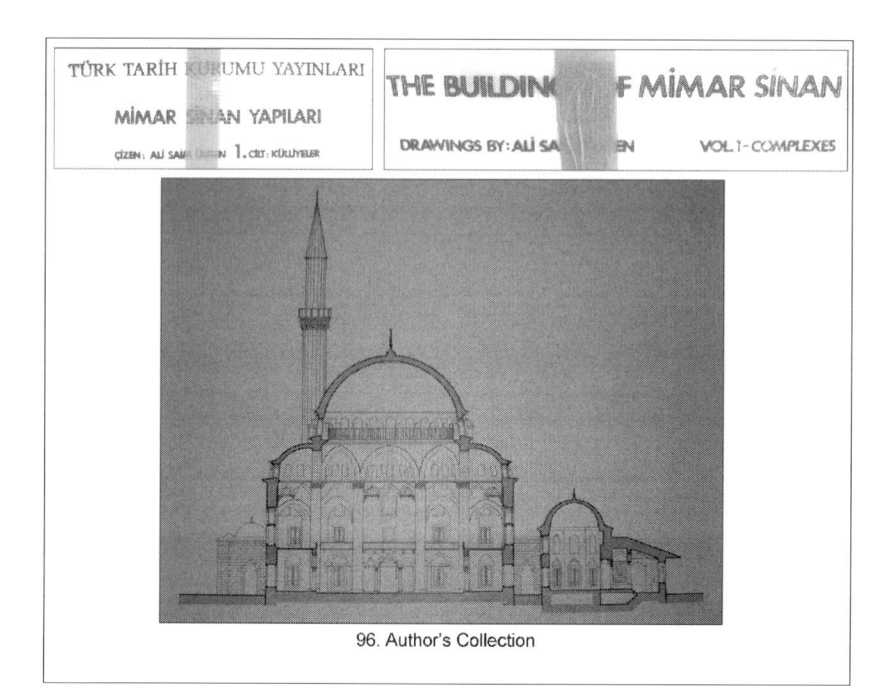

THE ARCHITECTURAL REPRESENTATION OF ISLAM

95. 2006, Author's Collection

96. Author's Collection

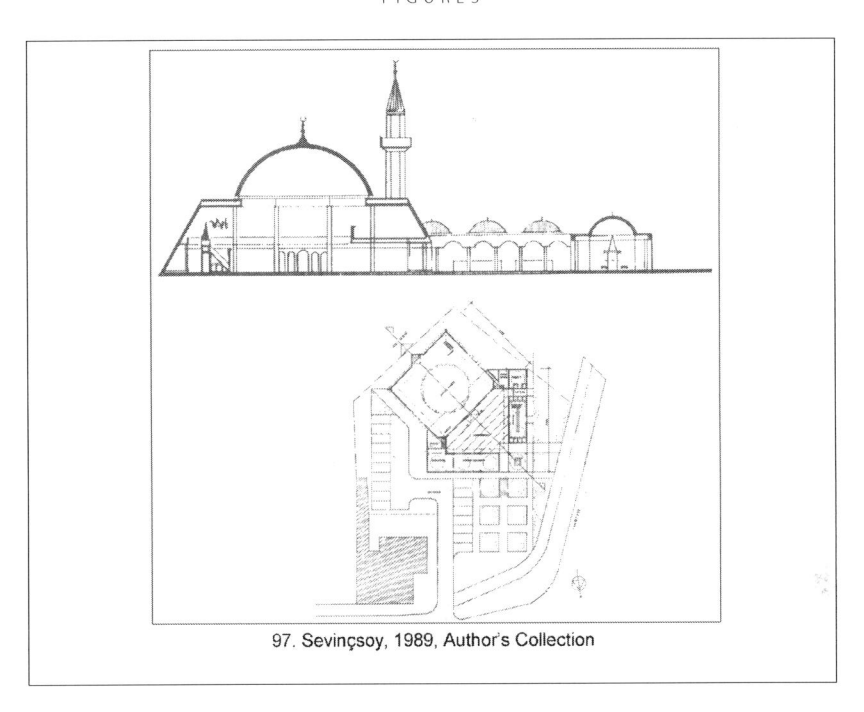

FIGURES

97. Sevinçsoy, 1989, Author's Collection

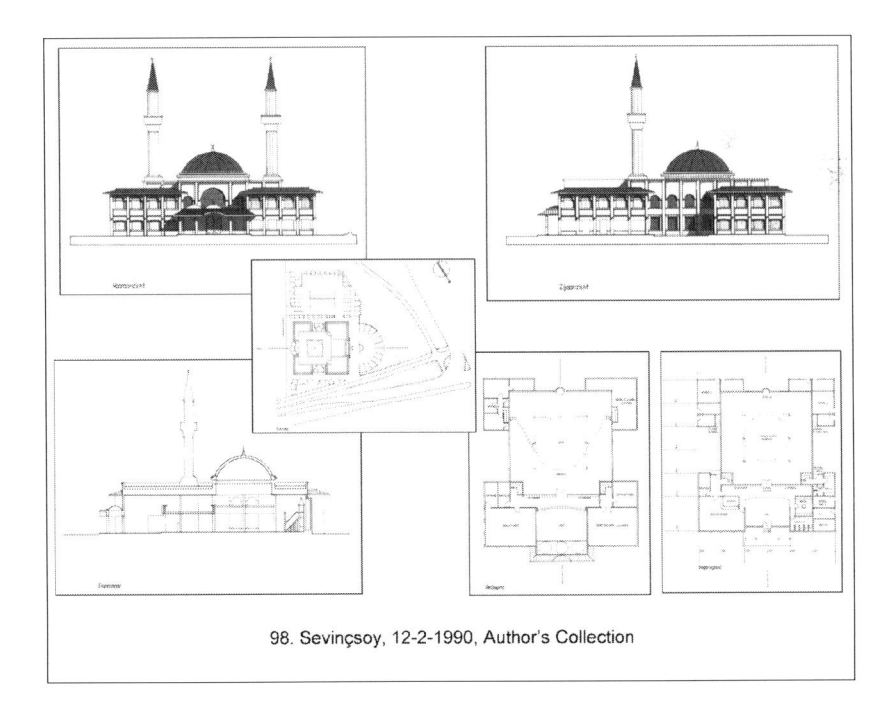

98. Sevinçsoy, 12-2-1990, Author's Collection

THE ARCHITECTURAL REPRESENTATION OF ISLAM

99. Bozdoğan 2001, p.273; Holod and Evin 1984, p.60

100. Sevinçsoy, undated, Author's Collection

FIGURES

101. Sevinçsoy, 11-2/10-5-1991, Author's Collection

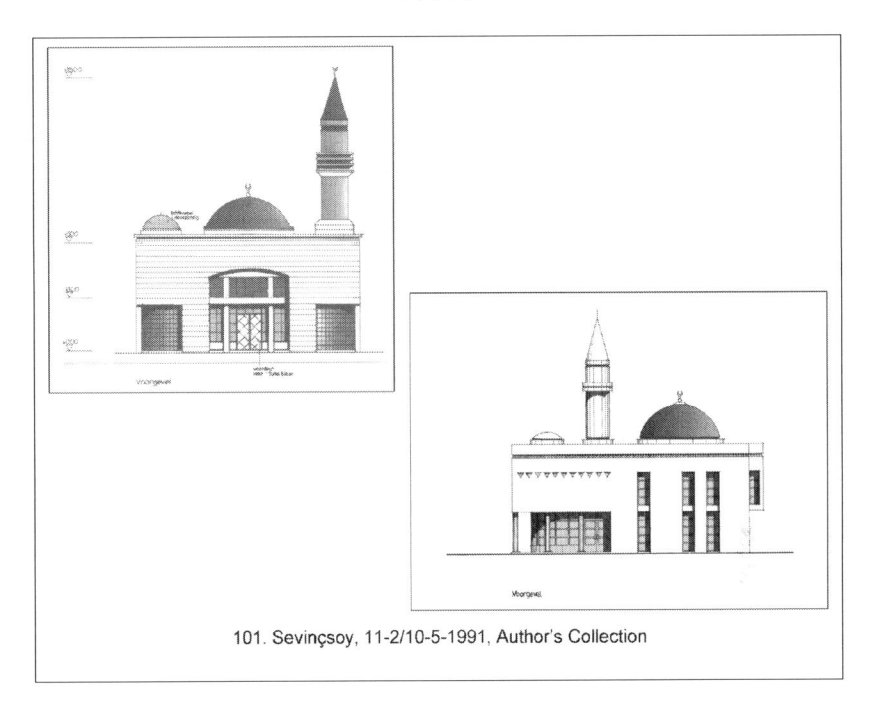

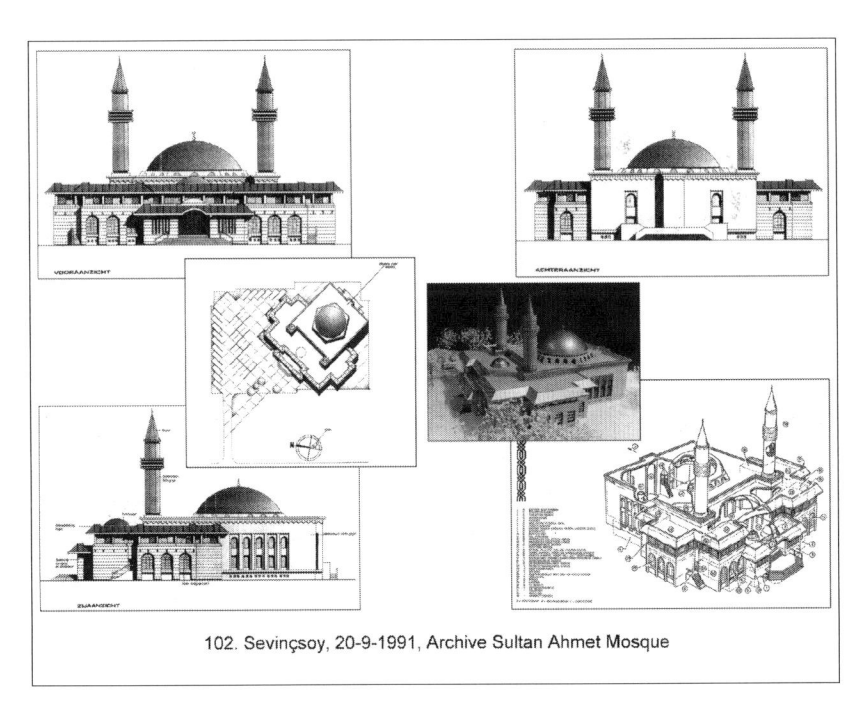

102. Sevinçsoy, 20-9-1991, Archive Sultan Ahmet Mosque

THE ARCHITECTURAL REPRESENTATION OF ISLAM

103. Sevinçsoy, 2-4-1992, Archive Municipality of Zaanstad

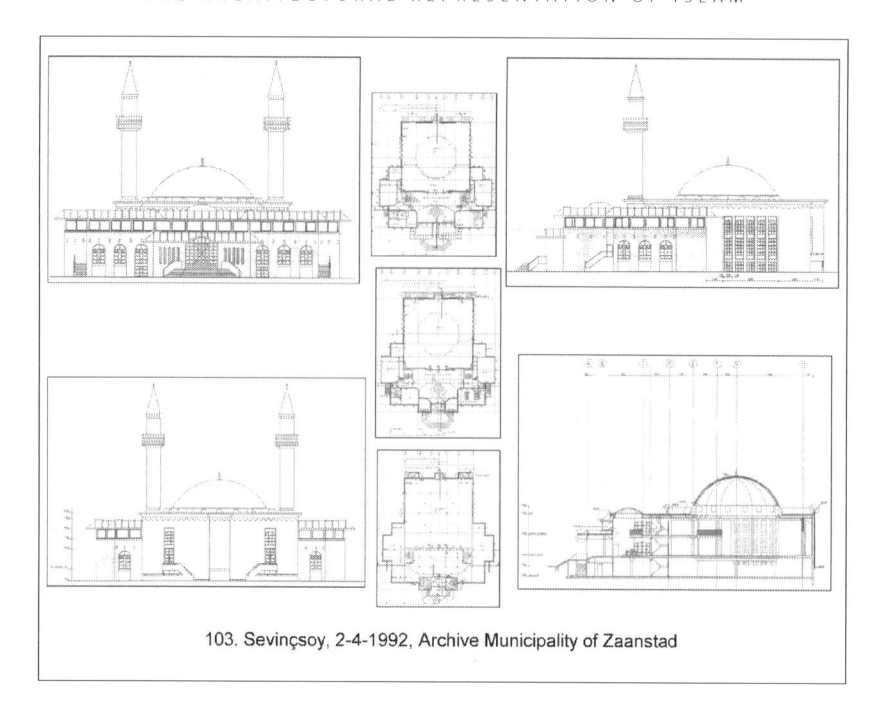

104. 1994, Archive Sultan Ahmet Mosque; Türkiye Diyanet Vakfi Yayinlari 1997, Cover

FIGURES

105. 2006, Author's Collection

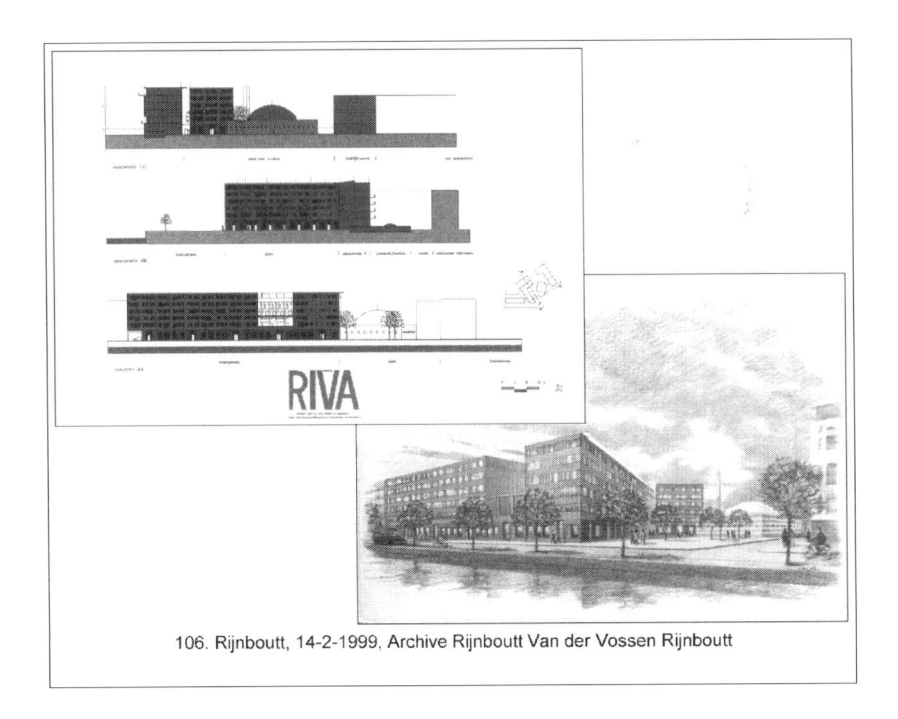

106. Rijnboutt, 14-2-1999, Archive Rijnboutt Van der Vossen Rijnboutt

THE ARCHITECTURAL REPRESENTATION OF ISLAM

107. Goodwin 1971, pp.343-344

108. Breitman, 9-1998, Archive Breitman & Breitman

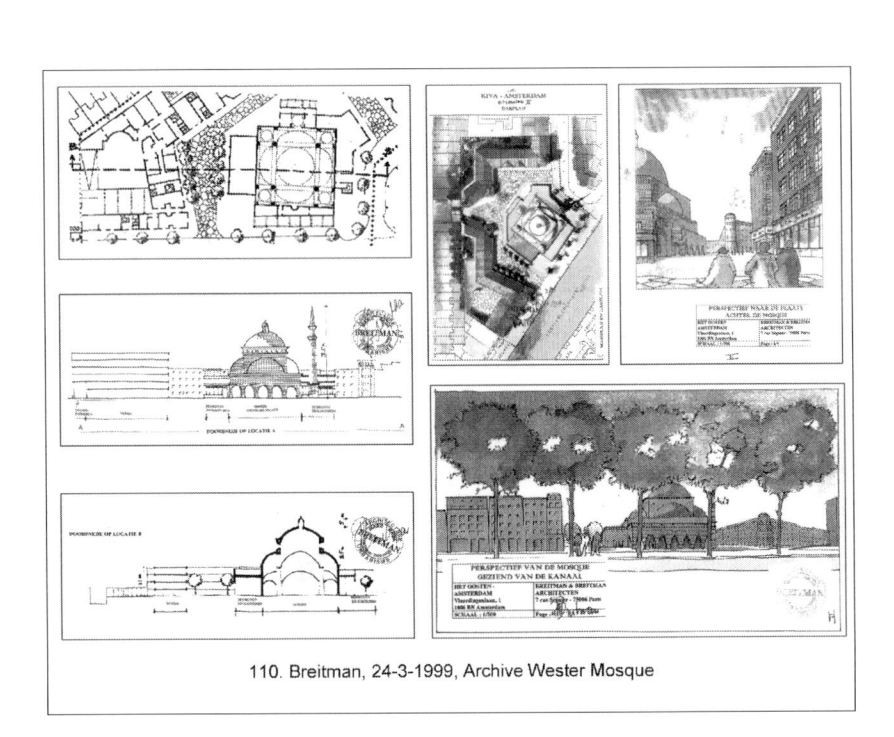

FIGURES

109. Breitman, 25-11-1998, Archive Wester Mosque

110. Breitman, 24-3-1999, Archive Wester Mosque

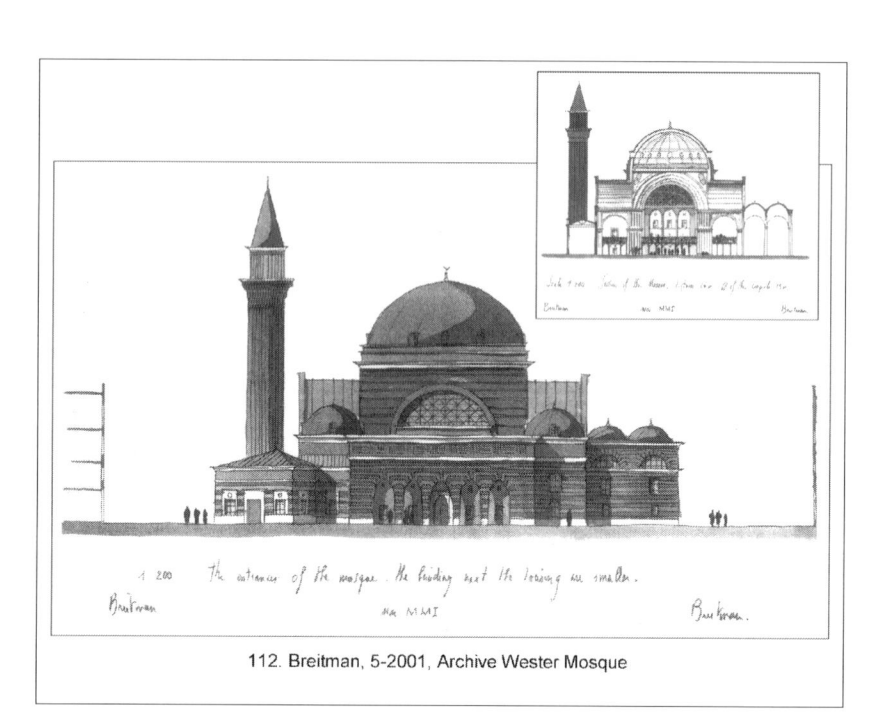

THE ARCHITECTURAL REPRESENTATION OF ISLAM

111. Vernooy, 22-10-2000, Archive 4DEE Architect

112. Breitman, 5-2001, Archive Wester Mosque

FIGURES

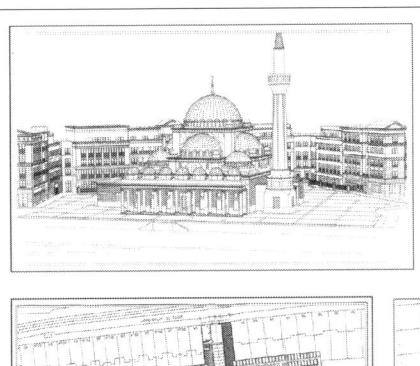

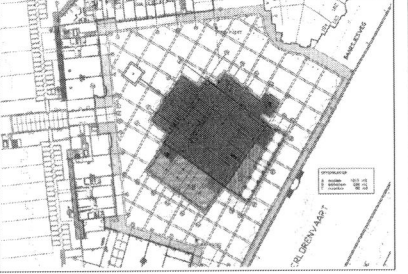

113. Breitman, 7-12-2001, Archive Het Oosten/Kristal

114. Goodwin 1971, pp.2, 262; www.anatolia.luwo.be/index.htm?Adana.htm&1

377

THE ARCHITECTURAL REPRESENTATION OF ISLAM

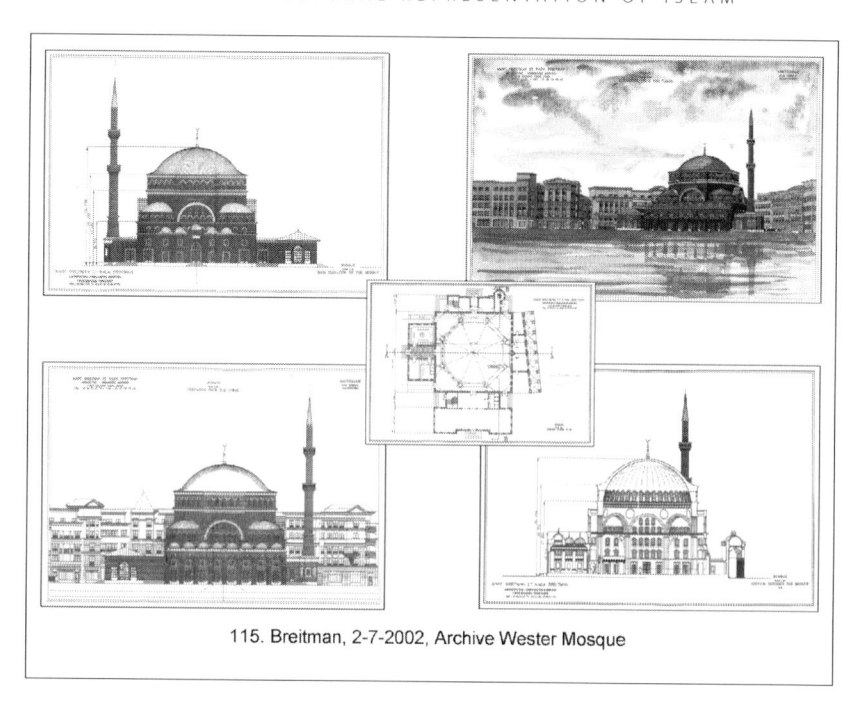

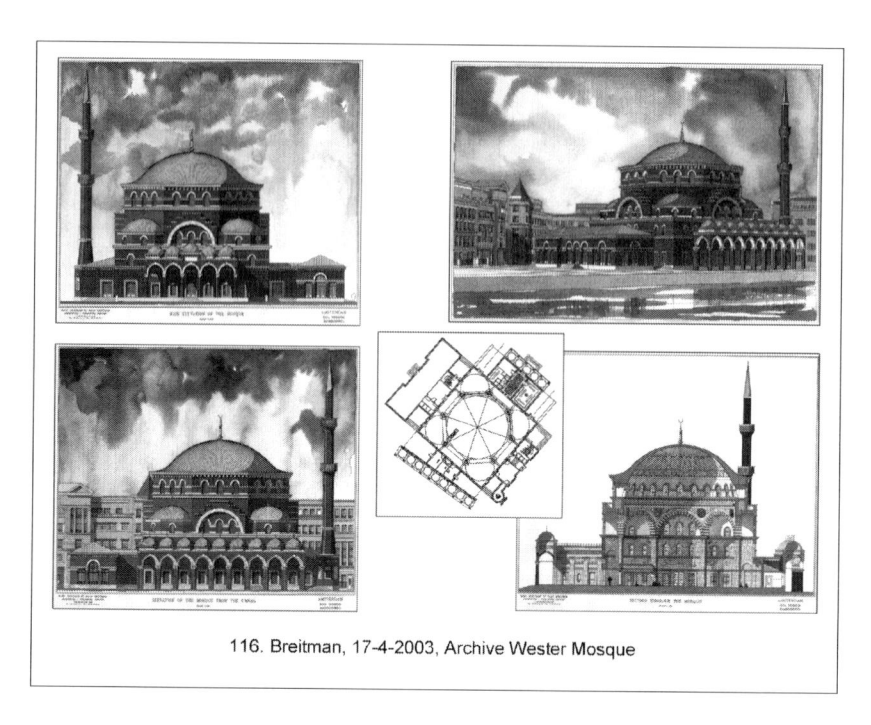

115. Breitman, 2-7-2002, Archive Wester Mosque

116. Breitman, 17-4-2003, Archive Wester Mosque

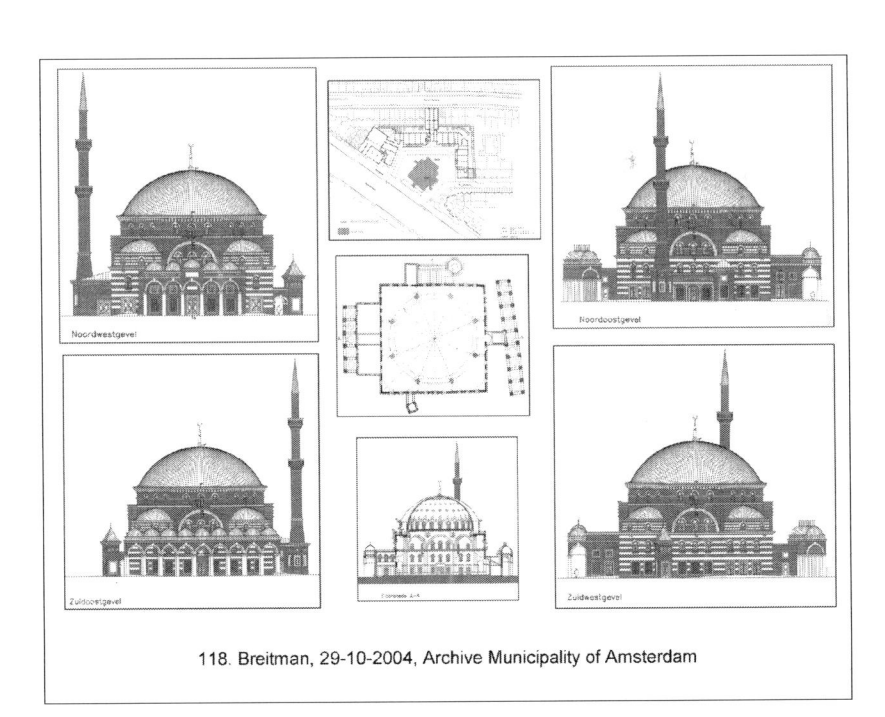

FIGURES

117. Breitman, 9-2004, Archive Wester Mosque

118. Breitman, 29-10-2004, Archive Municipality of Amsterdam

379

THE ARCHITECTURAL REPRESENTATION OF ISLAM

119. Archive Het Oosten/Kristal

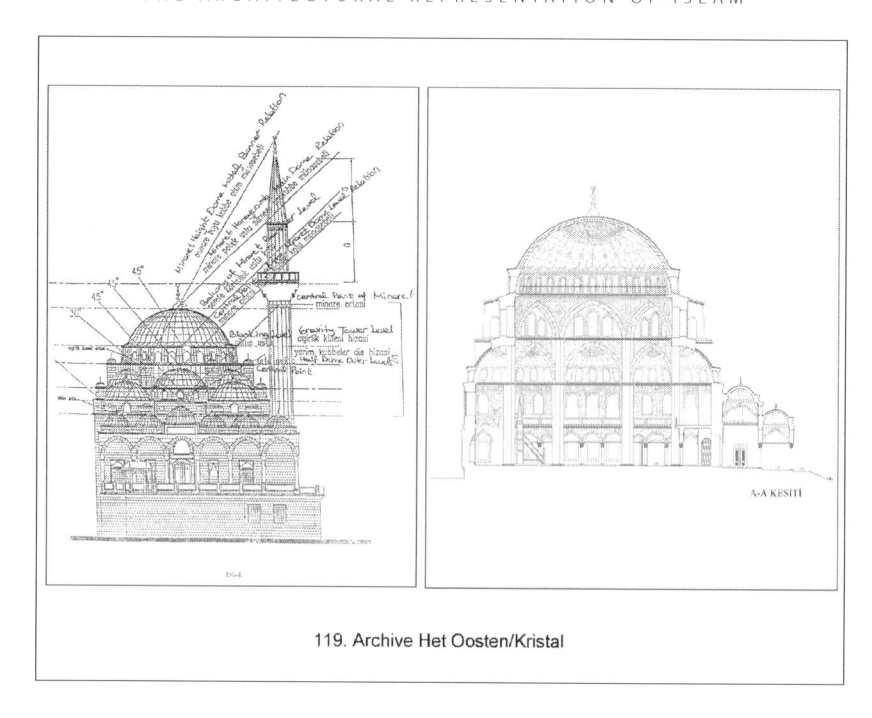

120. Archive Wester Mosque

FIGURES

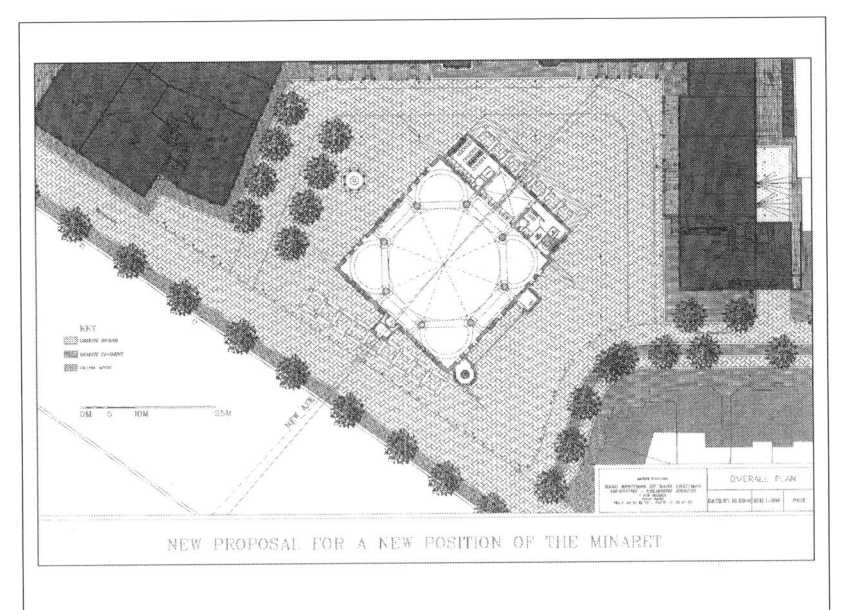

121. Breitman, 27-10-2005, Archive Breitman & Breitman

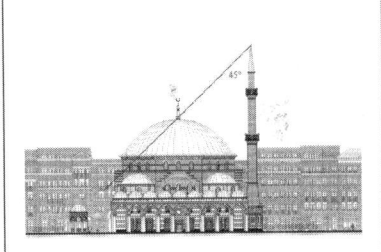

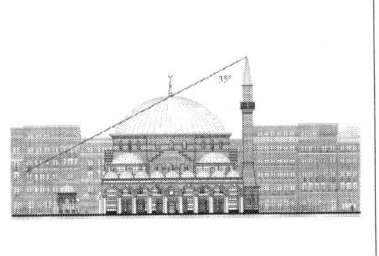

122. Archive Breitman & Breitman; Breitman, undated, Archive Breitman & Breitman

THE ARCHITECTURAL REPRESENTATION OF ISLAM

123. Archive Boon & Slagter

124. Sinaceur 1996, pp.10, 58-59

FIGURES

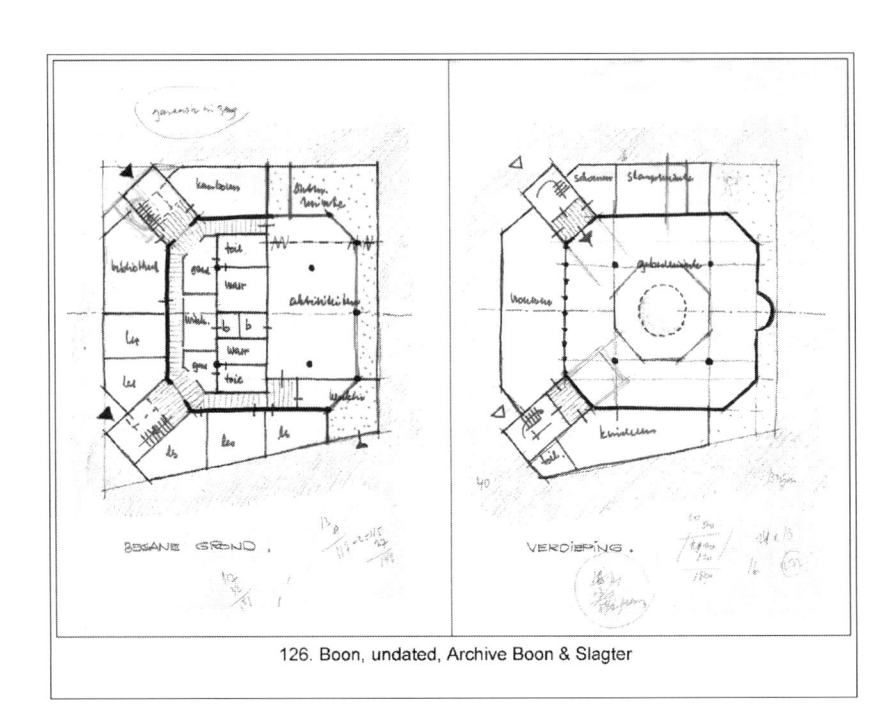

125. Boon, 30-1-1989, Archive Boon & Slagter

126. Boon, undated, Archive Boon & Slagter

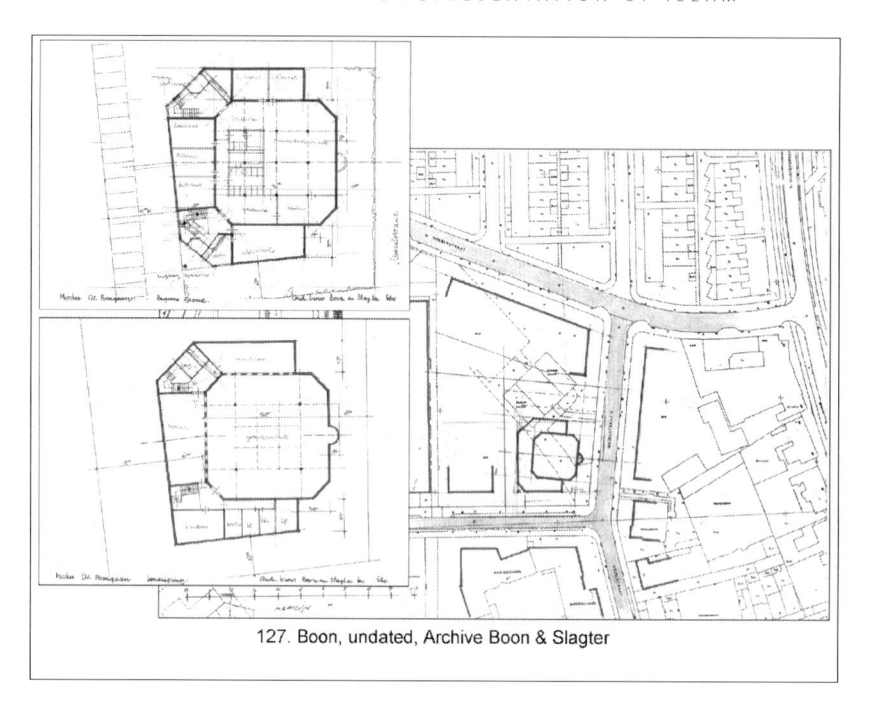

THE ARCHITECTURAL REPRESENTATION OF ISLAM

127. Boon, undated, Archive Boon & Slagter

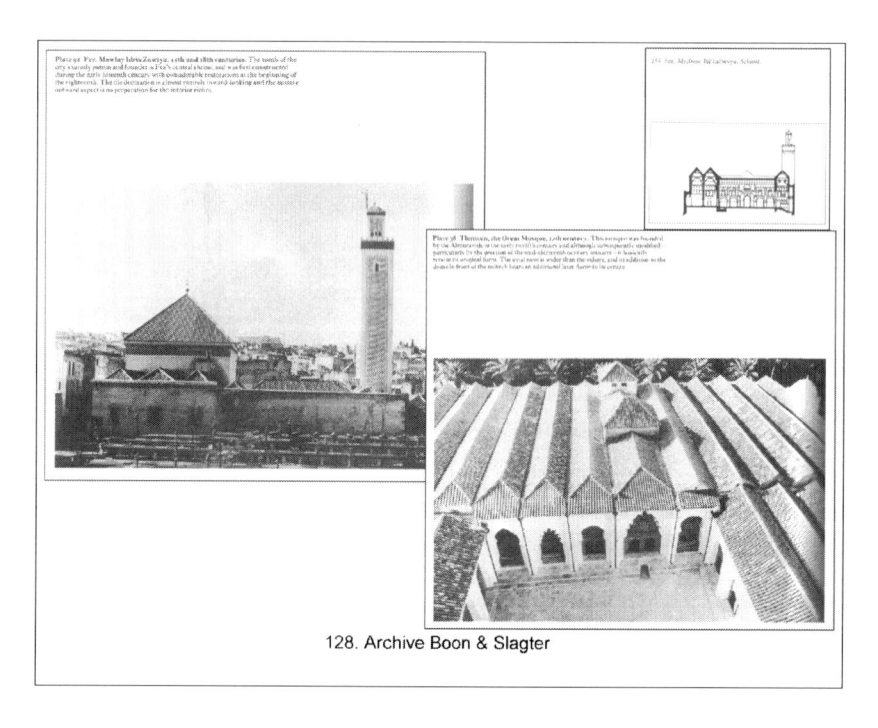

128. Archive Boon & Slagter

FIGURES

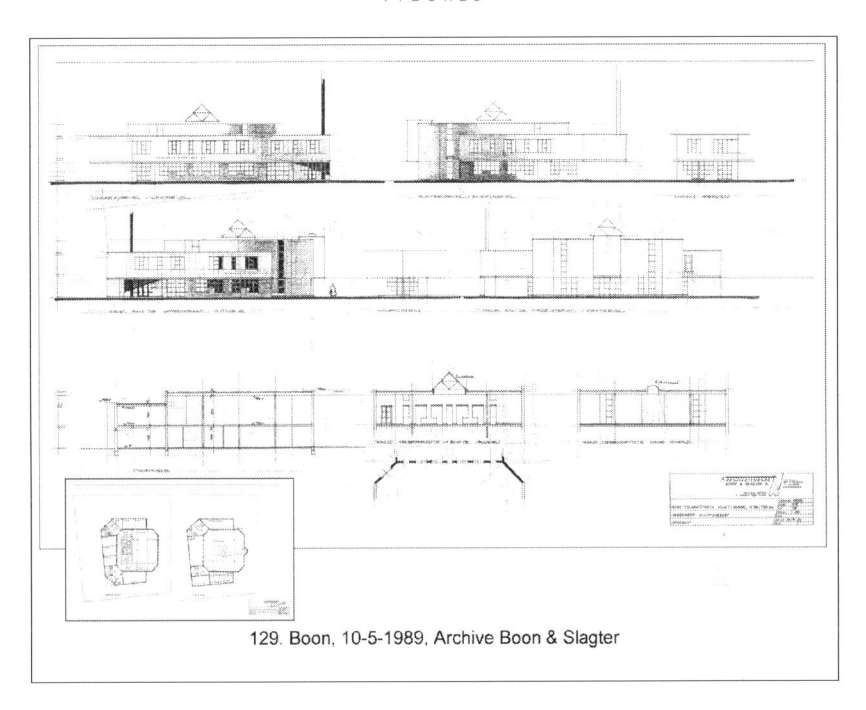

129. Boon, 10-5-1989, Archive Boon & Slagter

130. Archive Boon & Slagter

385

THE ARCHITECTURAL REPRESENTATION OF ISLAM

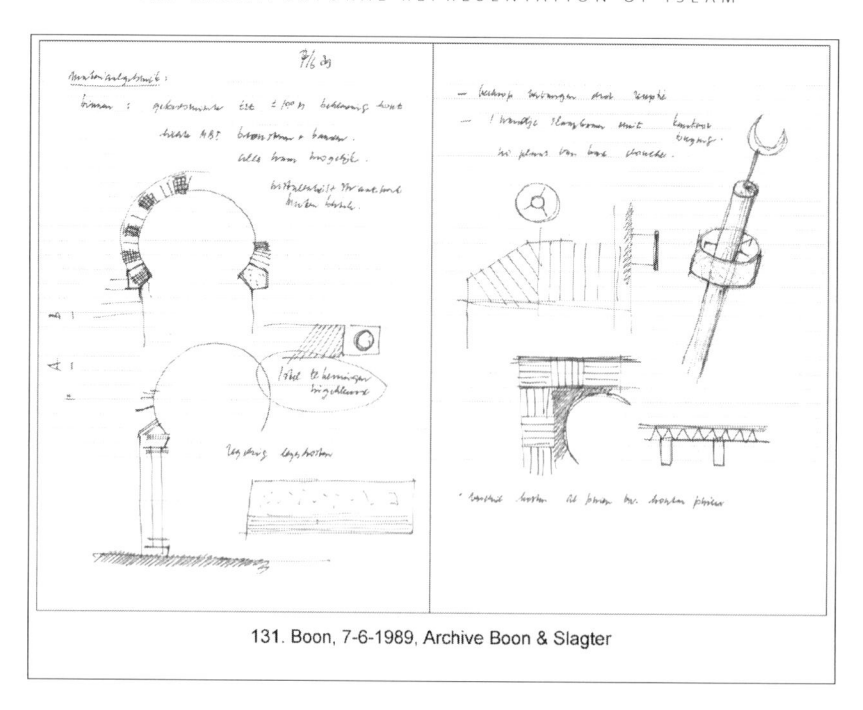

131. Boon, 7-6-1989, Archive Boon & Slagter

132. Archive Boon & Slagter

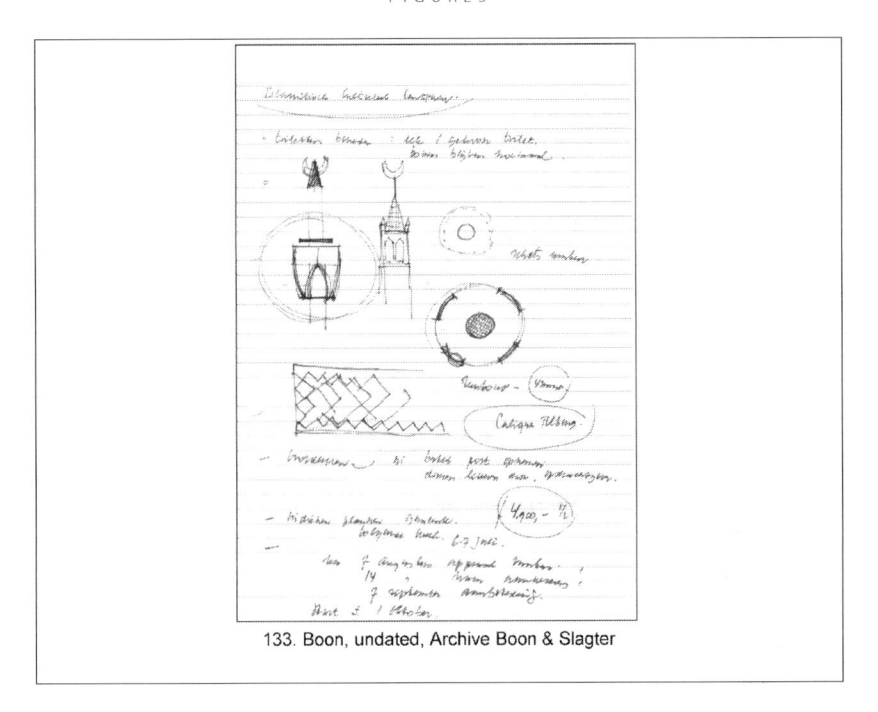

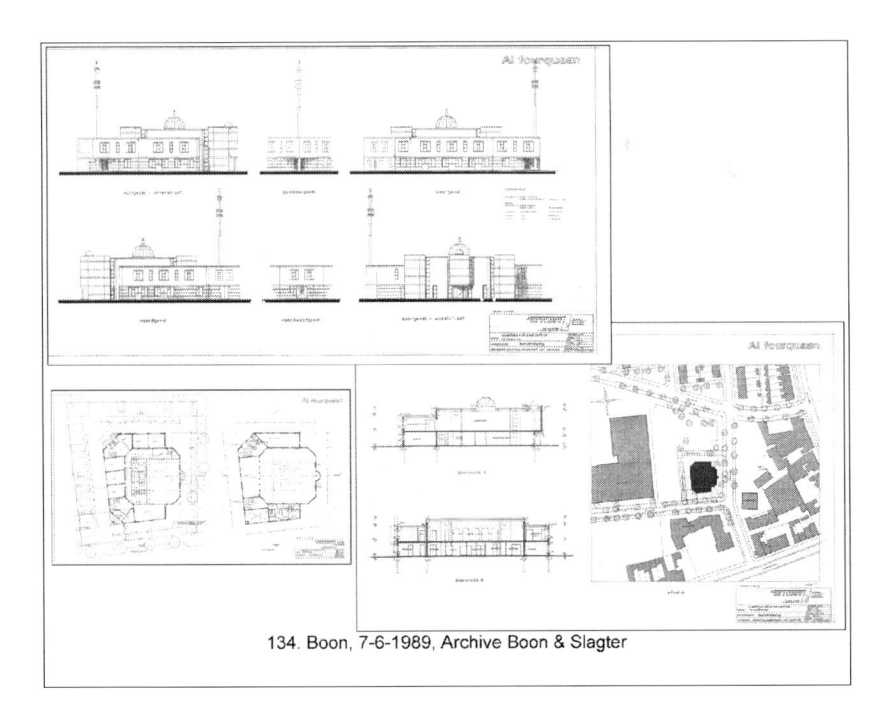

FIGURES

133. Boon, undated, Archive Boon & Slagter

134. Boon, 7-6-1989, Archive Boon & Slagter

THE ARCHITECTURAL REPRESENTATION OF ISLAM

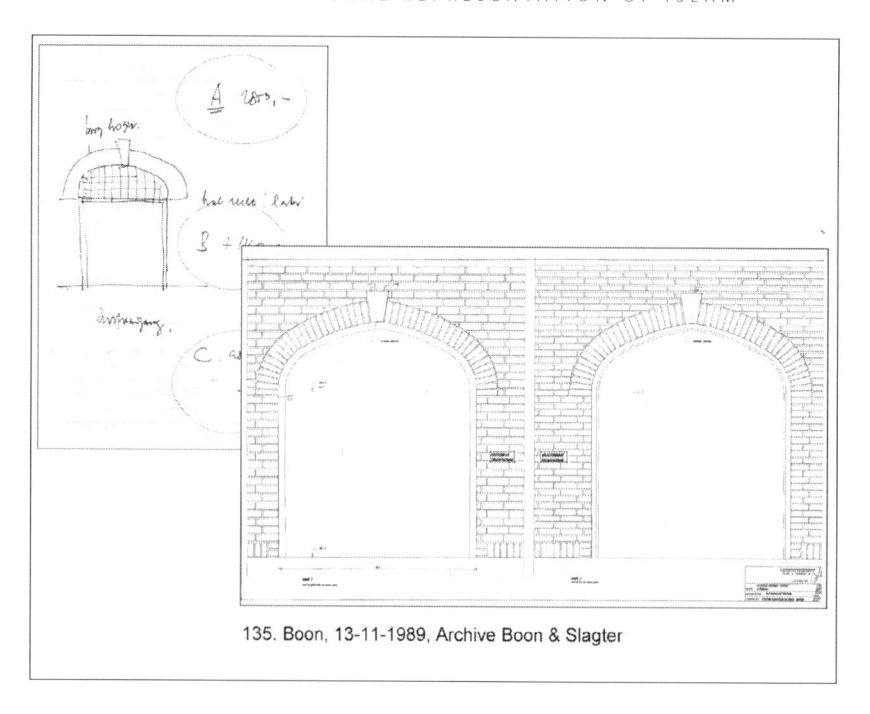

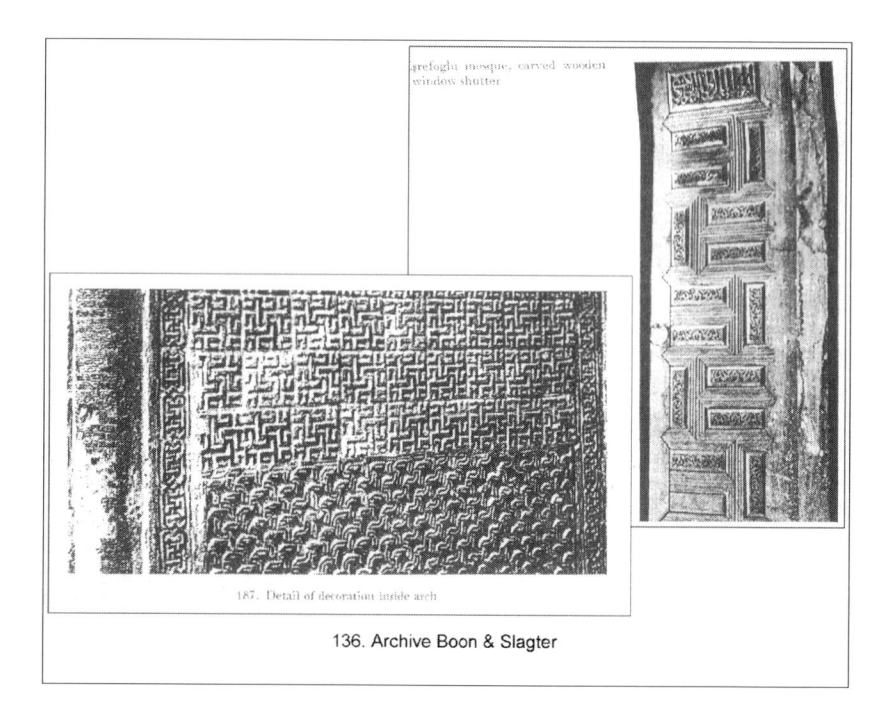

135. Boon, 13-11-1989, Archive Boon & Slagter

136. Archive Boon & Slagter

FIGURES

137. Boon, 1-1990, Archive Boon & Slagter

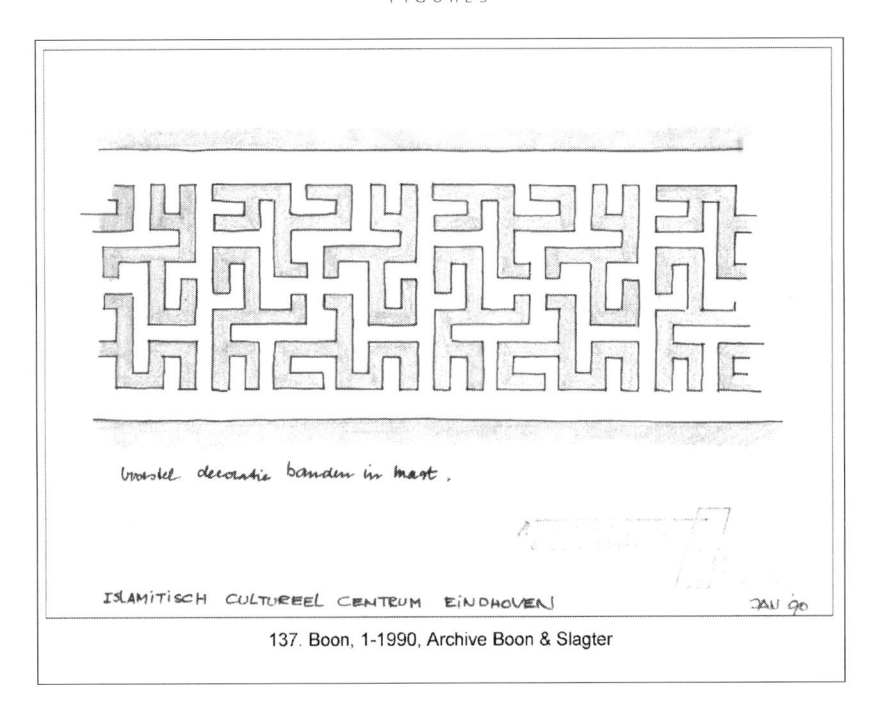

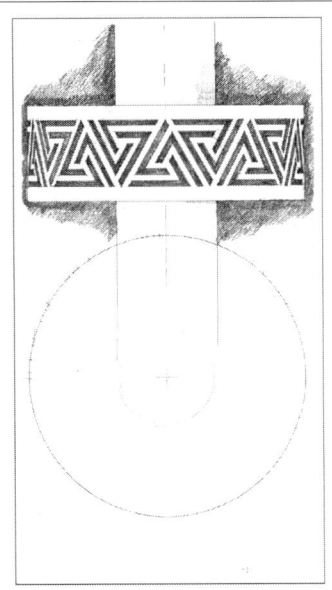

138. Archive Boon & Slagter; Boon, undated, Archive Boon & Slagter

139. Boon, 3-4-1990, Archive Boon & Slagter

140. Boon, undated, Archive Boon & Slagter

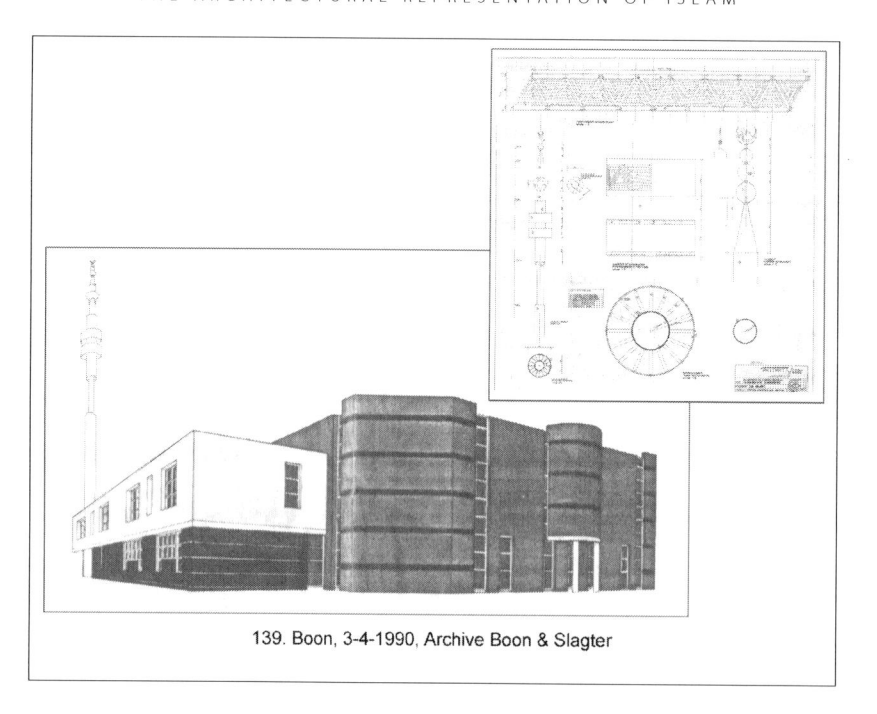

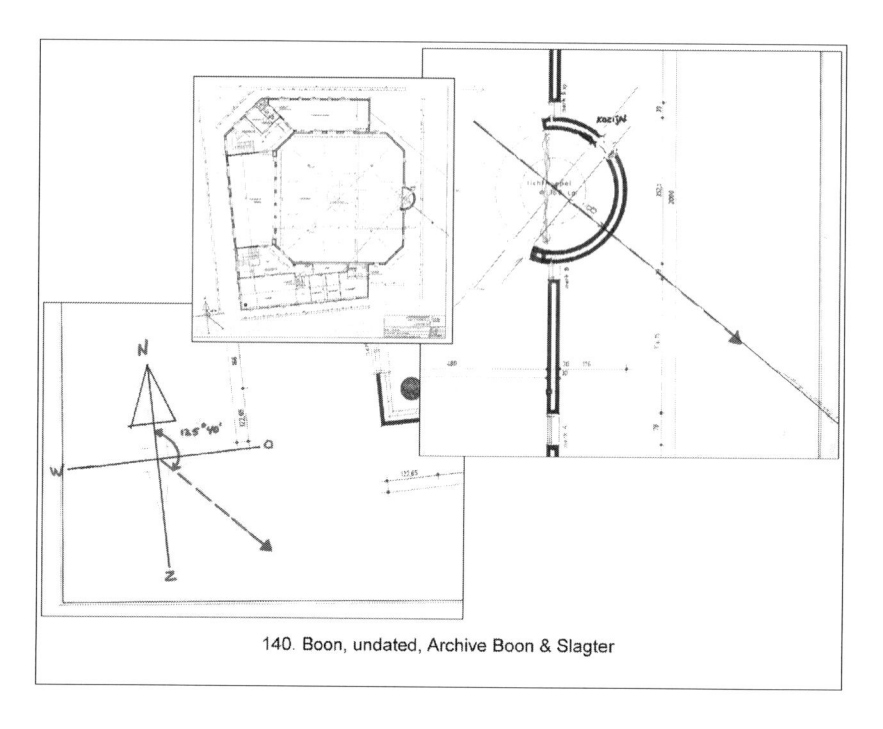

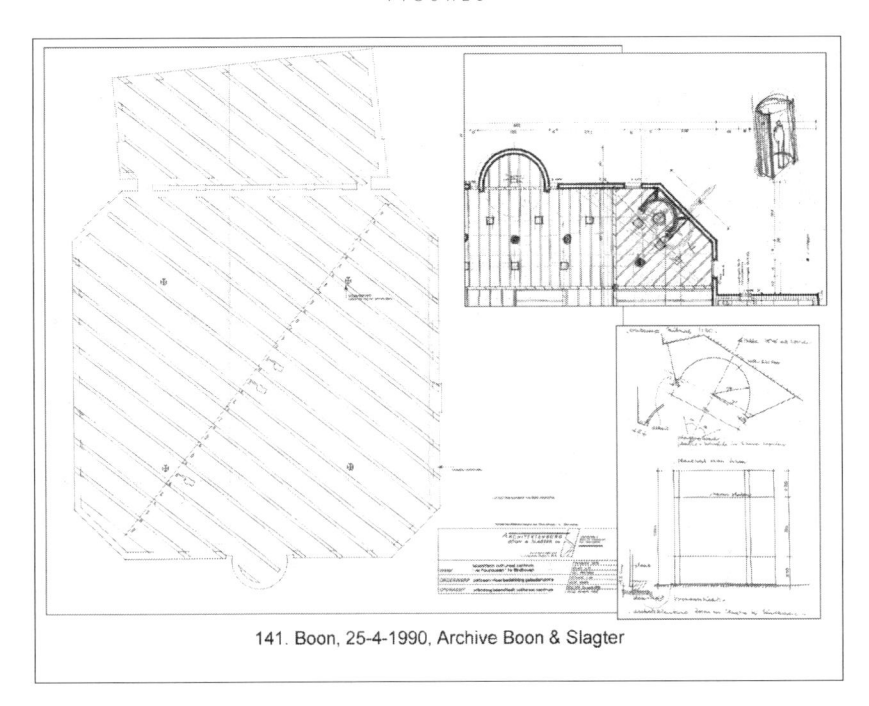

FIGURES

141. Boon, 25-4-1990, Archive Boon & Slagter

142. 2007, Author's Collection

THE ARCHITECTURAL REPRESENTATION OF ISLAM

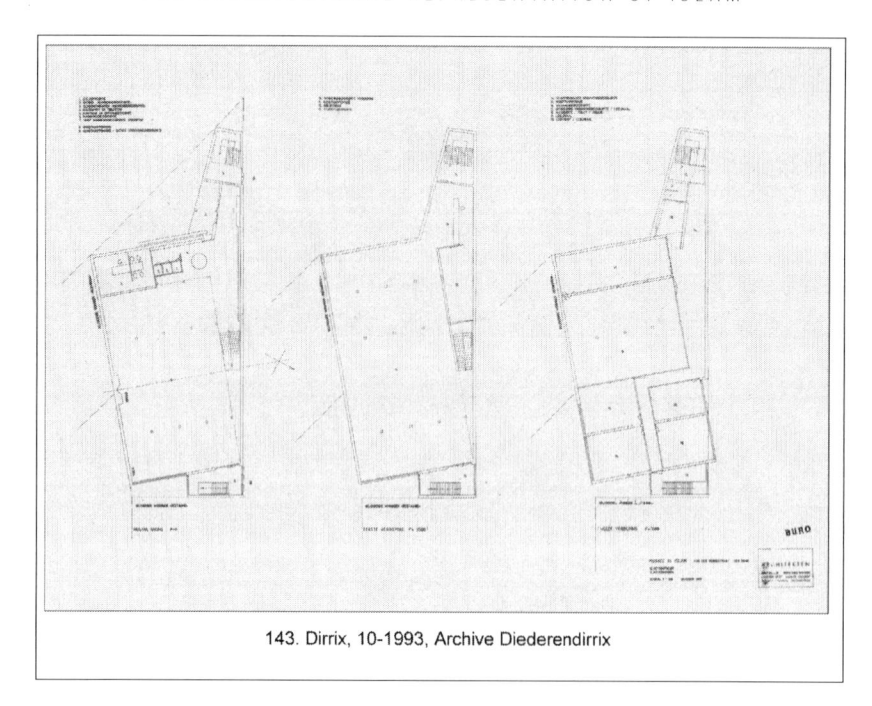

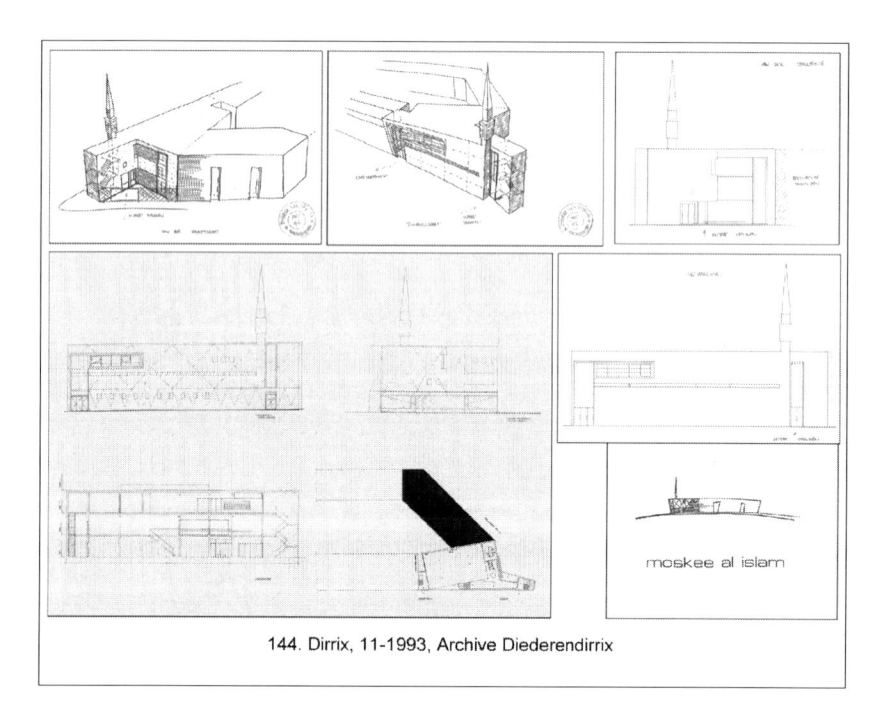

143. Dirrix, 10-1993, Archive Diederendirrix

144. Dirrix, 11-1993, Archive Diederendirrix

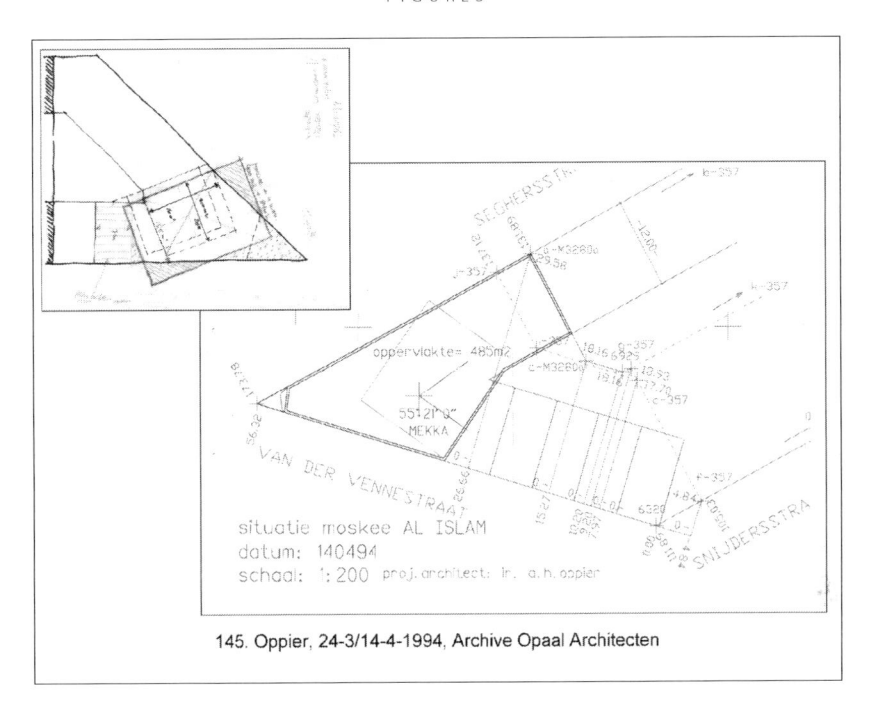

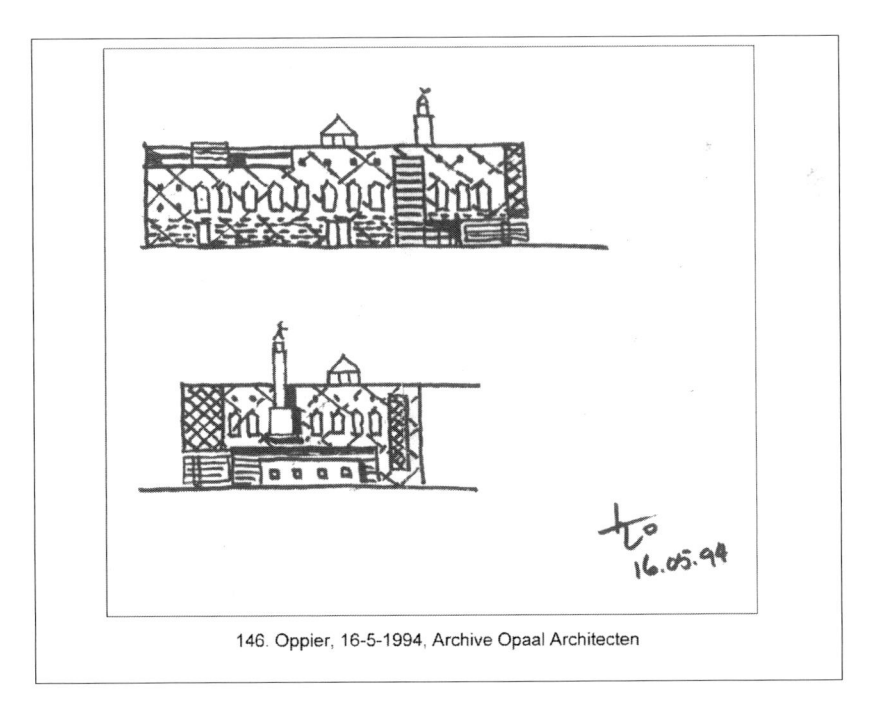

FIGURES

145. Oppier, 24-3/14-4-1994, Archive Opaal Architecten

146. Oppier, 16-5-1994, Archive Opaal Architecten

THE ARCHITECTURAL REPRESENTATION OF ISLAM

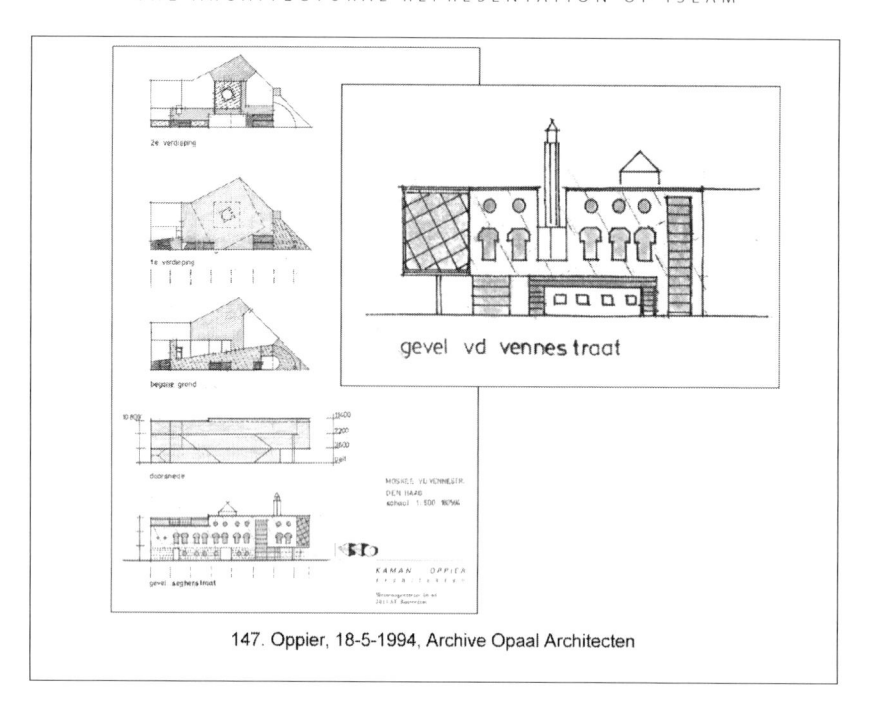

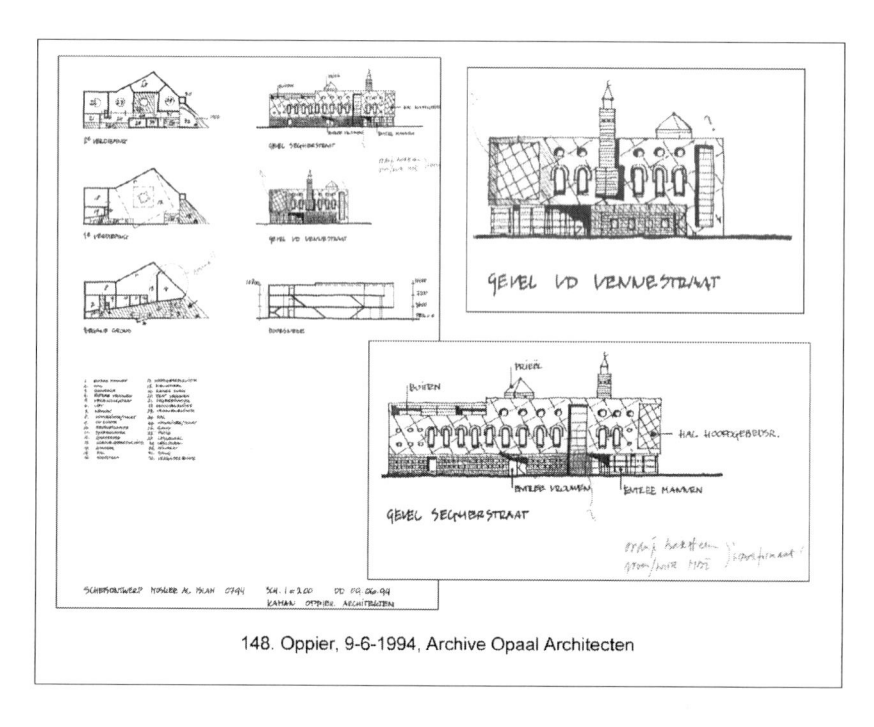

147. Oppier, 18-5-1994, Archive Opaal Architecten

148. Oppier, 9-6-1994, Archive Opaal Architecten

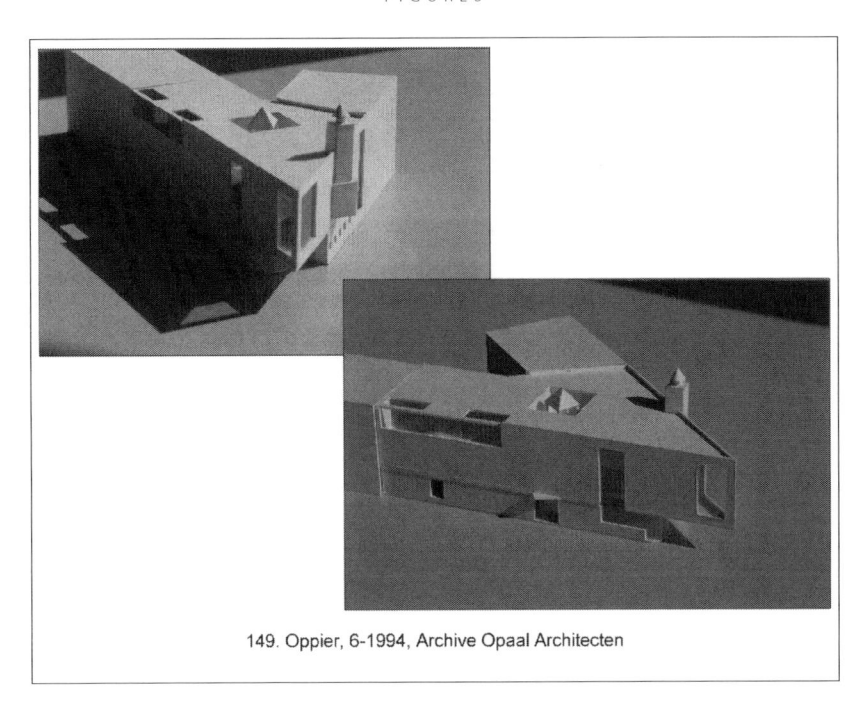

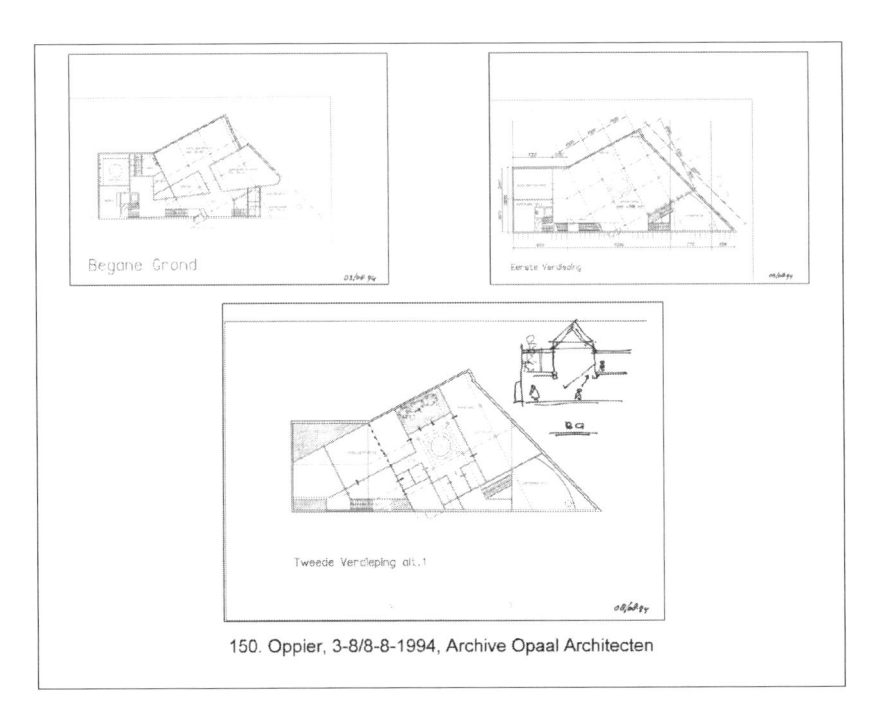

FIGURES

149. Oppier, 6-1994, Archive Opaal Architecten

150. Oppier, 3-8/8-8-1994, Archive Opaal Architecten

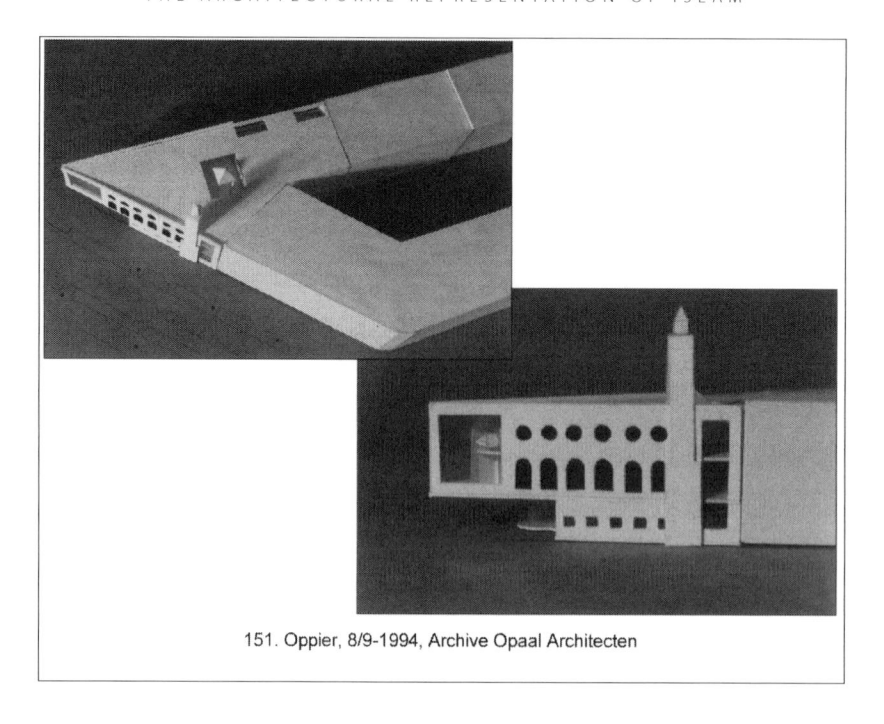

THE ARCHITECTURAL REPRESENTATION OF ISLAM

151. Oppier, 8/9-1994, Archive Opaal Architecten

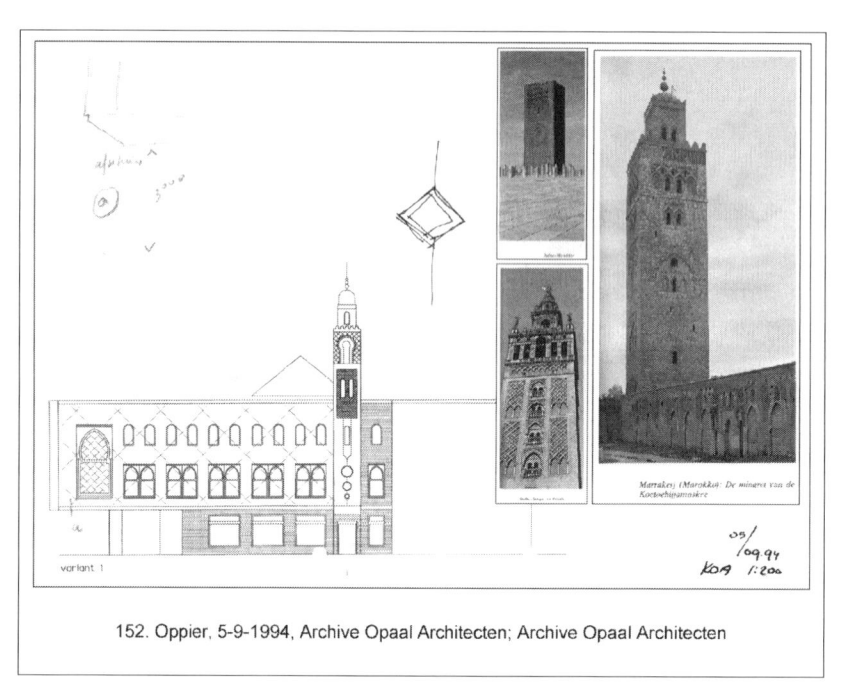

152. Oppier, 5-9-1994, Archive Opaal Architecten; Archive Opaal Architecten

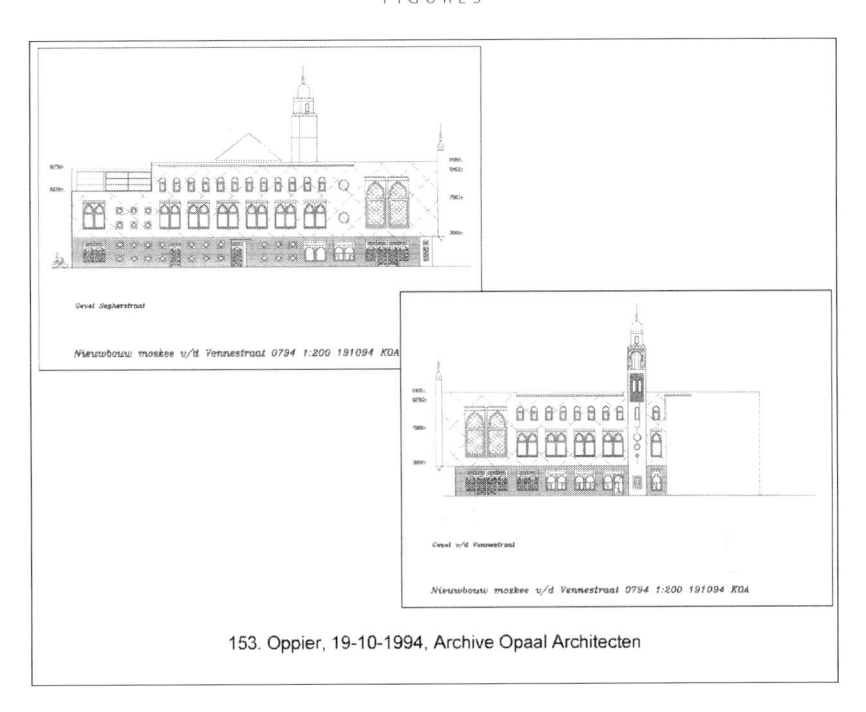

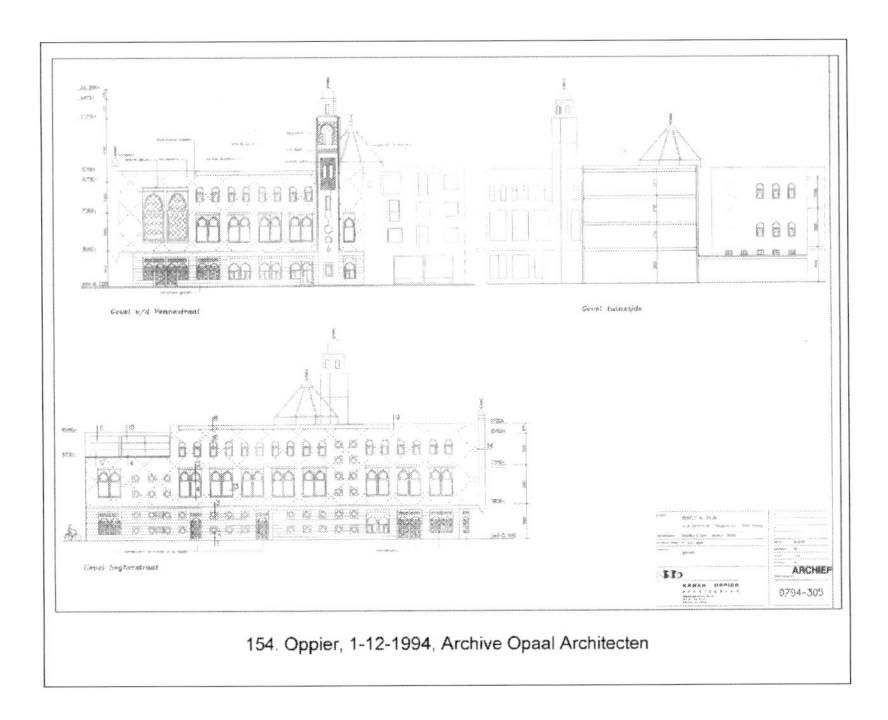

FIGURES

153. Oppier, 19-10-1994, Archive Opaal Architecten

154. Oppier, 1-12-1994, Archive Opaal Architecten

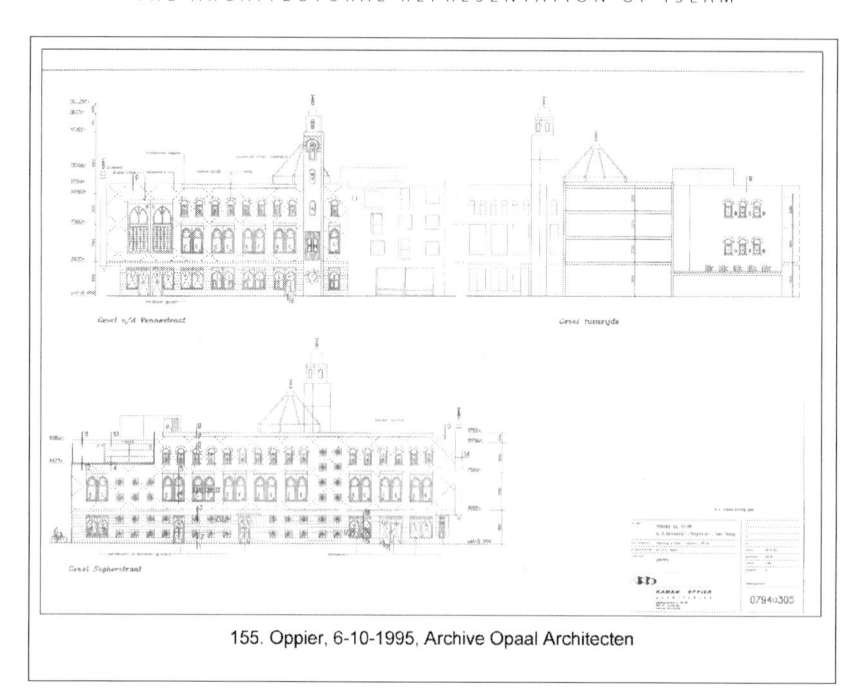

THE ARCHITECTURAL REPRESENTATION OF ISLAM

155. Oppier, 6-10-1995, Archive Opaal Architecten

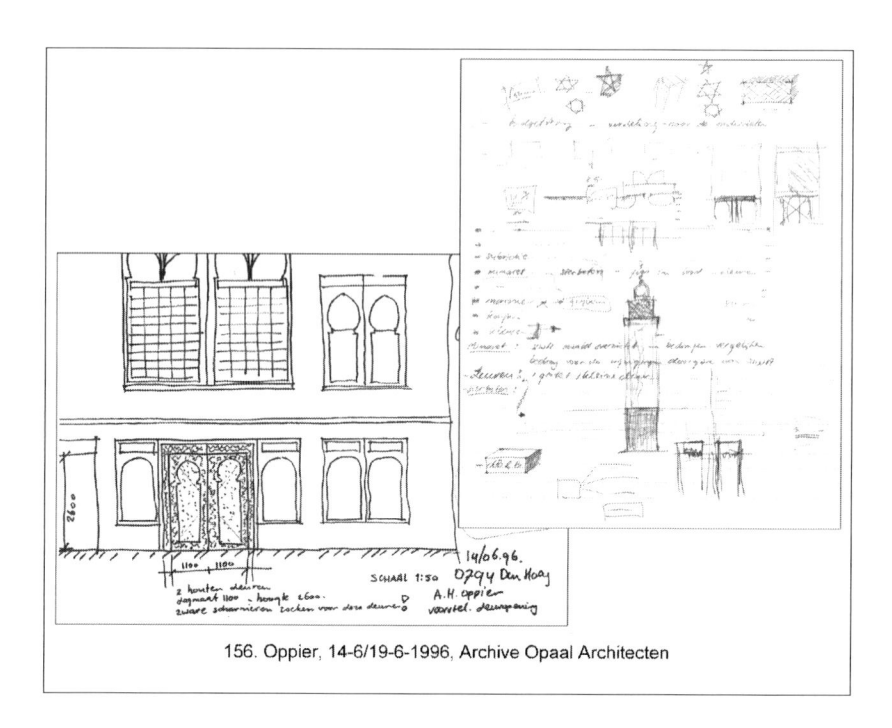

156. Oppier, 14-6/19-6-1996, Archive Opaal Architecten

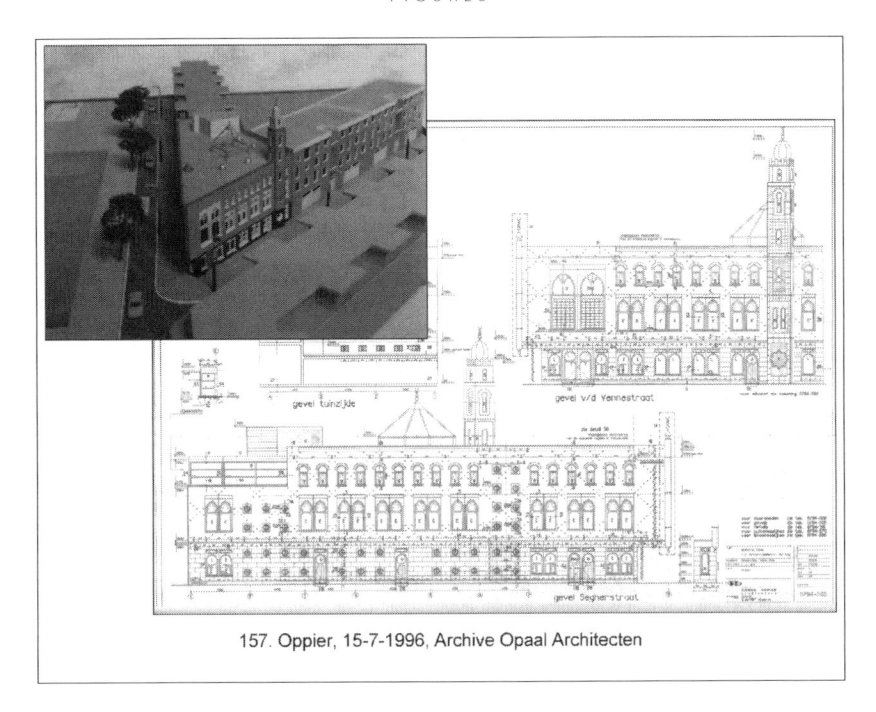

FIGURES

157. Oppier, 15-7-1996, Archive Opaal Architecten

158. 2007 (interior), Author's Collection; 1997 (exterior), Collection Oppier

THE ARCHITECTURAL REPRESENTATION OF ISLAM

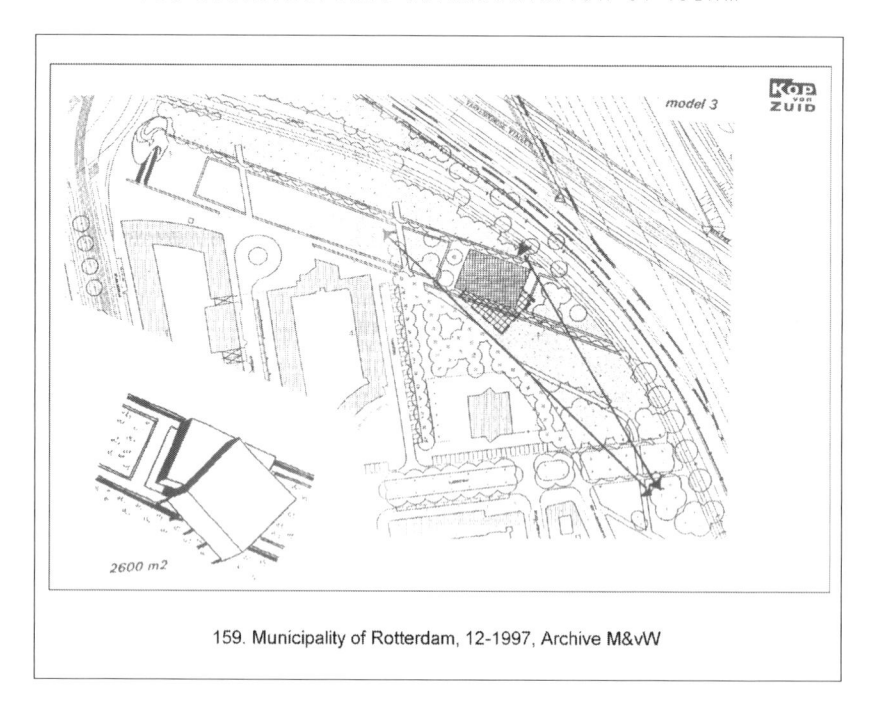

159. Municipality of Rotterdam, 12-1997, Archive M&vW

160. Ajdid, 1-2001, Archive M&vW

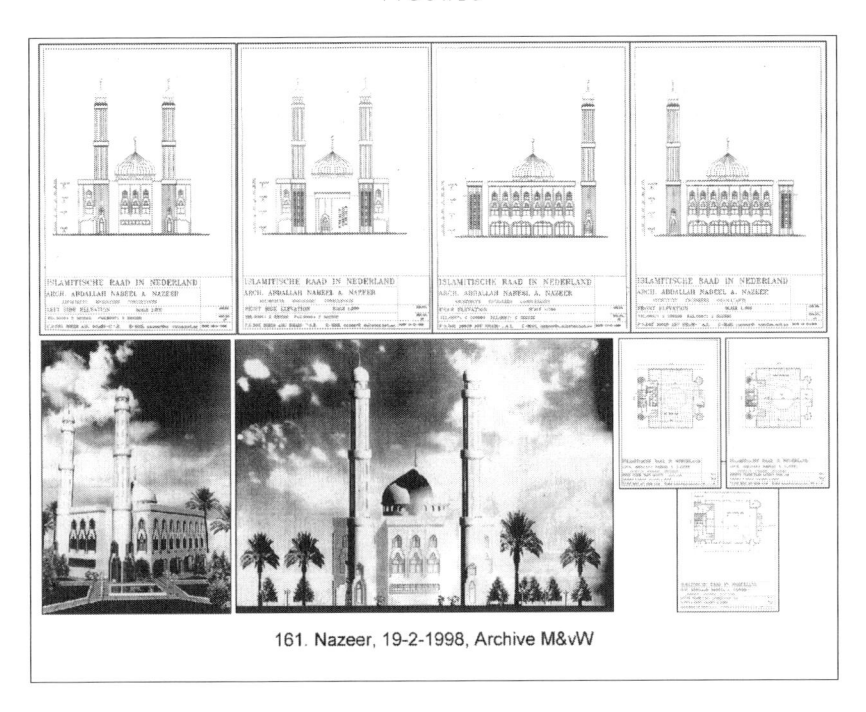

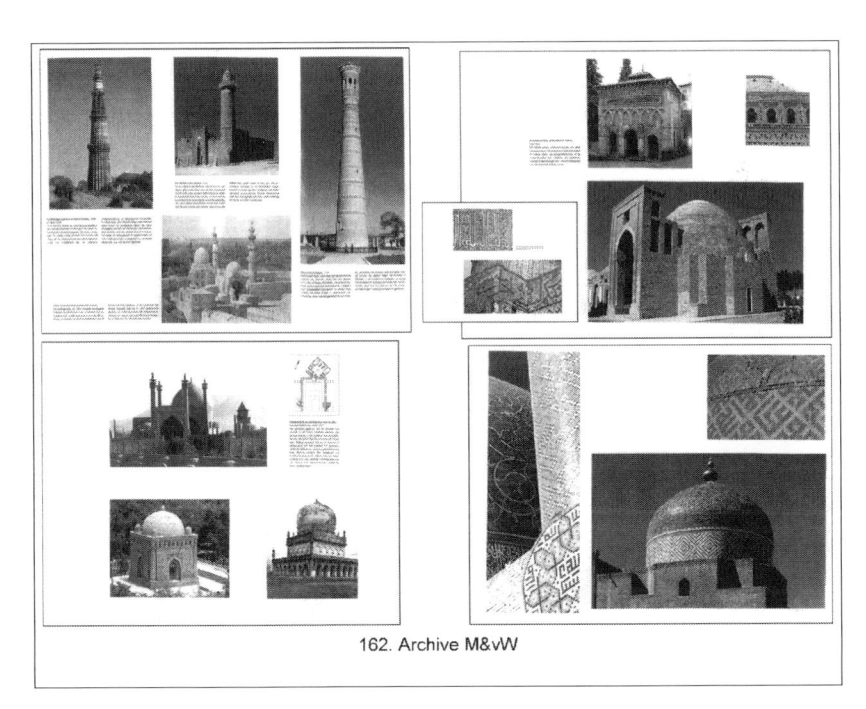

FIGURES

161. Nazeer, 19-2-1998, Archive M&vW

162. Archive M&vW

THE ARCHITECTURAL REPRESENTATION OF ISLAM

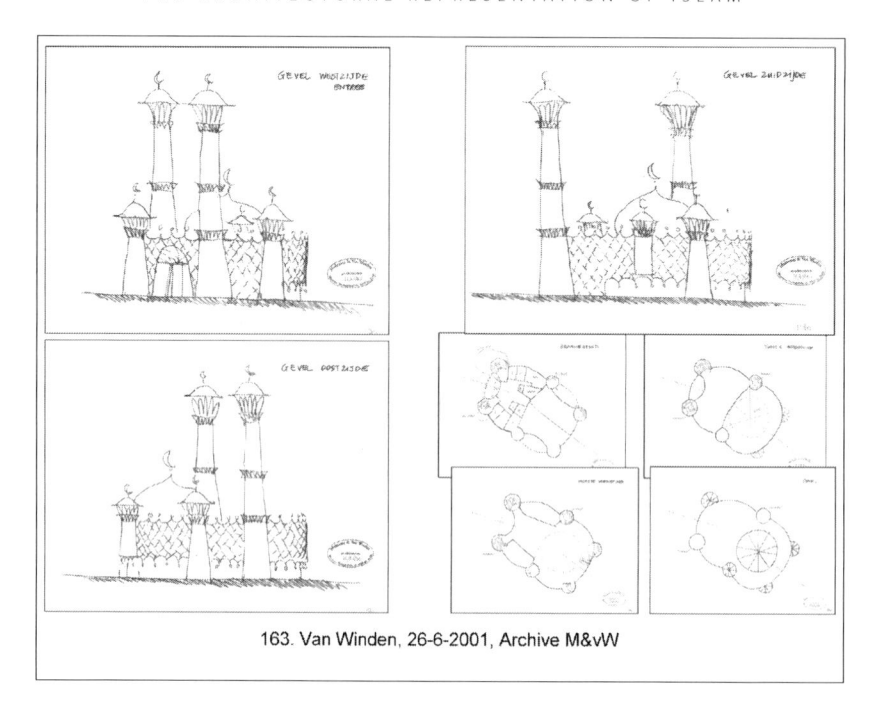

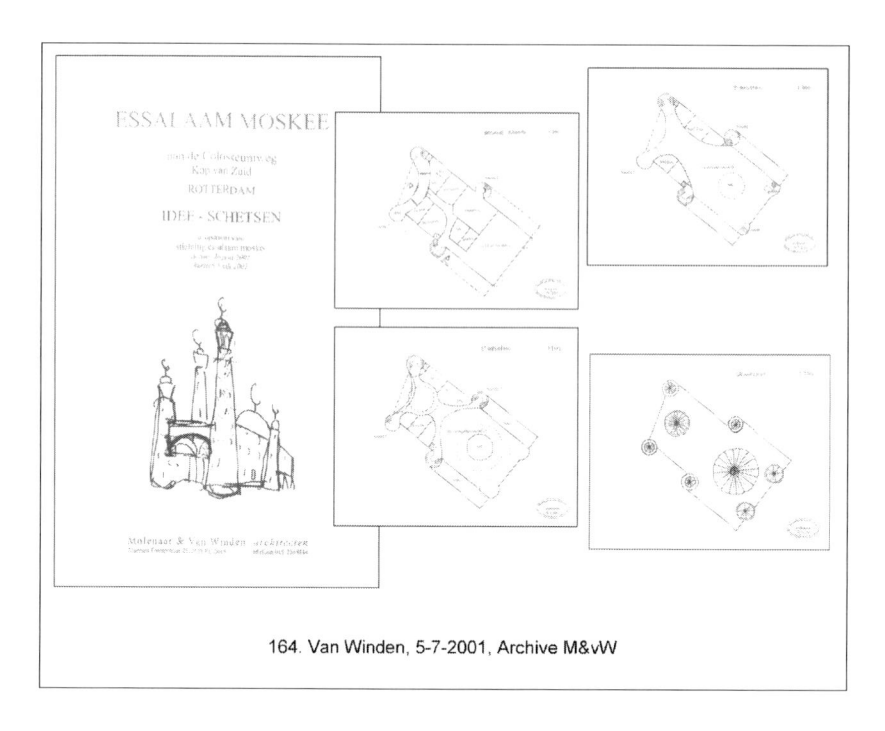

163. Van Winden, 26-6-2001, Archive M&vW

164. Van Winden, 5-7-2001, Archive M&vW

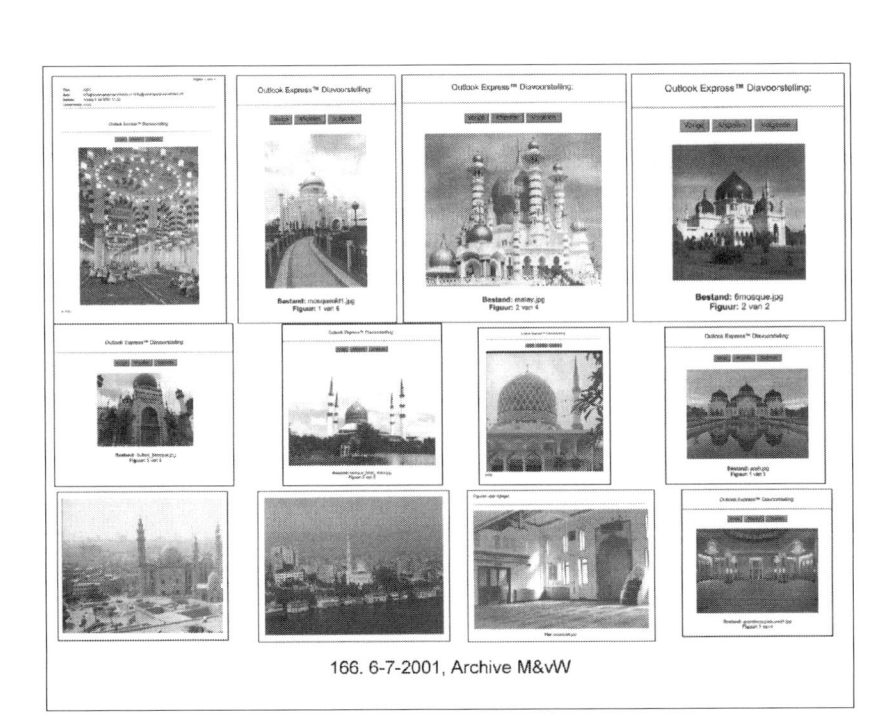

FIGURES

165. 5-7-2001, Archive M&vW

166. 6-7-2001, Archive M&vW

403

THE ARCHITECTURAL REPRESENTATION OF ISLAM

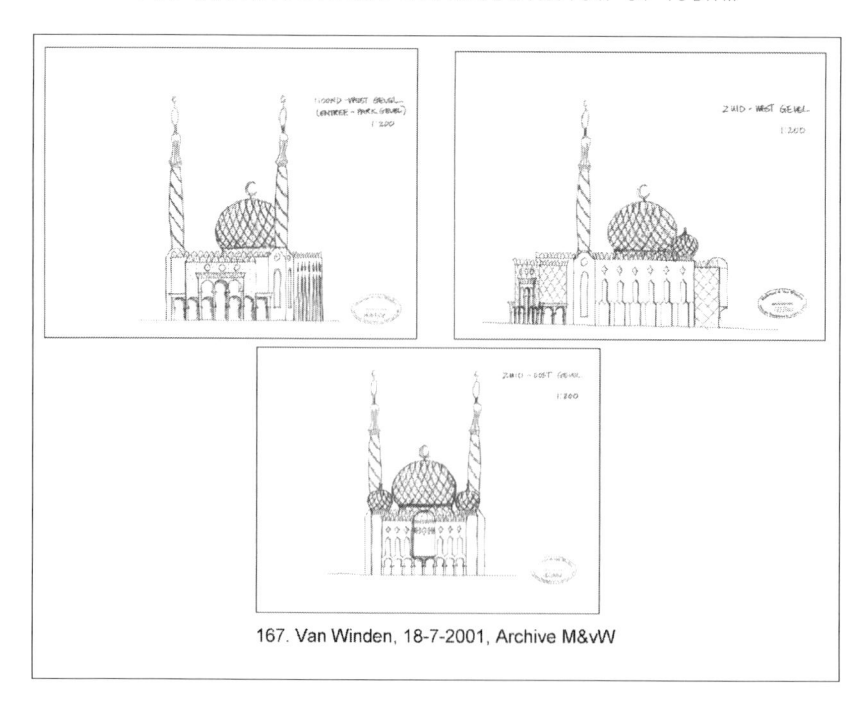

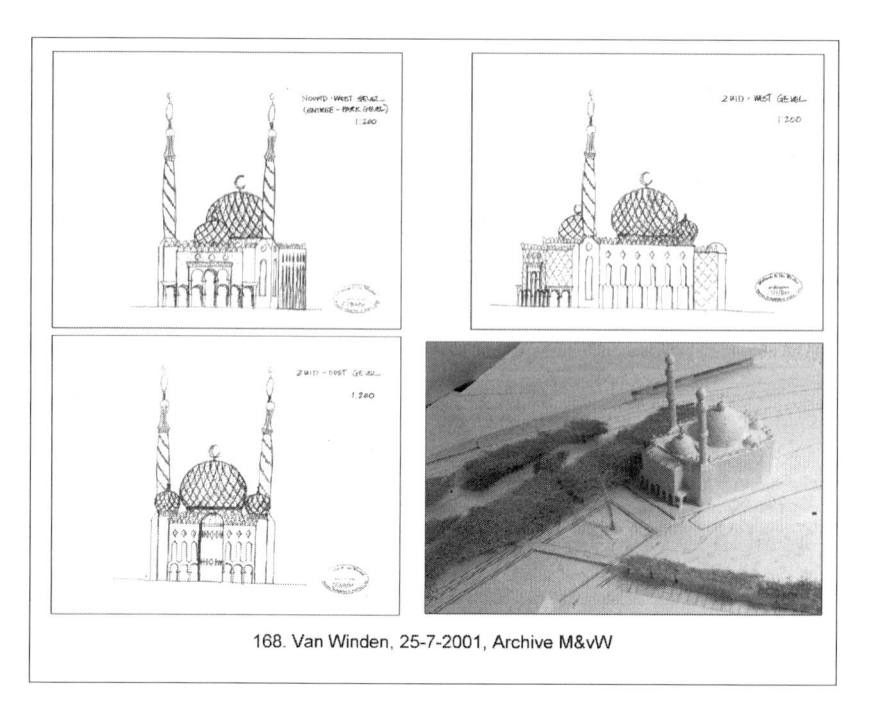

167. Van Winden, 18-7-2001, Archive M&vW

168. Van Winden, 25-7-2001, Archive M&vW

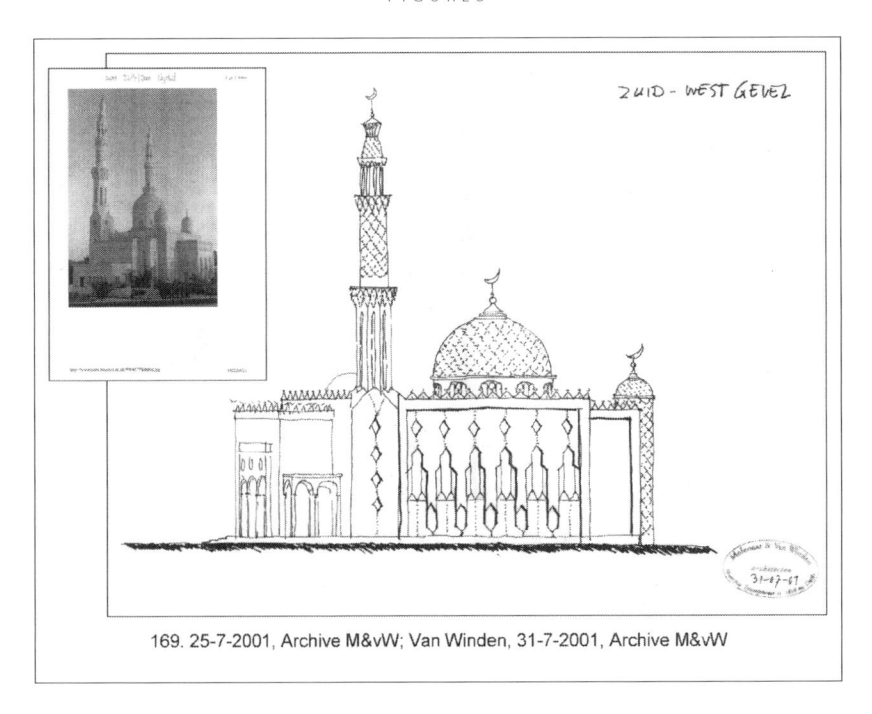

FIGURES

169. 25-7-2001, Archive M&vW; Van Winden, 31-7-2001, Archive M&vW

170. 1-8-2001, Archive M&vW

405

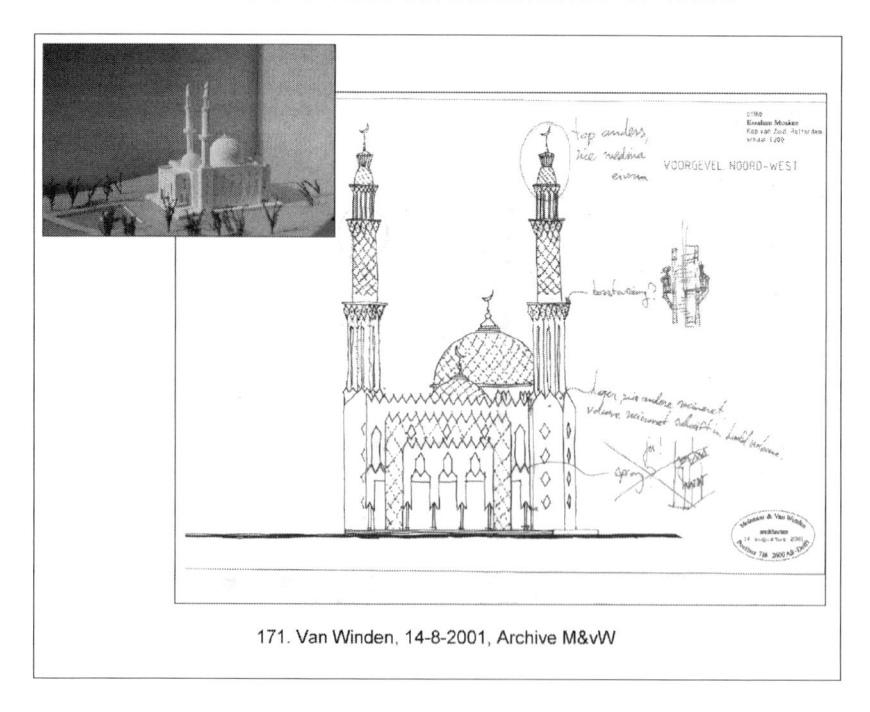

THE ARCHITECTURAL REPRESENTATION OF ISLAM

171. Van Winden, 14-8-2001, Archive M&vW

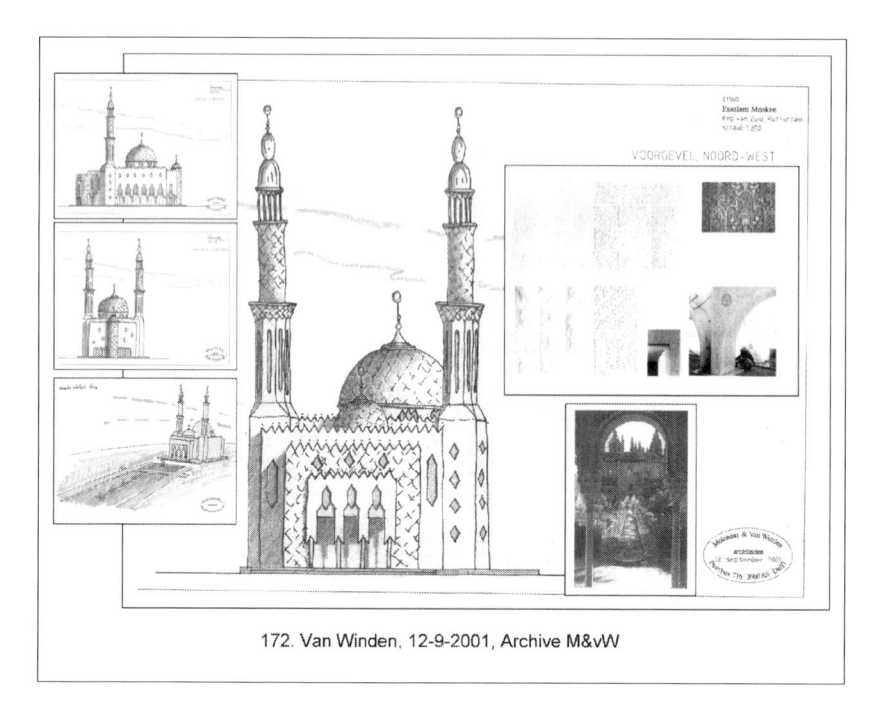

172. Van Winden, 12-9-2001, Archive M&vW

FIGURES

173. Van Winden, 11-2001, Archive M&vW

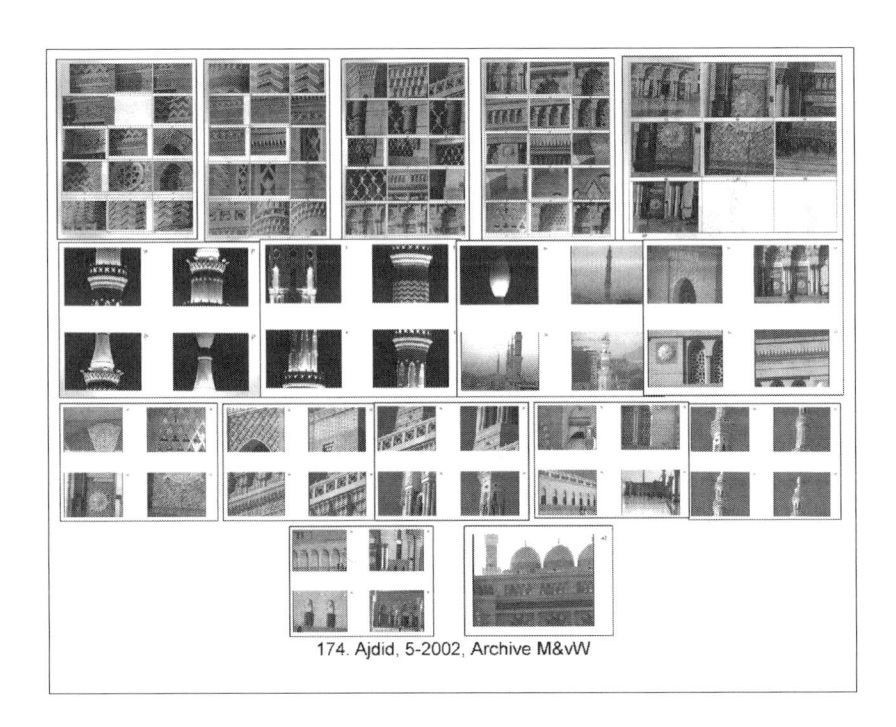

174. Ajdid, 5-2002, Archive M&vW

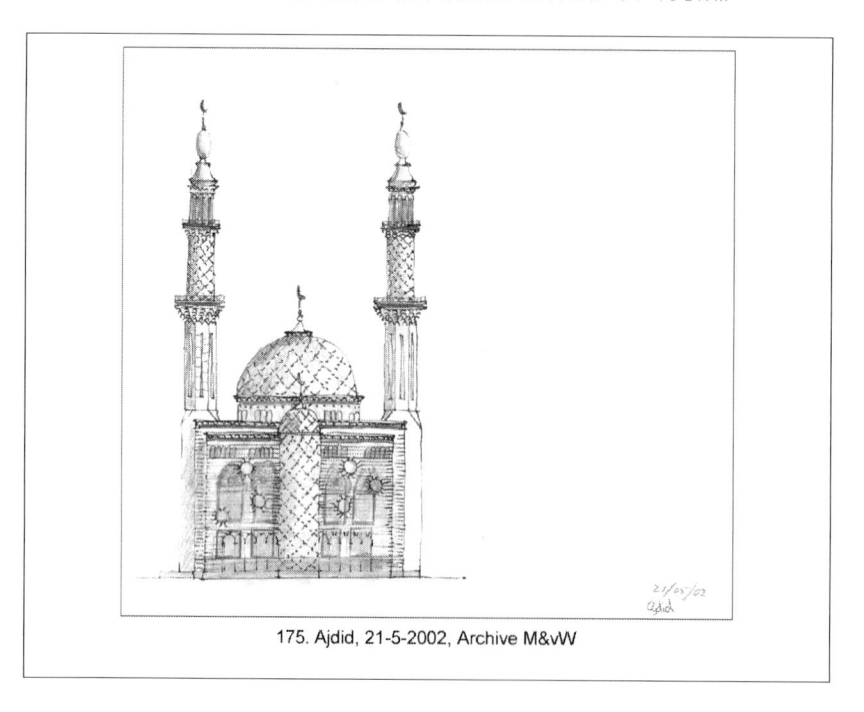

THE ARCHITECTURAL REPRESENTATION OF ISLAM

175. Ajdid, 21-5-2002, Archive M&vW

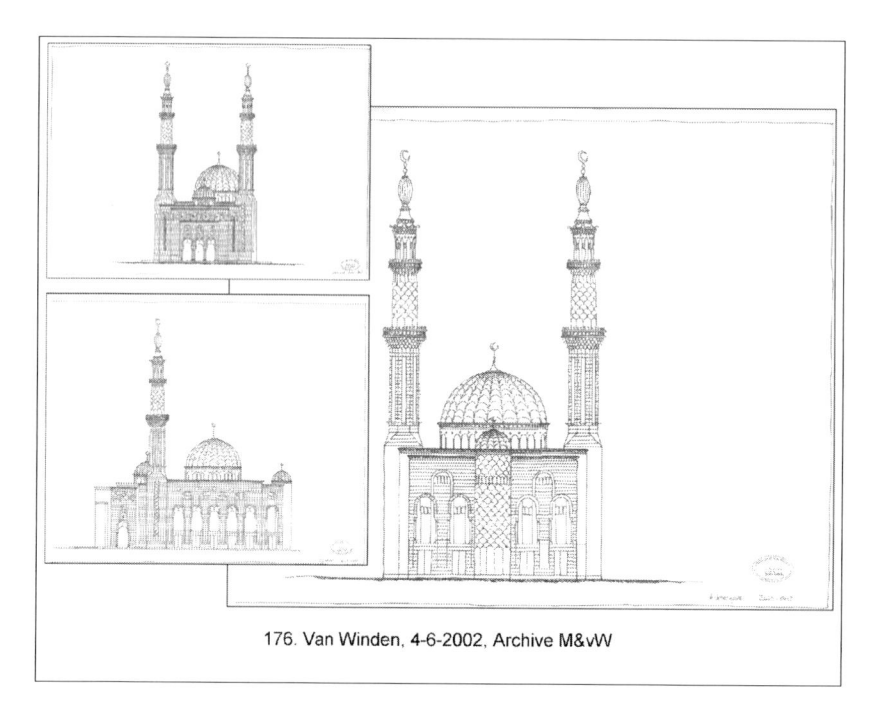

176. Van Winden, 4-6-2002, Archive M&vW

FIGURES

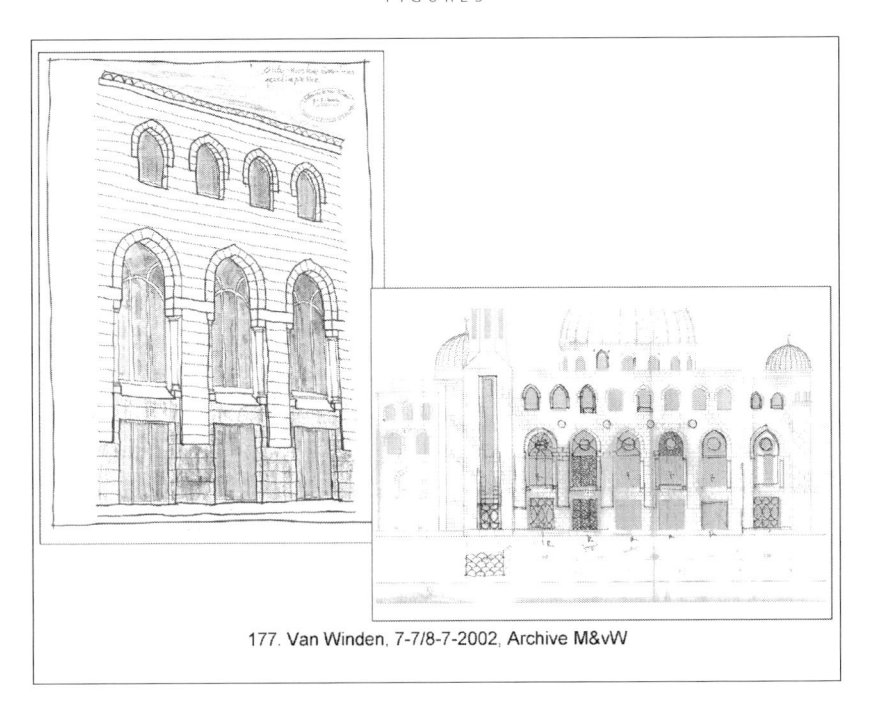

177. Van Winden, 7-7/8-7-2002, Archive M&vW

178. Ajdid, 11-7-2002, Archive M&vW

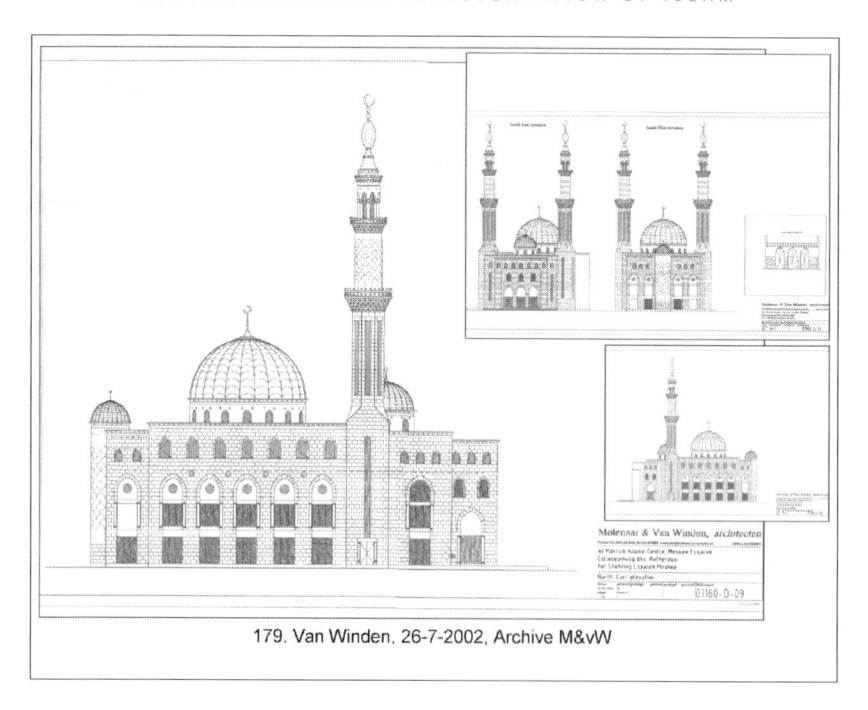

THE ARCHITECTURAL REPRESENTATION OF ISLAM

179. Van Winden, 26-7-2002, Archive M&vW

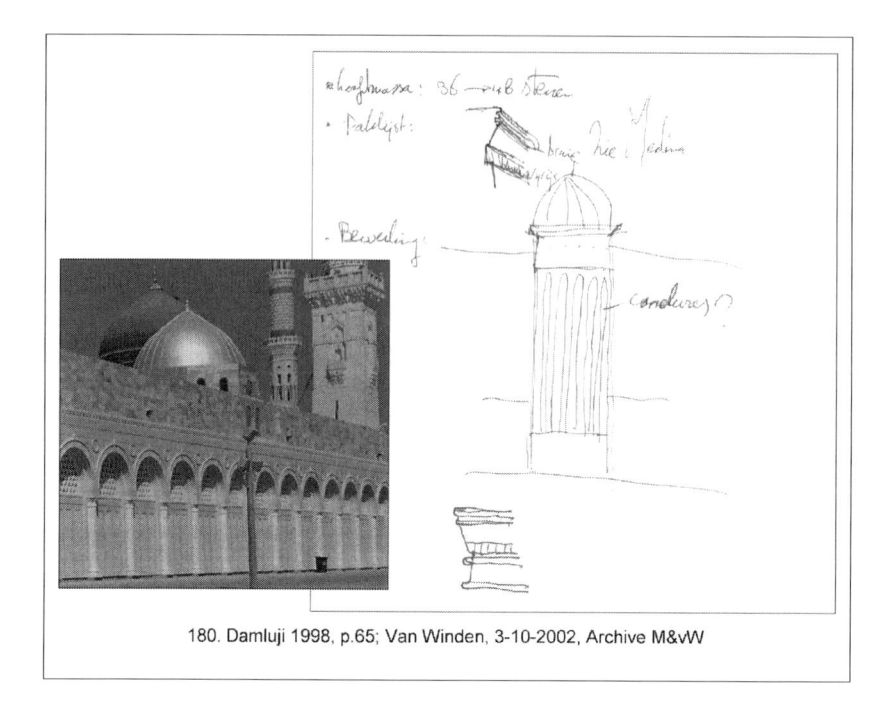

180. Damluji 1998, p.65; Van Winden, 3-10-2002, Archive M&vW

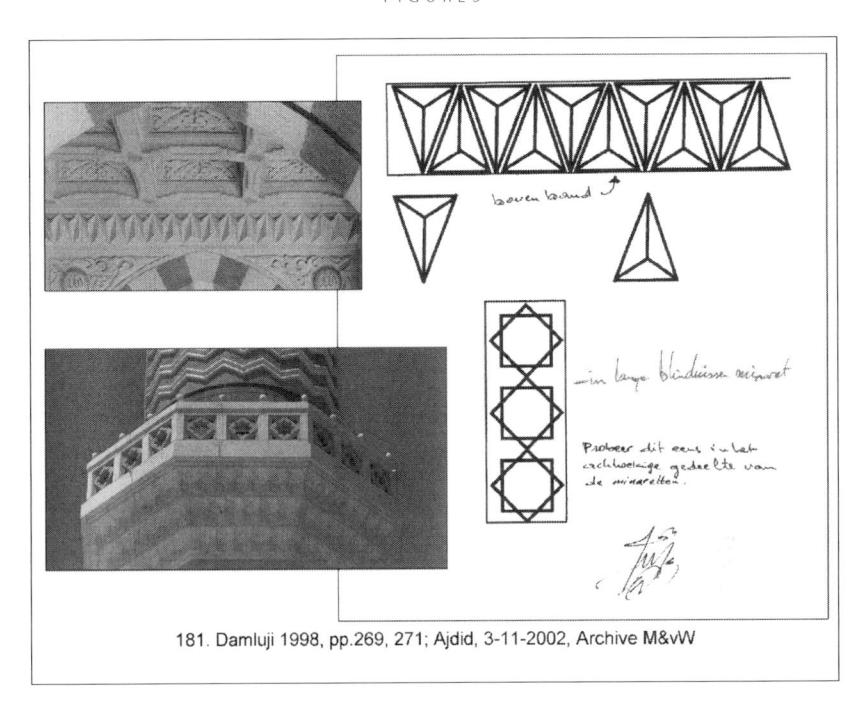

FIGURES

181. Damluji 1998, pp.269, 271; Ajdid, 3-11-2002, Archive M&vW

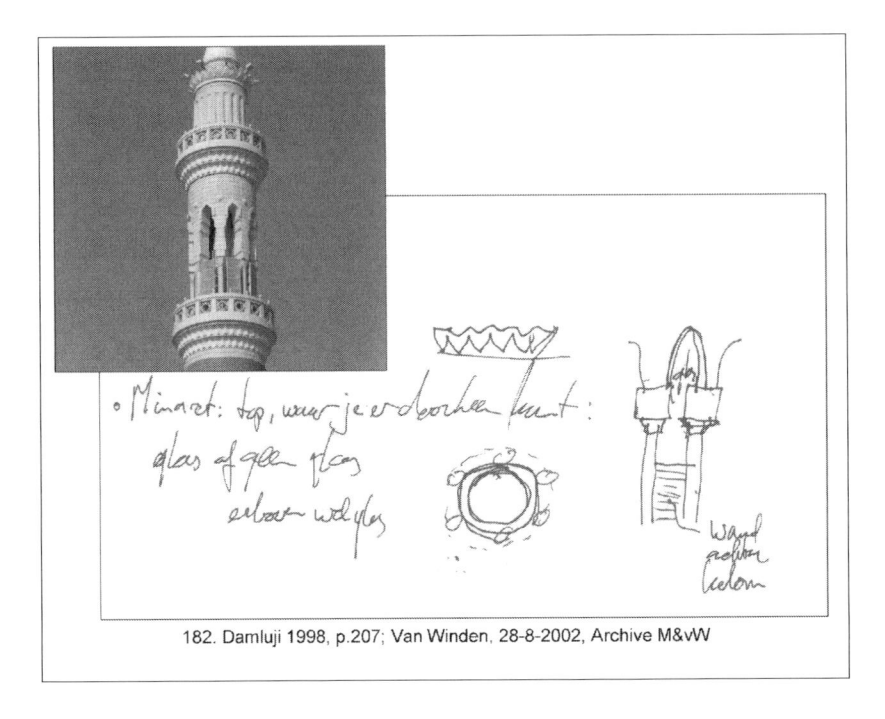

182. Damluji 1998, p.207; Van Winden, 28-8-2002, Archive M&vW

THE ARCHITECTURAL REPRESENTATION OF ISLAM

183. Van Winden, 3-12-2002, Archive M&vW

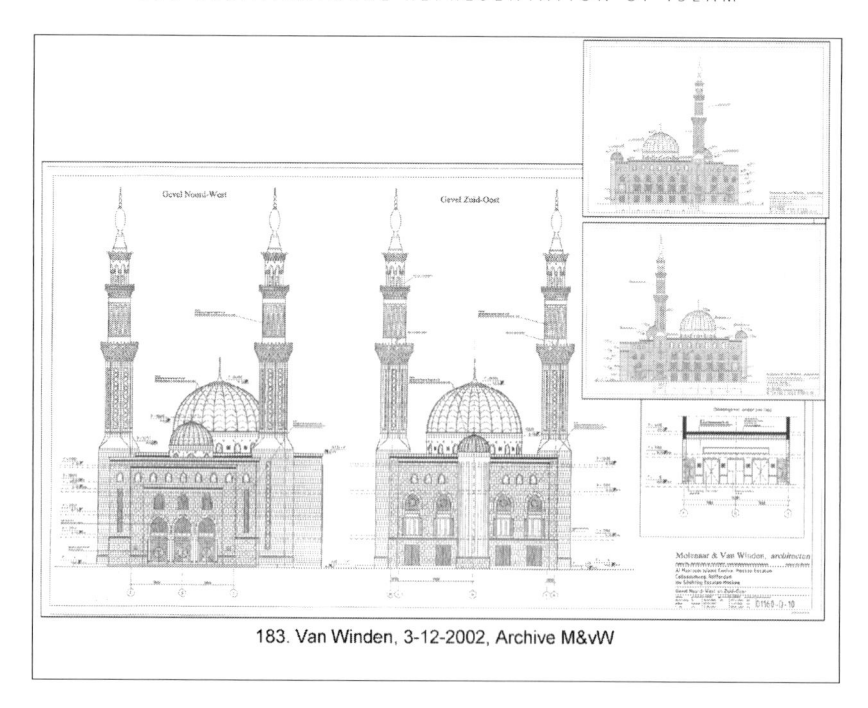

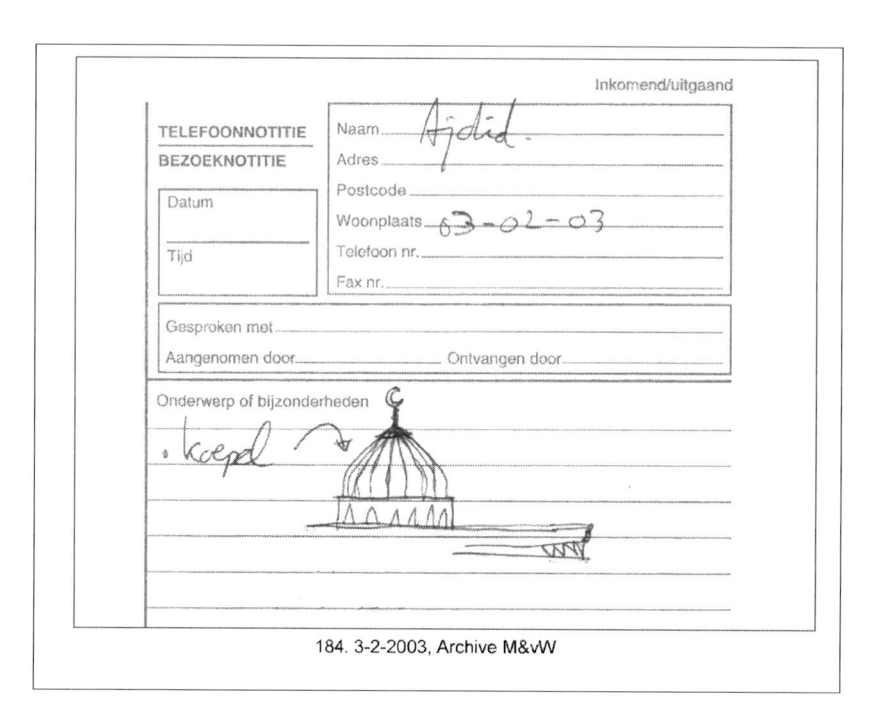

184. 3-2-2003, Archive M&vW

185. Van Winden, 25-2-2003, Archive M&vW

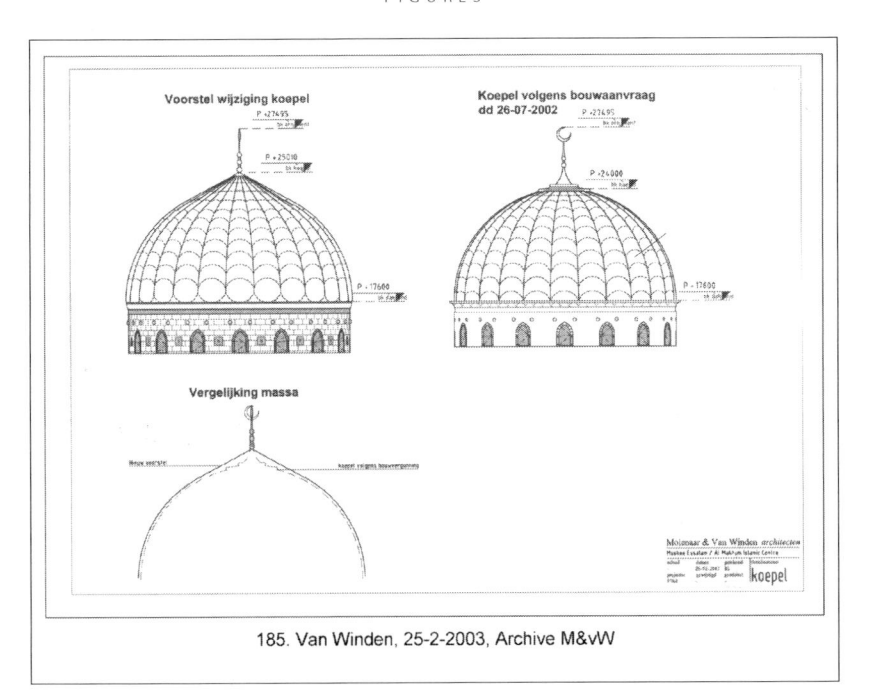

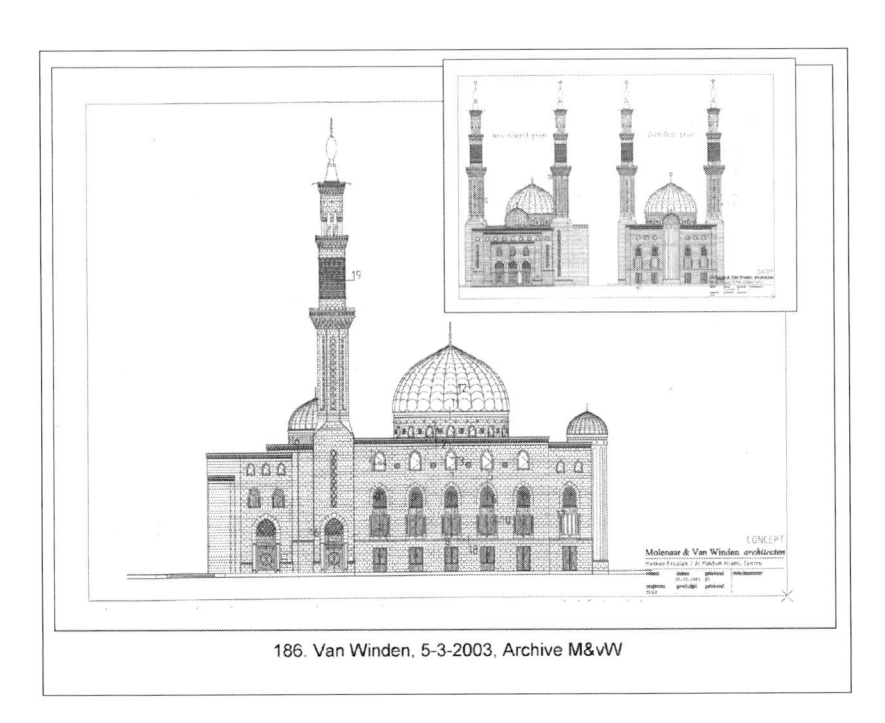

186. Van Winden, 5-3-2003, Archive M&vW

THE ARCHITECTURAL REPRESENTATION OF ISLAM

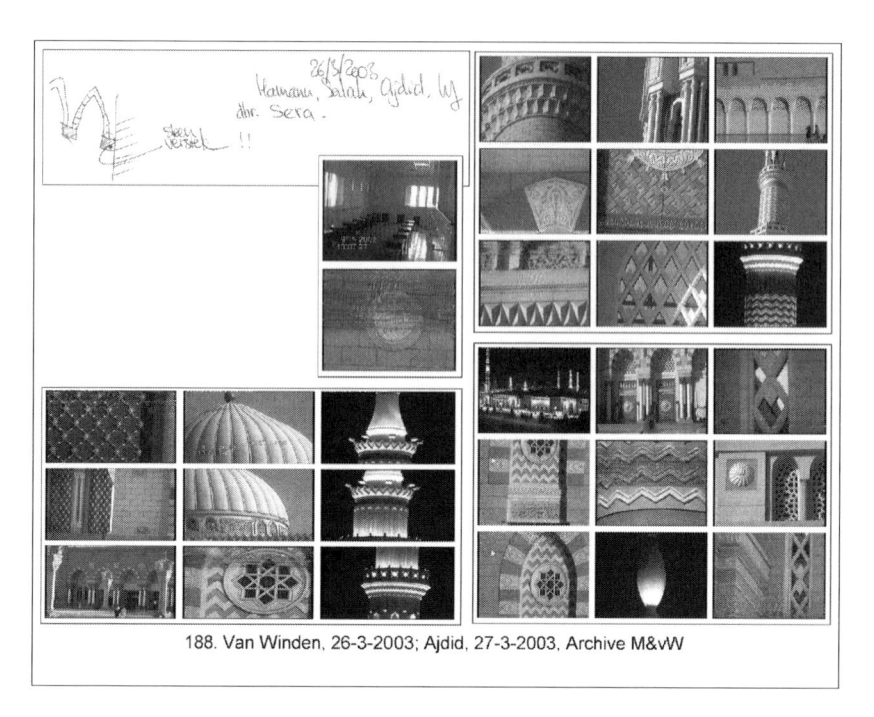

187. Van Winden, 25-3-2003, Archive M&vW

188. Van Winden, 26-3-2003; Ajdid, 27-3-2003, Archive M&vW

FIGURES

189. Van Winden, 1-4-2003, Archive M&vW

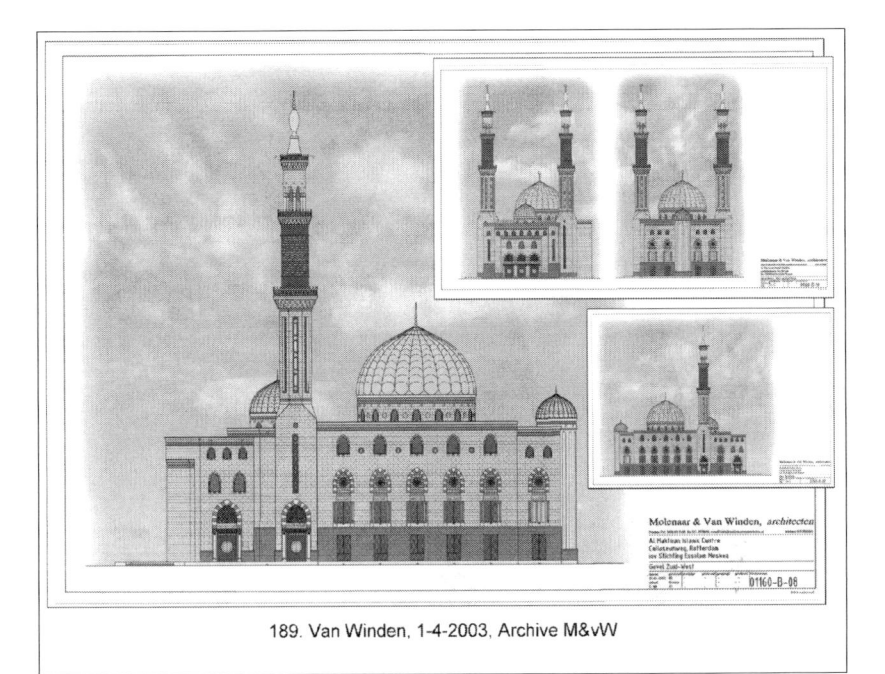

190. Van Winden, 2-4/8-4-2003, Archive M&vW

THE ARCHITECTURAL REPRESENTATION OF ISLAM

191. Franz Sill GmbH, www.al-maktoum.nl; Studio i2, www.i2.nl

192. 2008, Author's Collection

416

Printed in Great Britain
by Amazon